Index to Historic Preservation Periodicals

National Trust for Historic Preservation Library of the University of Maryland, College Park

National Trust Librarian	Sally R. Sims
General Editor	Hye Yun Choe
Indexers	Hope Headley
	Medea Ranck
	Brigid Rapp
	Cary Schneider
	Pamela Thurber
	Anne Twitchell
	Gloria Van Order
Serials Assistants	Susan A. Cox
	Nancy A. Kramer
Research Assistants	Patricia Aitken
	Etta Saunders

G.K. Hall & Co.
70 Lincoln St., Boston, Massachusetts 02111

ISBN 0–8161–0474–3

Table of Contents

Preface

The *Index to Historic Preservation Periodicals* is a compilation of the monthly listing of articles and ephemera that, since 1979, has been issued by the Library of the National Trust for Historic Preservation. Each month, the library's staff members have scanned several hundred publications for articles treating all aspects of historic preservation. The periodicals examined comprise those issued by international, national, regional, state, and local historic preservation organizations. Popular and scholarly serials that include material bearing on the historic preservation movement are considered as well. Indexers have also selected pamphlets, clippings, and brochures for inclusion in the list. The result has been a unique current-awareness tool for preservationists and a finding aid to the periodical and vertical file collections of the National Trust Library.

The National Trust for Historic Preservation Library (NTL) was transferred to the University of Maryland, College Park, in 1986. Now housed in the Architecture Library as a separate special collection, it is fully supported by and functions as a part of the University of Maryland College Park Libraries. An entirely new staff has been appointed; these personnel continue to produce a monthly update of articles and vertical file items of interest to historic preservation professionals, technicians, and scholars.

Periodical articles are entered in the *Index* as complete bibliographic citations, often accompanied by a brief annotation. Pamphlets, clippings and the like are designated ''VF'' and are maintained by subject in over 1700 vertical files in the library. This material represents the full spectrum of historic preservation topics: architecture, law, historical research; design review, interior treatments for historic buildings, restoration; real estate, fund raising, tax incentives; statewide historic preservation programs and federal policy matters. Today the *Index* contains over 6000 entries and the list of subjects has grown by half over the period 1979 to 1987.

A single subject heading is assigned to each citation in the *Index;* it is therefore often necessary to investigate more than one subject to complete a thorough search on a topic. For example, in consulting the *Index* for material on the adaptation of historic buildings for new uses, one should refer to ADAPTIVE USE as a general heading and also look for items under the specific type of building being studied, such as INDUSTRIAL BUILDINGS—ADAPTIVE USE or RAILROADS—STATIONS —ADAPTIVE USE.

The publication of this volume reflects a keen awareness on the part of G.K. Hall's editors that historic preservation is a dynamic force in the shaping of the American scene. And the foresight of the National Trust Library staff who began gathering entries for the *Index* in 1979 cannot be overstated. Particular credit is due Susan Shearer, Trust librarian from 1979 to 1984; and Cary Alan Schneider, immediate past librarian of the collection, under whose guidance the indexing process continued uninterrupted during the transfer of the library to the University of Maryland. Hearty appreciation is extended to Carol A. Jackson, director of information services at the National Trust, and to J. Jackson Walter, the Trust president. Mr. Walter's vision in placing the Trust's library in an academic setting, and in encouraging the University to make the *Index* commercially available to researchers and scholars, has gone far to promote awareness of the the historic preservation movement.

—Sally R. Sims, Librarian
National Trust for Historic Preservation Library
of the University of Maryland, College Park
November, 1987

A

AIA BULLETIN (Association for Industrial
        Archaeology)
*AIA MEMO (American Institute of Architects)
AIA NEWS (American Institute of Architects)
*AIC NEWSLETTER (American Institute for
    Conservation of Historic & Artistic Works)
ALRA BULLETIN (American Land Resource Assn.)
APT BULLETIN (Assn for Preservation
        Technology)
APT COMMUNIQUE (Assn for Preservation
        Technology)
*APVA NEWSLETTER (Assn for Preservation of
        Virginia Antiquities)
*APWA REPORTER (American Public Works
       Assn)
ASCHB NEWSLETTER (Assn for Studies in the
    Conservation of Hist. Bldgs)
ASCHB TRANSACTIONS
*ACCESS
ACQUISITIONS
ACTION
*ACTION ALERT
*AGORA
ALABAMA HERITAGE
ALASKA ASSOCIATION FOR HISTORIC PRESERVATION
*ALASKA HISTORY NEWS
ALBANY PRESERVATION REPORT
*ALL ABOARD
*ALLIANCE LETTER
ALLIANCE REVIEW, THE
*AMERICAN ART JOURNAL, THE
AMERICAN CANALS
AMERICAN HERITAGE SOCIETY (AMERICANA)
AMERICAN LAND FORUM
AMERICAN NEPTUNE
*AMERICAN PRESERVATION
*AMERICAN RIVERS
*AMERICAN SOCIETY FOR CONSERVATION
    ARCHAEOLOGY REPORT
*AMERICAN URBAN GUIDE NOTES
*AMERICAN VISIONS
ANCIENT MONUMENTS SOCIETY NEWSLETTER
ANNAPOLIS MERCURY
*ANNUAL REPORT (American Scenic & Historic
        Preservation Society)
*ANNUAL REPORTS (National Trust)
ANTIQUARIAN & LANDMARKS SOCIETY NEWSLETTER
*ANTIQUES WORLD
*APPALACHIA
*APPRAISAL JOURNAL, THE
ARCHAEOLOGICAL CONSERVANCY NEWSLETTER
ARCHAEOLOGY
*ARCHITECTURAL ANTIQUES & ARTIFACTS
    ADVERTISER
*ARCHITECTURAL FORUM
*ARCHITECTURAL HISTORY

*ARCHITECTURE MINNESOTA
*ARCHITECTURE PLUS
*ARCHIVES & HISTORY NEWS
ARIZONA PRESERVATION NEWS
ARKANSAS PRESERVATION
*ART & ANTIQUES
*ART & THE LAW
*ART HAZARDS NEWS
*ARTS & DECORATION
AVAILABLE FOR RESTORATION
AVISO

B

BAHA NEWS (Berkeley Architectural Her. Assn)
*BEEC REPORT (Built Environment Education)
*BEE (Bulletin of Environmental Education)
*BACK TO THE CITY NEWSREPORT
*BARBADOS NATIONAL TRUST NEWSLETTER
*BAY STATE HISTORICAL LEAGUE BULLETIN
*BERMUDA NATIONAL TRUST NEWSLETTER
*BETTER TIMES
*BIBLIOTEKA MUZEALNICTWA I CHRONY ZABYTKOW
BLUE PRINTS
BOSTON PRESERVATION ALLIANCE
BRACKET, THE
BRICK BULLETIN
*BRIEFS
*BROADSIDE NEWS OF HISTORIC WINDSOR
BROWNSTONER, THE
*BRUCEMORE
*BUILDING BLOCKS
*BUILDING CONSERVATION
*BUILDING DESIGN & CONSTRUCTION
*BUILDING NEWS
BUILDING RENOVATION
*BUILDING RESEARCH ESTABLISHMENT DIGEST
*BUILDING STONE MAGAZINE
*BUILDINGS
*BULLETIN OF HISTORICAL & TECHNICAL
        RESOURCES
BULLETIN OF THE KENTUCKY HISTORICAL
        SOCIETY
BULLETIN OF THE WASHINGTON METROPOLITAN
    CHAPTER OF THE AIA (See AIA BULLETIN)
BUNGALOW READER

C

*COPAR (Cooperative Psvn of Architectural
        Records, Library of Congress)
*COSCAA ACTIONS (Council of State
        Community Affairs)
CRM BULLETIN (U.S. Dept. of Interior,
        NPS Cultural Resources)

MICHIGAN HISTORIC DISTRICT NETWORK NEWS
*MICHIGAN HISTORICAL REVIEW
*MICRONESIAN PRESERVATION
*MINNESOTA PRESERVATION CONNECTION
MISSISSIPPI HISTORY NEWSLETTER
MISSOURI HERITAGE TRUST
MISSOURI PRESERVATION NEWS
MISSOURI SOURCE REVIEW
MISTLETOE LEAVES
*MONITOR
*MONTANA POST
MONTGOMERY COUNTY PRESERVATIONIST
*MONUMENTS HISTORIQUES
*MONUMENTUM
MOUNT VERNON: YESTERDAY, TODAY,
    TOMORROW
MOUNTAIN LIGHT, THE
*MUEMLEK VEDELEM
*MUNICIPAL ART SOCIETY NEWS
*MUSEOLOGIST
*MUSEUM
MUSEUM NEWS
MUSEUM OF CALIFORNIA (Oakland)

N
_____

NAHRO MONITOR (Nat'l Assn of Housing &
    Redevelopment Officials)
*NCPH NEWS (Nat'l Council on Public
    History; Boise, ID)
*NCPH NEWS (Morgantown, WV)
 NCSHPO NEWS (Nat'l Conference of State
    Historic Preservation Officers)
*NEH NEWS (Nat'l Endowment for the
    Humanities)
 NEMA NEWS (New England Museum Assn;
    formerly NEC NEWS)
*NOBSKA NEWS
*NATIONAL ALLIANCE OF PRESERVATION
    COMMISSIONS NEWS
*NATIONAL ASSOCIATION FOR OLMSTED PARKS
 NATIONAL ASSOCIATION FOR OLMSTED PARKS
    NEWSLETTER
*NATIONAL FISHERMAN
*NATIONAL HERITAGE NEWSLETTER
*NATIONAL MALL MONITOR
 NATIONAL NEIGHBORS
*NATIONAL PARK SERVICE PRESERVATION
    BRIEFS
*NATIONAL PARKS
*NATIONAL TRUST
*NATIONAL TRUST BULLETIN
*NATIONAL TRUST FOR SCOTLAND NEWS
 NATIONAL TRUST JOURNAL
 NATIONAL TRUST MAGAZINE
 NATIONAL TRUST OF AUSTRALIA NEWSLETTER
 NATIONAL TRUST QUEENSLAND JOURNAL
 NATION'S CITIES WEEKLY
*NATURE CONSERVANCY NEWS, THE
*NEIGHBORHOOD
*NEIGHBORHOOD IDEAS
*NEIGHBORHOOD PRESERVATION

NEIGHBORHOOD QUARTERLY
*NEIGHBORHOOD REINVESTMENT REPORT (formerly
    NEIGHBORHOOD & REHABILITATION REPORT)
*NEIGHBORHOOD WORKS, THE
 NETWORK
 NEW BEDFORD SOUNDINGS
 NEW JERSEY HISTORICAL COMMISSIONS NEWSLETTER
*NEW JERSEY HISTORY
*NEW MEXICO ARCHITECT
 NEW ORLEANS PRESERVATION IN PRINT (see
    PRESERVATION IN PRINT)
 NEW SOUTH CAROLINA STATE GAZETTE
 NEW YORK STATE COVERED BRIDGE SOCIETY
    NEWSLETTER
 NEW ZEALAND HISTORIC PLACES TRUST NEWSLETTER
*NEWPORT GAZETTE
*NEWS
 NEWS & VIEWS FROM THE PRESERVATION
    COMMUNITY
*NEWS FROM SCHLAES & CO.
 NEWS SERVICE
*NEWSLETTER (Commonwealth Preservation
    Council of Kentucky)
*NEWSLETTER (Louisville Historical League)
 NEWSLETTER (Municipal Art Society)
*NEWSLETTER (Preservation Society of New
    Port County)
*NEWSLETTER, THE   (San Antonio Conservation
    Society)
*NEWSLETTER (Society for the Preservation of
    Long Island Antiquities)
*NEWSLETTER (Western Interpreters Assn)
 NEWSREPORTER (see PIEDMONT ENVIRONMENTAL
    NEWSREPORTER)
*NINETEENTH CENTURY
 NORTH CAROLINA HISTORICAL REVIEW
 NORTH CAROLINA PRESERVATION (formerly
    NORTH CAROLINA PRESERVATIONIST)
*NORTHERN VIRGINIA HERITAGE
*NORTHWEST OHIO QUARTERLY
 NOTES ON VIRGINIA
*NOTIFICATIONS

O
_____

 OAK LEAVES
 OAKLAND HERITAGE ALLIANCE NEWS
*OCEANUS
*OCHRONA ZABYTKOW
 OCTAGON NEWSRELEASE, THE
 OHIO PRESERVATION
 OLD-HOUSE JOURNAL, THE
 OLD MILL NEWS
 OLD NEWS IS GOOD NEWS GAZETTE, THE
 OLD STURBRIDGE VISITOR
*OLD TIME NEW ENGLAND
 ORANGE EMPIRE RAILWAY MUSEUM GAZETTE
*OREGON DOWNTOWNS
*OUR TOWN WE CALL ST. MARY'S
 OUTLOOK IN HISTORIC CONSERVATION

VICTORIAN HOMES
VICTORIAN SOCIETY IN AMERICA (Washington
    Metro. Chapter)
VIEWPOINT
VIRGINIA PRESERVATION.

W

WASHINGTON COUNTY HISTORICAL SOCIETY
    EXPRESS
WASHINGTON INTERNATIONAL ARTS NEWSLETTER
*WASHINGTON LANDMARKS
WASHINGTON TRUST FOR HISTORIC
    PRESERVATION.
*WATER MONITOR
*WATERWAYS JOURNAL
WATERFRONT WORLD
*WEATHERVANE (See ALBANY PRESERVATION
    REPORT)
*WEEKSVILLE NEWSLETTER
WESTERN FOLKLORE
*WINTERTHUR NEWSLETTER
WISCONSIN MAGAZINE OF HISTORY
*WISCONSIN PRESERVATION (formerly NATIONAL
    REGISTER OF HISTORIC PLACES IN
    WISCONSIN NEWSLETTER)
*WOODEN BOAT
WOODROW WILSON BIRTHPLACE NEWSLETTER
*WORLD CULTURAL NEWSLETTER
WORLD INDUSTRIAL HISTORY
*WORLD MONUMENTS FUND NEWSLETTER
WRIGHT ANGLES
*WYOMING HERITAGE AND RECREATION

Y

YANKEE
*YESTERDAY'S NEWS

Z

ZONING NEWS

*No longer received by the National Trust Library.

ABANDONMENT OF PROPERTY

"Abandoned Houses Expropriation at Standstill."
New Orleans Preservation in Print. Nov. 1983.
p. 3.

ABANDONMENT OF PROPERTY

Leonhardt, Gay. "An Eye for Peeling
Paint." Landscape. Vol. 28, No. 2, 1985.
p. 23-25.

ACID RAIN

Brown, William M. "Maybe Acid Rain Isn't
the Villain." Fortune. May 28, 1984. pp. 170-
174.
Hudson Institute study finds natural origins
of acidity, not industrial. Current administration call for research may be correct.

ACID RAIN

"Acid Rain 'Sleeper'." Newsletter, World
Monuments Fund. Nov. 1985. p. 3.

ACID RAIN

"Court Orders EPA to Require States to
Reduce Acid Rain." Architecture. Sept. 1985. p.
56, 60.

ACID RAIN

D'Monte, Darryl. "Pollution Imperils the
Taj Mahal." Sierra. May/June 1984. pp. 48-9.

ACID RAIN

Matsumoto, Nancy. "Acid Rain, Pollution
Taking a Toll on Colonial Cemeteries." AGS
Newsletter, (Association for Gravestone Studies).
Vol. 9, No. 3, Summer 1985. p. 15.

ACID RAIN

Rhodes, Steven L. "Superfunding Acid Rain
Controls, Who Will Bear the Costs?" Environment.
Vol. 26, No. 6, July/August 1984. pp. 25-32.

ACID RAIN

Rodriguez, Anthony. "Acid Rain - the Silent
Threat." Boston Preservation Alliance Letter.
Vol. 6, No. 1, Apr. 1985. p. 7-8.

ACID RAIN--CANADA

Weaver, Martin. "The Rain that Eats Our
Cities". Canadian Heritage. Vol. 11, Issue
I, Feb./Mar. 1985. p. 24-31.

ADAPTIVE USE

"Architectural Landmarks." Progressive
Architecture. November 1981. Entire Issue.
PARTIAL CONTENTS: Papademetriou, Peter C.
Creme de Mint, Old U.S. Branch Mint, New Orleans--
McCue, George. Spirit from St. Louis, Wainwright
State Office Complex, St. Louis, Mo.--

ADAPTIVE USE

Baer, William C. "The Shadow
Market in Housing." Scientific American.
Vol. 255, No. 5, Nov. 1986. p. 29-35. (VF)

The addition of new housing units
through adaptive use.

ADAPTIVE USE

"The Bare Brick School".
Architectural Record. April 1975.
pp. 95-100.

ADAPTIVE USE

Baymiller, Joanna. "Sturdy Blacksmith
Shop Becomes a Children's Museum."
Architecture. Nov. 1986. p. 86-89.

Adaptive use in St. Paul, Minnesota.

ADAPTIVE USE

Beyard, Michael D. " When the Military Leaves Town." Urban Land. Vol. 46, No. 6. June 1987. pp. 6 - 9.

Conversion of an old military base into an industrial park.

ADAPTIVE USE

Building Design and Construction. October 1981. Partial Issue.

CONTENTS: Wright, Gordon. Sweetened Incentives Spark Reconstruction--Steinber, Susan. Warehouse Conjures Savings Out of Air--Miller, Michael J. Federal Building Opens its Doors to Private Offices--Keller, Karl P. Getting Class, Cutting Cost:Developers are Renovating Historic Buildings into Classy Hotels, at a Price Below What it Costs to Build New.

ADAPTIVE USE

Campbell. Robert. "Hospital Made into Apartments Flanked by Historicist Houses." Architecture. Nov. 1986. p. 75-77.

ADAPTIVE USE

Canty, Donald. "Building with a Checkered Past Renovated as a Museum." Architecture. Nov. 1986. p. 78-79.

Nineteenth century Denver finishing school adapted to Western Art Museum.

ADAPTIVE USE

Conrad, Barnaby III. "From Paris, With Love: A New Palace for Art now Shines on the Seine." Smithsonian. Vol. 17, No. 12, Mar. 1987. p. 82-95.

ADAPTIVE USE

"Corn Crib to Country Retreat." Architecture. January 1984. p. 87-89.

ADAPTIVE USE

Crosbie, Michael J. "Masterpiece Put to Suitable Use." Architecture. Nov. 1986. p. 45-47.

Adaptation of Frank Lloyd Wright's V.C. Morris Shop to an art gallery.

ADAPTIVE USE

Crosbie, Michael J. "Old Made New, New Amid Old, Etc." Architecture. November 1983. p. 48-57.

ADAPTIVE USE

"Designed for Delight." Traditional Homes. Vol. 3, No. 4, Jan. 1987, p.18-27.

A 17th-century pavilion has been restored and converted.

ADAPTIVE USE

Desson, Ken. "Improving With Age, Canada's Distilleries Reveal a Preservation Spirit." Canadian Heritage. May/June 1984. pp. 18-23.

ADAPTIVE USE

"An Elegant Station Identification." Commercial Renovation. Vol. 9, No. 2, Apr. 1987. p. 38-43.

Albany's Union Station adapted for use as corporate headquarters.

ADAPTIVE USE

"Facilitating the Arts." Design Arts. #2, 1981. pp. 59-100.

ADAPTIVE USE

Freeman, Allen. "Fine Tuning a Landmark of Adaptive Use." Architecture. Nov. 1986. p. 67-71.

San Francisco's Ghirardelli Square originally adapted from a chocolate factory has been modernized.

ADAPTIVE USE

Harra, Marilyn. "Conversion of obsolete buildings prove profitable". Challenge. January 1981. p. 4-10.

ADAPTIVE USE

"Housing, A Strong Demand for High-Density Apartments is a Result of Cost and Cultural Forces." Architectural Record. September 1977. pp. 111-126.

ADAPTIVE USE

Johnson, Robert B. "Historic Hostels/ Adaptive Use." 11593, Oct. 1979. pp. 1; 4-6.

ADAPTIVE USE

Ketchum, Morris. "Recycling and Restoring Landmarks: An Architectural Challenge and Opportunity." AIA Journal. September 1975. pp. 31-39.

ADAPTIVE USE

King, Brent. " The Design/Build Way." Building Renovation. Vol. 4, No. 3. May/June 1987. pp. 41 - 42
Conversion of a Victorian home in Halifax, Canada, into apartments.

ADAPTIVE USE

Knight, Carleton. "Housing Wrought from Other Building Types." Architecture. October 1983. pp. 66-77.

ADAPTIVE USE

Maupin, Florence M. "Les Halles des Beoufs : industrial jewel." Place. Vol. 6, No. 4, July/August 1986. p. 18-19.

A Parisian cattle market built in 1867 converted to an arts center.

ADAPTIVE USE

McKenna, Barrie. "Abused Home Survives Conversion." Building Renovation. Vol. 3, No. 5, Oct./Nov. 1986. p. 14. (VF)

Conversion of an abandoned Toronto mansion into the headquarters for a non-profit corporation.

ADAPTIVE USE

Melnick, Scott. "New Housing Projects Emerge from Abandoned Buildings." Building Design & Construction. Vol. 28, No. 2, Feb. 1987. p. 58-62.

ADAPTIVE USE

Miller, Hugh C. "Adaptive Use of Cultural Resources." Trends. Vol. 19, #2, 1982. pp. 18-22.

ADAPTIVE USE

Moore, Arthur Cotton. "Adaptive Abuse, Examining Some Perils (and to) the Preservation Movement." AIA Journal. Aug. 1979. pp. 58-66.

ADAPTIVE USE

"Multi-Use Convention Center in Adapted Hotel." The Rambler. Vol. 14, No. 1, Spr. 1987. p. 9.

1892 Americus, GA, Hotel adapted to convention center.

ADAPTIVE USE

"Museums and Adaptive Use". Museum News. September 1980. Entire issue.

ADAPTIVE USE

"New Life from Old Buildings." Architecture Minnesota. August/September 1981. pp. 44-51.

ADAPTIVE USE

"19th Century Brewery Will Be High-Tech Business Incubator." Urban Conservation Report. Vol. 10, No. 7, July 9, 1986. p. 3.

ADAPTIVE USE

"Preservation Is Prime Factor: 3 Large-scale Minneapolis Development Projects." Preservation Matters. Vol. 2, No. 11, Nov. 1986. p. 4.

ADAPTIVE USE

"Private-Public Partnership Restores Tifton Landmark." The Rambler. Vol. 14, No. 1, Spr. 1987. p. 10.

Conversion of hotel to civic center.

ADAPTIVE USE

"Radical Interior Changes Suggest New Directions for Re-use." Architectural Record. September 1980. p. 92-97.

ADAPTIVE USE

"Recycling: Another Route to More Productive Buildings." Architectural Record. December 1975. pp. 96-101.

ADAPTIVE USE

"Recycling Architectural Masterpieces- and Other Buildings Not So Great." Architectural Record. August 1977. pp. 81-92.

ADAPTIVE USE

"Remodeling and reuse". Progressive Architecture. November 1980. Entire issue.

ADAPTIVE USE

"Renovated Buildings find New Purpose." Architectural Record. June 1982. pp. 81-97.

INCLUDES: Six New Condominiums Replace a Paper Mill-- Classrooms for the Blind Occupy a Renovated Stable-- A Store Recycled as Offices Unites New and Old Downtowns.

ADAPTIVE USE

"Revitalization Brewing in Norristown, PA." Downtown Idea Exchange. Vol. 33, No. 23. Dec. 1, 1986. pp. 1-2.

ADAPTIVE USE

"Round Table: The Special Design and Specification Problems in Rehabilitation and Re-Use." Architectural Record. December 1982. pp. 28-35.

ADAPTIVE USE

Rutherford, Jindra. "From convent to co-op: historic site modifies usage." Housing Ontario. Jan./Feb. 1981. pp. 8-10.

ADAPTIVE USE

"Shopping Around Historic Structures." Yankee. March 1984. pp. 46-49, 60.

ADAPTIVE USE

Schreiner, Phil. "Quonsets Qualify As Office Rehab." Building Design & Construction. Vol. 27, No. 10, Oct. 1986. p. 94-95.

A Quonset bus terminal building converted to offices.

ADAPTIVE USE

"Spirited Hydro-Electric Revival." Architecture. January 1984. pp. 96-7.

ADAPTIVE USE

Steltzer, Alice C. " Springfield Recycles Motorcycle Block." Preservation News. Mar. 1987 p. 1, 13.

ADAPTIVE USE

"Sydney Restoration a Private Affair."
Public Innovation Abroad. Vol. 11, No. 2,
Feb. 1987. p. 2.
Historic Queen Victoria Building, originally
a market then offices, has been converted to a
shopping mall.

ADAPTIVE USE

"Trolley Barn Adapted for Rentals."
The Rambler. Vol. 14, No. 1, Spr. 1987. p. 10.

ADAPTIVE USE

"Urban Areas Can Turn Abandoned Rails Into
Public Trails." Urban Outlook. Vol. 9, No. 4.
Feb. 30 (sic), 1987. pp. 3-4.

ADAPTIVE USE--CASE STUDIES

Garrett, Billy. "Adaptive Use: The Superintendent's
Residence at Grand Canyon National Park," CRM Bulletin,
Vol. 17, No. 4, December 1984, pp. 6-7.

ADAPTIVE USE--CASE STUDIES

"In the Limelight: the Man Who Turns Churches
Into Discos." Business Week. Aug. 5, 1985. p.
68.

ADAPTIVE USE--CASE STUDIES

Keller, Karl. "How cold storage converted
to apartments." Building Design and Construction.
Feb. 1981. pp. 58-59.

ADAPTIVE USE--CASE STUDIES

Rubenstein, Hannah. "Preservation in
Perspective." HAC News. May-June 1981.
pp. 1-3.

CONTENTS: Billings Forge (factory complex)
The Linden (apartment building)

ADAPTIVE USE--CASE STUDIES

"Saving a Streamlined Cinema." "A Federal
Revival," and "The Grandeur That Was Harrisburg."
Architectural Record. June 1984. pp. 75-77.

Cinema in Klamath Falls, Oregon, Courthouse in East Cambridge, Mass. and Harrisburg
Capitol Complex.

ADAPTIVE USE--CASE STUDIES

Smith, Marcia Axtmann. "How Adaptive Use
Really Works: Renewed Museums Revisited." Museum
News. Vol. 63, No. 4, Apr. 1985. p. 12-29.

A planning checklist for adaptive use included as are new case studies.

ADAPTIVE USE--CASE STUDIES

"Special Modernization Issue." Buildings.
June 1981. Entire Issue.
CONTENTS: 400 North State Street, Chicago--
Landmark Center, Dallas--Baynard House, Wilming-
ton--Lowell Sun Building, Lowell--Wayland Building,
Providence--Tips on Modernization.

ADAPTIVE USE--CASE STUDIES--U.S.--MASSACHUSETTS--
BOSTON

"FNMA Breaks Financing Log-Jam in Boston
Rehab Project." Urban Conservation Report.
Vol. 5, No. 10. June 21, 1984. p. 3.

Lincoln Wharf Power Station rehab for
housing.

ADAPTIVE USE--CASE STUDIES--U.S.--MINNESOTA--
DULUTH--BREWERY

"Fitger's Brews Duluth Revitalization."
Minnesota Preservation Connection. April-May
1984. p. 3.

Brewery converted to housing.

ADAPTIVE USE--CASE STUDIES--WEST VIRGINIA--
INDUSTRIAL SITE

"UDAG Proves Difference Between Demolition
and Redevelopment." Community Development
Digest. No. 84-14. July 24, 1984. p. 11.

ADAPTIVE USE-- CHURCHES

"Once a Church: The Converted Long Island
Residence of Artist Philip Read." Interior
Design. August 1981. pp. 234-239.

ADAPTIVE USE --COMMERCIAL BUILDINGS

"The Bourse." National Mall Monitor.
March/April 1982. p. 36.

ADAPTIVE USE--COMMERCIAL BUILDINGS

Rubenstein, Hannah. "Reworking the Workplace." HAC News. July-August, 1981. p. 1.

ADAPTIVE USE--DEVELOPERS

Andrews, Jean. "The 1981 Top 50."
National Mall Monitor. November/December
1981. pp. 25-33.

ADAPTIVE USE--DEVELOPERS

Bidwell, Dennis. "Should we Work with a
Professional Developer?" Alliance Letter.
July-August 1982. pp. 10-11.

ADAPTIVE USE--DEVELOPERS

"Foundations as Developers? Editorial:
Private/Public Partnerships." Urban Design
International. March/April 1982. p. 9.

ADAPTIVE USE--DEVELOPERS

"He Digs Downtown: For Master Planner
James Rouse, Urban Life is a Festival." Time,
August 24, 1981. pp. 42-53.

ADAPTIVE USE--DEVELOPERS

Rosenberg, William G. "Downtown Adaptive
Reuse Project Signals New Public/Private
Partnership." Journal of Housing. August-
September, 1981. pp. 437-443.

ADAPTIVE USE--DEVELOPERS

"Roundtable on Rouse." Progressive
Architecture. July 1981. pp. 100-106.

ADAPTIVE USE--DEVELOPERS

"Urban Centers: NMM's Fourth Annual
Downtown Issue." National Mall Monitor.
September/October 1981. Vol. 11, No. 4.,
Partial Issue.
PARTIAL CONTENTS: Harborplace--Foxworthy, Randy.
Ingenuity is the Key to Financing Urban Centers--
Historic Preservation Integrates an Urban Mixed-
Use Complex--Wolf, Larry. The Magic Mix: Urban
Center Leasing is a Specialty Inself.--Treister,
Kenneth. Historical Perspective Invaluable in
Planning Rebirth of Lively Cities.

ADAPTIVE USE--DWELLINGS

"Congregate Living: A New Type of Elderly
Housing on Cape Cod Shows How Architectural Research
Can Enter the Realm of the Humane." Progressive
Architecture. August 1981. pp. 64-68.

ADAPTIVE USE--DWELLINGS

Giovannini, Joseph. "Los Angeles, American
Film Institute West Finds New Home." Federal
Design Matters. Fall 1981. p. 9.

ADAPTIVE USE--DWELLINGS

"The Mansion on Turtle Creek." Interior
Design. January 1982. pp. 218-233.

ADAPTIVE USE--ECONOMIC ASPECTS

"Atrium unlocks profit potential in
triad of historic buildings." Building
Design and Construction. March 1981.
p. 58-63.

ADAPTIVE USE--ECONOMIC ASPECTS

Breckenfield, Gurney. "The Rouse Show
Goes National." Fortune. July 27, 1981.
pp. 49-55.

ADAPTIVE USE--EUROPE

Council of Europe, A Future for Our Past. No. 22 - 1984, Entire Issue. Contains articles on adaptive use of churches, industrial buildings, farmhouses. 25 pp. Annual.

ADAPTIVE USE--INDUSTRIAL BUILDINGS

Levy, Francis. "The Granary; Imaginative Plan for Living in Philadelphia." Architectural Digest. Oct. 1979. pp. 135-138.

ADAPTIVE USE--INDUSTRIAL BUILDINGS

Rubenstein, Hannah. "Reworking the Workplace." HAC News. July-August, 1981. p. 1.

ADAPTIVE USE--INDUSTRIAL BUILDINGS

Schmertz, Mildred F. "An Old Brewery Born Again as the San Antonio Museum of Art." Architectural Record. June 1981. pp. 92-99.

ADAPTIVE USE--OFFICE BUILDINGS

McLaughlin, Herbert. "Some tips on evaluating renovation projects for office use." Architectural Record. Mar. 1979. pp. 73-75.

ADAPTIVE USE--PUBLIC BUILDINGS

Hamilton, Jeri. "Gainesville, Former Federal Building REstored and Recycled as Hippodrome Theater." Federal Design Matters. Fall 1981. p. 13.

ADAPTIVE USE--RAILROAD STATIONS

Jones, Larry. "Denver and Rio Grande Depot." Utah Preservation/Restoration. Vol. III, 1981. pp. 68-69.

ADAPTIVE USE--SPAIN

"Shipyard is Now Maritime Museum." Public Innovation Abroad. Vol. 11, No. 1, Jan. 1987. p. 7.

Spain's Royal Shipyards in Barcelona have been converted to a maritime museum.

ADAPTIVE USE--THEATERS

"An Art Deco Movie House of 1931 Transformed into a multi-use theater for the performing arts : The Paramount Arts Centre in Aurora, Illinois by Elbasani Logan Severin Freeman." Architectural Record, April 1979. pp. 130-133.

ADAPTIVE USE--THEATERS

Izenour, George C. "A Classic Revival Former College Chapel Provides 'Found Space' for a new theater, as does a once non-descript fifty-two-year-old auditorium: The Longstreet Theater, Columbia, South Carolina by W.S. Dowis and the Mayor Bob Carr Auditorium by Duer and Price." Architectural Record. Apr. 1979. pp. 134-140.

ADAPTIVE USE--THEATERS

"The New Madison Civic Center by Hardy Holzman Pfeiffer Associates." Architectural Record, July 1980. pp. 77-87.

ADAPTIVE USE--U.S.--CALIFORNIA--FRESNO

"Printing Plant Becomes A Club." Architecture. February 1984. pp. 50-53.

ADAPTIVE USE--U.S.--HAWAII

"CJS Group Architects: Enhancing the Old with New Design." Historic Hawai'i. Vol. 13, No. 3, Mar. 1987. p. 6.

ADAPTIVE USE--U.S.--HAWAII

Leineweber, Steven. "Historic Bank Space now Home to Slick Honolulu Magazine." Historic Hawai'i. Vol. 13, No. 3, Mar. 1987. p. 5.

ADAPTIVE USE--U.S.--HAWAII

    Peacock, Nancy. "Nature Conservancy Offices Redesigned." Historic Hawai'i. Vol. 13, No. 3, Mar. 1987. p. 7.

ADAPTIVE USE--U.S.--HAWAII

    "Working With the Past: Creative Offices through Adaptive Use." Historic Hawai'i. Vol. 13, No. 3, Mar. 1987. p. 4-8.

ADAPTIVE USE--U.S.--ILLINOIS--CHICAGO

    Marlin, William. "Architects spur rebirth of Chicago's historic Printing House Row." Architectural Record. Mar. 1980. pp. 89-96.

ADAPTIVE USE--U.S.--MARYLAND--BALTIMORE

    "From City College to Chesapeake Commons." The Phoenix. Vol. 6, No. 1, Fall 1985. p. 4-5.

ADAPTIVE USE--U.S.--MASSACHUSETTS--BOSTON

    Fisher, Thomas. "Graham Gund Associates Architect as Developer." Progressive Architecture. July 1985. p. 105-110.

    Revitalization of Bulfinch Square discussed.

ADAPTIVE USE--U.S.--MINNESOTA--ST. PAUL

    King, Shannon. "New Traffic for a Grand Station." Architecture Minnesota. Vol. 10, No. 2, March/April 1984. pp. 26-31.

ADAPTIVE USE--U.S.--OHIO--COLUMBUS

    "Sprucing Up the Old Neighborhood." Architectural Record. October 1984. p. 119.

    Pythian theater and an elementary school.

ADOBE

    "Adobe Conservation Research." The Getty Conservation Institute Newsletter. Vol. 2, No. 2, Spring 1987. p. 1-2.

Vertical File

ADOBE

    National Trust for Historic Preservation. The Preservation of Adobe Buildings: an Annotated Bibliography. Washington, D.C. Nov. 1986. 7p. (VF)

ADOBE HOUSES--CONSERVATION AND RESTORATION

    "All about Adobe." The Old-House Journal. December 1982. Front page.

ADOBE HOUSES--CONSERVATION AND RESTORATION

    Lewis, Billy C. "Architect & Adobe: Gil Sanchez has made a career out of restoring historic adobe buildings. His current project - a mission in California - is the largest yet." Americana. Vol. 12, No. 6, Jan./Feb. 1985. p. 43-49.

AERIAL PHOTOGRAPHY IN ARCHEOLOGY

    Potter, Stephen R., Ph.D. "Low Budget and Low Altitudes: Aerial Photography and Archeological Survey in Tidewater Virginia." NPS, CRM Bulletin. Vol. 7, No. 1, April 1984. pp. 3, 6-7.

AESTHETICS

    "Visual Resources". Environmental Comment. June 1980 (entire issue).

AESTHETICS

    Weingarden, Lauren. "Aesthetics Politicized: William Morris to the Bauhaus." Journal of Architectural Education. Vol. 38, No. 3, Spring 1985. p. 8-13.

AIR-CONDITIONING

Friedman, Robert. "The Air-Conditioned Century." American Heritage. Vol. 35, No. 5, August/September 1984. pp. 20-32.

AIR--POLLUTION

Maruca, Mary V. "Acid Rain: The Unknown Ingredient." Trends. Vol. 20, No. 2, 1983. pp. 32-33.

AIR--POLLUTION

Scholle, Stephen R. "Acid Desposition and the Materials Damage Question." Environment. Vol. 25, No. 8. October 1983. pp. 25-32.

AIR RAID SHELTERS--ADAPTIVE USE

"Aid Raid Shelters to Storage Vaults." Public Innovation Abroad. Vol. 10, No. 7, July 1986. p. 2.

AIRSPACE (LAW)

Schnidman, Frank. "Selling Air Rights Over Public Property." Urban Land. November 1981. pp. 3-9.

ALLEYS

Borchert, James. "Alley Landscapes of Washington." Landscape. No. 3, 1979. pp. 3-10.

ALMANACS

Musgrove, Stephen W. "The Almanac: Neglected Witness of the American Experience." SEMC Journal, November 1979. pp. 23-30.

AMERICAN INSTITUTE OF ARCHITECTS

AIA JOURNAL, Mid-August 1981. Entire Issue.

CONTENTS: The AIA Archives--The Basic Workings of the Institute--Contacts for Help at AIA--Glossary of Acronyms and Abbreviations--Directory of AIA Resources (Yellow Pages)--Materials Available Through Other Organizations--Books, Etc., toOrder Th: Through the Institute--Sources for AIA Contracts and Forms--Resources from Suppliers and Manufacturers.

AMERICAN INSTITUTE OF ARCHITECTS

"The Directory of AIA Resources." AIA Journal. April 1982. pp. 82-97.

AMUSEMENT PARKS

Journal of Popular Culture. Summer 1981. Partial Issue.

CONTENTS: King, Margaret j. The New American Muse: Notes on the Amusement/Theme Park--Nye, Russel B. Eight Ways of Looking at an Amusement Park--O'Brien, George M. The Parks of Vienna--Hildebrandt, Hugo John. Cedar Point: A Park in Progress--Neil, J. Meridith. The Roller Coaster: Architectural Symbol and Sign--King, Margaret J.

Journal of Popular Culture.continued

Disneyland and Walt Disney World: Traditional Values in Futuristic Form--Francaviglia, Richard V. Main Street U.S.A.: A Comparison/Contrast of Streetscapes in Disneyland and Walt Disney World--Johnson, David M. Disney World as Structure and Symbol: Re-Creation of the American Experience --Mechling, Elizabeth Walker and Jay. The Sale of Two Cities: A Semiotic with Marriott's Great America.

AMUSEMENT PARKS

Margolies, John. "Fanciful Fairways." Americana. Vol. 15, No. 2, May/June 1987. p. 80-81.

Miniature golf courses.

AMUSEMENT PARKS

Platania, Joseph. "The Sign of the Happy Clown: Looking back at Camden." Goldenseal. Vol. 13, No. 2. Summer 1987. pp. 9 - 18. Camden Park in Camden OH.

AMUSEMENT PARKS

Rinne, Katherine. "Disneyland: Urban Design in Southern California." Los Angeles Conservancy. Vol. 9, No. 3, May/June, 1987. p. 4-5

AMUSEMENT PARKS

Weaver, Susan M. "Rock Springs Park, a Panhandle Playground." Goldenseal. Vol. 11, No. 4, Winter 1985. p. 22-29.

AMUSEMENT PARKS--U.S.--CALIFORNIA

Burns, Jim and Peter Brand. "Building by the Sea: California." Architecture. June 1985. p. 76-85.

AMUSEMENT PARKS--U.S.--ILLINOIS--ROCK ISLAND

Carvey, Elizabeth. "Rock Island's Turn-of-the-Century Amusement Park". Historic Illinois. Vol. 7, No. 5, Feb. 1985. p. 1-5, 13.

History of now demolished "end of the (streetcar) line" amusement park west of Chicago detailed.

ANTIQUES

Lipson, Karin. "What is an Antique?" SEMC Journal. Nov. 1979. pp. 37-45.

ANTIQUES--COLLECTORS AND COLLECTING

Antiques World. October 1980.

ANTIQUES--COLLECTORS AND COLLECTING

Eyman, Scott. "Life of Americana's collectors-in-chief is a bowl of treasures." Smithsonian. November 1980. p.74-81.

APARTMENT HOUSES

Alpern, Andrew. "In the Manor Housed." Metropolis. March 1982. pp. 11-15.

APARTMENT HOUSES

Leopold, Allison Kyle. "Victorian Apartment Living." Victorian Homes. Vol. 6, No. 3. Summer 1987. pp. 14-19; 82-83.

APARTMENT HOUSES--U.S.--ILLINOIS--CHICAGO

Westfall, Carroll William. "The Golden Age of Chicago Apartments." Inland Architect. Nov. 1980. pp. 18-26.

APARTMENT HOUSES--U.S.--ILLINOIS--EVANSTON

McWilliams, Mary B. and Susan S. Benjamin. "Evanston's Suburban Apartment Buildings". Historic Illinois. Vol. 7, No. 5., Feb. 1985. p. 8-11.

APARTMENT HOUSES--U.S.--NEW YORK--BUFFALO

Kowski, Francis R. "Architectural History: the Red Jacket Building." Preservation Report. Vol. 7, No. 5. Sept./Oct. 1985. p. 11; 13.

APARTMENT HOUSES--U.S.--NEW YORK--NEW YORK CITY

Goldberger, Paul. "The Dakota, New York City." Antiques. Vol. CXXVI, No. 4, October 1984. pp. 842-852.

APARTMENTS--U.S.--NEW YORK STATE--NEW YORK CITY

Ruttenbaum, Steven. "Visible City." Metropolis. Jan./Feb. 1986, p. 47-49, 51.

The Beresford and San Remo luxury apartment buildings, designed by Emory Roth and constructed between 1928-30, are discussed.

AQUEDUCTS--U.S.--NEW YORK--FORT HUNTER

Ryan, J. Thomas. "Preservation of the Schoharie Creek Aqueduct". APT Bulletin XII, no. 2, p. 80-93.

ARCADES--U.S.--OHIO--SPRINGFIELD

"Hopeton Earthworks, Springfield Arcade Threatened." Ohio Preservation. Vol. 6, No. 1, Jan. 1986. p. 1.

APARTMENT HOUSES--U.S.--WASHINGTON, D.C.

"Apartment Building Survey to Aid Preservation and Development." DC Preservation League. Dec. 1985. p. 1-2.

ARCHAEOLOGY

"Archeology Round Up." Place. Vol. 4, No. 9, October 1984. p. 11.

ARCHAEOLOGY

"Artifacts Found in Downtown Construction Site." Albany Preservation Report. Vol. 5, No. 4. Spring 1986. p. 6.
Parts of a seventeenth century building and some household items found.

ARCHAEOLOGY

Berke, Debra. "Tangible Evidence of Intangible Resources: Ethnographic Objects in the National Park Service." NPS, CRM Bulletin. Vol. 7, No. 2, July 1984. pp. 12-16, 20.

ARCHAEOLOGY

Blades, Brooke; David Orr and Douglas Campana. "Historic Archeology and the Decorative Arts." CRM Bulletin. Vol. 8, No. 3 & 4, June/Aug. 1985. p. 14-15, 18.

ARCHAEOLOGY

Council of Europe. "The Heritage and Archaeology." A Future for Our Past. No. 23, 1984. Entire Issue. 29 p.

APARTMENT HOUSES--U.S.--NEW YORK--NEW YORK CITY

Epstein, Amy Kallman. "Multifamily Dwellings and the Search for Respectability: Origins of the New York Apartment House." Urbanism Past & Present. Summer 1980. p.29-39.

APARTMENT HOUSES--U.S.--NEW YORK--NEW YORK CITY

Fitch, James Marston. "Renovation of Alwyn Court, New York City: Restoring the Facades and Improving Public Spaces." Technology and Conservation. Summer 1980. pp. 24-27.

ARCHAEOLOGY

De Neergard, Margrethe. "Rescue Archaeology on the Thames." Archaeology. Vol. 40, No. 3, May/June 1987. p. 56-57.

Developers and Department of Urban Archaeology (London) are cooperating on the largest urban archaeological rescue operation.

ARCHAEOLOGY

"First U.S. Black Settlement said found by Archaeologists." Headquarters Heliogram. No. 184. Apr. - May 1987. p. 9.

ARCHAEOLOGY

Friedman, Robert. "Digging up the U.S." American Heritage. August/September 1983. pp. 34-47.

ARCHAEOLOGY

Gardiner, M.J. "Bringing an Island's Past Back to Life." Historic Places in New Zealand. No. 13, June 1986. p. 19-20.

Reconstruction of early Maori life through archaeological digs on Urupukapuka Island.

ARCHAEOLOGY

Gettys, Marshall. "Euro-American Historical Archaeology in Oklahoma." The Chronicles of Oklahoma. Winter 1981-82. pp. 448-464.

ARCHAEOLOGY

      Gramly, Richard Michael. "Eleven Thousand Years in Maine." Archaeology. November/ December 1981. pp. 32-39.

ARCHAEOLOGY

    "Highway Salvage Goldmine." Columns. Vol. 8, No. 1. Feb./Mar. 1987. pp. 4-6.
    Bachmann Site in Wisconsin is yielding important Indian artifacts.

ARCHAEOLOGY

    Hume, Ivor Noel. "Martin's Hundred: the Search Continues." Colonial Williamsburg. Vol. 8, No. 1, Autumn 1985. p. 5-14, 23.

ARCHAEOLOGY

    Hume, Ivor Noel. "Treasures from the Thames." Colonial Williamsburg. Vol. 9, No. 4. Summer 1987. pp. 35 - 42.
    Archaeological relics recovered from the shore of the Thames river in London.

ARCHAEOLOGY

    "Important Archaeological Finds at Jordan's Point." Tidings. Vol. 7, No. 3, Fall 1986. p. 8.

    17th century buildings located by archaeologist at Jordan's Point, VA.

ARCHAEOLOGY

    Interagency Resources Division, National Park Service. "Nomination of Archeological Propeties: Definition of National Register Boundaries for Archeological Properties." National Register of Historic Places Bulletin 12. Sept. 1985. 26 p.

ARCHAEOLOGY

    "Issues in Urban Archeology." Livability Digest. Winter 1982-83. Entire Issue.

    CONTENTS: Salvage Archeology and New Development--Community Image and Involvement-- Resource Preservation and Interpretation-- Learning from Abroad.

ARCHAEOLOGY

    King, Thomas F. "Preservation and Rescue; Challenges and Controversies in the Protection of Archaeological Resources." Journal of Field Archaeology. Spring 1979. pp. 108-111.

ARCHAEOLOGY

    Kwapil, Bryan W. "Coping With a Shady Past: Wickliffe Mounds Changes its Image from Pothunter's Dream to Viable Research Center." History News. Vol.42, No. 2, Mar./Apr. 1987. p. 13-17.

ARCHAEOLOGY

"Las Imagines Emerging." Preservation New Mexico. Vol. 4, No. 1, Spring 1987. p. 1.

Prehistoric rock art in Albuquerque has been placed on the National Register, and a National Monument is being considered.

ARCHAEOLOGY

Lees, Bill. "Highway Archaeology Salvage Program Investigates Great Bend Aspect Site." Kansas Preservation, Mar./Apr. 1987, Vol. 9, No. 3. p. 6-8.

ARCHAEOLOGY

Lovibund, David. "The Past in Danger." Country Life. Vol. 181, No. 23. June 4, 1987. p. 264.
Agriculture is damaging Britain's archaeological remains.

ARCHAEOLOGY

Mansberber, Floyd. "Relocation of Pioneer Bourbonnais Structure Prompts Archaeology Study." Historic Illinois. Vol. 9, No. 5, Feb. 1987. p. 1-5, 7.

ARCHAEOLOGY

McNulty, Deirdre. "Discovery Among the Ruins, The National Parks Reveal America's Ancient Peoples." National Parks. Vol. 58, No. 9-10. Sep./Oct. 1984. p. 17.

ARCHAEOLOGY

Michel, Mark. "A Race Against Time." Land Trusts' Exchange. Vol. 5, No. 2, Fall 1986. p. 1, 12-13, 16.

The work of the Archaeological Conservancy, the only land trust organization dedicated solely to the preservation of archaeologic sites in the U.S.

ARCHAEOLOGY

Nurse, Keith. "Candid Revelations." Country Life. Vol. 181, No. 33. Aug. 13, 1987. p. 77.
Excavation at Whithorn, Scotland, is revealing important information on Scotland's early Christian period, 850-1125.

ARCHAEOLOGY

"Prehistoric Village Saved." California Office of Historic Preservation Newsletter. Vol. 2, No.1, Feb. 1987, p. 3.

1400-year old cemetery discovered in Union City, CA.

ARCHAEOLOGY

Riess, Warren and Sheli O. Smith. "The Ship That Built a City." Sea History. No. 35, Spring 1985. p. 7-8.

The story of the excavation and recordation of the Ronson Ship discovered in January 1982 in the Wall Street Financial District is detailed.

ARCHAEOLOGY

Salwen, Bert. "Archaeology: Partnership in Historic Preservation." Journal of Field Archaeology, Fall 1979. pp. 365-366.

ARCHAEOLOGY

"SCA To Identify Commercial Archeology Sites for HABS/HAER." SCA News Journal. Vol 3, No. 1, Spring 1986. p. 1.

ARCHAEOLOGY

"17th Century Fort Believed Found in Pensicola Dig." Headquarters Heliogram. No. 183, Feb./Mar. 1987. p. 5.

ARCHAEOLOGY

Simon, Brona. "Important Site in Plymouth Protected from Development Impacts." Massachusetts Historical Commission Newsletter. Vol. 13, No. 1, Feb. 1987. p. 8.

Vertical File

ARCHAEOLOGY

Singleton, Theresa A. "Buried Treasure." American Visions. Vol. 1, No. 2, March/April 1986. p. 35-39. (VF)

Digs along the SouthCarolina and Georgia coasts reveal remains of slave dwellings and artifacts.

ARCHAEOLOGY

Wildensen, Leslie E. "Archaeology Leads to Frontiers of Knowledge." Colorado Heritage News. July 1985. p. 5, 7.

ARCHAEOLOGY--CASE STUDIES

"Cape Cod National Seashore Archeological Survey". CRM Bulletin. Vol. 8, No. 1, Feb. 1985. p. 12.

ARCHAEOLOGY--CASE STUDIES

Ferguson, T.J. "The Zuni Archeology Program: Cultural Resources Management at the Pueblo of Zuni". CRM Bulletin. December 1980. p.8-9.

ARCHAEOLOGY--CASE STUDIES

Harpster, James D. "Archeologists Unearthing Custer Battle Secrets." Council on America's Military Past, Headquarters Heliogram. No. 161, April-May 1984. p. 4.

ARCHAEOLOGY--CASE STUDIES

Martin, William and Bruce Hawkins. "Historic Archaeology: Understanding the Past through Pick and Shovel." Utah Preservation/Restoration. Vol. 3, 1981. pp. 64-65.

ARCHAEOLOGY--CASE STUDIES

Robinson, Paul. "Archaeology: Cove Lands Yield New Data." PPS News, Newsletter of the Providence Preservation Society. Vol. XXII, No. 3. p. 11.

ARCHAEOLOGY--CASE STUDIES

Thiessen, Thomas D. "Knife River Indian Villages Archeological Inventory: A Useful Management Tool." NPS, CRM Bulletin. Vol. 7, No. 1, Apr. 1984. pp. 8-9.

ARCHAEOLOGY--CASE STUDIES--U.S.--GEORGIA

Crook, Morgan R. Jr. "Evolving Community Organization on the Georgia Coast." Journal of Field Archaeology. Vol. 11, No. 3, Fall 1984. pp. 247-265.

ARCHAEOLOGY--CASE STUDIES--U.S.--GEORGIA-- MCINTOSH COUNTY

"Julianton Plantation Excavated." The Rambler, Newsletter of the Georgia Trust for Historic Preservation, Inc. Vol. 11, No. 4, Fall 1984. p. 10.

ARCHAEOLOGY--CASE STUDIES--U.S.--KANSAS

"Excavations at the Bell Site Provide New Information from South-Central Kansas." Kansas Preservation. Vol. VI, No. 6, September-October 1984. pp. 1-2.

ARCHAEOLOGY--CASE STUDIES--U.S.--NEVADA

Thomas, David H. "Three Generations of Archaeology at Hidden Cave, Nevada." Archaeology. Vol. 37, No. 5, September/October 1984. pp. 40-47.

ARCHAEOLOGY--CASE STUDIES--U.S.--NEW YORK

Feister, Lois M. "Material Culture of the British Soldier at 'His Majesty's Fort of Crown Point' on Lake Champlain, 1759-1783." Journal of Field Archaeology. Vol. 11, No. 2. Summer 1984. pp. 123-132.

ARCHAEOLOGY--CASE STUDIES--U.S.--OHIO

White, John R. "Unearthing Quakertown." Archaeology, Vol. 38, No. 1, Jan./Feb. 1985, p. 26-31.

ARCHAEOLOGY--CASE STUDIES--U.S.--TENNESSEE-- JACKSON

Fielder, Nick. "Pinson Mounds Archaeological Work." Tennessee Heritage Alliance, Network. Summer 1984. No. 2. pp. 8-9.

ARCHAEOLOGY--CASE STUDIES--U.S.--VIRGINIA

"Archaeology at Mount Vernon." Notes on Virginia. No. 25, Fall 1984. p. 24.

ARCHAEOLOGY--CASE STUDIES--U.S.--VIRGINIA

"The Chesapeake Indians and Their Predecessors: Recent Excavations at Great Neck." Notes on Virginia. No. 24, Spring 1984. pp. 36-39.

ARCHAEOLOGY--CASE STUDIES--U.S.--VIRGINIA

Outlaw, Alain C. "Virginia's Vanishing Past." Notes on Virginia. No. 26, Spring 1985. p. 24-27.

ARCHAEOLOGY--CASE STUDIES--U.S.--VIRGINIA

"Revelations at Gloucester Point." Notes on Virginia. No. 25, Fall 1984. pp. 25-29.

ARCHAEOLOGY--FRANCE--PARIS

Velay, Phillippe et al. "The Archaeology of Early Paris." Archaeology. Vol. 38, No. 6. Nov./Dec. 1985. p. 26-32.

ARCHAEOLOGY--ISRAEL--JERUSALEM

Seelig, Michael and Julie. "Main Street, Jerusalem." Architectural Record. May 1985. p. 118-123.

Restoration of the Jewish Quarter in the Old City of Jerusalem discussed.

ARCHAEOLOGY--LAW AND LEGISLATION

King, Thomas F. "The United States has a Program to Save its Heritage, but How Effective is It?" Early Man. Summer 1981. pp. 5-12.

ARCHAEOLOGY--LAW AND LEGISLATION

Warren, Scott S. "Crackdown on Shard Thieves." National Parks. Vol. 58, No. 9-10, Sept./Oct. 1984. pp. 12-16.

ARCHAEOLOGY--LAW AND LEGISLATION--U.S.--KANSAS

Stein, Martin. "Review and Compliance Activities Link the Study of Archaeology to the Future." Kansas Preservation. Vol. 8, No. 2. Jan./Feb. 1986. pp. 3-4.

ARCHEOLOGY--LAW AND LEGISLATION--U.S.--MASSACHUSETTS

"Massachusetts Archaeological Landmarks: A New Program to Protect Sites", Massachusetts Historical Commission Newsletter, Vol. 10, No. 4, Fall 1984, pp. 6-7.

ARCHAEOLOGY--METHODOLOGY

Gero, Joan and Jim Mazzullo. "Analysis of Artifact Shape Using Fourier Series in Closed Forms." Journal of Field Archaeology. Vol 11, No. 3, Fall 1984. pp. 315-323.

ARCHAEOLOGY--METHODOLOGY

Light, John D. "The Archeological Investigation of Blacksmith Shops." IA, The Journal of the Society for Industrial Archeology. Vol. 10, No. 1, 1984. pp. 55-68.

ARCHAEOLOGY--METHODOLOGY

Pavlish, L.A. and P.W. Alcock. "The Case of the Itinerant Bone: The Role of Sedimentalogical and Geochemical Evidence." Journal of Field Archaeology. Vol. 11, No. 3, Fall 1984. pp. 323-331.

ARCHAEOLOGY--METHODOLOGY

Priess, Peter J. "Archeology and Restoration, a Question of Responsibilities." Bulletin, APT. Vol. 17, No. 3&4, 1985. p. 56-60.

ARCHAEOLOGY--METHODOLOGY

Read, Dwight W. "Sampling Procedures for Regional Surveys: a Problem of Representativeness and Effectiveness." Journal of Field Archaeology. Vol. 13, No. 4, Winter 1986. p. 477-491.

ARCHAEOLOGY, SALVAGE--U.S.--OREGON--PORTLAND

Thompson, Dick. "The Rejuvenation House Parts Company: Period Supplies for the Cottage or Mansion." Newsletter, Historic Preservation League of Oregon. No. 35, Winter 1985. p. 15.

ARCHAEOLOGY--TECHNIQUE

Chase, Philip G. "Whole Vessels and Sherds: An Experimental Investigation of Their Quantitative Relationships." Journal of Field Archaeology. Vol. 12, No. 2, Summer 1985. p. 213-218.

ARCHAEOLOGY--TECHNIQUE

Hagstrum, Mellissa B. "Measuring Prehistoric Ceramic Craft Specialization: A Test Case in the American Southwest." Journal of Field Archaeology. Vol. 12, No. 1, Spring 1985. p. 65-75.

ARCHAEOLOGY--TECHNIQUE

Levin, Aaron M. "Excavation Photography: a Day on a Dig." Archaeology. Vol. 39, No. 1, Jan./Feb. 1986. p. 34-39.

ARCHAEOLOGY--TECHNIQUE

Van Horn, D. M., J. R. Murray, and R. S. White. "Some Techniques for Mechanical Excavation in Salvage Archaeology." Journal of Field Archaeology. Vol. 13, No. 2. Summer 1986. pp. 239-244.

ARCHAEOLOGY--TECHNIQUE

Wynn, Jeffrey C. and Susan I. Sherwood. "The Self-Potential (SP) Method: An Inexpensive Reconnaissance and Archaeological Mapping Tool." Journal of Field Archaeology. Vol. 11, No. 2, Summer 1983. pp. 195-204.

Electromagnetic exploration.

ARCHAEOLOGY--TECHNIQUE--U.S.--GEORGIA

Garrison, Ervang et al. "Magnetic Prospection and the Discovery of Mission Santa Catalina de Guale." Journal of Field Archaeology. Vol. 12, No. 3, Fall 1985. p. 299-313.

ARCHAEOLOGY--U.S.--ARIZONA

"Archaeological Site Vandalism Trials Result in Convictions." Arizona Preservation News. Vol. 3, No. 4. Oct. 1986. p. 11.

ARCHAEOLOGY--U.S.--ARIZONA

Ciolek-Torrello, Richard. "A Typology of Room Function at Grasshopper Pueblo, Arizona." Journal of Field Archaeology. Vol. 12, No. 1, Spring 1985. p. 41-63.

ARCHAEOLOGY--U.S.--CONNECTICUT

Donohue, Mary M. & David A. Poirier. "Federal Tax Incentives and Industrial Archeology: The Connecticut Experience." Journal of the Society for Industrial Archeology. Vol. 12, No. 1, 1986. p. 1-10.

ARCHAEOLOGY--U.S.--DELAWARE

"Thompson's: Loss or Gain?" Canvas. Vol. 6, No. 2, 1987. p. 5.

An archaeological site has provided valuable information on early Delaware farms.

ARCHAEOLOGY--U.S.--FLORIDA--ST. AUGUSTINE

"Archeology in the Oldest City." Florida Preservation News. Mar. 1985. p. 7.

ARCHAEOLOGY--U.S.--ILLINOIS

Barr, Keith L. "Pattern in Archaeology of Historic Public Buildings in Illinois." Historic Illinois. Vol. 9, No. 3. Oct. 1986. pp. 6-7; 9.

ARCHAEOLOGY--U.S.--ILLINOIS

Wiant, Michael D. "Steps Toward Preserving the Past: How to Record Archaeological Sites in Illinois." Illinois Heritage Association Newsletter. Vol. 5, No. 1. Jan.-Feb. 1987. Technical Insert No. 25. 2 p.

ARCHAEOLOGY--U.S.--ILLINOIS

Yingst, James R. "Dana-Thomas House Focus of Archaeological Study." Historic Illinois. Vol. 10, No. 1. June 1987. pp. 1-4.

ARCHAEOLOGY--U.S.--KANSAS

Stein, Martin. "An Archaeologist's Notebook: the Development of Horticulture Characterizes the Middle Ceramic Period." Kansas Preservation. Vol. 7, No. 3, Mar./Apr. 1985. p. 8-9.

Sixth in a series on archaeology in Kansas and first in a five-part series on the Middle Ceramic period.

ARCHAEOLOGY--U.S.--KANSAS

Stein, Martin. "An Archeologists's Notebook: Eastern Influences Appear on the Plains during the Early Ceramic Period." Kansas Preservation. Vol. 7, No. 2, Jan./Feb. 1985. p. 7-8.

ARCHAEOLOGY--U.S.--KANSAS

Stein, Martin. "Prehistoric Settlements along the Missouri River Are Described." Kansas Preservation. Vol. 9, No. 2, Jan.-Feb. 1987. p. 6-7.

ARCHAEOLOGY--U.S.--MAINE

Spiess, Arthur. "Coastal Erosion Concerns Archaeologists." Maine Citizens for Historic Preservation Newsletter. Vol. 11, No. 2, Summer 1985. p. 4-5.

ARCHAEOLOGY--U.S.--MARYLAND

Clark, Wayne E. "Archaeology Along the Chesapeake Bay." Place. Vol. 5, No. 5, May 1985. p. 6-8.

ARCHAEOLOGY--U.S.--MARYLAND--BALTIMORE

"Digging for Silver in Fells Point." SWAP, The Newsletter of the Maryland Historical Trust. November 1984. pp. 1-4.

ARCHAEOLOGY--U.S.--MASSACHUSETTS--BOSTON

Thibault, Barbara. "Learn About Charlestown's Origins Through Historic Archaeology." Boston Preservation Alliance Letter. Vol. 6, No. 8, Sept. 1985. p. 4-5.

ARCHAEOLOGY--U.S.--MICHIGAN

"Michigan Archeology Leads to Reconstructed Sawmill." Society for Industrial Archaeology Newsletter. Vol. 13, No. 3 & 4. Fall & Winter 1984. p. 11.

ARCHAEOLOGY--U.S.--NEW HAMPSHIRE--PORTSMOUTH

Agnew, Aileen Button. "The Archeology of a Neighborhood: Deer Street, Portsmouth, New Hampshire." Historical New Hampshire. Vol. 40, Nos. 1 & 2, Spring/Summer 1985. p. 72-83. (VF)

ARCHAEOLOGY--U.S.--NEW MEXICO

"Spanish Colonial Village Ruins Donated." The Archaeological Conservancy Newsletter. Fall 1986. p. 1, 3.

Spanish colonial site in New Mexico donated to the Archaeological Conservancy.

ARCHAEOLOGY--U.S.--NEW YORK

Geismar, Joan H. "Digging into a Seaport's Past." Archaeology. Vol. 40, No. 1. Jan./Feb. 1987. pp. 30-35.

Archaeologists uncover the urbanization of lower Manhattan.

ARCHAEOLOGY--U.S.--NEW YORK--NEW YORK CITY

Riess, Warren C. "The Ship Beneath the City." Mariner's Museum Journal. Vol. 12, No. 3, 1985. p. 2-7.

The bow of the "Ranson", an 18th-century merchant ship, excavated and moved to the museum.

ARCHAEOLOGY--U.S.--NORTH CAROLINA--BLOSSOM'S
FERRY

Watts, Gordon P., Jr. "Investigating
Historic Blossom's Ferry, North Carolina."
Archaeology. Vol. 38, No. 5, Sept./Oct. 1985.
p. 26-33.

ARCHAEOLOGY--U.S.--OKLAHOMA--HARDESTY

Lees, William B. "Panhandle Town Unearthed:
The Archaeological and Historical Treasures of
Hardesty." The Chronicles of Oklahoma. Vol. 63,
No. 4, Winter 1985-1986. p. 377-395.

ARCHAEOLOGY--U.S.--PENNSYLVANIA

Hatch, James W. and Patricia E. Miller.
"Procurement, Tool Production, and Sourcing
Research at the Vera Cruz Jasper Quarry in
Pennsylvania." Journal of Field Archaeology.
Vol. 12, No. 2, Summer 1985. p. 219-230.

ARCHAEOLOGY--U.S.--TEXAS

"Cabe Mounds Preserved." The Archaeological
Conservancy Newsletter. Fall 1986. p. 2-3.

A preservation easement to the Archaeological
Conservancy has been made, thus protecting eight
Indian mounds in Texas.

ARCHAEOLOGY--U.S.--TEXAS--SAN ANTONIO

Anderson, Kenneth L. "Mission Project
Brings Praise from Park and Region." CRM
Bulletin. Vol. 9, No. 3, June 1986. p. 11-15.

Documentation of the four Spanish colonial
missions in San Antonio Historical Park by
HABS.

ARCHAEOLOGY--U.S.--TEXAS--SAN ANTONIO

"Dig Yields Rare Artifacts." The Medallion.
Vol. 22, No. 4, Apr. 1985. p. 1, 4.

ARCHAEOLOGY--U.S.--VIRGIN ISLANDS

Lundberg, Emily R. "Interpreting the
Cultural Associations of Aceramic Deposits in
the Virgin Islands." Journal of Field Archaeology. Vol. 12, No. 2, Summer 1985. p. 201-202

ARCHAEOLOGY--U.S.--VIRGINIA--ALEXANDRIA

"Alexandria Archeology." Early American
Life. Vol. 18, No. 2, April 1987. p. 39-40.

ARCHAEOLOGY--U.S.--VIRGINIA--CHARLOTTESVILLE

"Archaeological Excavations Aid Grounds
Restoration at Monticello." The Decorative Arts
Trust. Vol. 5, No. 2, Oct. 1985. p. 4-5.

ARCHAEOLOGY--U.S.--VIRGINIA--MONTICELLO

Glick, Edward M. "Preamble to Restoration."
History News. Vol. 39, No. 3, March 1984. pp.
12-15.

ARCHAEOLOGY--U.S.--WISCONSIN

"Highway Archeology, Historic Preservation,
and the DOT." Columns. Vol. 7, No. 1, Feb./Mar.
1986.

ARCHAEOLOGY AND HISTORY

D'Eramo, Domenic E. "Archeological
findings and the MBTA Red Line extension :
Harvard Square to Alewife Brook Parkway",
Public Works Historical Society Newsletter.
December 1980. p. 10-11.

ARCHAEOLOGY AND HISTORY

Davis, Hester A. "A Case of Limited
Vision? Archeology and Historic Preservation."
American Society for Conservation Archaeology
Newsletter. July 1980. p. 26-28.

ARCHAEOLOGY AND HISTORY

Schuyler, Robert L. "Excavation into the
Recent Past: historic archaeology adds new
dimensions to understanding the total sweep of
human development." Early Man. Autumn 1979.
pp. 1-3.

ARCHAEOLOGY AND HISTORY--U.S.--MARYLAND

King, Julia A. and Dennis J. Pogue. "St. Inigoes Manor: an Archaeological History." Chronicles of St. Mary's. Vol. 34, No. 4, Apr. 1986. p. 353-359.

ARCHAEOLOGY AND HISTORY

Mansberger, FLoyd. "Archaeological Investigations at Galena's Washburne House." Historic Illinois. Vol.9, No. 1, June 1986. p. 6-7, 9.

ARCHAEOLOGY AND HISTORY

Orser, Charles E. "Uniting Public History and Historical Archaeology." The Public Historian. Winter 1981. pp. 75-83.

ARCHAEOLOGY AND HISTORY

Schlereth, Thomas J. "Above-ground archaeology: discovering a community's history through local artifacts." Bay State Historical League Bulletin. Summer & Autumn 1980. p.1-5

ARCHAEOLOGY AND HISTORY--U.S.--GEORGIA-- ATLANTA

Dickens, Roy S., R. and William R. Bowen. "Problems and Promises in Urban Historical Archaeology: The MARTA Project". Historical Archaeology. Vol. 14, 1980. p. 42-57.

ARCHAEOLOGY AND HISTORY--U.S.--MAINE

Bradley, Robert L. Ph.D. "Historical Archaeology in Maine." Maine Citizens for Historic Preservation. Vol. 11, No. 3, Fall 1985. p. 6-7.

ARCHES

"Calder Arches Resurrected." Pasadena Heritage. Vol. 9, Nos. 3 & 4, Spring & Summer 1986. p. 4.

Arches, created by Alexander Calder, son of the famous mobile sculptor, in 1910 and saved when the Caltech building of which they were a part was demolished in 1971 have been made a part of a new laboratory complex.

ARCHES

Hill, John. "Horseshoe, Ogee, & Lancet Arches." Mistletoe Leaves. Vol. 17, No. 4, 1986 p. 6.

ARCHES

Spence, Keith. "New Life for Tired Arches." Country Life. Vol. 180, No. 4657. Nov. 20, 1986. pp. 1630-1631.

Restoration of English railway arches.

ARCHITECTS

Anderson, Barbara. "Preserving Old Buildings May Require Hiring an Architect." Kansas Preservation. Vol. 8, No. 3, March-April 1986. p. 3-4.

ARCHITECTS

"A Biographical Directory of Architects in Maine." George Burnham, Bradbury Johnson. Maine Citizens for Historic Preservation. Spring 1984 Newsletter.

ARCHITECTS

Ehrlich, George. "The Bank of Commerce by Asa Beebe Cross: 'A Building of the Latest Architecture.'" Journal of the Society of Architectural Historians. Vol. XLIII, No. 2, May 1984. pp. 168-172.

Kansas City, Missouri (1883). Modeled on Furness' Provident Life and Trust Company, Philadelphia.

ARCHITECTS

Landau, Sarah Bradford. "The Potter Brothers: High Victorian Gothic Specialists." Newsletter, Preservation League of New York State. Vol. 11, No. 1, Jan./Feb. 1985. p. 4-5.

ARCHITECTS

Lawhorn, Jonelle M. "Making Preservation a Specialization." Architecture. Nov. 1986. p. 116-119.

Architecture firms that specialize in historic preservation.

ARCHITECTS

Lee, Antoinette J. "The Supervising Architect's Office: Government Architects in the Victorian Era." The Victorian. Vol. 13, No. 1, 1985. p. 8-9.

ARCHITECTS

"Palliser, Palliser and Company." A Biographical Dictionary of Architects in Maine. Vol. 3, No. 8. 1986. 6 pp.

ARCHITECTS--ADAMS, GEORGE G.

Pfaff, Christine E. "George G. Adams: a noted Lawrence architect rediscovered." Essex Institute Historical Collections. July 1980. pp. 176 - 195.

ARCHITECTS--AIN, GREGORY

O'Brien, Michael. "Mar Vista's Modern Lnadmark." Los Angeles Conservancy. Vol. 9, No. 3, May/June 1987. p. 12.

Post-WWII housing in Mar Vista designed by Gregory Ain.

ARCHITECTS --AUSTIN, JOHN C.

"John C. Austin: Distinguished Architect, Private Man." Pasadena Heritage. Vol. VIII, No. 1, Spring 1984. pp. 5-6.

ARCHITECTS--DENNY, WILLIS FRANKLIN, II

"Know Your Georgia Architects: Willis Franklin Denny II." The Rambler. Vol. 13, No. 1. Winter/Spring 1986. p. 7.

ARCHITECTS--COLONNA, EDWARD

Eidelberg, Martin. "The Life and Work of E. Colonna: The Early Years." The Decorative Arts Society Newsletter. Mar. 1981. pp. 1-7.

ARCHITECTS--COHN, KIMBLE A.

Conroy, Connie. "Resurrecting the Past: Cohn Sparks Restorations." Inland Architecture. Jul./Aug. 1986. pp. 40-41.

St. Louis architect Kimble A. Cohn's involvement in the restoration of commercial buildings in St. Louis.

ARCHITECTS--CODMAN, OGDEN

Metcalf, Pauline C. "Ogden Codman, Jr.: A Clever Young Boston Architect." Nineteenth Century. Spring 1981. pp. 45-47.

ARCHITECTS -- CODMAN, OGDEN

Metcalf, Pauline C. "Elegance Without Excess: Ogden Codman in New York." Preservation League of New York State Newsletter. Vol. 12, No. 1. Winter 1986. pp. 4-5.

ARCHITECTS--CLARK, JOSEPH

Rice, Kym Snyder. "Kenmore in Fredericksburg, Virginia." Antiques. Mar. 1979. pp. 552-555.

ARCHITECTS--BRYANT, GRIDLEY J.F.

"Gridley J.F. Bryant. (1816-1899)." A Biographical Dictionary of Architects in Maine. Vol. 3, No. 9, 1986. 6 p.

ARCHITECTS--BRUGES, WILLIAM

Mordaunt, Crook, J. "William Bruges and the Dilemma of Style." Architectural Review. Jul. 1981. pp. 8-15.

ARCHITECTS--BONSACK, FREDERICK C.

"St. Louis Architects: Famous and Not So Famous." Landmarks Letter. Vol. 20, No. 5. Sep. 1985. p. 2.
Frederick C. Bonsack, architect.

ARCHITECTS--BENJAMIN, ASHER

"Asher Benjamin and American Architecture." Journal of the Society of Architectural Historians. Oct. 1979. pp. 244-270.
Three articles on aspects of Benjamin's works.

ARCHITECTS--BEASLEY, CHARLES

Weitze, Karen J. "Charles Beasley, Architect (1827-1913): Issues and Images." Journal of the Society of Architectural Historians. Oct. 1980. pp. 187-207.

ARCHITECTS--BIOGRAPHY--DICTIONARIES

"A Biographical Dictionary of Architects of Maine." Maine Preservation News. Vol. 12, No. 1, Spring 1986. [unpaged.]

ARCHITECTS--BARRY, WILLIAM E.

Murphy, Kevin. "William E. Barry, 1846-1932." A Biographical Dictionary of Architects in Maine. Vol. 1, No. 6, 1984. (In - Maine Citizens for Historic Preservation Newsletter, Fall 1984, Vol. 10, No. 3). 4 pp.

ARCHITECTS--BARBER, GEORGE F.

Reed, Roger G. "George F. Barber (1854-1915)." A Biographical Dictionary of Architects in Maine. Vol. 1, No. 4, June 1984. 4 pp. (In- Maine Citizens for Historic Preservation Newsletter, Vol. X, No. 2, Summer 1984.)

ARCHITECTS--DRISCOLL, CHARLES FRANCIS

Pomeroy, Eva Belle G. "Charles Francis Driscoll, Early Pasadena Architect." Pasadena Heritage, Vol. 10, No. 1, Feb. 1987, p. 5-7.

ARCHITECTS--EPPSTEIN, SAM

Tremaine, Pat. "Sam Eppstein Receives Preservation Award." Historic Milwaukee News. Vol. 4, No. 5. Summer 1986. pp. 3-4.

A Milwaukee architect awarded for his involvement in numerous preservation projects.

ARCHITECTS--EYRE, WILSON

Fahlman, Betsy. "Wilson Eyre in Detroit: the Charles Lang Freer House." Winterthur Portfolio. Autumn 1980. pp. 257-270.

ARCHITECTS--EYRE, WILSON

Teitelman, Edward. "Wilson Eyre in Camden: the Henry Genet Taylor House and Office." Winterthur Portfolio. Autumn 1980. pp. 229-255.

ARCHITECTS--FLAGG, ERNEST

Levy, Daniel A. "Bow-Cot and the Honeymoon Cottage: Two Experimental Stone Houses by New York Architect Ernest Flagg." Fine Homebuilding. Oct./Nov. 1981. No. 5. pp. 28 - 35.

ARCHITECTS--GILBERT, CASS

Murphy, Patricia. "Minnesota's Architectural Favorite Son." AIA Journal. Mar. 1981. pp. 74-77.

ARCHITECTS--GREENE, CHARLES S. AND D. HENRY MATHER

"The Robert R. Blacker House." Pasadena Heritage. Vol. 11, No. 1. Fall 1985. pp. 1-3.

ARCHITECTS--GREENE AND GREENE

Dillon, David. "Preservationists, Collectors Debate Stripping of Details." Architecture. Dec. 1985. p. 12.
The Blacker House Forum during the recent National Trust Annual Preservation Conference is discussed.

ARCHITECTS--GREENE AND GREENE

"Stripping of Greene & Greene House By New Owner Protested." Architecture. Aug. 1985. pp. 16; 20.

ARCHITECTS--GREENE, CHARLES M.

Miller, Charles. "The James House: Charles Greene's Masterpiece in Stone." Fine Homebuilding. No. 24. Dec. 1984/Jan. 1985. pp. 26-32.

ARCHITECTS--HAMMOND, JOHN HAYS (1888-1965)

O'Gorman, James F. "Twentieth-Century Gothic: The Hammond Castle Museum in Gloucester and its Antecedents." Essex Institute Historical Collections. Apr. 1981. pp. 81-104.

ARCHITECTS -- HEISTAD, HANS O.

"Hans O. Heistad, 1871-1945." A Biographical Dictionary of Architects in Maine. Vol. 3, No. 10. 1986. 6 pp.

ARCHITECTS--HUNT, RICHARD MORRIS

Ganelin, Susan Stein. "The Drawings of Richard Morris Hunt: Foundation Organizes Invaluable Collection of Prominent Architect's Work." American Preservation. Apr.-May 1979. pp. 18-25.

ARCHITECTS -- INGHAM, JOHN Q.

"John Q. Ingham: Versatile Southern Tier Architect." Newsletter, Preservation League of New York State. Vol. 10, No. 4, September-October 1984. pp. 4-5.

ARCHITECTS --ITTNER, WILLIAM BUTTS

"St. Louis Architects: Famous and Not So Famous (part 4), William Butts Ittner." Landmarks Letter. Vol. 20, No. 1, Jan. 1985. p. 4.

ARCHITECTS--JONES, EDWARD VASON

Williams, Roger M. "Edward Vason Jones; Architect and Classicist; to the Art of Restoration Architecture, He Brings..." Americana. Sep./ Oct. 1979. pp. 32 - 39.

ARCHITECTS--KAHN, LOUIS I.

LeCuyer, Annette. "Evaluation: Kahn's Powerful Presence at Exeter." Architecture. Feb. 1985. p. 74-79.

ARCHITECTS--KAHN, LOUIS I.

Lobell, John. "A Lucid Mystic Helped Transform our Architecture." Smithsonian. Jul. 1979. pp. 36-43.

ARCHITECTS--KAHN, LOUIS I.

Progressive Architecture. Dec. 1984. Entire issue.

ARCHITECTS--LE CORBUSIER

Jencks, Charles. "The Corb Industry." Blueprint. Issue 33, Dec.-Jan. 1987. p. 15-17.

1987 is the one hundredth anniversary of Le Corbusier's birth.

ARCHITECTS -- LE CORBUSIER

Martinelli, Antonio. "Corb in India." Blueprint. Issue 33, Dec.-Jan. 1987. p. 22-23.

Le Corbusier's private houses in India.

ARCHITECTS -- LIGHTOLER, TIMOTHY

Lane, Joan. "The Craftsman Architect: Timothy Lightoler of Warwick, 1727-71(?)." Country Life. Mar. 19, 1987. pp. 108-109.

ARCHITECTS--MACCLURE, SAMUEL

Segger, Martin. "Variety and Decorum: Style and Form in the Work of Samuel MacClure 1860-1920." Society for the Study of Architecture in Canada Bulletin. Apr. 1981. pp. 4-12.

ARCHITECTS--MAYBECK, BERNARD R.

Banham, Reyner. "The Plot Against Bernard Maybeck." Journal of the Society of Architectural Historians. Vol. 48, No. 1. Mar. 1984. pp. 33-38.

ARCHITECTS--MAYBECK, BERNARD R.

Reinhardt, Richard. "Bernard Maybeck." American Heritage. Aug./Sep. 1981. pp. 37-47.

ARCHITECTS--MAYBECK, BERNARD

Smith, Thomas Gordon. "Bernard Maybeck's Wallen II House." Fine Homebuilding. Apr./May 1981. pp. 18-25.

ARCHITECTS--MEACHAM, GEORGE F.

Reed, Roger G. "George F. Meacham, 1831-1917." A Biographical Dictionary of Architects in Maine. Vol. 1, No. 5, 1984. (In - Maine Citizens for Historic Preservation Newsletter, Fall 1984, Vol. 10, No. 3). 4 pp.

ARCHITECTS--MIES VAN DER ROHE, LUDWIG

Kimball, Roger. "Modernism and Mies." Architectural Record. Mar. 1986. pp. 73-77.

ARCHITECTS -- MIES VAN DER ROHE, LUDWIG

Lizon, Peter. "Miesian Revival: First Barcelona, Now Tugendhat Restored." *Architecture*. Nov. 1986. p. 12-13.

Mies van der Rohe's Tugendhat house has been restored.

ARCHITECTS--MIES VAN DER ROHE, LUDWIG

McSheffrey, Gerald R. "Architectural Education: Mies's Greatest Bequest." *Architectural Record*. Aug. 1984. pp. 47; 49.

ARCHITECTS--MIES VAN DER ROHE, LUDWIG

"Mies van der Rohe." *Inland Architect*. Vol. 30, No. 2. Mar./Apr. 1986. pp. 19-59.
Series of articles published in observance of his centennial.

ARCHITECTS--WRIGHT, FRANK LLOYD

Reinberger, Mark. "The Sugarloaf Mountain Project and Frank Lloyd Wright's Vision of a New World." *Journal of the Society of Architectural Historians*. Vol. 48, No. 1. Mar. 1984. pp. 38-53.

ARCHITECTS--WRIGHT, FRANK LLOYD

Reinberger, Mark. "Frank Lloyd Wright, 1867-1959." *A Biographical Dictionary of Architects in Maine*. Vol. 2, No. 10. 1985. In *Maine Preservation News*. Vol. 11, No. 4, Winter 1986. 4 p.

ARCHITECTS -- WRIGHT, FRANK LLOYD

Quinan, Jack. "The Architecture of Frank Lloyd Wright in New York State." *Preservation League of New York State Newsletter*. Vol. 12, No. 3, Summer 1986. p. 6-7.

ARCHITECTS--WRIGHT, FRANK LLOYD

Pfeiffer, Bruce Brooks. "The Archives of the Frank Lloyd Wright Memorial Foundation." *Frank Lloyd Wright Newsletter*. Vol. 4, No. 2. 1981. pp. 17-18.

ARCHITECTS -- WRIGHT, FRANK LLOYD

Perez- Pena, Christine, "Ennis-Brown Revisited." *Los Angeles Conservancy*. Vol. 8, No. 6, Nov./Dec. 1986. p.3.

Frank Lloyd Wright's most monumental textile block house in California is in serious need of financial assistance for restoration.

ARCHITECTS--MIES VAN DER ROHE, LUDWIG

Seidel, Peter. "Mies Today: Thoughts of a Former Student." *Inland Architect*. Vol. 29, No. 2. Mar./Apr. 1985. pp. 46 - 50.

ARCHITECTS--MILLER, WILLIAM H.

Tomlan, Mary Raddant. "The Work of William H. Miller: Far Beyond Cayuga's Waters." *Newsletter, Preservation League of New York State*. Vol. 11, No. 3, May/June 1985. p. 4-5.

ARCHITECTS--MIZNER, ADDISON

Southworth, Susan. "The 'Boutiqueing of Joe's Alligator Farm: Addison Mizner and the Origins of Palm Beach Style." *Places*. Vol. 2, No. 3. p. 67-71.

ARCHITECTS--MIZNER, ADDISON

Thorndike, Joseph J., Sr. "Addison Mizner - What He Did For Palm Beach." *Smithsonian*. Vol. 16, No. 6. Sept. 1985. PP. 112-113.

ARCHITECTS --MONEO, RAFAEL

"Rafael Moneo." *Progressive Architecture*. Vol. 6, June 1986. p. 73-85.

Review of some of the earlier work of the Spanish architect.

ARCHITECTS -- MOORE, CHARLES

Littlejohn, David. "Wondrous Architecture of Charles Moore." *Smithsonian*. Vol. 15, No. 3, June 1984. pp. 54-64.

ARCHITECTS--PARRIS, ALEXANDER

Bishir, Catherine and Marshall Bullock. "Mr. Jones Goes to Richmond: A Note on the Influence of Alexander Parris' Wickham House." Journal of the Society of Architectural Historians. Vol. 48, No. 1. Mar. 1984. pp. 71-74.

ARCHITECTS--PARRIS, ALEXANDER

Norton, Bettina A. "The Massachusetts Bank Plans of Alexander Parris: An Essex Institute Discovery." Essex Institute Historical Collections. Jul. 1981. pp. 178-191.

ARCHITECTS --RENWICK, JAMES, JR.

Meltenry, Bannon. "James Renwick, Jr.: Institutional Architects in New York." Preservation League of New York State Newsletter. Vol. 13, No. 1, Winter 1987. p. 6-7.

ARCHITECTS--RICHARDSON, HENRY HOBSON

Hitchcock, Henry-Russell. "H. H. Richardson's New York Senate Chamber Restored." 19th Century. Spring 1980. pp. 44-47.

ARCHITECTS--RICHARDSON, HENRY HOBSON

O'Gorman, James F. "Documentation: An 1886 Inventory of H.H. Richardson's Library, and Other Gleanings from Probate." Journal of the Society of Architectural Historians. May 1982. pp. 150-155.

ARCHITECTS--RICHARDSON, HENRY HOBSON

Ochsner, Jeffrey Karl. "H.H. Richardson's Frank Willaim Andrews House." Journal of the Society of Architectural Historians. Vol. 48, No. 1. Mar. 1984. pp. 20 - 30.

ARCHITECTS--RICHARDSON, HENRY HOBSON

Russell, John. "Henry Hobson Richardson." American Heritage. Oct./Nov. 1981. pp. 48-59.

ARCHITECTS--RYDER, CALVIN

Reed, Roger G. "Calvin Ryder (1810-1890)." A Biographical Dictionary of Architects in Maine. Vol. 1, No. 3, February 1984. (In - Maine Citizens for Historic Preservation Newsletter, Summer 1984, Vol. X, No. 2.) 4 pp.

ARCHITECTS--SAARINEN, ELIEL

"Eliel Saarinen Studio, Bloomfield Hills, Michigan." Architectural Record. Sep. 1984. pp. 126-127.

ARCHITECTS--SAARINEN, ELIEL

Willis, Carol. "That Certain Something: The First 25 Years at Cranbrook." Architectural Record. June 1984. pp. 93-95.

ARCHITECTS--SCARPA, CARLA

"Carla Scarpa." Progressive Architecture. May 1981. Entire issue.

ARCHITECTS --SCHEIBLER, FREDERICK G.

"The Works of Frederick G. Scheibler, Jr." PHLF News, No. 101, Spring 1987, p. 3.

Survey of the work of an early 20th-century Pittsburgh architect.

ARCHITECTS--SUGDEN, WILLIAM LARNER

Powell, Ken. "Sugden's Morris Dance." Country Life. Vol. 181, No. 30. July 23, 1987. pp. 108-109.
The buildings of English architect William Larner Sugden (1850-1901).

ARCHITECTS--SULLIVAN, LOUIS HENRI

Krouse, Andrew. "The Guaranty Building." Friends of Terra Cotta. Vol. 3, No. 2. Summer 1984. pp. 1; 11.

ARCHITECTS--SULLIVAN, LOUIS HENRI

    Menocal, Narciso G. "The Bayard Building: French Paradox and American Synthesis." SITES. No. 13. 1985. pp. 4-24.

ARCHITECTS--SULLIVAN, LOUIS HENRI

    Stewart, Nancy H. "Landmark Survives and Thrives in Buffalo." Urban Land. May 1984. pp. 2-8.
    (Guaranty Building)

ARCHITECTS--SULLIVAN, LOUIS HENRI

    Weingarden, Lauren S. "The Colors of Nature: Louis Sullivan's Architectural Polychromy and Nineteenth-Century Color Theory." Winterthur Portfolio. Vol. 20, No. 4. Winter 1985. pp. 243-260.

ARCHITECTS--U.S.--GEORGIA

    "Know Your Georgia Architects: Daniel Pratt." The Rambler. Vol. 13, No. 2, Summer 1986. p. 15.

ARCHITECTS--U.S.--MAINE

    Goff, John V. "Arthur H. Vinal, 1854-1923." A Biographical Dictionary of Architects in Maine. Vol. 2, No. 6, 1985. (In Newsletter, Maine Citizens for Historic Preservation. Vol. 2, No. 4, 1985. 6 p.

ARCHITECTS--U.S.--MAINE

    Hennessey, William S. "Henry Van Brunt 1832-1903." A Biographical Dictionary of Architects in Maine. Vol. 2, No. 6, 1985. (In Newsletter, Maine Citizens for Historic Preservation, Vol. 11, No. 2, 1985). 4 p.

ARCHITECTS--U.S.--MAINE

    Kirker, Harold. "A Biographical Dictionary of Architects in Maine: Charles Bulfinch 1763-1844." Maine Citizens for Historic Preservation. Vol. 11, No. 3, Fall 1985. 6 p.

ARCHITECTS--U.S.--MAINE

    Landau, Sarah Bradford. "William Appleton Potter, 1842-1909." A Biographical Dictionary of Architects in Maine. Vol. 2, No. 11, 1985. In Maine Preservation News. Vol. 11, No. 4, Winter 1986. 4 p.

ARCHITECTS--U.S.--MAINE

    Morgan, William. "A Biographical Dictionary of Architects in Maine: Henry Vaughn, 1845-1917." Maine Citizens for Historic Preservation Newsletter. Vol. 10, No. 4, Winter 1985. Insert, 6p.

ARCHITECTS--U.S.--MAINE

    O'Gorman, James F. "Furness, Evans and Company." A Biographical Dictionary of Architects in Maine. Vol. 2, No. 9, 1985. In Maine Preservation News. Vol. 11, No. 4, Winter 1986. 4 p.

ARCHITECTS--U.S.--MAINE

    Reed, Roger C. "A Biographical Dictionary of Architects in Maine: Henry Richards, 1848-1949." Maine Citizens for Historic Preservation Newsletter. Vol. 10, No. 4, Winter 1985. Insert, 4p.

ARCHITECTS--U.S.--MAINE

    Reed, Roger G. "James Overlock, 1813-1906." A Biographical Dictionary of Architects in Maine. Vol. 2, No. 8, 1985. In Maine Preservation News. Vol. 11, No. 4, Winter 1986. 6 p.

ARCHITECTS--U.S.--MAINE

    Roth, Leland M. "McKim, Mead & White." A Biographical Dictionary of Architects in Maine. Vol. 2, No. 6, 1985. (In Newsletter, Maine Citizens for Historic Preservation. Vol. 2, No. 5, 1985). 6 p.

ARCHITECTS--U.S.--MAINE

    Shettleworth, Earle G. Jr. "A Biographical Dictionary of Architects in Maine: Peter W. Plummer, 1825-1873." Maine Citizens for Historic Preservation Newsletter. Vol. 10, No. 4, Winter 1985. Insert, 2p.

ARCHITECTS--U.S.--NORTH CAROLINA

Bishir, Catherine W., Peter Sandbeck, and Lynda V. Herzog. "North Carolina Architects and Builders: Hardy B. Lane and Sons." North Carolina Preservation. No. 64. Jul.-Aug. 1986. pp. 1-3.

ARCHITECTS--U.S.--SOUTH CAROLINA

Watson, Charles W. "Robert Mills, Architect, of South Carolina." Preservation Progress. Vol. 30, No. 3, May 1986. p. 1, 7-11.

ARCHITECTS -- WARNER, ANDREW JACKSON

Strayer, Betsy. "Andrew Jackson Warner: Leading Rochester Architect." Newsletter, Preservation League of New York State. Vol. 11, No. 4, July/Aug. 1985. p. 4-5.

ARCHITECTS--WRIGHT, FRANK LLOYD

Allen, James R. "Springfield's Dana-Thomas House." Historic Illinois. Oct. 1981. p. 2.

ARCHITECTS--WRIGHT, FRANK LLOYD

Brooks, H. Allen. "Frank Lloyd Wright and the Destruction of the Box." Journal of the Society of Architectural Historians. Mar. 1979. pp. 7-14.

ARCHITECTS--WRIGHT, FRANK LLOYD

Canty, Donald. "Clients'-Eye View of a Wright Classic." AIA Journal. Nov. 1981. p. 64.

ARCHITECTS--WRIGHT, FRANK LLOYD

Clarke, Jane H. "A Moving Violation?" Inland Architect. Vol. 29, No. 4. Jul./Aug. 1985. pp. 3-4.
The moving of the Wright gravesite is discussed.

ARCHITECTS--WRIGHT, FRANK LLOYD

Clausen, Meredith L. "Frank Lloyd Wright, Vertical Space, and the Chicago School's Quest for Light." Journal of the Society of Architectural Historians. Vol. 44, No. 1. Mar. 1985. pp. 66-74.

ARCHITECTS--WRIGHT, FRANK LLOYD

Connors, Joseph. The Robie House of Frank Lloyd Wright. Chicago: University of Chicago Press, 1984. 86p. (NA7238.C4C65)

ARCHITECTS--WRIGHT, FRANK LLOYD

"Deaths: Olgivanna Lloyd Wright, Guardian of the FLLW Legacy." Architecture. Apr. 1985. p. 29.

ARCHITECTS--WRIGHT, FRANK LLOYD

Heinz, Thomas A. "Frank Lloyd Wright's Art Glass: A Photo Essay." Frank Lloyd Wright Newsletter. First Quarter, 1981. pp. 6-19.

ARCHITECTS--WRIGHT, FRANK LLOYD

Heinz, Thomas A. "Frank Lloyd Wright's Jacobs II House." Fine Homebuilding. June/July 1981. pp. 20 - 27.

ARCHITECTS--WRIGHT, FRANK LLOYD

Heinz, Thomas A. "Historic Architecture: Frank Lloyd Wright." Architectural Digest. Oct. 1979. pp. 104-111; 160.

ARCHITECTS-- WRIGHT, FRANK LLOYD

"The House That Wright Built." Preservation League of New York State Newsletter. Vol. 12, No. 3, Summer 1986. p. 5.

Frank Lloyd Wright's Darwin D. Martin House in Buffalo.

ARCHITECTS--WRIGHT, FRANK LLOYD

Janke, R. Steven. "Martin House Celebrates Landmark Status." Preservation Report. Vol. 8, No. 6. Nov./Dec. 1986. p. 6.

One of Frank Lloyd Wright's prairie-style houses designated a National Historic Landmark.

ARCHITECTS--WRIGHT, FRANK LLOYD

Jordan, Wendy Adler. "Think Small Frank Lloyd Wright." Builder. January 1982. p. 135.

ARCHITECTS--WRIGHT, FRANK LLOYD

Kalec, Don and Ann Abernathy. "Frank Lloyd Wright's Oak Park Studio." Fine Homebuilding. No. 32. Apr./May 1986. pp. 60 - 66.

ARCHITECTS--WRIGHT, FRANK LLOYD

Meehan, Patrick J. "Frank Lloyd Wright's Lake Geneva Hotel." Frank Lloyd Wright Newsletter. Vol. 4, No. 2. 1981. pp. 6-10.

ARCHITECTS--WRIGHT, FRANK LLOYD

Mosteller, Michael. "The Towers of Frank Lloyd Wright." Journal of Architectural Education. Vol. 38, No. 2. Winter 1985. pp. 13 - 17.

ARCHITECTS--WRIGHT, FRANK LLOYD

Norton, Margaret Williams. "Japanese Themes and the Early Work of Frank Lloyd Wright." The Frank Lloyd Wright Newsletter. Vol. 4, No. 2. 1981. pp. 1-5.

ARCHITECTS--WRIGHT, FRANK LLOYD

"Rescuing the Willetts House." Progressive Architecture. Nov. 1983. p. 39.

ARCHITECTS--WRIGHT, FRANK LLOYD

Smith, Kathryn. "Frank Lloyd Wright, Holly- hock House, and Olive Hill, 1914-1924." Journal of the Society of Architectural Historians. Mar. 1979. pp. 15-33.

ARCHITECTS--WRIGHT, FRANK LLOYD

Sorkin, Michael. "Leaving Wright Enough Alone." Architectural Record. Mar. 1986. pp. 79-83.

Discussion of the proposed addition to the Guggenheim Museum in New York.

ARCHITECTS--WRIGHT, FRANK LLOYD

Taylor, Richard S. "Susan Lawrence, the Woman Who Hired Frank Lloyd Wright." Historic Illinois. Oct. 1981. p. 4.

ARCHITECTS--WRIGHT, FRANK LLOYD

Viladas, Pilar. "Invisible Reweaving - Storer House, Los Angeles, Calif." Progressive Architecture. Nov. 1985. pp. 112-117.

ARCHITECTS--WRIGHT, FRANK LLOYD

Wrobel, Peter. "Truth Against the World: the Psychological and Architectural Odyssey of Frank Lloyd Wright 1909-1929." SAH SCC Review. (Society of Architectural Historians, Southern California Chapter). No. 1, 1985. pp. 1-17.

ARCHITECTS--WRIGHT, FRANK LLOYD

Zalewski, Ellen. "Unity Temple." Historic Illinois. Vol. 7, No. 1. Jul. 1984. p. 6.

ARCHITECTS--YOUNG, THOMAS CRANE

"St. Louis Architects: Famous and Not So Famous (Part 3)." Thomas Crane Young. Landmarks Letter, Landmarks Association of St. Louis, Inc. Vol. 19, No. 6, November 1984. p. 3.

ARCHITECTURAL ACOUSTICS

Cavanaugh, William J. "Preserving the Acoustics of Mechanics Hall : a Restoration without Compromising Acoustical Integrity." Technology and Conservation. Fall 1980. p.24-28.

ARCHITECTURAL ACOUSTICS

Kaye, David H. "The Sound Amplification System for Mechanics Hall: a Design for Improving Speech Communication". Technology and Conservation. Fall 1980. p.29-30.

ARCHITECTURAL CRITICISM

Bloomer, Kent. "Shadows in Ruskin's Lamp of Power." Places. Vol. 2, No. 4, 1985. p. 61-66.

ARCHITECTURAL CRITICISM

Etlin, Richard A. "The Triumph of American Architecture". Humanities. Vol. 6, No. 1, Feb. 1985. p. 14-16.

ARCHITECTURAL CRITICISM--HISTORY

Lewis, Arnold. "A European Profile of American Architecture." Journal of the Society of Architectural Historians. Dec. 1978. pp. 265-282.

ARCHITECTURAL DESIGN

"Design Plagiarism Suit Settled." Architecture. Vol. 73, No. 11, November 1984. p. 38.

ARCHITECTURAL DESIGN

Hedman, Richard. "A Skyline Paved With Good Intentions." Planning. August 1981. pp. 12-18.

ARCHITECTURAL DESIGN

Longstreth, Richard W. "The Problem with 'Style'." The Forum, Bulletin of the Committee on Preservation, December 1984, Vol. 6, No. 1-2, in Newsletter, The Society of Architectural Historians. Vol. 29, No. 3, June 1985. 4 p.

ARCHITECTURAL DESIGN

Miller, Iris. "Design Seminar: An Urban Site." Journal of Architectural Education. Summer 1982. pp. 27-31.

ARCHITECTURAL DESIGN

"Responses to 'the Problem with "Style",' The Forum, Bulletin of the Committee on Preservation, Oct. 1985, Vol. 7, No. 1, in Newsletter, The Society of Architectural Historians. Vol. 29, No. 6, Dec. 1985. 2 p.

ARCHITECTURAL DESIGN

Sachner, Paul M. "Still Planning with the Poor: Community Design Centers Keep up the Good Works." Architectural Record. June 1983. pp. 126-131.

ARCHITECTURAL DESIGN--OLD/NEW BUILDINGS

Groat, Linda. "Measuring the Fit of New to Old: A Checklist Resulting from a Study of Contextualism." Architecture. Nov. 1983. pp. 58 - 61.

ARCHITECTURAL DESIGN--OLD/NEW RELATIONSHIP

"Architectural design citation: Stephen B. Jacobs & Associates." Progressive Architecture. Jan. 1981. pp. 152-152.

ARCHITECTURAL DESIGN--OLD/NEW RELATIONSHIP

"Architectural design citation: Swaney Kerns Architects, Robert Barber Anderson." Progressive Architecture. Jan. 1981. pp. 150-151.

ARCHITECTURAL DESIGN--OLD/NEW RELATIONSHIP

"Battle of the Styles in Spitalfields."
<u>Traditional Homes</u>. Vol. 3, No. 11. Aug. 1987.
p. 4.

ARCHITECTURAL DESIGN--OLD/NEW RELATIONSHIP

Campbell, Robert. "Evaluation: Boston's
John Hancock Tower in Context." <u>AIA Journal</u>.
Dec. 1980. pp. 18-25.

ARCHITECTURAL DESIGN--OLD/NEW RELATIONSHIP

Catt, Richard. "Marrying New to
Old." <u>Traditional Homes</u>. Sept. 1986.
p. 10-14.

Problems of adding to a traditional
house.

ARCHITECTURAL DESIGN--OLD/NEW RELATIONSHIP

"Classical Complexity." (Computer Science
Department Building, Columbia University)
<u>Architectural Record</u>. Mar. 1984. pp.126-133.

ARCHITECTUAL DESIGN--OLD/NEW RELATIONSHIP

"Commission Rejects Latest Proposal for St.
Bart's." <u>Architecture</u>. Aug. 1985. p. 12.

ARCHITECTURAL DESIGN--OLD/NEW RELATIONSHIP

"Context and Change." <u>Architecture</u>. Vol. 73,
No. 11. Nov. 1984. pp. 49-93.
The Tulsa Mid-Continental building, downtown
Roanoke, Washington, D.C., study of 73 archi-
tects on contextualism and projects in Rome,
Peabody library Danvers, Mass. featured in this
annual review.

ARCHITECTURAL DESIGN--OLD/NEW RELATIONSHIP

Dean, Andrea Oppenheimer. "Two Old
Schools Woven into an Office Complex."
<u>Architecture</u>. Nov. 1986. p. 60-63.

Sumner Center in Washington, D.C.
successfully meshes old and new buildings
and an artful use of landscaping.

ARCHITECTURAL DESIGN--OLD/NEW RELATIONSHIP

"Filling the Void, Center Ithaca, Ithaca,
New York." <u>Progressive Architecture</u>. Jul. 1982.
pp. 72-77.

ARCHITECTURAL DESIGN--OLD/NEW RELATIONSHIP

Gandee, Charles K. "A lesson in deportment:
Additions to Westover School, Middlebury,
Connecticut." <u>Architectural Record</u>. Feb. 1985.
pp. 124-133.
Science wing added to 1909 building originally designed by Connecticut's first woman
architect, Theodate Pope Riddle.

ARCHITECTURAL DESIGN--OLD/NEW RELATIONSHIP

Helmer, Paul. "Residential Infill Architecture." <u>Historic Kansas City Foundation Gazette</u>.
Mar./Apr. 1982. p. 6.

ARCHITECTURAL DESIGN--OLD/NEW RELATIONSHIP

"In the Center of Downtown Boston: A
Revitalized South Station as Transportation Hub."
<u>Architectural Record</u>. Jul. 1981. pp. 101-107.

ARCHITECTURAL DESIGN--OLD/NEW RELATIONSHIP

"Learning to Live with Landmarks." <u>Archi-
tectural Record</u>. Jul. 1982. pp. 82-85.

ARCHITECTURAL DESIGN--OLD/NEW RELATIONSHIP

"Linking Past and Present: The 'New'
Memorial Art Gallery." <u>The Landmark Society of
Western New York</u>. Vol. 25, No. 3. May 1987.
p. 5.
Expansion of art gallery, University of
Rochester.

ARCHITECTURAL DESIGN--OLD/NEW RELATIONSHIP

Miller, Nory. "The Boston Showroom."
<u>Progressive Architecture</u>. Jul. 1980. pp. 79-81.

ARCHITECTURAL DESIGN--OLD/NEW RELATIONSHIP

    Nairn, Janet. "Open-Air Pavillion is Centerpiece of Revitalized Historic Area." Architectural Record. Jun. 1981. pp. 100-103.

ARCHITECTURAL DESIGN--OLD/NEW RELATIONSHIP

    "The new Madison Civic Center by Hardy Holzman Pfeiffer Associates." Architectural Record. July 1980. pp. 77-87.

ARCHITECTURAL DESIGN--OLD/NEW RELATIONSHIP

    Perkin, George. "Context." Heritage Outlook. Nov./Dec. 1982. pp. 171-173.

ARCHITECTURAL DESIGN--OLD/NEW RELATIONSHIP

    "Porches: A Big Preservation Decision in Essex, New York." Blueprints. Vol. 5, No. 1. Spring 1987. p. 3.
    Issue of removing 80-year-old porches from 200-year-old houses.

ARCHITECTURAL DESIGN--OLD/NEW RELATIONSHIP

    "Public Housing Charleston Style." Architectural Record. Jul. 1983. p. 66.

ARCHITECTURAL DESIGN--OLD/NEW RELATIONSHIP

    "Quiet New Office Enhances an Historic District." Architectural Record. May 1980. pp. 93-96.

ARCHITECTURAL DESIGN--OLD/NEW RELATIONSHIP

    "Savannah Infill." AIA Journal. Jan. 1982. p. 36.

ARCHITECTURAL DESIGN--OLD/NEW RELATIONSHIP

    "Savannah Victorian District Design Competition." Architectural Record. Mar. 1982. pp. 44-45.

ARCHITECTURAL DESIGN--OLD/NEW RELATIONSHIP

    Schmidt, Wayne. "Contemporary Architecture in a Historic Setting." Preservation Progress (HLFI). Summer 1983. pp. 4-5.

ARCHITECTURAL DESIGN--OLD/NEW RELATIONSHIP

    Stanford, Virgil and Anna Smith. "Good Housing Comes in Small Packages: On Infill Lots in Des Moines." Planning. Dec. 1981. pp. 18-19.

ARCHITECTURAL DESIGN--OLD/NEW RELATIONSHIP

    Stein, Susan R. "French Ferociously Debate the Pei Pyramid at the Louvre." Architecture. May 1985. pp. 25; 31; 34; 40.

ARCHITECTURAL DESIGN--OLD/NEW RELATIONSHIP

    Whitaker, Craig. "Context and Cohesion: Martha's Vineyard." Skyline. Jul. 1982. pp. 22-23.

ARCHITECTURAL DESIGN--OLD/NEW RELATIONSHIP

    Worskett, Roy. "Conservation: the missing ethic." Monumentum. Jun. 1982. pp. 129-154.

ARCHITECTURAL DESIGN--OLD/NEW RELATIONSHIP-- AUSTRIA

    "Skillful and Intricate Addition to an Early Modern Monument." Architecture. Sep. 1984. pp. 166-169.

ARCHITECTURAL DESIGN--OLD/NEW RELATIONSHIP--
CANADA

Freeman, Allen. "Old and New Joined Around Significant New Public Spaces." Architecture. Sep. 1984. pp. 154-157.

ARCHITECTURAL DESIGN--OLD/NEW RELATIONSHIP--
CZECHOSLOVAKIA--PRAGUE

"Office Building Stylishly Completes Historic Square." Architecture. Sep. 1984. p. 115.

ARCHITECTURAL DESIGN--OLD/NEW RELATIONSHIP--
GERMANY--FRANKFURT

"Frankfurt: New and Old." Progressive Architecture. Mar. 1985. pp. 24; 26.

ARCHITECTURAL DESIGN--OLD/NEW RELATIONSHIP--
U.S.--CALIFORNIA--SAN FRANCISCO

Crosbie, Michael J. "Condominiums that Respect a Historic Hill's Character." and Nesmith, Lynn. "Complex Reflects Its Site's Colorful Past and Neighbors." Architecture. Mar. 1985. p. 144-149.

ARCHITECTURAL DESIGN--OLD/NEW RELATIONSHIP--U.S.--
CALIFORNIA--SAN FRANCISCO

Freeman, Allen. "Dual Act of Integration: Mei Lun Yuen Housing in San Francisco." Architecture. Vol. 74, No. 7. Jul. 1985. pp. 54-55.

ARCHITECTURAL DESIGN--OLD/NEW RELATIONSHIP--U.S.--
COLORADO--DENVER

Gaskee, Margaret. "Denver Distilled." Architectural Record. Sep. 1985. pp. 126-135. The renovation of the Tabor Block (c.1880).

ARCHITECTURAL DESIGN--OLD/NEW RELATIONSHIP--U.S.--
CONNECTICUT--HARTFORD

"Hartford Approves Tower Over Goodwin Building, Takes a New Look at Bonus System." Urban Conservation Report. Vol. 10, No. 2. Feb. 6, 1986. p. 4.

ARCHITECTURAL DESIGN--OLD/NEW RELATIONSHIP--U.S.--
ILLINOIS--CHICAGO

Granacki, Victoria. "Blending Old and New: Adaptive Use in Chicago and the Changing Nature of the Outer Downtown Core." Urban Design International. Vol. 6, No. 1. Summer 1985. pp. 30-33.

ARCHITECTURAL DESIGN--OLD/NEW RELATIONSHIP--U.S.
MASSACHUSETTS--BOSTON

"Building in Historic Districts: Quality Worth the Expense." Urban Land. Vol. 44, No. 8. Aug. 1985. pp. 15-17.
An interview with Boston architect Richard J. Bertman.

ARCHITECTURAL DESIGN--OLD/NEW RELATIONSHIP--U.S.
--MAINE--PORTLAND

"Rooftop Additions on Portland's Historic Buildings." Landmarks Observer. Vol. 12, No. 6, Nov./Dec. 1985. p. 1, 8-9.

ARCHITECTURAL DESIGN--OLD/NEW RELATIONSHIP--U.S.--
MASSACHUSETTS--BOSTON

Boles, Daralice D. "Assessing a Winner: Church Court Condominiums, Boston, Mass." Progressive Architecture. 2:85. pp. 88-93.

ARCHITECTURAL DESIGN--OLD/NEW RELATIONSHIP--U.S.
MASSACHUSETTS--BOSTON

Kay, Jane Holtz. "Bad Reviews in Boston." Progressive Architecture. Mar. 1985. pp. 27-28.
Proposed Downtown and Back Bay Philip Johnson and John Burgee buildings opposed by preservationists.

ARCHITECTURAL DESIGN--OLD/NEW RELATIONSHIP--U.S.--
NEW JERSEY--MOORESTOWN

Crosbie, Michael J. "Firehouse Inserted Discreetly Into a Victorian Main Street." Architecture. Oct. 1985. pp. 70-71.

ARCHITECTURAL DESIGN--OLD/NEW RELATIONSHIP--U.S.--
NEW YORK--NEW YORK CITY

Smith, C. Ray. "Pier 17 Pavilion Completes New York's South Street Seaport." Architecture. Nov. 1985. p. 20.

ARCHITECTURAL DESIGN--OLD/NEW RELATIONSHIP--U.S.--
NEW YORK--NEW YORK CITY

Viladas, Pilar. "Graves' Whitney Plans."
Progressive Architecture. Jul. 1985. p. 23.

ARCHITECTURAL DESIGN--OLD/NEW RELATIONSHIP--U.S.--
VIRGINIA--ALEXANDRIA

"An Eminent Neo-Victorian Along the Potomac."
Architectural Record. Sep. 1985. p. 57.

ARCHITECTURAL DESIGN--OLD NEW RELATIONSHIP

"Projects Portfolio, Robert A. M. Stern,
Architects." Progressive Architecture. Dec. 1983.
pp. 29-34.

ARCHITECTURAL DESIGN--OLD/NEW RELATIONSHIP

Wiseman, Carter. "Good Neighbor Policy."
Architectural Record. July 1984. pp. 86-95.

ARCHITECTURAL DESIGN--U.S.--CALIFORNIA--PACIFICA

"Land Use Ordinance Precluding 'Monotonous'
Developments, Detrimental Uses Upheld." Housing
& Development Reporter. Vol. 13, No. 10, July
29, 1985. p. 181-182.

ARCHITECTURAL DESIGN--WASHINGTON, D.C.

Gaskie, Margaret. "Neo-Eclecticism on the
Potomac." Architectural Record. July 1984.
pp. 96-107.

ARCHITECTURAL DRAWING

"Extant Recording - The Use of Templates
in Recording Historic Stuctures. The McKinlay
House, West Flamborough, Ontario, Canada."
APT Communique. Vol. XIII(2), April 1984, Technical Notes 1. pp. 9-10.

ARCHITECTURAL DRAWINGS

Earl, John. "Measured Drawing:
The Survey of London Tradition."
Transactions. Vol. 7, 1982. pp. 19-
26.

ARCHITECTURAL DRAWINGS--U.S.--MASSACHUSETTS--
BOSTON

Moss, Stanley. "Twentieth Century Building
Plans at the Boston Public Library." Boston
Preservation Alliance Letter. Vol. 6, No. 9,
Oct. 1985. p. 1, 3-4.

ARCHITECTURAL FIRMS

Ellis, Charlotte and Martin Meade. "R & R
Renewal." Architectural Review. Vol. 180,
No. 1078. Dec. 1986. pp. 40-46.

Reichen & Robert, French architectural firm
that specializes in conversion.

ARCHITECTURAL FIRMS--U.S.--KANSAS--KANSAS CITY

Hagedorn, Martha. "Kansas City Architectural
Firm Leaves Rich Legacy." Kansas Preservation.
Vol. 8, No. 1, Nov./Dec. 1985. p. 4.

Firm of William Warren Rose and David B.
Peterson practicing in Kansas City between 1909
and 1926 responsible for Old City Hall and
Argentine Carnegie Library.

ARCHITECTURAL LIBRARIES

Cederholm, Tess. "Boston Public Library."
Boston Preservation Alliance Letter. Vol. 6,
No. 8, Sept. 1985. p. 3-4.

ARCHITECTURAL REVIEW BOARDS

Kinney, John W. "Letters, More on
Aesthetic Regulation." North Carolina
Architect. November-December 1982. pp. 15-16.

ARCHITECTURAL REVIEW BOARDS

Kull, Ronald. "Making Maintenance an
Equal Part of the Design Process." Environmental
Comment. August 1981. pp. 11-15.

ARCHITECTURAL REVIEW BOARDS

Shirvani, Hamid. "Urban Design Through Review Process." Environmental Comment. Aug. 1981. pp. 4-10.

ARCHITECTURE--BERMUDA

Ives, Vernon A. " Bermuda's Unique Architecture. " Antiques. Aug. 1979. pp. 341-352.

ARCHITECTURAL REVIEW BOARDS

Thomas, Martha. "Color Those Houses Historic." Yankee. March 1984. p. 13.

ARCHITECTURE--CONSERVATION AND RESTORATION

"Lasers and Photo-flash Adapted to Construction Work." Architectural Record. September 1979. p. 34.

ARCHITECTURE--CONSERVATION AND RESTORATION-- CASE STUDIES

"Heritage..." Architecture. Feb. 1986. p. 54-65.

Description of rehab of carriage houses in Detroit, a jewelry factory in Providence, R.I., a New Haven office building, the Hurt building in Atlanta, and a Greek Revival building in Chester, Conn.

ARCHITECTURE--CONSERVATION AND RESTORATION-- GREAT BRITAIN

Saunders, Matthew. "Architectural Conservation: An Apology and Historical Perspective." Transactions of the Ancient Monuments Society. Vol. 30, 1986. p. 219-225.

ARCHITECTURE--CONSERVATION AND RESTORATION--STUDY AND TEACHING

Jamieson, Walter. "Architectural Conservation Training in Canada." Urbanism Past and Present, Summer 1979. pp. 46-49.

ARCHITECTURE--DETAILS

Caviglia, Rita. "Local Law No. 10 and the Disappearing Cornice." Progressive Architecture. November 1982. pp. 29-30.

ARCHITECTURE--DETAILS

Cunnington, Pamela. "Architectural Detail." Traditional Homes. Vol. 3, No. 4, Jan. 1987, p. 55-59.

Dating houses using architectural details.

ARCHITECTURE--DETAILS

Daniel, Christopher St. J. H. "Shedding a Glorious Light: Stained-Glass-Window Sundials." Country Life. Feb. 26, 1987 p. 72-75.

ARCHITECTURE--DETAILS

Day, Nancy R. "A Clearing-House for Victorian Crafts." Americana. Vol. 15, No. 1, Mar./Apr. 1987. p. 37-41.

A Victorian crafts cooperative in San Francisco.

ARCHITECTURE--DETAILS

Jabs, Carolyn. "Antiques from Architecture." Americana. March/April 1982. pp. 44-49.

ARCHITECTURE--DETAILS

"A Schoolyard History, Newly Revised and Expanded." Architectural Record. August 1982. pp. 90-91.

ARCHITECTURE--DETAILS--DICTIONARIES

"A Glossary of Old-House Parts : Exterior Features of Pre-1920 Houses." Old-House Journal, May 1979. pp. 53-56.

Note: Includes line drawings.

ARCHITECTURE--EXHIBITIONS

"Exhibit Chronicles 2 Centuries of City Hall Architecture." Nation's Cities Weekly. November 8, 1982. p. 1 & 4-5.

ARCHITECTURE --EXHIBITIONS

Hughes, Ellen Roney. "Rowhouse, A Baltimore Style of Living." Museum News. January/February 1982. pp. 68-72.

ARCHITECTURE--EXHIBITIONS

Leslie, Stuart W. "Exhibit Review, The Urban Habitat: The City And Beyond." Jul. 1982. pp. 417-429.

ARCHITECTURE--EXHIBITIONS

Wright, Helena C. Exhibit Reviews: "HABS: The First Fifty Years (1933-1983) - An Exhibition at the Library of Congress, Washington, D.C." Technology and Culture. Vol. 26, No. 2, Apr. 1985. p. 253-256.

ARCHITECTURE--EXHIBITIONS--GREAT BRITAIN

Harris, John and Susan R. Stein. "The Architect and the Interior: Drawings of British Country Houses." Antiques. Vol. 129, No. 1, Jan. 1986. p. 232-239.

ARCHITECTURE--HANDBOOKS, MANUALS, ETC.

Crosbie, Michael J. "From "Cookbooks" to "Menus": the Transformation of Architecture Books in Nineteenth-Century America." Material Culture. Vol. 17, No. 1, Spring 1985. p. 1-23.

ARCHITECTURE--HANDBOOKS, MANUALS, ETC.

Poore, Patricia. " Pattern Book Architecture : is yours a mail-order house?" Old-House Journal. December 1980. p. 183, 190-191.

ARCHITECTURE--HISTORY

Labine, Clem. "Post-Victorian Domestic Architecture, The Neo-Colonial House." The Old-House Journal. Vol. XII, No. 4, May 1984. pp. 73-77.

ARCHITECTURE--HISTORY

"Olympiad Architecture: 1896 to Present." Pasadena Heritage. Vol. VIII, No. 1, Spring 1984. p. 11.

ARCHITECTURE--HISTORY--GREAT BRITAIN

"A Missing Link Revealed." Traditional Homes. Vol. 3, No. 11. Aug. 1987. p. 4 - 5.
Rare building type, smoke-bay house, discovered.

ARCHITECTURE--HISTORY--U.S.

Nooter, Eric. "Colonial Dutch Architecture in Brooklyn." de HALVE·MAEN. Vol. 60, No. 1. June 1987. pp. 12 - 16.

ARCHITECTURE--HISTORY--U.S.--ALASKA

"Pattern Books in Alaska?" Heritage. No. 26, Oct.-Dec. 1985. p. 3.

ARCHITECTURE--HUMAN FACTORS

Gordon, Jean and Jan MacArthur. "Living Patterns in Antebellum America as Depicted by Nineteenth-Century Women Writers." Winterthur Portfolio. Vol. 19, Nos. 2&3. Sum./Aut. 1984. pp. 177-192.

ARCHITECTURE--MEASUREMENT

"Seminar on the Recording of Buildings, March 31st 1982, Reports." Transactions. Vol. 7, 1982. pp. 9-17.

ARCHITECTURE--POLAND--19TH CENTURY

Poplawska, Irena & Stefan Muthesius. "Poland's Manchester : 19th-Century Industrial and Domestic Architecture in Lodz." Journal of the Society of Architectural Historians. Vol. 45, No. 2, June 1986. p. 148-160.

ARCHITECTURE--RESEARCH

Glenn, Patricia Brown and Emily Woodward. "How to Research the History of Your House." Historic Kansas City Foundation Gazette. July-August 1982. p. 4.

ARCHITECTURE--RESEARCH

Journal of Architectural Education. May. 1979.

Brown, Denise Scott. On formal analysis as design research.--Cowan, Henry. Aesthetic concepts and scientific research.--Nivola, Constantine. Le Corbusier: research directed toward poetry.

ARCHITECTURE--STUDY AND TEACHING

Architecture Minnesota. Sep./Oct. 1979

Several articles; bibliography.

ARCHITECTURE--STUDY AND TEACHING

Eriksen, Aase. "Recent Developments in Built Environmental Education." Environmental Comment, April 1979. pp. 7-10.

ARCHITECTURE--STUDY AND TEACHING

Charney, Wayne Michael and John W. Stamper. "Nathan Clifford Ricker and the Beginning of Architectural Education in Illinois." Illinois Historical Journal. Vol. 79, No. 4. Winter 1986. pp. 257-266.

ARCHITECTURE--STUDY AND TEACHING

Inland Architect, September 1979.

Entire Issue.

ARCHITECTURE--STUDY AND TEACHING

Salzman, Stanley. "Architectural education: What is the National Institute for Architectural Education all about?" Architectural Record. Feb. 1986. pp. 55-57.

ARCHITECTURE--STUDY AND TEACHING

"Teaching Children about Architecture." The Indiana Preservationist. No. 4, 1986. p. 3.

Resources available from Historic Landmarks Foundation of Indiana for teaching children about architecture.

ARCHITECTURE--UNITED STATES

"American Architecture Center Formed at Columbia University." AIA Journal. June 1983. p. 24.

ARCHITECTURE--U.S.--CALIFORNIA--CARMEL

Jeffers, Donnan. "Historic Houses: Robinson Jeffers, The Writer's Rugged and Poetic Tor House in Carmel, California." Architectural Digest. July 1981. pp. 112-119.

ARCHITECTURE--U.S.--CALIFORNIA--LOS ANGELES-- LOS ANGELES CENTRAL LIBRARY

"L.A. Central Library: Future Uncertain." Progressive Architecture. July 1981. pp. 42-46.

ARCHITECTURE--U.S.--IOWA--IOWA CITY

Lafore, Laurence. "American Classic." The Palimpset. Jan.-Feb. 1981. pp. 2-9.

ARCHITECTURE--U.S.--MARYLAND

350 Years of Art & Architecture in Maryland. College Park, MD: University of Maryland, 1984. 248p. (N6530.M3T43)

ARCHITECTURE--U.S.--MASSACHUSETTS--STOCKBRIDGE--
NAUMKEAG

Moffett, Anne D. and Warren C. "Naumkeag,
a Berkshire Landmark." The Antiques Magazine.
July 1981. pp. 136 - 146.

ARCHITECTURE--U.S.--MINNESOTA--MINNEAPOLIS

"A Survey of Important Architecture in
Minneapolis/St. Paul/The Neighborhoods and
Suburbs". Architecture Minnesota. April/May
1981. Entire Issue.

ARCHITECTURE--U.S.--NEW JERSEY--PRINCETON

Greiff, Connie. "Morven Drumthwacket,
The Spirit of New Jersey." New Jersey History.
Fall-Winter, 1980. pp. 175-190.

ARCHITECTURE--U.S.--NEW YORK--NEW YORK CITY

Metropolis: The Architecture and Design
Magazine of New York. Vol. 1, No. 1, July 1981.

ARCHITECTURE--U.S.--NEW YORK--NEW YORK CITY--
WOOLWORTH TOWER

Gaskie, Margaret F. "The Woolworth Tower:
A Technology Revisited, A Material Understood,
A Landmark Restored." Architectural Record.
Mid-August 1981. pp. 90-95.

ARCHITECTURE--U.S.--SOUTHWEST

Architecture. March 1984. Entire Issue.

ARCHITECTURE--U.S.--UTAH--BEAVER

Bonar, Linda L. "The Influence of the
Scots Stonemasons in Beaver, Utah." Utah
Preservation/Restoration. Vol. III, 1981.
pp. 54060.

ARCHITECTURE--U.S.--UTAH--SALT LAKE CITY--
FORT DOUGLAS

Vail, Cindy. "Fort Douglas: A Story of
Survival." Utah Preservation/Restoration.
Vol. 3, 1981. pp. 26-33.

ARCHITECTURE--U.S.--UTAH--SALT LAKE CITY--SALT
LAKE TEMPLE

Hamilton, Charles Mark. "The Salt Lake
Temple-A Monument to a People." Utah Preservation/
Restoration. Vol. III, 1981. pp. 6-18.

ARCHITECTURE, ART DECO

Architecture. December 1983. Entire
Issue.

ARCHITECTURE, ART DECO

Towers, Walter. "The Art Deco House."
Old House Journal. Vol. 13, No. 1,
Jan.-Feb. 1985. p. 13-19.

ARCHITECTURE, COLONIAL

Upton, Dell. "Vernacular Domestic Architecture
in Eighteenth Century Virginia." Winterthur
Portfolio. Summer/Autumn 1982. pp. 95-

ARCHITECTURE, COLONIAL--UNITED STATES

Carson, Cary, Norman F. Barka, William M.
Kelso, Garry Wheeler Stone, and Dell Upton.
"Impermanent Architecture in the Southern
American Colonies." Winterthur Portfolio.
Summer/Autumn 1981. pp. 135-196

ARCHITECTURE, COLONIAL--UNITED STATES

Schroeder, Roger. "Rhode Island Stone-
Ender: A 17th-century Style House Planned and
Built Under the Practiced Eye of a Sculptor."
Fine Homebuilding. December 1981/January 1982.
pp. 42-47.

ARCHITECTURE, COLONIAL--U.S.--MASSACHUSETTS

Sweeney, Kevin M. "Mansion People: Kinship, Class, and Architecture in Western Massachusetts in the Mid-Eighteenth Century." Winterthur Portfolio. Vol. 19, No. 4, Winter 1984. p. 231-255.

ARCHITECTURE, COMMERCIAL

Bayer, Linda. "Commercial Brick Was 20th C. Small Business Style." The Preservation Report, Alabama Historical Commission. Vol. XII, No. 1, July/August 1984. pp. 3-4.

ARCHITECTURE, COMMERCIAL

Lohof, Bruce A. "Hamburger Stand: Industrialization and the American Fast-Food Phenomenon." Journal of American Culture, Fall 1979. pp. 519-533.

ARCHITECTURE, COMMERCIAL--ADAPTIVE USE

"Narrow and Urbane." Progressive Architecture. September 1982. pp. 190-191.

ARCHITECTURE, DOMESTIC

Berger, Terry. "The Flounder House Myths." The Soulard Restorationist. Vol. 11, Issue 1, Feb. 1, 1986. p. 14.

ARCHITECTURE, DOMESTIC

Bibber, Joyce K. "Laying the Foundation for the American Dream." Landmarks Observer (Portland, Maine). March-April 1983. pp. 6-7.

ARCHITECTURE, DOMESTIC

Etlin, Richard A. "A Paradoxical Avant-Garde: Le Corbusier's Villas of the 1920's." Architectural Review. Vol. 181, No. 1079, Jan. 1987. p. 21-32.

ARCHITECTURE, DOMESTIC

"Getting to Know Your Early Twentieth-Century Neighborhood." Conserve Neighborhoods. July-August, 1982. Entire Issue.

ARCHITECTURE, DOMESTIC

Harvey, Thomas. "Mail-Order Architecture in the Twenties." Landscape. Vol. 25, no. 3, 1981. pp. 1-9.

ARCHITECTURE, DOMESTIC

Heisner, Beverly. "Harriet Morrison Irwin's Hexagonal House: An Invention to Improve Domestic Dwellings." The North Carolina Historical Review. April 1981. pp. 105-123.

ARCHITECTURE, DOMESTIC

Kahn, Renee Kahn. " Post-Victorian Domestic Architecture, The American Foursquare." The Old-House Journal. February 1982. pp. 29-32.

ARCHITECTURE, DOMESTIC

Labine, Clem. "The Homestead House." The Old-House Journal. March 1982. pp. 55-57.

ARCHITECTURE, DOMESTIC

Labine, Clem. "The Princess Anne House, Post-Victorian Domestic Architecture." The Old-House Journal. July 1982. pp. 135-137.

ARCHITECTURE, DOMESTIC

Labine, Clem. "The Romantic English Revival." The Old-House Journal. May 1983. pp. 81-83.

ARCHITECTURE, DOMESTIC

    Poore, Patricia. "Post-Victorian Houses." <u>The Old House Journal</u>. Vol. 14, No. 1, Jan/Feb. 1986. p. 24-26.

ARCHITECTURE, DOMESTIC--ADAPTIVE USE

    "A Little Corporate Commitment." <u>Architectural Record</u>. May 1983. pp.114-119.

ARCHITECTURE, DOMESTIC

    Snyder, Tim. "The Montauk Association Houses: a Century Ago, these Summer Cottages Signaled the Birth of Shingle Style." <u>Fine Homebuilding</u>. No. 37, Feb./Mar. 1987. p. 52-55.

ARCHITECTURE, DOMESTIC

    Tudor, Phoebe. "The Development of the Shotgun House." <u>New Orleans Preservation in Print</u>. Vol. 14, No. 2, Mar. 1987. p. 4-5.

ARCHITECTURE, DOMESTIC--CONSERVATION AND RESTORATION

    <u>Victorian Homes</u>. Winter 1982. Vol. ,1, No. 1.

ARCHITECTURE, DOMESTIC--CONSERVATION AND RESTORATION--PERIODICALS

    <u>Home Restoration</u>. New Oxford, Pa. : Cyme. Bimonthly. 1980-

    "Everyperson's guide to total home restoration".

ARCHITECTURE, DOMESTIC--CONSERVATION AND RESTORATION--U.S.--NEW YORK --LONG ISLAND

    Wolfe, Kevin. "Into the Manor Bought." <u>Metropolis</u>. May 1985. p. 26-31, 34-35.

    Preservation of estates on Long Island's North Shore discussed.

ARCHITECTURE, DOMESTIC--DESIGNS AND PLANS

Upton, Dell. "Pattern Books and Professionalism: Aspects of the Transformation of Domestic Architecture in America, 1800-1860.", <u>Winterthur Portfolio</u>, Vol. 19, No. 2/3, Summer/Autumn 1984, pp. 107-150.

ARCHITECTURE, DOMESTIC--19th CENTURY

    Stapleton, Constance. "A Town Blessed by Buildings: Marshall, Michigan." <u>Americana</u>. May/June 1979. pp. 42-47.

ARCHITECTURE, DOMESTIC--SECURITY MEASURES

    Helmer, Paul. "Security for the Older Home." <u>Historic Kansas City News</u>. Aug./Sept. 1980. p. 2-3.

ARCHITECTURE, DOMESTIC--U.S.--ALABAMA

    Jones, Harvie, F.A.I.A. "Settlement of Northern Alabama Coincided with Federal Period." <u>The Preservation Report</u>. Vol. 13, No. 3, Nov./ Dec. 1985. p. 3-4.

ARCHITECTURE, DOMESTIC--U.S.--CALIFORNIA

    Ford, Larry R. "The Enduring Romantic Cottage: Rethinking Historic Preservation." <u>Landscape</u>. Vol. 29, No. 2, 1986. p. 17-23.

    The Spanish cottage of the 1920's continues to be popular and livable in California.

ARCHITECTURE, DOMESTIC--U.S.--CALIFORNIA--SAN FRANCISCO

    Nelson, Christopher H. "South of Market Street: a Brief Guide to Its Architecture, Part II." <u>Heritage Newsletter</u>. Vol. 13, No. 3, Oct. 1985. 8 p.

ARCHITECTURE, DOMESTIC--U.S.--VIRGINIA--CAMDEN

    Howland, Richard H. " Portfolio: Camden" <u>19th Century</u> Winter 1979. p. 40-44.

ARCHITECTURE, TROPICAL

Homes, Nicholas H. III, "Gulf Coast Developed Unique Architecture." Archifeature, The Preservation Report, Alabama Historical Commission. Vol. XII, No. 3, November/December 1984. pp. 304.

ARCHITECTURE, ROMANESQUE

Massey, James C. and Shirley Maxwell. "Reading the Old House: the Romanesque Revival-- A.K.A. Richardsonian Romanesque." The Old House Journal. Vol. 14, No. 1, Jan./Feb. 1986. p. 32- 33.

ARCHITECTURE, QUEEN ANNE--U.S.--KANSAS

Cawthon, Richard J. "Kansas Has Many Examples of Queen Anne Residential Architecture." Kansas Preservation. Vol. 7, No. 2, Jan./Feb. 1985. p. 1-4.

ARCHITECTURE, MODERN--20th CENTURY--U.S.--NEW YORK--ALBANY

Draper, G. Stephen. "Winchester Gables: Pine Hills Spanish Homes." Albany Preservation Report. Spring 1985. p. 8-9.

ARCHITECTURE, MODERN--20TH CENTURY

Todd, James W., Gregory J. Friess, and Douglas R. Porter. "Colonial Village, Arlington, Virginia; Agreement on a Multi-Interest/Multi- Use/Multi-Phase Redevelopment." Urban Land. April 1984. pp. 8-14.

ARCHITECTURE, MODERN--TWENTIETH CENTURY

The Third Annual Review of Recent World Architecture. Architecture. Sep. 1984. Entire Issue.

ARCHITECTURE, MODERN--20TH CENTURY

Huxtable, Ada Louise. "The Troubled State of Modern Architecture". Architectural Record. January 1981. p. 72-79.

ARCHITECTURE, MODERN--20th CENTURY

Gordon, Barclay F. "The Fagus Factory: Contemporary Design Seventy Years Later." Architectural Record. July 1981. pp. 114-117.

ARCHITECTURE, MODERN--20TH CENTURY

Brown, Denise Scott. "A Worm's Eye View of Recent Architectural History." Architectural Record. February 1984. pp. 69-81.

ARCHITECTURE, MODERN--19TH CENTURY--U.S.

Bishir, Catherine W. "Jacob W. Holt, an American Builder." Winterthur Portfolio. Spring 1981. p. 1-31.

ARCHITECTURE, MODERN--19th CENTURY

Elstein, Rochelle S. "William Washburn and the Egyptian Revival in Boston." Old-Time New England. Vol. LXX, 1980. p. 63-81.

ARCHITECTURE, MODERN--17th-18th CENTURIES

Gerson, Martha Blythe. "A Glossary of Robert Adam's Neo-Classical Ornament" Architectural History: Journal of the Society of Architectural Historians of Great Britain. Vol. 24, 1981. pp. 59-82.

ARCHITECTURE, INDUSTRIAL--CONSERVATION AND RESTOR- ATION--U.S.--MONTANA--ANACONDA

Shayt, David H. "Big Stack Makes Tall Order for IA Preservationists." Society for Industrial Archeology Newsletter. Vol. 13, No. 3 & 4, Fall & Winter 1984. p. 13.

ARCHITECTURE, GEORGIAN

Guiness, Desmond and Walter Smalling Jr. (photographer). "The Rescue of Castletown; Volunteer Efforts Help Preserve This Irish Georgian Masterpiece." American Preservation. Nov./Dec. 1979. pp. 23-30.

ARCHITECTURE, VICTORIAN

Capen, Judith M. "If It's Victorian, What Style Is It?" Capitol Hill Restoration Society, Inc. News. May 1986. p. 8.

ARCHITECTURE, VICTORIAN

Capen, Judith M. "What Style Is It?" Capitol Hill Restoration Society Inc. News. Nov. 1986. pp. 4-5.

Architectural styles of the Victorian era.

ARCHITECTURE, VICTORIAN

Kosmer, John. "Redondo Redo : In Southern California's Redondo Beach, a Modest Victorian House Becomes a Showcase of Victorian Design." Victorian Homes. Vol. 6, No. 3. Summer 1987. pp. 20 - 27.

ARCHITECTURE, VICTORIAN

McNamara, Sarah. "The Rise and Fall of the Mansard Roof." Old-House Journal. Vol. XII, No. 7, August-September 1984. pp. 131, 152-5.

ARCHITECTURE, VICTORIAN

Rodgers, Patricia H. "Cambridge Carriage Houses: Lake View Avenue." Nineteenth Century Summer 1979. pp. 44-47.

ARCHITECTURE, VICTORIAN

Spigel, G. Thomas and Cecelia M. Spigel. "Restoring a Queen Anne House in Portville, New York." Victorian Homes. Vol. 6, No. 3. Summer 1987. pp. 38 - 43.

ARCHITECTURE, VICTORIAN--CONSERVATION AND RESTORATION

Lockwood, Charles. "Specialists in Restoring Victoriana." Americana, January/February, 1980. pp. 50-56.

ARCHITECTURE, VICTORIAN--ENGLAND--LONDON

Casson, Sir Hugh. "Albertland." Places. Vol. 1, No. 3, 1984. pp. 39-45.

ARCHITECTURE, VICTORIAN--U.S.--CONNECTICUT-- FENWICK

Little, Christopher. "Summer Place." Places Vol. 1, No. 3, 1984. pp. 62-72.

ARCHITECTURE, VICTORIAN--U.S.

Kowsky, Francis R. "Frederick Clark Withers: High Victorian Gothic Architect." Preservation League of New York State Newsletter. Vol. 10, No. 2. Mar./Apr. 1984. pp. 4-5.

ARCHITECTURE--U.S.--CALIFORNIA--SAN FRANCISCO

"Chinatown." Heritage Newsletter. (Foundation for San Francisco Architectural Heritage). Vol. 14, No. 1. Apr. 1986. (inset, 4 p.)

Chinatown architecture.

ARCHITECTURE, VICTORIAN--U.S.--KANSAS

"Italianate Architecture Was Leading Residential Style in the 1860s and 1870s." Kansas Preservation. Vol. VI, No. 6, September-October 1984. pp. 5-7.

ARCHITECTURE AND ENERGY CONSERVATION

"Early Alabama Builders Designed for a Hot Climate." The Preservation Report (Alabama). September/October 1983. p. 4.

ARCHITECTURE AND ENERGY CONSERVATION

"Energy." Special double issue. Journal of Architectural Education. Vol. 37, No. 3 & 4, Spring/Summer 1984. Entire issue.

ARCHITECTURE AND ENERGY CONSERVATION

Galt, George. "There's oil in them thar walls." Canadian Heritage. October 1981. p.28-32.

ARCHITECTURE AND ENERGY CONSERVATION

Progressive Architecture, April 1979. Note: Entire issue devoted to the subject of energy conservation; includes a bibliography of information sources.

ARCHITECTURE AND ENERGY CONSERVATION

Watson, Donald. "The Energy Within the Space Within." Progressive Architecture. July 1982. pp. 97-102.

ARCHITECTURE AND ENERGY CONSERVATION

Webber, Andrew. "Energy Prospects Require New Planning Considerations in Housing and Community Development Fields." Journal of Housing. May 1979.

ARCHITECTURE AND THE HANDICAPPED

Molloy, Larry. "One Way to Comply with Section 504 : A List of Suggested Publications and Procedures for Making a Museum Accessible to the Handicapped." Museum News, March-April 1979. pp 24-28.

ARCHITECTURE AND THE HANDICAPPED

Morningstar, Cathy D. "504 Impact and Implementation." SEMC Journal, November 1979. pp.46-51.

ARCHITECTURE AND THE HANDICAPPED

"Wheelchairs and Doric Columns: When Buildings are Being Rehabilitated, the Problems of the Disabled Should Be Remembered." Heritage Canada. Aug. 1979. p. 29.

ARCHITECTURE AND THE HANDICAPPED

Wiggins, Betty. "Colonial Williamsburg and the Handicapped--What's Happening?". Colonial Williamsburg Today. Spring, 1980. p. 9-11.

ARCHIVES

Dearstyne, Bruce W. "The Records Wasteland: What do state records programs need to break their 'cycle of poverty'?" History News. Vol. 40, No. 6, June 1985. p. 18-22.

ARCHIVES

Summerville, James. "First Aid for Local Government Records." History News. Vol. 40, No. 6, June 1985. p. 23.

ARCHIVES

Thurman, Sybil. "The 'News-American' Legacy." Maryland Today. Mar. 1987. p. 1-3.

One of Maryland's oldest daily newspapers, the News-American, has donated its archives to the University of Maryland.

ARCHIVES--U.S.--ILLINOIS

Moore, Karl. "Saving Illinois's Historical Local Records: the Illinois Regional Archives Depository System." Illinois Heritage Association Technical Insert No. 18. Nov./Dec. 1985. 4 p.

ARCHIVES, ARCHITECTURAL

"The Committee for the Preservation of Architectural Records Moves On." Architectural Record. Aug. 1979. pp. 77-82.

ARCHIVES, ARCHITECTURAL

Hoffer, William. "Buildings on File: America's Antique Buildings Live on in the Archives of the Historic American Buildings Survey, now beginning its second half-century." Americana. Vol. 13, No. 1, Mar./Apr. 1985. P. 90-93.

ARCHIVES, ARCHITECTURAL

Rambusch, Catha Grace and Carol Herselle Krinsky. "A Plan for America's Architectural Records." Visual Resources: An International Journal of Documentation. Fall1980/Winter 1981. p.188-192.

ARCHIVES, ARCHITECTURAL

"Recording in the National Parks." CRM Bulletin. Vol. 8, No. 2, Apr. 1985. p. 5-6.

ARKANSAS--ATCHISON

Snow, Nan. "Atchison: an Arkansas town learns the basics of preservation to save its grand Victorians." American Preservation. July/August 1980. p.9-22.

ARMORIES

"Hyattsville Castle Converted to Mall." Center City Report. June 1983. p. 5.

ARSENALS--U.S.--MASSACHUSETTS--HINGHAM

Schroeder, Alfred K. "Rise and Fall of Hingham Ammo Depot." Periodical (Council on America's Military Past). Vol. 13, No. 2, W.N. 51. pp. 53-56.

ARSENALS--U.S.--PENNSYLVANIA--PHILADELPHIA

"Major razing in Frankford Plan." Head-quarters Heliogram. No. 174, Jan./Feb. 1986. p. 1-12 and editorial, p. 2.

ARSON

"Arson Ravages Boston's Neighborhoods." Alliance Letter. September 1982. Entire Issue.

ARSON

"Arsonists Threaten Historic Structures." The Medallion. June 1982, p. 3

ARSON

Baldwin, Susan. "A Forty-Second Street Saga." City Limits. Mar. 1981. pp. 4-7.

ARSON

Tatsuno, Sheridan. "Stopping Arson." Planning. July 1979. pp. 25-27.

ARSON

Wright, Connie. "Public-Private Teams Douse Arsonists." Nation's Cities Weekly. August 23, 1982. pp. 5-6.

ARSON INVESTIGATION

Rich, Joan. "Conference Looks for Answers to Arson Problem." PPS News (Providence Preservation Society.) Vol. XXII, No. 3, November-December 1984. p. 4.

ARSON--U.S.--ARKANSAS--LITTLE ROCK

Heinbockel, C.S. "While History Burns." Quapaw Quarter Chronicle. Vol. 12, No. 6, Dec. 1985/Jan. 1986. p. 1, 10.

ART

Blumenthal, Diane H. "Images of America's Past, the Catalog of American Portraits Documents 70,000 Paintings in Historical Agencies and Museums Across the Country." History News. Vol. 39, No. 11, November 1984. pp. 31-32.

ART--COLLECTORS AND COLLECTING

Wellemeyer, Marilyn. "How Not To Get Stung by Art." Fortune. Apr. 15, 1985. p. 171-173.

ART, MODERN--19TH CENTURY

Houston, Jourdan. "Extravagant art that embellished our Gilded Age". Smithsonian May 1980. p. 108-117

ART--U.S.

"American arts at Yale University." Antiques. June 1980. pp. 1273-1336.

ART, MODERN--19TH CENTURY

Appleton, Carolyn and Jan Huebner. "Nineteenth Century American Art at the University of Texas at Austin." Antiques. Vol. CXXVI, No. 5, November 1984. pp. 1234-1243.

ART, MUNICIPAL

Lorenzen, Lee. "California Public Art Ordinances." Zoning News. May 1987. pp. 2 - 3.

ART AND STATE

Gutheim, Frederick. "Architecture and the Reagan Administration." Architectural Record. April 1981. p. 98-105.

ART CENTERS

"Building for the Arts." Architectural Record. April 1981. p. 118-135.

ART CENTERS

Clack, George. "Footlight Districts." The Cultural Post. January/February 1982. pp. 1 6.

ART CENTERS

Jacobson, Dorothy and Michael J. Pittas. "Cultural Planning: A Common Ground for Development." American Arts. January 1982. pp. 22-24.

ART CENTERS

Sinclair, Stephen. "Spirit Square: How Charlotte, North Carolina, revitalized its downtown by converting an abandoned church into an arts center." Cultural Post. Sept/Oct. 1980. p. 18-21

ART CENTERS

Sinclair, Stephen. "When it Comes to the Arts, Winston-Salem Means Business." The Cultural Post. January/February 1982. pp. 12-15.

ART DECO

Aslet, Clive. "Stepped Back and Laid Back." Country Life. Mar. 12, 1987. p. 94-95.

Art deco architecture in Maimi, Florida.

ART DECO--U.S.--NORTH CAROLINA--WINSTON-SALEM

"Deco Landmark Augmented." Architecture. May 1984. pp. 216 - 221.

ART INDUSTRIES AND TRADE, SHAKER

The Clarion, Fall 1979.

Several articles on Shaker Industries, furniture and lifestyle.

ART MUSEUMS

Gebhard, David. "Harmonious Addition to an 'Arcadia'." Architecture. Feb. 1987. p. 54-57.

Addition to the Huntington Library and Art Gallery.

ART MUSEUMS--U.S.--CALIFORNIA--SACRAMENTO

West, Richard V. "Edwin Bryant Crocker's Art Gallery in Sacramento". 19th Century. Winter 1979. p. 34-39.

ART MUSEUMS--U.S.--ILLINOIS--EVANSTON

Sokol, David M. "The Terra Museum of American Art, Evanston, Illinois." Antiques. Vol. CXXVI, No. 5, November 1984. pp. 1156-1169.

ART NOUVEAU

Bayer, Patricia. "Flowing, Curving, Glowing, Art Nouveau." Antiques World. October 1981. pp. 24-33.

ART OBJECTS--CONSERVATION AND RESTORATION

Byrne, Gregory. "Ethnographic and Decorative Arts Conservation: a Comparison of Approaches." CRM Bulletin. Vol. 8, No. 3 & 4, June/Aug. 1985. p. 3, 5-6.

ARTIFICIAL SIDING

Anderson, Barbara. "Synthetic Siding Detrimental to Historic Buildings." Kansas Preservation. Vol. 8, No. 1, Nov./Dec. 1985. p. 6-7.

ARTIFICIAL SIDING

"The Case for Synthetic Materials" and "Cost Comparison for Painting and Siding a Home in Heritage Square." Michigan Historic District Commission Network Newsletter. Sep. 1983. pp. 1-2.

ARTIFICIAL SIDING

Conway, Brian D. " The Case Against Substitute Siding" The Old-House Journal April 1980. p. 37 and 44-46.

ARTIFICIAL SIDING

Jagger, Allan. "Vinyl and Aluminum Siding: The Truth Behind the Cover-Up." Landmarks Observer. Vol. 13, No. 2, Mar./Apr. 1986. p. 12-13.

ARTIFICIAL SIDING

Pilling, Ron. "Removing Formstone and Other Indignities." The Old-House Journal. September 1982. pp. 179-182.

ARTIFICIAL SIDING

"Synthetic Siding." Culture and History (West Virginia). March/April 1984. p. 10.

ARTIFICIAL SIDING

Widell, Cherilyn E. "Vinyl Siding Problems Confronted" 11593. February/March 1980. p.4-5.

ARTISTS

Curry, David P. "Whistler and Decoration." Antiques. Vol. CXXVI, No. 5, November 1984. pp. 1186-1199.

ARTISTS

DeVeer, Elizabeth. "Willard Metcalf in Cornish, New Hampshire." Antiques. Vol. CXXVI, No. 5, November 1984. pp. 1208-1215.

ARTISTS

Hill, May B. "Artists by Themselves: Portraits of Artists from the National Academy of Design." Antiques. Vol. CXXVI, No. 5, November 1984. pp. 1170-1174.

ARTISTS

Hjalmarson, Birgitta. "Thomas Hill." Antiques. Vol. CXXVI, No. 5, November 1984. pp. 1200-1207.

ARTISTS

Husch, Gail E. "David Maitland Armstrong." Antiques. Vol. CXXVI, No. 5, November 1984. pp. 1175-1185.

ARTISTS

Sill, Gertrude G. "John Haberle, Master of Illusion." Antiques. Vol. CXXVI, No. 5, November 1984. pp. 1127-1133.

ARTISTS' STUDIOS

Royer, Charles. "Seattle." American Arts. January 1982. p. 20.

ARTS AND CRAFTS MOVEMENT

Abercrombie, Stanlty. "Furnishings: George Mann Niedecken, Craftsman of the Prairie School." AIA Journal. November 1981. pp. 80-83.

ARTS AND CRAFTS MOVEMENT

Chase, Laura. "Eden in the Orange Groves, Bungalows & Courtyard Houses of Los Angeles." Landscape. Vol. 25, no. 3, 1981. pp. 29-36.

ARTS AND CRAFTS MOVEMENT

Flaherty, Carolyn. "The Craftsman House." The Old-House Journal, November 1979. pp. 121, 123-125.

ARTS AND CRAFTS MOVEMENT

Kalberer, Julie. "Tiffany Glass is Discovered in Providence." PPS News. September-October, 1981. pp. 6-7.

ARTS AND CRAFTS MOVEMENT

"Living With Antiques: A Collection in Upstate New York." Antiques. Vol. 128, No. 1, July 1985. p. 120-124.

William Morris wallpapers displayed.

ARTS AND CRAFTS MOVEMENT

Love, Jeannine. "Blanche Ostertag: Another Wright Collaborator." Frank Lloyd Wright Newsletter Vol. 4, No. 2, 1981, pp. 17-18.

ARTS AND CRAFTS MOVEMENT

Richards, Nancy. "The Far-Reaching Influence of Gustav Stickly: Mission Furniture in Utah". Utah Preservation/Restoration. Vol 2/Issue 2 1980. pp. 38 - 47.

ARTS AND CRAFTS MOVEMENT

Smith, Mary Ann. "Gustav Stickley: Master Craftsman Designer". Newsletter, Preservation League of New York State. Vol. 10, No. 6, Nov./Dec. 1984. p. 4-5.

ARTS AND CRAFTS MOVEMENT

Strebeigh, Fred. "Pleasure in Creation." American Heritage. Vol. 38, No. 5. Jul./Aug. 1987. pp. 82 - 89.
Arts and Crafts Movement reaches its 100th anniversary.

ARTS AND CRAFTS MOVEMENT--U.S.--MICHIGAN--
DETROIT

Novak, Celeste. "PEWABIC: a Vehicle for
Symbolism of the Arts and Crafts Movement."
Chronicle, Historical Society of Michigan. Vol.
21, No. 3, Autumn 1985. p. 2-7.

Ornamental patterns of Pewabic Pottery
decorate the Union Trust (Guardian) Building of
1929 in Detroit.

ARTS AND CRAFTS MOVEMENT--U.S.--NEW JERSEY--
PARSIPPANY-TROY HILLS

Benton, R. Bruce. "Stickley's Craftsman
Farms: a Preservation Priority." Preservation
Perspective NJ. Vol. 4, No. 6, Sept./Oct. 1985.
p. 1-2.

ARTS--PLANNING

"Cultural Planning." Livability Digest.
Spring 1982. pp. 34-45.

ASBESTOS

Donovan, Brian. "Confronting the Asbestos
Problem." Rehab Notes. Vol. 10, No. 2, Mar. 1986.
p. 4.

ASSOCIATIONS, INSTITUTIONS, ETC.

Longsworth, Nellie L. "Preservation
Action: Building a Preservation Constituency:"
CRM Bulletin. Vol. 9, No. 5, Oct.-Dec. 1986.
p. 11.

ASSOCIATIONS, INSTITUTIONS, ETC.

"The Maryland Historical Society: a New Look
at an Old Association." The Montgomery County Preservationist. Vol. 2, No. 2, Oct./Nov. 1986. p. 1,
6.

ASSOCIATIONS, INSTITUTIONS, ETC.

"Office of Preservation." Humanities.
Vol. 7, No. 3, June 1986. p.34.

The activities of the National Endowment
for the Humanities's Office of Preservation are outlined.

ASSOCIATIONS, INSTITUTIONS, ETC.

Schultz, William T. "Privately Managing a
Public Resource." Land Trusts' Exchange. Vol. 5,
No. 2, Fall 1986. p. 8-9.

The Ohio Historical Society manages a system
of historic, natural, and archaeological sites
in Ohio.

ASSOCIATIONS, INSTITUTIONS, ETC.--BUILDINGS

"Plans for Masonic Building."
Colorado Heritage News. October 1983.
p. 6.

ASSOCIATIONS, INSTITUTIONS, ETC.--MANAGEMENT--
(BOARDS)

Unterman, Israel and Richard Hart Davis.
"The Strategy Gap for Not-For-Profits." and
Vilberg, Alan. "Making Boards Work Better."
Museum News. June 1984. pp. 38-46.

AUDIO-VISUAL MATERIALS

Malan, Nancy E. "Producing Professional
Quality Slide Shows: A Systematic Approach."
AASLH Technical Report 2. 1985. 19 p.

AUDIO-VISUAL MATERIALS

O'Neill, John R. "A Guide to Overhead
Transparencies." Audio Visual Directions. July
1981. p. 14.

AUDIO-VISUAL MATERIALS

Rushton, William F. "Videotex: Wave of
the Future." Planning. September 1982. pp. 21-
24.

AUDITORIUMS--CONSERVATION AND RESTORATION

Kirlazis, Judith. "Roosevelt's Auditorium."
Inland Architect, September 1979. pp. 12-14.

AUTOMOBILE PARKING

Bond, James H. "Downtown Parking Problems Can Be Solved." Center City Report. August 1981. pp. 3-4.

AUTOMOBILE PARKING

Gaffney, David H. "Parking in Painesville." APWA Reporter. August 1981. p. 25.

AUTOMOBILES

"A Buyer's Market for Collector Cars." Business Week. June 18, 1984. pp. 120-2.

AUTOMOBILES

Conant, Alan. "City's Automotive Heritage Not Confined to Motor Speedway." The Indiana Preservationist. No. 2. May 1987. pp. 4 - 5. Auto showrooms in Indianapolis.

AUTOMOBILES

Long, Nancy. "Six New National Historic Landmarks Include Motor Speedway." The Indiana Preservationist. No. 2. May 1987. p. 4.

AUTOMOBILES--HISTORY

Lewis, David L. "Ford's (Henry) Michigan Homes." Chronicle, The Quarterly Magazine of the Historical Society of Michigan. Vol. 20, No. 2, Summer 1984. pp. 20-21.

AUTOMOBILES--SERVICE STATIONS--CONSERVATION AND RESTORATION--U.S.--MISSISSIPPI-- CORINTH

"Abandoned Gas Station Gets New Lease on Life." Commercial Renovation. August 1984. pp. 46-47.

BANK BUILDINGS

"Kate Mantilini Restaurant." Progressive Architecture. Jan. 1987. pp. 96-97. Conversion of a commercial bank into a 24-hour restaurant in Beverly Hills, CA.

BANK BUILDINGS

Morgan, William T. "Strongboxes on Main Street: Prairie-style banks". Landscape. 1980. vol.24, no.2. p. 35-40.

BANK BUILDINGS--AUSTRALIA

Eltham, Pater. "Gracious Old Lady of Queen Street." Heritage Australia. Vol. 5, No. 1, Autumn 1986. p. 2-5.

Brisbane's National Australia Bank building is outstanding example of High Victorian, Classical Revival bank architecture.

BANK BUILDINGS--CONSERVATION AND RESTORATION

"A Proper Bostonian." Architectural Record. July 1983. pp. ;28-135.

BANK BUILDINGS--CONSERVATION AND RESTORATION-- U.S.--FLORIDA--PALM BEACH

"First National Gets 'The Palm Beach Look.'" Commercial Renovation. August 1984. pp. 40-43.

BANK BUILDINGS--CONSERVATION AND RESTORATION--U.S.--MASS.--EAST CAMBRIDGE

"The East Cambridge Savings Bank". Architectural Record. April 1979. pp. 97-102.

BANKS AND BANKING

"New Development Bank Program Operating." Downtown Idea Exchange. July 15, 1982. pp. 3-4.

BARNS

Coffey, Brian. "Nineteenth-Century Barns in Geauga County, Ohio." Pioneer America. Dec. 1978. pp. 53-63.

BARNS

"In the Cathedrals of the Fields, Canadian Barns Reflect the Astonishing Inventiveness of Their Forgotten Builders." Canadian Heritage. August/September 1984. pp. 30-36.

BARNS

Kamin, Blair. "Architecture of Round Barns Is Linked to History." The Bracket. New Series, Vol. 2, No. 2, Spring 1986. p. 4-5.

BARNS

Korab, Balthazar, photographer. "Barns." American Preservation. Jun.-Jul. 1979. pp. 22-35.

BARNS

Schultz, LeRoy G. "Tobacco Barns." Goldenseal. Vol. 11, No. 4, Winter 1985. p. 60-64.

BARNS

Taylor, Lucy. "A Place for Memories-- The Leatherman Barn of Hardy County." Goldenseal. Winter 1981. pp. 50-56.

BARNS--ADAPTIVE USE

Doubilet, Susan. "Wine in a Manger: UKZ Architects of Ithaca, NY, insert a templelike structure in a barn to provide facilities for a winery." Progressive Architecture. Apr. 1985. p. 98-101.

BARNS--ADAPTIVE USE

"A New Use for an Old Stable." Historic Places in New Zealand. No. 15, Dec. 1986. p. 6.

A stable was converted to an art gallery.

BARNS--ADAPTIVE USE

Worne, Janet. "Born-Again Barns." Country Magazine. March 1981. p. 32-33.

BASEBALL PARKS

Neilson, Brian James. "Dialogue with the City: the evolution of baseball parks." Landseape. Vol. 29, No. 1, 1986. p. 39-47.

BATHING POOLS

Dawes, John. "Bathing Build." Traditional Homes. July 1986. p. 41-46.

Technical aspects of pool installation.

BATHROOMS

Curtis, Giles. "Sanitarian Saga." Traditional Homes. April 1986. p. 104-111.

History of the bathroom.

BATHROOMS

Monich, Joni. "Bathrooms with Character." The Old-House Journal. June 1982. pp. 127-129.

BEACHES
"Beach Access". Environmental Comment. March 1980. Entire issue.

BEDROOMS

Garrett, Elisabeth Donaghy. "The American Home, Part III: The Bedchamber." <u>Antiques</u>. pp. 612-625.

BILLBOARDS

"Billboards Remain Despite Highway Beautification Law". <u>Architecture</u>. Feb. 1985. p. 32.

BILLBOARDS

McMahon, Edward T. "Opinion." <u>Place</u>. Vol. 4, No. 10, November 1984. pp. 8-10.

BILLBOARDS

"New Federal Legislation to Restrict Billboards Proposed." <u>Architecture</u>. Jan. 1986. p. 18, 84.

BILLS, LEGISLATIVE

Barnes, William. "British Enterprise Zones: A Look at 2 Years Experience." <u>Nation's Cities Weekly</u>. September 10, 1984. Vol. 7, No. 37. p. 7.

BILLS, LEGISLATIVE

"Estate Tax Law is Changing Again." <u>Business Week</u>. May 7, 1984. pp. 156-7, 160.

BILLS, LEGISLATIVE

Hawkins, Benjamin M. "The Impact of the Enterprise Zone on Urban Areas." <u>Growth & Change</u>. Vol. 15, No. 1, January 1984. pp. 35-40.

BILLS, LEGISLATIVE

"1983 Jobs Act Preserves Historic Resources Creates New Employment Opportunities." <u>Pennsylvania Preservation</u>. Spring/Summer 1984. pp. 3-6

BILLS, LEGISLATIVE

"Senate Tax Bill Would Reduce Rehab Credits." <u>Urban Conservation Report</u>. Vol. VIII, No. 7, April 24, 1984. pp. 1-3.

BILLS, LEGISLATIVE

"Tax-Exempt Leasing: The House and Senate Bills." <u>Urban Conservation Report</u>. Vol. VIII, No. 7, April 24, 1984. p. 3.

BILLS, LEGISLATIVE

Williams, Chuck. "Columbia Gorge Legislation Stalled in Senate." <u>American Rivers</u>. Vol. 13, No. 2, June 1985. p. 8-9.

National Park designation for the area under discussion.

BILLS, LEGISLATIVE--TAX INCENTIVES

"House, Senate Approve Tax Bills Affecting Development Bonds, UDAG, Enterprise Zones." <u>Community Development Digest</u>. No. 84-8, April 24, 1984. pp. 8-9.

BILLS, LEGISLATIVE--U.S.--CALIFORNIA

"Legislation Introduced, Task Force Recommendations Take Shape." <u>California Preservation</u>. Vol. 8, No. 2, April 1984. p. 4.

BILLS, LEGISLATIVE--U.S.--CALIFORNIA--SAN FRANCISCO

"Proposals to Weaken Landmark Ordinance Defeated." <u>Heritage Newsletter</u>. Vol. 13, No. 1, Spring 1985. p. 1, 3.

BIRTHPLACES

Kahn, David M. "The Theodore Roosevelt Birthplace in New York City." Antiques, July, 1979. pp. 176-181.

BOAT BUILDING

Lipke, Paul. "Some subtle changes are afoot in the wooden boat kingdom". National Fisherman. April 30, 1980. p. 82-84.

BOAT BUILDING

Dayee, Frances S. "Craftsman's art is legacy of boatbuilding ancestors." National Fisherman. Apr. 30, 1980. pp. 86-87.

BONDS

Santucci, R.M. "How Do Bonds Perform?" Cost Cuts. Vol. 3, No. 2, Nov. 1985. p. 6-7.

How bonding works, if a contractor defaults.

BREWERIES--ADAPTIVE USE

"Refurbishment with Flair." Waterfront World. Vol. 5, No. 4, July/August 1986. p. 7.

London's Courage Brewery, a decorative Victorian structure nearly 200 years old, being converted to luxury apartments.

BRICK--CONSERVATION AND RESTORATION

Collier, Richard. "Guidelines for Restoring Brick Masonry." Parks. Vol. 8, No. 4. Jan./Feb. 1984. pp. 15-21.

BRICK WALLS

Ritchie, T. "Notes on Dichromatic Brickwork in Ontario." APT Bulletin. (Vol. XI, #2) 1979. pp. 60-75.

BRICK WALLS

Santucci, R.M. "There's No Big Trick to Repairing Old Brick." Cost Cuts. Vol. 3, No. 2, Nov. 1985. p. 1-3.

BRICK WALLS

Watson, Penelope S. "Eighteenth Century Patterned Brickwork in Connecticut." The Connecticut Antiquarian. Vol. XXXVI, No. 1, June 1984. pp. 4-12.

BRICKLAYING

Pilling, Ron. "Brick Walks". Old-House Journal. July 1980. p.73, 78-79.

BRICKMAKING

Walters, William D. "Nineteenth Century Midwestern Brick." Pioneer America. September 1982. pp. 125-136.

BRICKS

The Association for Preservation Technology Bulletin, number 3 1979.

Several articles on such topics as repointing, brick making and brick detail.

BRICKS

Graves, Jim. "History Under Your Feet." Blueprints. Vol. 5, No. 1. Spring 1987. p. 4.
Marking of brick; International Brick Collectors Association.

BRICKS

Hammond, Carol. "The Decorative, Durable Brick." Americana. July/August 1984. pp. 80-82.

BRICKS

Roth, Ron. "Masonry Building Materials: Brick". The Brownstoner. Vol. 16, No. 1, Jan. 1985. p. 1-6.

BRICKWORKS--U.S.--ILLINOIS

WAlters, William D., Jr. " Abandoned Nineteenth Century Brick and Tile Works in Central Illinois: An Introduction from Local Sources". Industrial Archaeology Review. Winter 1979-80. p. 70-80.

BRIDGE CONSTRUCTION

Snow, Richard F. "American Characters: Herman Haupt." American Heritage. Vol. 36, No. 2, Feb./Mar. 1985. p. 54-55.

BRIDGES

"Carlyle's General Dean Suspension Bridge." Historic Illinois. Vol. 9, No. 5, Feb. 1987. p. 14.

BRIDGES

"Colorado's Historic Bridges." Colorado Preservation. Winter 1987. p. 3.

BRIDGES

Desson, Ken and Norman Ball. "Good Connections." Canadian Heritage. October/ November 1984. pp. 18-22.

BRIDGES

Gibb, James. "Role of a Covered Bridge." Empire State Courier. Vol. 21, No. 3, Nov. 1986. p. 4-5.

BRIDGES

Kashdan, Sandra. "Bridges Light up across Continent." Waterfront World. Vol. 6, No. 1, Jan./Feb. 1987. p. 1, 4-5.

Lighting of bridges.

BRIDGES

Konkle, Joseph E. "Iron Bridges Need Saving." Indiana Covered Bridge Society Newsletter. Vol. 23, No. 2, April 1986. p. 1-3.

BRIDGES

Magaziner,Henry J. "The Rebirth of an Engineering Landmark." APT Bulletin. Vol. 18, No. 4, 1986. p. 52-64.

Restoration of the Delaware Aqueduct, the oldest remaining wire suspension structure in the U.S.

BRIDGES

"Roebling Aqueduct Restored." American Canals. Bull. No. 58, Aug. 1986. p. 1, 3.

BRIDGES

Schmitt, Robert C. "Historic Hawaiian Bridges." Historic Hawai'i News. October 1981. pp. 4-5.

BRIDGES

Society for Industrial Archeology Newsletter, January & March 1979.

Note: Articles on historic bridges and bridge engineering.

BRIDGES, CONCRETE--U.S.--MASSACHUSETTS

Clark, Edie. "The Bridge Blooms Again." Yankee. Vol. 49, No. 6, June 1985. p. 78-85, 104-105.

A trolley bridge has served as a community garden for over 50 years.

BRIDGES, CONCRETE--U.S.--OREGON

Eisemann, Eric. "Bye Bye Alsea Bay Bridge." Newsletter, Historic Preservation League of Oregon. No. 35, Winter 1985. p. 5-6.

BRIDGES--CONSERVATION AND RESTORATION

Anderson, Kenneth C. "Helping our bridges span the ages". Public Works Historical Society Newsletter. June 1980. p. 6-7.

BRIDGES--CONSERVATION AND RESTORATION

Closs, Christopher W. "The Failure to Preserve the Bellows Falls Bridge." Society for Industrial Archeology Newsletter. Winter 1983. pp. 1-3.

BRIDGES--CONSERVATION AND RESTORATION

"County and Consultants Rehabilitate Bridges." APWA Reporter. March 1982. pp. 22-24.

BRIDGES--CONSERVATION AND RESTORATION

Dinitz, Arthur M. and Russell Ferri. "Rehabilitating Bridges with Polymer Concrete." APWA Reporter. Aug. 1985. p. 13.

BRIDGES--CONSERVATION AND RESTORATION

Doyle, Judith. "Wollaston Bridge : Restoration of a New Zealand Designed and Built Bridge." Heritage Australia. Vol. 5, No. 1, Autumn 1986. p. 40-41.

BRIDGES--CONSERVATION AND RESTORATION

Doyle, Richard. "Neshanic Bridge Restoration." NJ Preservation Perspective. Vol. 4, No. 4, May/June 1985. p. 6.

BRIDGES--CONSERVATION AND RESTORATION

Silverman, Jane. "Rainbow Arch Bridge preserved through oral history". Public Works Historical Society Newsletter. March 1981. p.3-4.

BRIDGES--CONSERVATION AND RESTORATION--CALIFORNIA

"Colorado Bridge." Pasadena Heritage. Vol. VIII, No. 1, Spring 1984. p. 3.

BRIDGES--GREAT BRITAIN

Beazley, Elisabeth. "The Menai Suspension Bridge, 1819-26 and Britannia Bridge, 1845-50." Transactions of the Ancient Monuments Society. Vol. 29. p. 36-62.

BRIDGES--HISTORY

Crockett, Bernice Norman. "Across the Muddy Red." The Chronicles of Oklahoma. Winter 1983-84. pp. 340-363.

BRIDGES--HISTORY--U.S.--CALIFORNIA--SAN FRANCISCO

Crosbie, Michael J. "The Background of the Bridges: Two Famed Spans Raced for Records in the Depths of the Depression." Architecture. Mar. 1985. p. 150-157.

Golden Gate and Bay Bridges discussed.

BRIDGES--HISTORY--U.S.--MONTANA

Quivik, Fredric L. "Montana's Minneapolis Bridge Builders." IA, The Journal of the Society for Industrial Archeology. Vol. 10, No. 1, 1984. pp. 35-54.

BRIDGES--U.S.--CONNECTICUT--EAST BERLIN

Darnell, Victor. "Lenticular Bridges from East Berlin, Connecticut." IA. Vol. 5, No. 1. 1979. pp. 19-32.

BRIDGES--U.S.--IOWA--SIOUX CITY

Bowers, Martha and Hans Muessig. "Spanning the Missouri." The Palimpset. Jan.-Feb. 1981. pp. 14 - 25.

BRIDGES--U.S.--MICHIGAN--DETROIT

Naylor, Bob. " The Building of the Ambassador Bridge". Chronicle. Winter 1980 p.4-9.

BRIDGES--U.S.--NEW YORK

"Covered Bridges of New York State." Empire State Courier. Vol. 21, No. 2. Jul. 1986. pp. 7-10.

BRIDGES--U.S.--NEW YORK--NEW YORK

Salwen, Peter. "Visible City: A Selection of Bridges Around Manhattan." Metropolis. June 1985. p. 30-33.

BRIDGES, IRON AND STEEL

"Dynamite, Murky Deals Claim Big Bridges in MN, NY." Society for Industrial Archeology Newsletter. Vol. 14, No. 1, 1985. p. 1-2.

BRIDGES, IRON AND STEEL

Herbst, Rebecca. "Bridge Relocated through Impressive Cooperative Effort." Colorado Heritage News. July 1985. p. 6.

BRIDGES, IRON AND STEEL--MAINTENANCE AND REPAIR

Apostolos, John A. "Stopping Corrosion in its Tracks." APWA Reporter. Mar. 1986. p. 12-13.

BRIDGES, IRON AND STEEL--MAINTENANCE AND REPAIR

McLaughlin, David. "The Repair of a Cast-Iron Bridge over the Kennet and Avon Canal, Sydney Gardens, Bath." Transactions. Vol. 5, 1980. pp.30-33.

BRIDGES, MASONRY, CONCRETE--U.S.--NEW YORK

Chamberlin, William P. "The Cleft-ridge Span: America's First Concrete Arch/" IA, The Journal of the Society for Industrial Archeology. Vol. 9, No. 1, 1983. pp. 29-44.

BRIDGES, TRUSS

Leon, Hortense. "Spanning the Decades: A Look at Chicago's Fascinating Bridges." Inland Architecture. Jan./Feb. 1980. pp. 23-27.

BRIDGES, TRUSS

Perry, Wayne. "Sketches of the Childs Truss." Covered Bridge Topics. Vol. 44, No. 3, Summer 1985. p. 8-11.

BRIDGES, TRUSS--CONSERVATION AND RESTORATION

"New Arch Saves Old Bridge." APWA Reporter, (American Public Works Association). June 1984. p. 21.

BRIDGES, TRUSS--TENNESSEE PROGRAM

Hudson, Patricia. "Adopt a Bridge." Americana. July/August 1984. p. 20.

BRONZES--CONSERVATION AND RESTORATION

Veloz, Nicolas F. "Cleaning Up the Bronze in the National Park Service." CRM Bulletin. Vol. 9, No. 1, Feb. 1986. p. 2-3.

BROWNSTONE--CONSERVATION AND RESTORATION

Latham, Sarah. "Restoring Brownstone Facades: Techniques for Repairing and Replacing 19th-century Architectural Elements." Fine Homebuilding. October/November 1981, No. 5. pp. 36-39.

BUILDING

Allen, Henry. "There'll be Some Changes in the City When the Cranes Come Soaring In." Smithsonian. Vol. 16, No. 6, Sept. 1985. p. 44-53.

Use of giant cranes change the way buildings are constructed.

BUILDING--HISTORY

Lounsbury, Carl. "The Building Process in Antebellum North Carolina." The North Carolina Historical Review. October 1983. pp. 431-456.

BUILDING--HISTORY

National Building Museum. Blueprints. Vol. 1, No. 1., Summer 1981. 12 p.

BUILDING--HISTORY

"Our First 75 Years." Buildings. September 1981. Entire Issue.

CONTENTS: Shullaw, Susan. A Close Encounter of the 75th Kind--Henrich, Craig. Multi-Family Housing: The Early Years--Henrich, Craig. Advertising Aids Industry Growth--The Ohio Building at 75: A Diamond in the Rough is Restored.

BUILDING --HISTORY--U.S.--LOUISIANA--NEW ORLEANS

Van Tilburg, Mark W. "Researching the History of New Orleans' Buildings and Houses." New Orleans Preservation in Print. Vol. 13, No. 7, Sept. 1986. p. 8-9.

Research resources described.

BUILDING, STONE

Higgins, William J. "Stone Finishing Marks." The Association for Preservation Technology Bulletin. pp. 11-34.

BUILDING, TERRA-COTTA--U.S.--NEW YORK--NEW YORK CITY

Sliney, Diane Jones. "NY Landmark: Made in NJ." Preservation Perspective NJ. Vol. 4, No. 5, July/Aug. 1985, p. 1-2.

Materials for NY's Woolworth Building made in Perth Amboy, NJ by the Atlantic Terra Cotta Company.

BUILDING INSPECTION

Fidler, John. "Non-Destructive Surveying Techniques for the Analysis of Historic Buildings." Transactions. Vol. 5, 1980. pp. 3-10.

BUILDING INSPECTION

LePatner, Barry B. "Caveat Architectus: Facade Inspection and the Design Professional." Architectural Record. Vol. 169, No. 9, July 1981. pp. 57, 59, 61.

BUILDING INSPECTIONS

Anderson, Barbara and Terry Marmet. "Annual Inspections Recommended for Historic Buildings." Kansas Preservation. Vol. 8, No. 2, Jan./Feb. 1986. p. 5-7.

BUILDING LAWS

Antell, Jim. "Building Codes in Rehab Projects." Building Design & Construction. Vol. 27, No. 8, Aug. 1986. p. 84-85.

BUILDING LAWS

"Bradbury Building Endangered." Progressive Architecture. July 1981. p. 42.

BUILDING LAWS

"Building and Zoning Codes Updated Under New Proposals." The Neighborhood Works. January 1982. pp. 16-17.

BUILDING LAWS

"Governor Signs Rehab Building Codes Bill." The Rambler, Newsletter of the Georgia Trust. Vol. 11, No. 3, Summer 1984. p. 7.

BUILDING LAWS

"Historic Preservation and Building Codes." The Brownstoner. December 1981. p. 5.

BUILDING LAWS

"The New Generation of Building Codes." Urban Outlook. Vol. 7, No. 15, Aug. 15, 1985. p. 2-3.

BUILDING LAWS

Nolon, John R. "Housing rehabilitation and code enforcement : effective strategies require integrated efforts." Journal of Housing. February 1981. p. 80-87.

BUILDING LAWS

Overberg, Paul. "Uniform Fire Code: a Preservation Perspective." Preservation Perspective NJ. Vol. 4, No. 6, Sept./Oct. 1985. p. 6-7.

BUILDING LAWS

"Possible Breakthrough for Old Buildings at BOCA Meeting." Urban Conservation Report. Vol. VIII, No. 10, June 21, 1984. p. 4.

BUILDING LAWS

"Regulating Existing Buildings". APT Bulletin. Vol. XIII, No. 2 1981. Entire issue.

BUILDING LAWS

"Rehab Code Near Reality for Ohio." Ohio Preservation. Vol. IV, No. 8, October 1984. p. 1.

BUILDING LAWS

Tise, Larry E. and A.J. Capling. "Building regulation and historic preservation". APWA Reporter. December 1980. p.11-15.

BUILDING LAWS

Zgolinski, Al. "Cracking the Codes." Museum News, January-February, 1979. pp. 52-55. "While controlling energy waste, building codes must take into account the special requirements of the cultural community."

BUILDING LAWS--U.S.--WISCONSIN

"Wisconsin's Historic Building Code Goes into Effect." Wisconsin Preservation. Vol. 10, No. 6. Nov./Dec. 1986. pp. 1-2.

New code allows a cost-effective approach to preservation and restoration of historic buildings.

BUILDING LAWS--U.S.--NORTH CAROLINA

Burns, Norma DeCamp. "Preservation Appendix for State Building Code Adopted." North Carolina Preservation. No. 57, June/July 1985. p. 5.

BUILDING MATERIALS

Adams, Clare W. "Avoid Common Renovation Mistakes: Synthetic Siding." New Orleans Preservation In Print. Vol. 13, No. 9, Nov. 1986. p. 10-11.

BUILDING MATERIALS

Bero, John. "Asbestos." The Landmark Society of Western New York. Vol. 24, No. 6. Nov. 1986. p. 8.

Index to Historic Preservation Periodicals

BUILDING MATERIALS

"Brickwork Craft Training." Brick Bulletin.
No. 2, 1986. p. 22-23.

BUILDING MATERIALS

Hughes, Richard. "Material and
Structural Behaviour of Soil
Constructed Walls." Monumentum.
September 1983. pp. 175-188.

BUILDING MATERIALS

Poore, Jonathan. "Weatherstripping Entry
Doors." Old-House Journal. Vol. 19, No. 10,
Dec. 1986. p. 470-471.

BUILDING MATERIALS

"Preserving Historic Materials."
Architecture. Nov. 1986. Sivinski, Valerie A.
'Ferrous Metals.' p.108-109; Botsai, Elmer E
'Wood.' p. 109-110; Rosen, Shira. 'Sandstone'
p. 111-112; Smith, Baird M. 'Limestone,
Granite, and Marble.' p. 112-113.

BUILDING MATERIALS

"'Product Data Report.' Buyers Guide: A
Directory of Products & Services for Art and Ar-
chitectural Analysis, Preservation/Restoration,
Protection and Documentation." Technology &
Conservation. Vol. 8, No. 4, Winter 1983. Entire
Issue. 40 p.

BUILDING MATERIALS

Smith, Bradley T. "Substitute Materials for
Deteriorated Metal Building Components: The
Rehabilitation of a Country Courthouse in
Southern Georgia." APT Bulletin. Vol. 13, No.
4, 1981. pp. 19-26.

BUILDING MATERIALS

"Wood Siding: Real or Fake?" The Montgomery
County Preservationist. Vol. 2, No. 3. Dec.
1986/Jan. 1987. pp. 3; 8.

Owner of historic house advised not to
replace wood siding.

BUILDING MATERIALS--CONSERVATION & RESTORATION

Phillips, Morgan W. " Consolidation of
Porous Materials: Problems & Possibilities
of Acrylic Resin Techniques". Technology &
Conservation. Winter 1979. pp. 42-46.

BUILDING TRADES--U.S.--NORTH CAROLINA

Bishir, Catherine W. "Black Builders in
Antebellum North Carolina." The North Carolina
Historical Review. Vol. LXI, No. 4, October 1984.
pp. 423-462.

BUILDINGS, BATHING

Powers, Alan. "Watery Palaces." Traditional Homes. June 1986. p. 10-15.

History of bathing buildings.

BUILDINGS--CLEANING

"The Business of Cleaning." Canadian
Heritage. February-March, 1983. pp. 25-31.

BUILDINGS--CLEANING

"Cleaning External Surfaces of
Buildings." Building Research Establishment
Digest. Digest 280. 8 pp.

BUILDINGS--CLEANING

Fidler, John. "Cleaning Buildings."
Traditional Homes. Vol. 3, No. 10. July 1987.
pp. 28 - 30.
Masonry cleaning methods.

BUILDINGS--CLEANING

"Graffiti Gobbler for Walls Yearning to be
Free." Urban Innovation Abroad. Vol. 8, No. 4,
April 1984. p. 4.

56

BUILDINGS--CLEANING

"Maintenance is Preservation: Cleaning Methods Reviewed." The Medallion. Vol. 24, No. 4, Apr. 1987. p. 4.

BUILDINGS--CLEANING

Marmet, Terry. "Water Cleaning May Be Appropriate on Historic Masonry." Kansas Preservation. Vol. 7, No. 5, July/Aug. 1985. p. 1-2.

BUILDINGS--CLEANING

Moss, Elizabeth. "Graffiti: Neighborhoods Fight Urban Scrawl." Conserve Neighborhoods. No. 53, Nov./Dec. 1985. p. 1-3.

BUILDINGS--CLEANING

Spry, Alan H. "The Defence Against Graffiti: Anti-Graffiti Coating for Heritage Targets." Heritage Australia. Spring 1985. p. 42-45.

BUILDINGS--CLEANING

Veloz, Nick. "Graffiti: an Introduction with Examples." Technical Note 6, Communique. Vol. 14, No. 5. pp. 9-10.

BUILDINGS--CONSERVATION AND RESTORATION

Brenner, William. "Housing Rehabilitation: Research Needs for the Eighties." APT Bulletin. Vol. XIV, No. 2, 1982. pp. 35-43.

BUILDINGS--CONSERVATION AND RESTORATION--PERIODICALS

Building Conservation. "Building Conservation, published monthly, is available free to approved readers holding a senior position in the professional, contracting or industrial areas of repair, renovation, restoration, reconstruction and rehabilitation of building structures and infrastructures or to readers outside the above terms of control, by annual subscription..."

BUILDINGS--DESTRUCTION

"It Takes Guts to Build But Also to Demolish." Urban Innovation Abroad. Vol. 8, No. 4, April 1984. p. 1.

Demolition prize offered by French Urban and Rural League.

BUILDINGS--ENERGY CONSERVATION

Ambrosino, Michael. "Energy Conservation at the Cooper-Hewitt Museum : Renovation/Retrofitting for Improved Mechanical System Efficiency." Technology & Conservation, Spring 1979. pp. 32- 34.

BUILDINGS--ENERGY CONSERVATION

Elder, Betty Doak. "Energy! Historical Agencies make a Special Case". History News. May 1980. p. 5-7.

BUILDINGS--ENERGY CONSERVATION

Matthai, Robert A. "Energy Conservation & Management." Technology & Conservation. Spring 1978. pp. 12-20.

BUILDINGS--ENERGY CONSERVATION

Matthai, Robert A. "The Energy Crisis: It's Our Move." Museum News. November/December 1977. pp. 46-51.

BUILDINGS--ENERGY CONSERVATION

Miller, Hugh C. "Energy Management Planning: A Systematic Approach for Museums & Historic Buildings." Technology & Conservation, Fall 1979. pp. 16-22.

BUILDINGS--ENERGY CONSERVATION

"Special Energy Issue." The Old-House Journal. September 1981. Entire Issue.

CONTENTS: DiDonno, Ron. Is The Old House Ready for Solar?--Blandy, Tom. Energy Audits, Consultants, and Contractors--Labine, Clem. Energy-Saving Fundamentals--Bucher, Wm. Ward. Heating Alternatives--Stephen, George. Radiator Covers.

BUILDINGS--MAINTENANCE

"Historic Presidio Maintenance Plan." Progressive Architecture. January 1984. pp. 156-158.

BUILDINGS--MAINTENANCE

Skelton, James. "The PMI-An Alternative to Crises Management." APT Bulletin. Vol. 14, No. 3, 1983. pp. 34-37.

BUILDINGS--MECHANICAL EQUIPMENT

Gannes, Stuart. "The Bucks in Brainy Buildings." Fortune. December 24, 1984. pp. 132-144.

New Developments in communications and environmental systems.

BUILDINGS--PROTECTION

Crosby, Anthony. "A Preservation Monitoring System at Tumacacori National Monument." APT Bulletin, number 2 1978. pp. 47-76

BUILDINGS--REPAIR AND RECONSTRUCTION

"Diagnosis of Sick Buildings." Urban Outlook. Vol. 8, No. 10. May 30, 1986. pp. 2-4.

BUILDINGS--REPAIR AND RECONSTRUCTION

"Facts and Figures about Rehab." Urban Conservation Report. Special Report, August 24, 1983. Entire Issue.

BUILDINGS--REPAIR AND RECONSTRUCTION

Gordon, Douglas and M. Stephanie Stubbs. "The Mechanics of Building Rebirth." Architecture. Nov. 1986. p. 100-107.

Solutions to frequently encountered rehabilitation problems.

BUILDINGS--REPAIR AND RECONSTRUCTION

Syvaness, Bob. "Installing Baseboard." Fine Homebuilding. No. 34. Aug./Sep. 1986. pp. 40-41.

BUILDINGS--REPAIR AND RECONSTRUCTION--ECONOMIC ASPECTS

Kidd, Philip E. "Value of Nonresidential Rehabilitation will Double by Mid-1980's." Architectural Record. Oct. 1979. pp. 61.

BUILDINGS--REPAIR AND RECONSTRUCTION

Miller, Hugh C. " A Health Maintenance Program for Older Buildings." Architecture. Nov. 1986. p. 96-99.

BUILDINGS--REPAIR AND RECONSTRUCTION

"Old Gutters." Old-House Journal. Vol. 15, No. 2, Mar./Apr. 1987. p. 24-33.

Special section on problems with traditional gutter systems.

BUILDINGS--REPAIR & RECONSTRUCTION

"Renovation Case No. 35. Long Distance Planning." Traditional Homes. Vol. 3, No. 11. Aug. 1987. pp. 20 - 26.
The owners of a Georgian House in Somerset devise renovation while abroad and return to work over the years to achieve their goals.

BUILDINGS--REPAIR AND RECONSTRUCTION

"Stabilizing San Antonio's Spanish Colonial Missions." Texas Heritage. Fall 1983. pp. 6-7.

BUILDINGS--REPAIR AND RECONSTRUCTION

"Unusual Techniques Solve Unusual Problems." Montgomery County Preservationist . Vol. 2, No. 5, Apr./May 1987. p. 1, 7-8.

Problems and solutions in restoring a 19th century house.

BUILDINGS--REPAIR AND RECONSTRUCTION--
TECHNIQUE

Fidler, John A. "Glass-Reinforced
Plastic Facsimiles in Buildings
Restoration." APT Bulletin.
Vol. 14, No. 3, 1983. pp. 21-25.

BUILDINGS, OCTAGONAL

Massey, James C. & Shirley Maxwell.
"Octagons and Hexagons and Other Multi-
Faceted Eccentricities." Old-House
Journal. June 1986. p. 228-231.

BUILDINGS, OCTAGONAL--U.S.--MISSISSIPPI--NATCHEZ

Kennedy, Roger G. "Longwood: the Untimely
Octagonal." American Heritage. Vol. 36, No. 6,
Oct./Nov. 1985. p. 100-106.

BUILDINGS, PREFABRICATED

Fleming, Dolores. "One Order Brought
It All, A Morgantown Mail-Order House."
Goldenseal. Summer 1982. pp. 36-42.

BUILDINGS, PREFABRICATED

Halpin, Kay. "Sears, Roebuck's Best-Kept
Secret." Historic Preservation. September,
October, 1981. pp. 24-29.

BUNGALOWS

Ewing, Abigail. "The American Bungalow:
a 20th-Century Bestseller." Landmarks/Observer.
Vol. 12, No. 4, July/Aug. 1985. p. 10-12.

BUNGALOWS

"Fate of Vista Bungalows Still in Question."
Pasadena Heritage. Vol. 10, No. 1, Feb. 1987. p. 2.

BUNGALOWS

Moffat, Gary. "The Chicago Bungalow."
Old-House Journal. Vol. 15, No. 1, Jan./
Feb. 1987. p. 32-37.

BUNGALOWS

Poore, Patricia. "The Bungalow and Why We
Love It So." The Old House Journal. Vol. 13,
No. 4, May 1985. Entire issue.

BUNGALOWS

Szlizewski, Elizabeth. "Is there a bungalow on your block?" Historic Richmond, Inc.
Vol. 14, No. 1, Spring 1986. p. 2-4.

BUNGALOWS--U.S.--CALIFORNIA--PASADENA

"Vista Bungalows." Pasadena Heritage.
Vol. 9, Nos. 3&4. Spring & Summer 1986. p. 8.

Seventeen bungalows along the Vista Arroyo
in Pasadena boarded up for many years have been
announced by their owner, the General Services
Administration, to soon be available for
restoration for rehabilitation.

CALIFORNIA--LOCKE

Castle, Allen. "Locke: A Chinese
Chinatown." Pacific Historian. Spring 1980.
p. 1-7.

CALIFORNIA--LOS ANGELES

Lafer, Steven. "L.A. redux". Planning.
January 1981. p. 10-12.

CALIFORNIA--LOS ANGELES--GOVERNOR PIO PICO'S
ADOBE

Winter, Robert. "Historic Houses:
Governor Pio Pico's Adobe." Architectural Digest.
September 1981. pp. 170-176.

CALIFORNIA--OAKLAND

Mathes, Wayne A. and Frances Hayden Rhodes. "The Camron-Stanford House in Oakland, California." Antiques. Vol. CXXV, No. 4, April 1984. pp. 880-885.

CALIFORNIA--RIVERSIDE--MISSION INN

Johnson, Cecil E. "California's Other Castle: Riverside's Mission Inn Struggles to Recapture Some of Its Old Magic." American Preservation. Vol. 4, #2. pp. 49-54.

CALIFORNIA--SAN FRANCISCO

Williams, George A. "Fine Points of the San Francisco Plan." Planning. February 1984. pp. 12-15.

Also includes: Adams, George. "A Last-Ditch Effort to Save Downtown San Francisco. pp. 4-11.

CAMPSITES, FACILITIES, ETC.--U.S.--MICHIGAN

Karamanski, Ted. "The History and Preservation of the 'Great Camps' in Northern Michigan." Chronicle. Vol. 21, No. 1, Spring 1985. p. 23-25, 31.

CAMPUS PLANNING--U.S.--CALIFORNIA--DAVIS

"Trouble in Davis." California Preservation. Vol. 10, No. 3, July 1985. p. 6.

CAMPUS PLANNING--U.S.--KANSAS

Longstreth, Richard. "From Farm to Campus: Planning, Politics, and the Agricultural College Idea in Kansas." Winterthur Portfolio. Vol. 20, No. 2/3, Summer/Autumn 1985. p. 149-179.

CAMPUS PLANNING--U.S.--SOUTH CAROLINA--CHARLESTON

Bishop, Gregory S. "A Tribute to the College of Charleston's Progress in Preservation." Preservation Progress. Vol. 29, No. 4. May 1985. pp. 4-6.

CAMPUS PLANNING--U.S.--VIRGINIA--CHARLOTTES-VILLE

Woods, Mary N. "Thomas Jefferson and the University of Virginia: Planning the Academic Village." Journal of the Society of Architectural Historians. Vol. 44, No. 3, Oct. 1985. p. 266-283.

CANADA--ALBERTA

Cowan, Trudy. "How They're Saving Alberta's Past." Canadian Heritage. August/September 1984 pp. 13-17.

CANADA--MONTREAL--ARCHITECTURE

Charney, Melvin. "The Montrealness of Montreal: formation and formalities in urban architecture". Architectural Review. May 1980. p.299-302.

CANADA--QUEBEC CITY

Ross, Ken. "Where the River Has Walls, If Quebec City Makes the World Heritage List, It Will Be Because the City is a Vital Link Between New World and Old." Canadian Heritage. August/September 1984. pp. 18-23.

CANALS

Boelio, Bob. "12 Miles to Oblivion: The Clinton-Kalamazoo Canal." Chronicle, Quarterly Magazine of the Historical Society of Michigan. Vol. 20, No. 3, Fall 1984. pp. 22-3.

CANALS

Hadfield, Charles. "Evolution of the Canal Inclined Plane." American Canals. Bull. No. 58, Aug. 1986. p. 4-9.

CANALS

Manella, Susan. " Penna. Canal Locks Un-Earthed." American Canals. No. 61. May 1987.

CANALS

Meek, Thomas. "A Plan to Save the White-water Canal." _American Canals_. Bulletin No. 57. May 1986. pp. 4-5.

CANALS

Stockdale, Judith M. "Protecting a Living Landscape." _Place_. May 1983. pp. 1-3.

CANALS

Trout, W.E. III. "Cracking a Canal Engineer's Code." _American Canals_. No. 60, Feb. 1987. p. 3, 7.

CANALS--CONSERVATION AND RESTORATION

Amon, James C. "Delaware and Raritan Canal. _New Jersey Historical Commission Newsletter_. June 1983. pp. 5-6.

CANALS--CONSERVATION AND RESTORATION

Slaton, Deborah. "Esprit de Corridor: Re-navigating the Illinois and Michigan Canal." _Inland Architect_. Vol. 29, No. 5, Sept./Oct. 1985. p. 37-40.

CANALS--CONSERVATION AND RESTORATION--CANADA

Passfield, Robert W. "The Role of the Historian in Reconstructing Historic Engineering Structures: Parks Canada's Experience on the Rideau Canal, 1976-1983." _IA_, The Journal of the Society for Industrial Archaeology. Vol. 11, No. 1, 1985. pp. 1-28.

CANALS--CONSERVATION AND RESTORATION--U.S.--NEW YORK

Connors, Dennis J. "Last Tender's House on Erie Canal." _Society for Industrial Archeology Newsletter_. Vol. 13, No. 3 & 4, Fall & Winter 1984. p. 10.

CANALS--CONSERVATION AND RESTORATION--U.S.--PENNSYLVANIA

Whyte, Larry E. "Schuylkill Canal Restoration." _American Canals_. No. 52, Feb. 1985. p. 8.

CANALS--GREAT BRITAIN

Hughes, S.R. "The Swansea Canal: Navigation and Power Supplier". _Industrial Archaeology Review_. Winter 1979-80. p. 51-69.

CANALS--HISTORY

Schwantes, Carlos A. "Promoting America's Canals: Popularizing the Hopes and Fears of the New American Nation. Journal of American Culture, Winter 1978. pp. 700-712.

CANALS--U.S.--ILLINOIS

Fogarty, David. "Jewels of the Rust Belt." _Sierra_. Vol. 70, No. 5, Sept./Oct. 1985. p. 35-36, 39-40.

The Illinois and Michigan Canal National Heritage Corridor is discussed.

CANALS--U.S.--ILLINOIS

Lamb, John H. "I & M Canal National Heritage Corridor." _American Canals_. No. 54, Aug. 1985. p. 6.

CANALS--U.S.--MASSACHUSETTS

Holmes, Amanda. "The Cape Cod Canal." _American Canals_. No. 54, Aug. 1985. p. 11.

CANALS--U.S.--MASSACHUSETTS--LOWELL

Bedard, Marie Ellen. "The Canalway at Lowell." _American Canals_. No. 56, Feb. 1986. p. 1-2.

CANALS--U.S.--NEW YORK STATE

"Erie Canal - 160 Years Old!" <u>American Canals</u>. No. 53, May 1985. p. 3-6.

CANALS--U.S.--VERMONT

Proper, David. "Bellows Falls Canal." <u>American Canals</u>. No. 54, Aug. 1985. p. 9.

CANOES

Orr, Gordon D. "Restoration of Wood/Canvas Canoe." <u>APT Bulletin</u>. Vol. XV, No. 2, 1983. pp. 20-26.

CAPITOLS

Morrissey, Charles T. "The Vermont State-house in Montpelier." <u>Antiques</u>. Vol. CXXVI, No. 4, October 1984. pp. 891-899.

CAPITOLS (CITIES)--U.S.--CONNECTICUT

Bloom, Larry. "Hartford, Connecticut." <u>Yankee</u>. Vol. 49, No. 4. Apr. 1985. pp. 60-66; 134-136.

CAPITOLS (CITIES)--U.S.--WASHINGTON, D.C.

Dillon, David. "Old Outshines New in Pennsyl-vania Avenue Renewal." <u>Architecture</u>. May 1984. pp. 62; 64.

CAPITOLS--CONSERVATION AND RESTORATION

"Capitol Plan Approved." <u>Preservation Report</u>. Summer 1982. p. 1.

CAPITOLS--CONSERVATION AND RESTORATION

"Capitol Restoration Work Continues." <u>Architecture</u>. October 1984. p. 35.

CAPITOLS--CONSERVATION AND RESTORATION

"The Order and the Awe, State Capitol, Sacramento, California." <u>Progressive Architecture</u> July 1982. pp. 80-89.

CAPITOLS--CONSERVATION AND RESTORATION

Seale, William. "Glowing Revival for 'Most Beautiful Room in America'." <u>Smithsonian</u>. November 1981. pp. 146-152.

CAPITOLS--CONSERVATION AND RESTORATION

"Staff Specialists Conduct Paint Research at State Capitol." <u>Carolina Comments</u>. Vol. 33, No. 4, July 1985. p. 99-100.

CAPITOLS--CONSERVATION AND RESTORATION

"To California With Love; Restoration of the California Capitol is the Largest Such Effort in U.S. History. Its Unique Construction Procedures Are a Product of a Team Effort and Devotion." <u>Progressive Architecture</u>, November 1979. pp. 88-93.

CAPITOLS--CONSERVATION AND RESTORATION

Wilhite, Doyle. "Exterior Restoration of the West Virginia State Capitol: Cleaning and Structural Stabilization Procedures." <u>Technology & Conservation</u>, Spring 1979. pp. 14-16.

CAPITOLS--CONSERVATION AND RESTORATION--U.S.--ALABAMA

"Alabama Historical Commission Holds Con-ference on Capitol Restoration." <u>Capitol Preservation News</u>. Vol. 2, No. 2, June 1985. p. 4.

CAPITOLS--CONSERVATION AND RESTORATION--U.S.--
MASSACHUSETTS

Holtz, Paul. "Repair and Renovation of the
Massachusetts State House." Boston Preservation
Alliance Letter. Vol. 7, No. 1, Jan. 1986. p. 10.

CAPITOLS--CONSERVATION AND RESTORATION--U.S.--
MASSACHUSETTS

"SPNEA Reveals Architectural Discoveries in
a Report on the State House's Past." SPNEA News.
Series 38, Winter/Spring 1985. p. 5-6.

CAPITOLS--CONSERVATION AND RESTORATION--U.S.--
NEW YORK

"New York Opens Restored Executive Chamber."
Capitol Preservation News. Vol. 2, No. 2, June
1985. p. 3.

CAPITOLS--CONSERVATION AND RESTORATION--U.S.--
TEXAS

"Committee Hears Report on Capitol." The
Medallion. Vol. 22, No. 8, Aug. 1985. p. 1.

CAPITOLS--CONSERVATION AND RESTORATION--U.S.--
WISCONSIN

"Preservation of Wisconsin's First Capitol."
Wisconsin Preservation. Vol. 10, No. 1, Jan./
Feb. 1986. p. 8-9.

CAPITOLS--U.S.--ALABAMA

Holmes, Nicholas H., Jr. "The State Capitols of Alabama." The Preservation Report.
Vol. 12, No. 6, May/June 1985. p. 3-4.

CAPITOLS--U.S.--ILLINOIS

Moore, Evelyn R. "Constructing the Illinois
State House." Historic Illinois. Vol. 8, No. 5,
Feb. 1986. p. 10-12.

CAPITOLS--U.S.--LOUISIANA

"Capitol Complex Interpretive Center to Open."
Louisiana Preservation Alliance. Vol. 5, No. 2,
October 1985. p. 1-2.

CAPITOLS--U.S.--NORTH CAROLINA

Sanders, John L. "The North Carolina State
Capitol of 1840." Antiques. Vol. 128, No. 3,
Sept. 1985. p. 474-484.

CAPITOLS--U.S.--TEXAS

"Special Issue: the State Capitol."
The Medallion. Vol. 22, No. 2, Feb. 1985.
6p.

CAPITOLS--U.S.--WASHINGTON D.C.

"After Decades of Controversy Work Begins
on the West Front." Architecture, News. April
1984. p. 11.

CARIBBEAN

Brinkley, Frances Kay. "The Eastern Caribbean:
a museum on every island." Museum. No. 2, 1982.
pp. 127-129.

CARPENTRY--TOOLS

Law, Tom. "Site-Sharpening Saw Blades", Fine Homebuilding, No. 24, December 1984/January 1985, pp.
33-36.

CARPENTRY--TOOLS

Picton, Jim. "The Worm-Drive Saw", Fine Homebuilding,
No. 24, December 1984/January 1985, pp. 36-41.

CARPETS

Webster, Eric. "The Record of a Continuous Progress: The Nineteenth Century Development of John Crossley and Sons, Carpet Manufacturers of Halifax. Industrial Archaeology. Vol. 16, No. 1, Spring 1981. pp. 58-72.

CARIBBEAN

Dethefsen, Edwin. " "St. Eustatius' Archaeological Treasures." Place. May 1982. p. 1.

CAST IRON

Bidwell, T.G. "The Restoration and Protection of Structural and Decorative Cast Iron at Covent Garden." Transactions. Vol. 5, 1982. pp. 24-30.

CAST IRON

"Cast Iron Group Celebrates Fifteenth Anniversary." Newsletter, Preservation League of New York State. Vol. 11, No. 1, Jan./Feb. 1985. p. 3.

CAST IRON

Gayle, Margot. "Cast-Iron Masterpiece: Gothic Revival Tomb of President James Monroe." Nineteenth Century. Summer 1981. pp. 62-64.

CAST IRON FRONTS (ARCHITECTURE)

Fitch, James Marston. "The Case of the Purloined Building." Architectural Record. Jan. 1984. pp. 114-117.

CAST IRON FRONTS (ARCHITECTURE)--PAINT

Hawkes, Pamela W. "Paints for Architectural Cast Iron." APT Bulletin. Vol. 11, No. 1, 1979. pp. 17-36.

CAST-IRON FRONTS (ARCHITECTURE)--U.S.--NEW YORK-- NEW YORK CITY

"Bogardus Cast-Iron Building Designated N.Y.C. Landmark." Society for Industrial Archeology Newsletter. Vol. 14, No. 2, 1985. p. 13.

CASTLES

Nineteenth Century. Spring 1984, Vol. 9, No. 1-2. Entire Issue. Also contains Indices to previous Nineteenth Century issues.

CEILINGS

Lichtbau, Julia. "Restoring an Early Trompe L'oeil." Architecture. Nov. 1986. p. 33.

Restoration of the ceiling of Nantucket's Old South Church.

CEILINGS

Worthington, Miria. "Pressed Metal Ceilings in Western Australia." Heritage Australia. Vol. 5, No. 1, Autumn 1986. p. 31-32.

CEILINGS--CONSERVATION AND RESTORATION

Curtis, John Obed. "How to Save that Old Ceiling". Old House Journal. October, 1980. p. 131, 142-146.

CEILINGS--CONSERVATION AND RESTORATION

Tyler, James B. "Taking down a Ceiling Medallion". Old House Journal. August 1980. p. 95-97

CEILINGS--CONSERVATION AND RESTORATION

Wagner, Logan. "Rebuilding a Mudejar Ceiling." Fine Homebuilding. Apr./May 1985. p. 43-45.

CEILINGS, METAL

Bell, David L. "Offering a Variety of Patterns Overhead." Americana. Jul./Aug. 1979. pp. 52-59.

CEILINGS, METAL

The Old-House Journal. Mar. 1979. Several articles on tin ceilings.

CEMETERIES

Brown, Daniel A. "National Cemeteries: Unique Cultural Resources of the National Park Service." CRM Bulletin. Vol. 7, No. 3, October 1984. pp. 7, 9.

CEMETERIES

Caldwell, Shirley. "Historic Cemeteries of Dallas: The Greenwood Cemetery." Historic Dallas. Vol. 11, No. 1, Jan./Feb. 1987. p.7.

CEMETERIES

Christovich, Mary Lou. "Save Our Cemeteries: a 12 Year Retrospective." New Orleans Preservation in Print. Vol. 13, No. 8. Oct. 1986. p. 6.

CEMETERIES

Coones, Paul. "Kensal Greene Cemetery: London's First Great Extramural Necropolis." Transactions of the Ancient Monuments Society. Vol. 31, 1987. pp. 48-76.

CEMETERIES

"Grave Issues: The Historic Burying Ground Initiative." Boston Preservation Alliance. Vol. 8, No. 6. June 1987. p. 4.
Plans to restore sixteen historic cemeteries in Boston.

CEMETERIES

"Historic Cemeteries." Preservation New Mexico. Vol. 3, No. 4, Winter 1986. p. 3.

Cemeteries provide clues to town and landscape development.

CEMETERIES

Lemmon, Alfred E. "New Orleans' Treasure of Cemeteries." New Orleans Preservation in Print. Vol. 13, No. 8, Oct. 1986. p. 7-11.

CEMETERIES

Lenahan, Gaye. "Mountain View Cemetery 1863 - 1906." Oakland Heritage Alliance News. Vol. 7, No. 2. pp. 1 - 7.
Frederick Law Olmsted-designed cemetery.

CEMETERIES

The Medallion. Vol. 24, No. 4. Apr. 1987. pp. 2-3.
Special section on cemetery preservation.

CEMETERIES

Varoga, Craig. "City Hall's Everlasting Chore." New Orleans Preservation in Print. Vol. 13, No. 8, Oct. 1986. p. 12.

The care and preservation of New Orleans' cemeteries by the Department of Property Management.

CEMETERIES--CONSERVATION AND RESTORATION

"Cemeteries: 19th Century Funereal Planning." Alliance Letter. Vol. 5, no. 2, March 1984. pp. 3-4.

CEMETERIES--CONSERVATION AND RESTORATION

"Conservation Guidelines in Cemeteries Policy Paper." National Trust Magazine (National Trust of Australia, NSW). No. 33, Feb. 1986. p. 7-9.

CEMETERIES--CONSERVATION AND RESTORATION

Kallas, Phil. "Cemeteries: Our Outdoor Museums and Our Stewardship." Inscriptions. Vol. 14, No. 3, July 1985. p. 3-7.

CEMETERIES--CONSERVATION AND RESTORATION

Krontz, Marian. "Leaving no Stone Unturned: Procedures for Cleaning and Restoring a Graveyard." PAST (Pioneer America Society Transactions), 1979. pp. 81-95.

bibliography.

CEMETERIES--CONSERVATION AND RESTORATION

Moss, Elizabeth. "Community Cemeteries Make a Comeback." Conserve Neighborhoods. No. 50, July/Aug. 1985. p. 1-4, 6.

CEMETERIES--CONSERVATION AND RESTORATION

"Preserving Rural Burial Grounds." Massachusetts Historical Commission Newsletter. Fall, 1982. p. 10 & 13.

CEMETERIES--CONSERVATION AND RESTORATION

Smith, Harold. "Founder's Cemetery to be Restored... Preserved." Roswell Historic Preservation Commission News. Sep./Oct. 1983. p. 3.

CEMETERIES--CONSERVATION AND RESTORATION

Terrell, David and Van Jones Martin (Photographer). "Oakland Cemetery: Atlanta's Link with the Past is Being Preserved and Cherished." American Preservation. Nov.-Dec. 1979. pp. 41-48.

CEMETERIES--CONSERVATION AND RESTORATION-- CANADA--OTTAWA

Paine, Cecelia. "Restoration of the Billings Estate Cemetery." Bulletin, Association for Preservation Technology. Vol. XV, No. 4, 1983. pp. 60-65.

CEMETERIES--CONSERVATION AND RESTORATION--U.S.-- MASSACHUSETTS--BOSTON

Shea, Al. "Historic Burying Ground Initiative." Boston Preservation Alliance Letter. Vol. 6, No. 1. Jan. 1985. p. 3.

CEMETERIES--CONSERVATION AND RESTORATION--U.S.-- TENNESSEE--PULASKI

Abernathy, Robert A. "New Parks From Old Cemeteries." Trends. Vol. 21, No. 2, 1984. pp. 12-15.

CEMETERIES--CONSERVATION AND RESTORATION--U.S.-- TEXAS--JEFFERSON

"Historic Cemetery Revived." The Medallion. Vol. 22, No. 3, Mar. 1985. p. 3.

CEMETERIES--CONSERVATION AND RESTORATION--U.S.-- WISCONSIN

"State Legislature Considers Bill to Protect Burial Sites." Wisconsin Preservation. Vol. 9, No. 6, Nov./Dec. 1985. p. 1-2.

CEMETERIES--U.S.--MASSACHUSETTS--BOSTON

Humes, Roseanne Atwood. "Historic Burial Grounds Inventory." The Boston Preservation Alliance Letter. Vol. 5, No. 6. Jul./Aug. 1984. pp. 2-3; 8.

CEMETERIES--U.S.--MASSACHUSETTS--CAMBRIDGE

Zanger, Jules. "Mount Auburn Cemetery: the Silent Suburb" Landscape. 1980. vol.24, no.2, p. 23-28.

CEMETERIES--U.S.--MASSACHUSETTS--SALEM

Pitcoff, Rita L. "Greenlawn Cemetery: Salem's Botanical Garden." Essex Institute Historical Collections. Jan. 1981. pp. 43-53.

CEMETERIES--U.S.--MISSOURI--ST. LOUIS

Keller, Janet. "City Cemeteries."
St. Louis Home. March 1984. pp. 20-21, 52.

CEMETERIES--U.S.--NEW YORK--BROOKLYN--GREEN-WOOD

Remes, Naomi R. "The Rural Cemetery".
19th century. Winter 1979. p. 52-55.

CEMETERIES--U.S.--NEW YORK--NEW YORK CITY

Wolfe, Kevin. "Visible City: By commission-
ing the same architects who designed their houses
to build their mausoleums, Victorians proved, so
to speak, that you can take it with you."
Metropolis. Sept. 1985. p. 44-47, 50.

CEMETERIES--U.S.--NORTH CAROLINA

Mashburn, Rick. "Graveyard Gothics, the
Piedmont's One-Of-A-Kind Gravestones Have Caused
Much Speculation and Puzzlement." Americana.
Vol. 12, No. 4, November/December 1984. pp.
62-4.

CEMETERIES--U.S.--OHIO--CINCINNATI

Linden-Ward, Blanche and David C. Sloane.
"Spring Grove: the Founding of Cincinnati's
Rural Cemetery, 1845-1855." Queen City Heritage.
Vol. 43, No. 1, Spring 1985. p. 17-32.

CEMETERIES--U.S.--OHIO--CINCINNATI

Linden-Ward, Blanche and Alan Ward. "Spring
Grove: the Role of the Rural Cemetery in American
Landscape Design." Landscape Architecture. Vol.
75, No. 5, Sept./Oct. 1985. p. 126-131, 140.

CEMETERIES--U.S.--PENNSYLVANIA--PHILADELPHIA

Parrington, Michael and Daniel G. Roberts.
"The First African Baptist Church Cemetery, An
Archaeological Glimpse of Philadelphia's Early
Nineteenth-Century Free Black Community."
Archaeology. Vol. 37, No. 6, November/December
1984. pp. 26-32.

CENSUS

"Are the 'Gentry' Really Moving Back to the
City?" Business Week. June 4, 1984. pp. 12, 14.

Census data lacks evidence of this phenomena.

CENTRAL BUSINESS DISTRICTS

Alberts, Barry. "Lowell Gets Back on its
Feet." Urban Land. July 1984. p. 29.

CENTRAL BUSINESS DISTRICTS

Alexander, Laurence A. "Integrating the
New Downtown and the Old." Downtown Idea
Exchange. Vol. 33, No. 24, Dec. 15, 1986.
p. 4-6.

CENTRAL BUSINESS DISTRICTS

Alexander, Lawrence A. "Managing Downtowns
Effectively -- Part 1." Downtown Idea Exchange.
Vol. 32, No. 7, Apr. 1, 1985. p. 2-3.

CENTRAL BUSINESS DISTRICTS

Beauregard, Robert A. "Urban
Form and the Redevelopment of Central
Business Districts." Journal of
Architectural and Planning Research.
Vol. 3, No. 3, August 1986. p. 183-
198.

CENTRAL BUSINESS DISTRICTS

"Bringing Urban Glitter to Smaller Cities,
Developer Jim Rouse's Marketplaces Become
Riskier Ventures as They Pop Up in Gritty Industrial Areas." Business Week. July 23, 1984.
pp. 139-140, 144.

CENTRAL BUSINESS DISTRICTS

"Case Study: Pennsylvania Main Streets."
Downtown Idea Exchange. Vol. 31, No. 7, April 1,
1984. pp. 7-8.

CENTRAL BUSINESS DISTRICTS

"Development Checklist for Smaller Downtowns." Downtown Idea Exchange. Vol. 32, No. 7, Apr. 1, 1985. p. 6-7.

CENTRAL BUSINESS DISTRICTS

"Development Exactions and Downtown Development." Downtown Idea Exchange. Vol. 33, No. 14, July 15, 1986. p. 1-2.

CENTRAL BUSINESS DISTRICTS

Devine, David. "Using a Planning Consultant in Downtown Casa Grande, Arizona." Small Town. Vol. 14, No. 5, March-April 1984. pp. 9-13.

CENTRAL BUSINESS DISTRICTS

Fleming, Ronald Lee. "Why Merchants Renovate Storefronts." Home Again. No. 2. Spring 1984. pp. 20 - 23.

CENTRAL BUSINESS DISTRICTS

Francis, Mark. "Mapping Downtown Activity." Journal of Architectural and Planning Research. Vol. 1, No. 1, June 1984. pp. 21-35.

CENTRAL BUSINESS DISTRICTS

Grissett, Jim. "The View from Georgia, A Case for Downtown Development." National Mall Monitor. September/October 1984. Vol. 14, No. 4, pp. 72, 74, 149-150.

CENTRAL BUSINESS DISTRICTS

"Heritage Foundation Calls UDAg Program a 'Slush Fund' and Leveraging a Myth." Community Development Digest. No. 85-7, Apr. 2, 1985. p. 9.

CENTRAL BUSINESS DISTRICTS

"HHF to Serve as Umbrella for Main Street Program." Historic Hawaii News. Vol. 10, No. 7, July/August 1984. p. 1.

CENTRAL BUSINESS DISTRICTS

"How City Fathers Can Get More Entrepreneurial." Urban Outlook. Vol. 6, No. 5, August 15, 1984. pp. 2-3.

CENTRAL BUSINESS DISTRICTS

"Kansas' Own "Main Street Program" Helps Revive Downtowns." Local Economic Growth & Neighborhood Reinvestment Report. June 7, 1984. p. 4.

CENTRAL BUSINESS DISTRICTS

"Main Street Project Helps 7 Michigan Cities Set Goals for Economic Revitalization." Local Economic Growth and Neighborhood Reinvestment Report. 84-9. May 3, 1984. pp. 1-2.

CENTRAL BUSINESS DISTRICTS

"Main Street Wins Overwhelming Support of State Legislature." The Indiana Preservationist. No. 1, 1985. p. 1.

CENTRAL BUSINESS DISTRICTS

"Managing Downtown Effectively - Part 2." Downtown Idea Exchange. Vol. 32, No. 8, Apr. 15, 1985. p. 2-3.

CENTRAL BUSINESS DISTRICTS

"Marketplace/Festival Centers -- Are They Working?" Downtown Idea Exchange. Vol. 32, No. 7, Apr. 1, 1985. p. 3-4.

CENTRAL BUSINESS DISTRICTS

"100 Top Cities." National Mall Monitor. Vol. 14, No. 5, November/December 1984. pp. 37-187+.

Economic profiles of the nation's largest cities.

CENTRAL BUSINESS DISTRICTS

Paumier, Ceril B. "Design Elements for a Downtown Marketplace." Journal of Housing. May/June 1982.

CENTRAL BUSINESS DISTRICTS

Plowden, David. "Main Street, USA". (Photographic essay). American Photographer. July 1980. p. 50-63.

CENTRAL BUSINESS DISTRICTS

"A Prototype Downtown Survey- It's Got the Right Stuff." Downtown Idea Exchange. Vol. 34, No. 8, Apri. 15, 1987.

A sample shoppers' survey used in Jackson, MI.

CENTRAL BUSINESS DISTRICTS

Schwartz, Gail Garfield. "Developing Downtowns: Main Street Revitalization." Journal of Housing. Vol. 41, No. 4, July-August 1984. pp. 116-119.

CENTRAL BUSINESS DISTRICTS

"Setting Standards for Downtown." Downtown Idea Exchange. Vol. 31, No. 20, October 1984. pp. 1-2.

Draft Clearwater Florida. Downtown Property Standards Ordinance.

CENTRAL BUSINESS DISTRICTS

"Targeted Growth Planning Maximizes Local 'High Tech' Economic Potential." Local Economic Growth & Neighborhood Reinvestment Report. Apr. 19, 1984. p. 3.

CENTRAL BUSINESS DISTRICTS

"Ten Outstanding Projects Revitalizing Downtown Win Development Award Competition." Downtown Idea Exchange. Vol. 33, No. 16, Aug. 15, 1986. p. 1-8.

CENTRAL BUSINESS DISTRICTS

Toplivich, Ann. "Main Street Starts Work." Tennessee Heritage Alliance, Network. Summer 1984. No. 2. pp. 3-4.

CENTRAL BUSINESS DISTRICTS

Weisbrod, Glen. "Can Ma and Pa Compete Downtown? Business Impacts of Downtown Improvements." Urban Land. February 1983. pp. 20-23.

CENTRAL BUSINESS DISTRICTS

Weisbrod, Glen and Henry O. Pollakowski. "Effects of Downtown Improvement Projects on Retail Activity." Journal of the American Planning Association. Vol. 50, No. 2, Spring 1984. pp. 148-162.

CENTRAL BUSINESS DISTRICTS

Wright, Dorothy. "Will Redevelopment Threaten Historic Las Vegas." Preservation Association of Clark County newsletter. March-April 1986. p. 1-2.

A redevelopment plan approved by the Las Vegas City Council threatens historic district.

CENTRAL BUSINESS DISTRICTS--CASE STUDIES--U.S.-- TEXAS

"Special Texas Main Street Issue." Texas Historical Commission, The Medallion. Vol. 21, No. 12. Dec. 1984.

Entire issue.

CENTRAL BUSINESS DISTRICTS--CONSERVATION AND RESTORATION

Battle, Safford Levon. "Focus on... Richmond, Virginia." Journal of Housing. Vol. 43, No. 2. Mar./Apr. 1986. pp. 72-77.
Renovation of downtown Richmond.

CENTRAL BUSINESS DISTRICTS--CONSERVATION AND
RESTORATION

Broeske, Pat H. "Saving Downtown Anaheim."
Planning. Jan. 1980. pp. 19-22.

CENTRAL BUSINESS DISTRICTS--CONSERVATION AND
RESTORATION

Challenge! Feb. 1979.
Articles on commercial revitalization, fundraising for redevelopment, and commercial redlining..

CENTRAL BUSINESS DISTRICTS--CONSERVATION AND
RESTORATION

Cliff, Ursula. "Hudson, N.Y.: After Restoring
its Oldest Houses as a Historic Area, this River
Town Worked to Turn its Business District Around."
Urban Design. Fall 1978. pp. 40-43.

CENTRAL BUSINESS DISTRICTS--CONSERVATION
AND RESTORATION

Clinard, Susie. "Renewed Vitality
Seen for Five Oklahoma Towns." Mistletoe
Leaves. Vol. 17, No. 6, 1986. p. 4-5.

CENTRAL BUSINESS DISTRICTS--CONSERVATION AND
RESTORATION

Conserve Neighborhoods. Summer 1979.
Note: Entire issue; includes bibliography.

CENTRAL BUSINESS DISTRICTS--CONSERVATION AND
RESTORATION

DeVito, Mathias J. "Retailing plays key
role in downtown renaissance." Journal of Housing.
Apr. 1980. pp. 197-200.

CENTRAL BUSINESS DISTRICTS--CONSERVATION
AND RESTORATION

"Downtown Development Cases."
Downtown Idea Exchange. March 1, 1983.
p. 7.

CENTRAL BUSINESS DISTRICTS--CONSERVATION
AND RESTORATION

"Downtown Salem - Central Business
District Plan - Heritage Plaza East/West."
Landscape Architecture. September/
October, 1983. pp. 56-59.

CENTRAL BUSINESS DISTRICTS--CONSERVATION AND
RESTORATION

Engelbrecht, Peter and Charlotte Ames.
"Downtown Livability: Preservation and the Battle
for Public Awareness." Environmental Comment.
May 1979. pp. 13-15.
Case study of the preservation of Jamaica,
Long Island, with emphasis on the preservation
of the Valencia Theatre.

CENTRAL BUSINESS DISTRICTS--CONSERVATION
AND RESTORATION

"Five South Carolina Towns Selected for
Main Street Program." The New South Carolina
State Gazette. Vol. 17, No. 1, Summer 1984.
pp. 1-2.

CENTRAL BUSINESS DISTRICT--CONSERVATION
AND RESTORATION

Goss, K. David. "Heritage Plaza
East: Salem's Experiment in Urban Renewal."
Essex Insstitute Historical Collections.
October 1983. pp. 238-251.

CENTRAL BUSINESS DISTRICTS--CONSERVATION AND
RESTORATION

"Gov. Clinton Announces Five 'Main Street
Arkansas' Towns." DANCH Directions (Dept. of
Arkansas Natural and Cultural Heritage.)
Vol. III, Issue IV, Fall 1984. p. 4.

CENTRAL BUSINESS DISTRICT--CONSERVATION AND
RESTORATION

Kitner, Michael. "Downtown Renaissance: The
Improtance of Organization." Possibilities.
Jul. 1981. Vol. 6, No. 1. p. 1.

CENTRAL BUSINESS DISTRICTS--CONSERVATION AND
RESTORATION

"Main Street: a Roundup." Housing Ontario.
Jul./Aug. 1979. pp. 13-15.

CENTRAL BUSINESS DISTRICTS--CONSERVATION AND
RESTORATION

"Main Street Center Video Event Instructs
Towns on Attracting Downtown Development."
Community Development Digest. No. 84-18,
September 25, 1984. pp. 6-9.

CENTRAL BUSINESS DISTRICTS--CONSERVATION AND
RESTORATION

"Main Street: Downtown Forum '78: Expert
Warns Against the 'Romance of Restoration'."
Housing Ontario. Jan./Feb. 1979. p. 19.

CENTRAL BUSINESS DISTRICTS--CONSERVATION
AND RESTORATION

"Nine Downtowns Win Top Awards for
Revitalization." Downtown Idea Exchange.
April 15, 1983. pp. 1-7.

CONTENTS: Steuben Place, Chemainus,
Tampa City, Santa Rosa, Louisville,
Mud Island Park, Burlington, Milwaukee,
Saint Paul.

CENTRAL BUSINESS DISTRICTS--CONSERVATION
AND RESTORATION

"No Lost Causes: Three Strategies for
Salvaging Neighborhood Shopping Districts."
Planning. March 1983. pp. 12.

CONTENTS: Hall, Lawrence. New Haven, Private
Money First--Lurcott, Robert and Karen
LaFrance. Pittsburgh, Market Studies--
Dobbins, Michael. Birmingham, Design is the
Key.

CENTRAL BUSINESS DISTRICT--CONSERVATION
AND RESTORATION

Papsidero, Vincent A. and Howard F.
Wise. "Bringing Ohio Downtowns Back to
Life." Place. March 1983. pp. 6-8.

CENTRAL BUSINESS DISTRICT--CONSERVATION A
AND RESTORATION

"Preservationists Stress Public Role
for Downtown Renewal." Housing and
Development Reporter. March 28, 1983.
pp. 942-943.

CENTRAL BUSINESS DISTRICTS--CONSERVATION
AND RESTORATION

Prichard, Judith. "Warsaw Gets a
Head Start." Indiana Preservationist.
No. 2, April 1986. p. 2.

Downtown restoration of Warsaw, Indiana.

CENTRAL BUSINESS DISTRICT--CONSERVATION AND
RESTORATION

Robbins, Tom. "Putting Shops Back on
Main St." City Limits. Mar. 1981. pp. 20-22.

CENTRAL BUSINESS DISTRICTS--CONSERVATION
AND RESTORATION

"Small Pennsylvania Steel Town
Builds Downtown Strategy to Compete
with Suburban Malls." Economic Growth
and Revitalization. No. 86-15, August
12, 1986. p. 3-4.

Coatesville, Pa. to be revitalized
through rehabilitation.

CENTRAL BUSINESS DISTRICTS--CONSERVATION AND
RESTORATION

Smith, Kennedy. "Planning a Public Improvements Program." Main Street News. No. 14,
June 1986. p. 3.

CENTRAL BUSINESS DISTRICTS--CONSERVATION AND
RESTORATION

Sower, John. "Legal Measures Help to Insure
Success of Commercial Revitalization." Journal
of Housing. May 1979.

Note: "Ordinances requiring facade renovation
and management can be a powerful weapon in the
commercial rehabilitation battle."

CENTRAL BUSINESS DISTRICTS--CONSERVATION AND
RESTORATION

Stephens, George M. "Santa Cruz Cashes in on
Historic Commercial District Revitalization."
Urban Land. Oct. 1979. pp. 12-17.

CENTRAL BUSINESS DISTRICTS--CONSERVATION AND
RESTORATION

Stokvis, Jark R. "Why Can't a Downtown
Be More Like a Mall?" Urban Land. Vol. 43,
No. 9, September 1984. pp. 10-15.

Includes discussion of National Trust
participation in New Haven.

CENTRAL BUSINESS DISTRICT--CONSERVATION AND
RESTORATION

Vigil, Karen L. "'Rebirth' of Pueblo's
Union Avenue." Colorado Heritage News. October
1983. p. 5.

CENTRAL BUSINESS DISTRICTS--CONSERVATION
AND RESTORATION

"A Walk Around Metrocentre Mall."
Quapaw Quarter Chronicle. Vol. 13,
No. 3, June-July 1986. p. 6-7.

Many of the older, historically significant buildings of Little Rock's
Main Street are being restored.

CENTRAL BUSINESS DISTRICTS--CONSERVATION AND
                                RESTORATION

Wilcox, David A. "Attractions management is
key to a revitalized downtown's success." Journal
of Housing. Jul. 1980. pp. 377-382.

CENTRAL BUSINESS DISTRICTS--CONSERVATION AND
RESTORATION

Woodhouse, Linda R. "15,000 Participate
in Main Street America Teleconference." Nation's
Cities Weekly. September 24, 1984. p. 3.

CENTRAL BUSINESS DISTRICTS--CONSERVATION AND
RESTORATION--CANADA

Stewart, John. "Reviving Main Street."
Canadian Heritage. February 1981. p. 33-35.

CENTRAL BUSINESS DISTRICTS--CONSERVATION AND
RESTORATION--CASE STUDIES

Applebaum, Betsy. "Neighborhood Shopping
Streets Get Technical Assistance Boost." Conserve
Neighborhoods. Feb. 1986. p. 1-3, 6.

CENTRAL BUSINESS DISTRICTS--CONSERVATION
AND RESTORATION--CASE STUDIES

"Downtowns: Seven Good Bets".
Planning. May 1981. pp. 12-18.

CENTRAL BUSINESS DISTRICTS--CONSERVATION AND
RESTORATION--CASE STUDIES

"Upgrading Downtown: Harborplace, Baltimore,
Md.; Heritage Plaza East, Salem, Mass.; Station
Square, Pittsburgh, Pa." Urban Design
International. Nov./Dec. 1980. p. 8-33.

CENTRAL BUSINESS DISTRICTS--CONSERVATION AND
RESTORATION--CASE STUDIES--U.S.--NORTH CAROLINA

Swink, Rodney L. "Reviving North Carolina's
Downtowns: An Update on the Main Street Program."
North Carolina Preservation. Vol. 53. Oct./Nov.
1984. p. 3.

CENTRAL BUSINESS DISTRICTS--CONSERVATION AND
RESTORATION--ECONOMIC ASPECTS

Goodman, Linda and Janet Nutting. "A Tale of
Four Cities: Investment Activity in 'Dying' Downtowns." Urban Land. Vol. 44, No. 3, Mar. 1985.
p. 32-33.

Termed "staggering" the amount of investment
in Cleveland, Indianapolis, Detroit and Milwaukee
is analyzed.

CENTRAL BUSINESS DISTRICTS--CONSERVATION AND
RESTORATION--ECONOMIC ASPECTS

"Commercial Revitalization." Public/
Private Partnership for Revitalization. May 1982.
Entire Issue.

CENTRAL BUSINESS DISTRICTS--CONSERVATION AND
RESTORATION--ECONOMIC ASPECTS

"Advancing Centralized Retail Management"
and "Downtown Retail Leasing Strategies."
Downtown Idea Exchange. Vol. 33, No. 5, Mar. 1,
1986. p. 1-5.

CENTRAL BUSINESS DISTRICTS--CONSERVATION AND
RESTORATION--ECONOMIC ASPECTS

Ivey, Mark. "Will the World's Fair Cure
Those Basin Street Blues." Business Week.
May 7, 1984. pp. 22A + 22D.

ADAPTIVE USE

CENTRAL BUSINESS DISTRICT--CONSERVATION
AND RESTORATION--ECONOMIC ASPECTS

Meehan, Patrick. "Ways to Develop
a Cookbook Approach to Downtown Development."
Small Town. September-October 1983.
pp. 13-16.

CENTRAL BUSINESS DISTRICTS--CONSERVATION AND
RESTORATION--ECONOMIC ASPECTS

Robertson, Kent A. "Designing Downtown Re-
development Policy: the Problem of Knowledge."
Journal of Architectural and Planning Research.
Vol. 2, No. 2, June 1985. p. 129-139.

CENTRAL BUSINESS DISTRICTS--CONSERVATION AND
RESTORATION--ECONOMIC ASPECTS

"Special Study: Small Businesses--Key to
Downtown Strength." Downtown Idea Exchange.
Aug. 15, 1981. pp. 3-5.

CENTRAL BUSINESS DISTRICTS--CONSERVATION AND
RESTORATION--U.S.--COLORADO--DENVER

Ford, Chris. "The Future of Lower Downtown." Historic Denver News. Vol. 15, No. 3,
Mar. 1986. p. 1, 5.

CENTRAL BUSINESS DISTRICTS--CONSERVATION AND
RESTORATION--U.S.--INDIANA--FORT WAYNE

"The Courtyards." Progressive Architecture.
Jan. 1985. pp. 10-11.

CENTRAL BUSINESS DISTRICTS--CONSERVATION AND
RESTORATION--U.S.--INDIANA--INDIANAPOLIS

"New Indianapolis Revitalization Project."
Nation's Cities Weekly. Vol. 9, No. 6, Feb. 10,
1986. p. 6.

Plan to restore and reuse six landmark
buildings to create a new music hall, shopping
arcade and offices.

CENTRAL BUSINESS DISTRICTS--CONSERVATION AND
RESTORATION--U.S.--IOWA--ALBIA

Jenkins, Janet R. "The Cliffdwellers: Albia,
Iowa, Residents Reclaim Downtown Second Floors."
Small Town. Vol. 16, No. 4, Jan./Feb. 1986. p.
8-12.

CENTRAL BUSINESS DISTRICTS--CONSERVATION AND
RESTORATION--U.S.--NORTH CAROLINA--SHELBY

Jackson, Art and Hal Mason. "Shelby, N.C.:
Organizing for Success." Main Street News. No. 6
Sept. 1985. p. 1-3.

CENTRAL BUSINESS DISTRICTS--CONSERVATION AND
RESTORATION--U.S.--TEXAS

"Main Street Project: Cities Seek Revitalization." The Medallion (Texas Historical Commission). Vol. 21, No. 11, October 1984. p. 1.

CENTRAL BUSINESS DISTRICTS--CONSERVATION AND
RESTORATION--U.S.--TEXAS--STAMFORD

Butts, James and Linda Dalliston. "Stamford,
Tex.: the Time Was Right for Main Street." Main
Street News. No. 6, Sept. 1985. p. 4-6.

CENTRAL BUSINESS DISTRICTS--ECONOMIC ASPECTS

Alexander, Laurence A. "For Downtown Economic
Growth,High-Impact Planning Plus Cata.ytic Action."
Downtown Idea Exchange, Vol. 34, No. 7, Apr. 1987.
p. 2-3

CENTRAL BUSINESS DISTRICTS--ECONOMIC ASPECTS

Alexander, Laurence A. "The Future of Downtown Retailing and Retail Investments." Downtown
Idea Exchange, Vol. 34, No. 5, Mar. 1, 1987. p.
2-4.

CENTRAL BUSINESS DISTRICTS--ECONOMIC ASPECTS

Gruen, Nina J. "Public/Private Projects:
A Better Way for Downtowns." Urban Land. Vol. 45,
No. 8, Aug. 1986. p. 2-5.

CENTRAL BUSINESS DISTRICTS--ECONOMIC ASPECTS

"Lafayette [Louisiana] Organizes for
Downtown Action; Eight Committees Spearhead
the Work." Downtown Idea Exchange. Vol. 34,
No. 13. Jul. 1, 1987. pp. 4 - 5.
Among the eight committees are an Arts &
Cultural and Historic Preservation Committee.

CENTRAL BUSINESS DISTRICTS--ECONOMIC ASPECTS

Stokvis, Jack R. "Making Downtown Competitive
Again: The Promise of Centralized Retail Management." Urban Land. Vol. 46, No. 4. Apr. 1987.
pp. 7-11.

CENTRAL BUSINESS DISTRICTS--HISTORY--U.S.--
ILLINOIS--BLOOMINGTON

Koos, Greg and Wm. D. Walters, Jr. "Arson,
Accidents and Architecture: Downtown Blooming-
ton's Landscape Shaped by Fire." Historic
Illinois. Vol. 8, No. 1, June 1985. p. 1-4.

CENTRAL BUSINESS DISTRICTS--U.S.--ARKANSAS

"Fanfare for Main Street: New Cities Prepare and Original Cities Flourish." Directions. (Dept. of Arkansas Heritage). Vol. 5, Issue 3, Summer 1986. p. 4. (VF)

CENTRAL BUSINESS DISTRICTS--U.S.--ARKANSAS

"Main Street Program Update." Danch Directions. Vol. 4, No. 4, Fall 1985. p. 4.

CENTRAL BUSINESS DISTRICTS--U.S.-- ARKANSAS-- LITTLE ROCK

"A Better Idea in Little Rock." Urban Conservation Report. Vol. 9, No. 3. Mar. 1987. p. 7.

CENTRAL BUSINESS DISTRICTS--U.S.--ARKANSAS-- LITTLE ROCK

Guida, Louis. "Regina's Grand Closing Marked; Investors Have Plans for Main Street." The Quapaw Quarter Chronicle. Vol. 11, No. 2, April 1984. p. 1, 11.

TAX INCENTIVES

CENTRAL BUSINESS DISTRICTS--U.S.--CALIFORNIA-- GLENDALE

"Glendale Urban Design Study." Progressive Architecture. Jan. 1986. p. 118-121.

Winner of a P/A award.

CENTRAL BUSINESS DISTRICTS--U.S.--CALIFORNIA-- SAN FRANCISCO

Weitze, Karen. "Update on American Cities: Resurgent Sacramento--Downtown." The Society of Architectural Historians Newsletter. Vol. 30, No. 5, Oct. 1986, p. 5-7.

CENTRAL BUSINESS DISTRICTS--U.S.--CONNECTICUT-- NEW HAVEN

"New Haven Partnership Will Redevelop Old Business District." Urban Conservation Report. Vol. 8, No. 13. Jul. 20, 1984. p. 3.
First Trust Critical Issues Grant assists in two phases of this project.

CENTRAL BUSINESS DISTRICTS--U.S.--FLORIDA

"Florida Main Street Cities Are Goal-Oriented." Florida Preservation News. Vol. 2, No. 4, July-Aug. 1986. p. 8-9.

CENTRAL BUSINESS DISTRICTS--U.S.--FLORIDA

"Florida Main Street Cities Selected." Florida Preservation News. Mar. 1985. p. 1.

CENTRAL BUSINESS DISTRICTS--U.S.--GEORGIA

"Progress on Main Street." The Rambler. Newsletter of the Georgia Trust. Vol. 11, No. 3. Summer 1984. pp. 4; 6.

CENTRAL BUSINESS DISTRICTS--U.S.--GEORGIA-- ATLANTA

Arnold, Eddie J. "Historic Facade Program." Preservation Times, The Atlanta Preservation Center Newspaper. Vol. 4, No. 1, Summer 1984. pp. 1, 3.

CENTRAL BUSINESS DISTRICTS--U.S.--GEORGIA--ATLANTA

"Historic Preservation Main Street Program Revives Georgia University Town." Economic Growth & Revitalization Report. No. 86-17. Sep. 15, 1986. p. 2.

CENTRAL BUSINESS DISTRICTS --U.S.--ILLINOIS--CHICAGO

Freed, Robert. "Seeking a Sea Change: Can Chicago Redeem Its Ragtag Riverbanks?" Inland Architect. Sept./Oct. 1986. p. 30-35.

CENTRAL BUSINESS DISTRICTS--U.S.--ILLINOIS-- HIGHLAND PARK

Piper, Robert J. "Community Rehab + Urban Design = Economic Development." Inland Architect. Vol. 29, No. 2, Mar./Apr. 1985. p. 36-37.

CENTRAL BUSINESS DISTRICTS--U.S.--INDIANA

Bamberger, Rita J. and David W. Parham. "Indianapolis's Economic Development Strategy." Urban Land. Vol. 43, No. 11. Dec. 1984. pp. 12-18.

CENTRAL BUSINESS DISTRICTS--U.S.--INDIANA

"Indiana Main Street Gets Green Light." The Indiana Preservationist. No. 2 & 3, 1985. p. 4.

State passed program launched.

CENTRAL BUSINESS DISTRICTS--U.S.--INDIANA

"Welcome Back Main Street: Special Section on Downtown Revitalization", The Indiana Preservationist, No. 5, 1984, pp. 5-9.

CENTRAL BUSINESS DISTRICTS--U.S.--MARYLAND--BALTIMORE

Brickell, Sean. "The Brokerage: Upscaling History." National Mall Monitor. Vol. 14, No. 4, September/October 1984. pp. 60, 62, 123-4.

CENTRAL BUSINESS DISTRICTS--U.S.--MARYLAND--BALTIMORE

Lord, Courtney. "The Changing Face of Urban Retail." National Mall Monitor. Vol. 14, No. 4, September/October 1984. pp. 64, 66, 136-137.

CENTRAL BUSINESS DISTRICTS--U.S.--MICHIGAN--MUSKEGON

"Michigan City Transforms Street into Thriving Downtown Mall." Housing and Development Reporter. Vol. 11, No. 46, April 9, 1984. pp. 975-6.

CENTRAL BUSINESS DISTRICTS--U.S.--NEW YORK STATE--BUFFALO

Field, Scott and Bonnie Ott. "Mastering the Master Plans." Preservation Coalition of Erie County Preservation Report. Vol. 7, No. 5, Nov./Dec. 1985. p. 4-6.

CENTRAL BUSINESS DISTRICTS--U.S.--NORTH CAROLINA

Williams, Anne R. "Main Street--Everybody's Neighborhood." NC Arts. Summer '86. p. 8-9. (VF)

CENTRAL BUSINESS DISTRICTS--U.S.--NORTH CAROLINA SHELBY

Mason, S. Hal. "Shelby, North Carolina: A Main Street Case Study." Small Town. Vol. 15, No. 3, November-December 1984. pp. 4-8.

CENTRAL BUSINESS DISTRICTS--U.S.--OHIO--XENIA

Page, Clint. "Xenia, Ohio-10 Years Later Memory of Disaster Merges with Memory of Rebuilding." Nation's Cities Weekly. Vol. 7, No. 31, July 30, 1984. p. 3.

Vertical File

CENTRAL BUSINESS DISTRICTS--U.S.--PENNSYLVANIA

Foster, Teri. "Downtown Revitalization Brings New Businesses." Pennsylvanian. Vol. 25, No. 8. Aug. 1986. pp. 8-9. (VF)

CENTRAL BUSINESS DISTRICTS--U.S.--PENNSYLVANIA

Taylor, David L. "The New 'Main Street' in Pennsylvania Communities." Pennsylvanian. Vol. 25, No. 8. Aug. 1986. pp. 4-5; 17. (VF)

CENTRAL BUSINESS DISTRICTS--U.S.--PENNSYLVANIA--PITTSBURGH

Knack, Ruth E. "Pittsburgh's Glitter and Gloom." Planning. Vol. 51, No. 12, Dec. 1985. p. 4-11.

Vertical File

CENTRAL BUSINESS DISTRICTS--U.S.--PENNSYLVANIA--YORK

"Main Street Program Coming to York." Uncommon Sense. Vol. 9, No. 3, Summer 1986. p. 1, 3-4. (VF)

CENTRAL BUSINESS DISTRICTS--U.S.--RHODE ISLAND--
PROVIDENCE

Rich, Joan. "What Will Be The Future for
Westminster Center? Two New Studies Provide
Downtown Ideas." PPS News, Vol. XXII, No. 5,
November-December 1984, pp. 5-7.

University of Rhode Island planning and Harvard
University marketing study, supported by National
Trust-Providence Preservation Society grant,
discussed.

CENTRAL BUSINESS DISTRICTS--U.S.--TEXAS--AUSTIN

Williamson, Roxanne. "Update on American
Cities: Austin, Texas: A City in Crisis."
Newsletter, The Society of Architectural Historians.
Vo. 28, No. 6. Dec. 1984. pp. 3-4.

CENTRAL BUSINESS DISTRICTS--U.S.--WASHINGTON
STATE

"Main Street Coming to Washington."
The Washington Trust for Historic Preservation
Newsletter. April 1984. p. 1 & insert.

CENTRAL BUSINESS DISTRICTS--U.S.--WASHINGTON--
SEATTLE

"Seattle's Plan to Bring People Downtown."
Urban Conservation Report. Vol. VIII, No. 13,
July 31, 1984. p. 1.

CENTRAL BUSINESS DISTRICTS--U.S.--WASHINGTON--
VANCOUVER

"Redevelopment Keyed to Office Growth, Historic Themes and Transportation." Community
Development Digest. No. 84-8, April 24, 1984.
pp. 12-13.

CHAIRS

Talbott, Page. "Recliners and Sofa Beds,
A Search for Comfort." Nineteenth Century.
Summer 1981. pp. 51-53.

CHALK HOUSES--MAINTENANCE AND REPAIR

Pearson, Gordon. "Chalk Chambers." Traditional Homes. June 1986. p. 30-34.

Advice on maintenance and repair of chalk or
'cob' houses.

CHARITABLE USES, TRUSTS, AND FOUNDATIONS

Wilding, Suzanne. "New York's Own Private
Trust Fund." Town and Country. Vol. 139, No.
5064, Sept. 1985. p. 220-223.

Includes guide to the richest community
foundations in the U.S.

CHIMNEYS-MAINTENANCE AND REPAIR

Garrison, John Mark. "Relining Your
Chimney Flue." The Old-House Journal.
September 1982. pp. 177, 188-191.

CHINA--HISTORIC PRESERVATION

"Preservation in China." Progressive Architecture, November 1979. pp. 74-79.

Two articles.

CHRISTMAS

Gerhardt, Tom. "Decorating for an
Old-Fashioned Christmas". Old House Journal
Nov. 1980. p. 157, 172-174.

CHRISTMAS

Scharer, Laura Lynn. "Christmas Past :
how to decorate your historical tree".
History News. December 1980. p. 9-11.

CHRISTMAS--U.S.--SOUTH CAROLINA--COLUMBIA

Pearson, Katherine. "Columbia, South
Carolina's. Christmas Houses". Americana,
Nov-Dec. 1980, p.35-44.

CHURCH AND STATE

"Once more onto a religious battlefield:
A new proposal for the St. Bart's tower".
Architectural Record. Feb. 1985. p. 65.

CHURCH AND STATE--U.S.--NEW YORK--NEW YORK
CITY

"New Design for St. Bart's Tower Raises
Old Questions." Architecture. Mar. 1985.
p. 42, 44.

CHURCH ARCHITECTURE

Pastier, John. "An Evangelist of Unusual Architect-
ural Aspirations : After 20 Years in a Neutra Church,
Dr. Robert Schuller is building a Johnson Cathedral."
AIA Journal, May 1979. pp.48-55.

CHURCH ARCHITECTURE

Warren, William Lamson. "The Oxford
Meeting House." The Connecticut Antiquarian.
June 1981. pp. 4-8.

CHURCH ARCHITECTURE--ADAPTIVE USE--U.S.--
MASSACHUSETTS--FALL RIVER

"A neighborhood restored". Architectural
Record. Feb. 1985. p. 96-99.

Convent complex (NR) converted to housing
for the elderly and families.

CHURCH ARCHITECTURE--CONSERVATION AND RESTORATION

Dixon, John Morris. "Crusade Against
Preservation." (Editorial.) Progressive Architecture. March 1984. p. 7.

CHURCH ARCHITECTURE--GREAT BRITAIN

Stillman, Damie. "Church Architecture in Neo-
Classical England." Journal of the Society of
Architectural Historians. May 1979. pp. 103-119.

CHURCH ARCHITECTURE--U.S.--NEW YORK--ALBANY

Sinclair, Douglas L. "Trinity Episcopal
Church: Albany's Unknown Treasure." Albany
Preservation Report. Autumn 1985. p. 6-7, 9.

James Renwick, Jr. designed this church,
constructed in 1848.

CHURCH ARCHITECTURE--U.S.--NEW YORK--NEW YORK

Lowe, David Gerrard. "A Pilgrimage to New
York's Victorian Sanctuaries." The Victorian.
Vol. 13, No. 1, 1985. p. 1-2.

CHURCH DECORATION AND ORNAMENT--CONSERVATION
AND RESTORATION--EUROPE--ITALY--VENICE

Kessler, Herbert L. "Mosaics of San Marco.
Smithsonian. Vol. 15, No. 6, September 1984.
pp. 42-53.

CHURCHES

Anderson, Carson. "C[ultural] R[esources]
C[ommittee] Proposes New Landmark." Los Angeles
Conservancy. Vol. 9, No. 3, May/June, 1987. p.
5, 13.

First AME Zion Cathedral, Los Angeles.

CHURCHES

"Britain's Historic Churches: Conflict and
Reconciliation." National Trust of Australia,
Trust News. Vol. 13, No. 7, Feb. 1985. p. 11-
12.

CHURCHES

Cullen, Marygael. "Chapel from
French Colonial Period Discovered amid
Mississippi Artifacts." Dispatch
(Illinois State Historical Society).
Series 8, No. 2, March-April 1986. p. 4

CHURCHES

Cumberbatch, Kenneth. "Preservation
Profile: The Reformed Church of South Bush-
wick (Brooklyn, NY)." Common Bond. Vol. 2,
No. 4, Fall 1986. p. 2-4.

CHURCHES

Davis, Ann. "Masterpiece Financed by
Native Son." The Indiana Preservationist.
No. 5, 1986. p. 3.

An unusual art deco church was built
in 1937.

CHURCHES

"A Discreet Conversion." _Architectural Record_. August 1986. p. 96-99.

Structural changes for Charleston's neo-gothic Cathedral of St. John.

CHURCHES

Douthat, Carolyn. "Church Saga Continues." _Oakland Heritage Alliance News_. Vol. 7, No. 1, Apring1987. p. 8-9.

Interplay of Landmarks Advisory Board and Environmental Impact Review involving Fourth Church of Christ, Scientist, Oakland, CA.

CHURCHES

"Downtown Churches Getting Entrepreneurial." _Downtown Idea Exchange_. Vol. 31, No. 16, August 15, 1984. pp. 5-6.

CHURCHES

Dunlap, David W. "Conference Ponders Ways to Preserve Old Churches and Synagogues." _Newsletter_, Preservation League of New York State. Vol. 10, No. 3, May-June 1984. p. 1.

CHURCHES

"For the Record: Testimony in Opposition to Religious Properties Bill." _Preservation League of New York State Newsletter_. Vol. 10, No. 2, March-April 1984. pp. 1-3.

CHURCHES

Hanson, Michael. "Why the Church is Selling." _Country Life_. Vol. 171, No. 28. July 9, 1987. p. 132.
The Church of England is selling much of its property.

CHURCHES

Helmer, Paul. "The Preservation and Adaptive Use of Church Properties." _Historic Kansas City Gazette_. August/September, 1981. p. 6.

CHURCHES

"Historic Church Survey Completed." _Preservation New Mexico_. Vol. 3, No. 4, Winter 1986. p. 1.

Survey of historic New Mexico churches.

CHURCHES

"Historic Churches Symposium: Change in Emphasis in Building Preservation." National Trust of Australia, _Trust News_. Vol. 13, No. 7, Feb. 1985. p. 13.

CHURCHES

"Historic Religious Properties Awards Presented." _Newsletter_, Preservation League of New York State. Vol. 10, No. 3, May-June 1984. pp. 2-3.

CHURCHES

Jonnes, Jill. "To stay alive, big-city churches find new roles." _Smithsonian_, January 1981. p.107-118.

CHURCHES

Kroner, Walter M. "Energy and Religious Architecture." _Regional Conference of Historical Agencies_. Oct. 1981. Information Sheet #62.

CHURCHES

"Landmark Church v. Religious Freedom: Another Case Developing." _Urban Conservation Report_. Vol. 10, No. 11, Nov. 29, 1986. p. 2.

Church officials of the Fourth Presbyterian Church in Chicago disagree with preservationists on the desireability of landmark status for the church.

CHURCHES

Low-Beer, John R. "The Church and the Law." _The Livable City_. Vol. 11, No. 1. June 1987. pp. 8 - 9.

CHURCHES

"Rapprochment in Boston." Urban Conservation Report. Vol. 10, No. 11. Nov. 29, 1986. pp. 6-7. Demolition of the interior of the Church of the Immaculate Conception in Boston has been halted pending outcome of a landmark petition for the church.

CHURCHES

"Religious Architecture Survey." Place. Vol. 4, No. 9, October 1984. p. 13.

CHURCHES

"St. Bartholomew's Demolition, Development Plans Halted." Architecture. July 1984. p. 27.

CHURCHES

Shimoda, Jerry. "Pitching in to Preserve St. Benedict's, the Painted Church." Historic Hawaii News. Vol. 10, No. 6. June 1984. pp. 4-5.

CHURCHES

"Stalled Church Rehab Project Allowed to Proceed." Community Development Digest. No. 87-3, Feb. 3, 1987. p. 8.

CHURCHES

Sweet, Charles. "Father Blanchet Establishes the Church." The Table Rock Sentinel, Vol. 7, No. 2, Feb. 1987. p. 3-9.

Historical overview of St. Joseph's Catholic Church, Southern Oregon's oldest standing parish church.

CHURCHES--ADAPTIVE USE

"Architectural design citation : Graham Gund Associates". Progressive Architecture. January 1981. p. 154-155.

CHURCHES--ADAPTIVE USE

Glennan, Ellen Kenney. "The John Tarrant Kenney Hitchcock Museum, Riverton, Connecticut." Antiques. May 1984. pp. 1140-1147.

CHURCHES--ADAPTIVE USE

"Considerate Conversion." Traditional Homes. June 1986. p. 19-27.

A historic church converted into an unusual house.

CHURCHES--ADAPTIVE USE

"Redundant But Livelier than Ever." Heritage Outlook. January/February 1983. p. 19.

CHURCHES--ADAPTIVE USE--U.S.--MASSACHUSETTS-- BOSTON

Campbell, Robert. "Church Ruins Wall Condominiums." Architecture. May 1985. p. 256-261.

CHURCHES--ADAPTIVE USE--U.S.--MASSACHUSETTS-- BOSTON

Schmertz, Mildred. "Finding New Functions to Save a Landmark Form." Architectural Record. September 1984. pp. 134-139.

Charles Street Meeting House (N.R.), (1807), (Asher Benjamin).

CHURCHES--CANADA

McAleer, J. Philip. "St. Mary's (1820-1830)., Halifax: An Early Example of the Use of Gothic Revival Forms in Canada." Journal of the Society of Architectural Historians. Vol. 45, No. 2. June 1986. pp. 134-147.

CHURCHES--CONSERVATION AND RESTORATION

"Boston Greek Cathedral Restoration." The Boston Preservation Alliance Letter. Vol. 5, No. 3, April 1984. pp. 5-6.

CHURCHES--CONSERVATION AND RESTORATION

Browne, Henry J. "The Restoration of Mitchells Church, Culpepper County, Virginia." Notes on Virginia. No. 27, Fall 1985. p. 10-17.

CHURCHES--CONSERVATION AND RESTORATION

Kalman, Harold. "Restoration of the Chapel of the Rideau Street Convent." APT Bulletin. Vol. 18, No. 4, 1986. pp. 18-29.
A chapel in Ottawa, dismantled and salvaged when its convent was demolished in 1972, is undergoing restoration.

CHURCHES--CONSERVATION AND RESTORATION

"Renewing Old Churches." Preservation Report. Vol. 8, No. 5, Sept./Oct. 1986. p. 2-3.

CHURCHES--CONSERVATION AND RESTORATION--ENGLAND

Fawcett, Jane. "Greater Churches: Damage by Visitors." ASCHB Transactions. Vol. 9, 1984. p. 6-10.

CHURCHES--CONSERVATION AND RESTORATION--GREAT BRITAIN

Powell, Ken. "The Church and Conservation." Transactions of the Ancient Monuments Society. Vol. 30, 1986. p. 120-130.

CHURCHES--CONSERVATION AND RESTORATION--U.S.--ILLINOIS--CHICAGO

Clarke, Jane H. "The Glorification of St. James: a New Spirit Emanates From an Old Cathedral." Inland Architect. Vol. 29, No. 6, Nov./Dec. 1985. p. 19-22.

Arts and crafts interior uncovered and restored in church restoration.

CHURCHES--CONSERVATION AND RESTORATION--U.S.--NEW YORK STATE--BUFFALO

"Lancaster Residents Oppose Church Demolition." Preservation Report. Vol. 7, No. 5, Sept./Oct. 1985. p. 3.

CHURCHES--U.S.--CALIFORNIA--SAN FRANCISCO

Dehart, H. Grant. "Landmark Religious Buildings: Their Future." Heritage Newsletter. Vol. 13, No. 1, Spring 1985. p. 2-3.

CHURCHES--U.S.--DELAWARE--NEWCASTLE

"Risen from Ashes." Architectural Record. February 1984. pp. 108-111.

CHURCHES--U.S.--MAINE--PORTLAND

"Church Properties Face Uncertain Futures." Landmarks Observer. Vol. 12, No. 6, Nov./Dec. 1985. p. 4-5.

CHURCHES--U.S.--NEW YORK

Kay, Jane Holtz. "Faith and Form: Preserving New York's Religious Legacy." Preservation Report. Vol. 9, No. 1, Feb. 1987. p. 4-5, 11.

CITIES AND TOWNS

Barnes, Sandra. "Greenbelt- the Cooperative Spirit Lives On." The Region. Vol. 28, No. 1, Spring 1987. p. 26-28. (VF)

CHURCHES--U.S.--NEW YORK STATE--NEW YORK CITY

"St. Bart's Claims Economic Hardship in Third Application." Architecture. Oct. 1985. p. 16, 18.

CITIES AND TOWNS

Adams, Marcia. "Winona Lake Preserves Colorful History." The Indiana Preservationist. No. 4, 1986. p. 5.

Small Indiana town has many historically significant buildings including Bill Sunday's house and the tabernacle where he preached.

CITIES AND TOWNS

Carroll, Pam. "Greenbelt." Maryland. Vol. 19, No. 3, Spring 1987. p. 34-39.

History of experimental community, Greenbelt, Maryland.

CITIES AND TOWNS

Environmental Comment. May 1979.

Note: Articles from 5 member organizations of the Partners for Livable Places; on aspects of urban beautification and improvement.

CITIES AND TOWNS

Hoyt, Charles. "New Perceptions of Opportunity for Cities." Architectural Record, December 1979. pp. 114-119.

CITIES AND TOWNS

McGinn, Frank. "Ersatz Place: Variations on a Borrowed Theme: Small Towns Seek a Livelihood in Disguise." Canadian Heritage. Vol. 12, Issue 1, Feb./Mar. 1986. p. 25-29.

Examinations of "theme towns", including Solvang, California.

CITIES AND TOWNS

Talansky, Alan. "Turning The Lights Back on in Washington, D.C.'s Shaw District." Urban Land. Vol. 46, No. 5. May 1987. pp. 24 - 25.
Revitalization is beginning in Washington, D.C.'s Shaw District.

CITIES AND TOWNS

Walker, John O. "Life in a Greenbelt Community." USA Tomorrow. Vol. 2, No. 1. pp. 11-16. May 1987. (VF)

A description of life in the experimental community of Greenbelt, MD, in the 30's.

CITIES AND TOWNS

Ward, Richard C., Robert M. Lewis and S. Jerome Pratter. "St. Louis, A City Reborn." Urban Land. Vol. 46, No. 5. May 1987. pp. 14 - 19.

CITIES AND TOWNS--CIVIC IMPROVEMENT

Livability Digest. Spring 1982. Partial Issue.

Contents: What do Americans Want?--Open Space and Urban Design.

CITIES AND TOWNS--CIVIC IMPROVEMENT--U.S.--OHIO-- CLEVELAND

Leedy, Walter. "Updates on American Cities: Cleveland Architecture Now." Newsletter of the Society of Architectural Historians. Vol. 29, No. 1, Feb. 1985. p. 3.

CITIES AND TOWNS--CIVIC IMPROVEMENT--U.S.--PENN- SYLVANIA--HARRISBURG

Peirce, Neal R. "Harrisburg, Pa. on the mend with unique revival strategies." Nation's Cities Weekly. Vol. 8, No. 12, Mar. 25, 1985. p. 4.

CITIES AND TOWNS--CIVIC IMPROVEMENT--U.S.-- VERMONT

Therrien, Lois. "Letter from Burlington: A 'Rural' City Fights to Keep Its Personality." Business Week. Feb. 18, 1985. p. 26D, H, L.

CITIES AND TOWNS--CONSERVATION AND RESTORATION

Bond, Eugene H. "Lowell and Boston Host Development Forum." Place. September 1984. pp. 5-8.

International case examples applied to revitalization of aging industrial cities.

CITIES AND TOWNS--CONSERVATION AND RESTORATION

"Conservation of the Architectural Heritage and Urban Renaissance." A Future for Our Past. Information Bulletin 17, 1/1981. pp. 4-13.

CONTENTS: Feilden, Bernard and J. Jokilehto, Rehabilitation of Historic Buildings and Quarters-- Sandstrom, Christina. Social, Educational and Cultural Importance--Bartlet, Jacques and Yves Clossen. Analysis of the Architectural and Urban Heritage of the Historic Centre of the Town of Stavelot--Schimpff, Jean Marie. Identity and Growth of European Cities-Adapt or Go under.

CITIES AND TOWNS--CONSERVATION AND RESTORATION

Fleming, Ronald Lee. "Recapturing History: a Plan for Gritty Cities". Landscape. v.25, no.1, 1981. p. 20-27.

CITIES AND TOWNS--CONSERVATION AND RESTORATION

Giambastiani, Barbara J. "Syracuse Steps Up Preservation Development." Newsletter, Preservation League of New York State. Vol. 11, No. 4, July/Aug. 1985. p. 1-2.

CITIES AND TOWNS--CONSERVATION AND RESTORATION

Goetze, Rolf. "Citizen expectations can determine the success of local revitalization programs." Journal of Housing. April 1981. p. 205-212.

CITIES AND TOWNS--CONSERVATION AND RESTORATION

Lewis, Sylvia and Ron Cordon, photographer. "Redoing Chicago; HUD, the City and Private Architects are Jointly Funding a South Loop Renaissance." Urban Design International. Nov./Dec. 1979. pp. 28-29.

CITIES AND TOWNS--CONSERVATION AND RESTORATION

Papageorgiou-Venetas, Alexander. "The Nineteenth-Century Metropolitan City Quarters in Europe Criteria for Action on Their Integrated Conservation." Part II. Monumentum. Vol. 27, No. 1, March 1984. pp. 47-69.

CITIES AND TOWNS--CONSERVATION AND RESTORATION

Reed, Paula Stoner. "Hagerstown: a Renaissance in Western Maryland." The Phoenix. Vol. 5, No. 4, Summer 1985. p. 1-2.

CITIES AND TOWNS--CONSERVATION & RESTORATION

Schwartz, Gail Garfield, Ralph R. Widner, and John Shannon. "Revitalizing Inner Cities: A Trinational Perspective". Urban Innovation Abroad. March 1980.

CITIES AND TOWNS--CONSERVATION AND RESTORATION

Williams, Richard L. "Our Older Cities are Showing Signs of Age But Also Showing Signs of Fight: Second of a Series." Smithsonian. Jan. 1979. pp. 66-75.

CITIES AND TOWNS--CONSERVATION AND RESTORATION--
        CASE STUDIES

"Perth: Integrating Downtown Revitalization and Heritage Conservation." Housing Ontario. October 12, 1981. p. 12.

CITIES AND TOWNS--CONSERVATION AND RESTORATION--
        CASE STUDIES

Smith, Paul Bryan. "Conserving Charleston's Architectural Heritage." Town Planning Review. Oct. 1979. pp. 459-476.

CITIES AND TOWNS--CONSERVATION AND RESTORATION--
        CASE STUDIES

Weigard, Lynn. "League of California Cities Awards: Hanford tops competition with innovative ways to better service." Nation's Cities Weekly. Vol. 9, No. 7, Feb. 17, 1986. p. 3.

CITIES AND TOWNS--CONSERVATION AND RESTORATION--
        CASE STUDIES--U.S.--OKLAHOMA

Dallas, Sandra. "Guthrie's Revenge." Americana. Vol. 12, No. 4, September/October 1984. pp. 76-80, 82.

CITIES AND TOWNS--CONSERVATION AND RESTORATION
    --GERMANY--WEST BERLIN

Hoffman, Peter. "Report from West Berlin: An ambitious urban renewal plan is creating much-needed housing - and considerable controversy". Architectural Record. Feb. 1985. p. 67.

CITIES AND TOWNS--CONSERVATION AND RESTORATION--
    U.S.--CALIFORNIA--HOLLYWOOD

Carson, Theresa. "Letter from Hollywood: a Real Estate Story with a Happy Fade Out?" Business Week. Sept. 23, 1985. p. 28A, 28D.

CITIES AND TOWNS--CONSERVATION AND RESTORATION--
    U.S.--CONNECTICUT--NEW HAVEN

True, Conrad. "A Second Life for Ninth Square." Connecticut Trust for Historic Preservation News. Vol. 8, No. 2, Spring 1985. p. 2.

CITIES AND TOWNS--CONSERVATION AND RESTORATION--
U.S.--INDIANA--JEFFERSONVILLE

Niehaus, Charles R. "Historic Preservation
Comes to Jeffersonville, Indiana." Small Town.
Vol. 15, No. 5, Mar./Apr. 1985. p. 19-23.

CITIES AND TOWNS--CONSERVATION AND RESTORATION--
U.S.--MINNESOTA--ST. PAUL

Peirce, Neal R. "Renewing An Inner City
and Retaining Historic Character." Nation's
Cities Weekly. Vol. 8, No. 27, July 8, 1985.
p. 4.

CITIES AND TOWNS--CONSERVATION AND RESTORATION--
U.S.--MISSOURI--ST. LOUIS

Prost, Charlene. "Comeback City." Planning.
Vol. 51, No. 10, Oct. 1985. p. 4-10.

CHURCHES--CONSERVATION AND RESTORATION--U.S.--
NEW YORK--BUFFALO

Schaffner, Carolyn. "Landmark Designation
Sought For St. Mary of Sorrows." Preservation
Report. Vol. 8, No. 1, Jan./Feb. 1986. p. 1, 8.

CITIES AND TOWNS--CONSERVATION AND RESTORATION
--U.S.--PENNSYLVANIA--PITTSBURGH

"Lewis, David. "Urban Design in the
context of a changing economy: Pittsburgh as
a case study". Architectural Record. Feb.
1985. p. 79, 81.

CITIES AND TOWNS--ECONOMIC ASPECTS

"Economic Revitalization in
Small Cities." Developments. Spring 1983.
Entire Issue.

CITIES AND TOWNS--ECONOMIC ASPECTS

Odell, Rice. "Can We Afford to Maintain Our
Urban Infrastructure." Urban Land. January 1982.
pp. 3-8.

CITIES AND TOWNS--ECONOMIC ASPECTS

"Ontario Business Improvement Areas
Have a New Association." Housing Ontario.
October 12, 1981. p. 19.

CITIES AND TOWNS--ECONOMIC ASPECTS--U.S.--
MINNESOTA

Haas, Gregory. "Minnesota Star Cities
Lighting the Path of Economic Development."
Small Town. Vol. 16, No. 2, Sept./Oct. 1985. p.
12-15.

The State Star City Program requires the
formation of local development corporations.

CITIES AND TOWNS--ECONOMIC ASPECTS--U.S.--
MISSOURI--ST. LOUIS

Faltermayer, Edmund. "How St. Louis
Turned Less Into More." Fortune. Vol. 112, No.
14, Dec. 23, 1985. p. 44-58.

CITIES AND TOWNS--ECONOMIC ASPECTS--U.S.--TEXAS

Jones, Lonnie L. and Mike D. Woods.
"Determining the Impacts of New Industry on Small
Towns in Texas." Small Town. Vol. 16, No. 2,
Sept./Oct. 1985. p. 22-25.

CITIES AND TOWNS--ECONOMIC ASPECTS--U.S.--
VIRGINIA--ROANOKE

Wishneff, Brian and Douglas Eckel. "Roanoke,
Virginia: Revitalizing the Medium-Sized City."
Urban Land. Vol. 44, No. 11, Nov. 1985. p. 22-27.

CITIES AND TOWNS--GREAT BRITAIN

Country Life. Vol. 153, No. 4644, Aug. 21,
1986. (Historic Towns Number)

CITIES AND TOWNS--GROWTH

Environmental Comment. June 1979.
Note: Enitre Issue.

CITIES AND TOWNS--GROWTH

Sell, James L. and Ervin H. Zube. "Perception of and Response to Environmental Change." Journal of Architectural and Planning Research. Vol. 3, No. 1, Feb. 1986. p. 33-54.

A review of research literature organized in two sections: urban change, including literature on growth, urban renewal, historic preservation, gentrification and neighborhood conservation; rural change, including agriculture, rural development, and ⌢ energy production and development.

CITIES AND TOWNS--GROWTH--U.S.--MAINE

"Growth Management: a Means of Preserving Town Character." Landmarks Observer. Vol. 13, No. 2, Mar./Apr. 1986. p. 4-11.

An overview by the Greater Portland (Maine) Council of Governments, with reports from Freeport, Windham, South Portland, and Yarmouth.

CITIES AND TOWNS--HISTORY

Jackson, J. B. "The Vernacular City". Center (Center for the Study of American Architecture, University of Texas at Austin). Vol. 1, 1985. p. 26-43.

CITIES AND TOWNS--HISTORY

Schneider, John C. "Skid Row As An Urban Neighborhood, 1880-1960." Urbanism, Past and Present. Vol. 9, Issue 1, No. 17, Winter/Spring 1984. pp. 10-20.

CITIES AND TOWNS--HISTORY--U.S.--OHIO--CINCINNATI

Redman-Rengstorf, Susan. "To Better the Conditions: the Annexation Attempts of West College Hill." Queen City Heritage. Vol. 43, No. 1, Spring 1985. p. 3-16.

CITIES AND TOWNS--U.S.--CALIFORNIA--SAN DIEGO

Canty, Donald. "San Diego Gets an Exuberant New Downtown Development." Architecture. Nov. 1985. p. 16.

CITIES AND TOWNS--U.S.--CALIFORNIA--SAN DIEGO

Colburn, George A. "San Diego: Beyond Spit and Polish." Planning. Vol. 51, No. 11, Nov. 1985. p. 4-10.

CITIES AND TOWNS--U.S.--CALIFORNIA--SAN FRANCISCO

"San Francisco and Its Region." Architecture. Mar. 1985. p. 81-150.

A series of articles in focus on San Francisco and the Bay area including Allen Freeman, "An Explosion by the Waterfront;" Kathryn Anthony, "Public Perceptions of Recent Projects;" David Littlejohn, "Man and Nature in the Napa Valley⌢ : the Architecture of the Wine Country;" ⌢ (cont. on the next card)

"San Francisco and Its Region." Architecture. Mar. 1985. (card 2)

Reyner Banham, "The Greening of High Tech in Silicon Valley;" and Michael J. Crosbie, "The Background of the Bridges."

CITIES AND TOWNS--U.S.--CONNECTICUT--NEW HAVEN

"A Victory in the Downtown Struggle Against Regional Malls - New Haven Helps Block Mall Which Would Hurt Local Economy." Downtown Idea Exchange. Vol. 32, No. 22, Nov. 15, 1985. p. 1-4.

CITIES AND TOWNS--U.S.--ILLINOIS--CHICAGO

Urban Design International. Vol. 6, No. 1, Summer 1985. Entire Issue. 40 p.

CITIES AND TOWNS--U.S.--KENTUCKY--LOUISVILLE

Levitt, Rachelle L. "Louisville, Kentucky: A Commitment to Development." Urban Land. Vol. 44, No. 6, June 1985. p. 2-6.

CITIES AND TOWNS--U.S.--MASSACHUSETTS--ROWE

Gery, Michael E. C. "Rowe." Yankee. Vol. 49, No. 5, May 1985. p. 54-61.

CITIES AND TOWNS--U.S.--NEW MEXICO--LAS VEGAS

Dallas, Sandra. "Small Town, Big Ideas." Americana. Vol. 13, No. 3, July/Aug. 1985. p. 58-62.

CITIES AND TOWNS--U.S.--NEW YORK--NEW YORK CITY
--BROOKLYN

Van gelder, Lindsy. "Beautiful, Bountiful Brooklyn." Town and Country. Vol. 139, No. 5064, Sept. 1985. p. 225-233, 286-287.

CITIES AND TOWNS--U.S.--PENNSYLVANIA

Sutro, Suzanne. "Small Town Riverfront Revitalization: The Awakening of Bristol, Pennsylvania." Small Town. Vol. 17, No. 1, July-Aug. 1986. p. 16-23.

CITIES AND TOWNS--U.S.--MASSACHUSETTS--BOSTON

Ginna, Robert Emmett, Jr. "Boston Unchanging." Yankee. Vol. 49, No. 9, Sept. 1985. p. 164-171.

CITY PLANNING--PERIODICALS

Urban Design International. Nov./Dec. 1979.

Note: New bimonthly magazine from the Institute for Urban Design; covers aspects of city planning such as historic preservation, neighborhood revitalization, environmental factors, education, legislation, funding and energy.

CITY PLANNING--OPEN SPACES

Ramati, Raquel. "The Plaza as an Amenity." Urban Land. Feb. 1979. pp. 9-12.

CITIES AND TOWNS--U.S.--SOUTH CAROLINA--ABBEVILLE

"Abbeville - Prominent in S.C. History." The New South Carolina State Gazette. Vol. 18, No. 2. Winter 1986. pp. 1-2.

CITIES AND TOWNS--U.S.--TENNESSEE--NASHVILLE

Geniesse, Jane. "Nifty Nashville". Town and Country. Vol. 139, No. 5058, Mar. 1985. p. 154-163, 228.

CITIES AND TOWNS--U.S.--TEXAS--HOUSTON

Peters, James. "Houston Gets Religion." Planning. Vol. 51, No. 8, Aug. 1985. p. 4-11.

CITIES AND TOWNS--U.S.--TEXAS--SAN ANTONIO

Speck, Lawrence W. "A Diverse Culture, Memorable Places." Architecture. Mar. 1986. p. 44-55.

CITIES AND TOWNS--U.S.--VIRGINIA

Elias, Christopher. Special Advertising Section. "Richmond's Renaissance." Business Week. Sept. 30, 1985. p. 21-36.

CITIZEN PARTICIPATION

Francis, Mark. "Community Design." Journal of Architectural Education. Fall 1983. pp. 14-19.

CITIZEN PARTICIPATION

"Governor's 'Work Weeks' Encourage Local Preservation Efforts." Notes on Virginia. No. 29, Fall 1986. p. 34-36.

CITIZEN PARTICIPATION

Spaid, Donald. "Working With Neighborhood Groups to Develop Rehab Properties." Home Again. Summer 1984, No. 3. pp. 13-14.

CITY PLANNING

"Architect Dean Says Developers Threaten Virginia." Tidings. Vol. 7, No. 4, Winter 1987. p. 3.

CITY PLANNING

Birch, Eugenie L. and Douglass Roby. "The Planner and the Preservationist, An Uneasy Alliance." Journal of the American Planning Association. Vol. 50, No. 2, Spring 1984. pp. 194-207.

CITY PLANNING

"Creating Livable Winter Cities." Urban Outlook. Vol. 6, No. 9, May 15, 1984. pp. 4-5.

CITY PLANNING

"Developers Challenge 'Informal' Height Limit in Philadelphia." Architecture. July 1984. pp. 35, 37.

CITY PLANNING

Fuller, Larry Paul. "The Land, The City, and The Human Spirit: Building The Emerging American Landscape". Center (Center for the Study of American Architecture, University of Texas at Austin). Vol. 1, 1985. p. 64-69.

CITY PLANNING

Jacobs, Allen, and Donald Appleyard. "Toward an Urban Design Manifesto." APA Journal. Vol. 53, No. 1, Winter 1987, p. 112-120.

CITY PLANNING

Jacobs, Jane, and James W. Rouse. "Urban planning: its bias may determine our future. " Federal Design Matters. February 1981. p.1-2.

CITY PLANNING

"JAPA Index, 1958-1983." Journal of the American Planning Association. Autumn 1983. Entire Issue.

CITY PLANNING

Knack, Ruth E. "'Staking a Claim on Urban Design.' Questions of turf come to the fore as planners, architects and landscape architects take a renewed interest in the design of cities and towns." Planning. Vol. 50, No. 10, October 1984. pp. 4-11.

CITY PLANNING

Koch, Liz. "City Incentives Solder Brooklyn's Silicon Valley." City Limits. Vol. 12, No. 5, May 1987. p. 8-11.

Plans for a major high-tech center will affect a 10-block area of downtown Brooklyn.

CITY PLANNING

Langdon, Philip. "The Legacy of Kevin Lynch." Planning. Vol. 50, No. 10, October 1984. pp. 12-16.

CITY PLANNING

Mayo, Uames M. "Conflicts in Roles and Values for Urban Planners." Journal of Architectural and Planning Research. Vol. 1, No. 1, June 1984. pp. 67-77.

CITY PLANNING

Rand, George. "Crime and Environment: A Review of the Literature and Its Implications for Urban Architecture and Planning." Journal of Architectural and Planning Research. Vol. 1, No. 1, June 1984. pp. 3-19.

CITY PLANNING

Savitch, H.V. "Post Industrial Planning in New York, Paris, and London." APA Journal. Vol. 53, No. 1, Winter 1987. p. 80-91.

CITY PLANNING

"Urban Gateways: Symbolizing A Town's Character." Urban Outlook. Vol. 6, No. 9, May 15, 1984. p. 5.

CITY PLANNING AND REDEVELOPMENT LAW--U.S.--
CALIFORNIA--SAN FRANCISCO

Campbell, Robert. "Sweeping Downtown Plan
Approved in San Francisco." Architecture. Aug.
1985. p. 25; 27.

CITY PLANNING AND REDEVELOPMENT LAW--U.S.--NEW
YORK--ALBANY

"Historic Albany Wins New Look at Civic
Center Plan: State to Study Civic Center Plan:
Will Try to Find Alternatives to Demolishing
Historic Structures." Albany Preservation Report.
Jan. 1986. (Entire Issue)

CITY PLANNING--CASE STUDIES

Bailkin, Michael Caretnay. "Corporate
Initiatives in the Inner City." Urban Land.
Vol. 44, No. 10, Oct. 1985. p. 12-16.

CITY PLANNING--CASE STUDIES--U.S.--NEW YORK--
NEW YORK CITY

Jubak, Jim. "The Times Square Affair."
Sierra. Vol. 69, No. 6. Nov./Dec. 1984. pp. 14-
18.

CITY PLANNING--CASE STUDIES--U.S.--NEW YORK--
NEW YORK CITY

Russell, James S. "Golddiggers of '84?"
Architectural Record. October 1984. pp. 125,
127, 129, 131.

Times Square.

CITY PLANNING--CITIZEN PARTICIPATION

Hutcheson, John D. Jr. "Citizen Represen-
tation in Neighborhood Planning." Research
Report. Journal of the American Planning
Association. Vol. 50, No. 2, Spring 1984.
pp. 183-194.

CITY PLANNING--CITIZEN PARTICIPATION--U.S.--
COLORADO--DENVER

"Denver Partnership Establishes Private
Sector Unit to Manage, Help Plan Downtown."
Economic Growth and Revitalization Report.
No. 85-5, Mar. 12, 1985. p. 1-2.

CITY PLANNING--ECONOMIC ASPECTS

"Partnerships: New Models for Urban
Development." Urban Design International.
Fall 1982. Entire Issue.

CITY PLANNING--ECONOMIC ASPECTS--U.S.--GEORGIA--
COLUMBUS

"ACC's (American City Corporation) Two
Hundred and Forty-Two Million Dollar Revitalization Plan Adopted." Historic Columbus Foundation. Vol. 16, No. 3, Summer 1985. p. 2.

CITY PLANNING--ECONOMIC ASPECTS--U.S.--MARYLAND--
BALTIMORE

"How Baltimore Structured Redevelopment
Success." Nation's Cities Weekly. Vol. 8, No.
31, Aug. 5, 1985. p. 4-5.

CITY PLANNING--EVALUATION

Lucy, William. "Logue on Cities." Planning.
Vol. 51, No. 8, Aug. 1985. p. 12-16.

CITY PLANNING--HISTORY

Abbott, Carl. "Portland in the Pacific
War: Planning from 1940-1945." Urbanism Past
and Present. Winter/Spring 1981. pp. 12-23.

CITY PLANNING--HISTORY

Bauman, John F. "Visions of a Post-War
City: A Perspective on Urban Planning in
Philadelphia and the Nation, 1942-1945."
Urbanism Past and Present. Winter/Spring 1981.
pp. 1-11.

CITY PLANNING--HISTORY

Feiss, Carl. "The Foundations of Federal
Planning Assistance: a Personal Account of the
701 Program." Journal of the American Planning
Association. Vol. 51, No. 2, Spring 1985.
p. 175-184.

CITY PLANNING—HISTORY

Hill, David R. "Lewis Mumford's Ideas on the City." JAPA. Vol. 51, No. 4, Autumn 1985. p. 407-421.

CITY PLANNING—HISTORY

Kaplan, Barry J. "Andrew H. Green and the Creation of a Planning Rationale: The Formation of Greater New York City, 1865-1890. " Urbanism Past and Present. Summer 1979. pp. 32-39.

CITY PLANNING—HISTORY

Mandelbaum, Seymour J. "Historians and Planners: the Construction of Pasts and Futures." Journal of the American Planning Association. Vol. 51, No. 2, Spring 1985. p. 185-188.

CITY PLANNING—HISTORY

Silver, Christopher. "Neighborhood Planning in Historical Perspective." Journal of the American Planning Association. Vol. 51, No. 2, Spring 1985. p. 161-174.

CITY PLANNING—HISTORY

Speck, Lawrence. "The Hut, The Temple and the Tower: Toward an American Urbanism". Center (Center for the Study of American Architecture, University of Texas at Austin). Vol. 1, 1985. p. 6-25.

CITY PLANNING—HISTORY

"Symposium: Learning From the Past - the History of Planning." Journal of the American Planning Association. Vol. 51, No. 2, Spring 1985. 58 p.

Five articles.

CITY PLANNING—HISTORY

Wolfe, Margaret Ripley. "Changing the Face of Southern Appalachia, Urban Planning in Southwest Virginia and East Tennessee, 1890-1929." Journal of the American Planning Association. July 1981. pp. 252-265.

CITY PLANNING—HISTORY—U.S.—NEW YORK—NEW YORK CITY

Gelfand, Mark I. "Rexford G. Tugwell and the Frustration of Planning in New York City." Journal of the American Planning Association. Vol. 51, No. 2, Spring 1985. p. 151-160.

CITY PLANNING—HISTORY—U.S.—WASHINGTON—D.C.

Peterson, Jon A. "The Nation's First Comprehensive City Plan: a Political Analysis of the McMillan Plan for Washington, D.C., 1900-1902." Journal of the American Planning Association. Vol. 51, No. 2, Spring 1985. p. 134-150.

CITY PLANNING—MARYLAND—OXFORD

Hays, Alison. "Oxford, Maryland: A Small Town Rediscovers Planning." Small Town. May-June 1986. p. 4-9.

CITY PLANNING—OPEN SPACES

"New City and Town Common Program Established", Massachusetts Historical Commission Newsletter, Vol. 10, No. 4, Fall 1984, p. 7.

CITY PLANNING—OPEN SPACES

Nohl, Werner. "Open Space in Cities: Inventing a New Esthetic." Landscape. Vol. 28, No. 2, 1985. p. 35-40.

CITY PLANNING—STUDY AND TEACHING

Taylor, Caroline. "Understanding the City". Humanities. Vol. 6, No. 1, Feb. 1985. p. 18-19.

CITY PLANNING—U.S.—CALIFORNIA—LOS ANGELES

Flanagan, Barbara. "Redefining Downtown L.A.." Progressive Architecture. Mar. 1985. p. 22-23.

CITY PLANNING--U.S.--CALIFORNIA--LOS ANGELES

"Special Conference Issue: Tracking Changes in the City of the Future." Planning. Feb. 1986. Entire issue.

CITY PLANNING--U.S.--CALIFORNIA--SAN FRANCISCO

DeHart, H. Grant. "The Downtown Plan: Will It Stay Intact?" Heritage Newsletter (Foundation for San Francisco's Architectural Heritage). Vol. 12, No. 4. Fall 1984. p. 2.

CITY PLANNING--U.S.--CALIFORNIA--SAN FRANCISCO

Freeman, Allen. "An Explosion by the Waterfront" and Anthony, Kathryn. "Public Perceptions of Recent Projects." Architecture. Mar. 1985. p. 88-99.

CITY PLANNING--U.S.--CALIFORNIA--SAN FRANCISCO

Porter, Douglas R. "Downtown San Francisco's New Plan: Something for Everyone-Almost." Urban Land. Vol. 45, No. 2. Feb. 1986. pp. 34-35.

CITY PLANNING--U.S.--CALIFORNIA--SAN FRANCISCO

"Reshaping the San Francisco skyline: Seven current projects respond to the city's new downtown plan." Architectural Record. Mar. 1985. p. 58.

CITY PLANNING--U.S.--CALIFORNIA--SAN FRANCISCO

"San Francisco Downtown Plan." Progressive Architecture. Jan. 1986. p. 122-123.

Winner of a P/A award.

CITY PLANNING--U.S.--CALIFORNIA--SAN FRANCISCO

Woodbridge, Sally. "Commentary: San Fran Plan." Progressive Architecture. Dec. 1985. p. 33-34.

CITY PLANNING--U.S.--COLORADO--DENVER

Purdy, Lisa. "Historic Portion Key to Downtown Plan." Historic Denver News. Mar. 1985. p. 6.

CITY PLANNING--U.S.--INDIANA--INDIANAPOLIS

Robinson, Susan G. "Indianapolis Maximizes Its Assets." Place. Vol. 5, No. 4, Apr. 1985. p. 1-5.

CITY PLANNING--U.S.--MASSACHUSETTS--BOSTON

Kay, Jane Holtz. "The Limits of Growth: Boston's Downtown Plan." Progressive Architecture. Oct. 1985. p. 29-30.

CITY PLANNING--U.S.--MASSACHUSETTS--BOSTON

Padjen, Elizabeth S. "Envisioning Boston." Boston Preservation Alliance Letter. Vol. 7, No. 1, Jan. 1986. p. 1, 5-6.

CITY PLANNING--U.S.--NEW YORK--NEW YORK CITY

Karson, Robin. "Battery Park City Takes Manhattan." Landscape Architecture. Vol. 75, No. 4, July/Aug. 1985. p. 64-69.

CITY PLANNING--U.S.--NEW YORK--NEW YORK CITY

"On to the Next Challenge: A Crumbling Foundation." (Infrastructure.) Business Week. July 23, 1984. pp. 109-112.

CITY PLANNING--U.S.--NEW YORK--NEW YORK CITY

"Too Late for Times Square?" Progressive Architecture. October 1984. pp. 23-4.

CITY PLANNING--U.S.--OHIO--CINCINNATI

Merkel, Joyce. "Cincinnati." Landscape Architecture. Vol. 75, No. 5, Sept./Oct. 1985. p. 118-125.

A review of city planning and the architecture in Ohio's Queen City.

CITY PLANNING--U.S.--TEXAS--AUSTIN

Brown, Denise Scott. "Visions of the Future Based on Lessons From the Past". Center (Center for the Study of American Architecture, University of Texas at Austin). Vol. 1, 1985. p. 44-63.

CITY PLANNING--U.S.--TEXAS--FORT WORTH

Dillon, David. "Master Plan for Fort Worth Cultural District Revealed." Architecture. May 1984. p. 67.

CITY PLANNING--U.S.--TEXAS--HOUSTON

"Planning and Land Use Regs - From Houston." Urban Outlook. Vol. 7, No. 15, Aug. 15, 1985. p. 1-2.

CITY PLANNING--U.S.--WASHINGTON, D.C.

"The End of the Rhode(s)." Progressive Architecture. October 1984. pp. 25-6.

CITY PLANNING--U.S.--WYOMING--THERMOPOLIS

Crush, Teresa. "Thermopolis, Wyoming Developing a Comprehensive Downtown Plan." Small Town. Vol. 16, No. 2, Sept./Oct. 1985. p. 16-21.

CITY TRAFFIC

Dunphy, Robert. "Urban Traffic Congestion: A National Crisis." Urban Land. Vol. 44, No. 10, Oct. 1985. p. 2-7.

CLASSICISM IN ARCHITECTURE

Progressive Architecture. October 1981. p.71-109.

COASTAL ZONE MANAGEMENT

Environmental Comment. October 1980. Entire issue.

COASTAL ZONE MANAGEMENT--LAW AND LEGISLATION

Chasis, Sarah. "The Coastal Zone Management Act". APA Journal. April 1980. p. 145-153.

COLLECTIVE SETTLEMENTS--BIBLIOGRAPHY

Gyrisco, Geoffrey M. "Excavating Utopia: The Archaeology of American Communal Societies." 11593 Supplement. Oct. 1979. 7 pp.

COLLECTORS AND COLLECTING

Byrne-Dodge, Teresa. "Ima Hogg's Legacy." Americana. Vol. 13, No. 4, Sept./Oct. 1985. p. 34-35, 38.

COLONIAL REVIVAL

Gowans, Alan. "The Spanish Colonial Revival Style." The Old House Journal. October 1982. pp. 198-202.

COLOR

Bristow, Ian, "Prismatic Principles: 19th Century Colour Theory." Country Life, Apr. 9, 1987. p. 146-147.

COLOR IN ARCHITECTURE

Alderson, Caroline. "Recreating A 19th Century Paint Palette." APT Bulletin. Vol. XVI, No. 1, 1984. pp. 47-56.

Annotated bibliography.

COLOR IN ARCHITECTURE

Henning, Lisbeth. "Vivid Victorian Colors Not Suitable for All Styles." The Indiana Preservationist. No. 1, 1986. p. 5.

COLOR IN ARCHITECTURE

Jones, Larry. "Old House Paint Color Research". Utah: Preservation/Restoration. Vol. 2, Issue 2, 1980. pp. 80-81.

COLOR IN ARCHITECTURE

Kowsky, Francis R. "Jacob Wrey Mould: Master of Color." Newsletter, Preservation League of New York State. Vol. 11, No. 2, Mar./Apr. 1985. p. 4-5.

COLOR IN ARCHITECTURE

Lowe, Nancy. "Fashion and Technology Play a Role in Paint." The Quapaw Chronicle. Vol. 12, No. 7, Feb./Mar. 1986. p. 7, 10.

COLOR IN ARCHITECTURE

Moss, Roger W. "Colorful Victorians". Nineteenth Century. Spring 1981. pp. 26 - 30.

COLOR IN ARCHITECTURE

Old House Journal. April 1981. Entire issue.

COLUMNS

Leeke, John. "Exterior Wood Columns, Practical Repairs for Do-It-Yourselfers." The Old-House Journal. Oct. 1982. p. 195.

COLORADA--CRESTED BUTTE

Ristow, William. " Of Change and a Valley." The Cultural Post. March/April 1981. p.10-13.

COLORADO--GRAND JUNCTION

Brumgardt, John R. "Bringing it Together: Cross Orchards Project Offers Outstanding Example of Community Cooperation". History News. May 1981. pp. 40-43.

COLUMNS

Leeke, John. "Installing Architectural Columns." The Old-House Journal. June 1984, Vol. XII, No. 5. pp. 96-99.

COLUMNS

Leeke, John. "Shopping for Columns." The Old-House Journal. Vol. XII, No. 4, May 1984. pp. 71, 82-84.

COMMEMORATIVE PORCELAIN

Goldberg, Hayden. "The Architecture of Charles Bulfinch on Historical Blue Staffordshire: Part I: The Early Building, 1790-1807." Antiques. Vol. 128, No. 6, Dec. 1985. p. 1198-1205.

COMMERCIAL ARCHAEOLOGY

Cohen, Daniel. "For Food Both Cold and Hot, Put Your Nickels in the Slot." Smithsonian. Vol. 16, No. 10, Jan. 1986. p. 50-61.

The Automat, first opened by Horn and Hardhart in 1902, is discussed; only one survives today.

COMMERCIAL ARCHAEOLOGY

Cresswell, Catherine and William Widdowson. "The Golden Arches: Icon and Symbol." SCA News Journal. Fall 1986. p. 11-13.

COMMERCIAL ARCHAEOLOGY

"The Golden Arches Debate - should they be included in the State Register of Historic Places?" Connecticut Trust for Historic Preservation News. Winter 1981. p.1, 10-11.

COMMERCIAL ARCHEOLOGY

Jackson, Michael B. "McDonald's Museum Opens in Des Plaines, Illinois." SCA News Journal. Vol. 2, No. 6, Nov. 1985. p. 1-2.

First McDonald's restored to 1955 appearance.

COMMERCIAL ARCHAEOLOGY

Krim, Arthur. "McDonald's: One Up, One Down. SCA News Journal, Society for Commercial Archeology. Vol. 2, No. 4, September 1984. p. 1.

COMMERCIAL ARCHAEOLOGY

Luce, W. Ray. "White Castle and Preservation." SCA News Journal, Society for Commercial Archeology. Vol. 2, No. 4, September 1984. pp. 4-6.

COMMERCIAL ARCHAEOLOGY

MacDonald, Kent. "The Commercial Strip: From Main Street to Television Road." Landscape. Vol. 28, No. 2, 1985. p. 12-19.

COMMERCIAL ARCHAEOLOGY

Schlereth, Thomas J. "Doing History on the Road: the Above-ground Archaeology of the American Highway." Chronicle (Historical Society of Michigan). Vol. 20, No. 4, Winter 1985. p. 14-20.

Part two of a series, this article discusses U.S. Route 40 and the beginning of the Federal highway system.

COMMERCIAL ARCHAEOLOGY

Wolkomir, Richard. "Old McDonalds have a friend: his name is Liebs." Smithsonian. April 1981. p. 62-69.

COMMERCIAL ARCHAELOGY--U.S.--CALIFORNIA--LOS ANGELES

"Oldest McDonald's Considered for National Register Listing." Architecture, News. April 1984. p. 15, 18.

COMMERCIAL ARCHAEOLOGY--U.S.--INDIANA--INDIANA-POLIS

Dunn, Douglas. "Roadside Attraction Wins New Lease on Life." The Indiana Preservationist. No. 2 & 3, 1985. p. 13.

COMMERCIAL ARCHAEOLOGY--U.S.--NEW YORK--LONG ISLAND

Mansfield, Howard. "The Big Duck." Sites. XII. pp. 4-9.

COMMONS

Barker, James F. "Village Greens and Courthouse Squares." Place. September 1983. pp. 8-9.

COMMONS

"Living on the Green". Yankee. Vol. 49, No. 3, Mar. 1985. p. 92-100.

Six available properties on New England village greens shown.

COMMUNITY--STUDY AND TEACHING

Caldwell, Pamela. "Appreciating Our Built Environment." Trends. Winter 1979. pp. 21-22.

COMMUNITY DEVELOPMENT

"City Will 'Map' Blight to Plan Revitalization Strategies." Community Development Digest. No. 86-23, Dec. 2, 1986. p. 6-7.

Mapping of empty industrial buildings will allow new and expanding companies in Cleveland to rehab.

COMMUNITY DEVELOPMENT

Fennell, John. "Convert-to-Rent, Low-Rise Rehabilitation Two Most Popular Programs in Ontario." Building Renovation. Vol. 4, No. 2, Mar./Apr. 1987. p. 23.

COMMUNITY DEVELOPMENT

Hester, Randolph T. Jr. "12 Steps to Community Development", Landscape Architecture, Vol. 75, No. 1, Janaury/February 1985, pp. 78-85.

Preservation of "landstyles" and "lifescapes" discussed.

COMMUNITY DEVELOPMENT

Home Again, for Housing and Community Professionals. No. 1, Winter 1983.

COMMUNITY DEVELOPMENT

"Houston Economic Development Program Begins With Neighborhood Revitalization." Community Development Digest. No. 6, Mar. 17, 1987. p. 8-9.

COMMUNITY DEVELOPMENT

"Maryland Considers Taking Over Small Cities CD Block Grant Program." Community Development Digest. No. 4, Feb. 17, 1987, p.13.

COMMUNITY DEVELOPMENT

"Public/Private Management for Downtown Revitalization Triggers Downtown Success in Portsmouth, Virginia." Downtown Idea Exchange. Vol. 34, No. 6, Mar. 1987. p. 4-5.

COMMUNITY DEVELOPMENT

Schussheim, Morton J. "The Impact of Demographic Change on Housing and Community Development." The Appraisal Journal. July 1984. pp. 375-381.

COMMUNITY DEVELOPMENT

Stern, Jennifer. "Can Communities Shape Development?" City Limits. Vol. 12, No. 3, Mar. 1987. p. 12-15.

COMMUNITY DEVELOPMENT--CITIZEN PARTICIPATION

Didge, Willard K. "Citizen Participation Evolves from Low-level Start to Partnership Status in St. Paul." Journal of Housing, April 1979. pp. 217-219.

COMMUNITY DEVELOPMENT--ECONOMIC ASPECTS

"Bank Subsidiaries Are Bringing Capital, Expertise to Community Development Process." Local Economic Growth and Neighborhood Reinvestment Report. February 16, 1984. pp. 1-3.

COMMUNITY DEVELOPMENT--ECONOMIC ASPECTS

Casella, Sam. "Can TIF Help Your Community?" Center City Report. January 1983. pp. 4-6.

COMMUNITY DEVELOPMENT--ECONOMIC ASPECTS

Jefferys, Grady. "North Carolina Pilot Project Recruits Small Business." IDEA, Center City Report. June 1984. pp. 4-5.

COMMUNITY DEVELOPMENT--ECONOMIC ASPECTS

Patterson, Elizabeth. "Baltimore Bank Provides Neighborhood Resources." IDEA, Center City Report. June 1984. pp. 3,5.

COMMUNITY DEVELOPMENT--ECONOMIC ASPECTS

Rogel, Stuart L. "Utility Powers Community Development." Urban Land. January 1984. pp. 8-11.

COMMUNITY DEVELOPMENT--FEDERAL AID

"Administration Having Problems with CD Block Grant Targeting Proposal." Community Development Digest. No. 4, Feb. 17, 1987, p. 1-2.

COMMUNITY DEVELOPMENT--PERIODICALS

News Alert. Mar. 26, 1979. "A new communication service for NAHRO Agency members... the News Alert provides timely reports on important developments in program funding, program regulations, legislative activities, and policy formulation affecting housing and community development."

COMMUNITY DEVELOPMENT, URBAN

"Neighborhood Commercial Strips Offer Economic Growth Opportunities." Local Economic Growth and Neighborhood Reinvestment Report. August 4, 1983. pp. 1-2.

COMMUNITY DEVELOPMENT, URBAN--U.S.--NEW YORK-- NIAGARA FALLS

Propp, Jonathan. "A Neighborhood Revives in Niagara Falls." Place. Vol. 5, No. 3, Mar. 1985. p. 8-10.

COMMUNITY DEVELOPMENT, URBAN--U.S.--NORTH CARO- LINA--MANTEO

Hester, Randy. "Subconscious Landscapes of the Heart." Places. Vol. 2, No. 3. p. 10-22.

Process to document community life and values in context of overall development patterns described.

COMMUNITY DEVELOPMENT BLOCK GRANTS

Ehrmann, Michael M. and Ford, Douglas. "CD Rehabilitation: Analysis Reveals Dramatic Growth, Sucessful Local Programs." Journal of Housing. June 1981. pp. 330-337.

COMMUNITY DEVELOPMENT BLOCK GRANTS

Perlman, Konrad J. "New CD Regulations Make Planning Vital." Journal of Housing. Jan. 1980. pp. 27-32.

COMMUNITY DEVELOPMENT BLOCK GRANTS

Schultz, Fred. "Using Block Grant Money for People." Planning. Sep. 1979. pp. 26-28.

Note: On Baltimore's use of block grant money for community service programs.

COMMUNITY DEVELOPMENT CORPORATIONS

Bradford, Calvin. "Private Sector Initiatives and Public Sector Accountability, A Case Study of Contracting with City Venture." American Planning Association Journal. Summer 1983. pp. 326-335.

COMMUNITY DEVELOPMENT CORPORATIONS

Nolon, John R. "Innovative Joint Ventures: The Role of Residential Development Agencies." Journal of Housing. Jan./Feb. 1983. p. 13.

COMMUNITY DEVELOPMENT CORPORATIONS

Rash, James Dennis. "Privately Funded Redevelopment in North Carolina, A Business Proposition." Urban Land. October 1983. pp. 2-7.

COMMUNITY ORGANIZATIONS

"Directory of Useful Organizations." Conserve Neighborhoods. No. 54, Jan. 1986. Entire issue.

COMPANY TOWNS

Beauregard, Robert A. and Briavel Holcomb. "Dominant Enterprises and Acquiescent Communities: The Private Sector and Urban Revitalization." Urbanism Past and Present, Summer 1979. pp. 18-31.

COMPANY TOWNS

Crump, Nancy Carter. "Hopewell During World War I: The Toughest Town North of Hell." Virginia Cavalcade. Summer 1981. pp. 38-47.

COMPANY TOWNS

Krohe, James. "Utopia in Pullman." Americana. July/August 1981. pp. 45 - 50.

COMPANY TOWNS--CONSERVATION AND RESTORATION

"Preservation American Style; Support Historic Preservation--Drink at the Hotel Florence." Civic Trust News. Nov./Dec. 1979. pp. 6-7.

COMPANY TOWNS--U.S.--VERMONT--STRAFFORD

Clark, Edie. "Strafford." Yankee. Vol. 49, No. 10, Oct. 1985. p. 82-88, 174-178.

COMPANY TOWNS--U.S.--WASHINGTON STATE

Meyer, Bette E. "Red Row: Northern Pacific (R.R.) Housing on the Frontier." Landmarks, Magazine of Northwest History and Preservation. Vol. III, No. 2, Summer 1984. pp. 25-28.

COMPUTERS

Archaeological Assistance Division, National Park Service. Status Report on the National Archaeological Database. Jan. 20, 1987. 4p. (VF)

COMPUTERS

"CAD (Computer Assisted Design):The Wows and the Wherefores." Progressive Architecture. May 1984. pp. 135-172. (also two related articles)

COMPUTERS

"Computer-Aided Renovation." Commercial Renovation. Vol. 7, No. 4, Aug. 1985. p. 48-53.

COMPUTERS

"Computers and Preservation." Bulletin, The Association for Preservation Technology. Vol. 16, No. 2, 1984. Entire Issue. 22p.

Includes Nancy B. Brown, "Microcomputers: What, Why and How"; Barbara Wyatt, "The Computer- ization of Historic Preservation"; Herbert Gott- fried, "A Computer Program for Recording Historic Buildings Using the SPSS (Statistical Package for the Social Sciences) Program"; and Bruce MacDougal "National Register Computerization."

COMPUTERS

D'Amico, Philip and George Epstein. "Com- puter Equipment: How to Know What You Want." Part 2. Grantsmanship Center News. Vol. 13, No. 2, Issue 61, Mar./Apr. 1985. p. 20-27.

Vertical File
COMPUTERS

Farrel, Mary. Considerations Relating to Access to the National Register Information System (NRIS). Jun. 1986. 21p. (VF)

COMPUTERS IN PRESERVATION

"Using Computers Aids Downtown Facade Study." Downtown Idea Exchange. Vol. 34, No. 5, Mar. 1, 1987, p. 1-2.

Computer Aided Drafting and Design (CADD) system in Owen Sound, Ontario.

CONCRETE CONSTRUCTION--HISTORY

Gillespie, Ann. "Early Development of the Artistic Concrete Block: the Case of the Boyd Brothers." APT Bulletin. Vol. 11, No. 2, 1979. pp. 30-52.

Vertical File
COMPUTERS

Facts on Computerization of the National Register of Historic Places. Mar. 1987. 2 p. (VF)

COMPUTERS

Hicks, Ellen C. and Carolee Belkin Walker. "Streamlined Systems: Computers Make Museums Manageable." Museum News. Vol. 163, No. 6, Aug. 1985. p. 36-47.

COMPUTERS

Judge, W. James. "PARKMAN: A Computer Graphics Program for Cultural Resource Management." NPS, CRM Bulletin. Vol. 7, No. 1, April 1984. pp. 14-15, 18.

COMPUTERS

McDaniel, Dennis K. and Helen Tangires. "The 19th-Century McFaddin-Ward House Enters the Computer Age." History News. Vol. 40, No. 8, Aug. 1985. p. 14-17.

COMPUTERS

Mainfort Jr., Robert C. and Mary L. Kwas. "Make Way for Microcomputers: How to select a microcomputer for a small museum or historic site." History News. Vol. 41, No. 3, Mar. 1986. p. 23-28.

COMPUTERS

Merritt, Jim. "Where Old Computers Go." Americana. Vol 14, No. 2, May/June 1986. p. 39-41, 75.

Some historic computers have found a home in Boston's Computer Museum.

COMPUTERS

"'Quiet Revolution' Taking Place in the Way Localities Map/Plan Land Use." Community Development Digest, No. 7, Apr. 7, 1987. p. 8-11.

Computer mapping use in planning.

COMPUTERS

"The Society and Computers." Columns, Bimonthly Newsletter of the State Historical Society of Wisconsin. Vol. 5, No. 5, October/November 1984. pp. 4-6.

COMPUTERS--GREAT BRITAIN

Feilden, Sir Bernard. "A Plea for Computerized Listing." Transactions of the Ancient Monuments Society. Vol. 30, 1986. p. 67-68.

COMPUTERS--GREAT BRITAIN--LONDON

"Computer Monitoring of Protected Buildings." Urban Innovation Abroad. Vol. 9, No. 3, Mar. 1985. p. 2.

COMPUTERS IN PRESERVATION

"Preservation Data Management Network Forming." Urban Conservation Report. Vol. 9, No. 3, Mar. 1987. p. 5.

CONCRETE

"The Durability of Steel in Concrete: Part I Mechanism of Protection and Corrosion." Building Research Establishment Digest. #263, July 1982.

CONCRETE

Moore, Evelyn R. "Concrete in Illinois Newest Number in Preservation Series." Historic Illinois. Vol. 10, No. 2. Aug. 1987. p. 5.

CONCRETE

Smith, Raymond W. "Concrete Construction: Early Experiments in New York State." Preservation League of New York State Newsletter. March-April 1982. pp. 4-5.

CONCRETE--DETERIORATION

"Alkali Aggregate Reactions in Concrete," Building Research Establishment Digest. #258., February 1982.

CONCRETE--PRESERVATION

Scott, Gary. "Historic Concrete Preservation Problems at Fort Washington, Maryland." APT Bulletin number 2 1978. pp. 122-131.

CONCRETE CONSTRUCTION

Santucci, R.M. "Some Concrete Thoughts." Cost Cuts. Vol. 3, No. 5, March-April 1986. p. 1, 4-6.

"Pump lift" method saves money over traditional method for concrete repair.

CONCRETE CONSTRUCTION--DETERIORATION

"The Durability of Steel in Concrete: Part 2 Diagnosis and Assessment of Corrosion-Cracked Concrete." Building Research Establishment Digest. August 1982, #264. 8 pp.

CONCRETE CONSTRUCTION--MAINTENANCE AND REPAIR

Cotton, J. Randall. "Repairing Ornamental Concrete Block." The Old-House Journal. Vol. XII, No. 9, November 1984. pp. 201-204.

CONCRETE CONSTRUCTION--MAINTENANCE AND REPAIR

"The Durability of Steel in Concrete: Part 3. The Repair of Reinforced Concrete." Building Research Establishment Digest. Sep. 1982, No. 265. 8 p.

CONCRETE CONSTRUCTION--MAINTENANCE AND REPAIR

Prudon, Theodore. "Confronting Concrete Realities." Progressive Architecture. November 1981. pp. 131-137.

CONCRETE HOUSES

Cotton, J. Randall. "Ornamental Concrete Block Houses." Old-House Journal. October 1984. Vol. XII, No. 8 pp. 165, 180-183.

CONCRETE HOUSES--NETHERLANDS--AMSTERDAM

Metz, Tracy. "Amsterdam restores its 'concrete village' and a way of life." Architectural Record. Feb. 1986. p. 79.

CONDOMINIUM (HOUSING)

Navarro, Peter. "Rent Control and the Landlord's Loophole: Condominium Conversions in Cambridge, Mass." Urban Land. November 1980. p. 6-9.

CONSERVATION OF NATURAL RESOURCES

Franklin, Kay. "Protecting Nature's Design: A Case for Undeveloped Beachfront in the Indiana Dunes." Inland Architect. Sept./Oct. 1986. p. 36-39.

CONSERVATION OF NATURAL RESOURCES

"New Trust Policy Covers NSW Forests." National Trust Magazine (The National Trust of Australia, NSW). No. 35, June 1986. p. 9-11.

CONSERVATION OF NATURAL RESOURCES

Smith, Fiona. "Greening Australia". Heritage Australia. Vol. 5, No. 2. Winter 1986. p.18-19.

Reforestation program.

CONSERVATION OF NATURAL RESOURCES--LAW AND LEGISLATION

Connors, Donald L. and Michael E. High. "The Public Trust Doctrine: A Primer for the 1980s." Urban Land. Vol. 44, No. 3, Mar. 1985. p. 34-35.

CONSTRUCTION INDUSTRY

Santucci, R.M. "Securing the Site with Money in Mind." Cost Cuts. Vol. 2, No. 10, Aug. 1985. p. 1, 3-6.

Measures to take to secure a renovation site from theft.

CONSULTANTS

Davis, Barbara H. "How and Why to Hire a Consultant." The Grantsmanship Center News. March/April 1983. pp. 26-34.

CONVENTION FACILITIES

Graveline, Dan. "Convention Centers." Urban Land. July 1984. pp. 2-5.

CONVENTION FACILITIES

Official Meeting Facilities Guide. Spring 1981. 1034 p. (Reference shelf)

COPYRIGHT

Kirkpatrick, Nancy. "Rights and Reproductions in Art Museums." Museum News. Vol. 64, No. 3, Feb. 1986. p. 45-49.

CORNICE WORK

Garrison, John Mark. "Decorative Plaster Running Cornices." The Old-House Journal. Vol. XII, No. 10, December 1984. pp. 213-219.

CORNICES

Cecere, Joseph J. "Design and Wood Cornice Assembly." The Old House Journal. Vol. 13, No. 9, Nov. 1985. p. 190-194.

CORNICE WORK

Rossage, Mike. "Coping with Cornices." Traditional Homes. April 1986. p. 64-68.

How to make plaster moldings.

CORNICES

Poore, Jonathan. "Installing a Tin-Ceiling Cornice." Old-House Journal. Vol. 14, No. 9, Nov. 1986. p. 440.

CORPORATIONS

"Corporate Involvement in Preservation." Connecticut Trust for Historic Preservation. Spring 1983. Entire Issue.

CORPORATIONS

Fish, Michael. "The Alcan Move, It's More Than Seven Blocks From Place Ville Marie to Sherbrooke Street." Canadian Heritage. May/June 1984. pp 30-33.

Corporation uses historic buildings for headquarters.

CORPORATIONS, NONPROFIT

Andres, Susan. " A Primer on Mailing Lists." The Grantsmanship Center News. Sep./Oct. 1982. pp. 15-30.

CORPORATIONS, NONPROFIT

Basic Grantsmanship Library (7th edition), Grantsmanship Center News, Vol. 12, No. 3, September/December, 1984, pp. 37-50.

CORPORATIONS, NONPROFIT

Borof, Irwin J. "The Private Foundation Question: Problems and Solutions for CBO's." The Grantsmanship Center News. September/October 1983. pp. 32-36.

CORPORATIONS, NONPROFIT

Brinckerhoff, Peter C. "Tax Breaks for Not-for-Profits or How to Use the Tax Codes to Help Your Organization Thrive." The Grantsmanship Center News. January/February 1983. pp. 14-17.

CORPORATIONS, NONPROFIT

"Business Ventures for Nonprofits."
Conserve Neighborhood. Special Issue, 1986.
16p. (VF)

CORPORATIONS, NON-PROFIT

"Cut Costs by Sharing Staff." Economic Growth and
Revitalization. No. 7-1, Jan.13, 1987. p. 4.

CORPORATIONS, NONPROFIT

D'Amico, Phil. "How A Computer Thinks (And How It
Doesn't), first in "Computers for Nonprofits" series,
Grantsmanship Center News, Vol. 12, No. 3, September/
December 1984, pp. 25-31.

CORPORATIONS, NONPROFIT

"Fitting it Together: Managing State and
Local History." History News. March 1982.
Entire Issue.

CONTENTS: Gwirtzman, Lisa. Nonprofit Management
Control, Using Information About Money to Make
Better Decisions--Friedman, Renee. Museum People,
The Special Problems of Personnel Management in
Museums and Historical Societies--Hicks, George E.
Thinking Ahead, Long-Range Planning for the
Nonprofit Organization.

CORPORATIONS, NONPROFIT

Flanagan, Joan. "Raising Money From Members: Who
Needs What You Do?", Grantsmanship Center News,
Vol. 12, No. 3, September/December 1984, pp. 10-23.

CORPORATIONS, NONPROFIT

Gilbert, Julie Noel. "Coming to Terms with
the Tax Man." Museum News. September/October 1982.
pp. 18-23.

CORPORATIONS, NONPROFIT

Goldstein, Benjamin. "Opinion: Arts
Organizations Must Look Hard at Themselves before
the Leap into Entrepreneurial Activities." Place.
May 1982. p. 5.

CORPORATIONS, NONPROFIT

"Hostels Offer Free Memberships to Nonprofits."
Conserve Neighborhoods. No. 39. June 1984.
p. 377.

CORPORATIONS, NONPROFIT

"Illinois Heritage Association: A New
Preservation Service Organization." Historic
Illinois. Vol. 6, No. 6, April 1984. pp. 4-5,
13.

CORPORATIONS, NONPROFIT

Lord, James Gregory. "Marketing and the
Nonprofit Organization." History News.
October 1981. pp. 34-36.

CORPORATIONS, NONPROFIT

Matthews, Downs. "Keeping the Third Sector's
Purse Full." SEMC Journal, November 1979. pp. 31-
36.

CORPORATIONS, NONPROFIT

"Profit Making by Nonprofits, Part Two."
Grantsmanship Center News. March/April 1982.
pp. 24-41.

CORPORATIONS, NONPROFIT

Propp, Jonathan. "Partners Council Probes
Fiscal Innovation." Place. Vol. 4, No. 6,
June 1984. pp. 6-8.

CORPORATIONS, NONPROFIT

Reibel, Daniel B. "Partnership in
Historical Agencies." History News. March
1982. pp. 48-49.

CORPORATIONS, NONPROFIT

Salamon, Lester. "The Future of the Nonprofit Sector'", Grantsmanship Center News, Vol. 12, No. 3, September/December 1984, pp. 54-61.

CORPORATIONS, NONPROFIT

Williams, Roger M. "Why Don't We Set Up a Profit-Making Subsidiary?" Grantsmanship Center News. January/February 1982. pp. 14-23.

CORPORATIONS, NONPROFIT

Winkleman, Michael. "Nonprofits: At What Price Survival?" Metropolis. December 1981. pp. 18-19.

CORPORATIONS, NONPROFIT--ACCOUNTING

Kramer, Ira. "Fiscal Hygiene for Small Nonprofits", Place, January 1985, pp. 6-8.

CORPORATIONS, NONPROFIT--ACCOUNTING

Pizer, Laurence R. "How to Prepare (and Live With) a Budget." History News. March 1983. pp. 22-25.

CORPORATIONS, NONPROFIT--ECONOMIC ASPECTS

Adams, Katherine. "Great Fund Raisers." Conserve Neighborhoods. No. 50, July/Aug. 1985. p. 4-5.

CORPORATIONS, NONPROFIT--ECONOMIC ASPECTS

Connors, Jill. "Designer Show Houses." Americana. Vol. 13, No. 4, Sept./Oct. 1985. p. 22-28.

CORPORATIONS, NONPROFIT--ECONOMIC ASPECTS

"Directories of State and Local Grant-makers." Whole Nonprofit Catalog (Grantsmanship Center). Summer 1985. p. 24-25.

CORPORATIONS, NONPROFIT--ECONOMIC ASPECTS

Welch, Randy. "Lending Sources for Non-profits." Whole Nonprofit Catalog (Grantsmanship Center). Summer 1985. p. 34.

CORPORATIONS, NONPROFIT--MANAGEMENT

Ames, Peter J. "Guiding Museum Values: Trustees, Mission and Plans." Museum News. Vol. 163, No. 6, Aug. 1985. p. 48-52.

CORPORATIONS, NONPROFIT--MANAGEMENT

Callaghan, Christopher T. and William J. Whalen. "Cost Accounting for Non-Accountants." The Grantsmanship Center News. November/December 1981. pp. 27-33.

CORPORATIONS, NONPROFIT--MANAGEMENT

Davis, Kenneth A. "How Your Agency Can Organize A Conference." Grantsmanship Center News. Vol. 13, No. 2, Issue 61, Mar./Apr. 1985. p. 28-35.

CORPORATIONS, NONPROFIT--MANAGEMENT

Epstein, George. "How to Buy a Computer." Whole Nonprofit Catalog (Grantsmanship Center.) Summer 1985. p. 4-6, 11.

CORPORATIONS, NONPROFIT--MANAGEMENT

Flood, Gayle. "To Have or Have Not: The Pros and Cons of Membership Programs for Histori-cal Organizations and Museums." History News. Vol. 40, No. 5, May 1985. p. 12-17.

CORPORATIONS, NONPROFIT--MANAGEMENT

The Grantsmanship Center Whole Nonprofit Catalog, Winter 1984-85, Vol. 1, No. 1, Entire Issue.

"A Compendium of Sources and Resources for Managers and Staff of Nonprofit Organizations."

New Newsletter.

CORPORATIONS, NONPROFIT--MANAGEMENT

Gross, Susan. "Getting to the Source of Problems." The Grantsmanship Center News. March/April 1983. pp. 38-42.

CORPORATIONS, NONPROFIT--MANAGEMENT

Hemenway, Alic. "Working Together: Consortiums Can Save You Money." History News. April 1983. pp. 32-35.

CORPORATIONS,NONPROFIT--MANAGEMENT

"Marketing for Nonprofits." The Grantsmanship Center News. Nov./Dec. 1982. pp. 6-23.

Contents: Orr, Sam. Buzz Word or Good Idea--Andreasen, Alan R. Nonprofits: Check Your Attention To Customers--Stocker, Leslie E. Market Research Points Out Donor Perceptions--

CORPORATIONS, NONPROFIT--MANAGEMENT

Lincoln, Crawford. "What Historical Societies can Learn from the Profit Sector." History News. April 1981. p.38-39.

CORPORATIONS, NONPROFIT--MANAGEMENT

Mier, Robert and Wim Wiewel. "Business Activities of Not-for-Profit Organizations." American Planning Association Journal. Summer 1983. pp. 316-325.

CORPORATIONS, NONPROFIT--MANAGEMENT

Miller, Patricia L. "Fulfilling the Trust of Trusteeship". Illinois Heritage Association Newsletter. Vol. 3, No. 1, Jan./Feb. 1985. Technical Insert, 2p.

CORPORATIONS, NONPROFIT --MANAGEMENT

"Myths and Maxims about Boards of Directors." Conserve Neighborhoods. November-December, 1982. p. 254.

CORPORATIONS, NONPROFIT--MANAGEMENT

"Organizational Problems: Going to the Source." Conserve Neighborhoods. September/October 1982. 4 pp.

CORPORATIONS, NONPROFIT--MANAGEMENT

"Responsibilities and Duties of a Nonprofit Director." Whole Nonprofit Catalog (Grantsmanship Center.) Summer 1985. p. 30-31.

CORPORATIONS, NONPROFIT--MANAGEMENT

Tolles, Bryant F. "For the Board: How to Hire a Director." History News. Vol. 40, No. 3, Mar. 1985. p. 24-26.

CORPORATIONS, NONPROFIT--MANAGEMENT

Weber, William and Suzanne. "Long-Range Process Planning: The First Cut." The Grantsmanship Center News. Jul./Aug. 1982. pp. 24-35.

CORPORATIONS, NONPROFIT--MANAGEMENT--U.S.--NEW YORK

"League Expands Historic Sites Discount Program". Newsletter, Preservation League of New York State. Vol. 10, No. 6, Nov./Dec. 1984. p. 3.

League membership gives 10% discount on admission to participating historic sites.

CORPORATIONS, NONPROFIT--PERSONNEL MANAGEMENT

"National Council on Public History (NCPH), Ethical Guides for the Historian." NCPH Newsletter. Vol. 5, No. 1, Winter 1984-1985. p. 2.

COTTAGES

St. Marie, Satenig S. "Roseland Cottage." Victorian Homes. Vol. 5, Issue 3, Summer 1986. p. 24-31.

This Victorian cottage in Woodstock, Connecticut was visited by four U.S. presidents of the last century.

COSTUME

Carter, Virginia E. "How Williamsburg Keeps its Interpreters Looking Their Eighteenth-Century Best." Colonial Williamsburg Today. Summer 1981. pp. 14-19.

COSTUME--CONSERVATION AND RESTORATION

"An Introduction to Costume Care." Illinois Heritage Association Technical Insert. No. 16, July/Aug. 1985. 2 p.

COUNTRY HOMES

Ferro, Maximillian L. "Conserving Large Estates : Problems of Maintaining the Great Turn-of-the-Century Homes." Technology and Conservation. Fall 1981. pp. 22-27.

COUNTRY HOMES

Graham, Rosalyn. "Shelburne Farms Begins a New Era." Shelburne Farms Resources. Fall/Winter 1982. pp. 1; 4.

COUNTRY HOMES

Kaiser, Harvey H. "The Adirondack Rustic Style." The Old-House Journal. January-February, 1983. p. 1.

COUNTRY HOMES

Lawford, Vnlentine. "Historic Houses: The Locusts, Dutchess County Home of Mrs. Lytle Hull." Architectural Digest. Mar. 1979. pp. 59-65.

COUNTRY HOMES

Robinson, John Martin. "The Country Houses of Samuel Wyatt." Architectural Review. Oct. 1979. pp. 219-224.

COUNTRY HOMES--ADAPTIVE USE

Carter, Virginia. "A Virginia Landmark Becomes a Versatile Conference Center Now Distinguished by Its Elegance, Ambience, Facilities, and Location." Colonial Williamsburg Today. Spring 1982. pp. 12-15.

COUNTRY HOMES--ENGLAND

Jackson-Stops, Gervase. "Visions of Italy: the British Country House and the Grand Tour." Antiques. Vol. 128, No. 6, Dec. 1985. p. 1174-1189.

COUNTRY HOMES--GREAT BRITAIN

Shenker, Israel. "The Great English Country House Was Much More Than Merely Home." Smithsonian. Vol. 16, No. 7, Oct. 1985. p. 44-59.

COUNTRY HOMES--U.S.--NEW YORK--LONG ISLAND

Moonan, Wendy Lyon. "The One That Didn't Get Away." Town and Country. Vol. 139, No. 5061, June 1985. p. 187-194.

The article contains a list of great estates on Long Island and features "The Knole."

COURTHOUSES

Hagedorn, Martha. "Reno County Courthouse Exemplifies Art Deco Architecture." Kansas Preservation. Vol. 9, No. 4. May - June 1987. pp. 1, 3 - 4.

COURTHOUSES

"Carrollton Courthouse Square Historic District." Historic Illinois. Vol. 10, No. 2. Aug. 1987. pp. 12-13.

COURTHOUSES

"Jersey County Courthouse." Historic
Illinois. Vol. 9, No. 1, June 1986. p. 2-5.

COURTHOUSES

"Jonathan King, Ernest O. Moore,
Robert E. Johnson, Sally A. Guregian:
The Michigan Courthouse Study, Citation."
Progressive Architecture. January 1983.
pp. 144-146.

COURTHOUSES--CONSERVATION AND RESTORATION

Hardy, Janice and Anne Harman. "Courthouses
and Courthouse Squares Remain the Focal Points of
Georgia County Seat Towns." Small Town. May/June
1983. pp. 4-8.

COURTHOUSES--CONSERVATION AND RESTORATION

Reese, Teresa. "Converting and Conserving
Courthouses." Urban Design. Fall 1978. pp. 36-39.

COURTHOUSES--CONSERVATION AND RESTORATION--U.S.--
GEORGIA--CLEVELAND

"Festival Benefits Courthouse." The Rambler,
Newsletter of the Georgia Trust for Historic
Preservation, Inc. Vol. 11, No. 4. Fall 1984.
p. 9.

COURTHOUSES

Sabatini, William Q. "Luna County Court-
house--Deming, N.M." New Mexico Architecture.
Vol. 27, No. 6, Nov.-Dec. 1986. p. 10-15.

Renovation of a historic courthouse.

COURTHOUSES--CONSERVATION AND RESTORATION

"A Beaux-Arts Courthouse, Grand
Rapids, Michigan, will be turned into an
Arts Center as Part of Downtown Renovation."
Progressive Architecture. January 1976.
pp. 60-61.

COURTHOUSES--CONSERVATION AND RESTORATION--
U.S.--TEXAS

"Technique: Panels simulate slate
countertops in restored 1895 Texas courthouse". Commercial Renovation. Vol. 7,
No. 1, Feb. 1985. p. 26.

COURTHOUSES--CONSERVATION AND RESTORATION--U.S.--
TEXAS--Canyon

"THC, Officials Working to Preserve Courthouse",
The Medallion, Vol. 22, No. 1, January 1985, p.1.

COURTHOUSES--CONSERVATION AND RESTORATION--U.S.
--TEXAS--RANDALL COUNTY

"Randall County Courthouse: Bond Package
Defeated." The Medallion. Vol. 22, No. 4,
Apr. 1985. p. 6.

COVERED BRIDGES

Conwill, Joseph D. "Floor Surfaces in
Covered Bridges." Covered Bridge Topics. Vol.
44, No. 3, Summer 1985. p. 3-4.

COVERED BRIDGES

Konkle, Joseph E. "Cable Suspended Covered
Bridges." Newsletter, Indiana Covered Bridge
Society. Vol. 23, No. 1, Jan. 1986. p. 1-2.

COVERED BRIDGES

Sechrist, John. "Brownsville Bridge
on the Move Again." Indiana Covered
Bridge Society Newsletter. Vol. 23, No. 2,
April 1986. p. 1-2.

A bridge dismantled and moved to Indianapolis 12 years ago has been purchased by
the Columbus Dept. of Parks and Recreation
to replace a bridge destroyed by fire in
1985.

COVERED BRIDGES

Walther, Gary. "He Builds them to Last."
Americana. November/December 1982. pp. 40-46.

COVERED BRIDGES

> Williamson, Denise J. "Fetes for Bridges," *Americana*. Vol. 12, No. 4, September/October 1984. pp. 48-51.

COVERED BRIDGES--U.S.--NEW YORK

> Brainerd, Barbara. "Covered Bridges in the Catskills," *Covered Bridge Topics*. Vol. 44, No. 3, Summer 1985. p. 5-7.

COVERED BRIDGES--U.S.--OREGON

> "Gruenfeld, Debbie. "Oregon's Covered Bridges." Newsletter, *Historic Preservation League of Oregon*. No. 35, Winter 1985. p. 4-5.

COVERED BRIDGES--U.S.--PENNSYLVANIA

> Moll, Fred J. "Berks County False Front Portals." *Covered Bridge Topics*. Vol. 44, No. 3, Summer 1985. p. 12-13.

COVERED BRIDGES--U.S.--OREGON--STAYTON

> Dairy, Francis. "Jordan Bridge Finds a New Home." *Historic Preservation League of Oregon Newsletter*. No. 37, Summer 1985. p. 10-11.

CULTURAL PROPERTY, PROTECTION OF

> Burnham, Bonnie. "After the Earthquakes: Mexico City's Heritage at Risk." *Country Life*. Vol. 180, No. 4659, Dec. 4, 1986. p. 1806.

CULTURAL PROPERTY, PROTECTION OF

> Feilden, Bernard. "Examples of Appropriate and Inappropriate Technology in Conservation of Cultural Property." *Parks*. July-September, 1979. pp. 21-22.

CULTURAL PROPERTY, PROTECTION OF

> *Museum*, #1 1979.
>
> Issue on "Return and restitution of cultural property."

CULTURAL PROPERTY, PROTECTION OF

> Schmidt, J. David. "Freeze Drying of Historic/Cultural Properties: A Valuable Process in Restoration and Documentation." *Technology and Conservation*. Vol. 9, No. 1, Spring 1985. p. 20-26.

CULTURAL PROPERTY, PROTECTION OF

> "Towards an AAM Position on Repose for and Transfer of Cultural Property." *Aviso*. June 1986. p. 4-5.

CULTURAL PROPERTY, PROTECTION OF

> Wait, Walter. "The Development of a Regional Management System for Cultural Resources." *CRM Bulletin*. December 1980. p. 10-11

CULTURE--U.S.--NEW YORK

> Kenney, Alice P. "Neglected Heritage: Hudson River Valley Dutch Material Culture." *Winterthur Portfolio*. Vol. 20, No. 1, Spring 1985. p. 49-70.

DAMPNESS IN BUILDINGS

> "Rising Damp a Problem in Historic Buildings." *Kansas Preservation*. January-February, 1984. pp. 8-10.

DAMPNESS IN BUILDINGS

> "Rising damp in walls: diagnosis and treatment." *Building Research Establishment Digest*. January 1981. Digest 245.

DAMPNESS IN BUILDINGS

Schechtman, Jonathan T. "Bailing Out of Wet Basements." The Old House Journal. Vol. IX, No. 8, August 1981. pp. 169-173.

DAMPNESS IN BUILDINGS

Schechtman, Jonathan. "Wet Basements." Old House Journal. June 1981. p. 123.

DAMPNESS IN BUILDINGS

Victor, Dorothy. "House Notes-Spring Checklist: Diagnosis and Preventive Maintenance." The Landmark Society of Western New York. Vol. 25, No. 3, May 1987. p. 9.

DAMS--U.S.--MASSACHUSETTS--LAWRENCE

Molloy, Peter M. "Nineteenth-Century Hydropower: Design and Construction of Lawrence Dam, 1845-1848." Winterthur Portfolio. Winter 1980. pp. 315-343.

DAMS--U.S.--UTAH--MOUNTAIN DELL DAM

Jackson, Donald C. "John S. Eastwood and the Mountain Dell Dam." IA. Vol. 5, No. 1, 1979. pp. 33-48.

DECORATION AND ORNAMENT

Abercrombie, Stanley. "Ornament." AIA Journal. December 1980. p.26-31.

DECORATION AND ORNAMENT

"Decorative Screens." Architecture. April 1984. pp. 30-31.

DECORATION AND ORNAMENT

Howe, Katherine S. "Nineteenth-century American decorative arts." Antiques, March 1979. pp. 556-563.

DECORATION AND ORNAMENT

Matlack, Carol and Chad Slattery (photographer). "The Grammar of Ornament; a Bicycling Impresario Transforms Victorian Ceilings and Walls." American Preservation. Nov.-Dec. 1979. pp. 31-40.

DECORATIVE ARTS

Conger, Clement E. "Decorative Arts at the White House." Antiques. July, 1979. pp. 112-145.

DELAWARE--ODESSA--BUILDINGS

Hotchkiss, Horace L. "Odessa, Delaware: A Survey of its Buildings." Antiques. April 1981. p. 870-875.

DELAWARE--ODESSA--CORBIT-SHARP HOUSE

Chapple, Abby. " Odessa files its past." Country Magazine. December 1980. p.48-52.

DELAWARE--ODESSA--CORBIT-SHARP HOUSE

Sweeney, John A.H. "The Corbit-Sharp House in Odessa." Antiques. April 1981. p. 876-883.

DELAWARE--ODESSA--WILSON-WARNER HOUSE

Hotchkiss, Horace L. "The Wilson-Warner House in Odessa." Antiques. April 1981. p. 886-890.

DELAWARE--WINTERTHUR

Olmert, Michael. "In Winterthur's Splendid Rooms, Furnishing is Art." Smithsonian. May 1983. pp. 98-108.

DEMOLITION

Surprenant, Ann. "Demolition of Historic Properties." Massachusetts Historical Commission Newsletter, Vol. 13, No. 2, May 1987. p. 4-5.

DEPARTMENT STORES

Clausen, Meredith L. "The Department Store - Development of the Type." Journal of Architectural Education. Fall 1985. p. 20-29.

DEPARTMENT STORES--U.S.--OHIO--CLEVELAND

"Cleveland Downtown Landmark Reopens." Economic Growth and Revitalization Report. No. 85-24, Dec. 26, 1985. p. 6.

The Halle Department Store is refurbished as a mixed-use commercial/office building.

DEPARTMENT STORES--ADAPTIVE USE

Dory, Bill. "Library Votes for Downtown and Adaptive Use." The Indiana Preservationist. No. 1, 1986. p. 1.

DEPARTMENT STORES--U.S.--PENNSYLVANIA--PHILA-DELPHIA

Hine, Thomas. "Prospects Good for Renovation of Philadelphia Department Store." Architecture. Jan. 1986. p. 14, 16.

DESIGN

"Urban Environmental Design." Nation's Cities Weekly. July 27, 1981. pp. 5-8

CONTENTS: Moloney, Trudy G. National Conference Aimed at Guiding Development--Showley, Roger. City Sampler: San Diego--Hagar, Connie M. Linking Economic and Physical Growth--Byrd, Valeri A. Solar Systems Keep Funds in the City.

Vertical File
DESIGN CRITERIA

Architectural Guidelines: Shrewsbury (PA) Historic District. Historic York, 1986. 13p. (VF)

DESIGN CRITERIA

Brace, Paul. "Aesthetic Judgements on Urban Environments." Place. October 1982. pp. 1-5.

DESIGN CRITERIA

Crosbie, Michael J. "Is the Failure of the American City a Professional Failure?" Architecture. May 1984. pp. 49, 54, 58, 62.

DESIGN CRITERIA

Curtis, Debbie. "Coca-Cola Support for Main Street Design Assistance." The Rambler, Vol. 14, No. 1, Spring 1987. p. 7.

DESIGN CRITERIA

"Design Review Guidelines." Zoning News. June 1986. p. 1-3.

DESIGN CRITERIA

Moore, Arthur Cotton. "Adaptive Abuse: Examining some Perils of (and to) the Preservation Movement." AIA Journal. Aug. 1979. pp. 58-67.

DESIGN CRITERIA

Jacobs, Allan and Donald Appleyard. " Toward an Urban Manifesto." Journal of the American Planning Association. Vol. 53, No. 1, Winter 1987. p. 112-120.

DESIGN CRITERIA

Knight, Carleton, III. "Beauty and the Box: While Carefully Restoring an 1850's Hall, the Architects Added an Unsympathetic Modern Rear Addition Containing the Requisite Elevator and Stair Wells." Progressive Architecture. Nov. 1979, pp. 84-87.

DESIGN CRITERIA

Murphy, Jim. "A New Old Language; Daniel Solomon & Associates Has Designed Pacific Heights Townhouses in the San Francisco Vernacular with the Aim of Resolving Conflicts Between New Development Requirements and Preservation Ideals." Progressive Architecture, October 1979. pp. 54-59.

DESIGN CRITERIA

"Private Donors Fund Design Assistance." The Preservation Report. Vol. 14, No. 2, April/May 1987. p. 1.

Alabama Main Street towns receive funding for interns to prepare rehab proposals.

DESIGN CRITERIA

Stephens, Suzanne. "Tradition of the New." Skyline. December 1981. pp. 4-5.

DESIGN CRITERIA

Stephens, Suzanne. "Zoning for Context : Upper Madison." Skyline. December 1981. p. 6.

DESIGN CRITERIA

Zotti, Ed. "Design Reviews That Work." Inland Architect. Sept./Oct. 1986. p. 50-52.

DESIGN CRITERIA--NEW YORK--ALBANY

Special issue on CHARC (Capitol Hill Architectural Review Commission), Preservation Guidelines. The Weathervane. April/May 1980.

DESIGN CRITERIA--U.S.--KENTUCKY

"Planning Commission Considers Design Review Role." Preservation Press, Preservation Alliance of Louisville and Jefferson County. Vol. X, No. 1, Spring 1984. p. 6.

DEVELOPMENT RIGHTS TRANSFER

Brennan, Henry H. "An Architectural View of Air Rights Transfer in New York." Urban Land. November 1983. pp. 34-35.

DEVELOPMENT RIGHTS TRANSFER

"Do Developer Bonuses Undermine TDR's?" Urban Conservation Report. Vol. 10, No. 2, Feb. 6, 1986. p. 1-2.

Discussion of the Music Hall Theater, a 1929 movie palace in Seattle.

DEVELOPMENT RIGHTS TRANSFER

"The Future of Transferable Development Rights." Environmental Comment. April 1978. Entire Issue.

CONTENTS: Richman, Hershel and Kendig, Lane. Transferable Development Rights-A Pragmatic View--Basile, Ralph. Central City Landmark Preservation Without TDR--Schnidman, Frank. TDR: A Tool for More Equitable Land Management.

DEVELOPMENT RIGHTS TRANSFER

Levy, David E. 'TDRs in the Legal System." Florida Environmental and Urban Issues. Vol. 13, No. 4, July. p. 12-16.

DEVELOPMENT RIGHTS TRANSFER

Levy, David E. "Transferable Development Rights (TDRs)." Florida Environmental and Urban Issues. Vol. 13, No. 1, Jan. 1986. p. 12-15, 24-25.

DEVELOPMENT RIGHTS TRANSFER

Masterson, William F. "Considerations in Structuring TDR Programs." Urban Land. Vol. 44, No. 10, Oct. 1985. p. 29.

DEVELOPMENT RIGHTS TRANSFER

"Montgomery County Maryland TDR is Under Attack." Farmland Notes. Vol. 6, No. 6. June 1987. p.1.

Montgomery County, MD, Transfer of Development Rights program is under attack by landowners in receiving areas.

DEVELOPMENT RIGHTS TRANSFER

Poole, Samuel E. III. "TDR in Practice: The New Jersey Pinelands", Urban Land, Vol 43, No. 12, December 1984, pp. 34-35.

DEVELOPMENT RIGHTS TRANSFER

Purdy, Lisa and Peter D. Bowes. "Denver's Transferable Development Rights Story." Real Estate Issues. Spring/Summer 1982. pp. 5-8.

DEVELOPMENT RIGHTS TRANSFER

Raymond, George M. "Structuring the Implementation of Transferable Development Rights." Urban Land. July/August 1981. pp. 19-25.

DEVELOPMENT RIGHTS TRANSFER

"TDR Ordinance Passes!" Historic Denver News. February 1982. p. 3.

DEVELOPMENT RIGHTS TRANSFER--LAW AND LEGISLATION

Purdy, Lisa and Peter D. Bowes. "An Update on Denver's TDR Ordinances." Real Estate Issues. Vol. 10, No. 1, Spring/Summer 1985. p. 1-5.

DEVELOPMENT RIGHTS TRANSFER--U.S.--CALIFORNIA--LOS ANGELES

"TDRs in Los Angeles." Urban Land. Vol. 44, No. 2, Feb. 1985. p. 26.

DINERS (RESTAURANTS)

Jackson, Donald Dale. "The American Diner is in Decline, Yet More Chic than Ever." Smithsonian. Vol. 17, No. 8, Nov. 1986. p. 94-103.

DINERS (RESTAURANTS)

Riggs, Rollins. "In Search of Top Dog." Yankee. Vol. 49, No. 5, May 1985. p. 30-39.

DINERS (RESTAURANTS)--U.S.--CALIFORNIA

"The Liberty Bell - A Great American Diner." California Preservation. Vol. 11, No. 1, Jan. 1986. p. 6.

Threatened National Register eligible property in California.

DINING ROOMS

Clark, Clifford E., Jr. "The Victorian Dining Room, and how it came to be." Architecture Minnesota. Vol. 11, No. 3, May/June 1985. p. 42-45, 101.

DINING ROOMS

Freeman, John Crosby. "Late Victorian Dining Rooms." Old-House Journal. Vol. 14, No. 3, April 1986. p. 123-127.

DINING ROOMS

Garrett, Elisabeth D. "The American Home, Part IV: The Dining Room." Antiques. Vol. CXXVI No. 4, October 1984. pp. 910-922.

DINING ROOMS

Ruhling, Nancy A. "Furnishing the Dining Room." Victorian Homes. Vol. 5, Issue 3, Summer 1986. p. 20-23

DISCRIMINATION IN INSURANCE

Cassidy, Robert. "Insurance Firms Begin to Erase their Red Lines." Planning. August, 1979. pp. 22-23.

DISCRIMINATION IN MORTGAGE LOANS

Cassidy, Robert. "Home Insurers Are New Target In Continuing Redlining Battle." AIA Journal. May 1979. pp. 28-31.

DISCRIMINATION IN MORTGAGE LOANS

O'Connor, Philip R. "Urban Insurance : Plan in Illinois Helps Prevent Redlining of Older Neighborhoods." Journal of Housing, June 1979. pp. 317-319.

DOOR FITTINGS

Hines, Spencer. "Restoring My Mechanical Doorbell." The Old House Journal. Vol. 13, No. 7, Aug./Sept. 1985. p. 151.

DOORS

Basehore, Judith. "Wooden Screen Doors." Historic Preservation League of Oregon Newsletter. No. 37, Summer 1985. p. 14.

DOORS

"Screen Door Patterns". Old-House Journal. July 1980. p.80-81.

DOORS

Wallace, Alasdair G.B. "A Breath of Fresh Air: Making a Victorian Screen Door." Fine Homebuilding. No. 36, Dec. 1986/Jan. 1987. p. 39-41.

DOORS--MAINTENANCE AND REPAIR

Poore, Jonathan. "How to Fix Old Doors." Old-House Journal. June 1986. p. 222-227.

DOWNING, ANTOINETTE

Wyss, Bob. "She's Still Saving Old Houses." Yankee. April 1984. p. 78-81, 136-139.

DRAPERY

Fales, Martha Gandy. "A nineteenth-century guide to making curtains." Antiques. March 1981. p. 682-685.

DRAPERY

Flaherty, Carolyn. "How to make Victorian Drapery". Old House Journal. May 1980. p.57-59.

DRIVEWAYS

Shepherd, Nicola. "Paving the Way." Traditional Homes. Vol. 3, No. 2, Nov. 1986. p. 84-86.

An inexpensive driveway that complements an old house.

DWELLINGS--ADAPTIVE USE

"From Suburban Blight to Mixed-Use Delight." Architectural Record. July 1982. pp. 78-81.

DWELLINGS--ADAPTIVE USE

"A Gift House is no Gift Horse." Urban Innovation Abroad. February 1978. p. 5.

DWELLINGS--ADAPTIVE USE

Harding, Kerry. "House Weathers Transition from Private Home to Quarters for 100." The Indiana Preservationist. November/December 1983. p. 9.

DWELLINGS--ADAPTIVE USE

Jamieson, Syd. "Shared-Living Project." Challenge (HUD). March 1979. p. 21.

DWELLINGS--ADAPTIVE USE

Maxwell, Shirley. "High Tech in a High Victorian." Old-House Journal. Vol. 15, No. 1, Jan./Feb. 1987. p. 20-23.

A 24-room house converted to an architectural firm office, living space for the architects family and a separate apartment.

DWELLINGS--ADAPTIVE USE

"Mrs. McClelland's House as Model." Architectural Record. July 1982. pp. 86-87.

DWELLINGS--CONSERVATION AND RESTORATION

DiGaetano, Louis S. and Kathleen Haugh. "Rebuilding a Fire-Damaged House." Fine Homebuilding. August/September 1981. pp. 16-20.

DWELLINGS--ADAPTIVE USE

Walter, Ralph L. "Restoration of Two 19th Century McKim Mead and White Townhouses: Regaining Past Ambiance While Meet Modern Modern Commercial Needs." Technology and Conservation. Winter 1981. pp. 18-24.

DWELLINGS--CONSERVATION AND RESTORATION

Hallock, Terry and Beverly. "Assessing the Health of a House." Yankee. July 1981. p. 70.

DWELLINGS--CONSERVATION AND RESTORATION

Hallock, Terry and Beverly. "Getting a Good Foundation." Yankee. Nov. 1981. p. 114.

DWELLINGS--ENERGY CONSERVATION

Labine, Clem. "The Energy-Efficient Old House." The Old-House Journal. September 1977. pp. 97-107.

DWELLINGS--ENERGY CONSERVATION

"Portland's Energy Conservation Urban Demonstration House". The Neighborhood Works. April 25, 1980. p.13.

DWELLINGS--REMODELING

Labine, Clem. "The Interpretive Restoration." Old-House Journal. Apr. 1979. pp. 37-45.

DWELLINGS--REMODELING

Sherman, Joe. "Lessons Learned at the Clapp House: If you can't afford to restore a home, reviving it may be the next best thing." Fine Homebuilding. No. 32, Apr./May, 1986. p. 56-59.

Describes moving and rehabilitation of an 1845 vernacular Greek Revival style house in Montgomery, VT.

DWELLINGS--RESEARCH

Rhodes, Elizabeth. "Tracing the Roots of One's House." Landmarks. Summer, 1981. p. 36.

DWELLINGS--SECURITY MEASURES

Miner, Margaret. "Old-House Security or How to Keep the Bad Guys Out." The Old House Journal. November 1981. p. 245.

EARTH SHELTERED HOUSES

Bowman, Ian. "Repair and Maintenance of Earth Buildings." Historic Places in New Zealand. No. 15, Dec. 1986. p. 18-21.

EARTH SHELTERED HOUSES--U.S.--INDIANA

Miles, Mark. "Unique House Shows Wright's Influence." The Indiana Preservationist. No. 3, 1984. p. 5.

EARTHQUAKES AND BUILDINGS

Baratta, Alessandro. "The Role of Historical Data in Assessing Seismic Safety of Old Buildings: the Likelihood Approach." ICOMOS/Information. N. 2, Apr./June 1985. p. 14-23.

EARTHQUAKES AND BUILDINGS

Freeman, Michael et al. "Building Damage Severe but Spotty in Mexico City Quake." Architecture. Nov. 1985. p. 11-12.

EARTHQUAKES AND BUILDINGS

Helfant, David Benaroya. "Seismic Retrofits." Fine Homebuilding. No. 29, Oct./Nov. 1985. p. 34-38.

EARTHQUAKES AND BUILDING

Wong, Marcy Li. "Architectural Strategies in Seismic Design." Architectural Record. Feb. 1986. p. 136-143.

Features the seismic upgrading of the History Corner, Stanford University, Palo Alto, California, originally built in 1904.

EARTHWORKS (ARCHAEOLOGY)

Brown, Jeffrey L. "Earthworks and Industrial Archeology". IA. Vol. 6, no. 1, 1980. p. 1-8.

EARTHWORKS (ARCHAEOLOGY)

Kassler, Elizabeth B. "An Eye on the Moundscape." Inland Architect. Vol. 29, No. 2, Mar./Apr. 1985. p. 4-5.

EARTHWORKS (ARCHAEOLOGY)--U.S.--ILLINOIS

Iseminger, William R. "Excavations at Cahokia Mounds." Archaeology. Vol. 39, No. 1, Jan./Feb. 1986. p. 58-59.

EARTHWORKS (ARCHAEOLOGY)--U.S.--OHIO

"Hopeton Earthworks, Springfield Arcade Threatened." Ohio Preservation. Vol. 6, No. 1, Jan. 1986. p. 1.

EARTHWORKS (ARCHAEOLOGY)--U.S.--WEST VIRGINIA

"The Mound Builders-Adena Culture", Culture and History, Vol. 1, No. 3, January-February-March 1985, p. 29.

EASEMENTS

Avery, Jonathan H. "Valuing Preservation Easements: As charitable contributions are they fact or fancy?" Real Estate Finance. Vol. 2, No. 4, Winter 1986. p. 85-88.

EASEMENTS

Brown, Warren. "A Park with a View: The Value of Easements to the Historic Scene." Courier. Vol. 31, No. 8, Aug. 1986. p. 10-11.

EASEMENTS

Chicago, Ernst and Whinney. "Donating Historic Facade Easements." Landmarks Preservation Council of Illinois. Vol. 15, No. 3, May-June 1986. p. 5.

Tax Court approved substantial value for a donated facade easement.

EASEMENTS

"Conservation Easements." ALRA Bulletin.
Vol. 1, No. 1, Mar./Apr. 1987. p. 1-2.

EASEMENTS

"Conservation Easements: Improving
Their Effectiveness." Land Trusts Exchange. Vol.4, No. 4, Spring 1986.
p. 14-17, 22.

EASEMENTS

Denhez, Marc McC. "What Exactly Are
Covenants? They're One Way to Protect Vintage
Buildings." Canadian Heritage. August/September
1984. pp. 5-7.

EASEMENTS

"Does a Historic Easement Have Value?"
"IRS May Be Targeting Easements." Urban
Conservation Report. Vol. VIII, No. 13, July
20, 1984. pp. 4-5.

Washington, D.C. IRS field study found
average sale price of houses with historic
easements higher than those without.

EASEMENTS

"Easement Evaluation Questions Being
Answered." Piedmont Environmental Council
Newsreporter. Nov. 1986. p. 1-2.

Virginia's open space easement program.

EASEMENTS

"Easement's Year." Historic Denver News.
Vol. 15, No. 9, Sept. 1986. p. 12.

Advantages in donating facade and conservation easements before the end of 1986.

EASEMENTS

"Five Preservation Easements Donated to the
Virginia Historic Landmarks Board." Notes on
Virginia. No. 29, Fall 1986. p. 32-33.

EASEMENTS

"Foundation Easement Activity Becoming
'Hot Stuff'." The Heritage News. (Utah).
Vol. 20, No. 5, Nov. 1986. p. 1.

EASEMENTS

"From Inns to Plantations, Easements Protect the Treasured Past." North Carolina Preservation. No. 62, March-April 1986. p. 1-2

EASEMENTS

"HRH Easements Committee Hard at Work."
Hudson River Heritage Newsletter. Vol. 12, No. 1,
Feb. 1987. p. 4-6.

Hudson River Heritage seeks to preserve
significant architecture and unspoiled open space.

EASEMENTS

"Historic Preservation Guaranty
Offers Free Service." North Carolina
Preservation. March 1983. Tear Off.

EASEMENTS

Holmes, Robert J. "Conservation Easement:
At Last, Preservation Pays." Urban Land.
November 1982. pp. 3-8.

EASEMENTS

"IRS Issues Final Rules on Easements." American Farm Land. Vol. 6,
No. 2, March-April 1986. p. 3

EASEMENTS

Mott, William Penn. "Park
Service Encourages Greater Use of
Easements." Journal of the Land
Trust Exchange. Vol. 4, No. 4,
Spring 1986. p. 8-9.

EASEMENTS

"New Easement Requirements." Pasadena Heritage. Vol. 9, No. 3 & 4, Spring & Summer 1986. p. 11.

EASEMENTS

Piersma, Paul. "MHT Services Preservation Easements." Missouri Preservation News. Vol. 10, No. 1, Summer 1986. p. 10.

Vertical File
EASEMENTS

"Preservation Easement Program." Maine Citizens for Historic Preservation. 1986. 5p. (VF)

EASEMENTS

"Preservation Easements." (Part I of a three part series.) The Boston Preservation Alliance Letter. Vol. 5, No. 3, April 1984. pp. 1, 4-5, 10-11.

EASEMENTS

"Preservation Easements under Fire." Architectural Record. Mar. 1985. p. 33.

EASEMENTS

Roddewig, Richard J. and Jared Shlaes, MAI. "Preservation Easements Reconsidered: An Alternative Approach to Value." The Appraisal Journal. July 1984. pp. 325-347.

EASEMENTS

Russell, Joel. "Escrow Easements: Harnessing Economic Self-Interest." Land Trusts' Exchange. Vol. 5, Nos. 3&4. Winter 1987. pp. 4-5.

EASEMENTS

Thomsen, Thomas. "How a Preservation Easement Helped Save 45 Park Street, Portland." Maine Preservation News. Vol. 12, No. 1, Spring 1986. p. 1. 7.

Vertical File
EASEMENTS

Thompson, Edward. "Local Planning Efforts to Encourage Private Land Conservation." Zoning and Planning Law Report. Vol. 9, No. 4. Apr. 1986. pp. 25-31. (VF)

EASEMENTS

"Tools for Preserving Lake Forest's Visual Character: Easements Offer Tax Breaks for Property Owners." Lake Forest Preservation Foundation Newsletter. Fall 1986. p. 5-6.

EASEMENTS

"Virginia Historic Landmarks Board Receives Six New Easement Donations." Notes on Virginia. No. 30. Spring 1987. pp. 3 - 5.

EASEMENTS

"Wisconsin has New Uniform Conservation Easement Act." Wisconsin Preservation. July 1982. pp. 1-2.

Vertical File
EASEMENTS

Wyatt, William R. "Historic Facade Easements and Their Tax Advantage." South Dakota Municipalities. Vol. 54, No. 11, May 1986. p. 8-9. (VF)

EASEMENTS--U.S.--CALIFORNIA

"Foundation Sets Up Easement Program". California Preservation. Vol. 10, No. 1, Jan. 1985. p. 2.

EASEMENTS--U.S.--PENNSYLVANIA--PHILADELPHIA PROGRAM

Hern, Mary Ellen. "Facades Forever." Americana. Jul./Aug. 1984. p. 21.

EASEMENTS, FACADE

"Historic Facade Easements." Preservation Perspective (NJ). Vol. 5, No. 2, Jan./Feb. 1986. p. 1-2.

EASEMENTS, FACADE--U.S.--CALIFORNIA

"Easements - The Skin Trade." California Preservation. Vol. 11, No. 1, Jan. 1986. p. 3.

EASEMENTS, FACADE--U.S.--NEW YORK

Lowenstein, William. "Facade Easement: Hudson Urban Renewal Agency takes New Approach to Historic Renewal and is Achieving Economic and Racial Integration in Historically Rehabilitated Area." Journal of Housing: March 1974. pp. 120-123.

EASEMENTS, SCENIC

"Conservation: 39 ZD--Maryland." Land Use Law & Zoning Digest. Vol. 39, No. 1, Jan. 1987. p. 26.

A conservation heritage fund established to permit acquisition of conservation easements.

EASEMENTS, SCENIC

"IRS Issues Final Rules on Conservation Easements." Housing and Development Reporter. Vol. 13, No. 36, Jan. 27, 1986. p. 705-706.

EASEMENTS, SCENIC

"Open Spcae Easement Status Report." Piedmont Environmental Council Newsreporter. June 1982. Entire Issue.

EASEMENTS, SCENIC

"Report on 1985 National Survey of Government and Non-Profit Easement Programs." Land Trusts Exchange. Vol. 4, No. 3, Dec. 1985. Entire issue.

EASEMENTS, SCENIC

Wiechec, Elizabeth. "Subordinating Mortgages to Conservation Easements." Land Trusts' Exchange. Vol. 5, No. 2, Fall 1986. p. 14-15.

ECLECTICISM IN ARCHITECTURE

Classical America IV. 1977. Articles on various Beaux-Arts buildings, architects and interior decoration.

ECONOMIC ASSISTANCE, DOMESTIC

Barnes, William. "Cautions from Britain: The EZ Answer Proves Elusive." Urban Innovation Abroad. May 1982, Special Supplement. Entire Issue.

ECONOMIC ASSISTANCE, DOMESTIC

Berger, Renee and R. Scott Fosler. "Public-Private Partnership: The British Experience." Urban Innovation Abroad. November 1982 (Special Supplement). Entire Issue.

ECONOMIC ASSISTANCE, DOMESTIC

Doty, John G. "TVA Helping Preserve Tennessee's Past." Tennessee Heritage Alliance, Network. Summer 1984. No. 2. pp. 7-8.

ECONOMIC ASSISTANCE, DOMESTIC

"Enterprise Zone Designation More Important than Actual Tax Incentives, Study Suggests." Economic Growth & Revitalization Report. No. 86-16, Aug. 28, 1986. p. 5.

ECONOMIC ASSISTANCE, DOMESTIC

"Enterprise Zones." Urban Land. Vol. 45, No. 7, July 1986. p. 27-28.

ECONOMIC ASSISTANCE, DOMESTIC

"Enterprise Zones Are Making out." Urban Outlook. Vol. 8, No. 24, Dec. 30, 1986. p. 4-5.

ECONOMIC ASSISTANCE, DOMESTIC

Freund, Eric. "Enterprise Zones and Historic Preservation: Friends or Foes?" Historic Illinois. December 1983. pp. 12-15.

ECONOMIC ASSISTANCE, DOMESTIC

Gilpin, John. "Project to Commemorate the CCC [Civilian Conservation Corps]." Tennessee Heritage Alliance, Network. Summer 1984. No. 2. pp 6-7.

ECONOMIC ASSISTANCE, DOMESTIC

Mier, Robert. "Enterprise Zones: A Long Shot." Planning. April 1982. pp. 10-14.

ECONOMIC ASSISTANCE, DOMESTIC

O'Hara, Frank. "Risks Equal Rewards in Enterprise Zone Programs." Journal of Housing. November 1981. pp. 545-548.

ECONOMIC ASSISTANCE, DOMESTIC

Robbins, Tom. "Combat Over the Enterprise Zones." City Limits. May 1982. pp. 20-23.

ECONOMIC DEVELOPMENT

"America's Cities Aren't Giving Up on the High-Tech Dream." Business Week. Jan. 13, 1986. p. 123-124.

ECONOMIC DEVELOPMENT

Center, Joe and Wendy Grover. "City-Owned Property: Source of Quick Cash or Neighborhood Jobs and Services?" City Limits. Vol. 12, No. 5. May 1987. pp. 17-19.

ECONOMIC DEVELOPMENT

"Commerce Department Backs Preservation." California Office of Historic Preservation Newsletter. Vol. 2, No. 1, Feb. 1987. p. 1.

ECONOMIC DEVELOPMENT

"A Decade of Livability: Partners' Ten-Year Report." Place. Vol. 6, No. 7, Jan.-Feb. 1987. p. 10-14.

Summary of a Partners for Livable Places report on 16 cities.

ECONOMIC DEVELOPMENT

"Economic Revitalization in Sandy: A Closer Look." The Heritage News (Utah). Vol. 21, No. 2, Feb. 1987, p. 6.

ECONOMIC DEVELOPMENT

Gregerman, Alan S. "Federal, State, and Local Economic Development Initiatives." Urban Land. Jul. 1984. pp. 21-25.

ECONOMIC DEVELOPMENT

"High Technology and Economic Development Planning." Journal of the American Planning Association. Vol. 50, No. 3, Summer 1984. Entire Issue.

ECONOMIC DEVELOPMENT

Howell, James M. and Carolyn J. Schwenker.
"A Survey of Leveraging in Older Cities."
Urban Land. December 1980. p. 6-11.

ECONOMIC DEVELOPMENT

Howland, Libby. "PSDOS: Private Sector
Development Organizations." Urban Land. Vol. 44,
No. 12, Dec. 1985. p. 30-31.

ECONOMIC DEVELOPMENT

Mullin, John R., Jeane H. Armstrong and
Jean S. Kavanagh. "From Mill Town to Mill Town:
the Transition of a New England Town From a
Textile to a High Technology Economy." JAPA.
Vol. 52, No. 1, Winter 1986. p. 47-59.

ECONOMIC DEVELOPMENT

Moore, Carole M. "UGA Study Thumbs
up on Rehabilitation." The Rambler. Vol.
13, No. 3, Autumn 1986. p. 11.

A study by the Center for Business and
Economic Studies at the University of
Georgia shows that historic preservation
and rehabilitation are not incompatible.

ECONOMIC DEVELOPMENT

Pryde, Paul L. "Dimensions and Benefits of
Development Loan 'Discounting'." Nation's Cities
Weekly. Vol. 9, No. 12, Mar. 24, 1986. p. 5-6, 8.

Special report exploring some of the loan
"Discounting" techniques cities can use to
leverage existing UDAG loans.

ECONOMIC DEVELOPMENT

"The Pursuit of High Growth (Not Necessarily
High Tech) Firms: A Local Strategy Guide." Local
Economic Growth and Neighborhood Reinvestment
Report. No. 84-16, August 23, 1984. pp. 1-2.

ECONOMIC DEVELOPMENT

Rooney, Diane. "Enterprise Development in
Small Cities: How 4 Communities Implemented
Creative Solutions." Nation's Cities Weekly. Vol.
9, No. 1 , Jan. 6, 1986. p. 3-4.

ECONOMIC DEVELOPMENT

"Small Town Officials Advised to Base Plans
on Community Assets, Local Support." Housing
and Development Reporter. Vol. 13, No. 36, Jan.
27, 1986. p. 694.

Summary of a National League of Cities
workshop at which Scott Gerloff, Director of
National Main Street Center, was panelist.

Vertical File
ECONOMIC DEVELOPMENT

Walter, J. Jackson. "Historic Preservation
and Economic Development." Bell Atlantic Quarterly.
Vol. 3, No. 1. Spring 1987. 12 p. (VF)

ECONOMIC DEVELOPMENT--GREAT BRITAIN--SARK

Foote, Timothy. "How to Keep the 20th Century Mostly at Bay." Smithsonian. Vol. 17, No.
2, May 1986. p. 93-105.

Sark, a tiny island in the English Channel, is
successfully staving off autombiles, transistors,
paved roads and other modern "improvements".

ECONOMIC DEVELOPMENT--NEW ZEALAND

"What Sort of City Will Auckland Be?" Historic Places in New Zealand. No. 14, Sept. 1986.
p. 11-12.

ECONOMIC DEVELOPMENT--U.S.--CONNECTICUT

Buttman, Mark. "A 'Yale Connection' Brings
New Hope to An Old City." Business Week.
October 29, 1984. pp. 32D-H.

ECONOMIC DEVELOPMENT--U.S.--MAINE--FREEPORT

Dodson, James. "Look What's Happening to
Freeport!" Yankee. Vol. 50, No. 3, Mar. 1986.
p. 90-101, 124-132.

125 new businesses are attracted to
Freeport, Maine in three years.

ECONOMIC DEVELOPMENT--U.S.--TEXAS--DALLAS

Sandberg, Leif A. "Diversity Through History."
Urban Design International. Vol. 7, No. 1. Fall
1986. pp. 15-17.

Dallas is committed to historic preservation
while rapid development continues.

ECONOMIC POLICY--ITALY

Hatch, C. Richard. "Italy's Industrial Renaissance: Are American Cities Ready to Learn". Urban Land. Vol. 44, No. 1, Jan. 1985. p. 20-23.

EDUCATION

Lang, John. "Built Environment Project." Bulletin of Environmental Education. April 1981. pp. 9 - 14.

EDUCATION

Sandford, Herbert A. "Environmental Maps as a Resource for Environmental Studies." Bulletin of Environmental Education. May 1981. pp. 4-5.

EGYPTIAN REVIVAL (ARCHITECTURE)--U.S.--ILLINOIS

Ward, Michael. "Pharaohs and Facades: The Egyptian Revival Style in Illinois." Historic Illinois. Vol. 7, No. 3, October 1984. pp. 8-11.

ELECTRIC WIRING

Gerhardt, Tom H. "Old-House Intercoms; Buzzers, Beepers, Buttons & Bells." The Old-House Journal, October 1979. pp. 112-115.

ELECTRIC   WIRING

"Routing Wiring: How to Get From Here to There with Very Little Plaster Repair." The Old House Journal. Vol. 13, No. 8, Oct. 1985. p. 161, 168-170.

How to place wiring without disturbing finished building surfaces.

ENERGY CONSERVATION

"Books with Energy Hints." The Preservation Report (Alabama). Sep./Oct. 1983. p. 3.

ENERGY CONSERVATION

"Energy Conscious Redesign". Research and Design. Summer 1980. p. 5-7, 16.

ENERGY CONSERVATION

"Energy Savings." St. Louis Home. Sept. 1985. p. 17-32.

Eight short articles.

ENERGY CONSERVATION

"Glass-Covered Street Reduces Energy Use." Urban Innovation Abroad. Vol. 8, No. 5, May 1984. pp. 4-5.

ENERGY CONSERVATION

Ice Melter Newsletter. No. 23, Mar. 1987. 10p. (VF)

Reducing energy costs in religious buildings.

ENERGY CONSERVATION

Klabin, Don. "Tomorrow's energy from yesterday". Progressive Architecture. April 1980. p. 130-135.

ENERGY CONSERVATION

McClendon, Bruce W. and Ray Quay. "Targeted Energy Conservation Strategies in Galveston, Texas". Urban Land. June 1980. p. 19-22.

ENERGY CONSERVATION

Old House Journal. September 1980. Special Energy Issue.

ENERGY CONSERVATION

"Promoting Energy Conservation and Old-House Preservation." Home Again. No. 4, Autumn 1984. pp. 10-12.

Energy Education Center, Portland, Maine.

ENERGY CONSERVATION

Series of articles on insulation, windows, solar heat, how to pay for retrofit, water heating energy investment guide, and energy efficient systems. St. Louis Home. September 1984. pp. 21-31, 33-39.

ENERGY CONSERVATION

"Uncommon sense: a look at 8 recent redesign projects,...". Research and Design. Summer 1980. p. 8-15.

ENERGY CONSERVATION

Weaver, Martin E. "Nuts and Bolts: Energy Efficiency in Old Buildings." Canadian Heritage. February 1981. p.56-58.

ENERGY CONSERVATION

Wells, Betty L. "Energy Conservation, A Development Strategy for All Communities." Small Town. Vol. 15, No. 3, November-December 1984. pp. 20-22.

ENERGY CONSERVATION

Wise, Christopher T., AIA. "Saving Energy II: Storm Windows." New Bedford Soundings. Vol. 10, No. 3, Fall 1985. p. 13-15.

ENGINEERING

Jones, Larry. "Do You Need An Engineer?" Old House Journal. Vol. XIII, No. 1, Jan.-Feb. 1985. pp. 21-23.

ENGRAVED GLASS

Denison, Chris. "Etched Glass: Duplicating This Ornate Glass Entry Required a Combination of Sandblasting, Screen-Printed Masks and an Acid Bath," Fine Homebuilding, No. 24, December 1984/January 1985, pp. 52-53.

ENVIRONMENT--STUDY AND TEACHING

Trends, Winter 1979.

Note: Articles on educational issues in the fields of energy, conservation, preservation and government.

ENVIRONMENTAL PLANNING

Wrenn, Douglas. "Computer-Assisted Land Development." Environmental Comment. October 1981. pp. 4-7.

ETHNIC GROUPS

Bates, Craig. "Native Americans." National Parks. Vol. 59, No. 9-10, Sept./Oct. 1985. p. 12-15.

ETHNIC NEIGHBORHOODS

Coquillette, Judith. " Boston's Chinatown: A Treasure Worth Saving. " Boston Preservation Alliance Letter. Vol. 8, No. 7. Jul./Aug. 1987. p. 7.

EUROPE--HISTORIC PRESERVATION

"Proceedings of the Seminar on Architecture and Historic Preservation in Central and Eastern Europe New York, NY, 28-30 November 1975." Journal of the Society of Architectural Historians. May 1979. pp. 123-175.

EXCAVATIONS (ARCHAEOLOGY)

Schoeffler, William H. "Archaeologists Find Winthrop's 'Great House' in Charlestown Excavations." Nexus. Vol. 3, No. 2, April 1986. p. 61, 64-65.

A tavern that served a Massachusetts Governor Winthrop's "Great House" in 1630 uncovered.

EXHIBITION BUILDINGS

Peters, James. "After the Fair: What Expos Have Done for their Cities." Planning. July/ August, 1982. pp. 13-19.

EXHIBITIONS

Carpenter, Charles H. Jr. "The Way We Were: An Exhibition Review." Winterthur Portfolio. Vol. 20, No. 1. Spring 1985. pp. 71-80.

"Design Since 1945" at the Philadelphia Museum of Art, 10/16/83 - 1/8/84, given detailed review.

EXHIBITIONS

Caswell, Frank A. and Marguerite E. "Wisconsin at the World's Columbian Exposition of 1893." Wisconsin Magazine of History. Vol. 67, No. 4, Summer 1984. pp. 243-262.

EXHIBITIONS

Edwards, Alice. "The Portable Exhibit: Increasing Your Audience." Illinois Heritage Association Technical Insert. No. 15, May/June 1985. 2 p.

EXHIBITIONS

Rogow, Pamela. "Communicating Another Dimension." The Grantsmenship Center News. September/October, 1982. pp. 32-39.

EXHIBITIONS

Ruffins, Faith Davis. "The Exhibition as Form: an Elegant Metaphor." Museum News. Vol. 64, No. 1, Oct. 1985. p. 54-59.

EXHIBITIONS--U.S.--NEW YORK--NEW YORK CITY

Nevins, Deborah. "High Styles: American Design in the Twentieth Century." Antiques. Vol. 128, No. 4, Oct. 1985. p. 770-778.

EXHIBITS

"'An Open Land: Photographs of the Midwest, 1852-1982': Exhibition Invites New Appreciation of Midwest Land." Terrain (Open Lands Project). Vol 7, No. 1. pp. 1-3.

EXHIBITS

Rogow, Pamela. "History at the Mall." History News. March 1983. pp. 36-38.

FACADES

AIA Journal. October 1981. Entire issue on building "skins".

FACADES

Burns, Kathryn, Kathleen Frazier and William Frazier. "Making Facade Improvement Programs Work: it takes more than money." Main Street News. No. 12, April 1986. p. 1-4.

FACADES

Conway, Terry. "Retention of Heritage Streetscapes: The New Myer Centre, Queen Street." National Trust Queensland Journal. Apr. 1987. pp. 4 - 5.
Historic facade is retained in new development.

FACADES

Dehart, Grant. "A Trend Toward 'Facadism'- San Francisco Deserves Better." Heritage Newsletter. Summer 1982. p. 5.

FACADES

"Facade Improvement Program." The Queen City Quarterly (Historic Staunton Foundation). Vol. 12, No. 2, Apr. 1985. p. 5.

FACADES

"Facades-Saving Face?" National Trust Magazine, The National Trust of Australia (NSW). No. 31, Sept. 1985. p. 6-8.

The article summarizes presentations at a seminar on facadism, including one which recommended 6 guidelines for the incorporation of a facade into a new project.

FACADES

"HLF Provides Assistance for Downtown Facade Improvements." Historic Lexington Foundation. Vol. 5, No. 2. Winter 1986. p. 1.

FACADES

Lowe, Nancy. "A Bird's-eye View of Old Facades." The Chronicle. Vol. 13, No. 3, June-July 1986. p. 4.

FACADES

Nagy, Chris. "Magnet Foolproof Detector of Cast Iron." The Indiana Preservationist. No. 4, 1986. p. 6.

Method for detecting and restoring cast iron facades.

FACADES

Saunders, Matthew. "Facadism." Transactions of the Ancient Monuments Society. Vol. 30, 1986. p. 227-240.

FACADES

Vonier, Thomas. "Saving Face." Progressive Architecture. June 1983. pp. 41-43.

FACADES--AUSTRALIA

"Facades and the Future." National Trust (Australia/NSW) Magazine. No. 30, June 1985. p. 5.

The announcement of a National Trust Seminar entitled "Saving Face" called to discuss and develop Trust policy toward "facadism."

FACADES--U.S.--NEW YORK--NEW YORK CITY

"To preserve and Protect an Architectural Legacy." Architectural Record. Sept. 1985. p. 53.

FACADES--U.S.--OREGON--PORTLAND

Reed, Roger G. "A Century of Portland Storefronts As Seen Through Period Images." Landmarks Observer. Vol. 13, No. 4, July-Aug. 1986. p. 6-7.

FACADES--U.S.--PENNSYLVANIA--YORK

"Rediscovering York's Facades." Uncommon Sense. Vol. 9, No. 3. Summer 1986. pp. 2-3.

Many of York, Pa.'s facades are being uncovered in connection with the city's Facade Easement Program.

FACADES--U.S.--VIRGINIA--STAUNTON

"Facade Improvement Plan: A Review." The Queen City Quarterly. Vol. 13, No. 2, April 1986. p. 4-5.

FACADES--U.S.--WASHINGTON, D.C.

Freeman, Allen. "Old Facades Fronting for New Construction: Some Startling Conjunctions in the Nation's Capital." Architecture. November 1983. p. 68-71.

FACTORIES--ADAPTIVE USE

Barnes, W. Anderson. "Ghirardelli Square: Keeping a First First." Urban Land. Vol. 45, No. 5, 1986. p. 6-10.

Upgrading of historic buildings, formerly a chocolate factory, in San Francisco.

FACTORIES--ADAPTIVE USE

Melnick, Scott. "Adaptive Reuse Creates a Design Center in N.Y.C." Building Design & Construction. Vol. 27, No. 10, Oct. 1986. p. 72-73.

Conversion of a factory/warehouse into showroom space in New York City.

FAIRS

Douglas, William Lake. "An Event of Place, This Year's World Exposition Animates the Warehouse District in New Orleans." Land-scape Architecture. Vol. 74, No. 4, July/August 1984. pp. 48-55.

FAIRS

"In New Orleans, Warehouses and 'Forms From an Idealized World.'" Architecture. July 1984. pp. 10-12, 16, 20, 23.

FAIRS

Perrin, Noel. "The Old State Fair, Still What It Used to Be - Even More." Smithsonian. Vol. 16, No. 6, Sept. 1985. p. 96-109.

FAIRS

Smith, Herbert L. Jr. "The New Orleans Fair: Post-Mod Confronts Hi-Tech." Architectur-al Record. July 1984. pp. 73-85.

FAIRS

"Summer of 1904." Saint Louis Home. July 1984. p. 15.

FAIRS--U.S.--LOUISIANA--NEW ORLEANS

Anzalone, Kerry et al. "Something Old, Something New, An Analysis of the Buildings at the Fair." New Orleans Preservation in Print. Vol. 11, No. 8, October 1984. pp. 3-7.

FARM BUILDINGS

Davis, Ann. "Survey Find: It's Not Hip to be Square." The Indiana Preservationist. No. 2. May 1987. p. 2.
Six round barns by Kindig Builders in Fulton County, Indiana.

FARM BUILDINGS

"A Good Stand of Buildings." The Maine History News. Vol. 21, No. 4, Oct. 1985. p. 8-9, 11.

FARM BUILDINGS

"Making Connections: Architecture, Living Things, and the Good Earth." Architecture Minnesota. November/December 1983. pp. 21-43,
PARTIAL CONTENTS: The Intuitive Good Sense of the Prairie Homesteaders--Peterson, Fred W. Architecture on the Frontier: A Purely Expedient Idea--The Virtuous Farmstead.

FARM BUILDINGS

Schultz, LeRoy G. "West Virginia Silos." Goldenseal. Vol. 10, No. 3, Fall 1984. pp. 20-25.

FARM BUILDINGS

"Study of Rural Architecture Under Way." Kansas Preservation. July-August 1983. pp. 3-4.

FARM BUILDINGS

Tishler, William H. and Tony Soluri. "Historic Houses: Wisconsin's Finnish Farmsteads." Architectural Digest, May 1979. pp. 78-85.

FARM BUILDINGS--CONSERVATION AND RESTORATION

Randell, Geoffrey. "Rural character maintained in farm buildings conversion." Building Conservation. February 1980. p.23-25.

FARM BUILDINGS--U.S.--CALIFORNIA--NAPA VALLEY

Littlejohn, David. "Man and Nature in the Napa Valley: the Architecture of the Wine Country." Architecture. Mar. 1985. p. 100-109.

FARM BUILDINGS--U.S.--VIRGINIA

Hildebrand, Paul Jr. "Cultivating a Farm for the Arts." *Place*. Vol 4, No. 5, May 1984. pp. 6-8.

Cultural planning in rural Staunton, Va.

FARMHOUSES

Vargas, Robert L. "Grand Chaquard: An American Remodels a 17th Century French Farmhouse and Barn." *Fine Homebuilding*. No. 33, June/July 1986. p. 63-67.

FARMS

"AFT Purchase Bid Saves Bay State Farm." *American Farm Land*. Vol. 6, No. 2, March-April 1986. p. 3.

American Farmland Trust made successful bid to save a western Massachusetts farm from developers. Will sell a conservation easement over to the State.

FARMS

Conrat, Maisie and Richard. "The American Farm". *American Preservation*. May/June 1980, p. 24-30.

FARMS

Mattson, G.A. "What Small Town Residents Should Know About Farmland Preservation Alternatives." *Small Town*. July-August 1982. pp. 15-18.

FARMS--CONSERVATION AND RESTORATION

Brown, Warren Lee. "What to Do About Grandfather's Place: Lessons for Landsavers Who Are Landowners, Too." *American Land Forum*. Vol. 5, No. 4, Fall 1985. p. 55-59.

FARMS--CONSERVATION AND RESTORATION

"Current State Farmland Protection Activities." *Farmland Notes*. Vol. 6, No. 1, Jan. 1987. 1p. (Insert)

Table showing state-by-state farmland protection techniques.

FARMS--CONSERVATION AND RESTORATION

Emery, David. "Re-creating the Pettengill Farmscape." *Landmarks Observer* (Portland, Maine). March-April, 1983. pp. 8-9.

FARMS--CONSERVATION AND RESTORATION

"Highlights of 1986 State Activities in Farmland Protection." *Farmland Notes*. Vol. 6, No. 1, Jan. 1987. p. 1-4.

FARMS--CONSERVATION AND RESTORATION

"International Farmland Protection Focus: Australia." *Farmland Notes*. Vol. 6, No. 3, Mar. 1987. p. 3.

FARMS--CONSERVATION AND RESTORATION

Kinzler, Andrew and Ritter, George. "Twilight Zoning in New Jersey." *Urban Land.* December 1983. pp. 7-11.

FARMS--CONSERVATION AND RESTORATION--U.S.--New YORK

Shirvani, Hamid and David MacLeod. "Farmland Preservation in New York State." *Small Town*. Vol. 15, No. 5, Mar./Apr. 1985. p. 10-18.

FEDERAL AID TO CITIES

"CD Block Grants: Grantees Not Penalized for Complying with Expired Rehab Escrow Account Criteria." *Community Development Digest*. No. 87-10. May 19, 1987. p. 4.

FEDERAL AID TO CITIES

"55 Projects Gain $87.49 Million in Urban Development Action Grants." *HUD News Release*. No. 86-11, Feb. 6, 1986. 16 p.

FEDERAL AID TO CITIES

"Historic Preservation Continues
to be a Popular UDAG-assisted Activity."
Community Development Digest. July 12,
1983. pp. 11-12.

FEDERAL AID TO CITIES

"If Gramm-Rudman Triggers: a State-By-State
Analysis." Rehab Notes. Vol. 10, No. 2, Mar.
1986. p. 1, 6.

A summary of CDBG and UDAG cuts are
reported on a state-by-state basis.

FEDERAL AID TO CITIES

"Latest UDAG Grants Again Demonstrate
Program's Importance to Preservation."
Urban Conservation Report. Vol. 10, No. 11,
Nov. 29, 1986. p. 6.

FEDERAL AID TO CITIES

"President's Budget Proposal Targets
Housing, CD Programs for Cuts." NAHRO Monitor.
Vol. 8, No. 3, Feb. 15, 1986. p. 1-2.

FEDERAL AID TO CITIES

Todd, Reggie. "HUD Publishes Rules for
Housing Development Grants," "How the Program
Works." Nation's Cities Weekly. June 18, 1984.
p. 8.

FEDERAL AID TO COMMUNITY DEVELOPMENT

Aiken, David. "UDAG: 'An Effective and
Proven Asset' in Aiding Cities." Nation's
Cities Weekly. Vol. 9, No. 8, Feb. 24, 1986.
p. 5, 8.

FEDERAL AID TO COMMUNITY DEVELOPMENT

"Bond Financing and New Development Grants
Not an Easy Marriage, Officials Say." Housing
and Development Reporter. Vol. 11, No. 46, April
9, 1984. pp. 955-6.

FEDERAL AID TO COMMUNITY DEVELOPMENT

"Budget Mixed on Issues of Interest
to the Profession." Architecture. Mar. 1985.
p. 44, 51, 85.

FEDERAL AID TO COMMUNITY DEVELOPMENT

"CDBG Program: Statutory Changes and
Administrative Interpretations." Housing Law
Bulletin. Vol. XIV, Issue 4, July/August 1984.
pp. 5-6.

FEDERAL AID TO COMMUNITY DEVELOPMENT

"Changes Considered for Altering Distribu-
tion of CDBG and UDAG Funds." Community Development Digest. No. 84-11, June 12, 1984. pp.
1-2.

FEDERAL AID TO COMMUNITY DEVELOPMENT

Doctrow, Jerry L. "Rental Rehabilitation:
A Practitioner's View." Journal of Housing.
May/June 1984. pp. 72-4.

How landlords perceive public programs.

FEDERAL AID TO COMMUNITY DEVELOPMENT

"Extra Rental Aid for Very-Low-Income
Tenants Envisioned for HoDAG Programs." Housing
and Development Reporter. Vol. 11, No. 46, April
9, 1984. pp. 969-70.

FEDERAL AID TO COMMUNITY DEVELOPMENT

Knapp, Richard. "UDAG v. HoDag: How Do They
Compare as Housing Subsidy Mechanisms?", Urban
Land, Vol. 43, No. 12, December 1984, pp. 30-31.

FEDERAL AID TO COMMUNITY DEVELOPMENT

"Fiscal 1984 Funding Allocations for HUD
Rental Rehabilitation Grant Program." Housing
and Development Reporter. Vol. 11, No. 46,
April 9, 1984. pp. 987-993. Table by State.

FEDERAL AID TO COMMUNITY DEVELOPMENT

Fulton, William. "HUD at 20 Faces a Midlife Crisis." Planning. Vol. 51, No. 11, Nov. 1985. p. 12-18.

FEDERAL AID TO COMMUNITY DEVELOPMENT

"Funds for New Housing Programs Remain on Senate Hold." Community Development Digest. No. 84-8, April 24, 1984. pp. 7-8.

FEDERAL AID TO COMMUNITY DEVELOPMENT

"HODag: Not Much Time Between Rules and Application Deadline." Urban Conservation Report. Vol. VIII, No. 7, April 24, 1984. p. 4.

FEDERAL AID TO COMMUNITY DEVELOPMENT

McCarthy, Bill. "CDBG: a Shining Past - a Clouded Future." Nation's Cities Weekly. Vol. 9, No. 8, Feb. 24, 1986. p. 4, 7.

FEDERAL AID TO COMMUNITY DEVELOPMENT

Mielnik, Randy and Marc Smith. "Marion, Ohio CDBG Evaluation Strategy." Small Town. Vol. 15, No. 1, July/August 1984. pp. 24-27.

FEDERAL AID TO COMMUNITY DEVELOPMENT

"Proposed Eligible Areas List Sparks Controversy Over Housing Development Grants." Community Development Digest. No. 84-8, April 24, 1984. pp. 3-7.

FEDERAL AID TO COMMUNITY DEVELOPMENT

"Most Communities Stay with HUD Formula, Despite Drop Below Rehab Program Minimum." Community Development Digest. No. 86-14, July 22, 1986. p. 8.

Most communities whose formula amounts under HUD's Rental Rehabilitation Program fall below $50,000 minimum choose

, con't on next card....

(card 2)

FEDERAL AID TO COMMUNITY DEVELOPMENT

to stay with formula rather than take option of seeking funds for state programs.

FEDERAL AID TO COMMUNITY DEVELOPMENT

"Refinancing Restrictions on FHA Multifamily Rehab Projects Removed." Housing and Development Reporter. Vol. 11, No. 46, April 9, 1984. p.973.

FEDERAL AID TO COMMUNITY DEVELOPMENT

"Rehab Category Heads List of Deficiencies Found in CDBG Monitoring Visits." Community Development Digest. No. 84-14. Jul. 24, 1984. pp. 1-3.

Problems of local community development rehab programs discussed. Difficulty determining National Register eligible properties to meet environmental review requirements prompting HUD to prepare guide 'to help local officials under-stand historic preser-   vation procedures.' (to be published at   ( ) the end of 1984.

FEDERAL AID TO COMMUNITY DEVELOPMENT

"Rental Rehab Grant Rules Raise Questions Among HUD, Local and State Officials." Housing and Development Reporter. Vol. 11, No. 46, April 9, 1984. pp. 967-8.

FEDERAL AID TO COMMUNITY DEVELOPMENT

"Rental Rehab Program to Begin in Another Month." Community Development Digest. No. 84-8, April 24, 1984. pp. 1-3.

FEDERAL AID TO COMMUNITY DEVELOPMENT

"Rental Rehab Rules Finished; New York City to Get Largest Formula Grant." Housing and Development Reporter. Vol. 11, No. 46, April 9, 1984. pp. 952-954.

FEDERAL AID TO COMMUNITY DEVELOPMENT

"Supplemental Bill Allocating $1.5 Billion for HUD Held Up in Senate." Housing and Development Reporter. Vol. 11, No. 46, April 9, 1984. pp. 954-5.

FEDERAL AID TO COMMUNITY DEVELOPMENT

Woodhouse, Linda. "Infusion of Federal Funds was Key to this City's Revitalization." Nation's Cities Weekly. Vol. 9, No. 8, Feb. 24, 1986. p. 6-7.

Focuses on Charleston, W.Va.

FEDERAL AID TO COMMUNITY DEVELOPMENT

Wright, Gordon. "How government funds helped with innovative reconstruction." Building Design and Construction. March 1981. p.50-51.

FEDERAL AID TO COMMUNITY DEVELOPMENT--U.S.-- INDIANA--FORT WAYNE

Leonard, Craig. "Partnership Fuels Facade." The Indiana Preservationist. No. 3, 1984. p. 1.

FEDERAL AID TO HISTORIC SITES

"Chairman Testifies for Preservation Appropiation." Preservation. Vol. 11, No. 1, Spring 1986. p. 6.

Bob Vice, Chairman of the Board of Directors of Preservation Alliance testified before the House Subcommittee on Interior of the Committee on Appropriations on the 1987 appropriations request for the National Historic Preservation Fund.

FEDERAL AID TO HISTORIC SITES

Maxwell, Shirley. "A Beginner's Guide to Preservation Fed Regs." The Old-House Journal. June 1984, Vol. XII, No. 5. pp. 91, 101-103.

FEDERAL AID TO HISTORIC SITES

"Preservation Fund Grant to Be Split." Headquarters Heliogram. No. 176, May-June 1986. p. 3.

The remaining FY-86 Historic Preservation Fund to be given to the states in two equal appointments, one during the third quarter, the second during the fourth quarter despite opposition from the Dept. of the Interior.

FEDERAL AID TO MUSEUMS

Chandler, Jerry G. "Match-Making." SEMC Journal, November 1979. pp. 16-22.

FEDERAL AID TO MUSEUMS

Shute, David A. "Working Group on Federal Museums Policy." Journal of the American Institute for Conservation, Autumn 1978. pp. 52-57.

FEDERAL AID TO THE ARTS

Design Arts 1: Grants Recognition Program, the National Endowment for the Arts. Vol. 1, August 1980.

"A magazine encompassing: architecture, landscape architecture, urban design and planning, interior design, industrial design, graphic design, fashion design."

FEDERAL AID TO THE ARTS

York, Hildreth. "The New Deal Art Projects in New Jersey." New Jersey History. Fall/ Winter 1980. pp. 133-174.

FEDERAL BUILDING--CONSERVATION AND RESTORATION

Langlois, Henri A. "A Policy for the Conservation of Federal Heritage Buildings." APT Bulletin. Vol. 18, No. 1 & 2, 1986. p. 47 - 48 .

FEDERAL HOUSING PROGRAMS

Connerly, Charles E. Journal Forum: "Looking Back at HUD." JAPA. Vol. 51, No. 4, Autumn 1985. p. 461-483.

A major article on HUD's first twenty years by Robert C. Weaver its first Secretary, and a series of shorter comments.

FEDERAL HOUSING PROGRAMS

"Environment Review Procedures for the Community Development Block Grant, Rental Rehabilitation and Housing Development Grant Programs (24CFR58)." Housing and Development Reporter. Vol. 12, No. 11, August 6, 1984. pp. 9-24.

FEDERAL HOUSING PROGRAMS

Pols, Cynthia. "NLC sues HUD and OMB on Deferral of Housing Funds." Nation's Cities Weekly. Vol. 9, No. 8, Feb. 24, 1986. p. 1, 10.

FENCES

Boulton, Alexander O. "Good Fences." American Heritage. Vol. 38, No. 2, Feb./Mar. 1987. p. 90-94.

FENCES

Ciampa, Thomas D. and Nancy Goldenberg. "Restoration of the Centennial Fence at Washington's Headquarters State Historic Site." APT Bulletin. Vol. 14, No. 3, 1982. pp. 26-35.

FENCES

Freeman, John Crosby. "Fences & Gates." The Old-House Journal. Vol. 14, No. 2, Mar. 1986. p. 78-81.

FENCES

Herman, Frederick. "Fences." The Old-House Journal. Feb./Mar. 1979.

FENCES

McIntosh, Alistair. "Wood Picket Fences." Landscape Architecture. Vol. 77, No. 1, Jan./Feb. 1987. p. 112-114.

FENCES

Pilling, Ron. "'Forge's Fancy Iron Fence". Old-House Journal. February 1981. p.37-40.

FERRIES

Bolberg, Sara. "New York Ferryboats: Three and a Half Centuries in the Harbor." Seaport. Vol. 16, No. 2, Fall 1982. p. 10-17.

FINANCE

"Alexandria, Virginia, To Sell, Lease Back, Old Torpedo Factory." Urban Conservation Report. April 15, 1983. p. 5.

FINANCE

Chu, Franklin J. "Financing Real Estate in the Public Securities Market." Real Estate Finance. Vol. 1, No. 4, Winter 1985. p. 29-34.

FINANCE

"Community Development Loan Funds Are Becoming Popular As a Place to Invest." Economic Growth & Revitalization. No. 86-22, Nov./25, 1986. p. 2-3.

FINANCE

"Conservancy Offers Grants for Older Religious Properties." Preservation League of New York State Newsletter. Vol. 12, No. 3, Summer 1986. p. 3.

FINANCE

Dowall, David E. "Applying Real Estate Financial Analysis to Planning and Development Control". JAPA, American Planning Association. Vol. 51, No. 1, Winter 1985. p. 84-94.

FINANCE

"Dusting Off Tax Increment Financing as an Alternative Development Tool." Local Economic Growth and Neighborhood Reinvestment Report. No. 84-20, October 18, 1984. pp. 1-3.

FINANCE

"Financing Rehab Development Without Federal Subsidies." Home Again. Summer 1984. No. 3. pp. 10-12.

FINANCE

Friedman, Stephen B. "Local Incentives for Revitalization." Center City Report. July 1981. pp. 1-4.

FINANCE

"Getting into the Development Game, Investors Don't Love Old Buildings, So You Must Show Them How They Will Make Money on Your Rehab Project." Home Again. Summer 1984, No. 3. p. 15.

FINANCE

Gross, Martin M. "Shared Development of Historic Sites." The Appraisal Journal. Vol. LII, No. 4, October 1984. pp. 519-527.

FINANCE

"Historic Theater Gets Endowment Through 'Lease-Leaseback' in Tacoma, Washington." Urban Conservation Report. April 15, 1983. p. 6-7.

also: "Impending Sale-Leasebacks in Buffalo, New York, Too." p. 7.

FINANCE

Howell, Joseph T. "Project Syndication: How it Works." Journal of Housing. Vol. 41, No. 4, July-August 1984. pp. 105-111.

FINANCE

"Investors Find a New Home: Small-Town Main Streets." Business Week. August 6, 1984. pp. 71-72.

National Trust Main Street Program highlighted.

FINANCE

Laughlin, Mary. "An Introduction to Limited Partnership Bonds: Surety bonds are replacing letters of credit as an effective way to guarantee investor payments." Real Estate Finance. Vol. 1, No. 4, Winter 1985. p. 44-50.

FINANCE

Merritt, E.W. "Tax Increment Financing can Aid Redevelopment." Center City Report. May 1982. pp. 1-2.

FINANCE

"New Hampshire Program Helps Towns to Reduce Substandard Housing Conditions." Community Development Digest. No. 86-14. July 22, 1986. pp. 4-5.

State Planning Office emphasizing housing rehabilitation with its small cities CD block grant funds.

FINANCE

Ochs, Michael. "Interest Rate Protection for the Real Estate Developer." Real Estate Finance. Vol. 1, No. 4, Winter 1985. p. 7-16.

FINANCE

Porter, Douglas R. "The Rights and Wrongs of Impact Fees." Urban Land. Vol. 45, No. 7, July 1986. p. 16-19.

FINANCE

Schulwolf, James C. "Real Estate Securities Developments: An update on statutory and regulatory changes and proposals." Real Estate Finance. Vol. 1, No. 4, Winter 1985. p. 78-80.

FINANCE

Sears, Cecile. "S & Ls: A Changing Source of Real Estate Capital". Urban Land. Vol. 44, No. 1, Jan. 1985. p. 11-15.

FINANCE

Sears, Cecil E. "ULI Survey Examines Real Estate Development Finance." Urban Land. Vol. 43, No. 9, September 1984. pp. 2-5.

FINANCE

"ULI Roundtable Discusses the Future of Development Finance." Urban Land. Vol. 43, No. 9, September 1984. pp. 36-7.

FINANCE--CANADA

Smythe, Mary Ann. "Work Hard for the Money." Canadian Heritage. Vol. 12, Issue 3, Aug.-Sept. 1986. p. 42-44.

Finding financing for small scale restoration projects.

FIRE PREVENTION

Cohn, Bert M. "Fire Safety in Recycled Buildings: Establishing the Level of Protection Equivalent to Code Requirements." Technology and Conservation. Summer 1980. p. 40-45.

FIRE PREVENTION

"Fire Breaks" Progressive Architecture. Nov. 1986. p.116-121.

Fire safety in historic buildings.

FIRE PREVENTION

Fischer, Walter R. "Fire Safety Systems: Protecting Our Treasures from Threat of Fire." Technology and Conservation. Fall 1976. pp. 14-17.

FIRE PREVENTION

Lynch, Michael P. "Preventing Fire During Construction Projects." Common Bond. Vol. 2, No. 4, Fall 1986. p. 4-8.

FIRE PREVENTION

Neave, Charles. "The Equinox House (Manchester, Vt.) Fire." Yankee. Vol. 49, No. 5, May 1985. p. 14-15.

FIRE PREVENTION

Schur, Susan E. "Fire Protection at Mount Vernon: Incorporating Modern Fire Safety Systems into an Historic Site." Technology and Conservation. Winter 1980. p. 18-25.

FIRE PREVENTION

"A Sensing Approach Smokes Out Possible Threats to Historic Structures." Technology and Conservation. Summer 1981. pp. 9-13.

FIRE PREVENTION

Shepherd, Nicola. "When History Goes up in Flames." Traditional Homes. Sept. 1986. p. 84-89.

Fire prevention in historic buildings.

FIRE PREVENTION

Shepherd, Nicola. "Smoke Without Fire." Traditional Homes. Vol. 3, No. 1, Oct. 1986. p. 52-57.

Modern fire protection equipment for the traditional house.

FIRE PREVENTION

"Smoke Control in Buildings: Design Principles." Building Research Establishment Digest. Digest 260. April 1982.

FIRE PREVENTION

Tiszkus, Alphonse T. and E.G. Dressler. "Fire Protection Planning for Cultural Institutions". Technology and Conservation Summer 1980. p. 18-23.

FIREHOUSES--ADAPTIVE USE

Huemer, Christina. "Visible City." Metropolis. May 1986. p. 47-49.

Victorian firehouses of New York City.

FIREHOUSES--US--COLORADO--DENVER

"Neighborhood Guardians." Historic Denver News. Vol. 14, No. 1, Jan. 1985. p. 4-5.

FIREPLACES

Weck, Egon. "A Better Fireplace." Americana, January/February 1980. pp. 66-70.

FIRES

"A Part of Nashville's Heritage Lost.... The Historic Register. Vol. 8, Winter 1986. p. 1

Fire destroyed four historic buildings in a historic district of Nashville. Preservationist's effort to save facades failes and the buildings were demolished.

FLOOD DAMAGE PREVENTION

Geis, Donald and Barry Steeves. "Designing Against Flood Damage: a research project yields some guidelines". AIA Journal. November 1980. p. 52-58.

FLOOR COVERINGS

Blackman, Leo and Deborah Dietsch. "Linoleum, How To Repair It, Install It,and Clean It." The Old-House Journal. February 1982. pp. 36-38.

FLOOR COVERINGS

Brown, Marjorie. "Creating a Floor Cloth." Colonial Homes. September/October 1981. p. 134.

FLOOR COVERINGS

Kahn, Eve. "Finding Linoleum." Old-House Journal. Vol. 19, No. 10, Dec. 1986. p. 478-481.

FLOORS--MAINTENANCE AND REPAIR

Fidler, John. "Dirty Business." Traditional Homes. June 1986. pp. 72-75.

How to remove stains from different kinds of traditional floors.

FLOORING

Freeman, Jane. "The Reproduction of a Colonial Floor". The Old-House Journal April 1980. p. 42-43

FLOORS--MAINTENANCE AND REPAIR

Fossel, Peter V. "Refinish an Old Floor." Americana. Vol. 13, No. 4, Sept./Oct. 1985. p. 85-88.

FLOORS--MAINTENANCE AND REPAIR

Herman, Frederick. "Refinishing Floors : Think Twice Before Sanding". Old-House Journal. February 1981. p. 27, 44-45.

FLOORS--MAINTENANCE AND REPAIR

Poore, Patricia. "Fixing Old Floors: Repairing and replacing floorboards, Part 3." Old-House Journal. Mar.1981. pp. 61-63.

FLOORS--MAINTENANCE AND REPAIR

Poore, Patricia. "Sanding a Parquet Floor". Old House Journal. November 1980. p. 168-171.

FLOORS, WOODEN

Henning, Lisbeth. "Softwood floors: to sand or not to sand?" The Indiana Preservationist. No. 1, 1985. p. 6.

FLOORS, WOODEN--MAINTENANCE AND REPAIR

O'Donnell, Bill. "Reconditioning Floors."
The Old House Journal. Vol. 13, No. 10, Dec. 1985.
p. 201, 218-219.

Restoration of parquet floor without power
sanding described.

FLOORS, WOODEN--MAINTENANCE AND REPAIR

Orcutt, Georgia. "The Truth About Wood
Floors." Yankee. Vol. 49, No. 6, June 1985.
p. 110-115.

A discussion of whether or not to sand
floors.

FLOORS, WOODEN--MAINTENANCE AND REPAIR

Poore, Patricia. "Picking a Floor Finish".
The Old House Journal. May 1981. pp. 107 - 113.

FLORIDA--KEY WEST

Maxa, Kathleen. "Key West". American
Preservation. May/June 1980. p. 9-23.

FLORIDA--MIAMI BEACH--ART DECO DISTRICT

Johnson, Janis. "Good Times and Bad for
Art Deco on Miami Beach Strip." Smithsonian.
December 1982. pp. 58-67.

FLORIDA--MIAMI BEACH--ART DECO HISTORIC DISTRICT

Curtis, James R. "Lament for an Art Deco
Landmark." Landscape. Vol. 27, No. 1, 1983.
pp. 40-46.

FLORIDA--MIAMI BEACH

Morton, David. "Miami Beach: Yesterday,
today, and tomorrow". Progressive Architecture.
August 1980. p. 60-65.

FLORIDA--PALM BEACH

Kay, Jane Holtz. "Mizner's Eden: Will
the Paradise Created by Palm Beach's Flamboyant
Architect Survive?" American Preservation.
Vol. 4, #2. pp. 35-48.

FOLK ART

"Grassroots Artist: Grandma Prisbrey."
KGAA News. Vol. 4, no. 1, Winter 1983-84.
pp. 1-3. (NTHP PSF grant awarded in 1983 to
Preserve Bottle Village.)

FOLK ART--CONSERVATION AND RESTORATION

Wolf, Gary K. "The Merry-go-round at Tilden
Park; About to be Sold for its Parts, it Was
Saved by a Spirited Community and Restored by Pros
Named Fraley." Americana. Sep./Oct. 1979.
pp. 44-51.

FOLKLORE

Teske, Robert Thomas. "Folk Studies and
Historic Preservation." PAST (Pioneer America
Society Transactions), 1979. pp. 71-80.

FOOD

Rawlings, Sandra. "More Than Just Another
Fad,...Popcorn,...A Favorite American Snack Since
Ancient Indians." Americana. Vol. 12, No. 4,
September/October 1984. pp. 70-73, 122-123.

FORTIFICATION

Buecker, Thomas R. "The Lingering Death--
And Preservation--of Old Fort Sidney." Periodical
(Journal of the Council on America's Military
Past). Vol. 14, No. 1, March 1986. p. 17-30.

FORTIFICATION

McDougall, Terry. "Adventures in the Fur
Trade, Lower Fort Garry Opens its Gates to the
19th Century." Canadian Heritage. May/June
1984. pp. 24-29.

FORTIFICATION

Nickels, Marilyn W. "Guns Over the Potomac." (Fort Foote, Md.) CRM Bulletin. Vol. 7, No. 3, October 1984. pp. 4-5.

FORTIFICATION--ADAPTIVE USE

"Watertown Arsenal Now Retail Mall." Headquarters Heliogram. Dec. 1983. p. 4.

FORTIFICATION--U.S.--ALASKA

Jaunal, Jack W. "Bringing Ft. Egbert to the 'Outside'".Periodical. Vol. 14, No. 2, June 1986. p. 20-25.

Parts of an Alaskan fort has been restored.

FORTIFICATION--U.S.--GEORGIA--SAVANNAH

Cumberland, Donald R. Jr. "A Solution to Fort Pulaski's Preservation Dilemma." CRM Bulletin. Vol. 8, No. 5, Oct. 1985. p. 6-8.

Solutions to problems of a historic structure and artifacts suffering from high humidity, temperature and salt-air discussed.

FORTIFICATION--U.S.--MARYLAND

Kimmel, Ross M. "Fort Frederick Wall: Analysis and Stabilization." Bulletin, The Association for Preservation Technology. Vol. 16, No. 2, 1984. p. 32-43.

FORTIFICATION--U.S.--TEXAS

"Citizens Rally Behind Fort (Fort Davis)." The Medallion, Vol. 22, No. 4, Apr. 1985. p. 5.

FORTS

"Commission Studying Ft. Stanton Program." Headquarters Heliogram. No. 185. June 1987. p. 3.

Plans to restore Ft. Stanton in Lincoln County, N.M. are under study.

FORTS--U.S.--PENNSYLVANIA--PHILADELPHIA--FORT MIFFLIN

Liggett, Barbara and Sandra Laumark. "The Counterfort at Fort Mifflin." APT Bulletin. Vol. 11, No. 1, 1979. pp. 37-74.

FOUNDATIONS

Garrison, John Mark. "Fundamental Techniques for Foundation Shoring and House Jacking." The Old-House Journal. January-February, 1983. pp. 19-23.

FOUNDATIONS--CONSERVATION AND RESTORATION

Aldrich, Harl P. "Preserving the Foundations of Older Buildings: the Importance of Groundwater Levels." Technology & Conservation. Summer, 1979. pp. 32-40

FRAMING (BUILDING)

"Traditional house framing." Old-House Journal. December 1980. p. 197-199.

FRENCH, DANIEL CHESTER

Richman, Michael. "Daniel Chester French and Henry Bacon: Public Sculpture in Collaboration, 1897-1908." The American Art Journal. Summer 1980. pp. 46-64.

FUNDRAISING

"Adopt a Brick." Economic Growth & Revitalization Report. No. 87-88. Apr. 28, 1987. p. 4.

Fundraising program for restoration of historic monument in Santa Fe.

FUNDRAISING

"After the Federal Budget Cuts: Challenges and Opportunities for Philanthropy and What Business Expects from the Nonprofit Sector." The Grantsmanship Center News. March/April 1982. pp. 13-23.

FUND RAISING

Elliott, Don and Maurice Gordon. "The Fund Raiser - How to Establish an Annual Giving Campaign." <u>History News</u>. Vol. 39, No. 4, April 1984. pp. 26-28.

FUND RAISING

"Fund Raising Events." <u>Illinois Heritage Association Technical Insert</u>. No. 11. 2 pp. In <u>Illinois Heritage Association Newsletter</u>. Vol. 2, No. 5, September-October 1984.

FUNDRAISING

Grasty, William K and Sheinkopf, Kenneth G. "The Annual Fund." <u>The Grantsmanship Center News</u>. September/ October 1983. pp. 8-29.

FUND RAISING

Guzman, Carol. "Corporate Giving: An Overview, Private Corporations Will Fund Neighborhood Groups That "Give" A Little to Reach Their Goals." <u>Home Again</u>. Summer 1984, No. 3. pp. 16-17.

FUNDRAISING

Lant, Jeffrey L. "An Introduction to Capital Campaigns." <u>The Grantsmanship Center News</u>. March/April 1983. pp. ;9-25.

FUNDRAISING

Limpert, John. "Marketing Challenges in Cultural Fund Raising." <u>Museum News</u>. May/June 1982. pp. 51-60.

FUNDRAISING

Mittenhal, Stephen. "The Perfect Gift: Examples of Noncash Corporate Philanthropy." <u>The Grantsmanship Center News</u>. September/October 1983. pp. 50-54.

FUND RAISING

Mott, William Penn. "Singing the Philanthropic Blues: Raising Money Can Be Good for Your Financial Health." <u>Courier</u>. Vol. 31, No. 3, Mar. 1986. p. 6-7.

FUND RAISING

"New Ways to Raise IA (Industrial Archeology) $." <u>Society for Industrial Archeology Newsletter</u>. Vol. 14, No. 2, 1985. p. 1.

FUND RAISING

Poleshuck, Walter S. "Corporate Fund Raising." <u>Museum News</u>. March/April 1982. pp. 9-20.

FUND RAISING

"Professional Fund Raising." <u>Community Development Digest</u>. No. 87-10. May 19, 1987. p. 9-10.

Richmond, VA, establishes profit-making corporation to raise funds for housing development groups.

FUNDRAISING

Prospecting: How to Research Funding Sources. <u>Conserve Neighborhoods</u>. No. 45, Feb. 1985. p. 1-3, 6.

FUNDRAISING

"Public/Private Partnerships, a 1980s Approach to Urban Problems." <u>Neighborhood Ideas</u>. January 1982. Entire Issue.

FUNDRAISING

Scribner, Susan and Florence Green. "Asking for Money." <u>The Grantsmanship Center News</u>. March/April 1983. pp. 9-17.

FUND RAISING

Sinclair, Stephen. "Why Business Gives to the Arts." The Cultural Post. November/ December, 1981. pp. 1-5.

FUND RAISING

Snapp, Terry. "Turning Land Into Cash, A New Fund Raising Strategy." Neighborhood Ideas. June 1982. p. 101.

FUND RAISING

Sommerville, Bill. "Where Proposals Fail." Grantsmanship Center News. January/February 1982. pp. 24-25.

FUNDRAISING

Sweeney, Tim and Seltzer, Michael. "Fundraising Strategies for the Hard Times." The Neighborhood Works. February 1982. pp. 11-20.

FUND RAISING

Toscano, James V. "Development Comes of Age." Museum News. January/February 1982. pp. 61-67.

FUNDRAISING

Weiser, Paul R. "Prime Numbers: A Guide to Telephone Fundraising." The Grantsmanship Center News. July/ August 1983. pp. 30-40.

FURNITURE

Antiques, May 1979.

Note: Several articles on various styles of American furniture from the sixteenth through the nineteenth centuries.

FURNITURE

"Biedemeier Furniture." Victorian Homes. Vol. 5, Issue 4, Fall 1986. p. 34-37.

FURNITURE

Cotton, Randall J. "Furniture Architecture." Old-House Journal. Vol. 15, No. 2, Mar./Apr. 1987. p. 39-47.

Guide to period furniture.

FURNITURE

Frelinghuysen, Alice Cooney. "The Renaissance Revival Parlor in the Metropolitan Museum of Art." Antiques. Vol. 128, No. 1, July 1985. p. 118-119.

FURNITURE

Ruhling, Nancy A. "Hunzinger Furniture." Victorian Homes. Vol. 6, Issue 1, Winter 1987. p. 30-33.

FURNITURE

Seibels, Cynthia. "How to Restore Iron and Brass Beds." Americana. Vol. 15, No. 1, Mar./Apr. 1987. p. 63-66.

FURNITURE

Shepherd, Nicola. "Seating Arrangements." Traditional Homes. Sept. 1986. p. 76-80.

Traditional kitchen chairs.

FURNITURE

Stamm, Richard. "Victorian Mechanical Tables." The Victorian. Vol. 14, No. 2. Summer 1986. pp. 8-9.

Vertical File

FURNITURE

U.S. Dept. of State. The Diplomatic Reception Rooms. Washington, D.C. 1986. 16 p. (VF)

FURNITURE

Woolley, Martin. "Disguise or Display?" Traditional Homes. Vol. 3, No. 1, Oct. 1986. p. 62-67.

Problems of blending modern technology (TVs, VCRs, audio equipment) with traditional interiors.

FURNITURE--COLLECTORS AND COLLECTING

Connors, Jill. "Antiques Forums: Where the experts and collectors meet and mingle." Americana. Vol. 12, No. 6, Jan./Feb. 1985. p. 96-98.

FURNITURE--COLLECTORS AND COLLECTING

"The George Alfred Cluett Collection of American Furniture." Historic Deerfield Quarterly. Vol. 23, No. 2, Spring 1985. p. 1.

New collection to open in Historic Deerfield September 16, 1985.

FURNITURE--COLLECTORS AND COLLECTING

Kent, Margaret. "The Show and the Showman." Early American Life. Vol. 17, No. 4, Aug. 1986. p. 52-57, 71-72.

Exhibit of American furniture at the Wadsworth Atheneum that demonstrates woodworking techniques of the 17th and 18th centuries.

FURNITURE--COLLECTORS AND COLLECTING

Martin, Rebecca. "Past Masters: Israel Sack made a fortune by seeing early the craft in fine old American furniture", American Heritage, Vol. 36, No. 2, February/March 1985, pp. 36-47.

FURNITURE--COLLECTORS AND COLLECTING

Schmertz, Mildred. "Design for Diplomacy." Architectural Record. Vol. 173, No. 12, Oct. 1985. p. 152-161.

The Diplomatic Reception Rooms at the Department of State featured.

FURNITURE--CONSERVATION AND RESTORATION

Sherin, Richard W. "The Whitening of Furniture Finishes." RCHA Technical Information Sheet #75. April 1985. 4 p.

FURNITURE--HISTORY--18th CENTURY

Donegan, Frank. "In the Marketplace: Blockfront Furniture." Americana. Vol. 12, No. 6, Jan./Feb. 1985. p. 76-78.

FURNITURE--HISTORY--18th CENTURY

Forman, Benno M. "The Chest of Drawers in America, 1635-1730: the Origins of the Joined Chest of Drawers." Winterthur Portfolio. Vol. 20, No. 1, Spring 1985. p. 1-30.

FURNITURE--HISTORY--18th CENTURY

Trent, Robert F. "The Chest of Drawers in America, 1635-1730: A Postscript." Winterthur Portfolio. Vol. 20, No. 1, Spring 1985. p. 31-48.

FURNITURE--HISTORY--20th CENTURY

Hunter-Stiebel, Penelope. "Surpassing Style, Four Art Deco Masters: Ruhlmann, Dunand, Marinot, and Puiforcat." Antiques. Vol. 128, No. 4, Oct. 1985. p. 732-743.

FURNITURE MAKING

Ettema, Michael. "Technological Innovation and Design Economics in Furniture Manufacture." Winterthur Portfolio. Summer/Autumn 1981. pp. 197-223.

FURNITURE PAINTING--U.S.--NEW ENGLAND

Kirk, John T. "The tradition of English painted furniture; part 1: the experience in colonial New England." Antiques. May 1980 p. 1078-1083

FURNITURE PAINTING--U.S.--NEW YORK

O'Donnell, Patricia Chapin. "Grisaille decorated kasten of New York." Antiques. May 1980. pp. 1108-1111.

FURNITURE, REGENCY

Davidson, Marshall B. "Duncan Phyfe: Fulton Street Craftsman." Seaport. Fall 1981. pp. 22-27.

FURNITURE, SHAKER

Williams, Roger M. "Western Shaker Furntiure: One Man's Collection." Americana, March-April 1979. pp. 50-55.

FURNITURE--U.S.

Antiques. May 1981. Entire issue.

PARTIAL CONTENTS: Labeled New York furniture at the New York State Museum, Albany; Branded and stamped New York furniture; Decorated board chests of the Connecticut River valley; the Manney collection of Belter furniture.

FURNITURE--UNITED STATES

Lyle, Charles T., and Philip D. Zimmerman. "Furniture of the Monmouth County Historical Association." Antiques. Jan. 1980. pp. 186-205.

FURNITURE--U.S.--MASSACHUSETTS--BOSTON

Cooke, Edward S., Jr. "The Boston Furniture Industry in 1880." Old-Time New England. Vol LXX, 1980. p. 82-98.

FURNITURE--U.S.--MASSACHUSETTS--NORTHAMPTON

Keno, Leigh. "The windsor-chair makers of Northampton, Massachusetts, 1790-1820." Antiques. May 1980. p. 1100-1107.

FURNITURE--U.S.--NEW ENGLAND

Peladeau, Marius B. "A Hadley chest reconsidered." Antiques. May 1980. pp. 1084-1086.

FURNITURE--U.S.--NEW ENGLAND

Brown, Michael K. "Scalloped-top furniture of the Connecticut River valley." Antiques. May 1980. p. 1092-1099.

FURNITURE--U.S.--PENNSYLVANIA--PHILADELPHIA

Catalano, Kathleen and Richard C. Nylander. "New attributions to Adam Hains, Philadelphia furniture maker". Antiques. May 1980. p. 1112-1117.

FURNITURE--U.S.--RHODE ISLAND

Monahon, Eleanore Bradford. "The Rawson family of cabinetmakers in Providence, Rhode Island." Antiques. July 1980. p. 134-147.

FURNITURE--U.S.--RHODE ISLAND

Monkhouse, Christopher. "American furniture recently acquired by the Museum of Art, Rhode Island School of Design." Antiques. July 1980. p. 126-133.

GARAGES

"Aesthetics of Parking Lots and Parking Structures." Zoning News. Sept. 1986. p. 1-2.

GARAGES

Bergmann, Richard. "A Compatible Garage." Old-House Journal. Vol. 19, No. 10, Dec. 1986. p. 482.

Case study of a garage designed to be compatible with an old house.

GARAGES

Cotton, J. Randall. "The Great American Garage, Part I." Old-House Journal. Vol. 14, No. 7, Sept. 1986. p. 328-335.

GARAGES

Cotton, J. Randall. "The Great American Garage. Part II." Old-House Journal. Vol. 14, No. 8, Oct. 1986. p. 382-390.

GARAGES

Sinclair, Doug. "Albany's Carriage Houses." Albany Preservation Report. Vol. 5, No. 6, Fall 1986. p. 8-10.

GARDEN CITIES

Birch, Eugenie Ladner. "Radburn and the American Planning Movement." Journal of the American Planning Association. October 1980. p.424-439.

GARDEN CITIES

Winkleman, Michael. "Jackson Heights." Metropolis. March 1982. pp. 23-25.

GARDEN ORNAMENTS AND FURNITURE

Snyder, Ellen Marie. "Victory over Nature: Victorian Cast-Iron Seating Furniture." Winterthur Portfolio. Vol. 20, No. 4, Winter 1985. p. 221-242.

GARDEN ORNAMENTS AND FURNITURE

Phillips, Collin. "Precast Concrete Gnomes, Parody Standard Specification: Gnome Series." APT Bulletin. Vol. 14, No. 3, 1982. pp. 42-45.

GARDEN STRUCTURES

Favretti, Rudy. "Arbors and Trellises. Americana, May/June 1979. pp. 48-54.

GARDEN STRUCTURES

"Greenhouses, Conservatories and Garden Structures." Old-House Journal. Vol. 13, No. 3. Apr. 1985. p. 68.

GARDENS

Bynum, Flora Ann. "Landscape Maintenance." North Carolina Preservation. No. 65, Sept.-Oct.-Nov. 1986. p. 2.

Maintenance of gardens and grounds of restored houses and villages.

GARDENS

"City Botanic Gardens to be Restored." National Trust Queensland Journal. Dec. 1986. p. 13.

Restoration of botanic gardens in Brisbane, Australia.

GARDENS

Gribbin, Thomas & Judith Tulloch. "Ardgowan--The Restoration of an Island Garden." APT Bulletin. Vol. 18, No. 1 & 2, 1986. p. 99-105.

GARDENS

Krebs, Wolfgang. "The Historic Parks of Cleves and Their Restoration." Journal of Garden History. Vol. 6, No. 4, Oct./Dec. 1986. p. 376-388.

GARDENS

Kunst, Scott G. "Landscape & Gardens." Old-House Journal. Vol. 14, No. 3, April 1986. p. 125-135.

Simple home landscapes based on those of medieval England and colonial America.

GARDENS

Lawford, Valentine. "Gardens: A Touch of Europe; Formalism and Classicism in Upstate New York." Architectural Digest. Oct. 1979. pp. 78-83.

GARDENS

Paca-Steele, Barbara, and St. Clair Wright. "The Mathematics of an Eighteenth Century Wilderness Garden." Journal of Garden History. Vol. 6, No. 4, Oct./Dec. 1986. p. 299-320.

GARDENS--CONSERVATION AND RESTORATION

"ATR Completes Landscape Plan." Directions (Department of Arkansas Natural and Cultural Heritage). Fall 1983. p. 3.

GARDENS--CONSERVATION AND RESTORATION

Bynum, Flora Ann. "Historic Horticulture: Landscape Restoration New Thrust in Preservation." North Carolina Preservation, No. 61, Jan./Feb. 1986. p. 12-13.

GARDENS--CONSERVATION AND RESTORATION

Sales, John. "The Philosophy and Practice of Garden Preservation." Bulletin, APT. Vol. 17, No. 3&4, 1985. p. 61-64.

GARDENS--CONSERVATION AND RESTORATION--GREAT BRITAIN

Spencer, Christopher. "Unearthing Flower-beds." Traditional Homes. Mar. 1986. p. 74-79.

Restoration of a 1913 design in England by the eminent Edwardian garden designer, Gertrude Jekyll.

GARDENS--ENGLAND

Jacques, David. "Historic Garden Con-Servation." The Planner. Nov. 1986. p. 14-17.

Garden conservation in England.

GARDENS--HISTORY

Bassett, Thomas J. "Reaping on the Margins: a Century of Community Gardening in America." Landscape. Vol. 25, No. 2.pp. 1-7.

GARDENS--HISTORY

Brinton, David. "The Secrets of a Victorian Garden Told." Silver Queen Preservation News. Vol. 15, No. 1, July 1985. p. 6.

The decorative gardens of Frank S. Scott discussed.

GARDENS--HISTORY

Lundgren, Edward. "Public Gardens - A Victorian Ideal." Canadian Heritage. Vol. 2, No. 3, July/Aug. 1985. p. 14-19.

GARDENS--HISTORY

Martin, Peter. "Visions and Revisions in Historic Area Gardens." Colonial Williamsburg Today. Summer 1981. pp. 2-6.

GARDENS--HISTORY

Seaton, Beverly. "Gardening Books for the Commuter's Wife, 1900-1937." Landscape. Vol. 28, No. 2, 1985. p. 41-47.

GARDENS--HISTORY

Woodbridge, Kenneth. "Rise and decline of the garden knot." Architectural Review. June 1979. pp. 324-329.

GENEALOGY

Moeller, Josephine F. "Preserving Family History." Illinois Heritage Association. Vol. 5. No. 3. May - June 1987. Technical Insert no. 27.

GEORGIA--COLUMBUS

Snow, Nan. "Columbus: a combination of historic preservation and adaptive reuse has transformed this Georgia City." American Preservation. January/February 1981. p.44-57.

GERMANY--BERLIN--HISTORIC PRESERVATION

"The World of Conservation: An Interview with Ludwig Deiters." Monumentum. Vol. 27, No. 1, March 1984. pp. 3-17.

GHOST TOWNS

Dallas, Sandra. "Colorado's Ghost Towns and Mining Camps." Colorado Heritage News. Aug. 1985. p. 7-8.

GLASS

"Architectural Glass: History and Conservation." Association for Preservation Technology Bulletin. Vol. 13, No. 3, 1981. Entire issue.

CONTENTS: Byrne, R.O. Conservation of Historic Window Glass--Rambusch, V.B.A. Preservation and Restoration of Leaded Glass Windows--Yorke, D.A. Materials for Conservation for the Twentieth Century: The Case for Structural Glass--Taylor, Jr. T.H. Architectural Glass Repair: A Case Study

GLASS

Dietsch, Deborah. "Let There be Light, Again." Progressive Architecture. November 1982. pp. 129-133.

GLASS, ORNAMENTAL

"Hadley Square's (St. Louis) Egyptian Lobby Makes It All Worthwhile: Vitrolite glass tiled lobby is relocated and restored to its original magnificent look in conversion". Commercial Renovation. Vol. 7, No. 1, Feb. 1985. p. 40- .

GLASS, ORNAMENTAL

Lawrence, Wade. "Duluth's Tiffany Windows." Architecture Minnesota. Vol. 11, No. 4, July/Aug. 1985. p. 3, 62-63.

GLASS CONSTRUCTION

Bergmann, Richard. "Reconstruction of the Lockwood-Mathews Mansion Museum Conservatory." APT Bulletin. Vol. 14, No. 3, 1982. pp. 3-6.

GLASS CONSTRUCTION

"Restoring a Victorian botanical conservatory." Architectural Record. October 1980. p.72-77.

GLASS CONSTRUCTION--U.S.--CALIFORNIA--SAN FRANCISCO--STANFORD COURT

"Stanford Court under glass: a series of linked conservatories transparently adds 3,000 square feet." Interior Design. Apr. 1980. pp. 226-229.

GLASS PAINTING AND STAINING

Bordes, Marilynn Johnson. "Stained Glass of Tiffany and LaFarge in the Met's New Wing." 19th Century. p. 36-38. Autumn 1980

GLASS PAINTING AND STAINING

Clark, Willene B. "Gothic Revival Stained Glass of William Jay Bolton: A Preservation Project and Census." Nineteenth Century. Summer 1981. pp. 30-34.

GLASS PAINTING AND STAINING

Fleet, Rachael. "History Through Rose-Colored Windows; Odyssey of 42 Stained Glass Windows with the State Seals of the 1889 Union." Challenge! Sep. 1979. pp. 6-11.

GLASS PAINTING AND STAINING

Gaca, Fred J. "Buyer Beware, Seeing Through Bad Stained Glass." The Old-House Journal. March 1982. p. 53.

GLASS PAINTING AND STAINING

Janetski, Joyce Athay. "Louis Comfort Tiffany: Stained Glass in Utah." Utah Preservation/Restoration. Vol. III, 1981. pp. 20-25.

GLASS PAINTING AND STAINING

Millard, Richard. "Stained Glass Preservation: Guidelines for Repair and Restoration." Technology & Conservation, Spring 1979. pp. 36-41.

GLASS PAINTING AND STAINING

Murphy, Barbara. "Splendor in Glass". Utah: Preservation/Restoration. Vol. 2/ Issue 2 1980. pp. 46 - 47.

GLASS PAINTING AND STAINING

Sloan, Julie L. "Documentation of Stained Glass Window Restoration, Church of St. Ann and The Holy Trinity, Brooklyn, N.Y." APT Bulletin. Vol. 15, No. 1, 1983. pp. 12-19.

GLASS PAINTING AND STAINING

Swash, Caroline. "Glowing Panes." Traditional Homes. April 1986. p. 51-59.

Stained glass techniques; suppliers, artists, museums.

GLASS PAINTING AND STAINING-CONSERVATION AND
                                      RESTORATION

"American Decorative Window Glass, 1860 - 1890." Blueprints. Vol. 5, No. 1. Spring 1987. pp. 5 - 6.
    Discussion of Victorian Stained Glass, in connection with exhibit of decorative window glass at the National Building Museum.

GLASS PAINTING AND STAINING--CONSERVATION AND
    RESTORATION

Field, A. Scott. "Preservation Coalition Saves Windows from St. Mary's." Preservation Report. Vol. 9, No. 1, Feb. 1987. p. 1-2.

GLASS PAINTING AND STAINING--CONSERVATION AND
    RESTORATION

"A Fitting Solution for On-Site Window (Stained Glass) Restoration." Technology & Conservation. Fall 1983, Vol. 8, No. 3. pp. 5-8.

GLASS PAINTING AND STAINING--U.S.--GEORGIA

"Stained Glass Survey Underway in State." The Rambler, Newsletter of the Georgia Trust for Historic Preservation. Vol. 12, No. 4, Fall/ Winter 1985. p. 5.

GLASS PAINTING AND STAINING--CONSERVATION AND
    RESTORATION

Sloan, Julie. "Restoring Stained Glass Treasures." Home Again. No. 2, Spring 1984. pp. 10-14.

    --CHURCHES--U.S.--NEW YORK--BROOKLYN
    (St. Ann and Holy Trinity (1844), Minard Lafever, architect)

GLASS PAINTING AND STAINING--CONSERVATION AND
    RESTORATION

Ramsbusch, Viggo Bech. "The Lead Cames of Stained Glass Windows: Purpose, Problems, and Preservation Procedures." Technology & Conservation. Fall 1983, Vol. 8, No. 3. pp. 46-49.

GLASS PAINTING AND STAINING--CONSERVATION AND
RESTORATION.

Lynch, Michael F. "Stained Glass Restoration." APT Bulletin. Vol. 18, No. 4, 1986. p. 8-9.

GLASS PAINTING AND STAINING--CONSERVATION AND RE-
STORATION

Harper-Hinton, Reginald. "Stained Glass Restored." Historic Places in New Zealand. No. 14, Sept. 1986. p. 20-23.

    Restoration of the stained glass windows at the Canterbury Provincial Government Buildings in Christchurch.

GLASSWARE

Elbert, E. Duane. "American Pattern Glass." Technical Insert, No. 19, Jan./Feb. 1986. 4 p. Illinois Heritage Association Newsletter, Vol. 4, No. 1, Jan./Feb. 1986.

GLASSWARE

Tanenhaus, Ruth Amdur. "Frederick Carder: Innovations in Glass." <u>Antiques World</u>. October 1981. pp. 34-39.

GOODHUE, BERTRAM GROSVENOR (1869-1924)

Shipsky, James. "Goodhue's Serene Rewarding Museum." <u>AIA Journal</u>. March 1982. pp. 64-71.

GOTHIC REVIVAL (ARCHITECTURE)

Massey, James C. and Shirley Maxwell. "The Gothic Revival." <u>The Old-House Journal</u>. Vol. XII, No. 10, December 1984. pp. 226-7.

GOTHIC REVIVAL (ARCHITECTURE)--CONSERVATION AND RESTORATION

Dallas, Sandra. "Mining Camp Victorian: Hamill House: a Mining Magnate Bought the House in 1874 as a Status Sumbol. It is now Part of a Preservation Program that will Show How all Echelons Lived in this Rocky Mountain Town." <u>Americana</u>. Sep.-Oct. 1979. pp. 52-57.

GOVERNOR'S MANSIONS--U.S.--COLORADO

"Restoration Planned for Governor's Mansion." <u>Colorado Heritage News</u>. Nov. 1985. p. 4.

Master plan for restoration of 1908 structure to begin.

GRAINING

Witsell, Becky. "Wood Grainer Plies Skills in Quarter." <u>Quapaw Quarter Chronicle</u>. Spring 1981. p.10-11.

GREAT BRITAIN--CHESTER--HISTORIC PRESERVATION

Insall, Donald W. "Conservation in Action." <u>Urban Innovation Abroad</u>. May 1983. p. 2 & 4.

GREEK REVIVAL (ARCHITECTURE)

Schipa, Gregory. "A Greek Revival Restoration." <u>Fine Homebuilding</u>. February/ March 1981. p.48-51.

GREEK REVIVAL (ARCHITECTURE)

Roper, James H. and Van Jones Martin (photographer). "Eutaw; a Treasure of Greek Revival Architecture Distinguishes This Alabama Community." <u>American Preservation</u>. Nov./Dec. 1979. pp. 49-59.

GREEK REVIVAL (ARCHITECTURE)--U.S.--KANSAS

Cawthorn, Richard J. "Greek Revival Architecture is Rare in Kansas." 4th in a series on the architecture of Kansas. <u>Kansas Preservation</u>. Vol. VI, No. 5, July-August 1984. pp. 4-6.

GREENBELTS

Kunofsky, Judith and Larry Orman. "Greenbelts and the Well-Planned City." <u>Sierra</u>. Vol. 70, No. 6, Nov./Dec. 1985. p. 42-48.

GREENBELTS

Nelson, Arthur C. "A Unifying View of Greenbelt Influences on Regional Land Values and Implications for Regional Planning Policy." <u>Growth and Change</u>. Vol. 16, No. 2, Apr. 1985. p. 43-48.

GREENHOUSES

"The Committee for the Restoration of Phipps Conservatory." <u>PHLF News</u>. No. 96, Winter 1985/86. p. 8.

GREENHOUSES--GREAT BRITAIN

"Crystal Pavilions." <u>Traditional Homes</u>. Jan. 1986. p. 8-15.

GUIDEBOOKS

Fondersmith, John. "Guides to Cities."
American Urban Guidenotes. Vol. 3, No. 4, September 1984. Entire Issue. 12 p.

GUIDEBOOKS

"New Wave of Architectural Guidebooks."
American Urban Guidenotes. Vol. 4, No. 1, Dec. 1985. Entire Issue.

GUIDEBOOKS--PERIODICALS

American Urban Guidenotes. Summer 1979.

A new quarterly "Newsletter of Guidebooks," although its major emphasis will be on urban guidebooks, the newsletter will also provide information on a wide range of guidebook developments.

GUIDEBOOKS--U.S.--NEW YORK--NEW YORK CITY

Alpern, Andrew. "A Guide to Guidebooks."
Metropolis. July/Aug. 1985. p. 34-35.

HALF-TIMBERED HOUSES

Lynch, Bruce. "The Popular English Revival Style." The Old-House Journal. July 1983. pp. 117-120.

HANDICAPPED

Access. A new periodical published by the Arts & Special Constituencies Project/National Endowment for the Arts. (issue number one, June 1980)

HANDICAPPED

James, Marianna S. "One Step at a Time: How Winterthur Approaches Program Accessibility." History News. July 1981. pp. 10 - 15.

HANDICAPPED

Molloy, Larry. "Museum Accessibility: The Continuing Dialogue." Museum News. November/December 1981. pp. 50-57.

HANDICAPPED

"Museums and Disabled Persons." Museums. Vol. XXXIII, No. 3, 1981. Entire Issue.
PARTIAL CONTENTS: Gee, Maureen. The Power to Act--Treff, Hans-Albert. Educating the Public--Heath, Alison. Common sense, patience and enthusiasm.

HANDICAPPED

Reque, Barbara. "What You Can Do for the Blind for $108.86: Chicago Historical Society Provides and Innovative Program." History News. July 1981. pp. 16 - 19.

HARBORS

Wallace, David A. "An Insider's Story of the Inner Harbor." Planning, September 1979. pp. 20-24.

Note: On Baltimore's harbor.

HAWAII--HONOLULU--IOLANI PALACE

"Victorian Setting for Hawaiian Royalty."
AIA Journal. March 1982. pp. 79-83.

HEATING

Alexander, Laurence A. "District Heating Returns to Downtown as Economic Development Tool." Downtown Idea Exchange. Vol. 31, No. 20, October 1984. pp. 305.

HEATING

Capen, Judith M. "Staying Warm in Old Houses, Part 2." News, Capitol Hill (D.C.) Restoration Society, Dec. 1985. p. 4-5.

HEATING

"District Heating Re-Emerges as Economic Development Tool." Urban Outlook. Vol. 6, No. 5, August 14, 1984. pp. 3-6.

HEATING

Estoque, Justin. "Heating and Cooling Robie House." APT Bulletin. Vol. 19, No. 2, 1987. p. 38-51.

HEATING

Labine, Roland A. "Fine-Tuning A Hot Water Heating System : Radiator Adjustments Save Energy". Old-House Journal. November 1980. p.166-167.

HEATING

Labine, Roland A. "Making an Old Furnace Oil-efficient." Old-House Journal. December 1980. p.189.

HEATING

Robinson, Jeremy. "Tuning Up a Steam Heating System." Old House Journal. November 1981. pp. 252-256.

HIGHWAY PLANNING--CITIZEN PARTICIPATION

"Proposed Elevated Highway Vigorously Opposed in Mobile." Architecture. Vol. 73, No. 11, November 1984. pp. 33, 38.

HISTORIC AMERICAN BUILDINGS SURVEY--ARKANSAS

Carfagno, Jaci. "HABS Team in State for First Time Since Great Depression." DANCH Directions (Dept. of Arkansas Natural and Cultural Heritage). Vol. III, Issue IV, Fall 1984. p. 4.

HISTORIC BUILDINGS

Eckardt, Allison M. "The John Jay Homestead State Historic Site, Bedford, New York." Antiques. Jul. 1979. pp. 166-175.

HISTORIC BUILDINGS

Handler, Mimi. "About the Thomas Huckins House." Early American Life. Vol. 17, No. 4, Aug. 1986. p. 58-65.

HISTORIC BUILDINGS

Henning, Lisbeth. "Before-You-Buy Tips For Old-House Hunter." The Indiana Preservationist, Historic Landmarks Foundation of Indiana. No. 2, 1984. p. 9.

HISTORIC BUILDINGS

"House Tours: The Backbone of Fund Raising." Economic Growth & Revitalization Report. No. 86-19, Oct. 14, 1986. p. 5-7.

HISTORIC BUILDINGS

Lewis Taylor. "The Permanence of Oak Hill: Former Estate of President James Monroe." Architectural Digest. May 1979. pp. 62-69.

HISTORIC BUILDINGS

"Sites, A Literary Magazine on Buildings, Places & Monuments."

HISTORIC BUILDINGS

Thornton, Christopher. "Using Historic Settings for Special Occasions." Heritage Scotland. Vol. 3, No. 4, Winter 1986. p. 12.

HISTORIC BUILDINGS--ADAPTIVE USE--FRANCE

Simounet, Roland. "Picasso Palais." Architectural Review. Vol. 153, No. 1073, July 1986. p. 19-25.

Conversion of a 17th century mansion to a museum.

HISTORIC BUILDINGS--AUSTRALIA

"The National Trust of South Australia in the Jubilee 150 Year 1986." Heritage Australia. Vol. 5, No. 1, Autumn 1986. p. 23-30.

Fifteen historic buildings are pictured and discussed.

HISTORIC BUILDINGS--CANADA

Cameron, Christina. "Canadian Inventory of Historic Building." APT Bulletin. Vol. 18, No. 1 & 2, 1986. p. 49 - 53.

HISTORIC BUILDINGS--CANADA

Pettit, Barbara. "Teetering on the Pacific Rim." Canadian Heritage. May/June 1986. p. 14-19.

Development is endangering Vancouver's historic buildings.

HISTORIC BUILDINGS--CONSERVATION & RESTORATION

AE Concepts in Wood Design. July-August 1981. Entire issue.

HISTORIC BUILDINGS--CONSERVATION AND RESTORATION

Adams, Clare W. "Avoiding Common Renovation Mistakes. Part I: Interiors." New Orleans Preservation in Print. Vol. 13, No. 7, Sept. 1986. p. 7.

HISTORIC BUILDINGS--CONSERVATION AND RESTORATION

Alexander, David. "Reviving Hue --Vietnam's Broken Heart on the River of Perfumes." Smithsonian. Vol. 17, No. 3, 1986. p. 44-55.

The buildings and tombs of Hue, former imperial capital of Vietnam, are being restored

HISTORIC BUILDINGS--CONSERVATION AND RESTORATION

"Architectural Lankmarks." Progressive Architecture. Nov. 1981. Entire issue.

Partial Contents: Back to Basics, San Francisco de Asis, Ranchos de Taos, N.M.--The Altes Museum Renewed--The Best of Both Worlds, Helmsley Palace Hotel and Urban Center, N.Y.--Down and Dirty in 1917, Hallidie Building, San Francisco--Wrighting Wrongs? Arizona Biltmore Hotel, Phoenix, Az.

HISTORIC BUILDINGS--CONSERVATION AND RESTORATION

"Bank to Restore Rare Mansion." Historic Denver News. Vol. 15, No. 6. June 1986. p. 1.

Restoration of the Croke-Patterson-Campbell Mansion with its "Chateauesque" style.

HISTORIC BUILDINGS--CONSERVATION AND RESTORATION

Bergmann, Richard and Lynn Hamilton. "Restoration of the Lockwood-Mathews Mansion: Preserving a Masterpiece of Craftsmanship." Technology & Conservation. Winter 1982. pp. 14-25.

HISTORIC BUILDINGS--CONSERVATION AND RESTORATION

Boles, Daralice D. "Teaching Architecture." Progressive Architecture. Sept. 1986. p. 128-131.

A Columbia University building designed by McKim, Mead & White renovated into a fine arts center.

HISTORIC BUILDINGS--CONSERVATION AND RESTORATION

Bruno, Andrea. "Le Minaret de Jam, Afghanistan." Monumentum. September 1983. pp. 189-200.

HISTORIC BUILDINGS--CONSERVATION AND RESTORATION

Buttolph, Betty Yarbrough. "After Eleven Years of Old-House Living I've Got Some Pet Theories of Preservation." Old-House Journal. Vol. 14, No. 3, April 1986. p. 113-116.

HISTORIC BUILDINGS--CONSERVATION AND RESTORATION

"Congress Starts Preservation Study." Headquarters Heliogram. No. 178, Aug. 1986. p. 1.

GAO will review preservation plans for federally owned historic buildings.

HISTORIC BUILDINGS--CONSERVATION AND RESTORATION

Doermann, Elisabeth W. "Restoration of Electrical Systems in the James J. Hill House: Support of Historic Interpretation in an Adaptive-Use Site." APT Bulletin. Vol. 18, No. 3, 1986. p. 56-74.

HISTORIC BUILDINGS--CONSERVATION & RESTORATION

Feilden, Bernard M. "Presentation of Historic Buildings". Parks. April/May/June 1980. p.11-15.

HISTORIC BUILDINGS--CONSERVATION & RESTORATION

Floyd, Candace. "Coming full circle : a master restorationist trains a new generation of craftsmen." History News. July 1980. p.9-12

HISTORIC BUILDINGS--CONSERVATION AND RESTORATION

Goody, Nancy. "Rehabilitation and Tax Act Certification." Albany Preservation Report. Dec. 1982. pp. 7-11.

HISTORIC BUILDINGS--CONSERVATION AND RESTORATION.

"Harris Terrace." The National Trust Journal (Queenland, Australia). June 1986. p. 22.

A brick building built in the 1860's in an early Australian Victorian terrace style has been restored and renovated.

HISTORIC BUILDINGS--CONSERVATION AND RESTORATION

Howard, James Murray. "Restoration of Jefferson's Pavilions." Notes on Virginia. No. 29, Fall 1986. p. 11-14.

Restoration of the pavilions at the University of Virginia.

HISTORIC BUILDINGS--CONSERVATION AND RESTORATION

Kerski, Michael J. "Preserving Hartford's Architecture: Restoration Progress Firsthand." Conservancy News. Vol. 3, No. 6. Jan./Feb. 1987. pp. 1; 5; 11.

HISTORIC BUILDINGS--CONSERVATION AND RESTORATION

Kissel, Joanne. "The Rehabilitation of the Harris House : Preservation from the Owner's Perspective." Dimensions. Winter 1986. p. 2-6.

HISTORIC BUILDINGS--CONSERVATION AND RESTORATION

Lewis, Raymond. "Waverly Cottage: the Shone-Charley House." The Table Rock Sentinel. Nov. 1986. p. 21-27.

Vertical File
HISTORIC BUILDINGS--CONSERVATION AND RESTORATION

Mahoney, Paula. "Loving Care by Homeless Workers Helps Restore Derelict Mansion." Western City. Vol. 62, No. 9. Sep. 1986. pp. 12-15. (VF)

HISTORIC BUILDINGS--CONSERVATION AND RESTORATION

McCormick, Keith and Barbara. "Reviving a Revival: Uncovering the Past of a St. Paul Gem." Architecture Minnesota. Vol. 12, No. 3, May/June 1986. p. 38, 41.

Rehabilitation of a historically significant Greek Revival house.

HISTORIC BUILDINGS--CONSERVATION AND RESTORATION

McNamara, Sarah. "Summerizing the Victorian House." The Old-House Journal. June 1984. Vol. XII, No. 5. pp. 104-105.

HISTORIC BUIDINGS--CONSERVATION AND RESTORATION

Preston, Irene. "For People Who Belong in Old Houses; Live-in-a-Landmark; Alabama's Unusual Preservation Program Helps Families Restore Old Homes for Living." Americana. Nov./Dec. 1979. pp. 38-43.

HISTORIC BUILDINGS--CONSERVATION AND RESTORATION

Restoration Products News. V.1, n.1 October 1980. Published by the Old-House Journal Corp.

HISTORIC BUILDINGS--CONSERVATION AND RESTORATION

Schultz, Danielle L. "Mind Over Matter, Psychologically Surviving a Restoration." The Old-House Journal. Vol. XII, No. 4, May 1984. pp. 80-81.

HISTORIC BUILDINGS--CONSERVATION AND RESTORATION

Sherwood, Glenn V. "Preserving Historic Buildings Makes Sense." Colorado Heritage News. July 1986. p. 7.

HISTORIC BUILDINGS--CONSERVATION AND RESTORATION

"Survival Plan." Traditional Homes. July 1986. pp. 19-29.

Money generated by the conversion of a Palladian mansion to houses and cottages helped defray the cost of roof and other repairs.

HISTORIC BUILDINGS--CONSERVATION AND RESTORATION-- CANADA

"Faithful Restoration." The Canadian Architect. Vol. 31, No. 8, Aug. 1986. p. 25-29.

Month-by-month restoration of a private men's club shown in detailed illustrations.

HISTORIC BUILDINGS--CONSERVATION AND RESTORATION--GERMAN DEMOCRATIC REPUBLIC

Magirius, Heinrich. "The Reconstruction of the State Opera House in Dresden." Monumentum. September 1983. pp. 165-174.

HISTORIC BUILDINGS--CONSERVATION AND RESTORA- TION--U.S.--ALABAMA

"Fendall Hall Returns to Victorian Era Splendor." The Preservation Report. Vol. 13, No. 8, Sept./Oct. 1986. p. 1, 3.

HISTORIC BUILDINGS--CONSERVATION AND RESTORATION-- U.S.--ALABAMA--HUNTSVILLE

Callahan, Nancy. "Saving Harrison Brothers." Americana. Vol. 13, No. 1, Mar./Apr. 1985. p. 11.

Historic hardware store purchased by Historic Huntsville Foundation.

HISTORIC BUILDINGS--CONSERVATION AND RESTORA- TION--U.S.--COLORADO--DENVER

"Ford House to Be Restored As Black American West Museum." Historic Denver News. Vol. 15, No. 7, July 1986. p. 6.

The house of Denver's first Black woman physician to be restored.

HISTORIC BUILDINGS--CONSERVATION AND RESTORATION-- U.S.--GEORGIA

"FCF Undertakes Its Largest Project: 'Lion House' to be Stabilized." Historic Columbus Foundation. Vol. 18, No. 1, Winter 1987. p. 1-4.

HISTORIC BUILDINGS--CONSERVATION AND RESTORA- TION--U.S.--ILLINOIS--EVANSTON

"Mansion Metamorphosis." Commercial Renovation. Vol. 8, No. 4, Aug. 1986. p. 32-39.

Restoration of the Chateauesque head- quarters of the Evanston (IL) Historical Society.

HISTORIC BUILDINGS--CONSERVATION AND RESTORA- TION--U.S.--ILLINOIS--OAK PARK

Brenner, Douglas. "Wright at Home Again." Architectural Record. Sept. 1986. p. 118-125.

Restoration of the Frank Lloyd Wright Home and Studio, Oak Park, Illinois.

HISTORIC BUILDINGS--CONSERVATION AND RESTORATION--U.S.--MASSACHUSETTS--REHOBOTH

Kirk, John T. "Restoring the Daniel Bliss house: historical accuracy and personal vision". Antiques. Vol. 127, No. 2, Feb. 1985. p. 438-453.

HISTORIC BUILDINGS--CONSERVATION AND RESTORATION-- U.S.--NEW YORK

"Restoration of Montgomery Place Preserves Livingston Legacy." Preservation League of New York State Newsletter. Vol. 12, No. 4. Fall 1986. p. 7.

HISTORIC BUILDINGS--CONSERVATION AND RESTORATION --U.S.--NEW YORK--NEW YORK CITY

Strasser, Peter et. al. "Restoring a Greek Revival Townhouse." Fine Homebuilding. No. 29, Oct./Nov. 1985. p. 62-67.

Interior restoration work on 1837 townhouse described.

HISTORIC BUILDINGS--CONSERVATION AND RESTORATION
--U.S.--RHODE ISLAND--NEWPORT

"Winter Work." Newport Gazette. No. 101,
Feb. 1985. p. 10-11.

HISTORIC BUILDINGS--CONSERVATION AND RESTORATION
--U.S.--WASHINGTON, D.C.

"First Phase of Pension Building Renovation
for Museum Finished". Architecture. Feb. 1985.
p. 26-7, 32.

HISTORIC BUILDINGS--CONSERVATION AND RESTORATION
--U.S.--WASHINGTON, D.C.

"Restoration of White House Uncovers Ex-
quisite Carvings." Architecture. Vol. 73,
No. 11, November 1984. p. 14.

HISTORIC BUILDINGS--GREAT BRITAIN

Aslet, Clive. "Princely Dwellings : Houses of the Royal Younger
Sons." Country Life. Vol. 180, No.
4640, July 24, 1986. p. 216-221.

Houses occupied by the younger sons of
the Royal Family from the Hanoverian
accession to the early 20th century.

HISTORIC BUILDINGS--FRANCE

Nicot, Guy. "Le Palais de l'Elysee,
L'architecture." Monuments Historiques.
No. 132, Avril-Mai 1984. pp. 65-84.

HISTORIC BUILDINGS--MAINTENANCE AND REPAIR

Crosby, Anthony. "Preservation Maintenance in the Southwest." APT Bulletin. Vol.
18, No. 3, 1986. p. 48-55.

Maintenance important to prevent expen-
sive restoration and loss of irreplaceable
fabric.

HISTORIC BUILDINGS--GUIDELINES

"The National Register." Iowa Historian.
Vol. 1, No. 2, Apr. 1987. p. 4-6.

Eligibility guidelines for the National
Register of Historic Places.

HISTORIC BUILDINGS--LAW AND LEGISLATION

"New Law for Old Buildings." Preservation Report. Vol. 8, No. 3, May/
June 1986. p. 4

Buffalo, N.Y., Common Council passed
updated landmarks preservation bill.

HISTORIC BUILDINGS--MAINTENANCE AND REPAIR

Marmet, Terry. "Caring for Historic
Masonry Buildings: Proper Repair Treatments
Help Preserve Older Masonry Buildings."
Kansas Preservation. Vol. 8, No. 5, July-
Aug. 1986. p. 6-8.

HISTORIC BUILDINGS--PERIODICALS

Historic Houses, February 1979.

Note: A new newsletter of the Historic House Association of America. It includes articles on the
activities of the Association and articles on topics
of interest to owners of historic houses. It also
includes reviews of books and pamphlets.

HISTORIC BUILDINGS--RESEARCH

Baxter, Robert W. "Architectural Research, A
Brief Overview." Heritage West. Vol. 8, No. 2,
Summer 1984. pp. 16-17.

HISTORIC BUILDINGS--RESEARCH

Ellsworth, Lucius F. and Linda V.
"House-Reading: How to Study Historic Houses
as Symbols of Society". History News. May 1980.
p. 9-13.

HISTORIC BUILDINGS--RESEARCH

McGuckian, Eileen. "Researching & Dating Your
Historic House." The Montgomery County Preservationist. Vol. 2, No. 2, Oct./Nov. 1986. p. 7-8.

HISTORIC BUILDINGS--RESEARCH

Pearce, Sally. "Researching the History of
Your Home." Colorado Heritage News. Mar. 1986,
p. 5.

Emphasis on resources in Colorado.

HISTORIC BUILDINGS--RESEARCH

"Researching Your House History."
Old-House Journal. Vol. 15, No. 1, Jan/
Feb. 1987. p. 48-53.
Baker, David. 'Title Searching.' p.
48-51.
Romano, Deborah. 'Other Sources.' p.51.
Wolsiffer, Kathleen. 'The Library of
Congress.' p. 52-53.

HISTORIC BUILDINGS --RESEARCH

Tite, Graham. "Dating from Documents."
Traditional Homes. Vol. 3, No. 2, Nov. 1986.
p. 46-51.

The use of 18th and 19th century records
for dating historic buildings.

HISTORIC BUILDINGS--RESEARCH

Tite, Graham. "Dating from Domesday."
Traditional Homes. Vol. 3, No. 1. Oct. 1986.
pp. 78-83.

Relevance of the Domesday Books and other
early records to the dating of buildings constructed
much later.

HISTORIC BUILDINGS--RESEARCH--U.S.--VIRGINIA

Chambers, S. Allen. "HABS in Virginia: 52
Years of Documenting the Commonwealth's Architecture." Notes on Virginia. No. 26, Spring 1985.
p. 8-15.

HISTORIC BUILDINGS--SECURITY MEASURES

Swearingen, David. "Old-House Security. Part I:
Perimenter Security." Old-House Journal. Vol.14,
No.9, Nov. 1986. p.429-433.

HISTORIC BUILDINGS--SECURITY MEASURES

Swearingen, David. "Old-House Security,
Part Two: Locks & Alarms." Old-House Journal.
Vol. 19, No. 10, Dec. 1986. p. 472-475.

HISTORIC BUILDINGS--U.S.--CALIFORNIA

Hess, Alan. "Monsanto House of the
Future." Fine Homebuilding. No. 34, Aug./
Sept. 1986. p. 70-75.

A plastic house built in the 1950's
turned out not to solve structural problems
more efficiently and inexpensively than
houses built of more traditional materials.

HISTORIC BUILDINGS--U.S.--CALIFORNIA--LOS ANGELES

"Octagon House." L.A. Architect. July 1986.
p. 3.

The historic Longfellow octagon house to be
moved to Heritage Square historical park.

HISTORIC BUILDINGS--U.S.--CALIFORNIA--SAN FRANCISCO

"Heritage Wins Protection for Old Wells Fargo
Building." Heritage Newsletter. (Foundation for
San Francisco Architectural Heritage). Vol. 14,
No. 1. Apr. 1986. p. 1.

San Francisco's Downtown Plan allows a one time
opportunity to appeal the ratings of buildings
under the Plan.

HISTORIC BUILDINGS--U.S.--GEORGIA

"Architecture Profile: The Boddie House."
The Rambler, Vol. 13, No. 4, Winter 1987. p. 12.

HISTORIC BUILDINGS--U.S.--GEORGIA

Jablonski, Michael. "Visit Georgia's Sites:
The Vann House." The Rambler. Vol. 13, No. 4,
Winter 1987. p. 14.

HISTORIC BUILDINGS--U.S.--HAWAII

"Ali'iolani Hale: Restoring Hawaii's Judicial
History." Historic Hawaii. Vol. 13, No. 2, Feb. 1987.
p. 8-9.

HISTORIC BUILDINGS--U.S.--ILLINOIS--CHICAGO

"What's Happening in Chicago? The Partial
Designation Crisis." Landmarks Preservation Council
of Illinois. Vol. 16, No. 2, Mar./Apr. 1987.

HISTORIC BUILDINGS--ILLINOIS--EVANSTON

Yant, Gwen Sommers. "Evanston Landmark
Estate to be Redeveloped." The Commissioner (IL).
May 1987. p. 4-5.

The two-acre Wilson Estate in Evanston Lakeshore
Historic District example of public /private
cooperation.

HISTORIC BUILDINGS--U.S.--KENTUCKY

Godbey, Marty. "Whitehaven's Miraculous
Rebirth." Victorian Homes. Vol. 6, Issue 1,
Winter, 1987. p. 50-55.

A restored colonial revival mansion in
Paducah, KY, now a tourist center.

HISTORIC BUILDINGS--U.S.--LOUISIANA

Bacot, H. Parrott. "Kent Plantation House
in Alexandria, Louisiana." Antiques. July 1984.
pp. 134-141.

HISTORIC BUILDINGS--U.S.--LOUISIANA--NEW ORLEANS

Chretia, John. "Historic Goodrich-Stanley House
Offers Contemporary Livability." New Orleans
Preservation in Print. Vol. 14, No. 4, May 1987
p. 12-13.

HISTORIC BUILDINGS--U.S.--LOUISIANA--NEW ORLEANS

Walters, Jonathan. "Landmarks of Democracy."
New Orleans Preservation in Print. Vol. 14, No. 4
May 1987. p. 8-11.

HISTORIC BUILDINGS--U.S.--MAINE

"Maine Citizens for Historic Preservation 1982
Historic Properties Studies." Summer 1982.

HISTORIC BUILDINGS--U.S.--MAINE--KETTERY POINT

"Lady Pepperrell Forever." Yankee, Vol.
49, No. 1, January 1985, pp. 142-146.

HISTORIC BUILDINGS--U.S.--MARYLAND

"Milimar: Montgomery County's Oldest House?"
Montgomery County Preservationist. Vol. 2, No. 5,
Apr./May 1987. p. 3.

HISTORIC BUILDINGS--U.S.--MARYLAND

"Under the Dome." The Designer Specifier. Vol. 28,
No. 358, Feb. 1987. p. 17-18.

America's oldest stockbrockerage firm, Baltimore's
Alex Brown & Sons, restored by Michael Asner Associates.

HISTORIC BUILDINGS--U.S.--MARYLAND--MONTGOMERY COUNTY

"Montgomery's Oldest Houses."(Part I) The
Montgomery County Preservationist. Vol. 2, No. 2.
Oct./Nov. 1986. pp. 1; 4-5.

HISTORIC BUILDINGS--U.S.--MARYLAND--MONTGOMERY
COUNTY

"Montgomery's Oldest Houses" (Part II) The
Montgomery County Preservationist. Vol. 2, No. 3,
Dec. 1986/Jan. 1987. p. 1, 6.

HISTORIC BUILDINGS--U.S.--MARYLAND--MONTGOMERY COUNTY

"Montgomery's Oldest Houses." (Part III)
The Montgomery County Preservationist. Vol. 2,
No. 4. Feb./Mar. 1987. pp. 1; 7.

HISTORIC BUILDINGS--U.S.--MASSACHUSETTS

Crosbie, Michael J. "Richardson Library
Returned to its Original Luster."
Architecture. Nov. 1986. p. 72-74.

Austin Hall at Harvard Law School,
designed by Henry Hobson Richardson, has
been restored.

HISTORIC BUILDINGS--U.S.--MASSACHUSETTS

Hall, Ruth B. "The Mayflower Society
Museum, Plymouth Massachusetts." (Edward
Winslow House.) Antiques. August 1984.
pp. 294-302.

HISTORIC BUILDINGS--U.S.--MASSACUSETTS

Monagan, Charles. "In Search of the Oldest
House." Yankee. July 1986. p. 84-89, 132.

The Balch House and the Fairbanks House vie for
the title of oldest house in Massachusetts.

HISTORIC BUILDINGS--U.S.--MASSACHUSETTS

"The Oldest House on Nantucket Observes Its three Hundredth Birthday." Historic Nantucket. Vol. 34, No. 2, Oct. 1986. p. 7-13.

HISTORIC BUILDINGS--U.S.--MASSACHUSETTS--BOSTON

Detwiller, Frederic C. "The Evolution of the Shirley-Eustis House." Old-Time New England. Vol. LXX, 1980. p.17-30.

HISTORIC BUILDINGS--U.S.--MASSACHUSETTS--CAMBRIDGE

Stachiw, Myron O. "Cultural Change in Cambridge: The Cooper-Frost-Austin House and its Occupants". Old-Time New England. Vol. LXX, 1980. p. 31-44.

HISTORIC BUILDINGS--U.S.--MASSACHUSETTS--SALEM

Tolles, Bryant F. Jr. "Living With Antiques: The Putnam-Balch House, Salem, Massachusetts." Antiques. Vol 127, No. 1. Jan. 1985. pp. 277-283.

Vertical File
HISTORIC BUILDINGS--U.S.--NEVADA

Comstock Driving Tour/Virginia City Walking Tour. Comstock, NV: Comstock Historic District Commission, 1986. (VF)

HISTORIC BUILDINGS--U.S.--NEW HAMPSHIRE--PLAIN-FIELD

"To Be Sorted Later." Yankee. Vol. 49, No. 10, Oct. 1985. p. 142-151.

The Oaks, now for sale, home of painter Maxfield Parrish, featured.

HISTORIC BUILDINGS--U.S.--NEW JERSEY

Lyle, Charles T. "Buildings of the Monmouth County Historical Association." Antiques. Jan. 1980. pp. 176-185.

HISTORIC BUILDINGS--U.S.--NEW YORK--NEW YORK

Alpern, Andrew. "A Walk up Fifth Avenue." Metropolis. Sept. 1986. p. 56-59.

HISTORIC BUILDINGS--U.S.--NEW YORK--STATEN ISLAND

Picaid, Joseph M. "Visible City: Five Greek Revival Houses on Staten Island." Metropolis. June 1986. pp. 46-48.

HISTORIC BUILDINGS--U.S.--NORTH CAROLINA--EDENTON

Cheeseman, Bruce S. "The Survival of the Cupola House: 'A Venerable Old Mansion'." The North Carolina Historical Review. Vol.63, No. 1, Jan. 1986. p. 40-73.

HISTORIC BUILDINGS--U.S.--OHIO

"Volunteers Help Find Ohio's Past." Ohio Preservation. Vol. 6, No. 6, June 1986. p. 1

Inventories of 300 older buildings and archaeological sites in 16 Ohio communities were made during Ohio's first Survey Saturday, May 17.

HISTORIC BUILDINGS--U.S.--OHIO--CINCINNATI

Appel, Susan K. "Building and Beer: Brewery Architecture of Cincinnati." Queen City Heritage. Vol. 44, No. 2, Summer 1986. p. 3-20.

HISTORIC BUILDINGS--U.S.--PENNSYLVANIA--CHESTER COUNTY

Cook, Claudia. "Living over the Store." Early American Life. Vol. 17, No. 5, Oct. 1986. p. 12-21.

An 18th-century inn, a forge, and a county store, the oldest continuing store in America, are located in Chester County, Pa.

HISTORIC BUILDINGS--U.S.--VIRGINIA

Hodges, Mary Ellen N. "Camden: Another Look Seventeen Years after Registration." Notes on Virginia. No. 29, Fall 1986. p. 21-25.

HISTORIC BUILDINGS--U.S.--VIRGINIA

"The Virginia Landmarks Register." Notes on Virginia. No. 29, Fall 1986. p. 4-10.

HISTORIC BUILDINGS--U.S.--VIRGINIA--ALEXANDRIA

Handler, Mimi. "Alexandria Houses and Gardens." Early American Life. Vol. 18, No. 2, April 1987. p. 16-32.

HISTORIC BUILDINGS--U.S.--VIRGINIA--FAIRFAX COUNTY

Chittenden, Betsy. "A Brief Tour of Historic Buildings in Western Fairfax County." Fairfax Chronicles. Vol. 9, No. 3, Aug./Oct. 1985. p. 1, 4-5.

HISTORIC BUILDINGS--U.S. GOVT--NATIONAL PARK SERVICE

McDonald, Travis C. "Historic Structures of the National Park Service." CRM Bulletin. Mar. 1981. pp. 1-2; 8-9.

HISTORIC DISTRICTS

"BEWARE the Cable TV Wires." PPS News, Newsletter of the Providence Preservation Society. Vol. XXII, No. 2, March/April 1984. p. 3.

HISTORIC DISTRICTS

"Historic District Rehab and Davis-Bacon: a Cautionary Tale." Urban Conservation Report. Vol. 10, No. 11, Nov. 29, 1986. p. 3-4.

Disagreement over application of Davis-Bacon rules in Albany, N.Y.

HISTORIC DISTRICTS

Jamieson, Walter. "Creating Alberta's First Historic Area in Fort Macleod." Monumentum. September 1983. pp. 221-232.

HISTORIC DISTRICTS

LeClaire, Anne D. "Historic Districting: pregnant town issue of the '80's." Yankee. March 1981. p. 86-96.

HISTORIC DISTRICTS

Maryland Association of Historic District Commissions newsletter

new
from November 1982

HISTORIC DISTRICTS

Moore, Evelyn. "Lebanon Historic District." Historic Illinois. Vol. 9, No. 5, Feb. 1987. p. 8-9.

HISTORIC DISTRICTS

Niehaus, Charles. "The Historic District: Making Preservation Effective on a Local Level." First of two parts. The Indiana Preservationist, Historic Landmarks Foundation of Indiana. No. 2, 1984. pp. 1-2.

HISTORIC DISTRICTS

"NYC Designation: A Chance to Think." Progressive Architecture. November 1981. pp. 42-51.

HISTORIC DISTRICTS

"Second Avenue- Tough Decisions for Nashville." History-Gram. No. 41, Fall 1986/Winter 1987. p. 1-2.

Development threatens Nashville historic district.

HISTORIC DISTRICTS

Stipe, Robert. "Local Preservation Legislation: Questions and Answers." Preservation League of New York State. Technical Series/No. 8. 4 pp.

HISTORIC DISTRICTS--ARGENTINA--CORDOBA

"A City to Be Seen and Read." Architectural Record. July 1984. pp. 114-121.

HISTORIC DISTRICTS--CANADA

"Donut Shop No Sweet Affair." Preservation Action. Oct. 1986. p. 2.

A franchise donut shop refuses renovation design that would be compatible with the surrounding historic buildings.

HISTORIC DISTRICTS--CONSERVATION AND RESTORATION

Baymiller, Joanna. "St. Paul's Lowertown in Progress." Progressive Architecture. Oct. 1982. p. 56.

HISTORIC DISTRICTS--CONSERVATION AND RESTORATION--GEORGIA

"Restoration Underway on Jekyll." The Rambler, Newsletter of the Georgia Trust. Vol. 11, No. 3, Summer 1984. pp. 9, 11.

HISTORIC DISTRICTS--CONSERVATION AND RESTORATION

"Parks Open in Great Falls Historic District." Society for Industrial Archeology Newsletter. Summer 1982. pp. 1 & 9.

HISTORIC DISTRICTS--CONSERVATION AND RESTORATION

"Historic Districts." Progressive Architecture. November 1982. pp. 89-119. Entire Issue.
CONTENTS: Deco Rating(Miami Beach)--Low Gloss (Saratoga Springs)--New Goods in Old Tins(Granville, Island, Vancouver)--Oldham, Sally. The Rewards of Preservation--Goldstein, Barbara. Opulance on Olive (Oviatt Building, Los Angeles)--Richardson Restored (Senate Chambers, State Capitol, Albany, N.Y.).

HISTORIC DISTRICTS--CONSERVATION AND RESTORATION

Edwards, David. "Two Virginia Historic Districts: a study in collaborative effort." Notes on Virginia. No. 27, Fall 1985. p. 29-33.

HISTORIC DISTRICTS--CONSERVATION AND RESTORATION

Blake, Barbara. "Capitalizing the Charm of Wall Street." Discovery News. Vol. 1, No. 2, Spring 1986. p. 4-5.

HISTORIC DISTRICTS--CONSERVATION AND RESTORATION--U.S.--LOUISIANA--NEW ORLEANS

Hagstette, Kurt. "Lafayette Square Historic District." New Orleans Preservation in Print. Vol. 12, No. 8, Oct. 1985. p. 4-6.

HISTORIC DISTRICTS--ECONOMIC ASPECTS

"Scattered-Site Public Housing Generates Private Investment in Charleston Historic Area." Economic Growth and Revitalization. May 13, 1986. p. 5-6.

HISTORIC DISTRICTS--LAW AND LEGISLATION

"Preservation Ordinances Proliferate." Home Again. Summer 1984, No. 3. pp. 22-23.

HISTORIC DISTRICTS--LAW AND LEGISLATION--U.S.--FLORIDA--OCALA

"Ocala Approves Local Historic District." Florida Preservation News. Feb. 1985. p. 3.

HISTORIC DISTRICTS--LAW AND LEGISLATION--U.S.--TEXAS--DALLAS

Casey, Karen. "Conservation District Ordinance Readied." Historic Dallas. Vol. 9, No. 1, Jan./Feb. 1986. p. 5.

HISTORIC DISTRICTS--LAW AND LEGISLATION--U.S.--WEST VIRGINIA--HARPERS FERRY

Connors, Jill. "Dish Busters." Americana. Vol. 13, No. 1, Mar./Apr. 1985. p. 14.

Television radar dishes banned in historic town.

HISTORIC DISTRICTS--PLANNING--GERMANY--AUGSBURG

Hansjakob, Gottfried. "Konigsplatz Traffic Zone." Landscape Architecture. Vol. 75, No. 2, Mar./Apr. 1985. p. 52-55.

New transportation plan in medieval historic district described.

HISTORIC DISTRICTS--PLANNING--U.S.--SOUTH CAROLINA --CHARLESTON

"Extension of Old and Historic District Topic of January Meeting." Preservation Progress, (Preservation Society of Charleston). Vol. 29, No. 1, Jan. 1985. p. 1.

HISTORIC DISTRICTS--PLANNING--U.S.--SOUTH CAROLINA--CHARLESTON

"No Alternative Site for Charleston Courthouse Addition Says GSA." Urban Conservation Report. Vol. VIII, No. 13, July 31, 1984. p. 4.

HISTORIC DISTRICTS--PLANNING--U.S.--TENNESSEE-- RUGBY

"Rugby Colony Master Plan." Progressive Architecture. Jan. 1986. p. 108-113.

Winner of a P/A Award.

HISTORIC DISTRICTS--U.S.--ALABAMA

Hunter, Kevin. "From the Development Commission: the Leindauf District." Landmark Letter. Vol. 19, No. 2, 1986. pp. 14-16.

A historic district in Mobile, Alabama, is significant as an early 20th century suburb.

HISTORIC DISTRICTS--U.S.--ALABAMA--ATHENS

Caudle, Mildred W. "Protecting Athens, Alabama's Architectural Heritage". Small Town. Vol. 15, No. 4, Jan./Feb. 1985. p. 21-24.

HISTORIC DISTRICTS--U.S.--CALIFORNIA--HOLLYWOOD

"Hooray for Hollywood." California Preservation. Vol. 10, No. 3, July 1985. p. 1.

HISTORIC DISTRICTS, U.S.--CALIFORNIA--SAN DIEGO

"Chinese-American Thematic Historic District." Save Our Heritage Organization. Vol. 19, No. 5, May 1987. p. 4.

HISTORIC DISTRICTS--U.S.--CALIFORNIA-- SANTA BARBARA

Tuttle, Tom. "Santa Barbara's Landmark District: Brinkerhoff Avenue." Victorian Homes. Vol. 6, No. 3. Summer 1987. pp. 44 - 51.

HISTORIC DISTRICTS--U.S.--COLORADO--DENVER

"Baker District Passes State Review." Historic Denver News. Vol. 14, No. 9, Sept. 1985. p. 7.

Victorian Denver neighborhood to be nominated to National Register in October.

HISTORIC DISTRICTS--U.S.--FLORIDA

"Arts District Development Anchors Downtown." Downtown Idea Exchange. Vol. 34, No. 8, Apr. 15, 1987. p. 5

Lincoln Road Arts District, Miami, Florida.

HISTORIC DISTRICTS--U.S.--FLORIDA

Schaefer, Norah. "Morningside, Miami's New Historic District." Preservation Today (Dade Heritage Trust, Inc.). Vol. 1, No. 5, Spring 1985. p. 28-29.

HISTORIC DISTRICTS--U.S.--GEORGIA

Wolf, Janet C. "Applied Ethnography: Martin Luther King, Jr." CRM Bulletin. Vol. 10, No. 1, Feb. 1987. p. 5,7,8.

Conducting research for the MLK National Historic Site and Preservation District.

HISTORIC DISTRICTS--U.S.-GEORGIA--SAVANNAH

Horstmann, Neil W. "Proud Savannah." Place. Vol. 6, No. 9. May - June 1987. pp. 11 - 15.
Restoration of Savannah. (GA)

HISTORIC DISTRICTS--U.S.--HAWAII--OAHU

Wiig, Howard C. "Hale'iwa Slated to Become Historic District." Historic Hawaii News. Mar. 1984. pp. 2-3.

HISTORIC DISTRICTS --U.S.--ILLINOIS

O'Connell, Ed. " Edwardsville's LeClaire Historic District." Historic Illinois. Vol. 9, No. 3, Oct. 1986. p. 2-5.

An Illinois historic district significant for its social significance--it was designed as an ideal industrial community--rather than its architecture.

HISTORIC DISTRICTS--U.S.--ILLINOIS--ROCKTON

Moore, Evelyn R. "Rockton Historic District." Historic Illinois. Vol. 7, No. 4. Dec. 1984. pp. 12-13.

HISTORIC DISTRICTS--U.S.--KENTUCKY

"Tyler Settlement Rural Historic District." Preservation. Vol. 11, No. 1, Spring 1986. p. 1.

Kentucky to be one of only a few states to have a rural historic district listed in the National Register.

HISTORIC DISTRICTS--U.S.--LOUISIANA--NEW ORLEANS

Brooks, Jane S., Teresa Wilkenson and Alma H. Young. "Resolving Land Use Change in a Cooperative Mode the Jackson Brewery." Urban Land. June 1984. pp. 20-25.

HISTORIC DISTRICTS--U.S.--LOUISIANA--NEW ORLEANS

Cangelosi, Robert J., Jr. "Uptown National Register Historic District." New Orleans Preservation in Print. Vol. 12, No. 7, Sept. 1985. p. 11.

HISTORIC DISTRICTS--U.S.-LOUISIANA--NEW ORLEANS

McCabe, Carol. "The Vieux Carre of New Orleans." Early American Life. Vol. 18, No. 1. Feb. 1987. pp. 30-33; 76-77.

HISTORIC DISTRICTS--U.S.--MARYLAND

McCabe, Carol. "Annapolis, Maryland." Early American Life. August 1984. pp. 24-27, 70, 73.

HISTORIC DISTRICTS--U.S.--MASSACHUSETTS--DEERFIELD

Friary, Donald R. et al. "Introduction to Historic Deerfield." Antiques. Mar. 1985. p. 626-692.

HISTORIC DISTRICTS--U.S.--MASSACHUSETTS--BOSTON

Campoli, Lisa. "The Leather District." Boston Preservation Alliance Letter. Vol. 6, No. 1. Jan. 1985. pp. 3; 7-8.

HISTORIC DISTRICTS--U.S.--MICHIGAN

Channels, Newsletter of the Michigan Historic District Network. Vol. 1, No. 1. Feb. 1982.

HISTORIC DISTRICTS--U.S.--MINNESOTA--ST. PAUL

Hempl, Patricia. "Literary Landmarks." Architecture Minnesota. Vol. 10, No. 2, March/April 1984. pp. 50-51.

HISTORIC DISTRICTS--U.S.--MINNESOTA--ST. PAUL

"A Romantic Rowhouse Finds Its Past." Architecture Minnesota. Vol. 10, No. 2, March/April 1984. pp. 48-49.

HISTORIC DISTRICTS--U.S.--MINNESOTA--ST. PAUL

"St. Paul Living - Downstairs in a Summit Mansion, History in Detail." Architecture Minnesota. Vol. 10, No. 2, March/April 1984. pp. 40-43.

HISTORIC DISTRICTS--U.S.--MINNESOTA--ST. PAUL

Zahn, Thomas. "Can One of America's Best-Preserved Victorian Boulevards Remain That Way?" Architecture Minnesota. Vol. 10, No. 2, March/April 1984. p. 21.

HISTORIC DISTRICTS--U.S.--MINNESOTA--TAYLORS FALLS

King, Shannon. "On Angels Hill." Architecture Minnesota. Vol. 10, No. 4, July/August 1984. pp. 50-53.

HISTORIC DISTRICTS--U.S.--NEW JERSEY

Rothe, Leonard. "Plans for Historic District Move Ahead." Great Falls Newsletter. Spring 1987. p. 1, 5.

HISTORIC DISTRICTS--U.S.--NEW YORK--ALBANY

"Ten Broeck Historic District Expanded and Other Districts Nominated." Albany Preservation Report. Summer 1985. p. 15.

HISTORIC DISTRICTS--U.S.--NEW YORK--NEW YORK CITY

"Runs in the Silk Stocking." Metropolis. Aug./Sep. 1981. pp. 8-9.

HISTORIC DISTRICTS--U.S.--NORTH CAROLINA--CHARLESTON

Abbott, Shirley. "The Charleston Inheritance." American Heritage. Vol. 38, No. 3, Apr. 1987. p. 62-69.

Charleston's historic district.

HISTORIC DISTRICTS--U.S.--NORTH CAROLINA--CHARLOTTE--FOURTH WARD

"A Neighborhood Grows in Charlotte." Architecture. Oct. 1983. pp. 64-65.

HISTORIC DISTRICTS--U.S.--PENNSYLVANIA--PITTSBURGH

"The Fourth Avenue Historic District." PHLF News. No. 90, Summer 1986. p. 1.

Pittsburgh financial district.

HISTORIC DISTRICTS--U.S.--RHODE ISLAND--NEWPORT

Calvert, Catherine. "Christmas in Old Newport." Town and Country. Vol. 138, No. 5055, December 1984. pp. 189-201.

History of Newport and the efforts of the Newport Restoration Foundation are described.

HISTORIC DISTRICTS--U.S.--TEXAS--DALLAS

Gath, Jean. "West End Historic District, Dallas, Texas." Institute for Urban Design. Project Monograph. Vol. 2, No. 2. Sep. 1986. 8 p. (VF)

HISTORIC DISTRICTS--U.S.--UTAH

Notarianni, Philip. "The Tintic Mining District, Utah's Multiple Resource Historic District." Utah Preservation/Restoration. Vol. 2, No. 2, 1980. pp. 16 - 19.

HISTORIC DISTRICTS--U.S.--VIRGINIA--ALEXANDRIA

Morris, Philip. "QUEST Finds Alexandria, Va. A 'Special' Historic District." Architecture. May 1984. pp. 69, 71, 73.

Report of review team's findings.

HISTORIC DISTRICTS--U.S.--VIRGINIA--STAUNTON

"Staunton's National Register Districts." The Queen City Quarterly (Historic Staunton Foundation). Vol. 12, No. 2, Apr. 1985. p. 3-4.

HISTORIC FARMS

Main, Anita. "The New Vintners: As the American wine industry expands, grapes are now grown in the most unlikely - and historic - places." Americana. Vol. 12, No. 6, Jan./Feb. 1985. p. 50-52.

HISTORIC FARMS

Morain, Thomas. "In the American Grain: The Popularity of Living History Farms." *Journal of American Culture*, Fall 1979. pp. 548-557.

HISTORIC FARMS--NEW ENGLAND

"Our Farming Heritage on Display." *Yankee Magazine*. May 1984. pp. 46-60.

HISTORIC GARDENS

"The Gardens at Clermont." *Hudson River Heritage*. May 1984. p. 5.

HISTORIC GARDENS

Ries, Jane Silverstein. "Gardens of Tradition." *Historic Denver News*. Vol. 15, No. 4, April 1986. p. 8.

HISTORIC GARDENS

Williams, Richard L. "Jefferson: The Most Ardent Farmer in the State." *Smithsonian*. Vol. 15, No. 4, July 1984. pp. 68-77.

HISTORIC GARDENS--CONSERVATION AND RESTORATION

Batey, Mavis. "The Conservation and Restoration of Historic Gardens." *Transactions of the Ancient Monuments Society*. Vol. 28, 1984. pp. 114-122.

HISTORIC HOMES--NEW ENGLAND

"The Last of the Old Houses with Old-Fashioned Price Tags." *Yankee Magazine*, July 1984. pp. 126-130.

HISTORIC PRESERVATION

Ainslie, Michael. "Preservation takes on new directions." *Building Progress*. March 1981. p.2-3.

HISTORIC PRESERVATION

Bishir, Catherine W. "Making Value Judgments in State and Local Communities: What Does the Preservationist Need to Know?" *Newsletter, National Council on Public History*. Vol. 5, No. 4; Vol. 6, No. 1-2, 1985-1986. p. 1, 4-5.

HISTORIC PRESERVATION

Boles, Daralice D.; Thomas Fisher and Thomas Vonier. "What Price Success: P/A Round-table: Federal Government in Preservation." *Progressive Architecture*. Nov. 1985. p. 107-111, 140, 142.

Trust staffer Ian Spatz among panel of ten discussing the future of federal involvement in historic preservation.

HISTORIC PRESERVATION

Bruegmann, Robert. "What price preservation?" *Planning*. June 1980. p. 12-16.

HISTORIC PRESERVATION

Bullard, John. "Preservation in New Bedford." *CRM Bulletin*. Vol. 9, No. 5, Oct.-Dec. 1986. p. 12-13.

HISTORIC PRESERVATION

Bush, Bernard. "The New Jersey Historical Commission: A State Agency in Public History." *The Public Historian*. Fall 1981. pp. 33-44.

HISTORIC PRESERVATION

Chatfield-Taylor, Adele. "From Ruskin to Rouse: Heritage - Passion or Profit?" *Canadian Heritage*. Vol. 2, No. 3, July/Aug. 1985. p. 10-11.

HISTORIC PRESERVATION

"Cultural Heritage: International Campaigns." Panorama, Unesco Cultural Newsletter. No. 4, 1985. p. 2-5.

HISTORIC PRESERVATION

Datel, Robin. "Preservationists Profiled-- Recent Survey Results." California Preservation. January 1984. p. 9.

HISTORIC PRESERVATION

"A dialogue on conserving architectural landmarks." Journal of Housing. Mar. 1980. pp. 139-141.

Edited version of transcript of December 2, 1979 radio broadcast, WHN, New York. Brendan Gill and David Teitelbaum.

HISTORIC PRESERVATION

Elder, Betty Doak. "What Lies Ahead for the National Trust? An Interview with Michael Ainslie." History News. March 1981. pp. 8-13.

HISTORIC PRESERVATION

Ewalt, Donald H. and Gary R. Kremer. "The Historian as Preservationist: A Missouri Case Study." The Public Historian. Fall 1981. pp. 5-22.

HISTORIC PRESERVATION

Ford, Larry R. "The Burden of the Past, Rethinking Historic Preservation." Landscape. Vol. 28, No. 1, 1984. pp. 41-48.

HISTORIC PRESERVATION

Freed, Stacey. "Issues and Improvements at Walden Pond." Landscape Architecture. Vol. 76, No. 3, May/June 1986. p. 81.

HISTORIC PRESERVATION

Healy, Robert G. "Hallmarks of a New Decade in Land Use." Planning. July/August 1983. pp. 20-23.

HISTORIC PRESERVATION

Hild, Theodore W. "Directions in Historic Preservation." Historic Illinois. August 1983. pp. 12-13.

HISTORIC PRESERVATION

"Historic Preservation Resourcebook for Small Communities." Small Town. Vol. 13, No. 3. Nov./Dec. 1982. Entire issue.

Selected Contents: Lyle, Royster and Michael Lynn. Lexington, VA: Linking Preservation Planning and Tourism--Horstman, Neil. Defining a Role for Professionals in Small Town Preservation--Sillen, Elizabeth H. Public/Private Partnerships Provide Funding Alternatives.

HISTORIC PRESERVATION

"How Can You Tell If Your House Is Eligible for the National Register?" Miami Purchase Association for Historic Preservation. Jan.-Feb. 1987. p. 7.

HISTORIC PRESERVATION

Huxtable, Ada Louise. Goodbye History, Hello Hamburger. Washington, D.C.: Preservation Press, 1986. (NA705.H89)

HISTORIC PRESERVATION

Johnston, Douglas A. "Why Almost Everyone is Wrong about the Place of Historic Restorations and House Museums in Modern Historic Preservation Efforts." Carolina Comments. July 1982. pp. 93-97.

HISTORIC PRESERVATION

Kain, Roger. "Europe's Model and Exemplar Still?" Town Planning Review. October 1982. pp. 403-422.

HISTORIC PRESERVATION

Layman, Earle. "Genius Loci in Seattle: a Rationale for Preservation." Landmarks (Washington Trust). Vol. II, No. 3. pp. pp. 7-11.

HISTORIC PRESERVATION

Lowenthal, David. "Heritage--and Its Interpreters" Heritage Australia. Vol.5, No. 2. Winter 1986. p.42-45.

The author discusses the natural and built environment, for whom we interpret heritage, problems associated with visitors to historic sites, and authenticity.

HISTORIC PRESERVATION

Lyon, Elizabeth A. "Cultural and Environmental Resource Management: The Role of History in Historic Preservation." The Public Historian. Fall 1982. pp. 69-86.

HISTORIC PRESERVATION

McPherson, James W. "A U.S. Department of Historic Preservation?" The Heritage News. (Utah). Vol. 20, No. 6, Dec. 1986. p. 3.

HISTORIC PRESERVATION

Mikesell, Stephen D. "Historic Preservation that Counts: Quantitative Methods for Evaluating Historic Resources." The Public Historian. Vol. 8, No. 4, Fall 1986. p. 61-74.

HISTORIC PRESERVATION

Morrill, Dan L. "Keeping History in Historic Preservation." Small Town. July-August 1983. pp. 25-27.

HISTORIC PRESERVATION

Nicandri, David L. "Social Science Looks at Historic Preservation." Landmarks (Washington Trust). Vol. II, No. 3. pp. 11-12.

HISTORIC PRESERVATION

Niehaus, Charles. "Measuring Our Progress toward a Preservation Ethic." The Indiana Preservationist. No. 5, 1986. p. 1, 6.

HISTORIC PRESERVATION

O'Mara, W. Paul. "Make Preservation a Productive Partner in Change." Urban Land. January 198s. p. 27

(Michael Ainslie interview)

HISTORIC PRESERVATION

Pearce, Philip L. and Gianna M. Moscardo. "The Psychology of Heritage." Heritage Australia. Winter 1985. p. 42-43.

HISTORIC PRESERVATION

"Preservation and Restoration." Progressive Architecture. November 1984. Entire Issue.

Restorations in Buffalo, N.Y., Paris, Venice, Java, Rome, Tel Aviv and a discussion of Ruskin highlight this annual preservation review.

HISTORIC PRESERVATION

"Preservation and Reuse." Progressive Architecture. November 1983. Entire Issue.

HISTORIC PRESERVATION

"A Preservation Chronology for Staunton." The Queen City Quarterly. Vol. 13, No. 2, April 1986. p. 6-8.

Preservation 1970-1986 in the Virginia city.

HISTORIC PRESERVATION

"Preservation Has Its Pitfalls." Restoration Education Newsletter. Nov. 21, 1986. p. 2

Editorial in the Rockford, Illinois Register Star. of Nov. 8, 1986, critical of historic preservation.
Carlson, Gary. "Letter to the Editor." p. 2-4.
Response to the above editorial.

HISTORIC PRESERVATION--AFRICA

Mturi, Amini. "The Conservation of the African Architectural Heritage." Part 1. Monumentum. Vol. 27, No. 3, September 1984. pp. 181-197.

HISTORIC PRESERVATION--AFRICA

Mturi, Amini. "The Conservation of the African Architectural Heritage." Part 2. Monumentum. Vol. 27, No. 4, Dec. 1984. p. 275-284.

HISTORIC PRESERVATION--ALASKA

Stirling, Dale A. "Historic Preservation in the Aleutians." Periodical, Journal of the Council on America's Military Past. Vol. XIII, No. 1, Whole No. 50, May 1984. pp. 3-7.

HISTORIC PRESERVATION--BARBADOS

Jackson-Stops, Gervase. "A Future for a Colonial Past: Conservation in Barbados." Country Life. Sept. 25, 1986. p. 936-941.

Need for the Barbados National Trust to survey the island's sugar-cane plantation houses.

HISTORIC PRESERVATION--BIBLIOGRAPHY

Gamble, Robert S. "Sources of Information: A Bibliographical Essay." Advisory Council on Historic Preservation Report. March, 1979. 82p. (entire issue)

HISTORIC PRESERVATION--BIBLIOGRAPHY

"NPS Historic and Prehistoric Structure, Landscape Technical Bibliography." APT Bulletin. Vol. 16, No. 3 & 4, 1984. p. 75-78.

HISTORIC PRESERVATION--BIOGRAPHY

Hays, Laurie. "Carolyn Pitts Scouts Nations Landmarks- Sometimes to the Dismay of Developers." Wall Street Journal. Dec. 1, 1986.

HISTORIC PRESERVATION--BIOGRAPHY

"Preservation Awards Galore for Gutheim." The Montgomery County Preservationist. Vol. 2, No. 7. Jul./Aug. 1987. pp. 1, 4.
Frederick Gutheim receives two major awards and board appointment.

HISTORIC PRESERVATION--BIOGRAPHY

Rattner, Selma. "To Save the World We Built." American Heritage. Vol. 38, No. 3, Apr. 1987. p. 84-91.

An interview with preservationist James Marston Fitch.

HISTORIC PRESERVATION--BULGARIA--SOFIA

Stantcheva, Magdalina. "Museums in the street... Architectural heritage and contemporary town planning in Sofia". Museum. no.3, 1980. p.106-118.

HISTORIC PRESERVATION--CANADA

APT Bulletin. Vol. X, no.3, 1978. Special issue: Department of Indian and Northern Affairs, Canada.

HISTORIC PRESERVATION--CANADA

Dalibard, Jacques. "Why We Need a National Heritage Review." Canadian Heritage. Vol. 12, Issue 4, Oct.-Nov. 1986. p. 38-43.

HISTORIC PRESERVATION--CANADA

"The First Decade." Canadian Heritage. December 1982. pp. special insert, pp. i-ix.

HISTORIC PRESERVATION--CANADA--MONTREAL

London, Mark. "Can Gallic Charm Stop the Wrecking Ball?" Planning. Vol. 51, No. 3, Mar. 1985. p. 13-16.

HISTORIC PRESERVATION--CARIBBEAN

Montas, Eugenio Perez. "The CARIMOS Plan for Monuments and Sites in the Greater Caribbean." Monumentum. December 1983. pp. 265-280.

HISTORIC PRESERVATION--CASE STUDIES

Adams, Frank. "Rebirth of a Hotel." Utah Preservation/Restoration. Vol. III, 1981. pp. 66-67.

HISTORIC PRESERVATION--CASE STUDIES

Bouras, Charalambos. "Areas of Concern: Athens, The Parthenon." Monumentum. Vol. 27, No. 2, June 1984. pp. 109-121.

HISTORIC PRESERVATION--CASE STUDIES

Teixeira, Luiz Gonzaga. "Conservation in Action: Ouro Preto, Monument Town." Monumentum. Vol. 27, No. 2, June 1984. pp. 131-155.

HISTORIC PRESERVATION--CASE STUDIES

Williams, Roger M. "Old Merchant's House." Americana. September/October 1981. pp. 67-72.

HISTORIC PRESERVATION--CASE STUDIES--EGYPT

Ross, Ole. "Collaboration in Cairo: The Conservation of the Madrasa el Gawhariya." Monumentum. Vol. 27, No. 3, September 1984. pp. 211-233.

Danish-Egyptian project conserved Islamic religious building, c1440.

HISTORIC PRESERVATION--CONFERENCES

"The Willard Conference Special Report." Urban Conservation Report, Vol. 11, No. 2, Feb. 1987. whole issue.

HISTORIC PRESERVATION--CONGRESSES

Bulletin, The Association for Preservation Technology. Vol. 17, No. 3&4, 1985. Double Issue "Principles in Practice."

10 papers presented at the 1984 APT annual conference and 2 papers presented at the 1985 conference are published in this issue of conference proceedings.

HISTORIC PRESERVATION--CONGRESSES

"State Preservation Officers May Push Federal Program Changes." Urban Conservation Report. Vol. 11, No. 1. Jan. 1987. p. 5.

HISTORIC PRESERVATION--DEVELOPERS

Blackburn, Luci. "What Developers Think of Historic Preservation." Urban Land. November 1983. pp. 8-11.

HISTORIC PRESERVATION--DEVELOPERS

"Developers Discuss Historic Preservation." Urban Land. November 1983. pp. 12-13.

HISTORIC PRESERVATION--DIRECTORIES--NORTH CAROLINA

"Society Volunteers Ready to Assist." North Carolina Preservation. June/July 1982. pp. 3-5.

HISTORIC PRESERVATION--ECONOMIC ASPECTS

Abel, Betts. "The News About Preservation and Development is Not All Bad". Urban Land October 1980. p. 8-17.

HISTORIC PRESERVATION--ECONOMIC ASPECTS

Brown, Floy. "Historic Preservation promotes profits, widespread rehabilitation". Journal of Housing. October 1980. p. 513-517.

HISTORIC PRESERVATION--ECONOMIC ASPECTS

Cottrell, Debbie. "Battling Budget Cuts: the Texas Historical Commission Fights Hard Times with Economic Ammo." *History News*, Vol. 42, No. 3, May-June 1987. p. 6-8.

HISTORIC PRESERVATION--ECONOMIC ASPECTS

"Damonmill Square, Concord, Massachusetts." *Real Estate Finance*. Vol. 1, No. 3, Fall 1984, pp. 56-60.

Financing the certified historic rehabilitation of an abandoned textile mill.

HISTORIC PRESERVATION--ECONOMIC ASPECTS

"Developer's Dilemma--the Old Houses at Hallowell: Smart Builder Finds Preservation Works." *The Montgomery County Preservationist*. Vol. 2, No. 3. Dec. 1986/Jan. 1987. pp. 1, 4.

HISTORIC PRESERVATION--ECONOMIC ASPECTS

Dreimuller, A.P. and A.F. van Hooren. "Employment and the Restoration of Historic Buildings in the Netherlands." *A Future for Our Past*. No. 19, 1982. pp. 19-26.

HISTORIC PRESERVATION--ECONOMIC ASPECTS

Fennell, John. "Upgrading More Cost-Effective Option Than Demolition and New Construction." *Building Renovation*. Vol. 4, No. 3. May/June 1987. p. 26.

HISTORIC PRESERVATION--ECONOMIC ASPECTS

"Funding for Urban Design." *Urban Design International*. June 1981. Entire Issue.

HISTORIC PRESERVATION--ECONOMIC ASPECTS

Gay, Patricia H. "Historic Renovation As an Economic Stimulus." *New Orleans Preservation in Print*. Vol. 13, No. 7, Sept. 1986. p. 3.

HISTORIC PRESERVATION--ECONOMIC ASPECTS

Gilham, Allen F.E. " Local Authority Owned Historic Houses and the D.O.E. Project Cost Control Process." *Association for Studies in the Conservation of Historic Buildings Newsletter*. Aug. 1983. pp. 6-8.

HISTORIC PRESERVATION --ECONOMIC ASPECTS

"Historic Rehabs Boost Economy and Tax Revenues." *Urban Conservation Report*. Vol. VIII, No. 12, July 20, 1984. pp. 1-2.

Jared Shlaes & Co. study of benefits of preservation in Illinois.

HISTORIC PRESERVATION--ECONOMIC ASPECTS

Hitchings, Bradley. "Remodeling: the Time is Right." *Business Week*. Feb. 18, 1985. pp. 156-158.

HISTORIC PRESERVATION--ECONOMIC ASPECTS

Jones, David. "It Pays to Revitalize." *The Grantsmanship Center News*. July/August 1981. pp. 24-29.

HISTORIC PRESERVATION--ECONOMIC ASPECTS

Kopff, Gary J. "Real Estate Finance in 1980s." *California Preservation*. Summer 1982. pp. 8-12.

HISTORIC PRESERVATION--ECONOMIC ASPECTS

"Land Bank Begins Development Financing." *Center City Report*. August 1981. p. 9.

HISTORIC PRESERVATION--ECONOMIC ASPECTS

"A national surge of preservationist power." *Business Week*. Apr. 21, 1980. pp. 157-158.

HISTORIC PRESERVATION--ECONOMIC ASPECTS

"Neighborhood Gentrification: How Is It Working." Urban Outlook. Vol. 6, No. 5, August 15, 1984. p. 1.

HISTORIC PRESERVATION--ECONOMIC ASPECTS

Palermo, Nicholas Esq. "Jobs, Housing & Preservation." Boston Preservation Alliance Letter. Vol. 7, No. 1, Jan. 1986. p. 3, 7.

HISTORIC PRESERVATION--ECONOMIC ASPECTS

Prudon, Theodore H. M. "The Restoration Process: an Explanation of Costs." APT Bulletin Vol. 18, No. 4, 1986. p. 71-76.

HISTORIC PRESERVATION--ECONOMIC ASPECTS

"Rehab's Place in the Real Estate Market: Emerging Trends." Urban Conservation Report. Oct. 31, 1983. p. 6.

HISTORIC PRESERVATION--ECONOMICS

"Special Issue: The Impact of the Reagan Budget." Economics of Amenity News." April 6, 1981. Entire Issue.

HISTORIC PRESERVATION--ECONOMIC ASPECTS

Steller, Joseph D., Jr. "Preservationists as Developers". Urban Land. October 1980. p. 18-20.

HISTORIC PRESERVATION--ECONOMIC ASPECTS

"Study Committees Praise Preservation Economics." The Rambler. Vol. 13, No. 4. Winter 1987. pp. 1; 16.

Brief review of Georgia's Study Committees on Economic Development through Historic Preservation.

HISTORIC PRESERVATION--ECONOMIC ASPECTS

Thompson, Richard. "Old House Restoration Services: Authenticity on a Budget." Historic Preservation League of Oregon Newsletter. No. 42, Fall 1986. p. 12.

HISTORIC PRESERVATION--ECONOMIC ASPECTS

"Urban Gentrification Goes Industrial." Urban Outlook. Vol. 6, No. 13, July 15, 1984. pp. 1-2.

Dissatisfaction among small businesses forced out due to waterfront or factory revitalization.

HISTORIC PRESERVATION--ECONOMIC ASPECTS

"Wellesville School Rededicated: a Preservation Fund Success Story." Preservation Pennsylvania. Vol. 1, No. 3, Fall 1986. p. 1-2.

HISTORIC PRESERVATION--ECONOMIC ASPECTS

"What is the Economy Saying?" Livability Digest. Spring 1982. pp. 22-33.

HISTORIC PRESERVATION--ECONOMIC BENEFITS

"Special Issue: A Report on the Economics of Amenity Program." Economics of Amenity News. Vol. 2, No. 9. May 4, 1981. Entire Issue

HISTORIC PRESERVATION--EDUCATION

Neff, Jean Winnie. "Cooperative Programming for School Children." Regional Council of Historical Agencies. Vol. 16. No. 3. May 1987.

HISTORIC PRESERVATION--ENERGY CONSERVATION

Bazjanac, Vladimir. "Energy Analysis." Progressive Architecture. November 1981. p. 107.

HISTORIC PRESERVATION--ENERGY CONSERVATION

Harney, Andy Leon. "Adaptive Use: Saving Energy (and Money) As Well As Historic Buildings." AIA Journal. August 1974. pp. 49-54.

HISTORIC PRESERVATION--ENERGY CONSERVATION

Woodbury, Peter W. "Retrofitting Historic Structures." Trends. Vol. 19, #3, 1982. pp. 38-42.

HISTORIC PRESERVATION--FRANCE

France, Roger. "Aspects of Conservation Practice in France." Transactions. Vol. 7, 1982. pp. 42-47.

HISTORIC PRESERVATION--FUNDRAISING

Archer, Madeline C. "How to Pay for a Restoration." Americana. July/August 1983. pp. 27.

HISTORIC PRESERVATION--GRANTS

Archer, Madeline C. "Pay for a Restoration." Americana. July/August 1983. p. 27+.

HISTORIC PRESERVATION--GRANTS

"Historic Preservation Grants, Loans for Ohio Non-Profits Announced by National Trust." Housing & Development Reporter. Vol. 12, No. 20, October 8, 1984. p. 378.

HISTORIC PRESERVATION--GRANTS

Shettleworth, Earle G. "Maine's Historic Buildings Restoration Grants Program." Maine Preservation News. Vol. 11, No. 4, Winter 1986. p. 2.

HISTORIC PRESERVATION--GRANTS--U.S.--WISCONSIN

"Wisconsin Cities Set Up Preservation Grant, Loan Programs." Wisconsin Preservation. Vol. 10, No. 1, Jan./Feb. 1986. p. 12-13.

HISTORIC PRESERVATION--GREAT BRITAIN

Fidler, John. "Taking to the Streets." Traditional Homes. Mar. 1986. p. 98-99.

HISTORIC PRESERVATION--GREAT BRITAIN

"Ridley Lashes Conservation Movement." Architects' Journal. Vol. 184, No. 43, Oct. 22, 1896. p. 34.

England's environment secretary critical of preservationists.

HISTORIC PRESERVATION--GREAT BRITAIN

Turner, Phil. "Conserving Hampshire's Heritage." Heritage Education News. No. 19, Summer/Autumn 1986. p. 3.

Public Participation important to conservation of Hampshire, England.

HISTORIC PRESERVATION--HANDBOOKS, MANUALS, ETC.

Preservation League of New York State. Good Buildings, Good Times: A Manual of Program Ideas for Promoting Local Architecture. c. 1985. 56p. including index. (VF)

HISTORIC PRESERVATION--HISTORY

Connally, Ernest Allen. "Origins of the National Historic Preservation Act of 1966." CRM Bulletin. Vol. 9, No. 1, Feb. 1986. p. 7-10.

HISTORIC PRESERVATION--HISTORY

Coolidge, Nancy and Nancy Padnos. "William Sumner Appleton and the Society for the Preservation of New England Antiquities." Antiques. Vol. 129, No. 3, Mar. 1986. p. 590-595.

Special issue includes articles on SPNEA's collections, archives, and study houses (p. 596-661).

HISTORIC PRESERVATION--HISTORY

Hosmer, Charles B. "Preservation Comes of Age: From Williamsburg to the National Trust, 1926-1949." APT Bulletin. v.XII, no. 3, 1980. p. 20-27.

HISTORIC PRESERVATION--HISTORY

Kaynor, Fay Campbell. "Thomas Fileston Waterman: Student of American Colonial Architecture." Winterthur Portfolio. Vol. 20, No. 2/3, Summer/Autumn 1985. p. 103-147.

HISTORIC PRESERVATION--HISTORY

"Rebirth, Renewal and Restoration." Texas Heritage. Fall 1983. p.5.

HISTORIC PRESERVATION--HISTORY

Repellin, Didier. "Preservation Doesn't Mean an End to Progress", Heritage Newsletter (Foundation for San Francisco's Architectural Heritage), Vol. XII, No. 4, Fall 1984, p. 3.

HISTORIC PRESERVATION--HISTORY

Rogers, Jerry L. "National Historic Preservation Act - a Retrospective." CRM Bulletin. Vol. 9, No. 1, Feb. 1986. p. 1, 4.

HISTORIC PRESERVATION--HISTORY

Winks, Robin and Barry Mackintosh. "The Act of Self-Awareness." National Parks. Vol. 59, No. 9-10, Sept./Oct. 1985. p. 24.

A look at the Historic Sites Act (1935) on its 50th anniversary.

HISTORIC PRESERVATION--HISTORY--U.S.--MASSACHU-SETTS--BOSTON

Stone, Cynthia. "The Preservation of Old South Meeting House." The Boston Preservation Alliance Letter. Vol. 6, No. 5, May 1985. p. 1, 4.

HISTORIC PRESERVATION--HUNGARY

Boucher, Jack E. "Koszeg: Historic Preservation began centuries ago for this Hungarian town." American Preservation. May/June 1980. p. 31-42.

HISTORIC PRESERVATION--ISRAEL

Reilly, William K. "Conservation and Israel." Place. Vol. 6, No. 5, Sept.-Oct. 1986. p. 4-5.

HISTORIC PRESERVATION--KENYA

Pulver, Ann and Francesco Siravo. "Conservation in Kenya." Place. Vol. 6, No. 5, Sept.-Oct. 1986. p. 24-25.

The first conservation plan in eastern Africa will involve an island town, the oldest in Kenya.

HISTORIC PRESERVATION--LAW AND LEGISLATION

"Advisory Council Adopts Revised Review Regulations." Headquarters Heliogram. No. 178, Aug. 1986. p. 7.

The Advisory Council on Historic Preservation has adopted revised regulations governing the review process established in Section 106 of the National Historic Preservation Act.

HISTORIC PRESERVATION--LAW AND LEGISLATION

Ault, Barbara. "Know Your Rights: Preservation and the Law." Preservation Matters. Vol. 2, No. 12, Dec. 1986. p. 1.

HISTORIC PRESERVATION--LAW & LEGISLATION

"Chicago Gets New Landmarks Law." Landmarks Preservation Council of Illinois. Vol. 16, No. 3. May - June 1987. pp. 3 - 4.

HISTORIC PRESERVATION--LAW AND LEGISLATION

"City of Prescott Enacts Preservation Ordinance." Wisconsin Preservation. Vol 10, No. 3, May/June 1986. p. 2.

HISTORIC PRESERVATION--LAW AND LEGISLATION

"Congress's History Agenda Takes Shape."
History News Dispatch. Vol. 2, No. 4, Apr. 1987.
p. 1-2.

HISTORIC PRESERVATION--LAW AND LEGISLATION

Connally, Ernest Allen. "Origins of the
National Historic Preservation Act of 1966."
CRM Bulletin. Vol. 9, No. 1, Feb. 1986.
p. 7-10.

HISTORIC PRESERVATION--LAW AND LEGISLATION

Connally, Ernest Allen. "Origins of the
National Historic Preservation Act of 1966--
Part II." CRM Bulletin. Vol. 9, No. 2, April
1986. p. 9-14.

HISTORIC PRESERVATION--LAW AND LEGISLATION

"Conserving Nebraska's State-Owned
Buildings: New Law Offers Preservation
Alternatives, Preservation Opportunities."
Cornerstone. Vol. 7, No. 3, Fall 1986.
p. 1-2.

HISTORIC PRESERVATION--LAW AND LEGISLATION

"Court Refuses to Hear Challenge to Landmark
Designation of Cooper Homes." D.C. Preservation
League. Spring 1987. p. 5.

HISTORIC PRESERVATION--LAW AND LEGISLATION

Elder, Betty Doak. "Crossroads: Congress to
Decide Preservation's Future." History News.
April, 1980. p. 7-13.

HISTORIC PRESERVATION--LAW AND LEGISLATION

"Federal Historic Preservation Law: a
Summary." Wisconsin Preservation. Vol. 10, No. 1,
Jan./Feb. 1986. p. 4-7.

HISTORIC PRESERVATION--LAW AND LEGISLATION

Fowler, John. "Section 106 Process:
No Purgatory of Federal Preservation Review."
Urban Land. October 1980. p. 21-24.

HISTORIC PRESERVATION--LAW AND LEGISLATION

Gleye, Paul. "City Adopts Historic Treasure
Ordinance." The Bungalow Reader. No. 2. Feb.
1987. p. 6.

Pasadena, CA, has adopted a historic
preservation ordinance with strong financial
incentives.

HISTORIC PRESERVATION--LAW AND LEGISLATION

"Is Your Town Ready for a Preservation
Ordinance?" The Rambler. Vol. 14, No. 1.
Spring 1987. p. 13.

HISTORIC PRESERVATION--LAW AND LEGISLATION

"Middletown Struck Down on Appeal." Preservation
Perspective, Vol. 6, No. 3, Mar.-Apr. 1987. p. 1.

Middletown (NJ) historic preservation ordinance
is declared invalid by NJ appeals court.

HISTORIC PRESERVATION--LAW AND LEGISLATION

Murtagh, William. "The Preservation Act of
1966: 20 Years Later." CRM Bulletin. Vol.
9, No. 5, Oct.-Dec. 1986. p. 6-7.

HISTORIC PRESERVATION--LAW AND LEGISLATION

Nesmith, Lynn. "Religious Groups
Wage Legal Battles over Preservation Law."
Architecture. Nov. 1986. p. 16.

HISTORIC PRESERVATION--LAW & LEGISLATION

Netter, Edith M. "An Uncertain Future for
Housing Preservation Ordinances." Urban Land.
Vol. 46, No. 7. July 1987. pp. 34 - 35.

HISTORIC PRESERVATION--LAW & LEGISLATION

"New Code Guards Historic Buildings."
California Office of Historic Preservation Newsletter. Vol. 2, No. 3. Aug. 1987. p. 2.
    Amended California State Historic Building
Code requires that all state agencies must consult
with the SHBC Board before making decisions affecting State- or privately owned historic
buildings.

HISTORIC PRESERVATION--LAW AND LEGISLATION

"NJ Passes Enabling Legislation." Preservation
Perspective. Vol. 5, No. 3. Mar./Apr. 1986.
pp. 1-2.

    Legislation enabling New Jersey Municipalities to
empower local historic preservation commissions
passed.

HISTORIC PRESERVATION--LAW & LEGISLATION

"9 Steps to Successful Heritage Preservation."
Building Renovation. Vol. 4, No. 4. Jul. 1987.
p. 8.
    Recommendations adopted by Edmonton, Canada,
to promote preservation.

HISTORIC PRESERVATION--LAW AND LEGISLATION

Norton, Scott. "Vacant and Abandoned
Building Program Has Clout." New Orleans
Preservation in Print. Vol. 14, No. 5, June
1987. p. 12-13.

New Orleans new abandoned building program
has strict penalties to combat building neglect.

HISTORIC PRESERVATION--LAW & LEGISLATION

Powell, Ken. "Introducing the Ten-Year Rule:
New Listing of Modern Buildings." Country Life.
Vol. 181, No. 19, May 7, 1987. p. 116-118.

Britain's new ruling protects threatened
buildings over ten years old.

HISTORIC PRESERVATION--LAW AND LEGIS-
LATION

"Preservation Ordinance Updated."
The Plague. Vol. 7, May 1986. p. 7.

Alexandria, Va. plans to modify its
preservation ordinance.

HISTORIC PRESERVATION--LAW AND LEGISLATION

"Proposed IRS Rules Hit Non-profit Community."
History News Dispatch. Vol. 2, No. 5, May 1987.
p. 3.

HISTORIC PRESERVATION--LAW AND LEGISLATION

"Revision of Preservation Laws Needed."
Heritage Newsletter, Vol. 2, No. 3, May-June-July
1987. p. 2

HISTORIC PRESERVATION--LAW AND LEGISLATION

Rogers, Jerry L. "National Historic Preservation Act--a Retrospective." CRM Bulletin.
Vol. 9, No. 1, Feb. 1986. p. 14.

HISTORIC PRESERVATION--LAW AND LEGISLATION

Rosensaft, Menachem Z. "New York City
Landmarks Preservation Law as Applied to Radio
City Music Hall." Art & the Law. Vol. 4, No. 4,
1979. pp. 83-90.

HISTORIC PRESERVATION--LAW AND LEGISLATION

"Senate acts on historic preservation
amendments and reauthorization". Preservation
Action Alert. September 1980. p. 1-2.

HISTORIC PRESERVATION--LAW AND LEGISLATION

"Saving Sound Housing." City Limits. Vol.
11, No. 7, Aug./Sept. 1986. p. 7.

The Sound Housing Preservation Bill
passed by New York State Assembly.

HISTORIC PRESERVATION--LAW AND LEGISLATION

"Several Legislative Proposals Will Affect
Preservation Efforts." North Carolina Preservation. No. 67. Spring 1987. pp. 4 - 6.
    Several North Carolina legislative proposals
may affect preservation on the state level.

HISTORIC PRESERVATION--LAW AND LEGISLATION

Watts, W. David. "Historic Landmark
Designation Needs Accountability." Urban Land.
November 1980. p.18-19.

HISTORIC PRESERVATION--LAW & LEGISLATION--CANADA

Denhez, Marc. "Preservation Law, Building Codes, and Assorted Prognostications." APT Bulletin. Vol. XII, No.1, 1980. p.15-29.

HISTORIC PRESERVATION--LAW & LEGISLATION-- NATIONAL REGISTER

Archer, Madeline C. "How to List Your House on the National Register." Americana. July/ August 1984. pp. 77-8.

HISTORIC PRESERVATION--LAW AND LEGISLATION--U.S. --CALIFORNIA--PASADENA

"Treasure Ordinance Deserves Support." Pasadena Heritage, Members Alert. Feb. 1986. p. 1.

HISTORIC PRESERVATION--LAW AND LEGISLATION--U.S.-- NEW JERSEY

"First New Jersey Court Cases Overturn Ordinances." The Alliance Review. Vol. 2, No. 1, Jan./Feb. 1986. p. 1.

HISTORIC PRESERVATION--LAW AND LEGISLATION--U.S.-- NEW YORK

Feuer, Wendy E. "A Guide to the New York State Historic Preservation Act of 1980." Preservation League of New York State, Technical Series/No. 9. 4 p.

HISTORIC PRESERVATION--LAW & LEGISLATION-- U.S.-- NEW YORK

"Preservation and the Bond Act: Questions Answered." Preservation League of New York State Newsletter. Vol. 13, No. 2. Spring 1987. pp. 7 - 8.

The impact of New York State's "Environmental Quality Bond Act" on preservation.

HISTORIC PRESERVATION--LAW AND LEGISLATION--U.S.-- WASHINGTON, D.C.

"Review of the District's Preservation Ordinance." D.C. Preservation League. Dec. 1985. pp. 4-5.

HISTORIC PRESERVATION--LAW AND LEGISLATION--U.S.-- WISCONSIN

"New State Preservation Law Enacted." Wisconsin Preservation. May 1982. pp. 1-2.

HISTORIC PRESERVATION--NETHERLANDS

Van Voorden, F.W. "The Preservation of Monuments and Historic Townscapes in the Netherlands." Town Planning Review. October 1981. pp. 433-453.

HISTORIC PRESERVATION--NEW ZEALAND

"Incentives to Preserve." New Zealand Historic Places Trust. October 1982. p. 4.

HISTORIC PRESERVATION--PERIODICALS

Architectural Preservation Forum, February 1979. The SAH Forum is the new Bulletin of the Committee on Architectural Preservation, Society of Architectural Historians. Its purpose is to supplement the SAH News-letter as "an additional platform for the meaningful exchange of ideas and viewpoints on the many preservation issues which concern the Society."

HISTORIC PRESERVATION--PERIODICALS

Utah Preservation/Restoration. 1979

Note: New annual publication of the Utah State Historical Society, Preservation Section. "The publications goal is to become an information guide for the rehabilitation of old buildings for purposeful modern day use and comfort in Utah."

HISTORIC PRESERVATION--PLANNING

Edwards, Mark R. "The Computer as a Preservation Planning Tool: Maryland's Approach to Improving Resource Management." Technology & Conservation. Summer, 1979. pp. 18-25.

HISTORIC PRESERVATION--PLANNING

Reinhart, Marty and Susan Cianci. "Preservation and the Montgomery County Planning Board." The Montgomery County Preservationist. Vol. 2, No. 1, Aug./Sept. 1986. p. 1, 6.

HISTORIC PRESERVATION--PLANNING

"The 29th P/A Awards--Urban Design and Planning." Progressive Architecture, January 1982. pp. 172-189.
CONTENTS: Anderson Notter Finegold: Miami Beach Art Deco District Preservation and Development Plan--James Wood Burch & Assoc./John P. Gutting: Scott's Point, Guidelines for Change in Chester-Town, Md.--Davis Brody & Assoc. and Kwartler/Jones: N.Y. City Midtown Development Project Bulk Regulations--Venturi, Rauch & Scott Brown: Princeton Urban Design Study, Princeton, N.J.

HISTORIC PRESERVATION--POLITICAL PARTICIPATION

Upton, Dell. "The Architectural Historian and Public History", SAH Forum. December 1980.

HISTORIC PRESERVATION--RESEARCH

"Research First Award : Walter H. Moleski, Michael Rubin, ERG/Environmental Research Group." Progressive Architecture. January 1981. p. 106-109.

HISTORIC PRESERVATION RESEARCH

O'Malley, Leslie C. PhD. "Researching Local History." RCHA, Regional Conference of Historical Agencies, Technical Information. Vol. 14, No. 6, June 1984. Insert.

HISTORIC PRESERVATION--RESEARCH

"National Trust Quantifies Efforts in Report." Architecture. January 1984. p. 45.

HISTORIC PRESERVATION--RESEARCH

Shoptaufh, Terry. " Researching old buildings: using Sanborn maps". National Register of Historic Places in Wisconsin Newsletter. May 1980. p. 15-17.

HISTORIC PRESERVATION--RESEARCH--U.S.--PENNSYL-
VANIA--PHILADELPHIA AREA

Taylor, Beatrice K. "The G. Edwin Brumbaugh Papers - Documents for Future Study in Historic Preservation." Winterthur Newsletter. Vol. 31, No. 2, Summer 1985. p. 6-7.

HISTORIC PRESERVATION--SOCIETIES, ETC.

"Conserving America: How the U.S. Trust Faces New Challenges." Canadian Heritage. August/September 1981. pp. 14-17.

HISTORIC PRESERVATION--SOCIETIES

Watkins, T.H. "Trust and Civilisation," American Heritage. August/September, 1981. pp. 82-83.

HISTORIC PRESERVATION--STANDARDS

Ferro, Maximillian L. "Scrape vs. Anti-scrape: a Modern American Perspective." Bulletin, APT. Vol. 17, No. 3&4, 1985. p. 21-25.

HISTORIC PRESERVATION--STANDARDS

Hill, John. "Preservation Standards." Mistle-toe Leaves. Vol. 18, No. 2, 1987. p. 5.

HISTORIC PRESERVATION--STANDARDS

"Interior's Rehab Standards: Must New Additions Resemble Glass Boxes?" Urban Conservation Report. December 22, 1983. pp. 4-5.

HISTORIC PRESERVATION--STANDARDS

Jokilehto, Judda. "Authenticity in Restoration Principles and Practices." Bulletin, APT. Vol. 17, No. 3&4, 1985. p. 5-11.

HISTORIC PRESERVATION--STANDARDS

Lyon, Elizabeth A. "Architectural History and Preservation: the Need for Greater Professional Involvement". 11593. February/March 1980. p. 1, 5-7.

HISTORIC PRESERVATION--STANDARDS

Neil, J. Meredith. "Is There a Historian in the House? The Curious Case of Historic Preservation". The Public Historian. Winter 1980. p. 30-38.

HISTORIC PRESERVATION--STANDARDS

Null, Janet A. "Restorers, Villains, and Vandals." Bulletin, APT. Vol. 17, No. 3&4, 1985. p. 26-41.

HISTORIC PRESERVATION--STANDARDS

Pappas, Nicholas A. "Scrape and Antiscrape: Wherein We Explore the Treacherous Jungle Between these Two Extremes; Discover the Perils Hidden Therein; and Seek the Path to Eldorado." Bulletin, APT. Vol. 17, No. 3&4, 1985. p. 42-50.

HISTORIC PRESERVATION--STANDARDS

"Park Service in Washington Reverses Denver Office Denial of Rehab Credit." Urban Conservation Report. January 31, 1984. p. 4.

HISTORIC PRESERVATION--STANDARDS

Perkins, Bradford. "Preserving the Landmarks of the Modern Movement." Architectural Record. July 1981. pp. 108-113.

HISTORIC PRESERVATION--STANDARDS

Stovel, Herb. "Scrape and Antiscrape: False Idols on Main Street." Bulletin, APT. Vol. 17, No. 3&4, 1985. p. 51-55.

HISTORIC PRESERVATION--STANDARDS

Tschudi-Madsen, Stefan. "Principles in Practice." Bulletin, APT. Vol. 17, No. 3&4, 1985. p. 12-20.

HISTORIC PRESERVATION--STANDARDS

Wisley, Philip. "Rehabilitation Standard 4." Florida Preservation News. Vol. 3, No. 1, Jan./Feb. 1987. p. 6.

HISTORIC PRESERVATION--STUDY AND TEACHING

"Affiliates Design Workshop for Teachers." The Indiana Preservationist. No. 1, 1985. p. 2.

HISTORIC PRESERVATION--STUDY AND TEACHING

"Auburn-Opelika Heritage Education Program Cited." The Preservation Report. Vol. 14, No. 2, April/May 1987. p. 4.

Public school architectural heritage program in Alabama.

HISTORIC PRESERVATION--STUDY AND TEACHING

Bevitt, Emogene. "Skills... for Historical Architects." CRM Bulletin. Vol. 9, No. 4, Aug. 1986. p. 1-2, 4.

The National Park Service has initiated a Skills Development Plan for historical architects

HISTORIC PRESERVATION--STUDY AND TEACHING

"Building Trades Will Feature Historic Preservation in Apprenticeship Schools." Local Economic Growth and Neighborhood Reinvestment Report. September 9, 1983. p. 5.

HISTORIC PRESERVATION--STUDY AND TEACHING

"Fourth Graders Focus on Atlanta." The Rambler. Vol. 14, No. 1. Spring 1987. p. 14.

HISTORIC PRESERVATION--STUDY AND TEACHING

"Heritage Education." The Rambler. Vol. 14, No. 1, Spr. 1987. p. 14.

HISTORIC PRESERVATION-- STUDY & TEACHING

"Junior Historians: Students Save Landmarks." The Medallion. Vol. 24, No. 7.
Jul. 1987. p. 3.

HISTORIC PRESERVATION--STUDY AND TEACHING

"Heritage Education a Statewide Effort."
The Rambler, Newsletter of the Georgia Trust for
Historic Preservation. Vol. 12, No. 4, Fall/
Winter 1985. p. 7.

HISTORIC PRESERVATION--STUDY AND TEACHING

Lange, Linda. "Learning to care : how
Beaumont, Texas teaches kids to care about the
built environment." History News. July 1980.
p. 13-15.

HISTORIC PRESERVATION--STUDY AND TEACHING

Liebs, Chester H. "The University of Vermont's
Historic Preservation Education Program." Environmental
Comment, April 1979. pp. 12-15.

HISTORIC PRESERVATION--STUDY AND TEACHING

Lynch, Judith. "City Guides Aid in Preservation". HUD Challenge , February, 1980, p.4.

HISTORIC PRESERVATION--STUDY AND TEACHING

Miller, Hugh C., AIA. "Maintenance
Training for Historic Preservation: Is It a Dif-
ferent Ball Game?" NPS, CRM Bulletin. Vol. 7,
No. 2, July 1984. pp. 3-4, 7.

HISTORIC PRESERVATION--STUDY AND TEACHING

Oberlander, "Learning to Read a
Neighbourhood." Canadian Heritage,
October-November 1983. p. 44.

HISTORIC PRESERVATION--STUDY AND TEACHING

O'Conner, Grace. "Scavenger Hunt
Teaches Students About Architecture."
Preservation League of New York Newsletter.
September-October 1983. p. 3.

HISTORIC PRESERVATION--STUDY AND TEACHING

Papageorgiou-Venetas, Alexander. "New
Orientations in Environmental Planning and
Professional Training for Integrated Urban
Conservation." Town Planning Review.
April 1982. pp. 131-152.

HISTORIC PRESERVATION--STUDY AND
TEACHING

"Pittsburgh Heritage in Review."
and "Apprenticeship Reprise."
PHLF News. Fall 1983. p. 3.

HISTORIC PRESERVATION--STUDY AND TEACHING

"Preservation Education Involves Youth in
Discovery of Local Heritage: A Survey of Programs
Geared to Elementary, Middle and High School Students."
The Rambler. Summer 1981. p. 7

HISTORIC PRESERVATION--STUDY AND TEACHING

"Preservation Education: Using Neighborhood
Resources As Learning Experiences." California
Preservation. Vol.11, No. 4, Oct. 1986. p.5.

HISTORIC PRESERVATION--STUDY AND TEACHING

"Preservation Programs Enhance Universities
Curriculum." The Rambler (Georgia Trust).
Summer 1982. p. 6.

HISTORIC PRESERVATION--STUDY AND TEACHING

"Preservation School Unit Developed." The
Queen City Quarterly (Historic Staunton Foundation), Vol. 12, No. 2, Apr. 1985, p. 2.

HISTORIC PRESERVATION--STUDY AND TEACHING

"Research award : Olsen-Lytle Architects"
Progressive Architecture. January 1981. p.110-111.

HISTORIC PRESERVATION--STUDY AND TEACHING

Schur, Susan E. "Conservation Training
Profile: the National Trust Restoration
Workshop." Technology and Conservation,
Summer 1980. p. 36-39.

HISTORIC PRESERVATION--STUDY AND TEACHING

Searcy, Casey. "Georgetown's Guides
Capture the Historical Flavor of the Area."
The Silver Queen Preservation News. Vol. 15, No.
4, Mar. 1986. p. 1, 3.

Georgetown, Colorado program for fifth and
sixth graders to learn local history and landmark
preservation.

HISTORIC PRESERVATION--STUDY AND TEACHING

Stine, Mary Jo. "WPTC is one of a kind."
Courier. Vol. 31, No. 6, June 1986. p. 6-7.

Williamsport Preservation Training Center provides training in preserving historic properties.

HISTORIC PRESERVATION--STUDY AND TEACHING

."Teaching the Past for the Future." The
Landmark Society of Western New York. Vol. 25,
No. 3, May 1987. p. 3, 8.

Vertical File
HISTORIC PRESERVATION--STUDY AND TEACHING

Toward Promotion and Tenure: Guidelines for
Assessing the Achievement of a Preservation
Educator. A report by the Committee on Promotion
and Tenure of the National Council for Preservation submitted at its Annual Meeting, Baltimore, Maryland, Oct. 27, 1984. 7 p. (VF)

HISTORIC PRESERVATION--STUDY AND TEACHING

"Training the Stone-Masons of
Tomorrow." Heritage Outlook. January/
February 1983. p. 10.

HISTORIC PRESERVATION--STUDY AND TEACHING

Tramposch, William J. "A Really
Wonderful Month, The Williamsburg Seminar."
Museum News. February 1983. pp. 41-44.

HISTORIC PRESERVATION--STUDY AND TEACHING

Triem, Judy. "Experiencing a City: Kansas
City, Missouri--its Historical and Architectural
Significance." The Public Historian. Spring
1979. pp. 72-76.

Describes an internship for the National
Trust for Historic Preservation; the project
was to write a walking tour.

HISTORIC PRESERVATION--STUDYING AND TEACHING--
CASE STUDIES

"Canterbury Urban Studies Centre."
Bulletin of Environmental Education. August/
September, 1981. pp. 9-13.

HISTORIC PRESERVATION--STUDY AND TEACHING--
K-12

Gradis, Bernadette. "Young People
and the Heritage." A Future for Our Past.
No. 21, 1983. pp. 18-20.

HISTORIC PRESERVATION--STUDY AND TEACHING--U.S.--
GEORGIA--COLUMBUS

"Our Town." The Rambler, Newsletter of the
Georgia Trust for Historic Preservation. Vol. 11,
No. 4, Fall 1984. p. 11.

HISTORIC PRESERVATION--STUDY AND TEACHING--UNIVERSITIES
AND COLLEGES

Melnick, Robert and Richard Wagner. "Preservation
Eduation: Guidelines and Implementation of a Program."
APT Bulletin. (Vol. XI, #2) 1979. pp. 53-59.

HISTORIC PRESERVATION--STUDY AND TEACHING--
UNIVERSITIES AND COLLEGES

"The 1985 Yankee Intern Program: a Report
to Our Readers." Yankee. Vol. 50, No. 4, Apr.
1986. p. 174-175.

HISTORIC PRESERVATION--STUDY AND TEACHING--
UNIVERSITIES AND COLLEGES

"The 1984 Yankee Intern Program: A Report to our Readers". <u>Yankee</u>. Vol. 49, No. 3, Mar. 1985. p. 126-8.

HISTORIC PRESERVATION--STUDY AND TEACHING--
UNIVERSITIES AND COLLEGES--U.S.--HAWAII

"UH (University of Hawaii) Approves Preservation Program." <u>Historic Hawaii News</u>. June 1985. p. 1.

HISTORIC PRESERVATION--STUDY AND TEACHING--
U.S.--GEORGIA--TIFTON

"Educating a New Constituency: A Workshop." <u>The Rambler</u>, Newsletter of the Georgia Trust for Historic Preservation, Inc. Vol. 11, No. 4, Fall 1984. p. 10.

HISTORIC PRESERVATION--TECHNIQUE

Fisher, Charles E. "Temporary Protection of Historic Stairways During Rehabilitation Work." <u>NPS Preservation Tech Notes</u>, No. 1. 6 p.

HISTORIC PRESERVATION--TECHNIQUE

Fisher, Thomas. "Technics: Replacement Materials - the Sincerest Form of Flattery." <u>Progressive Architecture</u>. Nov. 1985. p. 118-123.

HISTORIC PRESERVATION--TECHNIQUE

Gustave, Peggy A. "A Look Inside: Recognizing Significant Interiors." <u>CRM Bulletin</u>. Vol. 8, No. 3 & 4, June/Aug. 1985. p. 24-27.

HISTORIC PRESERVATION--TECHNIQUE

Howard, Murray. "Craftsmanship at the University of Virginia." <u>APT Bulletin</u>. Vol. 18, No. 4, 1986. pp. 30-40.

HISTORIC PRESERVATION--TECHNIQUE

Menz, Katherine B. "Documenting the Historic Structure." <u>CRM Bulletin</u>. Vol. 8, No. 3 & 4, June/Aug. 1985. p. 6-7.

HISTORIC PRESERVATION--TECHNIQUES

"Organizing for Preservation: A Resource Guide." <u>Connecticut Trust for Historic Preservation News</u>. Fall 1982. pp. 6-8.

HISTORIC PRESERVATION--TECHNIQUE

"Organizing for Historic Preservation: A Resource Guide, Part II." <u>Connecticut Trust for Historic Preservation Newsletter</u>. Winter 1983. pp. 5-8.

HISTORIC PRESERVATION--TECHNIQUE

Pearson, Barbara E. "Photo Micrography and the Stanton House Restoration." <u>APT Bulletin</u>. Vol. 16, No. 3 & 4, 1984. p. 26-30.

The use of this tool for paint sample analysis in the reconstruction of building elements is described.

HISTORIC PRESERVATION--U.S.

Carlson, Alvar W. "An Analysis of Historic Preservation in the United States as Reflected by the National Register of Historical Places". <u>Journal of American Culture</u>. Summer 1980. p. 245-267.

HISTORIC PRESERVATION--U.S.

Cummings, Patricia J. "Standing for Sacred Places." <u>American Land Forum</u>. Vol. 7, No. 2, Mar./Apr. 1987. p. 12-14.

Preserving tribal sacred lands.

HISTORIC PRESERVATION--U.S.

Jones, Tonia. "National Register Misconceptions are Legion." <u>The Quapaw Quarter Chronicle</u>. Vol. 14, No. 3. June - July 1987. p. 12.
Criteria for determining National Register eligibility.

HISTORIC PRESERVATION--U.S.--ARKANSAS

"Arkansas Supports Open Space, Historic Preservation." Urban Conservation Report. Vol. 9, No. 3. Mar. 1987. p. 2.

Part of proceeds from new real-estate transfer tax earmarked for preservation fund.

HISTORIC PRESERVATION--U.S.--CALIFORNIA--LOS ANGELES

Goldstein, Barbara. "Los Angeles Restores." Progressive Architecture. Nov. 1985. p. 38, 40.

HISTORIC PRESERVATION--U.S.--CALIFORNIA-- SAN DIEGO

"Preservation-San Diego County." California Preservation. Vol. 12, No. 2. Apr. 1987. pp. 4-6.

Preservation activities in the Coronado-San Diego (CA) area.

HISTORIC PRESERVATION--U.S.--CONNECTICUT

"Connecticut Communities: Preservation on the Move." Connecticut Trust for Historic Preservation Newsletter. Winter 1983. 8 p.

HISTORIC PRESERVATION--U.S.--CONNECTICUT

"Connecticut's Attorney General Intervenes in Hartford Landmark Demolition." Urban Conservation Report. Vol. 9, No. 3, Mar. 1987. p. 3.

Controversy over Hartford's historic Goodwin Building.

HISTORIC PRESERVATION--U.S.--GEORGIA

DeLoach, Karen. "Black History Sites Surveyed in West Georgia." The Rambler. Vol. 13, No. 4. Winter 1987. p. 11.

HISTORIC PRESERVATION--U.S.--GEORGIA--ATLANTA

"Preservation Battles Spark Planning Effort in Atlanta." Urban Conservation Report. Vol. 10, No. 9, Sept. 30, 1986. p. 3-4.

HISTORIC PRESERVATION--U.S.--GEORGIA--ATLANTA

Segrest, Eileen B. "The Future of Preservation in Atlanta." Preservation Times. Vol. 6, No. 2. Fall 1986. pp. 1; 4.

HISTORIC PRESERVATION--U.S.--GEORGIA--THOMAS-VILLE

"Whole Town Bitten by Preservation Bug." The Rambler. Vol. 13, No. 2, Summer 1986. p. 24.

Thomasville, Georgia, has many restoration projects underway.

HISTORIC PRESERVATION--U.S.--HAWAII

"'Iolani Palace Restoration Update." Historic Hawai'i. Vol. 12, No. 10, Nov. 1986. p. 12-13, 16.

Restoration of the building and grounds of the official residence of Hawaii's last monarchs.

HISTORIC PRESERVATION--U.S.--HAWAII

Riznik, Barnes. "Changing Ideas and Forms of Preservation in Hawaii." Historic Hawaii News. July 1982. pp. 4-5.

HISTORIC PRESERVATION--U.S.--HAWAII--HONOLULU

"New Life for Downtown Honolulu." Historic Hawaii News. Mar. 1983. pp. 4-5.

HISTORIC PRESERVATION--U.S.--HAWAII--KOHALA

Holmes, Tommy. "Preserving Kohala's Heritage." Historic Hawaii. Vol. 12, No. 5, June 1986. p. 14-17.

HISTORIC PRESERVATION--U.S.--ILLINOIS

Berke, Arnold M. "Preservation Reaches the Heartland." Place. Feb. 1984. pp. 1-4.

HISTORIC PRESERVATION--U.S.--ILLINOIS

"Preservation Services Provides Vital
Service to Illinois' History." Dispatch from
the Illinois State Historical Society. Series
8, No. 3, May-June 1986. p. 5.

HISTORIC PRESERVATION--U.S.--INDIANA

Selm, William. "The Indiana Roof: a Star
is Reborn." The Indiana Preservationist. No.
4, 1986. p. 1.

A developer sought assistance of preservationists in restoring the interior of
the Indiana Roof Ballroom.

HISTORIC PRESERVATION--U.S.--MASSACHUSETTS--
BOSTON

"East Boston." Boston Preservation Alliance
Letter. Vol. 8, No. 7. Jul./Aug. 1987. p. 6.
A new historical society has formed to pro-
tect Boston's East Side.

HISTORIC PRESERVATION--U.S.--MASSACHUSETTS--
CAPE COD

Bradley, James. "Cape Cod Confronts Rapid
Development-Preservation Acitvities Intensify."
Massachusetts Historical Commission Newsletter.
Vol. 13, No. 1. Feb. 1987. pp. 1; 5.

HISTORICAL PRESERVATION--U.S.--MASSACHUSETTS --
CAPE COD

Friedburg, Betsy. "Cape Communities Escalate
Efforts to Protect Their Unique Heritage."
Massachusetts Historical Commission Newsletter.
Vol. 13, No. 1, Feb. 1987. p. 16, 11.

HISTORIC PRESERVATION--U.S.--MISSOURI

"Independence: Restoring and Preserving
Its 'Independent' Identity." Missouri Preservation News. Vol. 10, No. 2, Autumn 1986. p.
7-8, 11.

HISTORIC PRESERVATION--U.S.--MISSOURI

"Weston: Missouri Rivertown Restored to Its
Original Glory." Missouri Preservation News. Vol.
10, No. 2, Autumn 1986. p. 3-4.

HISTORIC PRESERVATION--U.S.--NEBRASKA

"Conserving Historic Places :
An overview of Nebraska's Preserva-
tion Office." Cornerstone : Historic
Preservation in Nebraska. Vol. 7,
No. 2, Summer 1986. p. 1-3.

HISTORIC PRESERVATION--U.S.--NEW YORK

"Beach Avenue Residents Petition for Preservation
District." The Landmark Society of Western New York.
Vol. 25, No. 2, Mar. 1987. p. 1.

HISTORIC PRESERVATION--U.S.--NEW YORK

McGregor, Robert Kuhn. "Historic Preservation in New York State." The Public Historian.
Vol. 7, No. 4, Fall 1985. p. 71-78.

HISTORIC PRESERVATION--U.S.--NEW YORK--NEW YORK CITY

Miller, Roy. "Big Business Preservation.
(New York: Wheeling and Dealing)." Architectural
Record. Oct. 1983. pp. 92-95.

HISTORIC PRESERVATION--U.S.--NEW YORK--NEW YORK CITY

"Streamlining Landmark Preservation."
Zoning News. Jul. 1986. p. 3.

New York City's 'Cooper Committee' issued
recommendations for revamping the city's Landmark
Preservation Commission's procedures.

HISTORIC PRESERVATION--U.S.--NORTH CAROLINA

Bishir, Catherine W. "Looking at North
Carolina's History through Architecture."
Carolina Comments. Mar. 1983. pp. 51-57.

HISTORIC PRESERVATION--U.S.--NORTH CAROLINA

" Easement Donated on Mount Carmel Baptist
Church." North Carolina Preservation. No. 67.
Spring 1987. pp. 16 - 17.

HISTORIC PRESERVATION--U.S.--NORTH CAROLINA

" Preservation Easement Given on Wall Street (N.C.) Rehab." North Carolina Preservation. No. 67. Spring 1987. p. 16.

HISTORIC PRESERVATION--U.S.--OHIO

"The Landmarks Committee of the Maumee Valley Historical Society 1968-1980" and "The Northwest Ohio Historic Preservation Office 1976-1981." Northwest Ohio Quarterly. Spr./Sum. 1982. Entire Issue.

HISTORIC PRESERVATION--U.S.--OHIO--CINCINNATI

Youkilis, Sanford. "Born-again preservationists." Planning. Oct. 1980. pp. 20-22.

HISTORIC PRESERVATION--U.S.--PENNSYLVANIA--PHILADELPHIA

"Adam's Evu." Progressive Architecture. Vol. 9, Sept. 1986. p. 145-147.

Robert Adam's Landsdowne House drawing room in the Philadelphia Museum of Art has recently been restored.

HISTORIC PRESERVATION--U.S.--PENNSYLVANIA--PITTSBURGH

Miller, Nory. "Big Business Preservation. (Pittsburgh: Virtuoso Preservationists.)" Architectural Record. October 1983. pp. 96-101.

HISTORIC PRESERVATION--U.S.--SOUTH

Wood, Ernest. "Preservation in the South : What It Has Done, Where It's Going." Southern Living. April 1986. p. 104-115.

HISTORIC PRESERVATION--U.S.--SOUTH CAROLINA--CHARLESTON

Groseclose, Bernard S., Jr. "Preservation Profile: Frances Ravenel Smythe Edmunds." Preservation Progress, Preservation Society of Charleston, Vol. 29, No. 4, May 1985. p. 3.

HISTORIC PRESERVATION--U.S.--SOUTH CAROLINA--CHARLESTON

Scardaville, Michael C. "The Selling of Historic Charleston." Preservation Progress. Vol. 30, No. 2, March 1986. p. 1, 6-11.

Selling the idea of historic preservation to Charlestonians not an easy task.

HISTORIC PRESERVATION--U.S.--TENNESSEE

Network. (Tennessee Heritage Alliance). Fall 1983, Number 1-

HISTORIC PRESERVATION--U.S.--TEXAS--GALVESTON

Miller, Nory. "Big Business Preservation. (Galveston: In-town Turnaround.)" Architectural Record. October 1983. pp. 102-105.

HISTORIC PRESERVATION--U.S.--TEXAS--SAN ANTONIO

Dillon, David. "The Alamo and Other Battles," Architecture. Mar. 1986. p. 62-69.

HISTORIC PRESERVATION--U.S.--VIRGINIA--WINCHESTER

Miller, Nory. "Big Business Preservation." (Winchester: No-frills Preservation.) Architectural Record. October 1983. pp. 106-109.

HISTORIC PRESERVATION--YEMEN

"Conserving the Traditional Architectrual Culture of Yemen." Architectural Record. September 1983. pp. 45-47.

HISTORIC PRESERVATION IN FOREIGN COUNTRIES

Aslet, Clive. "Home of Trust House Cuisine?" Country Life. Vol. 181, No. 23. June 4, 1987. pp. 266 - 268.
The National Trust for Scotland's historic kitchen reconstruction program.

HISTORIC PRESERVATION IN FOREIGN COUNTRIES

Burrman, Peter. "Conservation in Poland." Association for Studies in the Conservation of Historic Buildings [England] Transactions. Vol. 10, 1985. p. 37-47.

HISTORIC PRESERVATION IN FOREIGN COUNTRIES

Coney, Sandra. "'Radiant Living' for Auckland's Young Women." Historic Places in New Zealand. No. 16, Mar. 1987. p. 4-7.

The Auckland, NZ, YWCA.

HISTORIC PRESERVATION IN FOREIGN COUNTRIES

"Conservation of Mostar Old Town, Mostar, Yugoslavia." Architectural Record. Jan. 1987. pp. 98-99.

HISTORIC PRESERVATION IN FOREIGN COUNTRIES

De La Hey, Celia. "Monumental Wrenaissance." Country Life. Vol. 180, No. 4661. Dec. 18, 1986. pp. 1970-1971.

Restoration of Sir Christopher Wren's Ashton Memorial, Lancaster, England.

HISTORIC PRESERVATION IN FOREIGN COUNTRIES

Harris, Eileen. "So Rare, So Elegant: the Restored Grotto at Hampton Court House." Country Life. Vol. 180, No. 4661, Dec. 18, 1986. pp. 1956-1959.

Vertical File

HISTORIC PRESERVATION IN FOREIGN COUNTRIES

Higgs, Malcolm. "Glasgow Prefabs: a Suitable Case for Listing." Edinburgh Architecture Research. Vol. 13, 1986. p. 7-10. (VF)

HISTORIC PRESERVATION IN FOREIGN COUNTRIES

Hobhouse, Hermione. "Ninety Years of the Survey of London." Transactions of the Ancient Monuments Society, Vol. 13, 1987. p. 25-47.

HISTORIC PRESERVATION IN FOREIGN COUNTRIES

Hoskin, John. "Restoring Sukhothai Historical Park." Archaeology. Vol. 40, No. 2, Mar./Apr. 1987. p. 34-41.

Ruined city in Thailand focus of a 10-year restoration project.

HISTORIC PRESERVATION IN FOREIGN COUNTRIES

"Ipswich's [Queensland, Australia] Post Office Restored." National Trust Queensland Journal. Dec. 1986. p. 24.

HISTORIC PRESERVATION IN FOREIGN COUNTRIES

Jackson-Stops, Gervase. "Little Portugal in China: Conservation in Macau." Country Life. Vol. 181, No. 3, Jan. 15, 1987. p. 60-63.

HISTORIC PRESERVATION IN FOREIGN COUNTRIES

Lauritzen, Peter. Venice Preserved. London: Michael Joseph, 1986. 176p. (N6921.V5L38)

HISTORIC PRESERVATION IN FOREIGN COUNTRIES

Lim, William S. W. "Kuala Lumpur, Malaysia, Central Market- A Case Study for Adaptive Reuse." Place. Vol. 6, No. 8, Mar./Apr. 1987. p. 13-17.

HISTORIC PRESERVATION IN FOREIGN COUNTRIES

Lincoln, Helen. "Historic Drive-Brisbane to Toowoomba." National Trust Queensland Journal. Dec. 1986. p. 26-27.

HISTORIC PRESERVATION IN FOREIGN COUNTRIES

Powell, Ken. "What Future for the 'Coal Metropolis'?: the Conservation of Cardiff." Country Life. Vol. 180, No. 4653. Oct. 23, 1986. p. 1286-1288.

Historic preservation in Cardiff, Wales.

HISTORIC PRESERVATION IN FOREIGN COUNTRIES

   Richards, J.M. "Finland's Ironworking Heritage."
AA Files. No. 12, Summer 1986. p. 41-45.

Vertical File
HISTORIC PRESERVATION IN FOREIGN COUNTRIES

   The Undiscovered Gifts of the Caribbean.
Washington, D.C.: Partners for Livable Places, n.d.
Listing of Caribbean cultural resources. (VF)

HISTORIC PRESERVATION IN FOREIGN COUNTRIES

   "Venetian Love Affair." Foundation News. Vol. 27,
No. 6, Nov./Dec. 1986, p.18-24.

   HISTORIC PRESERVATION IN FOREIGN COUNTRIES

   Von Eckardt, Wolf. "Jerusalem the Golden."
Planning. Vol. 53, No. 2. Feb. 1987. pp. 24-
29.

   Ongoing efforts to preserve the character of
Jerusalem.

HISTORIC PRESERVATION IN FOREIGN COUNTRIES

   "Work to Restore Miss Traill's House." The
National Trust of Australia (NSW) Magazine. No.
38, Feb. 1987. p. 21.

   Restoration of historic house in Bathurst, NSW.

HISTORIC PRESERVATION IN FOREIGN COUNTRIES

   Worsley, Giles. "Rokeby Park, Yorkshire- I."
Country Life. Mar. 19, 1987. p. 74-79.

   18th century English estate.

HISTORIC PRESERVATION IN FOREIGN COUNTRIES--
RUSSIA

   Berton-Murrell, Kathleen. "The Fight to
Save Old Moscow: Rubble-Rousing Preservationists
Find a Friend in Gorbachev." The Washington
Post. Sunday, Mar. 29, 1987. p. C5.

HISTORIC SITES

   Ackelson, Mark C. "Threatened National Land-
marks-- an Opportunity for Land Trusts?" Land
Trusts' Exchange. Vol. 5, No. 2, Fall 1986. p.
12-13.

   A land trust worked with state and local
agencies and private citizens to protect a National Historic Landmark.

HISTORIC SITES

   Banks, William N. "Washington, New Hampshire
and Washington, Georgia." Antiques. Vol. CXXVI,
No. 6, December 1984. pp. 1398-1421.

   In addition, the 1984 Index appears in
this issue at pp. 1479-1518.

HISTORIC SITES

   "Homes of the Constitutional Era: Essays
in Preservation." Notes on Virginia. No. 30.
Spring 1987. pp. 6 - 21.
   Profiles of houses associated with Virginians
who played key roles in developing the Consti-
tution: Montpelier; Monticello; Stratford Hall;
Mount Vernon; Gunston Hall; Ashlawn-Highland;
Patrick Henry's Law Office at Red Hill.

HISTORIC SITES

   "The National Register of Historic Places: An
Index to Maryland's Past." Preservation Progress.
Vol. 1, No. 1, Winter 1986. p. 3-6

HISTORIC SITES

   Ward, Geoffrey C. "Eleanor Roosevelt
Drew Her Strength From Sanctuary Called Val-Kill."
Smithsonian. Vol. 15, No. 7, October 1984.
pp. 62-76.

HISTORIC SITES--ADMINISTRATION

   Mott, Wm. Penn Jr. "Entrance Fees: What
Should They Be?" Courier (NPS Newsletter). Vol.
30, No. 10, Oct. 1985. p. 11.

HISTORIC SITES--ADMINISTRATION

   Tise, Larry. "Coping with 'the Great
Declension', Pennsylvania Adopts New Strategies
to Manage its Historic Sites Economically."
History News. October 1982. pp. 12-18.

HISTORIC SITES--ADMINISTRATION

"Visitors Center Going Strong." <u>Wright Angles</u>. Oct./Dec. 1985. p. 2-3.

Oak Park Visitors Center directs tourists to sites in community served by 150 Foundation volunteers and financed by city.

HISTORIC SITES--CONSERVATION AND
    RESTORATION

Buchman, Sandra. "The Mitchell House, A Maryland Museum Combines History and Architecture to Tell the Story of a 19th-century Black Family." <u>History News</u>. February 1984. pp. 12-15.

HISTORIC SITES--CONSERVATION AND RESTORATION

Fitch, James Marston. "Visual Criteria for Historic Building Restoration: Determining Appropriate Repair/Cosmetic Treatments." <u>Technology & Conservation</u>. Winter 1978. pp. 10-15.

HISTORIC SITES--CONSERVATION AND
    RESTORATION

Jenison, Paul E. and Evans, Bryn E. "The Paul Revere and Moses Pierce-Hichborn Houses in Boston." <u>Antiques</u>. February 1984. pp. 454-461.

HISTORIC SITES--CONSERVATION AND RESTORATION

"Restoration and Living History: Low-Budget High-Quality Restoration (NB); Covered Bridge to Highlight Riverside Park (NH); Enlivening an Unfinished Fort (FL); Living History at Ft. Churchill (NV); Restored Stage Coach Inn (OR); Roving Interpreter (MD)." <u>Trends</u>. Summer 1979. pp. 17-22.

HISTORIC SITES--CONSERVATION AND RESTORATION--
    SCOTLAND

<u>Heritage Scotland</u> (National Trust for Scotland). Vol. 1, No. 2.

HISTORIC SITES--CONSERVATION AND RESTORATION--U.S.
    --CONNECTICUT--MIDDLEBURY

Duryee, Lawrence M. "General Rochambeau Slept Here; the Story of Breakneck Hill." <u>The Old House Journal</u>. Vol. 13, No. 2, Mar. 1985. p. 37-38.

HISTORIC SITES--CONSERVATION AND RESTORATION--U.S.--
Illinois--Springfield

Painter, George L. "Restoring the Lincoln Home Interior: An Interdisciplinary Approach," <u>CRM Bulletin</u>, Vol. 17, No. 4, December 1984, pp. 1-2, 4-5, 13.

HISTORIC SITES--INSURANCE

"Insurance Policy for Historic Homes." <u>The Old-House Journal</u>, February 1979. p. 14.

HISTORIC SITES--INTERPRETIVE PROGRAMS

Abercrombie, Stanley. "When a House Becomes a Museum." <u>AIA Journal</u>. August 1981. pp. 54-57.

HISTORIC SITES--INTERPRETATIVE PROGRAMS

Bailey, Mike. "Confederate Memorial Park Updates Interpretation." <u>The Preservation Report</u>. Vol. 13, No. 6, May/June 1986. p. 4

HISTORIC SITES--INTERPRETIVE PROGRAMS

Baker, Andrew and Warren Leon. "Old Sturbridge Village Introduces Social Conflict into its Interpretive Story." <u>History News</u>. Vol. 41, No. 3, Mar. 1986. p. 6-11.

HISTORIC SITES--INTERPRETATIVE PROGRAMS

"Interpretating Your Historic Building." <u>Culture & History</u>. Vol. 2, No. 3, April-May-June 1986. p. 27.

HISTORIC SITES--INTERPRETIVE PROGRAMS

George, Gerald. "The Great Drayton Hall Debate." <u>History News</u>. Jan. 1984. pp. 7-12.

HISTORIC SITES--INTERPRETIVE PROGRAMS

Elder, Betty Doak. "Drama for Interpretation." *History News*. June 1981. pp. 8-11.

HISTORIC SITES--INTERPRETIVE PROGRAMS

"Even Restorations Need Refurbishing." *The Herald*. Vol. 10, No. 2. pp. 4-10.

HISTORIC SITES--INTERPRETIVE PROGRAMS

Ferro, Maximilian L. "Planning for the Conservation of the Hay House: The Role of Infrastructure in House Museum Interpretation." *Technology and Conservation*. Fall 1982. pp. 40-48.

HISTORIC SITES--INTERPRETIVE PROGRAMS

Floyd, Candace. "Legend vs. History: Raynham Hall Redirects Interpretation from Romance to Documentary." *History News*. September 1981. pp. 14-15.

HISTORIC SITES--INTERPRETIVE PROGRAMS

Floyd, Candace. "A Sense of Pride: Cincinnati Neighborhoods Document their Histories." *History News*. October 1981. pp. 13-14.

HISTORIC SITES--INTERPRETIVE PROGRAMS

Floyd, Candace. "Upstairs, Downstairs: Minnesota Society Tells Story of James J. Hill House." *History News*. September 1981. pp. 10-13.

HISTORIC SITES--INTERPRETIVE PROGRAMS

Low, Shirley Payne. "Co-op History, How local historic sites can coordinate their interpretive plans." *History News*. November 1982. pp. 37-42.

HISTORIC SITES--INTERPRETIVE PROGRAMS

Nickerson, Ann T. "Teaching Hometown Heritage: Educators and Curators Work Together at Old Economy." *History News*. September 1981. pp. 16-18.

HISTORIC SITES--INTERPRETIVE PROGRAMS

Patterson, John. "Conner Prairie Refocuses its Interpretive Message to Include Controversial Subjects." *History News*. Vol. 41, No. 3, Mar. 1986. p. 12-15.

HISTORIC SITES--INTERPRETIVE PROGRAMS

"Park Techniques." *Parks*. July, August, September, 1981. pp. 16-23.

CONTENTS: Skinner, Barry. Waitangi Mangrove Forest Walkway--Foster, John. Countryside Commission for Scotland's Display Centre--Minimum Barrier.

HISTORICAL SITES--INTERPRETIVE PROGRAMS

O'Malley, Patricia M. "Humanizing Historic House Interpretation: Beyond the Decorative Arts." *The Bay State Historical League Bulletin*. Sum./Aut. 1981. pp. 1-4.

HISTORIC SITES--INTERPRETIVE PROGRAMS

Phillips, Charles. "The Missing Link: Can Interpretation Find a Home in Restored Neighborhoods?" *History News*. October 1981. pp. 9-12.

HISTORIC SITES--INTERPRETIVE PROGRAMS

"Recent Activities at Palace Complex Emphasize Furnishings." *Carolina Comments*. Vol. 33, No. 3, May 1985. p. 65-68.

Research leads to reinterpretation of furnishings and their arrangement at 18th century house.

HISTORIC SITES--INTERPRETIVE PROGRAMS

Reiss, Jim. "Judging the Voice of Your Museum, the Edison Institute Develops a Model Interpreter Evaluation Program." *History News*. Vol. 39, No. 11, November 1984. pp. 6-11.

HISTORIC SITES--INTERPRETIVE PROGRAMS

Sande, Theodore Anton. "Presenting the Truth About the Past," CRM Bulletin, Vol. 17, No.4, December 1984, pp. 1-3.

HISTORIC SITES--INTERPRETIVE PROGRAMS

Sellars, Richard West. "Vigil of Silence: The Civil War Memorials." History News. Vol. 41, No. 4, July/Aug. 1986. p. 19-21.

Lack of meaningful interpretation at historic battlefields.

HISTORIC SITES--INTERPRETIVE PROGRAMS

Tramposch, William J. "Put There to Spark" How Colonial Williamsburg Trains Its Interpretive Crew." History News. July 1982. pp. 21-23.

HISTORIC SITES--INTERPRETIVE PROGRAMS

Watson, Michael D. "NPS Interpretive Skills Training Program." Trends. Vol. 23, No. 2, 1986. p. 4-8.

HISTORIC SITES--INTERPRETIVE PROGRAMS

Worthen, William B. "Restoring the Restoration." History News. Vol. 39, No. 11, November 1984. pp. 6-11.

The Arkansas Territorial Restoration in Little Rock revises its interpretation of the frontier experience.

HISTORIC SITES--INTERPRETIVE PROGRAMS--U.S.-- NEW YORK--TARRYTOWN

Connors, Jill. "The New Nation." Americana. Vol. 13, No. 1, Mar./Apr. 1985. p. 12.

New interpretive program at Van Cortlandt Manor outlined.

HISTORIC SITES--INTERPRETIVE PROGRAMS--U.S.-- NEW YORK--TARRYTOWN

Haley, Jacquetta M. "Somewhere in Time: Van Cortlandt Manor Shifts the Focus of its Interpretation from Revolution to Nation Building." History News. Vol. 40, No. 5, May 1985. p. 6-11.

HISTORIC SITES--LAW AND LEGISLATION

"Proposed Historic Preservation Cuts Criticized at House Hearing." Housing and Community Development Reporter. Vol. 12, No. 42, Mar. 11, 1985. p. 794.

HISTORIC SITES--MANAGEMENT

Biallas, Rondall J. "Building Automation Systems at Iolani Palace-Honolulu, Hawaii." APT Bulletin. Vol. 13, No. 1. 1981. pp. 7-15.

HISTORIC SITES--MASTER PLANS

"Plans Unveiled for Ellis Island Restoration." Architectural Record. July 1984. p. 51.

HISTORIC SITES--U.S.--COLORADO

Mills, Gloria. "Ludlow Massacre Site Listed in Register." Colorado Heritage News. June 1986. p. 4.

Site of massacre precipitated by the 1913-14 Colorado coal strike has been named to the National Register.

HISTORIC SITES--U.S.--CONNECTICUT--HARTFORD

Taylor, Nick. "TheWhole Iceberg: Project Iceberg, as the recent renovation of the Wadsworth Atheneum was called, put most of the Wallace Nutting Collection and other treasures on public view." Americana. Vol. 12, No. 6. Jan. 1985. pp. 82-86.

HISTORIC SITES--U.S.--ILLINOIS

"The National Register of Historic Places in Illinois." Illinois Preservation Series, No. 6, June 1985. 16 p.

Illinois listings in the NR through 4/10/85.

HISTORIC SITES--U.S.--ILLINOIS--CAHOKIA

Iseminger, William R. "Cahokia: A Mississippian Metropolis" Historic Illinois April 1980. p. 1-7.

HISTORIC SITES--U.S.--KANSAS

Stein, Martin. "Sites in South Central Kansas Are Guides to Regional Diversity." Kansas Preservation. Vol. 8, No. 3, March-April 1986. p. 6-7.

HISTORIC SITES--U.S.--MASSACHUSETTS--NEW BEDFORD

Mayfield, Jared. "History and Hospitality in New Bedford." Yankee. Vol. 49, No. 8, August 1985. p. 28-35.

Vertical File
HISTORIC SITES--U.S.--NEVADA

A Guidebook to Nevada's Historic Markers. Carson City: Nevada Division of Historic Preservation and Archeology, n.d. (VF)

HISTORIC SITES--U.S.--NEW YORK

"Hyde Park, Franklin Delano Roosevelt National Historic Site." TPL Update (Trust for Public Land). No. 11, Fall 1984. p. 1.

HISTORIC SITES--U.S.--NEW YORK--NEW YORK CITY

"Old New York." Colonial Homes. Sep./Oct. 1981. pp. 102-119.

The Van Cortlandt Mansion--The Morris Jumel Mansion--The Avigail Adams Smith Museums--Fraunces Tavern.

HISTORIC SITES--U.S.--TENNESSEE

Wynn, Linda T. "Tennessee's State-Owned Historic Sites." The Courier (Tennessee Historical Commission). Vol. 25, No. 1, Oct. 1986. p. 4-5, 6, 8.

HISTORIC SITES--U.S.--TEXAS--SAN ANTONIO

von Schmidt, Eric. "The Alamo Remembered - from a painter's point of view." Smithsonian. Vol. 16, No. 12, Mar. 1986. p. 54-67.

HISTORIC SITES--U.S.--UTAH--EUREKA

George, Gerald. "Eureka, A Former Mining Town Strikes Gold...." History News. Vol. 39, No. 5, May 1984. pp. 15-19.

Tintic Historic Mining District.

HISTORIC STRUCTURES REPORTS

Biallas, Randall J. "Evolution of Historic Structure Reports." NPS, CRM Bulletin. Vol. 7, No. 1, April 1984. p. 19.

HISTORIC STRUCTURES REPORTS

Bulletin, APT. Vol. XIV, No. 4, 1982. Entire issue including:

Reed, P.S. "Documentation of Historic Structures."
Spiers, Tomas H. Jr. "Architectural Investigation and Analysis for Historic Structure Reports."
Gianopulos, Nicholas L., P.E. "Suggested Guidelines for the Structural Examination, Analysis and Evaluation ~ of an Historic Structure."
McCarthy, ( ) Thomas H. "Programming for Preservation."

HISTORIC STRUCTURE REPORTS

DeSamper, Hugh. "Partners in Preservation of a Historic Landmark: The Powder Magazine." Colonial Williamsburg. Vol. 9, No. 2, Winter 1986-87. p. 27-30.

HISTORIC STRUCTURES REPORTS

Mathien, Frances Joan. "Archeological Application of Historic Structure Reports." NPS, CRM Bulletin. Vol. 7, No. 1, April 1984. pp. 11, 19.

HISTORIC STRUCTURES REPORTS--U.S.--MASSACHUSETTS--BOSTON

"Preserving History." (State House, Austin Hall.) Architectural Record. October 1984. p. 117.

HISTORIC TREES

"Australia Protects Significant Trees." Urban Innovation Abroad. Vol. 8, No. 5, May 1984. p. 2.

HISTORIC TREES--AUSTRALIA--VICTORIA

"Register of Significant Trees of Victoria."
Trust News. Vol. 14, No. 2, Aug. 1985. p. 12-13.

HISTORICAL MARKERS--U.S.--ILLINOIS

"The State Historical Markers Program."
Dispatch, Illinois State Historical Society.
Series 6, No. 6, November-December 1984. p..4.

HISTORICAL MARKERS--U.S.--NORTH CAROLINA

Hill, Michael. "The Fiftieth Anniversary of
the North Carolina Highway Historical Marker
Program." Carolina Comments. Vol. 34, No. 2,
Mar. 1986. p. 59-63.

HISTORICAL MARKERS --U.S.--TEXAS

"Marker Project Launched." The Medallion.
Vol. 23, No. 5, May 1986. p. 1.

Effort to dedicate historical markers relating
to women.

HISTORICAL MUSEUMS

Riviere, Georges Henri. "Concerning the
creation of a musuem in a historic monument.
Museum. no.3, 1980. p. 104-105.

HISTORICAL RESEARCH

Bearss, Edwin C. "History Research: Getting
a Quality but Cost-Effective Product." CRM
Bulletin. Vol. 8, No. 6, Dec. 1985. p. 7-9.

HISTORICAL RESEARCH

Bradshaw, James Stanford. "The Use of
Newspapers in Historical Research." Chronicle,
The Quarterly Magazine of the Historical Society
of Michigan. Vol. 20, No. 2, Summer 1984.
pp. 18-19.

HISTORICAL RESEARCH

"House Hunting in Licking County (Ohio)."
American Heritage. Vol. 37, No. 2, Feb./Mar.
1986. p. 100-105.

HISTORICAL RESEARCH

Matteson, Ruth B. "How to Research Your
19th Century House: An Approach to Using Documentary Evidence." Conservancy News. Vol. 4,
No. 2. May/June 1987. p.3.

HISTORICAL RESEARCH

"A Ready Reference". CRM Bulletin.
Vol. 8, No. 1, Feb. 1985. (4p. insert)

A list of institutions to which
professionals in anthropology, historic
architecture, and museum activities can refer
for assistance.

HISTORICAL RESEARCH

Sturm, William. "The Oakland History
Room: Resource for the City's Buildings."
Oakland Heritage Alliance News. Vol. 6,
No. 4, Winter 1986-7. p. 1-5.

The Oakland Public Library's Oakland
History Room is a particularly fine resource
for the history of the city's architecture.

HISTORICAL SOCIETIES

Hartman, Hedy A. and Suzanne B. Schnell.
"Institutional Master Planning for Historical
Organizations and Museums." Technical Report II.
American Association for State and Local History.
(History News, Vol. 41, No. 6. Nov./Dec. 1986
insert.)

HISTORICAL SOCIETIES--VIRGINIA

Kimbrough, Janet C. "The Early History of
the Association for the Preservation of Virginia
Antiquities, a Personal Account." Virginia
Cavalcade. Autumn 1980. pp. 68-75.

HISTORICAL SOCIETIES

Richmond, Robert W. and Gerald George.
"Hard Times for America's Heritage, State Budget
Cuts Threaten History Work." History News.
April 1982. pp. 23-30.

HISTORIOGRAPHY

Phillips, Charles. "The Politics of State History: More and More, State Organizations are Forced to Play Politics with Culture." History News. Vol. 40, No. 9, Sept. 1985. p. 16-20.

HISTORIOGRAPHY

Tunnell, Curtis. "The Shape of the Eighties: Forty mini-trends in the state and local history field: Which ones affect you?" History News. Vol. 41, No. 3, Mar. 1986. p. 16-21.

HISTORY

Celsor, Sharon. "Preserving the Complete History." History News. Vol 39, No. 10, October 1984. pp. 6-9.

Preservationists, folklorists and social historians combine their research methods to document the architectural and humanistic histories of neighborhoods and sites.

HISTORY--U.S.--PENNSYLVANIA--PHILADELPHIA

Green, Anthony. "Philadelphia: the City that Gave Us a Nation." National Parks. Vol. 61, Nos. 3-4. Mar./Apr. 1978. pp. 24-29.

HISTORY

Kashdan, Sandra L. "Shaping America: Hispanic Heritage in the U.S. Environment." Place. Vol. 6, No. 6, Nov./Dec. 1986. p. 15-17.

HISTORY

Nunnally, Pat. "Iowa's Heritage Trail." American Land Forum. Vol. 7, No. 2, Mar./Apr. 1987. p. 23-27.

HISTORY--METHODOLOGY

Floyd, Candace. "The Historian in the Gray Flannel Suit." History News. Vol. 39, No. 5, May 1984. pp. 6-10.

HISTORY--METHODOLOGY

Phillips, Charles. "History's Hired Hands, Plain Talk About Writing Business Histories." History News. Vol. 39, No. 5, May 1984. pp. 11-14.

HISTORY--STUDY AND TEACHING

Martin, Dianne. "History goes Public." History News, May 1979. pp.121-143.

HISTORY--STUDY AND TEACHING

Pursell, Carroll W. "The Graduate Program in Public Historical Studies, University of California, Santa Barbara." APT Bulletin. v. XII, No. 3, 1980. p.127-129.

HISTORY--U.S.--CALIFORNIA

California: a Place, a People, a Dream. San Francisco: Chronicle Books, 1986. 158p. (F861. 5.C34)

Illustrated history of California.

HOME ECONOMICS

Garrett, Elisabeth D. "The American Home: Part VI: the Quest for Comfort: Housekeeping Practices and Living Arrangements the Year Round." Antiques. Vol. 128, No. 6, Dec. 1985. p. 1210-1223.

Vertical File

HOMELESSNESS

Trotsky, Judith. The NIMBY Syndrome. 1986. 33p. unpublished. (VF)

The problem of housing the homeless.

HOMESTEADING

"New York City Broadens Scope of Shopsteading Program." Housing and Development Reporter. July 4, 1983. pp. 103-104.

HOSPITALS

    Boyes, Lindy. "Tripler General Hospital:
Medical Veteran of the Islands." <u>Historic
Hawai'i</u>. Vol. 13, No. 5. June 1987. pp. 8 - 9.

HOSPITALS

    Brewer, Yvonne, and Scherer Easa. "A
Tale of Two Hospitals: Kapi'olani Medical
Center for Women and Children." <u>Historic Hawai'i</u>.
Vol. 13, No. 5. June 1987. pp. 6 - 7.

HOSPITALS

    "Hawai'i Medical Service Association."
<u>Historic Hawai'i</u>. Vol. 13, No. 5. July 1987.
pp. 15 - 16.

HOSPITALS

    Nikolaieff, George. "Kaiser Foundation
Hospital - Gone But Not Forgotten." <u>Historic</u>
<u>Hawai'i</u>. Vol. 13, No. 5. July 1987. pp. 16 - 18.

HOSPITALS

    Perry, Rachel. "One Doctor's Dream:
Straub Clinic and Hospital." <u>Historic Hawai'i</u>.
Vol. 13, No. 5. June 1987. p. 14.

HOSPITALS

    Spiker, Donda. "Kuakini Medical Center:
A Tradition of Caring." <u>Historic Hawai'i</u>.
Vol. 13, No. 5. June 1987. pp. 10 - 11.

HOSPITALS

    Yoshina, Cheryl. "St. Francis Medical
Center: A Mission of Love." <u>Historic Hawai'i</u>.
Vol. 13, No. 5. June 1987. pp. 12 - 13.

HOSPITALS--ADAPTIVE USE

    "Building Types Study 601: Hospital Planning,
An Unfinished Business." <u>Architectural Record</u>.
May 1984. pp. 129-145.

HOSPITALS--DESIGN AND CONSTRUCTION

    "L'architecture des hopitaux."
<u>Monuments Historiques</u>. No. 114. Entire Issue.

HOSPITALS--ADAPTIVE USE

    "Development Pressures Mount in Westchester."
and "A Tale of Two Hospitals: Utica and Buffalo."
<u>Newsletter</u>, Preservation League of New York
State. Vol. 10, No. 4, July-August 1984. pp. 1-3

HOSPITALS--ADAPTIVE USE

    "Upbeat ambience in downtown Baltimore: a
renovated restaurant and new cocktail lounge
designed by Rita St. Clair Associates, in a
hotel-turned-apartment complex." <u>Interior</u>
<u>Design</u>. Apr. 1980, pp. 242-245.

HOSPITALS--DESIGN AND CONSTRUCTION--U.S.--NEW
    JERSEY--BAYONNE

    Doubilet, Susan. "Pragmatic Ornamentalism."
<u>Progressive Architecture</u>. Mar. 1985. p. 78-81.

    Hospital modernization in traditional terms
depicted.

HOSPITALS--U.S.--MASSACHUSETTS

    Bennett, William. "The Genealogy of
Mass General." <u>American Heritage</u>. October/
November 1984. pp. 41-52.

HOTELS--EGYPT--CAIRO

    "Opulance on the Nile." <u>Architectural</u>
<u>Record</u>. June 1984. pp. 108-111.

HOTELS, TAVERNS, ETC.

"Bed & Breakfast." Economic Growth & Revitalization Report. No. 87-8. Apr. 28, 1987. p. 3.

Relaxation of historic preservation statutes in
Illinois will encourage more B & Bs.

HOTELS, TAVERNS, ETC.

"Classic Elegance Revived in Seattle's
Olympic Hotel." Architectural Record. December
1982. pp. 22-23.

HOTELS, TAVERNS, ETC.

Guida, Louis. "Capitalized At Last,
Capital Hotel to Open as Capital Hostelry."
The Quapaw Quarter Chronicle. November/
December 1983. p. 1.

HOTELS, TAVERNS, ETC.

Hathaway, Jim. "A History of the American
Drinking Place." Landscape. Vol. 29, No. 1,
1986. p. 1-9.

HOTELS, TAVERNS, ETC.

"Huntington Hotel." Los Angeles Conservancy.
Vol. 9, No. 3. May/Jun. 1987. p. 11.

Preservationist's attempts to save Huntington
Sheraton Hotel, Pasadena.

HOTELS, TAVERNS, ETC.

Hudson, Patricia L. "Appalachian Inns."
Americana. Vol. 13, No. 4, Sept./Oct. 1985.
p. 39-43, 104.

HOTELS, TAVERNS, ETC.

"The Huntington Hotel." Pasadena Heritage. Vol. 10,
No. 1, Feb. 1987. p. 4-5.

Excerpts from a presentation to Pasadena City
Board of Directors.

HOTELS, TAVERNS, ETC.

"Inns and Taverns Spotlight Vermont."
Americana. Vol. 15, No. 2, May/June 1987. p. 82-85

HOTELS, TAVERNS, ETC.

Lee, Madeline. "Santa Barbara's California
Craftsman Bed and Breakfast Inns." Victorian
Homes. Vol 6, No. 3. Summer 1987. pp. 52 - 54.

HOTELS, TAVERNS, ETC.

"Managing the Bed & Breakfast
Boom." Urban Outlook. Vol. 8, No. 15,
August 15, 1986. p. 4-5.

HOTELS, TAVERNS, ETC.

Maxwell, Shirley. "Supporting Your Old
House Obsession: Owning an Inn or B&B." The Old
House Journal. Vol. 13, No. 8, Oct. 1985. p. 171-
175.

HOTELS, TAVERNS, ETC.

Myers, Hyman. "The Restoration of the
Fairmont Hotel, Philadelphia: Regaining the
Building's Past Elegance while Modernizing
Systems." Technology and Conservation. Winter
1979. pp. 20-25.

HOTELS, TAVERNS, ETC.

O'Brien, Frank. "Hotel Faces Uncertain Future."
Building Renovation. Vol. 4, No. 2, Mar./Apr. 1987.
p. 6.

HOTELS, TAVERNS, ETC.

O'Mara, W. Paul. "The Queen Anne:
More than Just a 'Good Night's Sleep!."
Urban Land. May 1983. pp. 16-19.

HOTELS, TAVERNS, ETC.

    "The Redstone Inn: A Small, Elegant Hotel in Dubuque, Iowa." <u>Victorian Homes</u>. Vol. 5, No. 4. Fall 1986. pp. 71-73.

    A Victorian mansion becomes a bed and breakfast inn.

HOTELS, TAVERNS, ETC.--ADAPTIVE USE

    "A Star Is Born." <u>Commercial Renovation</u>. Vol. 8, No. 5, Oct. 1986. p. 45.

    Conversion of a movie theater lobby to a new cafe.

HOTELS, TAVERNS, ETC.--ADAPTIVE USE

    Thomas Ross. "Team Effort, Imagination Revive the Kenmore Hotel." <u>Building Design & Construction</u>. Vol. 27, No. 10, Oct. 1986. p. 80-81.

    Conversion of an abandoned hotel into offices in Albany N.Y.

HOTELS, TAVERNS, ETC.--ADAPTIVE USE--U.S.--MASSACHUSETTS--TOWNSEND

    Handler, Mimi. "A Habitable Antique." <u>Early American Life</u>. Vol. 17, No. 5. Oct. 1986. pp. 43-53.

    The Conant Tavern, an early 18th century landmark in Townsend, Mass. is now an antique dealer's store.

HOTELS, TAVERNS, ETC.--CANADA

    Brown, Dick. "More Than a Business." <u>Canadian Heritage</u>. Vol. 12, Issue 4, Oct-Nov. 1986. p. 15-20.

    Bed and breakfast business.

HOTELS, TAVERNS, ETC.--CONSERVATION AND RESTORATION

    Crandell, Dan. "Putting a Kelso Hotel to a New Use: An Example of Renovation for the Community." <u>Landmarks</u>. Summer 1981. p. 29.

HOTELS, TAVERNS, ETC.--CONSERVATION AND RESTORATION

    Greer, Nora Richter. 'Grande Dame Makes a Comeback." <u>Architecture</u>. Nov. 1986. p. 48-55.

    The restoration of the Willard Hotel in Washington, D.C.

HOTELS, TAVERNS, ETC.--CONSERVATION AND RESTORATION

    Hawley, Peter. "A Future for Downtown Hotels." <u>Possibilities</u>. Jul. 1980. pp. 1, 4-5.

HOTELS, TAVERNS, ETC.--CONSERVATION AND RESTORATION

    "The Huntington Hotel." <u>Pasadena Heritage</u>. Vol. 10, No. 1, Feb. 1987. p. 4-5.

    Defenders of the Huntington Hotel seeking to find a way to restore the hotel as an alternative to demolition.

HOTELS, TAVERNS, ETC.--CONSERVATION AND RESTORATION

    Lincoln, Sheryl J. "Single-room residential hotels must be preserved as low-income housing alternative". <u>JOH</u>. July 1980. p. 383-386.

HOTELS, TAVERNS, ETC.---CONSERVATION AND RESTORATION

    Marks, Dorothy Ames. "A Stately Willard Proudly Receives Guests Once More." <u>Smithsonian</u>. Vol. 17, No. 11, Feb. 1987. p. 79-89.

HOTELS, TAVERNS, ETC.--CONSERVATION AND RESTORATION

    McQuade, Walter. "There's A Small Hotel." <u>Fortune</u>. Apr. 1, 1985. p. 173-175.

HOTELS, TAVERNS, ETC.--CONSERVATION AND RESTORATION

    Roosevelt, Selwa. "The Fairfax Hotel: a gracious renovation in Washington, D.C." <u>Architectural Digest</u>. Apr. 1980. pp. 119-125.

HOTELS, TAVERNS, ETC.--CONSERVATION AND RESTORATION

    "UDAG Loss, Certification Problem, Beset Historic Hotel Project." Urban Conservation Report. Vol. 10, No. 3, Mar. 17, 1986. p. 5.

    Focus on Davenport Hotel in Spokane, Washington.

HOTELS, TAVERNS, ETC.--CONSERVATION AND RESTORA-
TION--BELGIUM--LIEGE

Brenner, Douglas. "En Rapport." Architectural Record. June 1985. p. 142-149.

16th Century Hotel Torrentius renovation
is described.

HOTELS, TAVERNS, ETC.--CONSERVATION AND RESTORATION--
U.S.--ALABAMA--MENTONE SPRINGS HOTEL

"Couple Was the Last Resort for Aging Hotel."
The Preservation Report, Alabama Historical
Commission. Vol. 12, No. 1. Jul./Aug. 1984.
p. 2.

HOTELS, TAVERNS, ETC.--CONSERVATION AND RESTORA-
TION--U.S.--GEORGIA--AUGUSTA

"Bon Air Revived as Elderly Housing."
The Rambler, Newsletter of the Georgia Trust
for Historic Preservation, Inc. Vol. 11, No. 4,
Fall 1984. p. 8.

McKim, Mead and White.

HOTELS, TAVERNS, ETC.--CONSERVATION AND RESTORA-
TION--U.S.--CALIFORNIA--SAN FRANCISCO

"As Good as Old." Commercial Renovation.
Vol. 7, No. 3, June 1985. p. 53.

HOTELS, TAVERNS, ETC.--CONSERVATION AND RESTORA-
TION--U.S.--MASSACHUSETTS--BOSTON

Dodson, James. "Still the Ritz." Yankee.
Vol. 49, No. 10, Oct. 1985. p. 94-101, 134-140.

HOTELS, TAVERNS, ETC.--CONSERVATION AND RESTORA-
TION--U.S.--MASSACHUSETTS--BOSTON

Miller, Kevin D. "The Lenox Hotel." Boston
Preservation Alliance Letter. Vol. 7, No. 1,
Jan. 1986. p. 12, 9.

HOTELS, TAVERNS, ETC.--CONSERVATION AND
RESTORATION--U.S.--NEW YORK--NEW YORK CITY

Gandee, Charles K. "The French
Connection: Morgans Hotel." Architectural
Record. Mar. 1985. p. 144-151.

HOTELS, TAVERNS, ETC.--CONSERVATION AND RESTORATION--
U.S.--OHIO--CINCINNATI

"Civic Centerpiece: The Carew Complex."
Progressive Architecture. Jan. 1985. pp. 43-44.

HOTELS, TAVERNS, ETC.--CONSERVATION AND RESTORA-
TION--U.S.--TEXAS--DALLAS

"December Reopening Planned for Renovated
Plaza Hotel." Historic Dallas. Vol. 7, No. 17,
Nov./Dec. 1985. p. 4.

HOTELS, TAVERNS ETC.--CONSERVATION AND RESTORATION--
U.S.--VERMONT--BARRE

"The Brandon Inn Sets a Precedent, Restored
1700's Inn is First in a Proposed 'Chain' of
Such Hostelries." Commercial Renovation.
Aug. 1984. pp. 28-33.

HOTELS, TAVERNS, ETC.--FRANCE--PARIS

Matthews, Tom. "Hotel Sale Restored."
Progressive Architecture. Nov. 1985. p. 35.

HOTELS, TAVERNS, ETC.--SINGLE-ROOM OCCUPANCY

Comerio, Mary. "Inside Chinatown's
Tiny Apartments." AIA Journal. April
1983. pp. 68-71.

HOTELS, TAVERNS, ETC.--U.S.--ARIZONA--PHOENIX

"Arizona Biltmore, Phoenix, Arizona, Frank
Lloyd Wright Foundation." Architectural Record.
Jul. 1980. pp. 116-121.

HOTELS, TAVERNS, ETC--U.S.--ARKANSAS--LITTLE ROCK

Heinbockel, C. S. "Lafayette Returns, Its
Lobby Grand Again." Chronicle, Quapaw Quarter
Association. Vol. 12, No. 1, Feb. 1985. p. 1,
10.

HOTELS, TAVERNS, ETC.--U.S.--CALIFORNIA--BALBOA

"Preservation Very Big in Balboa." California Preservation. Vol. 11, No. 1, Jan. 1986. p. 1.

Rehab of a 1930 Spanish Colonial Revival oceanfront hotel in Newport Beach by a partnership of professional basketball players.

HOTELS, TAVERNS, ETC.--U.S.--COLORADO--DENVER

"Barth Hotel (NR) Reopens." Historic Denver News. Vol. 14, No. 1. Jan. 1985. p. 3.

HOTELS, TAVERNS, ETC.--U.S.--FLORIDA

"Bed-and-Breakfast to Open in October." Florida Preservation News. Vol. 2, No. 3, May-June 1986. p. 14.

Six restored landmark wood structures will open in downown Miami.

HOTELS, TAVERNS, ETC.--U.S.--LOUISIANA--NEW ORLEANS

Giarrusso, Jerel M. "Time Stands Still at Historic Inns." New Orleans Preservation in Print. Vol. 13, No. 4, May 1986. p. 7.

HOTELS, TAVERNS, ETC.--U.S.--MINNESOTA--LAKE CITY

"Bed-and-breakfasting: a Classy Revival: the New State of a Stately Rivertown Home." Architecture Minnesota. Vol. 11, No. 4, July/Aug. 1985. p. 34-35.

HOTELS, TAVERNS, ETC.--U.S.--MINNESOTA--LAKE CITY

"Bed-and-breakfasting: In Tudor Style: a Lakeshore Mansion Sheds Its Private Past." Architecture Minnesota. Vol. 11, No. 4, July/Aug. 1985. p. 36-37.

HOTELS, TAVERNS, ETC.--U.S.--MISSOURI

Johnson, Cathy. "Missouri Country Inns." Early American Life. Vol. 17, No. 3. June 1986. pp. 32-39.

HOTELS, TAVERNS, ETC.--U.S.--NEW JERSEY

"Seaside Inns in Cape May." Victorian Homes. Vol. 5, Issue 3, Summer 1986. p. 62-63.

HOTELS, TAVERNS, ETC.--U.S.--NEW YORK--NEW YORK

Smith, Mary Ann. "The Metropolitan Hotel and Niblo's Garden: A Luxury Resort Complex in Mid-Nineteenth-Century Manhattan." 19th Century Winter 1979. p. 45-48.

HOTELS, TAVERNS, ETC.--U.S.--RHODE ISLAND-- NEWPORT

Bongartz, Roy. "Inn at Castle Hill". Americana. July/August 1980. p. 58-62.

HOTELS, TAVERNS, ETC.--U.S.--WASHINGTON, D.C.

Dunn, Donald H. (ed.). "Capital Ideas for a New Year's Vacation." Business Week. December 17, 1984. pp. 91-2.

HOUSE BUYING

Bongartz, Roy. "Would You Buy an Old Inn From This Man?" Americana. Vol. 12, No. 6, Jan./Feb. 1985. p. 59-62.

HOUSE BUYING

Fossel, Peter V. "Check Out An Old House: There are Many Steps to Take Before Buying." Americana. Vol. 13, No. 1, Mar./Apr. 1985. p. 16, 21-22.

HOUSE BUYING

"Inspecting the old house; a guide for buyers and owners." Utah Preservation/Restoration. 1979. pp. 31,38-39,42.

HOUSE FURNISHINGS

Olson, Sarah M. "The Historic Furnishings
Program," Courier. Vol. 31, No. 1, Jan. 1986.
p. 19-20.

HOUSE FURNISHING

Sweeney, Kevin M. "Furniture and the Domestic
Environment in Wethersfield, Connecticut, 1639-
1800", The Connecticut Antiquarian, Vol. XXXVI,
No. 2, December 1984, pp. 10-39.

HOUSING

"How Much Do Rehab, Adaptive Use,
Contribute to the Nation's Housing
Stock." Urban Conservation Report.
December 22, 1983. p.7.

HOUSING

Pommer, Richard. "The Architecture of Urban Housing in the United States during the Early 1930s".
Journal of the Society of Architectural Historians, December, 1978. pp. 235-264.

HOUSING

Stokes, Bruce. "Housing: The Environmental
Issues." Sierra. September/October 1982.
pp. 45-49.

HOUSING--FINANCE

Comings, William D., Jr. "Advice to
developers: multifamily rental housing can
be built." Journal of Housing. May 1980.
p. 258-261.

HOUSING--FINANCE

Miller, Anita. "Housing Finance Industry :
Needs Economic Policy, Deregulation, and Tax-exempt
Bond Limitations." Journal of Housing. July, 1979
pp. 354-356.

HOUSING--FINANCE

Sears, Cecil E. "Problems and Prospects
for Housing Finance." Urban Land. September 1982.
pp. 11-17.

HOUSING--LAW AND LEGISLATION

"1985 Developments in Housing Law."
Housing Law Bulletin. Vol. 15, Issue 6, Nov./
Dec. 1985. p. 1-7.

HOUSING--LAW AND LEGISLATION

"1978 Housing Legislation: an
Overview and Analysis." Journal of
Housing. January 1979. pp. 15-24.

HOUSING--LAW AND LEGISLATION--U.S.--CONNECTICUT
--HARTFORD

Tegeler, Philip and Rosalind Silverstein.
"Hartford Demands a Quid Pro Quo." Planning.
Vol. 51, No. 6, June 1985. p. 18-19.

HOUSING--REMOTE SENSING

Goldstein, Janice and William Hazard.
"Remote Sensing Assesses Housing and Heat Loss
in Houston." Practicing Planner, Mar. 1978.
pp. 7-9; 17.

HOUSING--U.S.--INDIANA

Owen, C. James and William L. Whited.
"Public-private ownership ; preservation
without gentrification." Planning.
Sept. 1980. p. 16-18.

HOUSING POLICY

"Essays On Social Housing." Progressive
Architecture. July 1984. pp. 82-87.

HOUSING POLICY

Evans, Sandra. "Lee Gardens Plans Readied, Arlington May Save 200 Housing Units." The Washington Post. Apr. 4, 1987. (VF)

HOUSING POLICY

Greer, Nora Richler. "The Homeless: An Urban Crisis of the 1980s." Architecture. Vol. 74, No. 7, July 1985. p. 56-59.

HOUSING POLICY

"Housing in the Koch Era." City Limits. Aug./Sept. 1985. Entire Issue. 39 p.

A review of the effects of property tax incentives for historic preservation, the elimination of single room occupancy housing, rent control and other housing policy in New York City over the last decade.

HOUSING POLICY

Listokin, David and Lizabeth Allewelt. "Housing Receivership: A National Remedy." Journal of Housing. Vol. 42, No. 1, Jan./ Feb. 1985. p. 21-24.

HOUSING POLICY

Myers, Phyllis. "Design Strategies for Housing the Elderly." Place. September 1984. pp. 8-10.

HOUSING POLICY

Todd, Reggie. "The Federal Housing Policy is in Disarray." Special Report, National League of Cities. Nation's Cities Weekly. Vol. 9, No. 8, Feb. 24, 1986. p. 3, 8.

HOUSING REHABILITATION

Anderson, Art. "The Rehab Corner." Neighborhood Quarterly. Vol. 6-2, Spring 1986. p. 2.

What to look for when considering housing rehabilitation.

HOUSING REHABILITATION

Beach, David. "The Right to 'a Decent Home': Creating Affordable Urban Housing." Conserve Neighborhoods. No. 67. Apr./May 1987. Entire issue.

HOUSING REHABILITATION

Benitez, A. William. "Cutting Costs in Your Rehab Program." Rehab Notes. Vol. 11, No. 1, Feb. 1987. p. 1-3.

HOUSING REHABILITATION

"A British Facelift for Inner Cities." Urban Innovation Abroad. August 1983. p. 5.

HOUSING REHABILITATION

"Community Development Groups Will Implement Major Housing Rehab Initiative." Community Development Digest. No. 87-3, Feb. 3, 1987. p. 15-16.

HOUSING REHABILITATION

D'Andrea, Nick. "Cost Saving Techniques." Rehab Notes. August 1981. pp. 4-8.

HOUSING REHABILITATION

"Estimating Rehab Costs: Some Guidelines." Rehab Notes. Vol. 10, No. 8. Sept. 1986. p. 4.

HOUSING REHABILITATION

Fisette, Paul. "On Jacking Old Houses: What To Do When Crooked Jambs and Sagging Joists Lose Their Charm." Progressive Builder. Vol. 12, No. 2, Feb. 1987. pp. 9-13.

HOUSING REHABILITATION

Hershey, Stuart S. "Section 312 Rehabilitation Loans: Alive and Well." Journal of Housing. Vol. 44, No. 2, Mar./Apr. 1987. p. 75-79.

HOUSING REHABILITATION

"Honeywell Subsidizes Neighborhood Rehab Near Minneapolis Headquarters." Housing and Development Reporter. May 23, 1983. p. 1141.

HOUSING REHABILITATION

Howell, Peter. "The Auctions: Going, Going.." City Limits. November 1982. pp. 21-25.

HOUSING REHABILITATION

"Impact of Rehabilitation on Housing Inventory is Overlooked, Says Report." Housing and Development Reporter. October 24, 1983. pp. 462-463.

HOUSING REHABILITATION

Johnson, William A. "Computer Usage: Housing Rehabilitation." Journal of Housing. Vol. 44, No. 2, Mar./Apr. 1987. p. 64.

HOUSING REHABILITATION

"Landmarks Initiates Home Ownership Program." PHLF News. No. 101, Spring 1987, p. 4.

Home Ownership for Working People Program (VMRI), Central North Side of Pittsburgh.

HOUSING REHABILITATION

Laufer, Pearl. "NIBS Creates Rehab Task Force." Cost Cuts. Vol. 4, No. 7. Jun./Jul. 1987. pp. 4 - 5.
The National Institute of Building Sciences' task force will study aspects of low-cost housing.

HOUSING REHABILITATION

McClellan, Peggy. "Urban Renaissance Through Rehabilitation." CRM Bulletin. Vol. 9, No. 5, Oct.-Dec. 1986. p. 14.

HOUSING REHABILITATION

"Massachusetts Multi-Jurisdiction Rehab Program Uses Small Cities CDBG Money." Community Development Digest. May 24, 1983. p. 9.

HOUSING REHABILITATION

Mayer, Neil S. "Conserving Rental Housing, A Policy Analysis." Journal of the American Planning Association. Vol. 50, No. 3, Summer 1984. pp. 311-325.

HOUSING REHABILITATION

"NLHA Urges Emphasis on Existing Housing Units to Provide Low-Income Rentals." Urban Outlook. Vol. 9, No. 4, Feb. 30 (sic), 1987. p. 5-6.

HOUSING REHABILITATION

"New Haven Section 8 Project to Yield $280,000 for Non-Profit Developer." Housing & Development Reporter. December 20, 1982. pp. 604-605.

HOUSING REHABILITATION

"The Perfect Partnership, 953 Pleasant Street Opens as Conservation/ Preservation Center." New Bedford Soundings. Winter 1983. pp. 1-2.

HOUSING REHABILITATION

"Rehab and Sale: Kenosha's Person-to-Person Approach." Stone Soup. Winter 1986/87. p. 16-18.

HOUSING REHABILITATION

Reilly, Jack. "Living without Asbestos." Old-House Journal. Vol. 15, No. 2, Mar./Apr. 1987. p. 34-38.

HOUSING REHABILITATION

Santucci, R. M. "Rehab's Triple Crown." Cost Cuts. Vol. 4, No. 4, Mar. 1987. p. 1-3.

Low cost, low maintenance materials for basic housing.

HOUSING REHABILITATION

"Savannah Historic District Project Uses Section 8, CD, UDAG, Equity Syndication." Housing and Development Reporter. January 17, 1983. pp. 694-695.

HOUSING REHABILITATION

Wallace, Andy. "Weathering the Old House." Old-House Journal. Vol. 14, No. 7, Sept. 1986. 338-343.

HOUSING REHABILITATION

"The Wrong Side of the Tracks." Traditional Homes. Sept. 1986. p. 18-27.

Railway cottages, due for demolition, were renovated instead.

Vertical File
HOUSING REHABILITATION--CANADA

Millward, Hugh A. and Donna D. Davis. "Housing Renovation in Halifax: 'Gentrification' or 'Incumbent Upgrading.'" Plan Canada. Vol. 26, No. 6, Aug. 1986. p. 148-155. (VF)

HOUSING REHABILITATION--ECONOMIC ASPECTS

Benitez, A. William. "Financing Alternatives in Rehabilitation." Rehab Notes. Vol. 10, No. 5, June 1986. p. 1

HOUSING REHABILITATION--CASE STUDIES

Boulter, Robert. "Rehabbing With Residents in Place." Home Again. No. 4, Autumn 1984. pp. 19-21.

Two Jubilee Housing projects in Adams-Morgan, Washington, D.C. are described.

HOUSING REHABILITATION--CASE STUDIES

McCormick, Delia. "Moderate Rehab-Some Early Section 8 Program Experiences." Challenge. Feb. 1981, pp. 4 - 10.

HOUSING REHABILITATION--FINANCE

Baldwin, Susan. "Reborn Sweat Equity Program Launched." City Limits. January 1982. p. 11.

HOUSING REHABILITATION--FINANCE

Benitez, A. William. "Financing Alternatives in Rehab : Part II." Rehab Notes. Vol. 10, No. 6, July 1986. p. 1, 6.

Discussion of CDBG funds and sweat equity.

HOUSING REHABILITATION--FINANCE

Benitez, A. William. "Home improvement loan program in Bellingham, Washington." Rehab Notes. June 1980. p. 1-4.

HOUSING REHABILITATION-FINANCE

"An Exaction that Really Works." Planning. October 1982. p. 6.

HOUSING REHABILITATION--FINANCE

"Housing Rehabilitation in Evansville, Indiana." Rehab Notes. July 1981. pp. 1 - 4.

HOUSING REHABILITATION--FINANCE

McCormick, Delia, "Section 8 moderate rehabilitation: a review of early program experiences". Journal of Housing. December 1980 p. 623-629.

HOUSING REHABILITATION--FINANCE

"Public/Private Participants Fund 10-Unit Rehab Project in Denver." Economic Growth & Revitalization Report. No. 86-13, July 15, 1986. p. 5.

HOUSING REHABILITATION--FINANCE

Quinn, Howard. "Good Housing Comes in Small Packages: In Aggressively Marketed Rehabs in Islip, Long Island." Planning. December 1981. pp. 18-19

HOUSING REHABILITATION--FINANCE

"Sweat Equity in South Shore." The Neighborhood Works. June 26, 1981. p. 1.

HOUSING REHABILITATION--FINANCE

Wiley, T. Michael. "Financing Redevelopment Projects." Journal of Housing. July/August 1982. pp. 108-11.

HOUSING REHABILITATION--HANDBOOKS, MANUALS, ETC.

"Property Owners as Contractors." Rehab Notes. August 1981. pp. 1-4.

HOUSING REHABILITATION--U.S.--GEORGIA

"Georgia Study Documents Economic Benefits of Historic Rehabs." Urban Conservation Report. Vol. 10, No. 9. Sep. 30, 1986. pp. 4-5.

HOUSING REHABILITATION--U.S.--SOUTH DAKOTA-- LEAD

Adams, Frank H. "A Stitch in Time: Rehabilitating Housing in Lead, South Dakota." Small Town. September-October 1980. p. 14-16

HOUSING, RURAL

Kidd, Susan. "Majorie Capel's Good Idea." American Land Forum. Vol. 5, No. 4, Fall 1985. p. 13-14.

National Trust Southern Regional Office Field Representative writes on the Anson County, N.C. housing rehabilitation program.

HOUSING, RURAL

Lapping, Mark B. "Changing Rural Housing Policies: Vermont's Mobile Home Zoning Law." Small Town. January-February, 1982. pp. 24-25.

ICCROM

"Questions and Viewpoints (ICCROM). ICCROM Newsletter. No. 9. pp. 6-9.

ILLINOIS--NEW SALEM

Holzer, Harold and Joseph C. Farber, "Here Lincoln Lived : New Salem and Springfield, Illinois." Antiques. February 1981. p. 424-437.

IMPLEMENTS, UTENSILS, ETC.

Lasansky, Jeannette. "Unusual Pennsylvania ironware". Antiques. February 1981. p. 438-444.

INDIANA--DUBOIS COUNTY--GREEN TREE HOTEL

Roberts, Warren E. "The Green Tree Hotel: A Problem in the Study of Ethnic Architecture." Pioneer America. September 1983. pp. 105-121.

INDIANS OF NORTH AMERICA--ARCHITECTURE

    Branstner, Susan M. "Excavating a Seventh-Century Huron Village." Archaeology. Vol. 38, No. 4, July/Aug. 1985. p. 58-59.

INDIANS OF NORTH AMERICA--ARCHITECTURE--CANADA
--BRITISH COLUMBIA

    McGhee, Robert, PhD. "In the Land of the Plank Houses." Canadian Heritage. May/June 1984. pp. 13-17.

INDUSTRIAL ARCHAEOLOGY--U.S.--NEW YORK--BUFFALO

    Banham, Reyner. "Buffalo Archaeological." Architectural Review. Feb. 1980. pp. 88-93.

INDUSTRIAL ARCHAEOLOGY

    Brady, Barry J. "Paterson, New Jersey: Birthplace of the American Industrial Revolution." Archaeology. September/October, 1981. pp. 22-29.

INDUSTRIAL ARCHEOLOGY

    Fannin, Minxie. "TICCIH (Fifth International Conference on the Conservation of Industrial Heritage-TICKY) Comes to Massachusetts." The Boston Preservation Alliance Letter. Vol. 5, No. 6, July/August 1984. pp. 4-5, 7.

INDUSTRIAL ARCHEOLOGY

    Ferns, S.L. "Electricity Supply and Industrial Archaeology." Industrial Archaeology. Vol. 17, No. 1, Spring. pp. 10, 19.

    POWER RESOURCES

INDUSTRIAL ARCHAEOLOGY

    "Historic Quarries to be Saved." Massachusetts Historical Commission Newsletter. Summer 1983. p. 6.

INDUSTRIAL ARCHAEOLOGY

    Industrial Archaeology. Vol. 16, No. 1, Spring 1981.

CONTENTS: Burt, Roger, Peter Waite and Michael Atkinson, Scottish Metalliferous Mining 1845-1913: Detailed Returns from the Mineral Statistics--Preece, Geoff, Salford Museum of Mining: A Unique Presentation of Coalmining History--Bowman, A.I. The Dockyard at Grangemouth--

INDUSTRIAL ARCHAEOLOGY

    Jackson, Michael. "Unwrapped Buildings." Historic Illinois. Vol. 10, No. 2. pp. 6-7.

INDUSTRIAL ARCHAEOLOGY

    Lankton, Larry D. and Terry S. Reynolds. "Industrialization and the Industrial Heritage in International Perspective: Lowell Conference on Industrial History; The International Conference on the Conservation of Industrial Heritage; and Conference of the Society for Industrial Archeology - Lowell, Cambridge, and Boston, Massachusetts, June 7-17, 1984." Technology and Culture. Vol. 26, No. 2, Apr. 1985. p. 268-274.

INDUSTRIAL ARCHAEOLOGY

    Mayse, Susan. "The Medalta Impasse." Canadian Heritage. Vol. 12, Issue 4, Oct.-Nov. 1986. p. 30-35.

    A large, abandoned pottery plant is being touted as a possible historic site.

Vertical File

INDUSTRIAL ARCHAEOLOGY

    "The New Industrial Archaeology." World Industrial History. No. 3, Summer 1986. p. 1-3. (VF)

    Rationale for industrial archaeology.

INDUSTRIAL ARCHAEOLOGY

    Parrington, Michael. "People in Public Works: Frederick Graff: Waterworks Engineer Par Excellence." APWA Reporter. Vol. 51, No. 9, September 1984. pp. 4-5.

    Draftsman to Latrobe on Philadelphia Waterworks Commission, later Superintendent of the Works.

INDUSTRIAL ARCHAEOLOGY

    Tompkins, Judith L. "Swan Song for a Dump in Bellevue, Michigan." Small Town. Vol. 14, No. 5, March-April 1984. pp. 4-8.

    MINES, OPEN-AIR MUSEUMS, VOLUNTEERS

INDUSTRIAL ARCHAEOLOGY

Wernick, Robert. "The Singular Vision of a Reincarnated Victorian Millwright." Smithsonian. Vol. 16, No. 7, Oct. 1985. p. 193-209.

The work of Robert Johnson, Rossville, Georgia in assembling 19th century machinery for National Museum of American History Mechanical and Civil Engineering Exibits.

INDUSTRIAL ARCHAEOLOGY

Yuskavitch, Jim. "Buried Treasure." Planning. Vol. 52, No. 10, Oct. 1986. p. 18-22.

Funding of urban archaeology projects.

INDUSTRIAL ARCHAEOLOGY--BIBLIOGRAPHY

"Current Bibliography in the History of Technology (1983)." Technology and Culture. Vol. 26, No. 2, Apr. 1985. p. 353-470.

Annual issuance of technologic titles.

INDUSTRIAL ARCHEOLOGY--BIBLIOGRAPHY

"Publications of Interest." A Supplement to Vol. 13, No. 1, Winter 1984. SIA Newsletter, Society for Industrial Archeology. Spring 1984.

INDUSTRIAL ARCHAEOLOGY--GREAT BRITAIN

Trinder, Barrie. "Industrial Archaeology in Britain". Archaeology. January/February 1981. p.8-16.

INDUSTRIAL ARCHAEOLOGY--STUDY AND TEACHING

Wright, Helena. "Insurance Mapping and Industrial Archeology." IA, the Journal of the Society for Industrial Archeology. Vol. 9, No. 1, 1983. pp. 1-19.

INDUSTRIAL ARCHAELOGY--U.S.--ILLINOIS

Hendrich, David. "Salt Processing at Gallatin County's Half Moon Lick." Historic Illinois. Vol. 6, No. 6, April 1984. pp. 1-3, 14.

INDUSTRIAL ARCHAEOLOGY--U.S.--MASSACHUSETTS--BOSTON

Howry, Jeffrey C. "Industrial Archeology in Greater Boston." Boston Preservation Alliance Letter. Vol. 6, No. 1, Apr. 1985. p. 1, 5-7.

Vertical File

INDUSTRIAL ARCHAEOLOGY--U.S.--NEW HAMPSHIRE

Starbuck, David R. "The Industrial Archeology of New Hampshire." Historical New Hampshire. Vol. 40, Nos. 1 & 2, Spring/Summer 1985. p. 84-99. (VF)

INDUSTRIAL ARCHEOLOGY--U.S.--NEW YORK--ROCKLAND LAKE

Scott, Peter. "The Knickerbocker Ice Company and Inclined Railway at Rockland Lake, New York." IA: The Journal of the Society for Industrial Archeology. Vol. 5, No. 1, 1979. pp. 7-18.

INDUSTRIAL BUILDINGS

Fesenmaier, Steve. "West Virginia-That'll Win Ya!--The Fesenmeier Brewery at Huntington." Goldenseal. Winter 1981. pp. 45-49.

INDUSTRIAL BUILDINGS--ADAPTIVE USE

"Clock Tower Apartments: From Drafting Boards to Drawing Rooms." Revitalization. December 1981. pp. 5-6.

INDUSTRIAL BUILDINGS--ADAPTIVE USE

DeLony, Eric N. "Trends in the Adaptive Use of Industrial Buildings." Society for Industrial Archeology Newsletter. Summer 1982. pp. 6-8.

INDUSTRIAL BUILDINGS--ADAPTIVE USE

DeLony, Eric N. "Trends in the Adaptive Reuse of Industrial Buildings, Brewery Houses a City's Art Treasures." Society for Industrial Archaeology Newsletter. Fall 1982. pp. 4-5.

INDUSTRIAL BUILDINGS--ADAPTIVE USE

"Design by Restoration, Haimes Lundberg Waehler Converts a New Jersey Mill into a Branch office that Blends the Contemporary with the Historic." Interior Design. Apr. 1982. pp. 220-223.

INDUSTRIAL BUILDINGS--ADAPTIVE USE

"Docklands Museum: Competition Results." Architectural Review. Vol. 181, No. 1080, Feb. 1987. p. 38-50.

Architectural competition held for conversion of a warehouse to a museum.

INDUSTRIAL BUILDINGS--ADAPTIVE USE

"Freight Depot Marketplace, Chattanooga, Tennessee". Real Estate Finance. Vol. 1, No. 4, Winter 1985. p. 62-67.

INDUSTRIAL BUILDINGS--ADAPTIVE USE

"From grain bins to hotel with government loan." Building Design and Construction. March 1981. p. 52-57.

INDUSTRIAL BUILDINGS--ADAPTIVE USE

Greer, William. " A Restoration Festival-- an illustrated talk on the potential for renovation and adaptive re-use of industrial buildings." Bay State Historical League Bulletin. Summer & Autumn 1980. p. 6-9.

INDUSTRIAL BUILDINGS--ADAPTIVE USE

"Medina Metamorphosis, Housing Scheme, Newport, IOW." Brick Bulletin. January 1984. pp. 3-8.

ARCHITECTURAL DESIGN--NEW/OLD RELATIONSHIP
ADAPTIVE USE--CASE STUDIES

INDUSTRIAL BUILDINGS--ADAPTIVE USE

"The Pursuit of Knowledge in Warehouse Lofts." Architectural Record. August 1982. pp. 88-89.

INDUSTRIAL BUILDINGS--ADAPTIVE USE

"Quaker Hilton: Novel Re-Use Strengthens CBD." Center City Report. January 1982. pp. 3-4.

INDUSTRIAL BUILDINGS--ADAPTIVE USE

"Renovation-Addition to Historic, Waterfront Site : Ocean Spray Cranberries, Inc., Plymouth, Massachusetts : Architects Moore-Heder Convert an Old 'Clam Factory' into a National Headquarters..." Architectural Record. August, 1979. pp. 73-76

INDUSTRIAL BUILDINGS--ADAPTIVE USE

"The Roak Block: Adaptive Re-Use Along the Androscoggin River." Landmarks Observer. March-April 1982. pp. 6-7.

INDUSTRIAL BUILDINGS--ADAPTIVE USE

"St. Anthony Main." Architectural Record. February 1979. pp. 130-132.

INDUSTRIAL BUILDINGS--ADAPTIVE USE

Smith, Penny Pence. "The Renaissance of Iwilei." Historic Hawai'i. Vol. 13, No. 3, Mar. 1987. p. 9-10.

Conversion of pineapple canneries to industrial condominiums.

INDUSTRIAL BUILDINGS--ADAPTIVE USE

"Tivoli Reopens in Style." Historic Denver News. Vol. 13, No. 9, October 1984. p. 1.

Brewery redesigned into retail space, including restaurants and movie theater.

INDUSTRIAL BUILDINGS--ADAPTIVE USE

Tuve, Richard L. "The San Antonio Museum of Art: the Adaptive Re-use of the Old Lone Star Brewery." Technology and Conservation. Winter 1980. p.26-31, 47.

INDUSTRIAL BUILDINGS--ADAPTIVE USE

Vaseff, James and Timothy J. King. "Action Plan for Historic Danville." <u>Urban Land</u>, December 1979. pp. 11-18.

INDUSTRIAL BUILDINGS--ADAPTIVE USE

"Warehouse rehabilitated into architect's offices". <u>Architectural Record</u> Mid-February 1981. p. 90-93.

INDUSTRIAL BUILDINGS--ADAPTIVE USE--BRAZIL

David, Theo. "Old Brick Factory Made into a Lively Recreation Center." <u>Architecture</u>. September 1984. pp. 180-1.

INDUSTRIAL BUILDINGS--ADAPTIVE USE--FRANCE

Fitch, James Marston. "Contrasting Pair of Restorations." <u>Architecture</u>. Oct. 1985. pp. 62-65.

Exteriors of railroad station and cattle hall restored and new interior uses developped.

INDUSTRIAL BUILDINGS--ADAPTIVE USE--FRANCE--PARIS

Boles, Daralice. "Paris Report: Progress at La Villette." <u>Progressive Architecture</u>. Nov. 1985. p. 47-49.

Slaughterhouse converted to park/museum.

INDUSTRIAL BUILDINGS--ADAPTIVE USE--U.S.--CALI- FORNIA--MONTEREY

Knight, Carleton III. "Purposeful Chaos on Cannery Row." <u>Architecture</u>. June 1985. p. 50- 59.

Hovden Cannery converted to Monterey Bay Aquarium.

INDUSTRIAL BUILDINGS--ADAPTIVE USE--U.S.-- CALIFORNIA--SAN FRANCISCO

Dean, Andrea O. "Architectural Offices in a Former Silverware Factory." <u>Architecture</u>. Mar. 1985. p. 140-141.

INDUSTRIAL BUILDINGS--ADAPTIVE USE--U.S.-- CONNECTICUT--NORWALK

"Refreshing Retrofit." <u>Architectural Record</u>. Jan. 1985. pp. 98-99.

INDUSTRIAL BUILDINGS--ADAPTIVE USE--U.S.--GEORGIA --COLUMBUS

DeLony, Eric. "The Columbus Iron Works - An Urban Tonic in the South." <u>Society for Industrial Archeology Newsletter</u>. Vol. 13, No. 3 & 4, Fall & Winter 1984. p. 1-2.

Fifth in a series on the adaptive use of industrial buildings.

INDUSTRIAL BUILDINGS--ADAPTIVE USE--U.S.-- MASSACHUSETTS--BOSTON

Haaland, Randi J. and Anthony C. Platt. "Pioneering Office Project in the Charlestown Navy Yard: Building 36 - Ironsides Place." <u>Boston Preservation Alliance Letter</u>. Vol. 6, No. 9, Oct. 1985. p. 4-5, 7.

INDUSTRIAL BUILDINGS--ADAPTIVE USE--U.S.--MASSACHU- SETTS--CHARLESTOWN

"A Navy Yard Refloated." <u>Architectural Record</u>. May 1984. pp. 156-161.

INDUSTRIAL BUILDINGS--ADAPTIVE USE--U.S.-- MICHIGAN--DETROIT

"Revitalized Riverfront on Tap for Detroit." <u>Architectural Record</u>. October 1984. p. 119.

Parke-Davis manufacturing complex.

INDUSTRIAL BUILDINGS--ADAPTIVE USE--U.S.-- MINNESOTA--DULUTH

King, Shannon. "Something's Brewing on the Waterfront." <u>Architecture Minnesota</u>. Vol. 11, No. 4. Jul./Aug. 1985. pp. 28-31.

Fitger Brewery (1890-1908) (NR) buildings adapted to inn, shops, restaurant, theater and brewing museum.

INDUSTRIAL BUILDINGS--ADAPTIVE USE--U.S.--MINNESOTA MINNEAPOLIS

Faricy, Richard. "From Munsingwear to Market Square." Architecture Minnesota. Vol. 2, No. 1. Jan./Feb. 1985. pp. 36-37.

INDUSTRIAL BUILDINGS--ADAPTIVE USE--U.S.--
MINNESOTA--MINNEAPOLIS

Mack, Linda. "An Energetic Revival of
Industrial Spirit: At Thresher Square, BRW Has
Fashioned a Solar-Age Factory for Design."
Architecture Minnesota. Vol. 11, No. 5, Sept./
Oct. 1985. p. 36-39.

INDUSTRIAL BUILDINGS--ADAPTIVE USE--U.S.--NEW YORK
ALBANY

Sahm, Heather. "Hinckel Brewery to be
Developped." Albany Preservation Report. Spring
1985. pp. 1-2.

INDUSTRIAL BUILDINGS--ADAPTIVE USE--U.S.--NEW
YORK--NEW YORK CITY

Doubilet, Susan. "Arch Support." Progressive
Architecture. Nov. 1985. p. 100-103.

Landmark asphalt plant in New York now a
recreational facility.

INDUSTRIAL BUILDINGS--ADAPTIVE USE--U.S.--OHIO--
COLUMBUS

"Former Warehouse with an Etched Facade and
Flamboyant Facilities." Architecture. Aug. 1985.
p. 79-81.

INDUSTRIAL BUILDINGS--ADAPTIVE USE--U.S.--OHIO--
CUYAHOGA VALLEY

Adelman, Edward H. AIA. "The Jaite Mill
Company Town: Adaptive Restoration as Park
Headquarters." CRM Bulletin. Vol. 8, No. 2,
Apr. 1985. p. 6, 10-14.

INDUSTRIAL BUILDINGS--ADAPTIVE USE--U.S.--
RHODE ISLAND--PROVIDENCE

"New Uses for Waterfront at Richmond,
Sq." PPS News, Newsletter of the Providence
Preservation Society. Vol. XXII, No. 2, March/
April 1984. p. 4.

INDUSTRIAL BUILDINGS--ADAPTIVE USE--U.S.--
TEXAS--DALLAS

McNevins, Kevin. "Turtle Creek Pump
Station Future Assured by Passage of Prop. 10."
Historic Dallas. Vol. 7, No. 17, Nov./Dec. 1985.
p. 6.

$415,000 bond issue adds to $750,000
privately raised to adapt station for Turtle
Creek Center for the Arts.

INDUSTRIAL BUILDINGS--ADAPTIVE USE--U.S.--
WASHINGTON--SEATTLE

"Scaling the Office Landscape." Architectural
Record. May 1984. pp. 162-167.

Pioneer Square Historic District warehouse
remodeling.

INDUSTRIAL BUILDINGS--CONSERVATION AND RESTORATION

"The End of an Era for D'Hanis Brick and
Tile Plant." The Medallion. Vol. 24, No. 7.
July 1987. p. 2.

INDUSTRIAL BUILDINGS--CONSERVATION AND RESTORATION

Heard, Robert. "Industrial Building
Revived by Conservation." The Neighborhood Works.
p. 19.

INDUSTRIAL BUILDINGS--CONSERVATION AND
RESTORATION

Kalman, Harold. "This Elevator is
Going Down." Canadian Heritage. February/
March 1984. ppl 18-24.

INDUSTRIAL BUILDINGS--CONSERVATION AND
RESTORATION

"New Hampshire Grantees Invest in
Mills to Prod Downtown Recovery."
Community Development Digest. January 24,
1984. pp. 5-6.

INDUSTRIAL BUILDINGS--CONSERVATION & RESTORATION

"The Steel Industry of Southwestern Pennsylvania."
PHLF News, No. 101, Spring 1987. p. 3.

Steel-site reconnaissance survey.

INDUSTRIAL BUILDINGS--CONSERVATION & RESTORATION

Tudor, Phoebe. "Louisiana's Historic Sugar
Industry." New Orleans Preservation in Print.
Vol. 14, NO. 4. May 1987. p. 4-6.

INDUSTRIAL BUILDINGS--CONSERVATION AND RESTORA-
TION--CASE STUDIES--U.S.--ILLINOIS

Dixon, John Morris. "Horwitz/Matthews
Rehabbing for Fun and Profit." Progressive
Architecture. July 1985. p. 87-94.

INDUSTRIAL BUILDINGS--CONSERVATION AND RESTORA-
TION--CASE STUDIES--U.S.--MASSACHUSETTS--
BOSTON

"Non-Profit Group Converting Boston Power
Plant to Condos in Public-Private Effort."
Housing and Development Reporter. Vol. 12,
No. 6, July 2, 1984. p. 111.

INDUSTRIAL BUILDINGS--CONSERVATION AND RESTORA-
TION--U.S.--MASSACHUSETTS--BOSTON

"Neighborhood Industrial Complex Lands Beer
Company For Abandoned Brewery." Economic Growth
& Revitalization. No. 86-3, Feb. 11, 1986.
p. 4-5.

Discussion of rehab project in an 1871
brewery complex in Boston.

INDUSTRIAL BUILDINGS--HISTORY--AUSTRALIA--
MELBOURNE

McConville, Chris. "Melbourne's Industrial
Heritage." Heritage Australia. Winter 1985. p.
37-39.

INDUSTRIAL BUILDINGS--HISTORY--U.S.--NEW
HAMPSHIRE--CONCORD

Taylor, William L. "The Concord (New
Hampshire) Gasholder: Last Intact Survivor
from the Gas-Making Era." IA, The Journal
of the Society for Industrial Archeology.
Vol. 10, No. 1, 1984. pp. 1-16.

INDUSTRIAL BUILDINGS--U.S.--CONNECTICUT--ROCK-
VILLE

Abbott, Ardis. "Historic Rockville Gains
Recognition." Connecticut Trust for Historic
Preservation News. Vol. 8, No. 2, Spring 1985.
p. 1.

19th century textile district listed on NR.

INDUSTRIAL DEVELOPMENT BONDS

"Alabama Law Encourages Private
Investment in Historic Preservation."
Local Economic Growth and Neighborhood
Reinvestment Report. February 17, 1983.
pp. 6-7.

INDUSTRIAL DEVELOPMENT BONDS

Dorfman, Robert S. "Industrial Development
Bond Financing." Real Estate Finance. Vol. 1,
No. 3, Fall 1984. pp. 26-31.

INDUSTRIAL DEVELOPMENT BONDS

Lincoln, Sheryl J. "Is there--and should
there be--a future for industrial revenue bonds?"
Journal of Housing. November 1981. pp. 535-
539.

INDUSTRIAL DEVELOPMENT BONDS

Marlin, Matthew R. "Evolution of a Subsidy:
Industrial Revenue Bonds." Growth and Change.
Vol. 16, No. 1, January 1985. p. 30-35.

INDUSTRIAL DEVELOPMENT BONDS

Squires, Gregory D. "Industrial Revenue
Bonds and the Deindustrialization of America."
Urbanism, Past and Present. Vol. 9, Issue 1,
No. 17, Winter/Spring 1984. pp. 1-9.

INDUSTRIAL DEVELOPMENT BONDS

"Tax Bills Would Restrict Tax-exempt
IDB Financing, Lessen Attractiveness of UDAG
Deals." Community Development Digest. No. 84-6.
March 27, 1984. p. 1-4.

INDUSTRIAL MUSEUMS

"The Working Past, America's Industrial
Heritage." History News. May 1982. Entire
Issue.

CONTENTS: Comp, T. Allan. The Best Arena,
Industrial History at the Local Level--Mullins,
Marsha and Geoffrey Huys. Industrial History on
Exhibit--Craig, Tracy Linton. Delicate Balance,
Hagley Museum Traces the Impact of Technology
and its Products on Society and the Individual.

INDUSTRIAL SITES

Flenley, Richard. "Derelict Land Becomes
Parkland at Stoke-on-Trent." Parks. July, August,
September, 1981. pp. 11-13.

INDUSTRIAL SITES--CONSERVATION AND
RESTORATION

DeLony, Eric. "Adaptive Reuse:
Lifeline of the Charlestown Navy Yard."
Society for Industrial Archeology Newsletter.
Winter 1983. pp. 6-7.

INDUSTRIAL SITES--CONSERVATION AND
RESTORATION

"Heritage State Parks." Urban
Design International. Spring 1983.
p. 31

INDUSTRIAL SITES--CONSERVATION AND RESTORATION

Jones, David H. "A Philosophy for Preservationists: Part I."
Bowie, Gavin. "A Philosophy for Preservationists: Part II." Industrial Archaeology.
Spring 1979. pp. 9-17.

INDUSTRIAL SITES--CONSERVATION AND RESTORATION

"Lowell National Cultural Park." Architectural
Record, September 1979. pp. 103-108.

INDUSTRIAL SITES--U.S.--CONNECTICUT--ROXBURY

Gordon, Robert B. and Michael S. Raber.
"An Early American Integrated Steelworks."
IA, The Journal of the Society for Industrial
Archeology. Vol. 10, No. 1, 1984. pp. 17-34.

INFORMATION SERVICES

Seligman, Daniel. "Life Will be Different When
We're All On-Line", Fortune, February 4, 1985,
pp. 68-70.

INFORMATION STORAGE AND RETRIEVAL SYSTEMS

"Computerization of Archaeological Data
Begins." Ohio Preservation. Vol. 5, No. 3,
Mar. 1985. p. 1

INFORMATION STORAGE AND RETRIEVAL SYSTEMS

Goodwin, Larry and Mary Ellen Conaway.
"The Micro and the Muse." Museum News. April
1984. pp. 55 - 63.

INFORMATION STORAGE AND RETRIEVAL SYSTEMS

"Library and Documentation."
ICCROM Newsletter. No. 9. pp. 18-20

INFORMATION STORAGE AND RETRIEVAL SYSTEMS

Megna, Ralph J. "Computer Basics for
Nonprofit Organizations." The Grantsmanship Center
News. July/August 1983. pp. 15-29.

INFORMATION STORAGE AND RETRIEVAL SYSTEMS

Megna, Ralph J. "Solving Big
Problems with Small Computers." Museum
News. October 1983. pp. 61-66.

INFORMATION STORAGE AND RETRIEVAL

"Paris Documentation Center On
Conservation Expands." Architecture,
(AIA Journal.) August 1983. p. 63.

INFORMATION STORAGE AND RETRIEVAL SYSTEMS

Rowland,Lisa. "Making Information Work
for Nonprofits." Place. pp. 10-11.

INFORMATION STORAGE AND RETRIEVAL
SYSTEMS

Sable, Martin. "Print-Format
Information Sources for Urban Research."
Urbanism Past and Present. Summer/Fall
1982. pp. 40-46.

INFORMATION STORAGE AND RETRIEVAL SYSTEMS

Sittler, Helen Bush. "Computers in Cultural Institutions: A Flexible Tool for Archival Use." Technology and Conservation. Fall 1976. pp. 24-28.

INFORMATION STORAGE AND RETRIEVAL SYSTEMS

Sowell, Joan L. "Historic Hi-Tech." Historic New Orleans Collection Newsletter. Vol. 3, No. 3, Summer 1985. p. 1-4.

Computers used to catalog museum collection.

INFORMATION STORAGE AND RETRIEVAL SYSTEMS

"Update: National Archeological Database." CRM Bulletin. Vol. 8, No. 2, Apr. 1985. p. 14-15.

INFORMATION STORAGE AND RETIEVAL SYSTEMS

Watson, John S. "Is there a Computer in your Future?" History News. August 1983. pp. 13-15.

INSULATION (HEAT)

Nelson, Carol Ann. "Saving Energy: Insulation." New Bedford Soundings. Vol. 10, No. 1, Winter 1985. p. 13-14.

INSULATION (HEAT)

Tye, Ronald P. "Retrofit Thermal Insulation: An Evaluation of Materials for Energy Conservation." Technology and Conservation, Fall 1979. pp. 36-42.

INSURANCE

Anderson, Robert Steven. "Management: Don't Think Becoming a Preservationist Relieves Liability Perils." Architectural Record. February 1984. pp. 29-31.

INSURANCE--ART

Babcock, Phillip H. and Marr T. Haack. "Plain-English Collections Insurance." Museum News. July/August 1981. pp. 22-25.

INSURANCE--HISTORIC SITE

Babcock, Phillip H. "Insure Against Employee Theft." History News. September 1981. p. 19.

INTERIOR DECORATION

Adler, David. "Historic Interiors: Frances Elkins". Architectural Digest. July/August 1980. p. 86-91.

INTERIOR DECORATION

Mooz, R. Peter. "The New Colonial Revolution: An Inside Account." Early American Life. Vol. 17, No. 3, June 1986. p. 54-61.

Recent research has revealed new information about colonial interiors.

INTERIOR DECORATION

"New interiors catch the spirit of the older buildings they transform". Architectural Record. May 1980. p. 85-92.

INTERIOR DECORATION

"1981-82 100 Interior Design Giants." Interior Design. January 1982. pp. 175-192.

INTERIOR DECORATION

Nylander, Jane C. "Bed Hangings, Part II: Field Beds." Early American Life. August 1984. pp. 49-53.

INTERIOR DECORATION

Pilling, Ron. "Creating a Victorian Bedroom." Victorian Homes. Vol. 6, Issue 1, Winter 1987. p. 44-49.

INTERIOR DECORATION

Poore, Patricia and Eve Kahn. "Post-Victorian Interiors." Old-House Journal. Vol. 15, No. 1, Jan./Feb. 1987. p. 54-58.

INTERIOR DECORATION--HISTORY

Bradbury, Bruce. "The Aesthetic Movement in England and America." Old-House Journal. Vol. XII, No. 7, August-September 1984. pp. 144-9.

INTERIOR DECORATION--HISTORY

MacDonald, Jacqueline A. "English Revival Interiors." The Old House Journal. Vol. 13, No. 7, Aug./Sept. 1985. p. 148-150.

INTERIOR DECORATION--19th CENTURY

Nineteenth Century, Spring 1979. Articles on decorative arts and architecture.

INTERIOR WALLS--U.S.--PENNSYLVANIA--MONTGOMERY COUNTY

Rastorfer, Darl. "Restoring Pattern." Architectural Record. Vol. 173, No. 12, Oct. 1985. p. 166-169.

Unique wall patterns found in restoration of 18th century Peter Wentz Farmstead by historic paint consultant Frank S. Welch and John Milner Associates.

IRON--CONSERVATION AND RESTORATION

Firth, M. and W.M. Williams. "An Architectural Example of Oxide Jacking." APT Bulletin. Vol. 13, No. 1, 1981.

IRON--CONSERVATION AND RESTORATION

"Iron Objects: Stop the Clock on Rust." History News. September 1981. p. 44.

IRON INDUSTRY AND TRADE

Schenck, Helen and Reed Knox. "Valley Forge: the Making of Iron in The Eighteenth Century." Archaeology. Vol. 39, No. 1, Jan./Feb. 1986. p. 26-33.

ITALY--FRIULI

Portoghesi, Paolo. "Rebuilding Friuli." Progressive Architecture. November 1983. pp. 114-118.

JEFFERSON, THOMAS

Bell, David. "Knowledge and the Middle Landscape: Thomas Jefferson's University of Virginia." Journal of Architectural Education. Vol. 37, No. 2, Winter 1983. pp. 18-26.

JEFFERSON, THOMAS

Fitch, James Marston. "THE LAWN, America's Greatest Architectural Achievement." American Heritage. Vol. 35, No. 4, June/July 1984. pp. 49-65.

University of Virginia Campus.

JOHNSON, PHILIP

"Castle in the Sky". Architectural Record. Feb. 1985. p. 63.

New "Jacobean inspired" tower planned for Chicago.

JOHNSON, PHILIP

Progressive Architecture. February 1984. Entire Issue.

KEEFE, CHARLES SCHOONMAKER, 1876-1946

Rhoads, William B. "Charles S. Keefe: Colonial Revivalist." Newsletter, Preservation League of New York State. Vol. 11, No. 5, Sept./Oct. 1985. p. 4-5.

KENNELS--ADAPTIVE USE

Allen, Nic. "Conservation at the Kennels." Traditional Homes. Apr. 1985. pp. 70-75.

KENTUCKY--LOUISVILLE--THE GALLERIA

"The Galleria: Synergy Reinforces Downtown." Center City Report. April 1983. p. 1.

KILNS

Ritchie, T. "A History of the Tunnel Kiln and other Kilns for Burning Bricks." APT Bulletin. v.XII, no. 3, 1980. p. 46-61.

KITCHENS

Carrell, Kimberley W. "Industrial Revolution and the Kitchen." Journal of American Culture. Fall 1979. pp. 488-499.

KITCHENS

"An Ironmaster's Kitchen." Traditional Homes. Vol. 3, No. 11. Aug. 1987. pp. 100 - 105; 122 - 124.
Preserving domestic detail from the Industrial Revolution.

KITCHENS

Kasper, Sharon. "Updating a Kitchen... Gently". Old-House Journal. January 1981. p. 11-13.

KITCHENS

Lantz, Louise K. "Victorian Kitchens." Nineteenth Century. Summer 1981. pp. 43-45.

KITCHENS

Monnich, Joni. "Re-Creating the 'Modern' Kitchen 1899-1930." The Old-House Journal. January-February, 1983. pp. 12-15.

KITCHENS

Ruhling, Nancy A. "A Landmark Kitchen." Victorian Homes. Vol. 6, No. 3. Summer 1987. pp. 60 - 63.
Restoration of 19th-century kitchen at Old Merchants House, Greenwich Village.

LABOR COSTS

Santucci, R.M. "The Wages of Work: How to Reduce the Effect of Davis-Bacon Requirements." Cost Cuts (The Enterprise Foundation). Vol. 2, No. 8, June 1985. p. 1-6.

LAMPS

Bourdon, David. "Antiques: The Radiance of Lamps." Architectural Digest. May 1979. pp. 92-97.

LAND USE

Chandler, William J. "Representing Land Trust Interests in the Nation's Capital." Land Trusts' Exchange. Vol. 5, Nos. 3&4, Winter 1987. p. 20-21.

LAND USE

Finkler, Earl L. and Frank J. Popper. "Finding Out Who Owns the Land." Planning. August 1981. pp. 19-22.

LAND USE

Knaap, Gerrit J. "Self-Interest and Voter Support for Oregon's Land Use Controls." Journal of the American Planning Association. Vol. 53, No. 1. Winter 1987. pp. 92-97.

LAND USE

Miner, Dallas D. "Coastal Zone Management and Farmland Preservation : Two Issues of Continuing Interest." Environmental Comment. Sep. 1979. pp. 4-7.

LAND USE--ENVIRONMENTAL ASPECTS

Duerksen, Christopher J. "Beyond Ecology and Economics: The Coming Aesthetic Revolution in Land Use Controls." Urban Land. Jan. 1986. p. 34-35.

LAND USE--ENVIRONMENTAL ASPECTS

Kolis, Annette. "Regulation: Where Do We Go From Here? Part 2." Urban Land. Feb. 1979. pp. 4-8.

LAND USE--ENVIRONMENTAL ASPECTS

Palmer, Arthur E. "Environmental Planning, Minimizing Land Use Confrontations." Small Town. Vol. 15, No. 1, July/August 1984. pp. 13-23.

LAND USE--ENVIRONMENTAL ASPECTS

Popper, Frank J. "Siting LULUs." Planning. April 1981. p. 12-15.

LAND USE, HISTORIC DISTRICT--U.S.--MASSACHUSETTS --BOSTON

"Suit Filed to Force Review of Boston High-Rise Project." Urban Conservation Report. Vol. 10, No. 3, Mar. 17, 1986. p. 4.

LAND USE--LAW AND LEGISLATION

"Ballots Cast on Growth and Environmental Controls." Zoning News. Dec. 1985. p. 1-2.

Summary of November ballots on initiatives concerning growth controls, land preservation, and locally unwanted land uses.

LAND USE--LAW AND LEGISLATION

Bassett, Timothy A. and Karl Seidman. "The Massachusetts Government Land Bank: A Model for Public Real Estate Development." Real Estate Finance. Vol. 1, No. 3, Fall 1984. pp. 48-55.

LAND USE--LAW AND LEGISLATION

Gordon, Dennis A. "The Development Guidance System: Hardin County, Kentucky Streamlines Land Use Regulations." Small Town. May-June 1986. p. 10-13.

LAND USE--LAW AND LEGISLATION

Klein, William R. "Nantucket Tithes for Open Space." Planning. Vol. 52, No. C, Aug. 1986. p. 10-13.

One-sixth of Nantucket Island is being set aside in a land bank paid for by real estate transfer taxes.

LAND USE--LAW AND LEGISLATION--U.S.--VERMONT

Daniels, Thomas L. and Mark B. Lapping. "Has Vermont's Land Use Control Program Failed? Evaluating Act 250." Research Report. Journal of the American Planning Association. Vol. 50, No. 4, Autumn 1984. pp. 502-508.

LAND USE--PLANNING

Churchman, Arza and Yona Ginsberg. "The Use of Behavioral Science Research in Physical Planning." Journal of Architectural and Planning Research. Vol. 1, No. 1. June 1984. pp. 57-66.

LAND USE--PLANNING

Elson, Martin. "Who Calls the Tune on the Green Belt?" Town & County Planning. No. 7/8, July/Aug. 1986. p. 203-204.

LAND USE--PLANNING

Higgins, Bryan. "The Sanderistas and a Metamorphosis of Burlington, Vermont." Places. Vol. 3, No. 2, 1986. p. 32-39.

LAND USE-PLANNING

"Federal Report Supports PEC"s 'Piedmont Reserve' Concept; Urges State/Local Action to Preserve America's Landscapes; Encourages Protection of Scenic Rivers and Roads." Piedmont Environmental Council Newsreporter. Apr. 1987. p. 1-3.

LAND USE--PLANNING

Kettlewell, Ursula. "Land Use Regulations As a Barrier to Business and Economic Development Perceived vs. Actual." The Appraisal Journal. Jul. 1984. pp. 399-419.

LAND USE--PLANNING

Kunofsky, Judith. "A Greenbelt for the Bay." American Land Forum. Vol. 6, No. 2, Spring 1986. p. 7-9.

Saving a three-and-a-half million acre greenbelt around the San Francisco Bay area.

LAND USE -- PLANNING

Metzger, Philip C. "Public-Private Partners Foster Land Conservation." Conservation Foundation Letter. July 1983. Entire Issue.

LAND USE--PLANNING

Morris, Wendy. "Historic Goldfields Under Threat." Trust News. (Victoria, Australia). Vol. 15, No. 4, Oct. 1986. p. 3-4.

LAND USE--PLANNING

Porter, Douglas R. "Montgomery County's Growth Fracas." Urban Land. Vol. 45, No. 6. June 1986. pp. 34-35.

LAND USE--PLANNING

Redfern, Roger A. "Mooresque Landscape: The Threat to Bleaklow." Country Life. Mar. 19, 1987. pp. 64-65.

England's Bleaklow moor is threatened by lack of management.

LAND USE--PLANNING

Winter, Gordon. "Green Votes and the Green Belt." Country Life. Vol. 180, No. 4656. Nov. 13, 1986. pp. 1510-1512.

Developers threaten the green belt that surrounds London.

LAND USE--PLANNING--CITIZEN PARTICIPATION

Rivkin, Malcolm D. "Negotiating With Neighborhoods: Managing Development Through Public/Private Negotiations." Urban Land. Jan. 1986. p. 15-19.

LAND USE PLANNING--CITIZEN PARTICIPATION

"The Scenic District Management Plan." Hudson River Heritage. May 1984. pp. 3-4.

LAND USE--PLANNING--U.S.--MASSACHUSETTS

"Massachusetts Government Land Banks." Urban Land. Vol. 44, No. 2, Feb. 1985. p. 26-27.

LAND USE--PLANNING--WESTERN U.S.

Shapira, Philip and Nancey Leigh-Preston. "Urban and Rural Development in the Western United States: Emerging Conflicts and Planning Issues." Journal of Architectural and Planning Research. Vol. 1, No. 1. June 1984. pp. 37-55.

LAND USE, RURAL

Beasley, Steven D., William G. Workman and Nancy A. Williams. "Estimating Amenity Values of Urban Fringe Farmland: a Contingent Valuation Approach: Note." Growth and Change. Vol. 17, No. 4, Oct. 1986. p. 70-78.

LAND USE, RURAL

Brumback, Barbara. "Conference Proceedings: Farms in Our Future? Farmland Protection Initiatives." Florida Environmental and Urban Issues. Part I: Vol. 13, No. 1, Jan. 1986. p. 7-11. Part II: Vol. 13, No. 4, July 1986. p. 17-20.

LAND USE, RURAL

Carbin, Richard. "Filling the Planning Void." Land Trusts' Exchange. Vol. 5, Nos. 3&4, Winter 1987. p. 6-7.

The use of land trusts to implement the land use planning process.

LAND USE, RURAL

"Connecticut Towns Move Forward with Various Farmland Protection Efforts." Farmland Notes. Vol. 5, No. 12, Dec. 1986. p. 3.

LAND USE, RURAL

Daniels, Thomas L. and Arthur C. Nelson. "Is Oregon's Farmland Preservation Program Working?" JAPA. Vol. 52, No. 1, Winter 1986. p. 22-32.

LAND USE, RURAL

"Farmland Preservation Debated in Boston." Urban Land. Vol. 44, No. 1, Jan. 1985. p. 28.

LAND USE, RURAL

Fricker, Jonathan. "Preserving Louisiana's Rural Heritage." New Orleans Preservation in Print. Vol. 13, No. 9, Nov. 1986. p. 8-9.

LAND USE, RURAL

Krieger, Linda. "Participating in Public Planning." Land Trusts' Exchange. Vol. 5, Nos. 3&4, Winter 1987. p. 8-9.

The Land Trust for Santa Barbara County, previously confining its activities to the private sector, has begun participating in the formulation of public policy.

LAND USE, RURAL

Krohe, James Jr. "Buy Now, Save Later: a Farmland Proposal." Planning. Vol. 52, No. 11, Nov. 1986. p. 12-16.

A proposal to preserve farmland by making it a part of the city.

LAND USE, RURAL

Langdon, Philip. "Platting to Save." Planning. Vol. 52, No. 7. July 1986. pp. 28-31.

Zero lot lines infill strategies, and other methods for making land development affordable.

LAND USE, RURAL

Melnick, Robert Z. "Landscape Thinking." CRM Bulletin. Vol. 8, No. 1, Feb. 1985. p. 1-3, 10.

LAND USE, RURAL

"Managing Growth in Culpeper." Piedmont Environmental Council Newsreporter. Sept. 1986. 5p. (entire issue)

Planning for rural land use in Culpeper, Va.

LAND USE, RURAL

Mulkey, David & Rodney L. Clouser. "Market and Market-Institutional Perspectives on the Agricultural Land Preservation Issue." Growth and Change. Vol. 18, No. 1, Winter 1987. p. 72-81.

LAND USE, RURAL

"New Twist for Farmland Protection in a California County." Farmland Notes. Vol. 5, No. 11, Nov. 1986. p. 3.

Creation of the Solano County Open Space and Farmland Foundation, which has been directed to maintain agricultural land around the city of Fairfield.

LAND USE, RURAL

Nielsen, David C. and Philip R. Pryde. "Providing for Rural Land in San Diego County." Urban Land. November 1980. p.10-17.

LAND USE, RURAL

"Rural Land Use Policies and Rural Poverty.'
Journal of the American Planning Association.
Vol. 50, No. 3, Summer 1984. pp. 326-333.

LAND USE, RURAL

Stone, Bill. "Plantation Heritage: Alive
and Hopeful at Waialua." Historic Hawai'i News.
Mar. 1984. pp. 4-5.

LAND USE, RURAL

Washbon, Wallace E. "How to Save Prime Farm-
lands." American Land Forum. Vol. 5, No. 4, Fall
1985. p. 11-13.

LAND USE, RURAL

Wright, Lloyd. "Farmland: What to Protect."
Planning. July/August, 1982. pp. 20-21.

LAND USE, RURAL--ENVIRONMENTAL ASPECTS

"PEC Proposes the Virginia Piedmont Reserve.'
Piedmont Environmental Council Newsreporter.
July 1984. Entire Issue. 5 p.

LAND USE, RURAL--PLANNING

"Density Transfer Procedure Approved by
Loudoun Planning Commission as it Sends Leesburg
Area Management Plan to Board." Piedmont Environ-
mental Newsreporter. September 1982. pp. 1-2.

LAND USE, RURAL--PLANNING

Gustafson, Greg C. and Thomas L. Daniels,
Rosalyn P. Shirack. "The Oregon Land Use Act,
Implications for Farmland and Open Space Protection."
Journal of the American Planning Association.
Summer 1982. pp. 365-373.

LAND USE, RURAL--PLANNING

Healy, Robert G. "Regulatory Review: Lots
or Crops: the Land Supply Dilemma." Urban Land.
Vol. 44, No. 2, Feb. 1985. p. 34-35.

LAND USE, RURAL--PLANNING--U.S.--COLORADO

Walker, Donald V.H. and Martin E. Zeller.
"Promoting Public/Private Initiatives for Preser-
vation: Colorado Open Lands." Urban Land. Vol. 44,
No. 11, Nov. 1985. p. 12-16.

LAND USE, RURAL--PLANNING--U.S.--VIRGINIA--
WATERFORD

Page, Jake. "Will Success Spoil Brigadoon:
How Waterford, Virginia is Trying to Save Its
Surround." American Land Forum. Vol. 5, No. 3,
Summer 1985. p. 44-49.

LAND USE, RURAL--U.S.--NEW YORK

"New York Examines Its Future Agricultural
Land Protection Needs." Farmland Notes. Vol. 5,
No. 4, April 1986. p. 1-2, 4.

LAND USE, URBAN

Benson, Virginia O. "The Rise of the Independent Sector in Urban Land Development."
Growth and Change. Vol. 16, No. 3, July 1985.
p. 25-39.

Case studies of nonprofits' involvement in
land development includes waterfront development,
historic preservation, large-scale land use
planning and neighborhood redevelopment.

LAND USE, URBAN

"Building Types Study 633: Urban
Infill." Architectural Record. Oct. 1986.
p. 89-95.

LAND USE, URBAN

Carlson, Cynthia J. and Robert J. Duffy.
"Cincinnati Takes Stock of Its Vacant Land."
Planning. Vol. 51, No. 11, Nov. 1985. p. 22-23,
26.

LAND USE, URBAN

Collens, Geoffrey. "New Parks for Barcelona." Landscape Design. No. 164, Dec. 1986. p. 15-17.

LAND USE, URBAN

Dorney, Robert S. "The Ecology and Management of Disturbed Urban Land." Landscape Architecture, May 1979. pp. 268-272.

LAND USE, URBAN

"Downtown's Outdoor Living Room." Downtown Idea Exchange. Vol 33, No. 16, Aug. 15, 1986. p. 2

Downtown open space wins out over proposed office building and has triggered extensive renovation of buildings in the area.

LAND USE, URBAN

"Facing the Issues of Open Space and Recreation in the Chicago Region." Torrain. Vol. 10, No.2, May/June 1986. p. 1-3.

LAND USE, URBAN

"If the New Fits, Spare It: Overcoming Hurdles to Infill Development." Urban Land. Vol. 44, No. 10, Oct. 1985. p. 30-31.

LAND USE, URBAN

"Low Income Housing: A Lesson from Amsterdam", Architectural Record, January 1985, pp. 134-143.

LAND USE, URBAN

"Numero Special consacre a l'amenagement des espaces collectifs en milieu ancien". Monumentum. 1979. Entire issue.

LAND USE, URBAN

Osmundson, Theodore. "LAs Champion Open Space Plan." Landscape Architecture. Vol. 76, No. 6, Nov./Dec. 1986. p. 60-61.

LAND USE, URBAN

"Program for City Revitalization." Terrain. Vol. 10, No. 2, May/June 1986. P. 4.

Creation of Chicago's "City Open Lands" program.

LAND USE, URBAN

Smart, Eric. "Making Infill Projects Work." Urban Land. Sept. 1985. p. 2-7.

LAND USE, URBAN

Trends, Fall 1978. Articles on open spaces, parks and landscape protection in urban areas as a means of urban revitalization and conservation.

LAND USE, URBAN

"Urban Space Targeted by Trust for Public Land." Urban Outlook. Vol. 6, No. 13, July 15, 1984. pp. 2-3.

Non-profit to acquire more urban property for parks.

LAND USE, URBAN--BELGIUM--LIEGE

"Renovation in Hors-Chateau." Architectural Record. June 1985. p. 150-155.

In-fill housing construction in old Liege described.

LAND USE, URBAN--ENGLAND

Keyes, John. "Controlling Residential Development in the Green Belt: a Case Study." The Planner. Nov. 1986. p. 18-20.

The green belt policy in Rochford, England.

LAND USE, URBAN--U.S.--SOUTH CAROLINA--CHARLESTON

Crosbie, Michael J. "Genteel Infill in a Genteel City." Architecture. Vol. 74, No. 7, July 1985. p. 44-48.

LANDMARKS

Baymiller, Joanna. "Should a 12-Year-Old Building Become a Historic Landmark." Architecture. August 1984. p. 11.

LANDMARKS

Lynes, Russell. "Landmarks - the Bright Side". Architectural Digest. February 1981. p.32-32f.

LANDMARKS

"One Person's Landmark...(Editorial)." Progressive Architecture. November 1982. p. 7.

LANDMARKS

"State Plans New Psych Building While Vacant Landmarks Decay." Preservation Report. Vol. 8, No. 5, Sept./Oct. 1986. P. 1-2, 13.

Henry Richardson buildings and Olmsted designed landscape are threatened.

LANDMARKS

Willette, Leo. "Interior Secretary Designates 11 National Historic Landmarks." Department of the Interior News Release. Apr. 29, 1985. 3 p.

LANDMARKS--CONSERVATION AND RESTORATION--U.S.-- NEW YORK--POUGHKEEPSIE

"Hudson Valley groups save Springside". Newsletter, Preservation League of New York State. Vol. 10, No. 6, Nov./Dec. 1984. p. 1-2.

LANDMARKS--CONSERVATION AND RESTORATION--U.S.-- NEW YORK--SENECA FALLS

West, Michael and Karlota M. Koester. "Right to Survive: Restoration of the Elizabeth Stanton Home." CRM Bulletin. Vol. 8, No. 2, Apr. 1985. p. 1, 4.

LANDMARKS--CONSERVATION AND RESTORATION--WASHINGTON-- D.C.

Knight, Carlton III. "The White House's Next Door Neighbor: the Robust Old Executive Office Building Undergoes Restoration." Architecture. Apr. 1985. pp. 80-87.

LANDMARKS--U.S.--CALIFORNIA--LOS ANGELES

Boles, Daralice D. "What To Do With the Watts Towers." Progressive Architecture. July 1985. p. 41.

LANDMARKS--U.S.--ILLINOIS--CHICAGO

"Landmark Controversy Stirs Criticism of Preservation Group." Urban Conservation Report. Vol. 10, No. 2, Feb. 6, 1986. p. 3.

The Landmarks Preservation Council of Illinois decides not to fight demolition plans for the Chicago's McCarthy Building.

LANDMARKS--U.S.--LOUISIANA

Poesch, Jessie. "Living with Antiques: the Poydras-Holden House in Louisiana." Antiques. Vol. 127, No. 4, Apr. 1985. p. 870-878.

LANDMARKS--U.S.--NEW HAMPSHIRE--CORNISH

Dryfhout, John H. "The Saint-Gaudens National Historic Site, Cornish, New Hampshire." Antiques. Vol. 128, No. 5, Nov. 1985. p. 982-985.

LANDMARKS--U.S.--NEW YORK--NEW YORK CITY

Berke, Arnold M. "A Competition Probes Times Tower's Future." Place. Vol. 5, No. 3, Mar. 1985. p. 1-5.

LANDMARKS--U.S.--NEW YORK--NEW YORK CITY

Duvert, Elizabeth. "Georgia O'Keeffe's Radiator Building: Icon of Glamorous Gotham." Places. Vol. 2, No. 2. p. 3-7.

Ramond M. Hood's Radiator Building, early twenties skyscraper, discussed.

LANDMARKS--U.S.--NEW YORK--NEW YORK CITY

"Favorite Landmark." Metropolis. Oct. 1985. p. 68-69.

LANDMARKS--U.S.--NEW YORK--NEW YORK CITY--QUEENS

Dudor, Helen. "Those Golden Years When Hollywood Was Way Back East." Smithsonian. Vol. 16, No. 8, Nov. 1985. p. 110-122.

The Astoria Studios, listed on the National Register of Historic Places, to be site of American Museum of the Moving Image.

LANDMARKS--U.S.--OKLAHOMA--TULSA

Knight, Carleton III. "Tulsa Tower's Historic Status Questioned by U.S. Park Service." Architecture. Oct. 1985. p. 15.

LANDMARKS--U.S.--NEW YORK STATE--TARRYTOWN

Butler, Joseph T. "Winter Holidays at Sleepy Hollow Restorations." Antiques. Vol. 128, No. 6, Dec. 1985. p. 1174-1189.

LANDMARKS--U.S.--VIRGINIA--ARLINGTON

Kennedy, Roger. "Arlington House, a Mansion That Was a Monument." Smithsonian. Vol. 16, No. 7, Oct. 1985. p. 156-166.

LANDMARKS--U.S.--WASHINGTON, D.C.--PENSION BUILDING

Goldberger, Paul. "The Pension Building, Home of the National Building Museum." Antiques. Vol. 128, No. 4, Oct. 1985. p. 724-731.

LANDMARKS--U.S.--WASHINGTON, D.C.--SUPREME COURT

Greenberg, Allan and Stephen Kiernan. "The United States Supreme Court Building, Washington, D.C. Antiques. Vol. 128, No. 4, Oct. 1985. p. 760-769.

LANDMARKS COMMISSIONS

"Dealing With Historic District Commissions.' Home Again. No. 4, Autumn 1984. pp. 14-15.

LANDMARKS COMMISSIONS

"New York Landmarks Head Reflects Broadened Constituency." Architecture. September 1983. pp. 12-16.

LANDMARKS COMMISSIONS--U.S.--ILLINOIS

Ward, Michael. "Six New Certified Local Governments Designated." Historic Illinois. Vol. 8, No. 5, Feb. 1986. p. 5-7.

Review of six historic preservation commissions in Illinois.

LANDMARKS COMMISSIONS--U.S.--INDIANA

"Local Ordinances and Commissions." The Indiana Preservationist. No. 1, 1982. pp. 6-7.

LANDMARKS COMMISSIONS--U.S.--LOUISIANA--NEW ORLEANS

Christorich, Mary Louise. "CBDHDLC (Central Business District Historic Landmarks Commission) Effectiveness." New Orleans Preservation in Print. Vol. 12, No. 8, Oct. 1985. p. 7.

LANDMARKS COMMISSIONS--U.S.--LOUISIANA--NEW ORLEANS

"Vieux Carre Commission Celebrates 50 Years." Preservation in Print. Vol. 13, No. 2, Mar. 1986. Entire issue.

LANDMARKS COMMISSIONS--U.S.--NEW YORK

"New Coalition for Landmarks Commissions."
Newsletter, Preservation League of New York
State. Vol. 11, No. 1, Jan./Feb. 1985. p. 2.

LANDMARKS COMMISSIONS--U.S.--NEW YORK--ALBANY

Opaka, Anthony. "Preservation History,
Albany's Historic Sites Commission." Historic
Albany Foundation, Inc., Albany Preservation
Report. May/June 1984. pp. 1-3.

LANDMARKS COMMISSIONS--U.S.--NORTH CAROLINA

Mayes, Thompson M. "Historic Properties
Commissions: Survey Assesses Performance, Needs."
North Carolina Preservation. No. 61, Jan./Feb.
1986. p. 10-11.

LANDSCAPE

APT Bulletin. Vol. 11, No. 4, 1979. Entire
Issue.
Tishler, W.H. "The Landscape: An Emerging
Historic Preservation Resource." pp. 9-25.
Goodman, J. A. "Turf Management at Drayton
Hall." pp. 26-30.

LANDSCAPE

Boyles, Fred. "Historic Landscaping: Moores
Creek National Battlefield." CRM Bulletin. Vol.
9, No. 4, Aug. 1986. p. 9-11.

LANDSCAPE

Coones, Paul and John Patten. The Penguin
Guide to the Landscape of England and Wales.
Middlesex, England: Penguin Books, 1986. 348p.
(DA650.C66P46)

LANDSCAPE

Fly, Everett L. and La Barbara Wigfall Fly.
"Ethnic Landscapes Come to Light." Landscape
Architecture. Vol. 77, No. 4. Jul./Aug. 1987
pp. 34 - 39.

LANDSCAPE

Melnick, Robert Z. "Cultural
Landscapes: An Emerging Concern for
Resource Managment." Trends. Vol. 20,
No. 2, 1983. pp. 24-26.

LANDSCAPE

"Olmsted Beseiged in Central Park" A Little
News. Winter 1986-87. p.2.

A proposed restaurant and bar is threatening
the integrity of Central Park.

LANDSCAPE

Warnock, Robert et al. "Vegetative Threats
to Historic Sites and Structures. " NPS, CRM
Bulletin. Vol. 7, No. 2. July 1984. pp. 11,
18-19.

LANDSCAPE

White, Dana. "Historic Landscapes: From
Conservation & Liberation to Restoration &
Reclamation." National Association for Olmsted
Parks Newsletter. Autumn 1986. p. 6-7.

LANDSCAPE--HISTORY

Bynum, Flora Ann. "Historic Horticulture:
designs and periods for historic landscapes."
North Carolina Preservation. No. 63, May-June
1986. p. 3.

LANDSCAPE--HISTORY

Bynum, Flora Ann. "Historic Horticulture:
documenting a landscaping program." North
Carolina Preservation. No. 62, March-April
1986. p. 3.

LANDSCAPE--HISTORY

Helphand, Kenneth I. "Landscape Films."
Landscape Journal. Vol. 5, No. 1, 1986. p. 1-8.

Discussion of the perception of landscape
through film.

LANDSCAPE--HISTORY

Landscape Architecture. January 1981.
Entire issue.

CONTENTS: Historic preservation leaps the
garden wall; Landscape preservation deserves a
broader meaning; Capturing the cultural landscape; Coping with a Visitor's Overrun;
Restoring a Pre-European Landscape; Changing
view from Mt. Vernon; How to protect the
historic look of Nantucket.

LANDSCAPE--HISTORY

Morrow, Baker H. "Old Landscapes, New Ideas:
New Mexico's Historic Landscape Architecture."
New Mexico Architecture. Vol. 26, No. 5, Sept./
Oct. 1985. p. 11-17.

New Mexico's historic preservation division
sponsors a State Registry of Historic Landscapes
protecting plazas with Spanish design influences
among other sites.

LANDSCAPE--HISTORY

Speake, James. "Sources for period
landscape researchers." Preservation
Report (Alabama Historical Commission).
November/December 1980. p. 2-3.

LANDSCAPE--HISTORY

Turner, Suzanne Louise. "Plantation Papers
as a Source for Landscape Documentation and
Interpretation: The Thomas Butler Papers."
APT Bulletin. v. XII, no.3., 1980. p.28-45.

LANDSCAPE--HISTORY

Upton, Dell. "White and Black Landscapes in
Eighteenth-Century Virginia." Places. Vol. 2,
No. 2. p. 59-72.

LANDSCAPE--U.S.--ILLINOIS

Watson, Daryl. "Dooryard Gardens in Early
Illinois, A Guide to Landscape Restoration."
Illinois Preservation Series, Illinois Department
of Conservation, Division of Historic Sites. No.
12 p.

LANDSCAPE ARCHITECTS

Balmori, Diana. "Beatrix Farrand: Pioneer
Landscape Architect." Newsletter, Preservation
League of New York State. Vol. 11, No. 6, Nov./
Dec. 1985. p. 4-5.

LANDSCAPE ARCHITECTS

Major, Judith K. "The Downing Letters: A.J.
Downing's Correspondence to John Jay Smith."
Landscape Architecture. Vol. 76, No. 1, Jan./Feb.
1986. p. 50-57.

LANDSCAPE ARCHITECTS

Nevins, Deborah. "The Triumph of Flora:
Women and the American Landscape, 1890-1935."
Antiques. Vol. 127, No. 4, Apr. 1985. p. 904-
922.

LANDSCAPE ARCHITECTS

Strong, Donna. "Beatrix Farrand Landscape
Gardener." Inland Architect. Vol. 30, No. 1,
Jan./Feb. 1986. p. 36-41.

LANDSCAPE ARCHITECTS

Tatum, George B. "Andrew Jackson Downing:
Nineteenth Century Tastemaker." Newsletter,
Preservation League of New York State, Vol. 10,
No. 4, July-August 1984. pp. 4-5.

LANDSCAPE ARCHITECTS--OLMSTED, FREDERICK LAW

Kucinski, Bernadine. "Niagara Reservation
Centennial." Preservation Report. Vol. 7, No. 5.
Sep./Oct. 1985. p. 4.

LANDSCAPE ARCHITECTS--OLMSTED, FREDERICK LAW

National Association for Olmsted Parks.
(Newsletter). v.1, no.1, Fall/Winter 1980-81.

LANDSCAPE ARCHITECTURE

Landscape Architecture. July, 1979. entire
issue.

Note: Awards issue; includes project information
on historic districts, urban design and conservation
of natural resources.

LANDSCAPE ARCHITECTS--OLMSTED, FREDERICK LAW

"Olmsted Parks: The Second Century."
Alliance Letter. Vol. 5, No. 2. Mar. 1984.
pp. 1, 4-5.

LANDSCAPE ARCHITECTURE

Agora. The newsletter of the Landscape
Architecture Foundation. First issue:
Autumn 1980.

LANDSCAPE ARCHITECTURE

Barry, Anthony. "The Best Cuts."
Traditional Homes. Vol. 3, No. 1, Oct.
1986. p. 46-49.

Creating topiary.

LANDSCAPE ARCHITECTURE

Benjamin, Susan S. "Highland Park's H. G.
Becker Estate." Historic Illinois. Vol. 9, No. 6,
Apr. 1987. p. 1-5, 7.

Only private estate designed by landscape
architect Jens Jenson that still retains its
meadow.

LANDSCAPE ARCHITECTURE

Crawford, Ian. "Visit to Wrest Park, Silsoe,
Bedfordshire, July 27th 1985." ASCHB Transactions.
Vol. 10, 1985. pp. 54-56.

LANDSCAPE ARCHITECTURE

Palace, Ruth G. "Romantic Suburb-
Residential Landscaping." Preservation Perspective NJ. Vol. III, No. 6, September/October 1984.
p. 6.

LANDSCAPE ARCHITECTURE

Fell, Derek. "Deerfield Maze." Garden Design. Vol. 5, No. 3, Autumn 1986. p. 26-28.

The maze at Hampton Court, England, is replicated at an estate in the Delaware Valley,
Pa.

LANDSCAPE ARCHITECTURE

Hubbard, William. "Reassessing the Art
of Landscape Design: Central Park as a Case Study.
Architectural Record. September 1984. pp. 69, 71
73, 75.

LANDSCAPE ARCHITECTURE

Kashdan, Sandy. "The D.C. Saga." Landscape Architecture. Vol. 77, No. 1, Jan./
Feb. 1987. p. 78-83, 120.

Landscape architecure in Washington, D.C.
from L'Enfant to the Olmsteds.

LANDSCAPE ARCHITECTURE

Kowsky, Francis R. "New York's Urban
Parks: the Legacy of Frederick Law Olmsted."
Preservation League of New York State News-
letter. Vol. 12, No. 4, Fall 1986. p. 8-9.

LANDSCAPE ARCHITECTURE

Lettieri, Linda Hittle. "Updating
Stanford's Inner Quad." Landscape Architecture. Vol. 76, No. 6, Nov./Dec. 1986.
p. 68-71.

An Olmsted design being updated.

LANDSCAPE ARCHITECTURE

Major, Judith K. "Surveying Professional Domains",
Landscape Architecture, Vol. 75, No.1, January/
February 1985, pp. 66-71.

The relationship between architecture and landscape architecture, as found in early journals
(19th century), explored.

LANDSCAPE ARCHITECTURE

"1984 ALSA Awards." Landscape Architecture.
Vol. 74, No. 5, Sept./Oct. 1984. pp. 43-101.

Includes the Recreation of Thomas Jefferson's
Garden Terrace and Grove at Monticello: Merit/De-
sign: Historic Preservation and Restoration,
p. 88; Hamlets of the Adirondacks: Merit/Planning
and Analysis, p. 94.

LANDSCAPE ARCHITECTURE

Osmundson, Theodore. "LAs Champion Open
Space Plan." Landscape Architecture. Vol.
76, No. 6, Nov./Dec. 1986. p. 60-61.

Landscape architects supporting open space
initiative in the South of Market Area of
San Francisco.

LANDSCAPE ARCHITECTURE

Palmer, J.F. et al. "Summary of the Landscape Architecture Needs Survey", Agora, Winter 1984, pp, 17-19.

LANDSCAPE ARCHITECTURE

"Primer: Plant Materials A Craftsman Landscaping." Pasadena Heritage. Vol. VIII, No. 1, Spring 1984. pp. 6-7.

LANDSCAPE ARCHITECTURE

"Seattle Parks and the Olmsted Tradition." Landmarks, Magazine of Northwest History and Preservation. Vol. III, No. 2, Summer 1984. pp. 2-5.

LANDSCAPE ARCHITECTURE

Steiner, Frederick R. and Kenneth R. Brooks. "Agricultural Education and Landscape Architecture." Landscape Journal. Vol. 5, No. 1, 1986. p. 19-32.

Discussion of the history of landscape architectural education in the U.S. beginning in the 19th century with the establishment of land-grant agricultural colleges.

LANDSCAPE ARCHITECTURE

Thacker, Christopher. "Unnatural Practices." Traditional Homes. Sept. 1986. p. 94-97.

On the history of topiary.

LANDSCAPE ARCHITECTURE

Trieb, Marc. "Topiary." Landscape Architecture. Vol. 76, No 7, July/Aug. 1986. p. 76-81.

LANDSCAPE ARCHITECTURE--HISTORY

Donahue, John. "Historic Landscaping." CRM Bulletin. Vol. 9, No. 2, April 1986. p. 1, 8.

LANDSCAPE ARCHITECTURE--U.S.--MAINE--PORTLAND

Brown, Barbara. "Baxter, Olmsted and Portland's 'Emerald Necklace'." Landmarks Observer. Vol. 12, No. 3, May/June 1985. p. 7-8.

LANDSCAPE ARCHITECTURE--U.S.--MASSACHUSETTS--BOSTON

Pearson, Danella. "Shirley-Eustis House Landscape History". Old-Time New England. Vol.LXX, 1980. p. 1-16.

LANDSCAPE ARCHITECTURE--U.S.--NEW JERSEY

Bonted, David W. "NJ's Olmsted Collection." Preservation Perspective NJ. Vol. III, No. 6, September/October 1984. pp. 1-2.

LANDSCAPE ARCHITECTURE--U.S.--NEW YORK--NEW YORK

Murphy, Jean Parker and Kate Burns Ottavino. "The Rehabilitation of Bethesda Terrace." APT Bulletin. Vol. 18, No. 3, 1986. p. 24-39.

Restoration of an area of New York's Central Park.

LANDSCAPE GARDENING--HISTORY

Howett, Catherine M. "Frank Lloyd Wright & American Residential Landscaping." Landscape. Vol. 26, No. 1, 1982. pp. 33-40.

LANDSCAPE GARDENING--HISTORY

Stilgoe, John R. "Privacy and Energy-Efficient Residential Site Design: An Example of Context." Journal of Architectural Education. Vol. 37, No. 3 & 4, Spring and Summer 1984. pp. 20-25.

LANDSCAPE PROTECTION

Alesch, Richard J. "Cultural Landscaping: Buffalo National River." CRM Bulletin. Vol. 9, No. 4, Aug. 1986. p. 7-9.

Vertical File

LANDSCAPE PROTECTION

Bland, David H. "The Local Land Trust: Formation and Operation." <u>Popular Government</u>. Vol. 52, No. 1, Summer 1986. p. 11-16, 47. (VF)

Vertical File

LANDSCAPE PROTECTION

Bryant, Christopher R. "Farmland Conservation and Farming Landscapes in Urban-Centered Regions: the Case of the Ile-de-France Region." <u>Landscape and Urban Planning</u>. Vol. 13, No. 4, Aug. 1986. p. 251-176. (VF)

LANDSCAPE PROTECTION

Christy, Stephen F. "Don't Let History Repeat Itself." <u>Land Trusts' Exchange</u>. Vol. 5, No. 2, Fall, 1986. p. 9, 16.

LANDSCAPE PROTECTION

Corbett, Marjorie. "Greenline Parks, Protecting America's Great Working Landscapes." <u>National Parks</u>. Jul./Aug. 1982. pp. 29-33.

LANDSCAPE PROTECTION

Firth, Ian J.W. "For Beauty or Business, Farmland Preservation on Villa, Estate and Plantation." <u>Landscape Architecture</u>. Jan. 1983. pp. 62-68.

LANDSCAPE PROTECTION

Duffus, Thomas R. "Planning to Beat the Bulldozer: Working from Your Criteria." <u>Land Trusts' Exchange</u>. Vol. 6, No. 1. Spring 1987. pp. 8 - 9, 18.

LANDSCAPE PROTECTION

Frondorf, Anne F., Michael Martin McCarthy, and Ervin H. Zube. "Quality Landscapes: Preserving the National Heritage." <u>Landscape</u>, number 1 1980. pp. 17-21.

Vertical File

LANDSCAPE PROTECTION

Kihn, Cecily Corcoran, et al. "Conservation Options for the Blackstone River Valley." <u>Landscape and Urban Planning</u>. Vol. 13, No. 2, May 1986. p. 81-99 (VF)

LANDSCAPE PROTECTION

"Landscape Preservation." <u>Bulletin, Association for Preservation Technology</u>. Vol. XV, No. 4, 1983. Entire Issue. 76 p. Including Toole, R.M. "Historic Landscape Architecture on the Hudson River Valley Estates," pp. 39-40. Marshall, J.M. "Computerization of Landscape Surveys," pp. 55-56. and Ellwand, Nancy. "Motherwell Homestead: Restoration of a Landscape," pp. 66-71.

LANDSCAPE PROTECTION

Melnick, Robert. "Preserving cultural and historic landscapes: developing standards." <u>CRM Bulletin</u>. March 1980. p. 1-2, 4-7.

LANDSCAPE PROTECTION

Monk, David. "Thoughts on Prairie Preservation." Technical Insert No. 14, <u>Illinois Heritage Association Newsletter</u>. Mar./Apr. 1985. 4 p.

Resource listing included.

LANDSCAPE PROTECTION

"New Landscape Department Created." <u>Hagley Museum and Library Newsletter</u>. Vol. 15, No. 1, Spring 1986. p. 1-2.

Hagley establishes landscape department to research and preserve the landscape at the historic site.

LANDSCAPE PROTECTION

"Olmstead Historic Landscape Preservation Program." <u>National Association for Olmsted Parks News Update</u>. 1986. p. 5.

LANDSCAPE PROTECTION

"Springside: Preserving a National Historic Landscape." <u>Preservation League of New York State Newsletter</u>. January-February 1984. pp. 2-3

LANDSCAPE PROTECTION

"Springside's Landscape to be Saved."
Hudson River Heritage News. Vol. 10, No. 1,
Feb. 1985. p. 3-4.

Only remaining example of Andrew Jackson
Downing's landscape work to be preserved.

LANDSCAPE PROTECTION

"Thoughtful Use of Our Hillsides."
Miami Purchase Association Newsletter.
Spring 1983. p. 3.

LANDSCAPE PROTECTION--LAW AND LEGISLATION

"Bill to List Olmsted Designs Meets
Resistance in Senate." Architecture. Mar. 1986.
p. 32, 35.

LANDSCAPE PROTECTION--LAW AND LEGISLATION

Simpson, John W. "The Emotional Landscape
and Public Law 95-87." Landscape Architecture.
May/June 1985, p. 60-63, 108-109, 112.

Legislative history of surface mining
reclamation proposals discussed.

LANDSCAPE PROTECTION--U.S.--NEW JERSEY

Preservation Perspective (NJ). Vol. III,
No. 3, March/April 1984. Entire issue.

LANDSCAPE PROTECTION--U.S.--VIRGINIA

"Microwave Tower Debates May Generate New
Government Policies." Piedmont Environmental
Council Newsreporter. Sept. 1985. p. 1-2.

Concern for scenic vistas and historic
areas, as well as health, expressed as entry of
companies into tele-communications field fuels
pressure for construction of more towers.

LAW--CASES--U.S.--GEORGIA

"Valley Landowners Powerful Against Utility."
The Rambler, Newsletter of the Georgia Trust.
Vol. 11, No. 3. Summer 1984. p. 8.

LAW--CASES--U.S.--MASSACHUSETTS--BOSTON

Campbell, Kenneth D. "Citizens File Two
Suits to Nullify B.R.A. Zoning on N.E. (New
England) Life Project." Boston Preservation
Alliance Letter. Vol. 6, No. 9, Oct. 1985.
p. 8, 6.

LE CORBUSIER

Herz-Fischler, Roger. "Le Corbusier's
'Regulating Lines' for the Villa at Garches
(1927) and Other Early Works." Journal of the
Society of Architectural Historians. Vol. XLIII,
No. 1, March 1984. pp. 53-60.

LEGISLATION

"Tax Credits for Montgomery County Landmarks." Maryland Association of Historic District Commissions. July-August 1984. p. 1.

County 10% credit for landmark rehabilitation enacted.

LEGISLATION--U.S.--ILLINOIS

Hild, Theodore. "Emergency Jobs Bill
in Illinois, A Mandate for Preservation."
Historic Illinois. Vol. 6, No. 6, April 1984.
pp. 8-10.

LEGISLATION--U.S.--OREGON

"Historic Preservation Task Force Legislation
Passed and Signed by Governor Victor Atiyeh."
Historic Preservation League of Oregon Newsletter.
No. 29. Winter 1983. [pp. 10-11].

LIBRARIES

"Central Library Renovation and Expansion
Plans Revealed." Los Angeles Conservancy.
Vol. 9, No. 3, May/June, 1987. p. 7, 10.

The 1926 Bertram Goodhue library, victim of
two arson fires in 1986, to be renovated by
Hardy Holzman Pfeiffer Associates.

LIBRARIES

"Rejuvenation for the Grand Dowager."
Architectural Record. August 1983.
pp. 74-79.

LIBRARIES--CONSERVATION AND RESTORATION

Dixon, John Morris & David Morton. "Beaux-Arts Burnished." Progressive Architecture. August 1986. p. 89-95.

Restoration of several rooms in the New York Public Library.

LIBRARIES--U.S.--WASHINGTON, D.C.

Belote, Julianne. "Voluminous Pleasures." Early American Life. Vol. 17, No. 3, June 1986. p. 46-51.

Library of Congress interior.

LIENS--U.S.--MISSOURI

McGrath, Roger. "Who's Getting Leined On?" St. Louis Home. Vol. 6, No. 2, Feb. 1986. p. 14-16.

Discussion of Missouri's mechanics lien law and recent lobbying efforts by "Remodeling Contractors to Revise the Lien Laws."

LIGHTHOUSES

Fischetti, David C. "Relocation of Cape Hatteras Lighthouse Makes Sense." North Carolina Preservation. No. 59, Oct./Nov. 1985. p. 3, 16.

LIGHTHOUSES

Glass, Christopher. "Lighthouse Conference, October 1985." Maine Preservation News. Vol. 11, No. 4, Winter 1986. p. 1, 6.

LIGHTHOUSES

Hague, Douglas B. "From Open Fires to Headlamp Arrays: Britain's Lighthouse Heritage." Country Life. Vol. 181, No. 18, Apr. 30,1987. p.134-135.

LIGHTHOUSES

"High Bid Wins It." Yankee Magazine. May 1984. pp. 142-146.

LIGHTHOUSES

"The Lantern Room." Keepers Log, Vol. 1, No. 1, Fall 1984, pp. 15-17.

LIGHTHOUSES

"Protecting the Protectors... Restoring Historic Lighthouses." Technology and Preservation. Spring 1983. pp. 9-13.

LIGHTHOUSES

Slaton, Deborah, Harry J. Hunderman and Jerry G. Stockbridge. "The Cape Hatteras Lighthouse: Diagnostics and Preservation." APT Bulletin. Vol. 19, No. 2, 1987. p. 52-60.

LIGHTHOUSES

Wheeler, Wayne. "America's First Lighthouse: Boston Light." Keepers Log, Vol. 1, No. 1, Fall 1984, pp. 1-5.

LIGHTHOUSES--U.S.--MAINE

Perrin, Stephen. "On Saving Maine's Lighthouses." Maine Citizens for Historic Preservation Newsletter. Vol. 11, No. 2, Summer 1985. p. 6-7.

LIGHTHOUSES--U.S.--MARYLAND--CHESAPEAKE BAY

Sands, John O. "Beacons of the Bay." The Mariners' Museum Journal. Vol. 13, No. 2. Summer 1986. pp. 1-2.

Chesapeake Bay Lighthouses.

LIGHTHOUSES--U.S.--NEW YORK

"New Life for Hudson River Lighthouses." Newsletter, Preservation League of New York State. Vol. 11, No. 6, Nov./Dec. 1985. p. 1-2.

LIGHTHOUSES--U.S.--NEW YORK

Vogel, Mike. "Lighthouse Weathers the Storm." Preservation Report. Vol. 8, No. 1, Jan./Feb. 1986. p. 11.

LIGHTHOUSES--U.S.--NEW YORK STATE--BUFFALO

"New Group Forms to Restore Lighthouses." Preservation Report. Vol. 7, No. 5, Sept./Oct. 1985. p. 3, 14.

LIGHTING

Bowers, Brian and David Woodcock. "Burning the Midnight Oil." Traditional Homes. Vol. 3, No. 1, Oct. 1986. p. 28-31.

Development and use of oil in table lamps.

LIGHTING

Cook, Melissa and Maximillian L. Ferro. "Electric Lighting and Wiring in Historic American Buildings: Guidelines for Restoration and Rehabilitation Projects." Technology and Conservation.   Spring 1983. pp. 28-48.

LIGHTING

Cox, Henry Bartholomew. "Plain and Fancy: Incandescence becomes a household word!" 19th century. p. 49-51. Autumn 1980.

LIGHTING

Garrett, Elisabeth Donaghy. "The American Home, Part II: Lighting Devices and Practices." Antiques. February 1983. pp. 408-417.

LIGHTING

Gilmore, Andrea M. "Preserving Historic Electric Lighting and Wiring at the Frederick Law Olmsted National Historic Site." APT Bulletin. Vol. 16, No. 3 & 4, 1984. p. 31-38.

LIGHTING

Melnick, Scott. "Lighting Adds Flash to Building Exteriors." Building Design & Construction. Vol. 27, No. 11. Nov. 1986. pp. 106-109.

LIGHTING

Myers, Denys Peter. "A Little Light on Gas." Nineteenth Century. Summer 1979. pp. 48-51.

LIGHTING--GREAT BRITAIN

Gaskin, Richard. "Candle to Crystal." Traditional Homes. Mar. 1986. p. 50-55.

LIGHTING, ARCHITECTURAL AND DECORATIVE

AIA Journal, September 1979.

Note: Entire issue on aspects of natural light in architecture.

LIGHTING, ARCHITECTURAL AND DECORATIVE

Hollenberg, Larry. "Saving More Than Face: Historic Lighting, the Gas Connection." The Soulard Restorationist. Vol. 10, No. 5, Sept. 15, 1985. p. 7.

LIGHTING, ARCHITECTURAL AND DECORATIVE

Jones, Larry. "Early Lighting". Utah: Preservation/Restoration. Vol. 2/Issue 2 1980. p. 34 -37.

LIGHTING, ARCHITECTURAL AND DECORATIVE

Rambusch, Viggo Bech. "Historic Interior Lighting: Recreating 19th Century Fixtures for Capitol Buildings." Technology and Conservation. Winter 1981. pp. 36-41.

LIGHTING, ARCHITECTURAL AND DECORATIVE

"A Report on Period Lighting."
Restoration Products News. April 1981.
p.3-8.

LIMESTONE--MAINTENANCE AND REPAIR

Ashurst, John. "The Cleaning and Treatment
of Limestone by the 'Lime Method'." Part II.
Monumentum. Vol. 27, No. 3, September 1984.
pp. 233-253.

LIMESTONE--MAINTENANCE AND REPAIR

Grisafe, David A. "Weathering of the Kansas
Capitol Building: A Study of Limestone
Deterioration." Technology and Conservation.
Spring 1982. pp. 26-31.

LINCOLN, ABRAHAM

Painter, George L. "Restoring the Historic
Scene at Lincoln Home." CRM Bulletin. Vol. 8,
No. 5, Oct. 1985. p. 1, 4.

The leasing program is being used for
houses surrounding Lincoln's Home in Springfield,
Ill.

LINCOLN, ABRAHAM, 1809-1865

Schwartz, Thomas. "State to Acquire Lincoln
Law Offices." Dispatch, Illinois State Historical
Society. Series 7, No. 4, July/Aug. 1985. p. 2-
4.

LITERARY LANDMARKS

Dodson, James. "The Man Who Found Thoreau."
Yankee. Vol. 49, No. 5, May 1985. p. 62-65,
116-123.

LITERARY LANDMARKS--CANADA--ONTARIO--DRESDEN

Boelio, Bob. "Uncle Tom's Cabin." Chronicle
(Historical Society of Michigan). Vol. 20, No. 4,
Winter 1985. p. 22-24.

LITERARY LANDMARKS--U.S.--CALIFORNIA--SAN FRANCISCO

Dawson, Dianne. "Eugene O'Neill NHS Opened
to Public." Courier (NPS Newsletter). Vol. 30,
No. 6. June 1985. p.3.

LITERARY LANDMARKS--U.S.--CONNECTICUT--HARTFORD

Landau, Sarah Bradford. "Mark Twains's
House in Connecticut." Architectural Review.
March 1981. p. 162-166.

LITERARY LANDMARKS--U.S.--MASSACHUSETTS--DANVERS--
OAK KNOLL

Zollo, Richard P. "Oak Knoll-Whittier's
Hermitage." Essex Institute Historical Collections.
Jan. 1981. pp. 27-42.

LITERARY LANDMARKS--U.S.--MINNESOTA--SAUK CENTER

Bourjaily, Vance. "Red Lewis' Town is
Kinder to Him than He Was to It." Smithsonian.
Vol. 16, No. 9, Dec. 1985. p. 46-57.

Profile of Sinclair Lewis' hometown which
was dealt a stinging portrait in his Main
Street.

LITERARY LANDMARKS--U.S.--MISSOURI--HANNIBAL

Curtis, James R. "The Most Famous Fence in
the World: Fact and Fiction in Mark Twain's
Hannibal." Landscape. Vol. 28, No. 5, 1985.
p. 8-14.

LIVING ROOMS

Freeman, John Crosby. "The Queen Anne
Parlor." The Old House Journal. Vol. 13, No. 9,
Nov. 1985. p. 181, 195-197.

LIVING ROOMS

McMurry, Sally. "City Parlor, Country
Sitting Room: Rural Vernacular Design and the
American Parlor, 1840-1900." Winterthur Portfolio.
Vol. 20, No. 4, Winter 1985. p. 261-280.

LOBBYING

Craig, Tracey Linton. "Champions of History, from Statehouses to Capitol Hill, Politicians Defend and Support Heritage Programs." History News. May 1983. pp.7-16.

LOBBYING

Summers, John. "How to Get a Bill Passed." Tennessee Heritage Alliance, Network. Summer 1984, No. 2. pp. 5-6.

LOCAL HISTORY

Dunlap, Carol. "A Joint Venture in Public History." Humanities. October 1981. p. 6.

LOCAL HISTORY

Larson, Sarah. "The Census and Community History: A Reappraisal." Prologue: Journal of the National Archives. Fall 1981. pp. 209-220.

LOCAL HISTORY--STUDY AND TEACHING

Floyd, Candace. "History at Every Corner: New York Project Takes Local History to Public Places." History News. July 1981. pp. 33 - 36.

LOCAL HISTORY--STUDY AND TEACHING

Schirmbeck, Peter. "The Museum of the City of Russelsheim-Council of Europe Award 1980." Museum, Vol. 33, No. 1, 1981. pp. 35- 50.

LOFTS

Hornick, Sandy. "New York Plays Robin Hood to Loft Industries." Planning. November 1982. pp. 18-21.

LOFTS

"Loft Tenants Get a Bill." City Limits. June-July 1982. pp. 28-30.

LOFTS--CONSERVATION AND RESTORATION

Warren, David. "Living Above the Shop." Heritage Outlook. November/December 1981. pp. 151-156.

LOG BUILDINGS

Barrick, Mac E. "The Log House as Cultural Symbol." Material Culture. Vol. 18, No. 1, Spring 1986. p. 1-19.

LOG BUILDINGS

Candelaria, Gary. "If These Walls Could Talk..." Courier. Vol. 32, No. 2, Feb. 1987. p. 18-19.

The Russian Bishop's House at Sitka, Alaska.

LOG BUILDINGS

"Hands-On Preservation with Hank Handler, Part II." The Montgomery County Preservationist. Vol. 2, No. 7. Jul./Aug. 1987. pp. 5 - 6.
Restoration of four log houses in Maryland.

LOG BUILDINGS

McKenzie, Molly. "Reconstructing the Cahokia Courthouse." Historic Illinois. Vol. 7, No. 1, June 1984. pp. 8-10.

LOG BUILDINGS

Spude, Robert R. "Preserving the Largest Log Cabin Community in North America." Courier. Vol. 32, No. 2, Feb. 1987. p. 17-18.

Research on the community of Chisana, Alaska.

LOG BUILDINGS--CANADA

Arnoti, Brigitta. "The Log House Tradition."
Canadian Heritage. Vol. 11, No. 4, Oct./Nov.
1985. p. 27-29.

LOG BUILDINGS--CONSERVATION AND RESTORATION

Haegler, Jeff. "Reconstructing a Log House."
Fine Homebuilding. No. 32, Apr./May 1986. p. 72-75.

Two-story log house built in 1865 in
Scarboro, Wisconsin was dismantled and reconstructed at a new site.

LOG BUILDINGS--CONSERVATION AND RESTORATION

McRaven, Charles. "Chinking Log Walls."
Fine Homebuilding. Apr./May 1985. p. 48-51.

LOG BUILDINGS--CONSERVATION AND RESTORATION

Oppel, Mary Cronan. "Log Houses."
Old House Journal. August 1980. p.85, 100-103.

LOG BUILDINGS--CONSERVATION AND RESTORATION

"Overwhelming Legislative Approval for
Sagamore Land Exchange." *Newsletter, Preservation League of New York State*. p. 3.

LOUISIANA--NATCHITOCHES

Roper, James H. "Natchitoches: Where a
strong preservation ordinanace protects
valuable buildings." *American Preservation*.
July/August 1980. p. 49-58.

LOUISIANA--NEW ORLEANS

Brooks, Jane A. and Deborah Weeter.
"Canal Place: A Clash of Values." *Urban Land*.
July 1982. pp. 3-9.

LUTYENS, SIR EDWIN

Stamp, Gavin. "The Rise and Fall of
Edwin Lutyens." *The Architectural Review*.
November 1981. pp. 311-318.

MAINE--CASTINE

Banks, William Nathaniel. "Castine, Maine,
and St. Andrews, New Brunswick, Canada."
Antiques. July 1980. p. 102-119.

MAINE--RUMFORD--STRATHGLASS PARK

Bourassa, Robert P. "Strathglass Park."
American Preservation. January/February 1981.
p. 9-20.

MANAGEMENT

Broenneke, Karen and Keith Petersen.
"Planning for Change, How Long-Range Planning
Can Benefit Historical Organizations of All
Sizes." *History News*. Vol. 39, No. 8, August
1984. pp. 12-17.

MANAGEMENT

Grove, Andrews. "How to Make Confrontation
Work for You." *Fortune*. July 23, 1984. pp.
73-75.

MANAGEMENT

Wyzbinski, Patricia. "An Overview of
Office Management Procedures." *Grantsmanship Center
News*. May/June 1981. pp. 59-73.

MAPS

Vogel, Robert M. "Quadrangular Treasure:
The Cartographic Route to Industrial Archeology."
IA Vol. 6, no.1, 1980 p. 25-54.

MAPS--HISTORY--U.S.--FLORIDA

Armstrong, Helen Jane. "University of Florida Libraries to Launch Sanborn Map Preservation Project." *Florida Preservation News*. Mar. 1985. p. 2-3.

MARBLE

Strangstad, Lynette. "How to Clean and Polish Marble." *The Old-House Journal*. Oct. 1982. pp. 208-211.

MARBLE--MAINTENANCE AND REPAIR

"Interior Marble Cleaned in Memorial Building." *Kansas Preservation*. September-October 1983. pp. 6-7.

MARITIME HISTORY

Carr, J. Revell. "Maritime Preservation in America-Coming of Age." *Trends*. Vol. 20, No. 2, 1983. pp. 16-19.

MARITIME LAW

Anzalone, Kerry J. "Maritime Preservation, Conflicting State and Federal Laws Engender Political and Legal Squalls in Stormy Confrontations to Gain Control Over Historic Shipwrecks." *New Orleans Preservation in Print*. Vol. 11, No. 7 September 1984. pp. 8, 16.

MARITIME PRESERVATION

APT Bulletin. Vol. 9, No. 1, 1987. Special Issue on Maritime Preservation. Special Section: APT Short Course: Maritime Preservation.

Anderson, Richard K., Jr. "Lifting Lines from the Schooner Wawona." p. 80-88.

MARITIME PRESERVATION

APT Bulletin. Vol. 9, No. 1, 1987. Special Issue on Maritime Preservation. Special Section: APT Short Course: Maritime Preservation.

Birkholz, Don. "The Role of Marine Surveys in Maritime Preservation." p. 44-45.

MARITIME PRESERVATION

APT Bulletin. Vol. 9, No. 1, 1987. Special Issue on Maritime Preservation. Special Section: APT Short Course: Maritime Preservation.

Brouwer, Norman. "The Role of Historical Research in Documenting Historic Vessels." p. 40-43.

MARITIME PRESERVATION

APT Bulletin. Vol.9, No. 1, 1987. Special Issue on Maritime Preservation. Special Section: APT Short Course: Maritime Preservation.

Darr, Bob. "Maritime Preservation Training Programs." p. 76-77.

MARITIME PRESERVATION

APT Bulletin. Vol. 9, No. 1, 1987. Special Issue on Maritime Preservation. Special Section: APT Short Course: Maritime Preservation.

Delgado, James P. "The National Register of Historic Places and Maritime Preservation." p. 34-39.

MARITIME PRESERVATION

APT Bulletin. Vol. 9, No. 1, 1987. Special Issue on Maritime Preservation Special Section: APT Short Course: Maritime Preservation.

Hewson, Dana. "Suggested Standards for the Maintenance of Historic Vessels." p. 72-75.

MARITIME PRESERVATION

APT Bulletin. Vol. 9, No. 1, 1987. Special Issue on Maritime Preservation. Special Section: APT Short Course: Maritime Preservation

Kortum, Karl. "Why Do We Save Ships?" p. 30-33.

MARITIME PRESERVATION

APT Bulletin. Vol. 9, No. 1, 1987. Special Issue on Maritime Preservation. Special Section: APT Short Course: Maritime Preservation.

Maounis, John. "Interpreting Historic Vessels." p. 62-65.

MARITIME PRESERVATION

APT Bulletin. Vol. 9, No. 1, 1987. Special Issue on Maritime Preservation.
McGrath, H. Thomas, James P. Delgado and Don Birkholz. "Historic Structure Report: Wapama." p. 4-9.

MARITIME PRESERVATION

APT Bulletin. Vol. 9, No. 1, 1987, Special Issue on Maritime Preservation. Special Section: APT Short Course: Maritime Preservation.

Morss, Strafford. "Preserving the Warships of World War II Battleship Cove as a Case History." p. 56-59.

MARITIME PRESERVATION

APT Bulletin. Vol. 9, No. 1, 1987. Special Issue on Maritime Preservation.

Murphy, Larry. "Preservation at Pearl Harbor." p. 10-15.

MARITIME PRESERVATION

APT Bulletin. Vol. 9, No. 1, 1987. Special Issue on Maritime Preservation. Special Section: APT Short Course: Maritime Preservation.

Neill, Peter. "Developing a National Cultural Policy for Maritime Preservation." p. 24-29.

MARITIME PRESERVATION

APT Bulletin. Vol. 9, No. 1, 1987. Special Issue on Maritime Preservation. Special Section: APT Short Course: Maritime Preservation.

Rybka, Walter. "Preserving Historic Vessels: A Long View of History." p. 46-52.

MARITIME PRESERVATION

APT Bulletin. Vol. 9, No. 1, 1987. Special Issue on Maritime Preservation. Special Section: APT Short Course: Maritime Preservation.

Rybka, Walter. "Suggested Standards for Replica and Reproduction Vessels." p. 66-71.

MARITIME PRESERVATION

APT Bulletin. Vol. 9, No. 1, 1987. Special Issue on Maritime Preservation. Special Section: APT Short Course: Maritime Preservation.

Steele, Peter. "Artifacts within Artifacts: Collections and Historic Vessels. p. 60-61.

MARITIME PRESERVATION

APT Bulletin. Vol. 9, No. 1, 1987. Special Issue on Maritime Preservation. Special Section: APT Short Course: Maritime Preservation.

Walker, David A. "The Application of Preservation Technology to Historic Ships." p. 53-55.

MARITIME PRESERVATION

APT Bulletin. Vol. 9, No. 1, 1987. Special Issue on Maritime Preservation.

Contents: Wall, Glennie Murray. "The National Maritime Initiative." pp. 2-3, 18.

MARITIME PRESERVATION

APT Bulletin. Vol. 9, No. 1, 1987. Special Issue on Maritme Preservation.

Weaver, Martin. "Fighting Rust." p. 16-18.

MARITIME PRESERVATION

APT Bulletin. Vol. 9, No. 1, 1987. Special Issue on Maritime Preservation. Special Section: APT Short Couse: Maritime Preservation.

"Conclusion: Toward a National Policy for Maritime Preservation." p. 78-79.

MARITIME PRESERVATION

Craig, Tracey Linton. "Seafaring Traditions Live On in Bath." Museum News. Vol. 64, No. 2, Dec. 1985. p. 60-65.

MARITIME PRESERVATION

"Florida Maritime Folklife Project." Folklife Center News. Vol. 9, Nos. 2 & 3, April-Sept. 1986. p. 2-3.

The Folklife Center is cooperating with the Bureau of Florida Folklife Programs on the Florida Maritime Cultural Heritage Survey.

MARITIME PRESERVATION

Hastings, Stephen. "Restoration of C.A. Thayer, 1983." CRM Bulletin. Vol. 7, No. 3, October 1984. pp. 10-11, 18.

MARITIME PRESERVATION

Kvarning, Lars-Ake and Erling Matz. "Designing a New Home for the Wasa." Place. January 1984. pp. 1-3.

MARITIME PRESERVATION

McGrail, Sean. "Need We Wreck the Past?"
Country Life, Apr. 16, 1987. p. 192-193.

Britain's neglect of its maritime heritage.

MARITIME PRESERVATION

"Preserving Our Maritime Heritage." Land Trusts'
Exchange. Vol. 5, No. 3, Fall 1986. p. 10.

The work of the Lighthouse Preservation Society.

MARITIME PRESERVATION

"Submarine Memorial Association." New Jersey
Historical Commission Newsletter. Vol. 17, No. 5,
Jan. 1987. p. 2.

MARKETING

Ensman, Richard. "Building a
Mailing List, An Introduction." The
Grantsmanship Center News. May/June 1983.
pp. 10-21.

MARKETING

"Marketing Old Neighborhoods." Conserve
Neighborhoods. No. 56, Mar. 1986. p. 1-3, 6-7.

MARKETING

"New Marketing Service is
Specially Tailored for Neighborhood
Business Areas." Local Economic Growth
and Neighborhood Reinvestment Report.
July 21, 1983. p. 4.

MARKETPLACES

"Contemporary Merchandising Principles
Revive an Historic Building Type: Market
House in Washington, D.C." Architectural
Record. October 1980. p. 96-99.

MARKETPLACES

Petrocci, Barbara. "The New Urban
Marketplace: Street Fairs and Farmers' Markets
Revisited." Journal of American Culture.
Fall 1981. pp. 163-168.

MARKETPLACES

"Planning the Urban Marketplace".
Architectural Record. October 1980. p. 90-95.

MARKETPLACES--CONSERVATION AND RESTORATION

Christensen, Terry. " A Sort of Victory,
Covent Garden Renewed." Landscape. Vol. 26,
No. 2, 1982. pp. 21-28.

MARKETPLACES--CONSERVATION AND RESTORATION

Thompson, Jane McC. "Boston's Faneuil Hall,
The Market's Multi-sensory Quality is a Magnet,
But It May Not be Easy to Maintain." Urban Design
International. Nov./Dec. 1979. pp. 12-14, 19,
30-31.

MARKETPLACES--CONSERVATION AND RESTORATION--U.S.-
-WASHINGTON--SEATTLE

Canty, Donald. "A Revived Market Maintains
Its Identity." Architecture. May 1985. p. 274-
281.

Pike Place Market (1907) discussed.

MARKETPLACES--U.S.--VIRGINIA

Brown, John C. "Citywide Implications of
Virginia's Festival Marketplaces: Norfolk's
Waterside and Richmond's 6th Street Marketplaces."
Journal of Architectural and Planning Research.
Vol. 3, No. 1, Feb. 1986. p. 79-85.

Discussion of project investment and minority
participation in a leading example of downtown
commercial revitalization, the festival marketplace. Two Enterprise Development Company
projects were analyzed.

MARKETS

Campbell, Thomas A., Jr. "Galena's
Market House." Historic Illinois. December
1980. p.1-3, 14.

MARKETS

Colley, David. "Farm Fresh and Friendly." _Americana_. Vol. 13, No. 3, July/Aug. 1985. p. 39-41.

Revival of farmer's markets discussed.

MARKETS

"The Farmer's Market, A Tradition Revived." _Pasadena Heritage_. Vol. VIII, No. 1, Spring 1984. p. 11.

MARKETS

Hunter, Patricia. "Making the Most of Urban Farmers Markets." _Place_. May 1982. pp. 8-10.

MARKETS

Kahn, Vivian. "Western Market Building." _Oakland Heritage Alliance News_. Vol. 7, No. 1, Spring 1987. p. 12.

MARKETS

Knecht, Gary. "Oakland's Wholesale Produce Market." _Oakland Heritage Alliance News_. Vol. 7, No. 1. Spring 1987. pp. 1-7.

MARKETS

Merrill-Corum, Vance. "Farmers Market Revival." _Center-City Report_. May/June 1987. p. 1.

MARKETS--ADAPTIVE USE

"Covent Garden restoration: Flower Market becomes Transport Museum". _Building Conservation_ February 1980. p. 30-32.

MARYLAND

Maryland Historical Magazine. 1954-1976 (missing scattered issues.)

MARYLAND--BALTIMORE

Paraschos, Janet Nyberg. "Baltimore:a mayor helps his city regain its pride through neighborhood power". _American Preservation_. July/August 1980. p. 23-38.

MARYLAND --BALTIMORE--INNER HARBOR

Clay, Grady. "On Baltimore's Inner Harbour." _Landscape Architecture_. November 1982. pp. 48-53.

MARYLAND--BALTIMORE--VERNACULAR ARCHITECTURE

Hayward, Mary Ellen. "Urban Vernacular Architecture in Nineteenth-Century Baltimore." _Winterthur Portfolio_. Spring 1981. p.33-63.

MASONRY

Charbonneau, Andre. "Notes sur la maconnerie de deux edifices militaires construits a Quebec au milius du XIXe siecle" _APT Bulletin_. V. XII, no. 3, 1980. p. 115-126.

MASONRY

Cotton, J. Randall. "Blasted! Now What?" _Old-House Journal_. Vol. 15, No. 1, Jan./Feb. 1987. p. 38-41.

How to deal with problems caused by sandblasting.

MASONRY

Ferro, Maximillian L. "The Russack System for Brick and Mortar Description: A Field Method for Assessing Masonry Hardness." _Technology and Conservation_. Summer 1980. p. 32-35.

MASONRY

Fidler, John. "Expert View: Spring Cleaning , Part I." Traditional Homes. Vol. 3, No. 5, Feb. 1987, p. 28-30.

Considerations necessary before cleaning masonry buildings.

MASONRY

Holtz, Paul. "Evaluating a Proposal or Specification for Masonry Repair." Massachusetts Historical Commission Newsletter. Vol. 13, No. 1, Feb. 1987. p. 10, 14.

MASONRY

Marmet, Terry W. "Caring for Historic Masonry Buildings." Kansas Preservation. Vol. 8, No. 4, May-June 1986. p. 3-5.

MASONRY

Marmet, Terry W. "Removal of Mortar from Historic Masonry Requires Care." Kansas Preservation. Vol. 9, No. 1, Nov./Dec. 1986. p. 2-4.

MASONRY

Mason, Glenn. "Sandblasting: Bane of Older Buildings." Historic Hawai'i. Vol. 12, No. 9, Oct. 1986. p. 8.

MASONRY

Matero, Frank G. and Jo Ellen Freese. "Notes on the Treatment of Oil and Grease Staining on a Masonry Surface." APT Bulletin, number 2 1978. pp. 132-141.

MASONRY

Miller, Charles. "From Boulders to Building Blocks: How a Traditional Stonemason Quarries and Dresses Sandstone." Fine Homebuilding. No. 35, Oct./Nov. 1986. p. 35-37.

MASONRY

Moore, Evelyn R. "Sandblasting Harmful to Historic Buildings." Historic Illinois. Vol. 9, No. 3, Oct. 1986. p. 10-11.

MASONRY

"Of Cobbles and Cobblestones...Upstate New York's Unique Architectural Legacy." The Landmark Society of Western New York. Vol. 25, No. 3, May 1987. p. 6-7.

MASONRY

Pearce, Christopher. "Faked Facades." Traditional Homes. Vol. 3, No. 1, Oct. 1986. p. 10-16.

Present and past use of stucco over brick to give the appearance of stone.

MASONRY

Poore, Patricia. "Stripping Exterior Masonry." Old House Journal. Vol. XIII, No. 1, Jan.-Feb. 1985. pp. 1, 26-29.

MASONRY

Potter, Robert. " The monitoring of crack movement with electronic equipment at St. Paul's Cathedral, London." Monumentum. Vol. 25, #3, September 1982, pp. 215-227.

MASONRY

"Read This Before You Clean Masonry!" Arizona Preservation News. Vol. 3, No. 4, Oct. 1986. p. 17.

MASONRY

Rooks, Tom. "Silica Aggregate Blasting." Conservancy News. Vol. 3, No. 5, Oct./Nov. 1986. p. 5.

The dangers of using sandblasting when cleaning buildings.

MASONRY

Staehli, Alfred M. "Appropriate Water Pressures for Masonry Cleaning." APT Bulletin. Vol. 18, No. 4. 1986. pp. 10-17.

MASONRY

Stockbridge, Jerry G. "Evaluating the Strength of Existing Masonry Walls." APT Bulletin. Vol. 18, No. 4, 1986. p. 6-7.

MASONRY

Tindall, Susan M. "Repointing Masonry: Why Repoint?" Old-House Journal. Vol. 15, No. 1, Jan./Feb. 1987. p. 24-26.

MASONRY

Ward, Tessa. "Forgotten Earth Relics of Early Settlement." Historic Places in New Zealand. No. 15, Dec. 1986. p. 12-15.

Some of the cob buildings of New Zealand are undergoing restoration.

MASONRY

Wheeler, Lorne. "Masonry Wall Deterioration: Plugging the Leaks." Building Renovation. Vol. 4, No. 2, Mar./Apr. 1987. p. 19.

MASONRY

Winkler, Erhard M. "The Measurement of Weathering Rates of Stone Structures." APT Bulletin. Vol. 18, No. 4, 1986. p. 65-70.

MASONRY

Woroch, Gregory S. "How to Repoint." Old-House Journal. Vol. 15, No. 1, Jan./Feb. 1987. p. 27-31.

MASONRY--CONSERVATION AND RESTORATION

"An Annotated Master Specification for the Repointing of Historic Masonry." APT Technical Notes 5, Communique. Vol. 14, No. 4, Aug. 1985. p. 9-10.

MASONRY--CONSERVATION AND RESTORATION

Bucher, Wm. Ward. "The Crack Detective: Beginning the Investigation". The Old House Journal. May 1981. p. 97.

MASONRY--CONSERVATION AND CONSERVATION

Bucher, Wm. Ward. "The Crack Detective, Part II: Lining Up Suspects." The Old House Journal. July 1981. pp. 155-159.

MASONRY--CONSERVATION AND RESTORATION

Bucher, Wm. Ward. "The Crack Detective : More Suspects." The Old-House Journal. Vol. IX, No. 8, August 1981. pp. 177-181.

MASONRY--CONSERVATION AND RESTORATION

Bucher, William Ward. "The Crack Detective, Planning Structural Repairs." The Old House Journal. December 1981. pp. 277-281.

MASONRY--CONSERVATION AND RESTORATION

"Cleaning Masonry : A Look at Water and Chemical Treatments." Canadian Heritage. December 1981. pp. 39-42.

MASONRY--CONSERVATION AND RESTORATION

Goody, Nancy H. "Cleaning Masonry Buildings: Considerations and Methods." Albany Preservation Report. September 1982. pp. 5-7.

MASONRY--CONSERVATION AND RESTORATION

Grimmer, Anne E. "Documenting the Condition and Treatment of Historic Building Materials." Technology and Conservation. Summer 1981. pp. 32-35.

MASONRY--CONSERVATION AND RESTORATION

Grissom, Carol and Norman Weiss. "A History and Guide to the Literature on Alkoxysilanes as used for the Conservation of Works of Art." Art and Archaeology Technical Abstracts. Vol. 18, No. 1. pp. 149-198.

MASONRY--CONSERVATION AND RESTORATION

Herman, Frederick. "Masonry Repointing." The Old-House Journal. June 1979. pp. 61-68.

MASONRY--CONSERVATION AND RESTORATION

Kreh, Richard T. "The Point of Repointing: Renewing tired masonry joints can bring an old brick building back to life." Fine Homebuilding. April/May 1981. p. 45-47.

MASONRY--CONSERVATION AND RESTORATION

Livingston, Richard A. "The Air Pollution Contribution to Stone Deterioration: Investigating the Weathering of the Bowling Green Custom House, N.Y. City." Technology and Conservation. Summer 1981. pp. 36-39.

MASONRY--CONSERVATION AND RESTORATION

Marshall, Philip C. "The Use of Pneumatic Tools in Repointing Historic Masonry." Tech Note 8, Communique, APT. Vol. 15, No. 1, Feb. 1986. p. 9-10.

MASONRY--CONSERVATION AND RESTORATION

"Repair and Maintenance of Masonry Buildings." Journal of Housing. January/February 1983. pp. 16-17.

MASONRY--CONSERVATION AND RESTORATION

"Repointing: An Annotated Master Specification for the Repointing of Historic Masonry." Technical Notes 5. Communique. Vol. 14, (2). p. 9-10.

MASONRY--CONSERVATION AND RESTORATION

"Repointing: An Annotated Master Specification for the Repointing of Historic Masonry." Technical Notes 5 cont'd. APT Communique. Vol. 14 (3), June 1985. p. 9-10.

MASONRY--CONSERVATION AND RESTORATION

Strangstad, Lynette. "Patching Limestone and Marble, A Step-by Step Guide." The Old-House Journal. Jul. 1982. p. 133.

MASONRY--CONSERVATION AND RESTORATION

Wescott, William F. "Technically Speaking: Restoring Historic Masonry and Stucco." Preservation Today (Dade Heritage Trust, Inc.). Vol. 1, No. 5, Spring 1985. p. 35-36.

MASONRY--MAINTENANCE AND REPAIR

Fidler, John. "Stabilising Stonework." Traditional Homes. Jul. 1986. pp. 62-64.

Repair and replacement of old masonry.

MASONRY--MAINTENANCE AND REPAIR

"Masonry Repairs." City Limits. June/July 1986. p. 3.

MASSACHUSETTS--BOSTON

Kay, Jane Holtz. " The 'Lost Boston -- and the Future". AIA Journal. Sept. 1980. p. 38-45.

MASSACHUSETTS--BOSTON

Planning. March 1981. Entire issue.

CONTENTS: Boston:Qualified success. -- Harvard and MIT:Where it all began. -- Neighborhood pride, neighborhood power.

MASSACHUSETTS--BOSTON--CITY HALL

Craig, Lois. "The Boston City Hall and its Antecedents." _AIA Journal._ SEpt. 1980. p. 46-52.

MASSACHUSETTS--LINCOLN--THE CODMAN ESTATE(The Grange)

Old Time New England. Vol. LXXI, Serial No. 258. Entire Issue.

CONTENTS : Adams, Thomas Boylston, The Codmans and Lincoln. -- Emmet, Alan. The Codman Estate -"The Grange : A Landscape Chronicle. -- Chapin, R. Curtis. The Early History and Federalization of the Codman House. -- Floyd, Margaret Henderson. Redesign of "The Grange" by John Hubbard Sturgis, 1862-1866. -- (continued on next card)

MASSACHUSETTS--LINCOLN--THE CODMAN ESTATE(The Grange)   (Card 2)

Metcalf, Pauline C. Ogden Codman, Jr. and "The Grange." -- Nylander, Richard C. Documenting the Interior of Codman House : The Last Two Generations. -- Redmond, Elizabeth. The Codman Collection of Pictu Pictures. -- Reichlin, Ellie. "Reading" Family Photographs : A Contextual Analysis of the Codman Photographic Collection. -- Howie, Robert L., Jr. Codman Connections : Portrait of a Family and Its Papers. --

MASSACHUSETTS--LOWELL

Hudon, Paul. "New Lowell Experiments." _Museum News._ November/December 1982. pp. 73-75.

MASSACHUSETTS--LOWELL-- MILLS

Fossel, Peter V. "The Mills of Lowell." _Americana._ January/February 1983. pp. 52-57.

MASSACHUSETTS--LYNN

"Fire Site 'Vital' to Rebirth, Says Second Lynn R/UDAT." _AIA Journal._ April 1982. p. 31.

MASSACHUSETTS--MARTHA'S VINEYARD

Banks, William Nathaniel. "The Wesleyan Grove Campground on Martha's Vineyard." _Antiques._ July 1983. pp. 104-115.

MASSACHUSETTS--SALEM--HOUSE OF SEVEN GABLES

Stevenson, Edward M. "House of the Seven Gables: Hawthorne's Memorial." _Antiques._ March 1984. pp. 666-672.

MASSACHUSETTS--WORCESTER--MECHANICS HALL

Ingwersen, John A. "Restoration of Mechanics Hall, Worcester, Massachusetts: Revitalizing a 19th century Cultural Center". _Technology and Conservation._ Fall 1980. p.16-23.

MATERIAL CULTURE

Schloreth, Thomas J. "Material Culture Research and Historical Explanation." _The Public Historian._ Vol. 7, No. 4, Fall 1985, p. 21-36.

MATERIAL CULTURE

"Special Issue: Material Culture Studies: A Symposium." _Material Culture._ Vol. 17, Nos. 2 & 3, Summer-Fall 1985. 46 p.

MEMORIALS

Fox, Phyllis G. "Waikiki War Memorial and Natatorium." _Historic Hawai'i._ Vol. 13, No. 1, Jan. 1987. p. 4-5

MEMORIALS

Harris, Neil. "The Battle for Grant's Tomb." _American Heritage._ Vol. 36, No. 5, Aug./ Sept. 1985. p. 70-79.

MERCANTILE BUILDINGS--CONSERVATION AND RESTORA-
TION

 "A Benign Urban Renewal Project in the City
of Brotherly Love." Architectural Record.
Apr. 1985. p. 71.

 Lit Brothers Store part of new Independence
Center.

MERCANTILE BUILDINGS--CONSERVATION AND
 RESTORATION

 Gluckin, Neil D. "Sprucing Up the Strand."
Americana. November/December 1981. pp. 50-57.

MERCANTILE BUILDINGS--U.S.--KANSAS

 Cawthon, Richard J. "Nineteenth Century
Commercial Architecture Displays a Variety of
Styles." Kansas Preservation. Vol. 7, No. 3,
Mar./Apr. 1985. p. 5-7.

 Ninth in a series on architecture in Kansas.

MERRY-GO-ROUND

 Fromkin, Jay N. "The Merry-Go-Round Rides
Again. Where to find carousels that have been
restored to midway condition." Americana.
July/August 1984. pp. 33-35, 85.

MERRY-GO-ROUND

"Parker Carousel Designated National Historic
Landmark." Kansas Preservation. Vol. 9, No. 4.
May - June 1987. p. 7.

MERRY-GO-ROUND

 Schwarz, Joel. "Menageries in the
Round: the remarkable efforts of Carol and
Duane Perron have made Portland, Oregon, the
city where the carousels are to be found."
Americana. Vol. 12, No. 6, Jan./Feb. 1985.
p. 66-71.

MERRY-GO-ROUND--U.S.--COLORADO

 Blevins, Terry W. "After the Ball: The
Kit Carson County Carousel." Small Town.
Vol. 15, No. 1, July/August 1984. pp. 4-12.

METAL-WORK

 Marmet, Terry. "Galvanized Metal: An
Important Building Material." Kansas Preservation
Vol. VI, No. 5, July-August 1984. pp. 8-9.

METAL-WORK--CONSERVATION AND RESTORATION

Marmet, Terry. "Galvanized Metal: Causes of Deterioration and Preservation Treatments.", Kansas
Preservation, Vol. VII, No. 1, November-December 1984.

METAL-WORK--CONSERVATION AND RESTORATION

 Fidler, John. "Any Old Iron."
Traditional Homes. Sept. 1986. p.
66-68.

 How to restore rusted ironwork.

METAL-WORK--CONSERVATION AND RESTORATION

 Edwards, Charles E. "A Process for
Duplicating Ornamental Castings for Historical
Buildings." Utah Preservation/Restoration.
Vol. III, 1981. pp. 72-73.

MICHIGAN--DETROIT

 Dewhurst, C. Kurt, Betty MacDowell and Marsha
MacDowell. "The Art of Julius and Gari Melchers."
Antiques. Vol. CXXXV, No. 4. April 1983.
pp. 860-873.

MICHIGAN--SAULT STE. MARIE--HISTORIC PRESERVA-
TION

Omoto, Sadayoshi. "Historic Preservation and
a Small Michigan Town." Small Town. May-June
1980. p. 16-19.

MILITARY ARCHITECTURE

 Clark, Tim. "Living in a Quonset Hut is
Like Eating Spam." Yankee. Vol. 49, No. 11,
Nov. 1985. p. 116-123, 192.

 Trustee Frederick Williamson featured in
this discussion of the architectural history of
the quonset hut.

MILITARY ARCHITECTURE--ADAPTIVE USE

"Former Military Bases Become Parks, Factories, Schools." Headquarters Heliogram. No. 173, Dec. 1985. p. 4.

MILITARY ARCHITECTURE--AUSTRALIA

"Historic RAAF Base Classified." Trust News. Vol. 13, No. 10, April 1985. p. 8-9.

MILITARY ARCHITECTURE--U.S.--CALIFORNIA--SAN FRANCISCO

Chandler, Robert J. "Ft. Alcatraz: Symbol of Federal Power." Periodical (Council on America's Military Past). Vol. 13, No. 2, W.N. 51. p. 27-47.

MILLS

Adams, Evan. "Rummel Mill, Remnant of Ohio's Settlement Period." Old Mill News. Vol. 15, No. 1, Winter 1987. p. 3-5.

MILLS

Andrew, J.H. "Coon Valley Mill." Old Mill News. Vol. 14, No. 3, Summer 1986. p. 15.

MILLS

Beardsley, Bradley. "New Hope Mills--Products the Natural Way." Old Mill News. Vol. 14, No. 3. Summer 1986. pp. 3-4.

A mill built in 1823 still grinds wheat and buckwheat flour.

MILLS

Crandall, Jim. "New Bedford's Mill Buildings--a Preservation Challenge." New Bedford Soundings. Vol. 11, No. 3, Fall 1986. p. 10-11.

MILLS

Giles, Colum and Ian H. Goodall. "Framing a Survey of Textile Mills: RCHME's West Riding Experience." Industrial Archaeology Review. Vol. 9, No. 1, Autumn 1986. p. 71-81.

The Royal Commission on the Historical Monuments of England's survey of textile mills.

MILLS

Hanson, Michael. "Where There's a Mill." Country Life. Vol. 181, No. 26. June 25, 1987. pp. 130 - 131.

MILLS

Hubbs, Robert. "The Poncelet Wheel--The Ultimate Undershot." Old Mill News. Vol. 14, No. 4, Fall 1986. p. 6-7.

MILLS

"List of Mills on the National Register of Historic Places." Old Mill News. Vol. 15, No. 1, Winter 1987. 15p. (Insert)

MILLS

"Oatlands Mill Project off to a 'flying start'." National Trust of Australia (Tasmania) Newsletter. No. 104, Dec. 1986. p. 1.

MILLS

Stidham, David. "Large Diameter Water Wheels in the U.S." Old Mill News. Vol. XII, No. 3, July 1984. pp. 8-9.

MILLS

Stidham, David. "Large Diameter Water Wheels in the U.S." Part II. Old Mill News. Vol. XII, No. 4, October 1984. pp. 10-12.

231

MILLS

Stidham, David. "Large Diameter Waterwheels Part IV (conclusion)." Old Mill News. Vol. 13, No. 2, Spring 1985. p. 5-7.

MILLS

Tidbury, Jane. "Flour and Flax." Traditional Homes. Vol. 3, No. 11. Aug. 1987. pp. 51 - 57.
The renovation of a seventeenth-century Irish farmhouse and its mills.

MILLS

"Where Are the Scenic Mills." Old Mill News. Vol. 14, No. 3, Summer 1986. p. 10-11.

Photos of scenic mills.

MILLS

"Where Are the Scenic Mills?" Old Mill News. Vol. 14, No. 4, Fall 1986. p. 12-14.

MILLS--ADAPTIVE USE

Cook, Marion. "Life in an Historic Old Mill." Old Mill News. Vol. XII, No. 3, July 1984. p. 14.

MILLS--ADAPTIVE USE

Dixon, John Morris; Thomas Fisher and Duralice D. Boles. "P/A Inquiry: New Products From Old Mills." Progressive Architecture. Nov. 1983. p. 94-99.

MILLS--ADAPTIVE USE

Earnshaw, Sally. "Mill Mutations." Traditional Homes. July 1986. p. 34-38.

Conversion of Shalford Mill to a family home accomplished with minimum disruption to the original features.

MILLS--ADAPTIVE USE

"Kahuku Sugar Mill Site to Reopen as Shopping Center." Historic Hawai'i. Vol. 13, No. 1, Jan. 1987. p. 18.

MILLS--ADAPTIVE USE

McGrain, John. "Lewis Mill Goes to Pottery." Old Mill News. Vol. XII, No. 2, April 1984. p. 5.

Solar panels heat National Register mill.

MILLS--ADAPTIVE USE

"Tax Credits, Innovative Leasing Help Nonprofit Group Transform Abandoned Mill." Local Economic Growth and Neighborhood Reinvestment Report. September 9, 1983. p. 6.

MILLS--ADAPTIVE USE--U.S.--MASSACHUSETTS-- UXBRIDGE

Knight, Carleton III. "Apartments in a Restored Rural Mill and an Intown Farmhouse." Architecture. Oct. 1985. p. 74-75.

MILLS--ADAPTIVE USE--U.S.--VERMONT--WINOOSKI

Ellenberger, William J. "Champlain Mill Makes News in Winooski." Society for Industrial Archeology Newsletter. Vol. 13, No. 3 & 4, Fall & Winter 1984. p. 10.

MILLS--CONSERVATION AND RESTORATION

Boelio, Bob. "Old Wolcott Mill." Chronicle, Historical Society of Michigan. Vol. 21, No. 3. Autumn 1985. pp. 8-10.

A 19th century gristmill will soon become the center of a new Metropark.

MILLS--CONSERVATION AND RESTORATION

Curtis, John O. "The Move and Restoration of the Hapgood Wool Carding Mill: A Case History from the 1960's". APT Bulletin. Vol.XII, no.1, 1980, p.31-51.

MILLS--CONSERVATION AND RESTORATION

McGuire, E. Barton Hall. "News and Notes From the Wye Miller." The Phoenix. Vol. 5, No. 4, Summer 1985. p. 3.

MILLS--CONSERVATION AND RESTORATION

Plater, R.C. "The Burwell-Morgan Mill, Millwood, Va." Old Mill News. Vol. 14, No. 2, Spring 1986.

MILLS--CONSERVATION AND RESTORATION

Watts, Martin. "The Repair and Restoration of Crowdy Mill, Devon." Industrial Archaeology. Vol. 17, No. 1, Spring. pp. 47-52.

MILLS--CONSERVATION AND RESTORATION--U.S.--MARYLAND

Getty, Joe. "New Developments at Old Union Mills." The Phoenix. Vol. 5, No. 3, Spring 1985. p. 6.

MILLS--U.S.--NEBRASKA

Paul, R. Eli and Thomas R. Buecker. "Beyond the Particular, Neligh Mills in Nebraska Becomes the Focus of A State-Wide Survey of the Milling Industry." History News. Vol. 39, No. 11, November 1984. pp. 27-30.

MILLS--U.S.--WEST VIRGINIA

Pauley, Michael J. "Grinding Grist: The Inner Workings of Mollohan Mill." Goldenseal. West Virginia Traditional Life. Vol. 10, No. 4. Winter 1984. pp. 13-17.

MILLWORK (WOODWORK)

"Reproducing Wood Mouldings." Technical Note 7, Communique. Vol. 14 (6), Dec. 1985. p. 9-10.

MINES

Rothfuss, Edwin L. "Keane Wonder Mine Structure Stabilization Project." CRM Bulletin. Vol. 7, No. 3, October 1984. pp. 1-2.

MINES--GREAT BRITAIN

Ayris, I. "Elemore Colliery and the Hetton Coal Company". Industrial Archaeology Review. Winter 1979-80. p. 6-35.

MINES--U.S.--COLORADO

"Campaign under Way to Preserve Crystal Mill [mine near Marble, Col.]." Colorado Heritage News. Apr. 1985. p. 5, 7.

MINNESOTA--MINNEAPOLIS--HENNEPIN AVENUE

"Learning from Las Vegas?" Progressive Architecture. July 1981. p. 31.

MINNESOTA--ST. PAUL--IRVINE PARK

Sanders, William D. "A Neighborhood Comes Home." Landscape Architecture. March 1982. pp. 61-65.

MINNESOTA--ST. PAUL--LOWERTOWN

Lu, Weimung. "A Private Corporation with a Public Purpose." PLACE. February 1982. pp. 6-7.

MINORITIES

Fleming, John E. "Taking Stock of Afro-American Material Culture." History News. Vol. 40, No. 2, Feb. 1985. p. 14-19.

MINORITIES

National Foundation on Historic Preservation in the Minority Community, Inc. Communique. Vol. 2, No. 1, April 1984.

MINORITIES--BLACKS

Gamble, Bob. "Black Builders Left Their Mark in Antebellum Alabama." The Preservation Report. Vol. 12, No. 6, May/June 1985. p. 5-6.

MINORITIES--BLACKS

History News. February 1981. Entire issue.

MINORITIES--BLACKS

"Nationwide: Black Restoration Projects." Communique, National Foundation on Historic Preservation in the Minority Community. Vol. 3, No. 3, Feb. 1986. p. 1.

MINORITIES--BLACKS--U.S.--GEORGIA--SAVANNAH

Orser, Charles E., Jr. "Artifacts, Documents and Memories of the Black Tenant Farmer." Archaeology. Vol. 38, No. 4, July/Aug. 1985. p. 48-53.

MINORITIES--HISPANIC

Woodward, Kenneth. "In Old San Antonio, Mestizaje Nurtures New American Way." Smithsonian. Vol. 16, No. 9, Dec. 1985. p. 114-127.

MISSIONS--U.S.--TEXAS--SAN ANTONIO

Suess, Bernhard J. "Portals of the San Antonio Missions." National Parks. Vol. 59, No. 7-8. July/August 1985. p. 10-13.

MISSOURI--ST. LOUIS

Harbatkin, Lisa. " Spirits Flow Strong in St. Louis." Urban Land. April 1980. p. 14-21.

MISSOURI--ST. LOUIS

Simril, Geoffrey. "St. Louis." American Arts. Jan. 1982. pp. 19-20.

MISSOURI--ST. LOUIS--LACLEDE'S LANDING

Shullaw, Susan M. "Laclede's Landing, Reviving the Spirit of St. Louis." Building. June 1981. pp. 60-66.

MODEL ORDINANCES, LANDMARKS--U.S.--PA--PHILA-DELPHIA

"Tougher Landmark Protection in Philadelphia." Urban Conservation Report. Vol. 9, No. 1, Jan. 24, 1985. p. 3.

MOLDINGS

Association for Preservation Technology Bulletin. Vol. 10, No. 4, 1978.

Articles on various aspects of architectural moldings.

MOLDINGS

Garrison, John Mark. "Running Plaster Mouldings." Old-House Journal. Vol. XII, No. 7, August-September 1984. pp. 136-141.

MOLDINGS

Gilmore, Andrea M. "Dating Architectural Moulding Profiles - A Study of Eighteenth and Nineteenth Century Moulding Plane Profiles in New England." APT Bulletin. No. 2, 1978. pp. 90-117.

MOLDINGS

Schiller, Barbara. "A Cake Decorator Method to Replace Plaster Mouldings." *The Old-House Journal*. July, 1979. pp. 80-82.

MONASTERIES--ADAPTIVE USE

"Monastery Reuse Under Discussion." *The Indiana Preservationist*. No. 1, 1986. p. 4.

MONUMENTS

Anderson, Grace. "Restoring the Statue of Liberty." *Architectural Record*. July 1984. pp. 128-135.

MONUMENTS

Craine, Clifford and John R. Dennis. "Preservation of Bronze Monuments." *Boston Preservation Alliance Letter*. Vol. 5, No. 6, July/August 1984. pp. 5-6, 8.

MONUMENTS

Crosbie, Michael J. "The Monument and the Mall." *Architecture*. December 1984. pp. 74-79.

MONUMENTS

Grossman, Elizabeth. "Architecture for a Public Client: The Monuments and Chapels of the American Battle Monuments Commission." *Journal of the Society of Architectural Historians*. Vol. XLIII, No. 2, May 1984. pp. 119-143.

MONUMENTS

"Statue Restoration May Have Ripple Effect." *The Indiana Preservationist*, Historic Landmarks Foundation of Indiana. No. 2, 1984. p. 1.

MONUMENTS--PRESERVATION

Allen, Frederick. "Saving the Statue." *American Heritage*. Vol. 35, No. 4, June/July 1984. pp. 97-111.

MONUMENTS--PRESERVATION

Chiles, James R. "Engineers Versus the Eons, or How Long Will Our Monuments Last?" *Smithsonian*. March 1984. pp. 56-67.

MONUMENTS--PRESERVATION

Sherrill, J. Charline. "Liberty Centennial Campaign." *St. Louis Home Magazine*. August 1984. pp. 50, 54.

MONUMENTS--PRESERVATION

"Technique-Remodeling America's Number-One Symbol is a Long, Slow Process." *Commercial Renovation*, Vol. 6, No. 6, December 1984, pp. 23-24.

MONUMENTS--PRESERVATION

Townsend, Samuel P. "'Battling the Bronze Disease.' North Carolina groups wage a clean up campaign for the monuments on Union Square." *History News*. Vol. 39, No. 9, September 1984. pp. 14-21.

MONUMENTS--PRESERVATION

Wainwright, Ian N.M. "Lichen Removal from an Engraved Memorial to Walt Whitman." *APT Bulletin*. Vol. 18, No. 4, 1986. p. 46-51.

MORGAN, JULIA

Olson, Lynne. "A Tycoon's Home Was His Petite Architect's Castle." *Smithsonian*. Vol. 16, No. 9, Dec. 1985. p. 60-71.

Hearst Castle at San Simeon, Cal. discussed.

MORTAR

Stewart, John and James Moore. "Chemical Techniques of Historic Mortar Analysis." APT Bulletin. Vol. 14, No. 1. pp. 11-16.

MORTGAGE LOANS

"Rehabilitation Mortgage Plan Worth a Try." The Quapaw Chronicle. Vol. 12, No. 7, Feb./Mar. 1986. p. 5.

MOTELS

Lancaster, Paul. "The Great American Motel." American Heritage. June/July 1982. pp. 100-108.

MOTOR BUS TRAVEL

Barone, Constance B. "Organizing A Bus Tour." Regional Conference of Historical Agencies. Vol. 14, No. 7, August 1984. Information Sheet #74.

MOVING OF BUILDINGS, BRIDGES, ETC

Dittmer, John. "Disassembling a Timber Frame House". Old House Journal. October 1980. p. 139-141.

MOVING OF BUILDINGS, BRIDGES, ETC.

Filipowicz, Diane H. "Historic-Buildings-To-Go?", North Carolina Preservation, Vol. 53, October-November 1984, p. 5.

MOVING OF BUILDINGS, BRIDGES, ETC.

Gagne, Cole. "Do you want to move a house?". Old House Journal. October 1981. p.219, 234-238.

MOVING OF BUILDINGS, BRIDGES, ETC.

"Historic Building Collections." The Medallion. Dec. 1983. (Special Issue) pp. 2-5.

Partial Contents: Maxson, Peter. Consider Options to Moving--Graves, Stan. Relocation, Use Experts, Analysis--Shull, Carol. Original Site Key to Listing--Gary, Grace. Building Collections Simplify Complexities of History.

MOVING OF BUILDINGS, BRIDGES, ETC.

"How to Move a Building." Historic Hawai'i. Vol. 12, No. 9, Oct. 1986. p. 13-15.

MOVING OF BUILDINGS, BRIDGES, ETC.

Lipton, S. Gregory. "Moving houses to new locations helps conservation and preserves neighborhood character." Journal of Housing. Mar. 1979. pp. 151-154.

MOVEMENT OF BUILDINGS, BRIDGES, ETC.

Lipton, S. Gregory and Rosaria F. Hodgdon. "House Moving: A Housing Resource." Environmental Comment. Jan. 1979. pp. 4-6.

MOVING OF BUILDINGS, BRIDGES, ETC.

"A Moving Experience." Pasadena Heritage. Vol. VIII, No. 1, Spring 1984. pp. 1-2.

MOVING OF BUILDINGS, BRIDGES, ETC.

Paraschos, Janet Nyberg. "How to Move a House: a Primer for the Courageous Few who Attempt Such a Project." American Preservation. Jun./Jul. 1979. pp. 5-6.

MOVING OF BUILDINGS, BRIDGES, ETC.

Powter, Andrew & Giovanni Castellarin. "Lifting and Moving Wooden Buildings : A Low Tech Approach." APT Bulletin. Vol. 18, No. 1 & 2, 1986. p. 87-93.

MOVING OF BUILDINGS, BRIDGES, ETC.

"Moving Historic Buildings." The Old-House Journal, November 1979. pp. 131.

MOVING OF BUILDINGS, BRIDGES, ETC.

"Relocating Historic Structures." Connecticut Trust for Historic Preservation News. Vol. 10, No. 1, Winter 1987. p. 3-4.

MOVING OF BUILDINGS, BRIDGES, ETC.

Slater, Margaret. "Historic Bridge Relocated." The Courier (Tennessee Historical Commission). Vol. 25, No. 1, Oct. 1986. p. 3.

A historic bridge was successfully moved 120 miles as part of the Tennessee Department of Transportation's Historic Bridge Relocation Program.

MOVING OF BUILDINGS, BRIDGES, ETC.

"Trucks Tow Texas Inn." APWA Reporter. Vol. 52, No. 6, June 1985. p. 21.

Fairmount Hotel in San Antonio moved by Emmert International of Clackamas, Oregon thought to be heaviest building ever moved.

MOVING OF BUILDINGS, BRIDGES, ETC.

Wagner, Charles. "On the Move." Traditional Homes. April 1986. p. 75-77.

Moving old buildings.

MOVING OF BUILDINGS, BRIDGES, ETC.--U.S.--MICHIGAN--MARQUETTE

Stratton, Robert E. "The Long Move of the Longyear House." Chronicle. Vol. 21, No. 1, Spring 1985. p. 2-5.

Stone house dissembled and moved from Marquette to Boston in 1903.

MOVING PICTURE THEATERS

"Glittering Splendor of Rialto Theater Restored." Architectural Record. December 1982. pp. 26-27.

MOVING PICTURE THEATERS

Gomery, J. Douglas. "The History of the American Movie Palace: Reading for Profit and Pleasure." Marquee. Vol. 16, No. 2, Second Quarter 1984. pp. 5-11.

MOVING PICTURE THEATERS

Larson, Jan. "Aurora Converts Old Fox Theatre Into Arts Center." Colorado Heritage News. Feb. 1984. p. 7.

MOVING PICTURE THEATERS

Long, Julian. "Born Again, The Revival of America's Movie Palaces." American Arts. Jan. 1983. pp. 22-26.

MOVING PICTURE THEATERS

Mylott, Jim. "The Robey Theater of Spencer--A Roane County Tradition." Goldenseal. Winter 1981. pp. 57-64.

MOVING PICTURE THEATERS

Schrenk, Lisa. "Birth of the Movies." Architecture Minnesota. Vol. 10, No. 6, November/December 1984. pp. 40-45+.

MOVING PICTURE THEATRES

Silag, William. "William Steele's Silent Music." The Palimpset. March - April 1981. pp. 45 - 55.

MOVING PICTURE THEATERS

"The Strand, Shreveport, Louisiana." Marquee. Vol. 18, No. 3, 1986. p. 13-15.

Restoration of the 60 year old movie theater.

MOVING PICTURE THEATERS

"A Vaudeville Palace Stages a Comeback." Architectural Record. Aug. 1983. pp. 92-95.

MOVING PICTURE THEATRES--CONSERVATION AND RESTORATION

Munsell, Ken. "Movie Palaces Live Again in Two Midwest Towns." Small Town. Jan./Feb. 1981. pp. 13 - 17.

MOVING PICTURE THEATERS--CONSERVATION AND RESTORA-
TION
"Restoration of the Seattle 5th Avenue Theatre." Architectural Record. Mid Feb. 1982. pp. 124-127.

MOVING PICTURE THEATERS--CONSERVATION AND RESTORATION

"Trio of theaters restores, preserves historic movie house." Building Design and Construction. March 1981. p. 64-69.

MOVING PICTURE THEATERS--U.S.--ILLINOIS--CHICAGO

"Special Issue on the Balaban and Katz Tivoli Theatre, Chicago, Ill." Marquee. Vol. 17, No. 4, Fourth Quarter 1985. Entire Issue.

MUMFORD, LEWIS

Filler, Martin. "Lewis Mumford: The Making of an Architectural Critic." Architectural Record. April 1982. pp. 116-123.

MUNICIPAL BUILDINGS--CONSERVATION AND RESTORATION

"City Hall Restoration Plan Moves Ahead." Architecture Minnesota. July/August 1981. p. 13.

MUNICIPAL BUILDINGS--CONSERVATION AND RESTORATION

Mack, Linda. "Reviving Pride in Mill (Minneapolis) City Hall." Minnesota Preservation Connection. April-May 1984. pp. 1, 3.

MUNICIPAL BUILDINGS--CONSERVATION AND RESTORATION--U.S.--WISCONSIN--OCONOMOWOC

"A Robust Old City Hall Given a New Skin and Spire." Architecture. Oct. 1985, p. 73.

MUNICIPAL BUILDINGS--U.S.--MINNESOTA--MINNEAPOLIS

Mack, Linda. "A Revealing Look Into City Hall's Past - And Future." Architecture Minnesota Vol. 10, No. 4, July/August 1984. pp. 30-33.

MUNICIPAL ENGINEERING

Centenari, Peter and Robert E. Nipp. "HUD Study Shows New Techniques for Utility Infra-structure Rehabilitation." U.S. Department of Housing and Urban Development News Release. HUD 85-32. 2 p.

MUNICIPAL LIGHTING--HOLLAND--AMSTERDAM

Multhauf, Lettie S. "Street Lighting in 17th-Century Amsterdam." Technology and Culture. Vol. 26, No. 2, Apr. 1985. p. 236-252.

MUSEUM CONSERVATION METHODS

"In Event of Flood Damage to Historic and Artistic Works." Regional Conference of Historical Agencies. April 1982. Information sheet #64.

MUSEUM CONSERVATION METHODS

Klock, Lawrence. "Climatic Controls for Furnished Historic Buildings." Trends. Vol. 20, No. 2, 1983. pp. 37-39.

MUSEUM CONSERVATION METHODS

Paine, Shelley Reisman. "Basic Conditions for Controlling Environmental Conditions in Historical Agencies and Museums." Technical Report 3, Technical Information Service, American Association for State and Local History. 15 p.

MUSEUM CONSERVATION METHODS

Raphael, Toby and Allen S. Bohnert. "Resolving a Preservation Problem at Mesa Verde". CRM Bulletin. Vol. 8, No. 1, Feb. 1985. p. 3-5, 11.

Archeologic collections management discussed.

MUSEUM CONSERVATION METHODS

Schur, Susan E. "Conservation Profile: Division of Museum Services, Harpers Ferry Center, NPS". Technology and Conservation. Fall 1980. p.32-41.

MUSEUM REGISTRATION METHODS

Elkins, Sandra. "What's In a Name?: Staff at the Strong Museum and Historical Organizations Across the Country Forge Ahead on a Revised Nomenclature for the Field." History News. Vol. 40, No. 8, Aug. 1985. p. 6-12.

MUSEUM STORES

Barsook, Beverly. "A Code of Ethics for Museum Stores." Museum News. January/February 1982. pp. 50-52.

MUSEUM STORES

Brown, Marion H. "Keeping an Eye on Each Other, the IRS and the Museum Store." Museum News. September/October 1982. pp/ 24-27.

MUSEUM STORES

Craig, Tracey Linton. "Packaging the Past, Winterthur Museum takes a Calculated Gamble on Reproducing its Collections for Sale." History News. July 1983. pp. 6-11.

MUSEUM STORES

Murphy, Suzanne Dupre. "Minding the Store." Museum News. October 1983. pp. 55-59.

MUSEUM TECHNIQUES

Appelbaum, Barbara and Himmelstein, Paul. "Planning for a Conservation Survey." Museum News. Vol. 64, No. 3, Feb. 1986. p. 5-14.

MUSEUM TECHNIQUES

Elder, Betty Doak. "Collecting the 20th Century." History News. November 1981. pp. 9-12.

MUSEUM TECHNIQUES

Floyd, Candace. "Too Close for Comfort: Museum Professionals Find That Collecting the Recent Past is a Delicate and Sometimes Dangerous Endeavor." History News. Vol. 40, No. 9, Sept. 1985. p. 8-14.

MUSEUM TECHNIQUES

Pardue, Diana. "Climate Control in Furnished Room Exhibits." CRM Bulletin. Vol. 8, No. 3 & 4, June/Aug. 1985. P. 20-21.

MUSEUM TECHNIQUES

Porter, Daniel R. "Current Thoughts on Collections Policy: Producing the Essential Document for Administering Your Collection, Technical Report 1, AASLH Technical Information Service, 12 p.

A glossary of terminology is included.

MUSEUMS

Coates, Joseph F. "The Future and Museums." Museum News. Vol. 62, No. 6, August 1984. pp. 40-46.

MUSEUMS

Baltierra, Miguel. "Rivera House Restoration." L.A. Architect. Feb. 1987. p. 4-6.

Muralist Diego Rivera's house in Mexico City has been restored and opened as a museum.

MUSEUMS

Mansfield, Howard. "The Ribbon across the Chair." Metropolis. July/August 1986. p. 24-27.

House museums assessment.

MUSEUMS

"The Growing Museum Movement, Chapter 1 of the Report of the Commission on Museums for a New Century." Museum News. Vol. 62, No. 6, August 1984. pp. 18-33.

MUSEUMS

Henshey, Lori. "The West Virginia State Farm Museum." Goldenseal. Vol. 12, No. 4, Winter 1986. p. 11.

MUSEUMS

"Inaugurating the Building Hall of Fame." Blueprints. Vol. 4, No. 2, Fall 1986. p. 13.

The National Building Museum will include a Hall of Fame.

MUSEUMS

"Mariner's Museum Will Get Monitor Artifacts." Headquarters Heliogram. No. 183, Feb./Mar. 1987. p. 4.

MUSEUMS

"New Canal Museum Dedicated." American Canals. Bulletin No. 59, Nov. 1986. p. 4.

C. Howard Heister Canal Center opened in Reading, PA.

MUSEUMS

Pisney, Raymond F. Review of Museums for a New Century. History News. Vol. 40, No. 9, Sept. 1985. p. 29-34.

MUSEUMS

"Port City Will Use Federal Grant to Build Historic Village for Swedish Celebration." Community Development Digest. No. 86-23. Dec. 2, 1986. p. 12.

Salem City, N.J. will build an authentic 17th century Swedish settlement which will eventually become a museum.

MUSEUMS

Riley, Sheila and Larry Boothby. "When Crystal Comes to Your House." History News. Vol. 41, No. 4, July/Aug. 1986. p. 14-18.

On-location filming provides revenue and recognition for historic house museums.

MUSEUMS

Schur, Susan E. " Museum Profiles: The Museum of Transportation & the Children's Museum, Boston." Technology & Conservation. Winter 1979. pp. 26-32.

MUSEUMS

Sukel, W. Mark. "The Evaluation of Museums." SEMC Journal, November 1979. pp. 1-9.

MUSEUMS

Widen, Larry. "Milwaukee's Dime Museum Era." Marquee. Vol. 18, No. 4, Fourth Quarter 1986. p. 3-8.

MUSEUMS--ACCREDITATION

Glickburg, Randi R. "Historic Sites and Accreditation." Museum News. November/December 1981. pp. 42-49.

MUSEUMS--ACCREDITATION

Hadwin, Mildred. "Small Museums &
Accreditation : the Ella Sharp Museum".
Museum News. November/December 1980. p.54-59.

MUSEUMS--ACCREDITATION

Museum News. September/Ocotber 1981.
Entire Issue.

CONTENTS: Beyond the Beginning: Accreditation
after 10 Years--Leavitt, Thomas W. Reaccreditation:
Learning from Experience--Norman, Joy Youmans.
How Museums Benefit--Wall, Alexander J.
Demystifying the Accreditation Process.

MUSEUMS--ACCREDITATION

Norman, Joy Youmans. "Reaccreditation:
How it Works and How it's Working." Museum
News. September 1982. pp. 63-68.

MUSEUMS--ADAPTIVE USE

Walker, Sybil. "Art Museum Architecture
on Exhibit." Museum News. September/October
1982. pp. 32-41.

MUSEUMS--ADAPTIVE USE

Pearce, Sally. "Renovation of Former State
Museum Planned." Colorado Heritage News. Mar.
1986. p. 5-6.

Listed in the National Register, the vacant
museum building will now serve as offices.

MUSEUMS--FIRE AND FIRE PREVENTION

Musgrave, Stephen W. "A New Look at
Fire Protection." Museum News. Vol. 62, No. 6,
August 1984. pp. 11-17.

2 pp. bibliography included.

MUSEUMS--INTERPRETIVE PROGRAMS

Gardner, Toni. "Learning from Listening:
Museums Improve Their Effectiveness Through
Visitor Studies." Museum News. Vol. 64, No. 3,
Feb. 1986. p. 40-44.

MUSEUMS--INTERPRETIVE PROGRAMS

Haines, Prudence Procter. "Volunteers and
Research." History News. Vol. 42, No. 1,
Jan./Feb. 1987. p. 21-25.

MUSEUMS--INTERPRETIVE PROGRAMS

Harvey, Bruce. "Inside the Treasure Houses."
History News, Vol. 42, No. 3, May-June 1987.
p. 16-18.

Helping American visitors interpret the English
National Trust Treasure Houses.

MUSEUMS--INTERPRETIVE PROGRAMS

Hood, Marilyn G. "Getting Started in
Audience Research." Museum News. Vol. 64, No.
3, Feb. 1986. p. 25-31.

MUSEUMS--INTERPRETIVE PROGRAMS

Munley, Mary Ellen. "Asking the Right
Questions.: Evaluation and the Museum Mission."
Museum News. Vol. 64, No. 3, Feb. 1986. p. 18-
23.

MUSEUMS--INTERPRETIVE PROGRAMS

Munro, Patricia and Glenn Porter. "The
Exhibit Challenge. Working With Consultants
May Improve the Odds for a Successful Exhibit."
History News. Vol. 39, No. 6, June 1984.
pp. 12-17.

MUSEUMS--INTERPRETIVE PROGRAMS

Smith, Jeffrey E. "Living With A Legend."
History News. Vol. 40, No. 11, Nov. 1985. p. 14-
19.

Interpretive planning at house in Akron,
Ohio in which abolitionist John Brown lived for
only a short time discussed.

MUSEUMS--MANAGEMENT

Arth, Malcolm. "The Changing Role of the
Mid-Level Manager." Museum News. July/August
1982. pp. 32-35.

MUSEUMS--MANAGEMENT

Brown, Ellsworth. "For the Board. 'Models for Board Responsibilities.'" History News. Vol. 39, No. 6, June 1984. pp. 27-30.

MUSEUMS--MANAGEMENT

Dillon, Phyllis. "Conservation Planning: Where can you find the Help You Need?" History News. Vol. 42, No. 4, Jul./Aug. 1987. pp. 10 - 15.

MUSEUMS--MANAGEMENT

Ganz, Paul. "To Charge or Not to Charge, 1984." Museum News. April 1984. pp. 41-45.

MUSEUMS--MANAGEMENT

Simerly, Robert. "Strategic Long-Range Planning." Museum News. July/August 1982. pp. 28-31.

MUSEUMS--MANAGEMENT

Slate, Jane. "A National Study Assesses Collections Management, Maintenance and Conservation." Museum News. Vol. 64, No. 1, Oct. 1985. p. 38-45.

MUSEUMS--MANAGEMENT

Weil, Stephen E. "MGR: (Methods/Goals/ Resources) A Conspectus of Museum Managment." Museum News. July/August 1982. pp. 22-27.

MUSEUMS--MANAGEMENT

Williams, David W. "How Museums Can Use Information Management Systems." History News. June 1981. pp. 37-40.

MUSEUMS--SECURITY MEASURES

Fuss, Eugene L. "Security in Cultural Institutions: Advances in Electronic Protection Techniques". Technology and Conservation. Winter 1979. pp. 34-37.

MUSEUMS--SECURITY MEASURES

Solon, Thomas E., AIA. "Security Panels for the Foster-Armstrong House." APT Bulletin. Vol. 16, No. 3 & 4, 1984. p. 70-73.

A window cover which allows ventilation for use in mothballing a building is described.

MUSEUMS--STUDY AND TEACHING

Museum News. July/August 1982. pp. 36-61. Partial Issue.

CONTENTS: McDonnell, Patricia J. Professional Development and Training in Museums--Chapman, Laura H. The Future and Museum Education--Fertig, Barbara C. Historians/Artifacts/Learners, the History Museum as Educator.

MUSEUMS--U.S.--DELAWARE--WILMINGTON--WINTERTHUR

Karp, Walter. "Henry Francis du Pont and the Invention of Winterthur." American Heritage. Apr./May 1983. pp. 86-97.

MUSEUMS--U.S.--NEW YORK--NEW YORK CITY

Williams, Roger M. "The Metropolitan Museum's American Wing". Americana. May/June 1980. p. 39-62.

MUSEUMS--U.S.--VIRGINIA--WILLIAMSBURG

Cooper, Wendy A. "New Showcase for Decorative Arts: Touring the Wallace Gallery," Colonial Williamsburg. Vol. 7, No. 4, Summer 1985. p. 13-20.

MUSEUMS--U.S.--VIRGINIA--WILLIAMSBURG

"The New DeWitt Wallace Decorative Arts Gallery at Colonial Williamsburg." Antiques. Vol. 128, No. 2, Aug. 1985. p. 266-269.

MUSEUMS--U.S.--WASHINGTON, D.C.

Applewhite, E.J. "It's Not All on the Mall - A Personal Look at Washington's Other Museums." Museum News. April 1984. pp. 20 - 31.

MUSEUMS--U.S.--WASHINGTON, D.C.

Vonier, Thomas. "National Building Museum Opens." Progressive Architecture. Nov. 1985. p. 23.

MUSEUMS AND THE HANDICAPPED

Coons, Valerie. "Talking up to the Deaf, An Update on Efforts to Promote Accessibility and Achieve Greater Sensitivity to the Needs of Handicapped Visitors." Colonial Williamsburg Today. Spring 1983. pp. 22-24.

MUSEUMS AND THE HANDICAPPED

Kenney, Alice P. "Open Door for the Handicapped." Historic Preservation. July-September 1978. pp. 12-17.

MUSEUMS AND THE HANDICAPPED

Museum News. January/February 1977. Entire Issue.

PARTIAL CONTENTS: Molloy, Larry. The Case for Accessiblity--Sunderland, Jacqueline. Museums and Older Americans--Kenney, Alice P. A Test of Barrier-Free Design.--Setting Priorities.

MUSEUMS AND THE HANDICAPPED

Palmer, Cheryl. "Accessibility for All." Semc Journal, March,1979. pp. 9-14.

Bibliography and list of relevant organizations.

MUSEUMS AND THE HANDICAPPED

Spinetto, Stephen. "Access for Persons with Disabilities to Historic Structures." The Boston Preservation Alliance Letter. Vol. 7, No. 4, April 1986. p. 1, 7.

MUSEUMS AND THE HANDICAPPED

"Trends in Serving Special Populations." Trends. Spring 1978. Entire Issue.
PARTIAL CONTENTS: NPS Guidelines for Serving Special Populations--Pomeroy, Barbara and Kathleen Zaccagnini. Recreation for Deaf People--Jones, Walter. Special Use Trail--Bultena, G. and Donald Field and Renee Renninger. Interpretation for Retired National Parkgoers.

MUSEUMS AND THE HANDICAPPED

Wiggens, Betty. "Colonial Williamsburg and the Handicapped." Colonial Williamsburg Today. Spring 1980. pp. 9-11.

MUSICAL INSTRUMENTS

Schrader, Arthur F. "Musical Instruments at Old Sturbridge Village." Antiques. Sep. 1979. pp. 583-591.

NATIONAL BUILDING MUSEUM

Cunningham, Maureen. "A Celebration of Architecture, A Tribute to the Mason's Craft." Trowel. Winter 1983. pp. 4-12.

NATIONAL ENDOWMENT FOR THE ARTS

"An Interview with Frank Hodsoll." American Arts. January 1982. pp. 4-9.

NATIONAL PARK SERVICE

Biallas, Randall. "Historic NPS Owned Concession Buildings." NPS, CRM Bulletin. Vol. 7, No. 2, July 1984. pp. 17, 20.

NATIONAL PARKS AND RESERVES

Albright, Horace. "Building the Ranger Mystique." National Parks. Vol. 60, No. 1-2, Jan./Feb. 1986. p. 18-25.

Former NPS Director Albright details the history of the Park Service and the park ranger.

NATIONAL PARKS AND RESERVES

Cahn, Robert. "Ellis Island." National Parks. Vol. 60, No. 7-8, July/Aug. 1986. p. 16-23, 30.

Controversy surrounding restoration of Ellis Island.

NATIONAL PARKS AND RESERVES

Cahn, Robert, ed. "Horace Albright Remembers the Origins." National Parks. Vol. 59, No. 9-10, Sept./Oct. 1985. p. 27-31.

Recollections of Stephen Mather and the beginning of the National Park Service.

NATIONAL PARKS AND RESERVES

"A Conversation with Interior Secretary Donald Hodel." National Parks. Vol. 59, No. 9-10, Sept./Oct. 1985. p. 8-9.

NATIONAL PARKS AND RESERVES

Corbett, Marjorie. "Protecting the New River Gorge." National Parks. March/April 1982. pp. 10-11.

NATIONAL PARKS AND RESERVES

Foresta, Ronald A. "America's Urban National Parks." Urbanism Past & Present. Vol. 9, No. 18, Issue 2, Summer/Fall 1984. p. 1-14.

NATIONAL PARKS AND RESERVES

Freeman, Judith. "Rustic Lodgings in a Grand Style." National Parks. Vol. 59, No. 11-12, Nov./Dec. 1985. p. 8-9.

NATIONAL PARKS AND RESERVES

"Introducing Decorative and Fine Arts." CRM Bulletin. Vol. 8, No. 3 & 4, June/Aug. 1985. Entire issue. 32 p.

Collections of NPS reviewed.

NATIONAL PARKS AND RESERVES

Knight, Carleton III. "The Park Service as Client: II, Shifting Emphasis Since WWII." Architecture. Dec. 1984. pp. 48-50.

NATIONAL PARKS AND RESERVES

"Law-Related Issues for Park and Recreation Managers." Trends. Vol. 21, No. 3, 1984. Entire issue.

NATIONAL PARKS AND RESERVES

Myers, Phyllis. "The Park Service as Client: The Early Days of Rustic Grandeur." Architecture. December 1984. pp. 42-47.

NATIONAL PARKS AND RESERVES

"Myths Concerning the HABS/HAER Documentation Program." Arizona Preservation News. Vol. 4, No. 1, Jan. 1987. p. 5-7.

NATIONAL PARKS AND RESERVES

Nowicki, Peter L. "National and Natural Park Protection in France." Parks. July, August, September 1983. pp. 4-6.

NATIONAL PARKS AND RESERVES

Pierce, Robert. "The National Park Trust, Private Help for Public Land." National Parks. Vol. 58, No. 9-10, Sept./Oct. 1984. pp. 18-19.

NATIONAL PARKS AND RESERVES

Recio, Maria E. "The Park Service Gets a Champion of Conservation." Business Week. July 8, 1985. p. 52.

William Penn Mott and NPS problems profiled.

NATIONAL PARKS AND RESERVES

"Urban Parks: Are they Successful or Unrealistic?" Conservation Foundation Letter. July 1982. Entire Issue.

NATIONAL TRUST

Zuill, William S. "The Bermuda National Trust." Antiques. Aug. 1979. p. 353.

NATIONAL PARKS AND RESERVES--INTERPRETIVE PROGRAMS

Wry, Brann J. "Recycling History with Urban Cultural Parks." Place. March 1982., pp. 6-9.

NATIONAL PARKS AND RESERVES--INTERPRETIVE PROGRAMS

"Interpretation." Trends. Vol. 22, No. 4, 1985. Entire Issue.

NATIONAL PARKS AND RESERVES--INTERPRETIVE PROGRAMS--U.S.--ALASKA

Holing, Dwight. "On the Last Frontier." Americana. Vol. 13, No. 2, May/June 1985. p. 54-59.

The restoration of Skagway, Alaska, a gold rush boom town in The Klondike Gold Rush National Historical Park, is described.

NATIONAL PARKS AND RESERVES--PLANNING

Eisemann, Eric. "Crater Lake Lodge Update: HPLO Team Visits Site." Historic Preservation League of Oregon Newsletter. No. 31, Summer 1984. p. 10.

NATIONAL PARKS AND RESERVES--PLANNING

Hamilton, John. "Mr. Mott Goes to Washington: a Sierra Interview." Sierra. Vol. 71, No. 1, Jan./Feb. 1986. p. 128-133.

NATIONAL PARKS AND RESERVES--PLANNING

Kahn, Jeffery. "Restoring the Everglades." Sierra. Sept./Oct. 1986. p. 38-43.

NATIONAL PARKS AND RESERVES--PLANNING

Staehli, Alfred. "Crater Lake Lodge Preservation Undecided." Historic Preservation League of Oregon Newsletter. No. 32, Fall 1984. pp. 8-9.

NATIONAL PARKS AND RESERVES--PLANNING

Staehli, Alfred M. "Crater Lake Lodge's Preservation Receives Verbal Commitment by NPS", Historic Preservation League of Oregon Newsletter, No. 33, Winter 1984, p. 6.

NATIONAL PARKS AND RESERVES--U.S.--ALASKA

Wayburn, Edgar. "Alaska Parks in Peril." Sierra. Vol. 70, No. 4, July/Aug. 1985. p. 24-26.

NATIONAL PARKS AND RESERVES--U.S.--MONTANA

Ferguson, Gary. "A Last Fierce Paradise." Sierra. Vol. 70, No. 4, July/Aug. 1985. p. 36-41.

The 75th Anniversary of Glacier National Park, Montana, celebrated in this article.

NATIONAL PARKS AND RESERVES--U.S.--OREGON--CRATER LAKE

"W. Franklin Arant and Will G. Steel and the Crater Lake Rumble." Table Rock Sentinel. Oct. 1985. p. 2-12.

Early history of the Crater Lake National Park detailed.

NATIONAL TRUST--GORDON GRAY

Greenya, John. "The Quiet Power of Gordon Gray." Historic Preservation. September/October, 1983. pp. 26-29.

NATIONAL TRUST--GREAT BRITAIN

Shenker, Israel. "A House Where Nothing Was Ever Thrown Away." Smithsonian. Vol. 16, No. 4. Jul. 1985. pp. 100-111.

NATIONAL TRUST--NATIONAL MAIN STREET CENTER

"Smaller Communities Successfully Use Self-help Approach to Revitalize their Downtowns." Local Economic Growth and Neighborhood Reinvestment Report. December 1, 1983. Partial Issue

NATIONAL TRUST FOR HISTORIC PRESERVATION

"J. Jackson Walter's Agenda as President of National Trust." Architecture. May 1985. p. 82-83.

NATIONAL TRUST FOR HISTORIC PRESERVATION

Knight, Carleton. "Fitch Gets Trust Award, Assesses Architect's Role in Preservation." Architecture. Feb. 1986. p. 10-11.

NATIONAL TRUST FOR HISTORIC PRESERVATION

"NEFSO Studies Preservation and New England Banks." Society for the Preservation of New England Antiquities. December 15, 1977. pp. 6-8.

NATIONAL TRUST FOR HISTORIC PRESERVATION

"A Successful Experiment" (Program Council.) History News. Vol. 39, No. 11, November 1984. p. 23.

NATIONAL TRUST FOR HISTORIC PRESERVATION

"What lies ahead for the National Trust: an interview with Michael Ainslie". History News. March 1981. p.8-13.

NATIONAL TRUST FOR HISTORIC PRESERVATION-- GRANTS

"A Maritime Heritage Preserved." American Heritage. April/May 1983. pp. 110-111.

NATIONAL TRUST FOR SCOTLAND

LaBastille, Anne. "The National Trust for Scotland." Parks. Vol. 8, No. 1. pp. 8-10.

NATURAL MONUMENTS

Kassler, Katrina. "Preserving our natural heritage." National Parks & Conservation. July 1980. p. 23-24.

NAVAL ARCHITECTURE--HISTORY

Bradley, Jesse N. " The ingenious Mr. Peck: America's first naval architect". National Fisherman . April 30, 1980. p. 88-90.

NEIGHBORHOODS

"Adopt a Block Program." Rehab Notes. Vol. 10, No. 4, May 1986. p. 3.

A Louisville neighborhood association targets blocks for rehabilitation and looks for investors.

NEIGHBORHOODS

Galperin, Ron. "Issues Forum: Neighborhood Focus." Los Angeles Conservancy. Vol. 9, No. 3, May/June 1987. p. 6-7.

South Carthay, L.A.'s second Historic Preservation Overlay Zone.

NEIGHBORHOODS

Goetze, Rolf and Kent W. Colton. "The Dynamics of Neighborhoods: a fresh approach to understanding housing and neighborhood change". APA Journal. April 1980. p.184-194.

NEIGHBORHOODS

"Neighborhood Buyouts and Sell Outs Threaten Area." Urban Outlook. Vol. 9, No. 1, Jan. 15, 1987, p. 1-3.

NEIGHBORHOODS

"Neighborhoods Take Lessons from Main Streets." Conserve Neighborhoods. No. 63, Dec. 1986. p. 1-8.

Entire issue examins neighborhood development in three cities: Cheyenne, WY; Knoxville, TN; South Side, Pittsburgh, PA.

NEIGHBORHOODS

Qualls, Shirley. "AHC Seeks Clues to Neighborhood Life." The Preservation Report (AL). Vol. 14, No. 1, Feb./Mar. 1987. p. 4-5.

Examining historic black neighborhoods.

NEIGHBORHOODS

Rafter, David O. "Neighborhood Planning: Arnstein's Ladder Applied." Planning. Jan. 1980. pp. 23-25.

NEIGHBORHOODS

Rohe, William M. and Lauren B. Gates. "When Cities Work with Neighborhoods." Planning. Vol. 52, No. 1, Jan. 1986. p. 24-29.

NEIGHBORHOODS

Solomon, Arthur P. and Kerry D. Vandell. "Alternative Perspective on Neighborhood Decline." APA Journal. Winter 1982. pp. 81-98.

NEIGHBORHOODS

Washington, Jennifer. "Neighborhood Inventory." Neighborhood Quarterly. Vol. 6-2, Spring 1986. p. 5.

NEIGHBORHOODS--CONSERVATION AND RESTORATION

Bernhard, Arlyne S. and Lachman, M. Leanne. "Milwaukee, Neighborhood Preservation in Action." Urban Land. December 1983. pp. 13-19.

NEIGHBORHOODS--CONSERVATION AND RESTORATION

Bodmer, Luis Alberto. "Houston's Harrisburg-Wayside: Enlisting the Private Sector in Inner-City Revitalization." Urban Land. Vol. 46, No. 1, Jan. 1987. p. 2-5.

NEIGHBORHOODS--CONSERVATION AND RESTORATION

Burton, Lydia and David Morley. "Neighborhood Survival in Toronto." Landscape. No. 3, 1979. pp. 33-40.

NEIGHBORHOODS--CONSERVATION AND RESTORATION

DeGiovanni, Frank F. "Patterns of Change in Housing Market Activity in Revitalizing Neighborhoods." Journal of the American Planning Association. Winter 1983. pp. 22-39.

NEIGHBORHOODS--CONSERVATION AND RESTORATION

Gale, Dennis E. "Prospects for Newly Revitalized Urban Neighborhoods." Urban Land. Vol. 44, No. 8, Aug. 1985. p. 34-35.

NEIGHBORHOODS--CONSERVATION AND RESTORATION

Hallman, Howard W. "Initiating Neighborhood Self-Help." Neighborhood Ideas. June 1981. pp. 132-134.

NEIGHBORHOODS--CONSERVATION AND RESTORATION

Harris, Jack. "The Context of Inner City Revitalization." Real Estate Issues. Fall 1982. pp. 8-13.

NIEGHBORHOODS--CONSERVATION AND RESTORATION

"Historic Arbor Hill Undergoes Rehabiliation."
Albany Preservation Report. Vol. 5, No. 5.
Summer 1986. pp. 1; 4-5.

Rehabilitation of a neighborhood involving
82 buildings.

NEIGHBORHOODS--CONSERVATION AND RESTORATION

Morford, Jana C. "Preserving a 'Special
Place:' The Lytle Park Neighborhood, 1948-
1976." Queen City Heritage. Vol. 44, No. 3,
Fall 1986. p. 3-22.

NEIGHBORHOODS--CONSERVATION AND RESTORATION

"Neighborhoods in the 1980's." Livable Digest.
Winter 1981-1982. Entire issue.

Taking Stock--Resources Old and New--Designs,
Plans and Objects.

NIEGHBORHOODS--CONSERVATION AND RESTORATION

"Neighborhood Revitalization." Journal of the
American Planning Association. Oct. 1979.

Entire issue.

NEIGHBORHOODS--CONSERVATION AND RESTORATION

Page, Clint. "Cementing Neighborhood
Partnerships, St. Paul Matches Funding with
Self-Help Projects." Nation's Cities Weekly.
June 27, 1983, p. 3.

NEIGHBORHOODS--CONSERVATION AND RESTORATION

Paraschos, Janet Nyberg. "Mt. Auburn:
Helping Residents take Pride in their Cincinnati
Neighborhood." American Preservation. Apr./May
1979. pp. 7-17.

NEIGHBORHOODS--CONSERVATION AND RESTORATION

Roper, James H. "Ah, Venice!: An Eccentric
Los Angeles Community Wants to Save its Dream of
Canals and Gondolas." American Preservation.
Apr./May 1979. pp. 26-37.

NEIGHBORHOODS--CONSERVATION AND RESTORATION

Stout, Gary and Orlo Otteson, "Neighborhood
Commercial Revitalization in St. Paul. HUD
Challenge. February 1980. p. 10.

NEIGHBORHOODS--CONSERVATION AND RESTORATION

Tourbier, Joachim. "Caring for Doylestown:
Capitalizing on Cultural Resources." Practicing
Planner. June 1979. pp. 36-38.

NEIGHBORHOODS--CONSERVATION AND RESTORATION

Westerman, Marty. "The Landed Non-Gentry--
The Revitalization of a Neighborhood." Resources.
Spring/Summer 1981. p. 20.

NEIGHBORHOODS--CONSERVATION AND RESTORATION

Winters, Christopher. "The Social Identity
of Evolving Nieghborhoods." Landscape. Vol. 23,
No. 1, 1979. pp. 8-14.

NEIGHBORHOODS--CONSERVATION AND RESTORATION--
CASE STUDIES

"Corporate-Sponsored Neighborhood Redevelop-
ment Succeeds in St. Louis." Local Economic
Growth & Neighborhood Reinvestment Report.
April 19, 1984. pp. 5-7.

RALSTON PURINA REDEVELOPMENT OF LA SALLE
PARK

NEIGHBORHOODS--CONSERVATION AND RESTORATION--
CASE STUDIES

Humphries, Barry K. "Renaissance: Rebirth
of a Neighborhood." Urban Land. January 1982.
pp. 9-17.

NEIGHBORHOODS--CONSERVATION AND RESTORATION--
CASE STUDIES

Lavicka, William L. "Restoring a Block in
Chicago." The Old-House Journal. Dec. 1979.
pp. 135-137.

NEIGHBORHOODS--CONSERVATION AND RESTORATION--
CASE STUDIES

"Rural Partnerships: Spunky Independent and
Proud." Stone Soup. Winter 1985. p. 14-15, 21.

Programs in East Valley, Vermont; Mabton,
Washington; and western New York State described.

NEIGHBORHOODS--CONSERVATION AND RESTORATION--ECONOMIC
ASPECTS

Gibson, Constance B. "In New Jersey, a State
Loan Program Helps Older Neighborhoods Survive."
Journal of Housing. July, 1979. pp. 357-360.

NEIGHBORHOODS--CONSERVATION AND RESTORATION--
ECONOMIC ASPECTS

Itzkowitz, Vicki. "Minnesota--Where the
Grassroots Approach Works." Challenge! Apr. 1979.
pp. 18-21.

Note: On state and federal programs for
community development.

NEIGHBORHOODS--CONSERVATION AND RESTORATION--
ECONOMIC ASPECTS

Mason, Hal. "Commercial Loan Pool Program
Aids Shelby , N.C." Center City Report. July 1982.
pp. 5-7.

NEIGHBORHOODS--CONSERVATION AND RESTORATION--
ECONOMIC ASPECTS

"Neighborhood Groups Develop Financial, Fund-
Raising Skills in Historic Areas." Economic
Growth and Revitalization Report. No. 85-24, Dec.
26, 1985. p. 2-3.

National Trust's ICVF program discussed;
Director Mark Weinheimer quoted.

NEIGHBORHOODS--CONSERVATION AND RESTORATION--U.S.
--INDIANA--LOGANSPORT (BANKER's ROW)

Gilman, Dennis S. "Preservation: How It
Changed an Indiana Neighborhood." Small Town.
Vol. 16, No. 1, July/Aug. 1985. p. 11-15.

NEIGHBORHOODS--ECONOMIC ASPECTS

"Baltimore Group Uses Video Tape As
Organizing Tool Against Displacement."
Economic Growth & Revitalization. No. 86-16,
Aug. 28, 1986. p. 4.

NEIGHBORHOODS--ECONOMIC ASPECTS

"'Defensible Space' Adopted." Economic Growth
and Revitalization Report. No. 87-4, Feb. 25,
1987. p. 5.

Vertical File

NEIGHBORHOODS--ECONOMIC ASPECTS

"Historic Preservation for Low-Income
Neighborhoods." PAS Memo. Feb. 1986. 4p. (VF)

NEIGHBORHOODS--ECONOMIC ASPECTS

Procter, Owen. "CCC Turns Tables on Deterioration
in Neighborhood South of Downtown." The Keystone.
Winter 1987. p. 4-5.

Neighborhood revitalization in Memphis.

NEIGHBORHOODS--LAW AND LEGISLATION

"Kentucky Mortgage Guaranty Fund for Proper-
ties in Designated Neighborhood Redevelopment
Zones." Local Economic Growth & Neighborhood
Reinvestment Report. April 19, 1984. p. 7.

NEIGHBORHOODS--LAW AND LEGISLATION

"Mortgage Insurance Fund Aids Neighborhoods." Local Economic Growth & Neighborhood
Reinvestment Report. April 19, 1984. p. 7.

NEIGHBORHOODS--LAW AND LEGISLATION

"Neighborhood Reinvestment Corporation Must
Focus on Survival in Fiscal 1985." Local Economic
Growth & Neighborhood Reinvestment Report. April
19, 1984. p. 7.

NEIGHBORHOODS--REVITALIZATION

"Two Birds With One Stone:Y-CATs'." Economic
Growth and Revitalization. No. 87-1, Jan. 13, 1987.
p. 5-6.

Youth employment program aids neighborhood
revitalization.

NEIGHBORHOODS--U.S.--CALIFORNIA--SAN FRANCISCO

Nelson, Christopher H. "Pacific Heights." Heritage Newsletter (The Foundation for San Francisco's Architectural Heritage). Vol. 14, No. 2, June 1986. Supplement. p. 1-4.

Thirty-six block area of San Francisco is one of the city's most historic residential districts.

NEIGHBORHOODS--U.S.--ILLINOIS--CHICAGO

Samuelson, Timothy. "Chicago's Black Metropolis." Historic Illinois. Vol. 9, No. 4. Dec. 1986. pp. 1-6.

NEIGHBORHOODS--U.S.--MINNESOTA--ST. PAUL

Propp, Jonathan. "Neighborhood Revitalization: St. Paul." Place. Vol. 6, No. 1, Jan./Feb. 1986. p. 16-17.

NEIGHBORHOODS--U.S.--NEW YORK--NEW YORK CITY

"Favorite Neighborhoods." Metropolis. Oct. 1985. p. 66-67.

NEIGHBORHOODS--U.S.--PENNSYLVANIA--PITTSBURGH

"Pittsburgh: Neighborhoods for Living." Conserve Neighborhoods. No. 56, Mar. 1986. p. 4-5, 7.

NEIGHBORHOODS--U.S.--TENNESSEE--MEMPHIS

Henderson, Stephanie. "Cooper Young District Recaptures Sense of Community." The Keystone (Memphis Heritage). Spring 1986. pp. 4-5.

NEOCLASSICISM (ARCHITECTURE)

"Ah Mediterranean! Twentieth Century Classicism in America." Center: a Journal for Architecture in America. Vol. 2, 1986. (Entire Issue)

NEOCLASSICISM (ARCHITECTURE)

Flaherty, Carolyn. "The Federal House." The Old-House Journal, January 1980. pp. 1, 4-6.

NEW HAMPSHIRE--CORNISH--CHARLES A. PLATT HOUSE

Morgan, Keith N. "Charles A. Platt's Houses and Gardens in Cornish, New Hampshire." Antiques. July 1982. pp. 117-129.

NEW JERSEY--CAPE MAY

Borja, Andrew D. "Restoring the Resort - Cape May." Urban Land. Vol. 43, No. 3, March 1984. pp. 22-25.

NEW MEXICO--PECOS

Kessell, John L. "The great temple at Pecos." Early Man. Autumn 1979. pp. 18-21.

NEW MEXICO--SHAKESPEARE

Brown, Patricia Leigh. "Shakespeare", American Preservation. January/February 1981. p. 21-28.

NEW YORK--ADIRONDACKS

Mooney, Elizabeth C. "Museum in the Mountains." Americana. March/April 1981. pp. 33 - 38.

NEW YORK--ADIRONDACKS

"A Place for All Seasons: A Photographic Portrait of Lake Placid, New York, in the pre-Olympic Age." American Heritage. December 1981. pp. 57-69.

NEW YORK--ALBANY--CHERRY HILL

Blackburn, Roderic H. "Historic Cherry Hill in Albany, New York". Antiques. April 1980. pp. 886-896.

NEW YORK--BROOKLYN--BROOKLYN BRIDGE

Berger, Horst. "Brooklyn Bridge at 100." Architectural Record. August 1983. pp. 118-127.

NEW YORK--CAZENOVIA

Hugill, Peter J. "Houses in Cazenovia: the effects of time and class." Landscape. 1980 vol.24, no.2. p. 10-15.

NEW YORK--COXSACKIE--BRONCK HOUSE

Hammond, Joseph W. "An Historical Analysis of the Bronck House, Coxsackie, New York". Halve Maen. Summer 1980. p.5-8, 17-18.

NEW YORK--ELLIS ISLAND

"Preservation Plans Set for Statue of Liberty, Ellis Island." Architecture. September 1983. pp. 16-17.

NEW YORK--HISTORIC PRESERVATION

Pierpont, Ruth Lawlor. "Sources of Funding for Preservation Projects." Preservation League of New York State-- Technical Series, No. 7.

NEW YORK--NEW YORK CITY

Ryder, Sharon Lee. "The Visible City." Metropolis. December 1981. pp. 23-25.

NEW YORK--NEW YORK CITY--BEDFORD-STUYVESANT

Robbins, Tom. "Restoring History in Bed-Stuy." City Limits. January 1981. p. 10-12.

NEW YORK--NEW YORK CITY--CHINATOWN

Lockwood, Charles. "A Summer's Walk Through Chinatown." Seaport. Summer 1981. pp. 21-27.

NEW YORK--NEW YORK CITY--ELLIS ISLAND

"Restoring the Isle of Tears." Progressive Architecture. February 1984. pp. 27-28.

NEW YORK--NEW YORK CITY--OLD MERCHANT'S HOUSE

"The Old Merchant's House: the saving and restoration of a Manhattan landmark". Interior Design. May 1980. p. 248-251.

NEW YORK--NEW YORK CITY--LEVER HOUSE

"Lever's Landmark Status Upheld; Demolition Threats Defended." AIA Journal. Apr. 1983. p. 17.

NEW YORK--NEW YORK CITY--ROCKFELLER CENTER

Allen, Gerald. "The Artist of the Center." American Heritage. October/ November 1982. pp. 98-107.

NEW YORK--NEW YORK CITY--SAILORS' SNUG HARBOR

Shur, Susan E. "Restoration Profile: Snug Harbor Cultural Center, Inc." Technology and Conservation. Spring 1981. pp. 32-41.

NEW YORK--NEW YORK CITY--SOUTH STREET SEAPORT

Canty, Donald. "New Meets Old in a Museum That Is a Neighborhood." Architecture. November 1983. p. 42-47.

NEW YORK-NEW YORK CITY--SOUTH STREET SEAPORT

"Some Last Words on South Street." Metropolis. March 1982. pp. 20-22.

NEW YORK--NEW YORK CITY--STATUE OF LIBERTY

"A Colossus Undertaking...Renewing Liberty's Exterior and Interior."
Technology and Conservation. Summer 1983. pp. 5-16

NEW YORK--NEW YORK CITY--TRIBECA

Winkleman, Michael. "The Visible City: A Tour of Tribeca's Residential Ripening." Metropolis. August/September, 1981. pp. 26-29.

NEW YORK--NEW YORK CITY--VILLARD HOUSES

"The Helmsley Palace." Interior Design. February 1981. pp. 206-217.

NEW YORK--NEW YORK CITY--VILLARD HOUSES

"The Latest Life of the Villard Houses". AIA Journal. February 1981. p. 68-73.

NEW YORK--NEW YORK CITY--VILLARD HOUSES

Rhodes, James W. "Preservation of the Villard Houses: Developing the Restoration/ Building Systems Upgrading Program." Technology and Conservation. Winter 1980. p.32-37, 46.

NEW YORK--NEW YORK CITY--VILLARD HOUSES

"The Villard Houses." Architectural Record. Mid-Feb. 1981. pp. 65-68.

NEW YORK--NEW YORK CITY--VILLARD HOUSES

Weber, William T. "Restoring the Landmark Interior at the Helmsley Palace Hotel: The Adaptation of the Villard Houses to Public Use." Technology and Conservation. Winter 1980. pp. 38-46.

NEW ZEALAND--HISTORIC PRESERVATION

Historic Places in New Zealand.

periodical shelf.

NORTH CAROLINA--ASHEVILLE--BILTMORE

Brendel-Pandich, Susanne. "Biltmore in Asheville, North Carolina". Antiques. April 1980. pp. 855-867.

NORTH CAROLINA--EDENTON

"Historic Edenton." Colonial Homes. January-February, 1982. pp. 72-101.

OFFICE BUILDINGS

Brown, Daniel C. "The D&F Tower Challenge, Developed as Office Condominiums, the Historic Daniels & Fisher Tower Sold Out, and is Considered a Success." Building Design & Construction. Apr. 1982. pp. 86-87.

OFFICE BUILDINGS

"Cantilevering Keeps Load Off Old Structure." Building Design & Construction. Apr. 1982. p. 28.

OFFICE BUILDINGS--ADAPTIVE USE

"Restoration Balanced with Profit Potential." Building Design and Construction. April 1982. pp. 100-101.

OFFICE BUILDINGS--CONSERVATION AND RESTORATION

"Adaptive Re-Use Provides Downtown Housing. Center City Report. March 1983. pp. 1-2.

OFFICE BUILDINGS--CONSERVATION AND RESTORATION

Hoster, Jay. "The Wyandotte: A Rehabilitation Effort." Urban Land. May 1979. pp. 3-8.

OFFICE BUILDINGS--CONSERVATION AND RESTORATION

"The Wainwright Building in St. Louis: Kudos for Saving a Landmark." Architectural Record. August 1981. p. 27.

OFFICE BUILDINGS--CONSERVATION AND RESTORATION-- U.S.--CALIFORNIA--LOS ANGELES

"The Wiltern, Part II Opens in L.A." Commercial Renovation. Vol. 6, No. 5, October 1984. pp. 48-53.

OFFICE BUILDINGS--CONSERVATION AND RESTORATION-- U.S.--PENNSYLVANIA--ERIE

"Revitalizing Expansion." Architectural Record. Jan. 1985. pp. 104-107.

OFFICE BUILDINGS--CONSERVATION AND RESTORATION-- U.S.--PENNSYLVANIA--PHILADELPHIA

"Insured Against Loss: Reliance Standard Life Insurance Company." Architectural Record. Apr. 1985. pp. 120-123.

OFFICE BUILDINGS--U.S.--MINNESOTA--ST. PAUL

"A St. Paul Icon Reclaimed." Architecture Minnesota. Vol. 10, No. 2, March/April 1984. pp. 32-35.

OFFICE BUILDINGS--U.S.--OREGON--PORTLAND

"Dayton Building Renovation, Portland Oregon", Portland Chapter/AIA 1984 Design Awards. Architectural Record. Feb. 1985. p. 76.

OHIO--CINCINNATI--RAILROAD TERMINALS

Roberts, Jim. "Cincinnati Union Terminal." Caboose Cable. February 1981. p.3-6.

OHIO--CINCINNATI--RAILROAD TERMINALS

Roberts, Jim. "Cincinnati Union Terminal." (Last of two-part series). Caboose Cable. March 1981. p.6-9.

OKLAHOMA--OKLAHOMA CITY--COLCORD BUILDING

Outlook in Historic Conservation. November/December 1980. Entire issue.

OPEN-AIR MUSEUMS

Albright, John. "Research to Planning to Operations: Grant-Kohrs Ranch National Historic Site." CRM Bulletin. Vol. 8, No. 2, Apr. 1985. p. 1-3.

OPEN-AIR MUSEUMS

Angotti, Thomas. "Planning the open-air museum and teaching urban history: the United States in the world context." Museum. No. 3, 1982. pp. 179-188.

OPEN-AIR MUSEUMS

Janssen, Quinith. "Old Time Farms." *Americana*. Vol. 12, No. 4, September/October 1984. pp. 110-117.

OPEN-AIR MUSEUMS

Karp, Walter. "Putting Worms Back in Apples." *American Heritage*. August/September 1982. pp. 33-43.

OPEN-AIR MUSEUMS

"A New Lease of Life." *Traditional Homes*. Vol. 3, No. 2. Nov. 1986. pp. 94-97.

The Weald and Downland Open Air Museum has moved 25 vernacular buildings to the museum.

OPEN-AIR MUSEUMS--U.S.--ILLINOIS--BISHOP HILL

Krone, James. "Sweden on the Prairie: Bishop Hill, Illinois." *Americana*. March/April 1981. pp. 64 - 70.

OPEN-AIR MUSEUMS--U.S.--MASSACHUSETTS--STURBRIDGE

Fossel, Peter V. "A New Sawmill for Old Sturbridge." *Americana*. Vol. 13, No. 1, Mar./Apr. 1985. p. 82-88.

OPEN-AIR MUSEUMS--U.S.--NEW JERSEY

Brilla, Kathy. "Howell Farm: Preserving Rural History"; Hunton, Gail. "Longstreet: Living History in Monmouth"; and Strathean, Nancy. "Fosterfields: Living History in Morris." *NJ Preservation Perspective*. Vol. 4, No. 4, May/June 1985. p. 1-2, 5, 7.

Living historical farms in New Jersey.

OPEN-AIR MUSEUMS--U.S.--VIRGINIA--WILLIAMSBURG

Dunn, Helen. "Mad House." *Americana*. Vol. 13, No. 1, Mar./Apr. 1985. p. 6.

Reconstructed first public mental hospital opened in March 1985.

OPEN-AIR MUSEUMS--U.S.--VIRGINIA--WILLIAMSBURG

"How the Royal Governor's Palace Became One of the Most Carefully Researched and Authentically Furnished Buildings of the Colonies." *Colonial Williamsburg Today*. Vol. III, Spring 1981. Entire Issue.

OPEN-AIR MUSEUMS--U.S.--VIRGINIA--WILLIAMSBURG

Karp, Walter. "My Gawd, They've Sold the Town." *American Heritage*. August/September, 1981. pp. 84-95.

OPEN-AIR MUSEUMS--U.S.--VIRGINIA--WILLIAMSBURG

Kukla, Jon. The Furnishings of the Governor's Palace at Williamsburg." *Virginia Cavalcade*. Summer 1981. pp. 20-31.

OPEN-AIR MUSEUMS--U.S.--VIRGINIA--WILLIAMSBURG

Pappas, Nicholas A. "The Public Hospital: Its Place in Williamsburg." *Colonial Williamsburg*. Vol. 7, No. 4, Summer 1985. p. 29-31.

OPEN-AIR MUSEUMS--U.S.--VIRGINIA--WILLIAMSBURG

Wenger, Mark R. "The Architecture of the Governor's Palace at Williamsburg. " *Virginia Cavalcade*. Summer 1981. pp. 13-19.

OPEN SPACES

Alexander, Lawrence A. "Downtown People Places: Encouraging Use, Avoiding Abuse." *Downtown Idea Exchange*. Vol. 34, No. 3, Feb. 1, 1987. p. 2-4.

OPEN SPACES

HUD Challenge. March 1980. Entire issue on urban open spaces.

OPEN SPACES

    Westbrook, John L. "Places of the Art." Place. Vol. 6, No. 5, Sept.-Oct. 1986. p. 14-15.

    Bethesda, Md. plan to produce public spaces with many amenities.

OPEN SPACES

    Woodcock, Janice and Beth Mountsier. "Planning and Design for Quality Open Space: Three Northwest Case Studies." UD Review. Vol. 9, No. 3. Summer 1986. pp. 18-25.

OPEN SPACES--CONSERVATION AND RESTORATION

    "Focus: Preservation of Open Green Spaces." Alliance Letter. Vol. 5, no. 2, March 1984. Entire issue.

OPEN SPACES--CONSERVATION AND RESTORATION

    Roper, H. James and Jack E. Boucher. "Waterford: Preserving Open Space is the Challenge Facing this Remarkable Community." American Preservation. Jun.-Jul. 1979. pp. 47-58.

OPERA HOUSES--U.S.--NEVADA--VIRGINIA CITY

    Loney, Glenn. "Ghosts Around Piper's Opera House in Virginia City, Nevada." 19th century. Autumn 1980. p. 52-54.

ORAL HISTORY

Brinkley, Ellen Hanson. "A Gift of the Past: Writing Family History," Goldenseal: West Virginia Traditional Life, Vol. 10, No. 4, Winter 1984, pp. 4-8.

ORDINANCES, MUNICIPAL

    "New Preservation Ordinance in Los Angeles Will Permit Designation of Local Preservation Zones." Landmark & Historic District Commissions. June 1979. pp. 1-2.

ORDINANCES, MUNICIPAL

    Niehaus, Charles. "Local Ordinance Often Controversial Issue." The Indiana Preservationist. No. 3, 1984. p. 4.

    (Second of three parts)

OREGON--JACKSONVILLE

    Slattery, Chad. " Jacksonville: Preservationists often may disagree in this picturesque little Oregon town, but they are never indifferent." American Preservation. May/June 1980. p. 43-58.

OREGON--PORTLAND

    "Prosperity Means Development, Livability." Center City Report. June 1981. pp. 1-3.

ORNAMENTAL HORTICULTURE

    Buckler, James R. "Victorian Horticulture: The Smithsonian Approach". Nineteenth Century. Spring 1981. pp. 53 - 61.

ORNAMENTAL HORTICULTURE

    Insinger, Wendy. "Going Out: Philadelphia : the Blooming Flower Show". Town and Country. Vol. 139, No. 5058, Mar. 1985. p. 94-104.

    History of event, held annually beginning in 1829, is described.

ORNAMENTAL HORTICULTURE

    Kunst, Scott G. "Carpet Bedding: Promiscuous Beds in the Victorian Landscape." Old House Journal. Vol. 13, No. 3, Apr. 1985. p. 53, 61-67.

ORNAMENTAL HORTICULTURE

    Maciejak, Dan. "Window Box Gardening." Old House Journal. June 1981. p. 133.

PAINT

Albee, Peggy A. "A Study of Historic Paint Colors and the Effects of Environmental Exposures on Their Colors and Their Pigments." APT Bulletin. Vol. 16, No. 3 & 4, 1984. p. 3-25.

PAINT

Black, David R. "Dealing with Peeling Paint." North Carolina Preservation. No. 66, Dec./Jan./Feb. 1987. p. 16-17.

PAINT

Bristow, Ian. "Repainting Eighteenth-Century Interiors." Transactions. Vol. 1, 1981. pp. 25-33.

PAINT

"Decorative Finishes." APT Bulletin. Vol. XVI, No. 1, 1984. Entire Issue. 60 p.

PAINT

Doonon, Nancy Locke. "Historic Exterior Paints, Guidelines for Establishing Whether a Sample Contains a Layer Original to the Building's Construction." APT Bulletin. Vol. XIV, No. 2, 1982. pp. 26-29.

PAINT

Elswick, Dan. "Preparing Historic Woodwork for Repainting Part 2- Thermal and Chemical Cleaning." The New South Carolina State Gazette. Vol. 19, No. 3, Spring 1987. p. 4-5

PAINT

"Exterior Paints." City Limits. Vol. 11, No. 8, Oct. 1986. p. 15.

PAINT

"Finishing Wood Exteriors." Progressive Builder. Vol. 12, No. 1, Jan. 1987. p. 11-20.

PAINT

Freeman, John Crosby. "Grand Illusions: Victorian House Painting Then and Now. Part One: Victorian Color Anxiety." Victorian Homes. Vol 6, No. 3. Summer 1987. pp. 64 - 67, 94.

PAINT

"Lead Poisoning: A Renovation Hazard, Part II-Safe Removal Procedures." The Landmark Society of Western New York. Vol. 25, No. 2, Mar. 1987. p. 9.

PAINT

Marshall, Philip and Eric Groves. "How to Paint Historic Buildings." Possibilities. June 1982. pp. 1-2.

PAINT

Masury, John W. "Hints on House Painting: or, Paints and Colors, and How to Use Them." Technology and Conservation. Vol. 9, No. 1, Spring 1985. p. 2, 14-19.

Excerpts from Mr. Masury's 1868 publication.

PAINT

Miller, Hugh C. "Historic Whitewash". CRM Bulletin. Vol. 8, No. 1, Feb. 1985. p. 9.

Recipes for whitewash for wood and stone and brick masonry given.

Vertical File

PAINT

O'Bright, Alan. "Exterior Woodwork, Number 2: Paint Removal from Wood Siding." Preservation Tech Notes. National Park Service, Sept. 1986. 6p. (VF)

PAINT

O'Donnell, Bill. "Unwanted Texture Finish: How to Get Rid of It." Old-House Journal. Vol. 14, No. 8, Oct. 1986. p. 374-381.

Removing paint and plaster texture finishes.

PAINT

"Paint Program Reopens." Neighborhood Quarterly. Vol. 6-2, Spring 1986. p. 6.

New Haven's Housepainting Program makes available to all homeowners in the area a 50 percent grant for house paint.

PAINT

"Painting Better." Journal of Housing Lab. No. 24. Journal of Housing. Vol. 43, No. 6, Nov./Dec. 1986. p. 252-253.

PAINT

"Painting up the Town." Economic Growth and Revitalization. No.86-13, Nov. 11, 1986. p.5-6.

Kansas City's neighborhood paint program that has involved 16,500 homes is linked to a weatherization program.

PAINT

"Painting Walls, Part 1: Choice of Paint." Building Research Establishment Digest. No. 197. 1982.

PAINT

"Painting Woodwork." Building Research Establishment Digest. May 1982. #261.

Vertical File
PAINT

Park, Sharon C. "Exterior Woodwork, Number 1: Proper Painting and Surface Preparation." Preservation Tech Notes. National Park Service. May 1986. 8 p. (VF)

PAINT

Phillips, M.W. "Acrylic Paints for Restoration: Three Test Applications." APT Bulletin. Vol. 15, No. 1, 1983. pp. 2-11.

PAINT

Phillips, Morgan W. "Brief Notes on the Subjects of Analyzing Paints and Mortars and the Recording of Moulding Profiles." APT Bulletin. No. 2, 1978. pp. 77-89.

PAINT

Phillips, Morgan W. and Brian Powell. "Several Experiences Using Lime Paste as a Cleaning Agent for Oil Paint." APT Bulletin. Vol. XIV, No. 2, 1982. pp. 30-34.

PAINT

"Stripping Paint." The Old-House Journal. December 1982. pp. 249-252.

PAINT

Perrault, Carole L. "Techniques Employed at the North Atlantic Historic Preservation Center for the Sampling and Analysis of Historic Architectural Paint and Finishes." APT Bulletin, number 2 1978. pp. 6-46.

PAINT

"Reproduction Paints by Dutch Boy." Charleston. Vol. 4, No. 3. Spring 1987. pp. 1; 3.

PAINT

Santucci, R.M. "Paint: For Savings, Keep It Simple." Cost Cuts. Vol. 3, No. 2, Nov. 1985. p. 1, 4-5.

PAINT

Street, Ann. "Lead Poisoning: A Serious Preservation Issue." PPS News (Providence Preservation Society). Vol. XXII, No. 3, November-December 1984. p. 3.

Discussion of safety techniques when removing lead-based paint.

PAINT

"Technical Assistance for Architectural Preservation." Arizona Preservation News. Vol. 4, No. 3. Jul. 1987. p. 10.
Guidelines to choosing colors for an historic building.

PAINT

Weaver, Martin. "New Paint and Old Distempers." Canadian Heritage. December 1981. p. 43.

PAINT

Weeks, Kay D. and Look, David W. "Paint on Exterior Historic Woodwork: Identification & Treatment of Surface Condition Problems." Technology & Conservation. Summer 1982. pp. 34-45.

PAINT

Welsh, Frank S. "Who Is an Historic Paint Analyst?: a Call for Standards." APT Bulletin. Vol. 18, No. 4, 1986. p. 4-5.

PAINT

Welsh, F.S. and Granquist, C.L. "Restoration of the Exterior Sanded Paint at Monticello." APT Bulletin. Vol. XV, No. 2, 1983. pp. 3-10.

PAINT

Zucker, Howard. "Paneling Flush Doors with Paint (Part II)." Victorian Homes. Vol. 6, Issue 1, Winter 1987. p. 60-62.

PAINT, FIREPROOF

Harp, Dale W. "Intumescent Paints: A Useful Component of Fire Protection Plans." Technology and Conservation. Spring 1981. pp. 30-31.

PAINT MATERIALS

Bock, Gordon H. "Yes, I Still Use Whitewash." The Old House Journal. Vol. 13, No. 2, Mar. 1985. p. 49.

PAINT MATERIALS

Penn, Theodore Zuk. "Decorative and Protective Finishes, 1750-1850, Materials, Process and Craft." APT Bulletin. Vol. XVI, No. 1, 1984. pp. 3-46.

Contains extensive bibliography.

PAINT REMOVERS

Himelick, Kirk J., "Methods of Refurnishing Interior Architectural Woodwork." Illinois Heritage Association Newsletter Technical Insert No. 7, Jan-Feb. 1984. 2 pp.

PAINT REMOVERS

Poore, Patricia. "Stripping Paint From Exterior Wood." The Old House Journal. Vol. 13, No. 10, Dec. 1985. p. 207-211.

Appropriate techniques under particular conditions discussed.

PAINT REMOVERS

"Take It All Off? Advice on When and How to Strip Interior Paintwork." Canadian Heritage. December 1983-January 1984. PP. 44-47.

PAINTED COUNTRY FURNITURE

Hogrefe, Jeffrey. "Painted Furniture: At Prices that are Still Reasonable but Rising Fast." Americana. May/Jun. 1979. pp. 16-21.

PAINTING

Hardingham, David. "Preparing for Painting: Part I." Old House Journal. October, 1980. p. 133-136.

PAINTING

"Painting Exterior Wood Surfaces." Landmarks Observer. Vol 13, No. 3, May-June 1986. p. 8-9, 11.

PAINTING--CONSERVATION AND RESTORATION

Berger, Gustav A. "Conservation of Large Canvas Paintings: the role of constant tension mounting systems." Technology and Conservation. Spring 1980. p. 26-31.

PAINTING--CONSERVATION AND RESTORATION

"Hue and Pry... to Determine an Historic Property's True Colors." Technology and Conservation. Fall 1982. pp. 5-8.

PAINTING--CONSERVATION AND RESTORATION

Jones, Larry and Harris, Louis. "The Culmer House: Restoration of Stencils and Wall Paintings". Utah: Preservation/Restoration. Vol. 2/Issue 2 1980. pp. 42 - 44.

PAINTING--HISTORY

"Old Painting Techniques Find New Uses." Commercial Renovation. Vol. 6, No. 5, October 1984. pp. 56-60.

PAPER--PRESERVATION

Hohler, Joanne. "Polyester Encapsulation." Illinois Heritage Association Technical Insert. No. 10, 1984. 4 p.

PAPER--PRESERVATION

Schur, Susan E. "Conservation Profile: The Northeast Document Conservation Center." Technology and Conservation. Fall 1982. pp. 32-39.

PARKING LOTS

"APA to Research Parking Lot Design." Zoning News. Sept. 1985. p. 1-2.

PARKING LOTS--U.S.--MONTANA--BUTTE

Cornish, Janet A. "Parking and Preservation: Solving a Dilemma in Butte, Montana." Preservation, Montana Historical Society Preservation Office. May/June 1985. p. 1-3.

PARKS

Carter, Robert A. "Douthat State Park Recognized As Historic Landmark." Notes on Virginia. No. 29, Fall 1986. p. 26-31.

PARKS

Cook, Jess. "Los Angeles Lands the Nation's Biggest 'Urban' Park, the Santa Monica Mountains National Recreation Area, but a battle is on Between Developers and Preservationists." Smithsonian, July, 1979. pp. 26-35.

PARKS

"Emerald Necklace Master Plan Proposal." Boston Preservation Alliance. Vol. 8, No. 6. June 1987. p. 5.
Olmsted parks in Boston.

PARKS

Ford, Larry and Ernst Griffin. "Chicano Park: Personalizing an Institutional Landscape." Landscape. Vol. 25, No. 2. pp. 42-48.

PARKS

Kowsky, Francis R. "Municipal Parks and City Planning: Frederick Law Olmsted's Buffalo Park and Parkway System." Reprinted from the *Journal of the Society of Architectural Historians*. Mar. 1987. (VF)

PARKS

Loughlin, Caroline and Catherine Anderson. *Forest Park*. St. Louis: Jr. League of St. Louis; Columbia: University of Missouri Press, 1986. (F474.S27F675)

PARKS

Maguire, Meg. "Saving City Parks." *Sierra*. October 1983. pp. 24-27.

PARKS

Maney, Susan. "A Century of Rochester's Parks." *The Landmark Society of Western New York*. Vol. 25, No. 2, Mar. 1987. p. 4.

100th anniversary of Rochester Park System.

PARKS

"Observation Tower." *Design* (National Park Service). Spring 1986. R-4996-R-5005.

Renovation of Cape Henlopen State Park (Delaware) observation tower.

PARKS

Osterhout, Marcia A. "The Urban Cultural Park System in New York." *Preservation League of New York State Newsletter*. Vol. 13, No. 2. Spring 1987. pp. 10 - 11.

PARKS

Parsons, Randall T. "The Grace Estate: a Case Study." *Land Trusts' Exchange*. Vol. 5, No. 2, Fall 1986. p. 6-7, 18.

The town of East Hampton, N.Y. joined forces with the Nature Conservancy and the North Bay Associates to preserve the 623-acre Grace Estate.

PARKS

"Restoration in Prospect Park." *A Little News*. Winter 1987. p. 1.

Building and landscape restoration in New York's Prospect Park.

PARKS

Silverman, Jane. "Three Urban Parks: 'Gateways' to America". *Urban Design International*. July/August 1980. p. 14-19.

PARKS

Stepenoff, Bonnie. "Pacesetting Recognition of State Park Architecture." *Missouri Preservation News*. Vol. 10, No. 1, Summer 1986. p. 1, 7-8.

Growing appreciation of the rustic bridges, shelters, lodges and other park buildings erected during the 1930's by federal relief works.

PARKS

Stone, Andrew. "The Parks that Never Were: New York's 1811 Plan." *City Limits*. Vol. 12, No. 2, Mar./Apr. 1987. p. 26-28.

PARKS

Stone, Kyle. "Rich Parks, Poor Parks." *City Limits*. Vol. 12, No. 4, Apr. 1987. p. 21-23.

Difficulties in obtaining funding for New York parks' upkeep.

PARKS

Worsley, Guy. "Planning into the 25th Century." *Traditional Homes*. Mar. 5, 1987. pp. 102-103.

Replanting Blenheim Park (England).

PARKS--CONSERVATION AND RESTORATION

Cromley, Elizabeth. "Riverside Park and Issues of Historic Preservation." *Journal of the Society of Architectural Historians*. Vol. 43, No. 3. Oct. 1984. pp. 238-249.

PARKS--CONSERVATION AND RESTORATION

"The First Historic Landscape Report for the Ravine." Landscape Architecture. September/October, 1983. pp. 70-73.

PARKS--CONSERVATION AND RESTORATION

McLaughlin, Charles C. "Frederick Law Olmsted's Parks: Antiques or Urban Necessities?" National Association for Olmsted Parks Newsletter. Fall/Winter 1980/81. p. 7-10.

PARKS--CONSERVATION AND RESTORATION

Meyer, Amy. "Revitalizing Urban Parks, Its Time to Restore Our Older City Parks." Sierra. November/December, 1982. pp. 38-41.

PARKS--CONSERVATION AND RESTORATION

Pierro, Lorraine. "Olmsted Hotspots." Preservation Report. Vol. 8, No. 1, Jan./Feb. 1986. p. 4-5.

PARKS--CONSERVATION AND RESTORATION

Ryan, Terry Warriner. "The Michigan Avenue/ Grant Park Partnership." Inland Architect. Vol. 30, No. 2, Mar./Apr. 1986. p. 17, 60.

A public/private partnership established for the restoration of Grant Park in Chicago.

PARKS--CONSERVATION AND RESTORATION--U.S.--NEW YORK--BUFFALO

Field, Scott. "Lawsuit Brought to Stop School in MLK Park." Preservation Report. Vol. 8, No. 1, Jan./Feb. 1986. p. 1, 6.

The Buffalo Friends of Olmsted Parks commence lawsuit, assisted with a $2,000 matching grant from the National Trust.

PARKS--INTERPRETIVE PROGRAMS

Sherfy, Marcella. "Honesty in interpreting the cultural past." Parks. Jan.-Mar. 1979. pp. 13-14.

PARKS--MANAGEMENT

Jubak, Jim. "The People and the Pinelands." National Parks. Vol. 58, No. 9-10, Sept./Oct. 1984. pp. 20-25.

PARKS--MANAGEMENT

U.S. DOI, NPS. Trends. Vol. 21, No. 1. Vandalism, 1984, Entire Issue.

Powers, Robert M. and David A. Rosen. "Central Park Graffiti Removal Program." pp. 20-24.

PARKS--MANAGEMENT

"User Fees and Charges." Trends, U.S. Department of the Interior, National Park Service Park Practice Program. Vol. 21, No. 4, 1984. Entire issue, 48 p.

PARKS--U.S. -ILLINOIS--CHICAGO--GRANT PARK

Fink, J. Theodore. "Grant Park's 150 years." Inland Architect. Mar. 1980. pp. 10-17.

PARKS--U.S.--MASSACHUSETTS--BOSTON

Heath, Richard. "The Centennial of Franklin Park." Boston Preservation Alliance Letter. Vol. 6, No. 1. Jan. 1985. pp. 4-5.

PARKS--U.S.--PENNSYLVANIA--PHILADELPHIA

Major, Judith K. "Fairmount Park's Changing Role in City Life: a 19th Century Philadelphia Landmark Adapts to 20th Century Uses and Values." Urban Land. Vol. 44, No. 2. Feb. 1985. pp. 18-21.

PARTNERS FOR LIVEABLE PLACES

"Partners Offers Consulting Services." Livability. Spring 1983. p. 8.

PARKS --U.S.--WASHINGTON, D.C.

Wolf, Dick. "Anacostia Park Site for New Prison: A Planning Catastrophe." Capitol Hill Restoration Society Inc. News. Sept. 1986. p. 4.

PEDESTRIAN FACILITIES

"History Via Skyways or History Versus Skyways?" Preservation Matters. Vol. 3, No. 1, Jan. 1987. p. 1.

Disagreement over whether or not skyways and historic buildings are incompatible.

PEDESTRIAN FACILITIES

Knack, Ruth Eckdish. "Pedestrian Malls: Twenty Years Later." Planning. December 1982. pp. 15-20.

PEDESTRIAN FACILITIES DESIGN

"Pedestrian Malls: Trial, Error, and Success." Downtown Idea Exchange. Vol. 34, No. 4, Feb. 15, 1987. p. 4-6.

PEDESTRIANS

"Downtown Pedestrianization: A Good Concept that's Getting Great." Downtown Idea Exchange. November 15, 1983. pp. 2-5. December 1, 1983. pp. 2-4.

PENNSYLVANIA--DOYLESTOWN--FONTHILL

Barnes, Roger. "Fonthill: Romanticism and Ingenuity Cast in Reinforced Concrete." Fine Homebuilding. December1981/January 1982. pp. 29-35.

PENNSYLVANIA--EPHRATA-- CLOISTERS

Kraft, John L. "Ephrata Cloister, an eighteenth-century religious commune". Antiques. October 1980. p. 724-737.

PENNSYLVANIA--PHILADELPHIA--BARTRAM'S GARDEN

Mower, D. Roger. "Bartram's Garden in Philadelphia." Antiques. March 1984. pp. 630-636.

PENNSYLVANIA--JIM THORPE

"Urban design and planning citation: Venturi, Rauch & Scott Brown." Progressive Architecture. January 1981. p. 98-99.

PENNSYLVANIA--PHILADELPHIA--GERMANTOWN

"Germantown 1683-1983." Antiques. Aug. 1983. Entire issue.

Hendrickson, Hope. Cliveden--Stoddary, Mary and Reed Engle. Stenton--Lloyd, Mark. Upsala--Lloyd, Sandra. Wyck--Fanelli, Doris. The Deshler--Morris House--Peterson, Karin. The Ebenezer Maxwell Mansion--Gill, Bruce Cooper. Grumblethorpe.

PENNSYLVANIA--PHILADELPHIA--PENNSYLVANIA ACADEMY

Myers, Hyman. "The Three Buildings of the Pennsylvania Academy." Antiques. March 1982. March 1982.

PENNSYLVANIA--PITTSBURGH

Lewis, David. "A Remarkable Renaissance: The City." American Arts. Jan. 1982. pp. 14-17.

PERFORMANCE ZONING

Frank, Michael J. "Performance Zoning: How it's doing in the place where it began." Planning. December 1982. pp. 21-24.

PEST CONTROL

Gagne, Cole. "Eureka: Solutions to the Pigeon Problem." Old House Journal. June 1981. p. 136.

PEST CONTROL

Labine, Clem. "Insects that Eat the House." Old House Journal. June 1981. p. 129.

PEST CONTROL

McGiffin, Robert F. Jr. "A Current Status Report on Fumigation in Museums and Historical Agencies." American Association for State and Local History Technical Report 4, 1985. 15 p.

Copy on Reference Shelf.

PEST CONTROL

"A Safe good riddance...to protect holdings from pest attack." Technology and Conservation. Vol. 9, No. 1, Spring 1985. p. 5-11.

PHOTOGRAMMETRY

Bell, John. "Underwater Stereo-photogrammetric Recording : A Pilot Project--Red Bay, Labrador." APT Bulletin. Vol. 18, No. 1 & 2, 1986. p. 113-114.

PHOTOGRAMMETRY

Thomas, W.M. "Photogrammetry: a modern survey method for conservationists." Building Conservation. January 1980. pp. 12-16.

PHOTOGRAPH COLLECTIONS

Brannan, Beverly. "Bell's Images, Organizing a Complex Photographic Collection." History News. March 1982. pp. 41-45.

PHOTOGRAPH COLLECTIONS

Noble, Geoffrey. "The Role of Photographic Archives in Conservation." Transactions. Vol. 7, 1982. pp. 27-41.

PHOTOGRAPHS

Clark, Jerry. "Computer Image Processing of the Huntsville Depot Photograph." APT Bulletin. Vol. 11, No. 1, 1979. pp. 13-16.

PHOTOGRAPHS

Fink, Daniel A. "Photographs from the Early Nineteenth Century." Nineteenth Century, Autumn 1979. pp. 34-42.

PHOTOGRAPHS

Jones, Harvie P. "Enhancement of Historic Photographs." APT Bulletin. Vol. 11, No. 1, 1979. pp. 4-12.

PHOTOGRAPHS--CONSERVATION AND RESTORATION

"Conservation of Photographic Collections, An Interview with Eugene Ostroff." Parks. Jan./Feb./Mar. 1982. pp. 17-21.

PHOTOGRAPHS--CONSERVATION AND RESTORATION

Jowers, Walter. "Making Photos Last...And Bringing Back the Old Ones." The Old House Journal. Vol. 13, No. 10, Dec. 1985. p. 213-215.

PHOTOGRAPHS--CONSERVATION AND RESTORATION

Taylor, Nick. Vanishing Georgia. Americana. September/October, 1983. pp. 75-79.

PHOTOGRAPHY

Conrad, James H. "Technical Leaflet #139, Copying Historical Photographs: Equipment and Methods." History News. August 1981.

PHOTOGRAPHY

Walther, Gary. "How to Photograph a Restoration: Advice from a Pro." Americana. Jan./Feb. 1980. pp. 20-23.

PHOTOGRAPHY, AERIAL

Schmidt, Ray. "Interpreting Images, A Slice at a Time." Bulletin, Association for Preservation Technology. Vol. XV, No. 4, 1983. pp. 57-9.

PHOTOGRAPHY, ARCHITECTURAL

Archibald, Margaret. "Positive Evidence: Using Photographs as Documents in Structural History." APT Bulletin. v.XII, no. 3, 1980. p.62-92.

PHOTOGRAPHY, ARCHITECTURAL

Franzen, David. "How to Photograph a Building for Documentation." Historic Hawai'i. Vol. 12, No. 9, Oct. 1986. p. 4-5.

PHOTOGRAPHY, ARCHITECTURAL

Freeman, Allen. "Architectural History on Film." Architecture. Feb. 1986. p. 66-69.

Exhibition of the work of Jack Boucher, Historic American Building Survey's photographer.

PHOTOGRAPHY, ARCHITECTURAL

"HABS Photo Project S[outh] C[arolina]." The New South Carolina State Gazette. Vol. 19, No. 2, Winter 1987. p. 7.

PHOTOGRAPHY, ARCHITECTURAL

"Historic Photography as a Research Tool for Capitol Restoration." Capitol Preservation News. Vol. 4, No. 1, May 1987, p. 3-4.

PHOTOGRAPHY, ARCHITECTURAL

Mann, Frederick M. "Photo Drawings: A Practical Alternative." APT Bulletin. Vol. 19, No. 2, 1987. p. 25-37.

Using scaled-rectified photography as an alternative to measured drawings.

PHOTOGRAPHY, ARCHITECTURAL

"Photographs preserve image of endangered properties." The Preservation Report. Vol. 13, No. 5, March/April 1986. p.3.

PHOTOGRAPHY, ARCHITECTURAL

Robinson, Erik. "Equipment and Techniques for Photo Documentation in Museums and Preservation Organizations." Illinois Heritage Association Newsletter. (Technical insert, No. 9, 1984.) Vol. 2, No. 3. May-June 1984.

PHOTOGRAPHY, ARCHITECTURAL

Wasserman, Abby. "Roger Sturtevant: Free Spirit with a Work Ethic." The Museum of California. Vol. 10, No. 3, Nov./Dec. 1986. p. 13-15.

The "father of architectural photography" profiled .

PHOTOGRAPHY, ARCHITECTURAL

Wexler, Clifford. "Photodocumentation, Developing a Portrait of Small Town America." Small Town. Vol. 15, No. 3, November-December 1984. pp. 15-19.

PHOTOGRAPHY--CONSERVATION AND RESTORATION

Ramer, Grant B. "A Stabilization Packaging Technique for Photographs." RCHA Technical Information, Information Sheet #17. June 1985. 4 p.

PLANTATIONS

Lytle, Sarah. "Middleton Place." Antiques. Apr. 1979. pp. 779-794.

PLANTATIONS

Schober, Maburl. "Lousiana's Cane River Plantations." Early American Life. Vol. 17, No. 3, June 1986. p. 20-27.

PLANTATIONS--CONSERVATION AND RESTORATION

Cheek, Mary Tyler. "Restoring and Furnishing Stratford." The Decorative Arts Trust, Vol. 4, No. 2, December 1984. Entire issue, 6 p.

PLANTATIONS--U.S.--LOUISIANA

Banks, William Nathaniel. "Louisiana Plantations, the Bayou Country." Antiques. Jul. 1984. pp. 102-118.

Includes National Trust property, Shadows-on-the-Teche.

PLANTATIONS--U.S.--VIRGINIA

Dunkley, Diane. "A New Look at Carter's Grove: Reviving the Colonial Revival." Colonial Williamsburg. Vol. 8, No. 1, Autumn 1985. p. 30-34.

PLANTS

Goeldner, Paul K., PhD. "Plant Life at Historic Properties." APT Bulletin. Vol. 16, No. 3 & 4, 1984. p. 67-69.

The threats of vegetation to historic resources discussed.

PLANTS

Robson, Eric. "Plant Collections in Trust Gardens." Heritage Scotland. Vol. 1, No. 4, Summer 1984. pp. 11-12.

PLASTER

Labine, Clem. "Paint Encrusted Plaster." Old-House Journal. Vol. XII, No. 6, July 1984. pp. 111, 124.

PLASTER

Worsham, Gibson. "Exterior Plaster Restoration at the Lord Morton House, Lexington, Kentucky." APT Bulletin. Vol. XIII, No. 4, 1981. pp. 27-33.

PLASTERING

Jowers, Walter. "Textured Plaster Finishes." The Old-House Journal. Vol. 14, No. 2, Mar. 1986. p. 75-77.

PLASTERING

"Plaster: a Primer on Techniques and Terms." Illinois Heritage Association Technical Insert. No. 17, Sept./Oct. 1985. 2 p.

PLASTERWORK

Boutwood, Jim. "Proud Plaster-work." Traditional Homes. July 1986. p. 41-46.

Restoration of pargetting.

PLASTERWORK

"The Plasterer's Art." Traditional Homes. Mar. 1986. p. 34-40.

PLASTERWORK

Todaro, John. "Molding and Casting Materials." Fine Homebuilding. February/March 1981. p.36-39.

PLASTERWORK--CONSERVATION AND RESTORATION

Fidler, John. "Save the Ceiling." Traditional Homes. Mar. 1986. p. 42-46.

PLASTERWORK--CONSERVATION AND RESTORATION

Flaherty, David. "A Craftsman Restores the Ornamental Plasterwork in the Old Merchants House." 19th Century. Autumn 1980. pp. 34-35.

PLASTERWORK--CONSERVATION AND RESTORATION

Ontario Heritage Foundation. "Repair of a Papered Plaster Wall at the Barnum House, Grafton, Ontario." Technical Notes 2, Communique. Vol. XIII.(3). pp. 9-10.

PLASTERWORK--CONSERVATION AND RESTORATION

Poore, Patricia. "What's Behind Sagging Plaster." The Old-House Journal. January-February, 1983. pp. 24-25.

PLASTERWORK--CONSERVATION AND RESTORATION

Phillips, Morgan W. "Adhesives for the Reattachment of loose Plaster". APT Bulletin v. XII, no.2,1980. p. 37-63.

PLASTERWORK--CONSERVATION AND RESTORATION

Wolf, Stephen L. "Improving Old Walls and Ceilings with Lining Materials." The Old House Journal. Vo. 13, No. 2, Mar. 1985. p. 39-41.

PLASTERWORK--CONSERVATION AND RESTORATION--U.S.--OREGON--PORTLAND

Staehli, Alfred M. "Scagliola: Restoration of an Antique Plaster Finish in the Portland City Hall, Oregon." Bulletin, The Association for Preservation Technology. Vol. 16, No. 2, 1984. p. 44-50.

PLASTERWORK, DECORATIVE

Garrison, John Mark. "Casting Decorative Plaster." The Old House Journal. Vol. 13, No. 9, Nov. 1985. p. 186-189.

PLASTERWORK, DECORATIVE

"Restoration Specialty: Ornamental Plaster for Restoration and Modern Designs Available through Special Process." Architectural Record. Mid-Oct. 1979. p. 14.

PLAZAS

Sanders, James. "Toward a Return of the Public Space: an American Survey." Architectural Record. Apr. 1985. p. 87-95.

PLAZAS--U.S.--MASSACHUSETTS--BOSTON

Chabrier, Yvonne V. "The Greening of Copley Square." Landscape Architecture. Vol. 75, No. 6, Nov./Dec. 1985. p. 70-76.

PLUMBING--REPAIRING

Lang-Runtz, Heather. "Plumbing Truths: An Introduction to Plumbing for the Older Home." Canadian Heritage. Vol. 11, No. 4, Oct/Nov. 1985. p. 44-47.

PLUMBING--REPAIRING

Lang-Runtz, Heather. "Plumbing Truths: an Introduction to Plumbing for the Older Home, Part II." Canadian Heritage. Vol. 11, No. 5, Dec. 1985 /Jan. 1986. p. 47-51.

POLLS

"Public Attitudes toward Housing, Preservation, Environment." Urban Conservation Report. Vol. 10, No. 7, July 9, 1986. p. 6.

Results of a Gallup poll.

POLLUTION

Fisher, Thomas R. "Pollution and historic structures." Connecticut Trust for Historic Preservation News. Winter 1981. p. 5.

PORCELAIN--COLLECTORS AND COLLECTING

    Donegan, Frank. "Historical Staffordshire: Middle-Class China Now Brings High-Class Price." Americana. Vol. 13, No. 1, Mar./Apr. 1985. p. 111-115.

PORCHES

    Cole, Roy F. "Restoring a Porch." Fine Homebuilding. April/May 1981. p.14-17.

PORCHES

    Freeman, John Crosby and Clem Labine. "In Praise of Porches." The Old-House Journal. Vol. IX, No. 8, August 1981. p. 167.

PORCHES

    Leeke, John. "Canvassing a Porch Deck." Old House Journal, Vol. 15, No. 3, May-June 1987. p. 28-31.

PORCHES

    Montgomery, Arnold. "The Art of Properly Proportioned Porches." Soulard Restorationist. Vol. 11, Issue 2, April 1, 1986. p. 10-11.

PORCHES

    "Porch Areas Require Care." The Medallion. Vol. 24, No. 7. Jul. 1987. p. 3.

PORCHES

    Rochlin, Davida. "The American Porch: a Look at Porches, and a Glossary of Types From Past to Present." Fine Homebuilding. No. 29, Oct./Nov. 1985. p. 47-50.

PORCHES--U.S.--MAINE--PORTLAND

    Taylor, Anthony. "The Triple Alliance: Portland's Three-Deckers Gain Respectibility." Landmarks/Observer. Vol. 12, No. 4, July/Aug. 1985. p. 8-9, 16.

    Tenement buildings with three-tiered porches discussed as style of architecture.

POST OFFICE BUILDINGS

    Pringle, Susan. "Significant U.S. Post Offices in New Jersey: 1900-1941." Preservation Perspective. Vol. 5, No. 3, March/April 1986. p. 4.

POST OFFICE BUILDINGS

    "Public, Private Sectors Combine to Rehabilitate Historic Government Building." Housing and Development Reporter. November 7, 1983. p. 496.

POST OFFICE BUILDINGS--ADAPTIVE USE

    "Akron's New Art Museum: A Model for Adaptive Re-Use." Architectural Record. February 1982. pp. 98-101.

POST OFFICE BUILDINGS--ADAPTIVE USE

    "City Declines CDBG Grant When David-Bacon Intervenes." Urban Conservation Report. Vol. 10, No. 3, Mar. 17, 1986. p. 1-2.

    Old post office building in Waterville, Maine, on National Register, is being converted into a mini-mall of shops and restaurants.

POST OFFICE BUILDINGS--CONSERVATION AND RESTORATION

    "The Old Post Office: Unique or Ubiquitous?" Progressive Architecture. February 1984. pp. 41-42.

POST OFFICE BUILDINGS--CONSERVATION AND RESTORATION

    Von Eckardt, Wolf. "A Preservation Victory Saves Washington's Old Post Office." Humanities. November 1983. pp. 26-27.

POST OFFICE BUILDINGS--U.S.--COLORADO--FORT
COLLINS

Albertson-Clark, Sherry. "Landmark Status
May Save Old Post Office." Colorado Heritage
News. Jan. 1986. p. 5-6.

POST OFFICE BUILDINGS--U.S.--WASHINGTON, D.C.

"Pennsylvania Avenue Projects Changed;
Post Office to Open." AIA Journal. November 1981.
pp. 21-25.

POSTCARDS

"America in a Post Card Mirror." Lake County
Museum Postcard Journal. Vol. 4, No. 1, Winter
1987. p. 1-2.

Curt Teich postcard collection.

POSTCARDS

Gettys, Marshall. "Historic Postcards as a
Tool of the Preservationist." Outlook in Historic
Preservation. November/December 1982.

POSTCARDS

Pfeifer, Jim. "Post Cards Chronicle Little
Rock's Architectural History." The Quapaw Quarter
Chronicle. Vol. 14, No. 3. June - July. p. 11.

POSTCARDS

Skaler, Robert M. "Victorian Postcards:
A Periscope on the Past." USA Tomorrow.
Vol. 2, No. 1, May 1987. (VF)

POSTCARDS

Skaler, Robert Morris. "Victorian Postcards: a Periscope on the Past." The Victorian.
Vol. 12, No. 3, 1984. p. 4.

POTTERY

Heath, Roger. "Bennington Pottery." Americana,
January/February 1980. pp. 28-33.

POTTERY

Trapp, Kenneth. "Rookwood and the Japanese
Mania in Cincinnati." Cincinnati Historical
Society Bulletin. Vol. 49, Spring 1981, No. 1.
pp. 51 -75.

POWER-PLANTS

Evers, Charles A. "Big Plans for Philly's
Fairmount." Society for Industrial Archeology
Newsletter. Vol. 13, No. 2, Summer 1984. pp.
1-2.

POWER-PLANTS

Heywood, Peter. "From Powerhouse to
Funhouse: A Reuse Proposal for Battersea Station."
Architectural Record. October 1984. p. 115.

PRAIRIE SCHOOL (ARCHITECTURE)

O'Donnell, Francis. "The Prairie School".
Humanities. Vol. 6, No. 1, Feb. 1985. p. 17-18.

PREFABRICATED HOUSES

Brett, Deborah L. "Manufactured Housing:
One Solution to Affordability." Nation's Cities
Weekly. August 27, 1984. Vol. 7, No. 35.
pp. 3, 6.

PREFABRICATED HOUSES

Henning, Lisbeth. "Magnets Handy in Metal
Landmarks." The Indiana Preservationist. No. 5,
1986. p. 7.

Lustion prefabricated metal houses built
in the late 1940s.

PREFABRICATED HOUSES

Schwartz, David M. "When Home Sweet Home Was Just a Mailbox Away." Smithsonian. Vol. 16, No. 8, Nov. 1985. p. 90-101.

Sears catalog houses discussed.

PREFABRICATED HOUSES

Snyder, Tim. "The Sears Pre-Cut: A Mail-Order House for Everyone." Fine Homebuilding. No. 28, Aug./Sept. 1985. p. 42-45.

PREFABRICATED HOUSES

Stevenson, Katherine Cole and H. Ward Jandl. Houses by Mail: a Guide to Houses from Sears, Roebuck and Company. Washingtin, D.C.: Preservation Press, 1986. 365p. (TH4819.P7S74)

PRESIDENTS--UNITED STATES

Plante, Christine M. and Lucinda Mullin. "Presidential Homes: In Stately Fashion." Town and Country. Vol. 139, No. 5061, June 1985. p. 117-127, 180, 183.

The article contains a guide to presidential homes.

PRINTING

Purcell, L. Edward. "Writing Printing Specifications : A Systematic Approach to Publications Management." AASLH Technical Leaflet. No. 142.

PRISONS--U.S.--MASSACHUSETTS--BOSTON

Larson, Leslie. "Letters to the Editor." Boston Preservation Alliance Letter. Vol. 7, No. 1, Jan. 1986. p. 2, 6-7.

A letter from the President of SAH/NE concerning testimony urging deletion of a requirement to demolish the Charles Street Jail (1848) (NR) when a new prison is constructed.

PROMOTION OF SPECIAL EVENTS

"Christmas Success Downtown: Making It Happen!" Downtown Promotion Reporter. August 1981. Entire Issue.

PROPERTY TAX

"Historic Homes Get Tax Relief." Historic Hawai'i News. February 1983. p. 1.

PUBLIC BUILDINGS--ADAPTIVE USE

Crouch, Elizabeth G. and Robert Olson. "The Grand Rapids Art Museum: The Adaptive Reuse of an Historic Federal Building." Technology & Conservation. Fall 1981. pp. 28-36.

PUBLIC BUILDINGS--ADAPTIVE USE

Thomas, Margaret A. " Sales with a String Attached: Historic Public Buildings Preserved through Legal Controls". Small Town. March-April 1980. p. 19-23.

PUBLIC BUILDINGS--CONSERVATION AND RESTORATION

"Governments in Reuse and Preservation." Progressive Architecture November 1983. pp. 85-107.

CONTENTS: Old Post Office, St. Louis--Philadelphia City Hall--Florida's Old Capitol, Tallahassee--State Department Reception Rooms, Washington, D.C.--Chenango County Courthouse, N.Y.

PUBLIC BUILDINGS--CONSERVATION AND RESTORATION

Hoagland, Alison K. "District Building Restoration." D.C. Preservation League. Spring 1986. p. 5.

Plans to restore the exterior and rehabilitate the interior of the District Building.

PUBLIC BUILDINGS--CONSERVATION AND RESTORATION

Inghram, Cheryl A. and Melanie Betz. "Preserving County Courthouses and City Halls." Small Town. Vol. 15, No. 6, May/June 1985. p. 4-11.

PUBLIC BUILDINGS--CONSERVATION AND RESTORATION

Johnson, Ken. "New Life for Old State Education Building." Preservation League of New York State Newsletter. Vol. 12, No. 4. Fall 1986. p. 3.

New York's State Education Building undergoing 14-stage renovation including repainting of intricate ceiling in original colors and conversion of the former State Museum into office space.

PUBLIC BUILDINGS--CONSERVATION AND RESTORATION

McGraw, Peter A. "The Old Post Office and Federal Building in Dayton, Ohio: A Case History of Restoration and Adaptive Use." APT Bulletin. pp. 55-64.

PUBLIC BUILDINGS--CONSERVATION AND RESTORATION

McGraw, Peter A. "The Rehabilitation of the Old Post Office, Dayton, Ohio: Restoring/ Renovating an Historic Building for Multi-Purpose Use." Technology & Conservation. Fall 1981. pp. 16-21.

PUBLIC BUILDINGS--CONSERVATION AND RESTORATION

Mortner, Anders. "Restoring the Riksdagshus in Stockholm." Progressive Architecture. May 1984. pp. 33, 36, 39.

PUBLIC BUILDINGS--CONSERVATION AND RESTORATION

Saunders, Ivan J. "The Restoration of Government House, Regina, Saskatchewan: An Historian's Perspective." APT Bulletin. v.XII, no. 3, 1980. p. 130-147.

PUBLIC BUILDINGS--CONSERVATION AND RESTORATION-- U.S.--UTAH--SALT LAKE CITY

"A Salt Lake City/County Building Update: Everybody Wins." Heritage News, Utah Heritage Foundation. Jan./Feb. 1985. p. 1.

PUBLIC BUILDINGS--U.S.--CALIFORNIA--PASADENA

Scheid, Ann. "Pasadena Civic Center - A Brief History - Part II." SAH SCC Review (Society of Architectural Historians, Southern California Chapter). No. 1, 1985. p. 18-24.

PUBLIC BUILDINGS--U.S.--GOVERNMENT

Oulahan, Richard. "Capital's Doughty Dowager Becomes a New Cinderella." Smithsonian. Vol. 16, No. 12, Mar. 1986. p. 84-95.

Restoration of the Old Executive Office Building.

PUBLIC BUILDINGS--U.S.--WASHINGTON D.C.

"Federal Support Waning for Pension Building Restoration." Architecture, News. April 1984. p. 12.

PUBLIC HOUSING

Challenge!. June 1979.

Note: Several articles on the benefits of public housing.

PUBLIC HOUSING--U.S.--CALIFORNIA--SAN FRANCISCO

Canty, Donald. "Combining Artistry and Compassion: Public Housing Remodeled for Senior Citizens in San Francisco." Architecture. Vol. 74, No. 7, July 1985. p. 49-53.

PUBLIC LANDS

McCurdy, Howard E. "Making Public Lands Private: An Issue of Politics." Urban Land. Vol. 43, No. 8, August 1984. pp. 21-25.

Vertical File
PUBLIC RELATIONS

Dyer, Mary W. "Public Affairs: What's Involved." American Association for State and Local History. Technical Report 8, 1986. 10p. (VF)

PUBLIC RELATIONS

Gornto, Mary M. "Festivals are Effective Promotion Tools." Center City Report. June 1981. pp. 10-11.

PUBLIC RELATIONS

Hart, Jennifer C. "Public Relations for Public Approval." Urban Land. Vol. 45, No. 2. Feb. 1986. pp. 19-21.

PUBLIC RELATIONS

Morrison, Larry. "Public Relations and Public Image." <u>Museum News</u>, January-February 1979. pp.26-33.

PUBLICITY

Costello, Anthony. "The Powers of the Press: Communicating Preservation C Concepts Through Local Newspapers." <u>Small Town</u>. January-February, 1983. pp. 18-21.

PUBLICITY

"Public Relations Techniques." <u>The Commissioner</u>. Jan. 1987. p. 3-4.

PUBLISHERS AND PUBLISHING

Elkins, Sandra. "History's New Face: Historical Organizations Are Turning to Popular Magazine Formats to Capture a Wider Audience." <u>History News</u>. Vol. 40, No. 10, Oct. 1985. p. 13-17.

QUILTING

Hayden, Dolores and Peter Marris. "The Quiltmaker's Landscape." <u>Landscape</u>. Vol. 25, no. 3, 1981. pp. 39-47.

QUILTING

Lipsett, Linda Otto. "The Lives of a Quilt." <u>Yankee</u>. Vol. 49, No. 12, Dec. 1985. p. 84-91, 116-117.

QUILTING

"Old Quilts -- Their Care, Repair, and Display." <u>Early American Life</u>. Vol. 17, No. 5, Oct. 1986. p. 37-38.

Vertical File

QUILTING

"Quilts: From the Mississippi Heartland." <u>American Visions</u>. Vol. 1, No. 3. p. 28-32. (VF)

Quilting skills link generations of Afro-Americans to one another.

RAILROAD BRIDGES--MAINTENANCE AND REPAIR--U.S.-- COLORADO--GEORGETOWN

Zimmermann, Karl. "To There and Back: A Million-Dollar Bridge Reconstruction Completes a Historic Railroad Circuit." <u>Americana</u>. Vol. 13, No. 1, Mar./Apr. 1985. p. 66-70.

RAILROADS

Jones, James B. "Early Railroad Development in Tennessee, 1830 - 1860." <u>The Courier</u>. Vol. 25, No. 3. June 1987. pp. 4 - 5.

RAILROADS

"Northeast Corridor: On the Right Track". <u>Environmental Comment</u>. January 1980. Entire issue.

RAILROADS

Vreeland, Susan. "Roundup: Going By Steam." <u>Americana</u>. Vol. 13, No. 2, May/June 1985. p. 34-37, 91.

Historic steam lines cataloged.

RAILROADS--BUILDINGS AND STRUCTURES

Stanford, Linda Oliphant. "Railway Designs by Fellheimer and Wagner, New York to Cincinnati." <u>Queen City Heritage</u>. Vol. 43, No. 3, Fall 1985. p. 2-24.

Designers of the art deco Cincinnati Union Terminal (1929) are featured.

RAILROADS--BUILDINGS AND STRUCTURES--ADAPTIVE USE

"Founded on Play." <u>Architecture Minnesota</u>. Vol. 12, No. 1, Jan./Feb. 1986. p. 32-33.

An 1885 train shed is restored and used as a children's museum in St. Paul's Bandana Square complex.

RAILROADS--CARS

  Morison, Elting E. "The Absolute All-Ameri-
can Civilizer." American Heritage. Vol. 36, No.
4, June/July 1985. p. 54-57.

  The Pullman car is discussed.

RAILROADS--CONSERVATION AND RESTORATION

  Monk, David. "The Role of Railroads in
Preservation." Illinois Heritage Association.
Technical Insert. No. 22, July-August. 1986. 2p.

RAILROADS--DIRECTORIES

  Willard, L.F. "Catching the Color By Rail."
Yankee. Vol. 49, No. 10, Oct. 1985. p. 38-49.

  Schedules for New England's historic and
scenic railroads.

RAILROADS--HISTORY

  Gibson, Ted. "Keeping Hawaii's Railroads
Rolling." Historic Hawaii News. Jan. 1985.
p. 4-5.

RAILROADS--HISTORY--U.S.--NEW YORK--NEW YORK
  CITY

  Robertson, Kent A. "The Use of Grand
Central Station as an Urban Redevelopment Tool."
Urbanism Past & Present. Vol. 9, No. 18, Issue
2, Summer/Fall 1984. p. 26-33.

RAILROADS--HISTORY--U.S.--NORTH CAROLINA

  Bishir, Catherine. "Location Book of the
Raleigh and Gaston Railroad." IA. Vol. 5, No. 1,
1979. pp. 49-59.

RAILROADS--HISTORY--U.S.--NORTH CAROLINA

  Trelease, Allen W. "The Passive Voice: The
State and North Carolina Railroad, 1849-1871."
The North Carolina Historical Review. Vol. LXI,
No. 2, April 1984. pp. 174-205.

RAILROADS--MAINTENANCE AND REPAIR

  "Kentucky Town Uses CD (Community Develop-
ment) to Save Railroad, Enterprise Zone to Stem
Job Losses." Housing & Development Reporter.
Vol. 12, No. 14, August 27, 1984. p. 271.

RAILROADS--RIGHT OF WAY

  Marsolan, Ernest F. "Development Opportun-
ties on Railroad Rights-of-Way: Promises and
Pitfalls." Urban Land. Vol. 45, No. 2, Feb. 1986.
p. 2-6.

RAILROADS--STATIONS

  Bohi, Charles W. and H. Roger Grant. "The
Country Railroad Station as Corporate Logo."
The Journal of Historic American Material Culture:
Pioneer America. Aug. 1979. pp. 117-129.

RAILROADS--STATIONS

  Finnegan, Thomas. "From Union Station to
Corporate Headquarters: Norstar Plaza in Albany."
Preservation League of New York State Newsletter.
Vol. 13, No. 1. Winter 1987. p. 3.

RAILROADS--STATIONS

  Kyper, Frank. "Let's Stop Burning up Our
Rail Heritage." Timber Transfer. Vol. 3, No. 1.
Feb.-Apr. 1986. p. 16.

RAILROADS--STATIONS

  Lane, George, Jr. "Passenger Trains Gone
But Main Street Depot Saved ... " Florida
Preservation News. Vol. 3, No. 4. Jul./Aug. 1987.
p. 6.

  Seaboard Coastline depot in Arcadia,
Florida.

RAILROADS--STATIONS

  "Railroad Station to Be Restored." The
Indiana Preservationist. No. 4, 1986. p. 5.

  A Madison, Indiana, railroad station will
become a museum.

RAILROADS--STATIONS--ADAPTIVE USE

"Chicago Station to Become Mixed-Use Center." Architectural Record. Nov. 1985, p. 67.

RAILROADS--STATIONS--ADAPTIVE USE

DeLony, Eric N. "Savannah's Central of Georgia Railroad Shops Targeted as Tourist, Convention Center." Society for Industrial Archaeology Newsletter. Spring-Summer 1983. pp. 12-13.

RAILROADS--STATIONS--ADAPTIVE USE

"Edwardian Elegance: Roger Sherman Associates and the History and Landmarks Foundation Created a Restaurant Masterpiece in Pittsburgh." Progressive Architecture. Nov. 1979. pp. 66-69.

RAILROADS--STATIONS--ADAPTIVE USE

Reisdorff, Jim. "Whistle Stopping: Small Town Railroad Depot Preservation in Nebraska." Small Town. July-August 1982. pp. 4-8.

RAILROADS--STATIONS--ADAPTIVE USE

Rowland, David. "Train Depot Arrives in Fayettville." North Carolina Preservation. No. 63. May-June 1986. p. 3.

Conversion of a Romanesque Revival style train station into a restaurant.

RAILROAD--STATIONS--ADAPTIVE USE

"Shopping Center Developer Moves to Historic Station." The Preservation Report (Ala.). May/June 1983. p. 3.

RAILROADS--STATIONS--ADAPTIVE USE

White, Jane. "New Life for a Landmark." Riverside Avondale Preservation. Oct. 1986. pp. 4-6.

The Henry M. Flagler railroad terminal in Jacksonville, Florida converted to a convention center.

RAILROADS--STATIONS--ADAPTIVE USE

Wright, Gordon. "Old Terminal Gets Back on Track." Building Design & Construction. Vol. 27, No. 10, Oct. 1986. p. 98-99.

The largest adaptive reuse project ever undertaken in the U.S. involved the conversion of St. Louis Union Station into hotel and retail store space.

RAILROADS--STATIONS--ADAPTIVE USE--U.S.-- MISSOURI--ST. LOUIS

"Making a Dream Come True." Commercial Renovation. Vol. 7, No. 6, Dec. 1985. p. 26-33.

RAILROADS--STATIONS--ADAPTIVE USE--U.S.-- MISSOURI--ST. LOUIS

Morton, David. "The Spirit of St. Louis." Progressive Architecture. Nov. 1985. p. 83-93.

RAILROADS--STATIONS--ADAPTIVE USE--U.S.--MISSOURI --ST. LOUIS

"Union Station on Track for Late Summer Opening." National Mall Monitor. May/June 1985. p. 70.

RAILROADS--STATIONS--CONSERVATION AND RESTORATION

Hodges, Gail. "The Station Renovation-- Together We Did It!" Lake Forest Preservation Foundation Newsletter. Spring 1986. p. 3.

The historic Chicago and North Western Railroad Station in Lake Forest(IL) is restored.

RAILROADS--STATIONS--CONSERVATION AND RESTORATION

Kubinszky, Mihaly. "La Reconstruction d'une Oeuvre d'Eiffel, le Hall de la Gare de l'Ouest a Budapest." Monumentum. September 1983. pp. 209-220.

RAILROADS--STATIONS--CONSERVATION AND RESTORATION

Mills, Michael. "RR Station Restoration: Elizabeth." Preservation Perspective NJ. Vol. 4, No. 3, Mar./Apr. 1985. p. 1.

RAILROADS--STATIONS--CONSERVATION AND RESTORATION

"N.E. Train Project : Offsetting the Demise of Railroads is this Improvement Project that Brings New Life to 15 Stations." Architectural Record. July, 1979. pp. 120-121.

RAILROADS--STATIONS--CONSERVATION AND RESTORATION

"Plans to Revive Washington's Union Station Announced." Architecture. October 1984. pp. 33, 35.

RAILROADS--STATIONS--CONSERVATION AND RESTORATION

"Washington's Union Station: At last back on the right track". Architectural Record. Feb. 1985. p. 59.

RAILROADS--STATIONS--CONSERVATION AND RESTORATION-- AUSTRALIA

"Ballarat Railway Station (1862) Restored." Trust News. Bol. 13, No. 11. June 1985. pp. 4-5.

RAILROADS--STATIONS--CONSERVATION AND RESTORATION-- CANADA

Murphy, Gavin. "Canada's Train Stations: Destination Oblivion or Protection." Canadian Heritage. Vol. 2, No. 3. Jul./Aug. 1985. pp. 28-33.

RAILROADS--STATIONS--CONSERVATION AND RESTORATION-- CANADA--TORONTO

Weaver, Martin E. "Union Station gets the Cinderella Treatment." Canadian Heritage. Vol. 2, No. 3. Jul./Aug. 1985. pp. 36-38.

RAILROADS--STATIONS--CONSERVATION AND RESTORATION-- U.S.--CALIFORNIA

"Caltrans Restores Station." California Preservation. Vol. 10, No. 1. Jan. 1985. p. 1.

RAILROADS--STATIONS--CONSERVATION AND RESTORATION-- U.S.--GEORGIA--COLUMBUS

"SOS Station in Distress." The Rambler, Newsletter of the Georgia Trust. Vol. 11, No. 3. Summer 1984. p. 1.

RAILROADS--STATIONS--U.S.--ILLINOIS--CHICAGO

Farrar, William G. "In Memoriam the Chicago and North Western Passenger Terminal 1908-?" Historic Illinois. Vol. 6, No. 6, April 1984. pp. 6-7.

RAILROADS--STATIONS--CONSERVATION AND RESTORATION --U.S.--ILLINOIS--CHICAGO

Slaton, Deborah. "Dearborn Station: Roman-esque Renaissance." Inland Architect. Vol. 29, No. 3, May/June 1985. p. 16.

RAILROADS--STATIONS--CONSERVATION AND RESTORA-TION--U.S.--INDIANA--HOBART

Christianson, Elin. "Historical Society Acts as Developer of Depot." The Indiana Preservationist. No. 6, 1984. p. 7.

RAILROADS--STATIONS--CONSERVATION AND RESTORA-TION--U.S.--MARYLAND--BALTIMORE

"Pennsylvania Station is Back on the Right Track." Commercial Renovation. August 1984. pp. 34-39.

RAILROADS--STATIONS--U.S.--MASSACHUSETTS--BOSTON

Bahne, Charles. "Boylston Station Update." Boston Preservation Alliance Letter. Vol. 7, No. 1, Jan. 1986. p. 11.

MBTA stripping of original fabric from 1897 NHL, one of the first two subway stations in America, stopped.

RAILROADS--STATIONS--U.S.--MINNESOTA--LITTLE FALLS

"Little Falls Depot on the Move?" Preservation Matters. Vol. 2, No. 2, Feb. 1986. p. 1.

Discussion of a train depot in Little Falls, Minn., designed by Cass Gilbert in 1899.

RAILROADS--STATIONS--CONSERVATION AND RESTORATION--
U.S.--MISSOURI--ST. LOUIS

"St. Louis Union Station Opens." Landmarks
Letter. Vol. 20, No. 5. Sep. 1985. p. 5.

RAILROADS--STATIONS--U.S.--WASHINGTON--SEATTLE

"Union Station Redevelopment." Progressive
Architecture. Jan. 1986. p. 125-127.

Winner of a P/A award.

RAILROADS--U.S.--COLORADO

Kyper, Frank. "Tale of Two Cities,
Part I: Durnago & Silverton." Timber
Transfer. Vol. 3, No. 2, May-June 1986.
p. 12.

RAILROADS--U.S.--ILLINOIS--CHICAGO

"Interurban Railroad History to be Pre-
Served." Courier (NPS Newsletter). Vol. 30,
No. 6, June 1985. p. 4.

Chicago South Shore and South Bend Railroad,
an electric interurban railline, to be preserved
under aegis of Indiana Dunes National Lake Shore.

RAILROADS--U.S.--NEW ENGLAND

"Timothy Mellon's Big Gamble on a Little
Business." Business Week. October 8, 1984.
pp. 191-192.

RANCHES--U.S.--ARIZONA

Linden, Patricia. "The Last Great Ranches
of Arizona." Town and Country. Mar. 1986. p. 139-
149.

REAL ESTATE BUSINESS

Curtis, Cathy. "Museums on the Move,
Creative Alternatives in Real Estate."
Museum News. June 1983. pp. 62-69.

REAL ESTATE BUSINESS

Gerell, Bob. "Creative Financing."
Historic Hawai'i News. November 1981. p. 6.

REAL ESTATE BUSINESS

Madsen, Stephany A. "Urban Timesharing."
Urban Land. February 1983. pp. 14-19.

REAL ESTATE BUSINESS

Real Estate Issues. Vol. 6, No. 1,
Spring/Summer 1981.

CONTENTS: McGuire, Chester C. Urban Revitalization
and Rent Control in the District of Columbia.

REAL ESTATE BUSINESS

Special Section: Real Estate Opportunities;
"Should You Get Involved in Real Estate Develop-
ment?"; Stewart, Perry. "Syndications: The Basics
for CBD's"; and Borof, Irwin J. "Structuring
Nonprofit's Role in Real Estate Syndications."
Goldman, John and Larry Green. "Law-Tech Revival:
A Shot in the Arm for Inner Cities." The Grants-
manship Center News. Vol. 12, No. 2, Issue 58,
Spring/Summer 1984. pp. 12-37, 64-66.

REAL ESTATE DEVELOPMENT

Dietsch, Deborah K. "Cooking with History."
Architectural Record. Jan. 1987. p. 84-93.

Washington Harbour, Washington D.C.'s
elaborate complex of offices, retail stores,
restaurants, and condominiums has created
controversy.

REAL ESTATE DEVELOPMENT

Porter, Douglas R. "Deal Making in Dallas."
Urban Land. Vol. 45, No. 2, Feb. 1986. p. 10-13.

REAL ESTATE INVESTMENT

Wetterer, Charles C. "Seeking High Yields
from Real Estate Partnerships: A model for
analyzing investor return from public programs".
Real Estate Finance. Vol. 1, No. 4, Winter
1985. p. 51-61.

REAL ESTATE MARKET

"Rehab's Place in the Real Estate Market: Emerging Trends." Urban Conservation Report. October 31, 1983. p. 6.

REAL PROPERTY--VALUATION

Barlow, Marc Phillip. "How to Make an Inspection." The Appraisal Journal. Vol. 53, No. 4, Oct. 1985. p. 606-616.

REAL PROPERTY AND TAXATION

Blumenberg, Anne. "Fees, please: Cutting and Coping with Settlement Costs." Cost Cuts (The Enterprise Foundation). Vol. 2, No. 8, June 1985. p. 1, 8-10.

REAL PROPERTY TAX--U.S.--HAWAII

Rohter, Sharlene. "The Lowdown on Historic Home Real Property Tax." Historic Hawaii News. Vol. 10, No. 10, November 1984. p. 9.

RECORDING AND REGISTRATION

Letellier, Robin. "Heritage Recording : An Essential Activity within the Conservation Process of Historic Resources." APT Bulletin. Vol. 18, No. 1 & 2, 1986. p. 109-112.

REGIONAL PLANNING

"Comparitive Perspectives on Public Participation." Town Planning Review. July 1981. pp. 257-297.

CONTENTS: Garner, J.F. Editorial Introducation--Fogg, Alan. Public Participation in Australia--Suetens, L.P. Public Participation in Belgium--Kimminich, Otto. Public Participation in the Federal Republic of Germany--Bjerken, M.T. Public Participation in Sweden--Callies, David. Public Participation in the United States--Garner, J.F. Editorial Postscript.

REINFORCED CONCRETE

Billington, David P. "Solomon Cady Hollister Colloquium: Perspectives on the History of Reinforced Concrete in the United States, 1904-1941: Princeton University, June 2, 1980." Technology and Culture. October 1981. 757-759.

RELOCATION (HOUSING)

Clay, Phillip L. "Managing the Urban Reinvestment Process." Journal of Housing. Oct. 1979. pp. 453-458.

RELOCATION (HOUSING)

"Development Without Displacement (A Theme for the 1980's)--Closing the Low-Income Housing Gap: The Case for Affordable Housing in Chicago." Chicago Rehab Network Reports. December 1981.

RELOCATION (HOUSING)

Kamens, Peg. "Fighting Displacement in Loisaida." City Limits. Vol. 12, No. 2. Feb. 1987. pp. 18-20.

RELOCATION (HOUSING)

Klibanow, Saul H. and Norman A. Katz. "Sensitive Relocation Plan Needed to Skirt Rehabilitation Program Delays, Problems." Journal of Housing. November 1981. pp. 540-544.

RELOCATION (HOUSING)

White, Sammis. "Displacement : Is It the Real Enemy?" Urbanism Past and Present. Summer/Fall 1981. pp. 21-29.

RELOCATION (HOUSING)

Witte, William A. "Reinvestment: The Federal Status." Journal of Housing. Oct. 1979. pp. 459-460.

RENTAL HOUSING

Mandel, Michael. "A Real Look at Rent Control." City Limits. Vol. 11, No. 5. May 1986. pp. 10-14.

Author debunks the idea that rent controls cause abandonment of buildings.

RENTAL HOUSING

O'Mara, W. Paul. "Rehab and Rentals: Producing a Long-term Gain from an Interim Marriage." Urban Land. February 1984. pp. 8-11.

RENTAL HOUSING--U.S.--WASHINGTON, D.C.

Bredemeier, Kenneth. "Washington's Rent Control Battle: Who Wins, Who Loses?" Urban Land, Vol. 44, No. 6, June 1985. p. 34-35.

RESORT BUILDINGS

Hanlin, Chris. "Two-Stepping Down the West Shore: Early Twentieth-Century Dance Halls Along Lake Michigan." Chronicle. Vol. 23, No. 1. May - June 1987. pp. 4 - 8.

RESORT BUILDINGS

McCormick, Nancy D. and John S. McCormick. Saltair. Salt Lake City: University of Utah Press, 1985 (GV1853.3.U825245)

An elaborate Moorish style resort on the Great Salt Lake dating from the 1890s burned down in 1970.

RESORT BUILDINGS--ENGLAND

Secrest, Meryle. "Bumptious Bath, the Town That Beau Nash Built." Smithsonian. Vol. 15, No. 8, November 1984. pp. 122-135.

RESORT BUILDINGS--U.S.--NEW YORK STATE--SARATOGA

"Race Track Renovations." Current Issues, Saratoga Springs Preservation Foundation, Inc. Vol. 9, Nos. 7-8, July/Aug. 1985. p. 2.

RESORT BUILDINGS --U.S. OREGON

Failing, Patricia. "Timberline Lodge". Americana, April, 1980. pp. 33-38.

RESORTS

Kimball, Michael. "Old Orchard Beach, Maine." Yankee. Vol. 51, No. 8. Aug. 1987. pp. 58 - 67; 106 - 107.

RESORTS

Todhunter, Rodger. "Banff and the Canadian National Park Idea." Landscape. Vol. 25, No. 2. pp.33-39.

RESORTS--U.S.--NEW YORK--SARATOGA SPRINGS

Broderick, Mosette Glaser. "Saratoga Springs, New York, the Queen of American Resorts." Antiques. Vol. 128, No. 1, July 1985. p. 96-110.

RESORTS--U.S.--NEW YORK--SARATOGA SPRINGS

"National Park Service Considers Casino For Landmark Status." Current Issues, Saratoga Springs Preservation Foundation, Inc. Vol. 9, No. 8, Nov./Dec. 1985. p. 4.

Focuses on Congress Park and the Canfield Casino.

RESTAURANTS, LUNCH ROOMS, ETC.

Hess, Alan. "The Origins of McDonald's Golden Arches." Journal of the Society of Architectural Historians. Vol. 45, No. 1. Mar. 1986. pp. 60-67.

RESTAURANTS, LUNCHROOMS, ETC.--CONSERVATION AND RESTORATION

O'Lear, Michael P. "McPreservation or McRenovation." Regional Conference of Historical Agencies. Vol. 14, no. 3. March 1984. pp. 1-4.

REVOLVING FUNDS

"CD, UDAG Revolving Loans Spark Unassisted Developement in Lynchburg." Housing and Development Reporter. March 28, 1983. p. 949.

REVOLVING FUNDS

Finger, Bill. "History for Sale." _Americana_. Vol. 15, No. 2, May/June 1987. p. 50-54.

Revolving fund of North Carolina; also a brief summary of such activity in other states.

REVOLVING FUNDS

"Governor Proposes Bonds for Preservation, Conservation." _PPS News_, Newsletter of the Providence Preservation Society. Vol. XXII, No. 2, March/April 1984. pp. 1, 6.

REVOLVING FUNDS

"HSDF Forms Revolving Fund to Provide Financing for Restoration." _Historic South Dakota_. Summer 1983. p. 1.

REVOLVING FUNDS

"Improvement Loan Funds: New Techniques, New Money." _Downtown Idea Exchange_. Vol. 32, No. 16, Aug. 15, 1985. p. 1-2.

REVOLVING FUNDS

Jones, Tommy. "Revolving Funds: A Revolution for Historic Preservation." _The Rambler_. Vol. 14, No. 1, Spr. 1987. P. 12.

REVOLVING FUNDS

King, Mary. "Lilly Endowment Grant Funds Creative New Housing Program." _The Indiana Preservationist_. No. 2, 1982. p. 10.

REVOLVING FUNDS

"Local Revolving Funds Make Preservation Happen." _North Carolina Preservation_. No. 64, July-Aug. 1986. p. 4-7.

REVOLVING FUNDS

MacDonell, Amy. "Assessing the Effect of the Revolving Fund." _Landmarks Observer_. Sep.-Oct. 1982. pp. 10-11.

REVOLVING FUNDS

Manget, Diane. "The Historic Faubourg St. Mary Corporation." _New Orleans Preservation in Print_. July 1983. p. 6.

REVOLVING FUNDS

"The Preservation Loan Program, San Francisco's Heritage Revolving Loan Fund Aids Low-Income Homeowners." _California Preservation_. Spring 1982. p. 8.

REVOLVING FUNDS

"Revolving Fund Assists Renovation of County Landmark." _Preservation Press_, Preservation Alliance of Louisville and Jefferson County. Vol. X, No. 1, Spring 1984. pp. 1, 4.

REVOLVING FUNDS

"Revolving Funds Can Keep Downtown Action Rolling." _Downtown Idea Exchange_. Vol. 33, No. 18, Sept. 15, 1986. p. 1-2.

REVOLVING FUNDS

Simon, Jeffrey. "Land Bank Deals Massachusetts New Developments." _Urban Land_. July 1982. pp. 10-17.

REVOLVING FUNDS--U.S.--CONNECTICUT--BRIDGEPORT

"'Adopt a House' Project Spurs Bridgeport Revitalization." _Stone Soup_. Winter 1985. p. 13.

Neighborhood Housing Service and Rotary Club joint effort described.

REVOLVING FUNDS--U.S.--CONNECTICUT--HARTFORD

"Revolving Fund Base Helps Hartford Group to Grow as Housing Rehabilitation Developer." Economic Growth & Revitalization. No. 86-4, Feb. 25, 1986. p. 1-2.

REVOLVING FUNDS--U.S.--NEW YORK--NEW YORK CITY

"Unusual Revolving Loan Fund Begins to Pay Out." Urban Conservation Report. Vol. VIII, No. 6, March 30, 1984. p. 4.

REVOLVING FUNDS--U.S.--RHODE ISLAND--PROVIDENCE

Schoettle, Clark. "Revolving Fund Adds New Neighborhood." PPS News. Jan./Feb. 1986. p. 3.

Update on the Providence Preservation Society Revolving Fund.

RHODE ISLAND--NEWPORT--CASINO

Gordon, Barclay F. "Newport is Host to a National Home for Court Tennis." Architectural Record. April 1981. p.106-111.

RHODE ISLAND--NEWPORT--CHATEAU-SUR-MER

Cherol, John A. "Chateau-sur-Mer in Newport, Rhode Island". Antiques. December 1980. p.1220-1225.

RHODE ISLAND--NEWPORT--KINGSCOTE

Cherol, John A. "Kingscote in Newport, Rhode Island". Antiques. Sept. 1980. p. 476-485.

RHODE ISLAND--PROVIDENCE

Brown, Patricia Leigh. "Providence: This New England Community is Thriving Again Thanks to a Citywide Preservation Movement." American Preservation. Vol. 4, #2. pp. 9-24.

RIVERS

"American Rivers Seeks Protection for Eight Rivers." American Rivers. Vol. 14, No. 3, Sept. 1986. p. 4-5.

RIVERS

Bowman, David. "Memphis Plans a Greenway for Wolf River." Place. Vol. 4, No. 6, June 1984. pp. 4-5.

RIVERS

"Federal Budget Cuts to Affect River Programs." River Conservation Update. Feb. 1986. p. 1.

RIVERS

"Interior Department 'unprotects' Rivers." American Rivers (American Rivers Conservation Council). Vol. 13, No. 1, Mar. 1985. p. 1, 10.

RIVERS

"Just Three of Twenty-Four Wild and Scenic Studies Recommend Protection." American Rivers. Vol. 13, No. 2, June 1985. p. 4.

RIVERS

Lynott, Mark J. "Past Patterns of Human Adaptation: Ozark National Scenic Riverways." NPS, CRM Bulletin. Vol. 7, No. 1, April 1984. p. 10.

RIVERS

Pontier, Glenn. "Impasse on the Upper Delaware." Planning. Vol. 50, No. 8, August 1984. pp. 14-21.

RIVERS

Primm, Alexander. "Heat on the River: A Look at the Wild and Scenic River System." American Land Forum Magazine. Fall 1983. pp. 52-59.

RIVERS

"Threatened Rivers of the Northwest." American Rivers (American Rivers Conservation Council). Vol. 13, No. 1, Mar. 1985. p. 6-8.

Fourth in a series of analyses of the nation's rivers.

RIVERS

Trends, Spring 1979.

Note: Issue on "Trends in Rivers and Trails."

RIVERS

Wagner, Mary. "Preserving Columbia Gorge and Its Tributaries." American Rivers. Vol. 14, No. 3, Sept. 1986. p. 6-7.

RIVERS--U.S.--CONNECTICUT

Clark, Edie. "The Colors of the River." Yankee. Vol. 49, No. 10, Oct. 1985. p. 102-109, 156-167.

The Connecticut River and structures along it discussed.

RIVERS--U.S.--MAINE

Neily, Sandra D. "The Most Threatened River in the Nation: Maine's West Branch Penobscot." American Rivers. Vol. 13, No. 2, June 1985. p. 1, 12.

RIVERS--U.S.--VIRGINIA

"Virginia River Policy Developed." Tidings. Vol. 7, No. 2. Summer 1986. p. 3.

ROADS

"Status Report: Protecting Scenic Roads." Piedmont Environmental Council Newsreporter. Jan. 1987. p. 3.

ROADS

Swerkstrom, Buz. "A Step Backward." Americana. Vol. 12, No. 6, Jan./Feb. 1985. p. 9.

Wisconsin Rustic Roads program described.

ROADS

Wilson, Richard Guy. "The Heyday of Highway and Bridge Building." Metropolis. Dec. 1986. p. 62-65.

Highways and bridges of the 1920's and 1930's.

ROADS--CONSERVATION AND RESTORATION--U.S.--COLORADO--DENVER

"History Being Restored to Speer." Historic Denver News. Vol. 15, No. 8, Aug. 1986. p. 1, 5.

Historic features along Speer Boulevard in Denver have been identified and the streetscape will be restored.

ROADS--HISTORY

Hokanson, Drake. "The Lincoln Highway." The Bracket, Iowa State Historical Department. Summer '83. pp. 2-5.

ROADS--HISTORY

Hokanson, Drake. "To Cross America, Early Motorists Took a Long Detour." Smithsonian. Vol. 16, No. 5, Aug. 1985. p. 58-65.

The Lincoln Highway, first transcontinental auto route detailed.

ROADS--HISTORY

Lay, K. Edward and Nathaniel Mason Pawlett. "Architectural Surveys Associated with Early Road Systems". APT Bulletin. V.XII no.2, 1980. p. 3-36.

ROADS--HISTORY

"San Francisco Supervisors Vote to Demolish Freeway." Architecture. Jan. 1986. p. 18.

ROADS--HISTORY

Schlereth, Thomas J. "Doing History on the Road: The Above-Ground Archaeology of the American Highway." Chronicle, Quarterly Magazine of the Michigan Historical Society of Michigan. Vol. 20, No. 3, Fall 1984. pp. 14-17.

ROADS--HISTORY

Schust, Sunny Maye. "Route 66 is Officially Wiped Off the Map." Nation's Cities Weekly. July 15, 1985. p. 6.

ROADS--LAW AND LEGISLATION

Miller, Arthur. "From Truck Route to Tour Road: A Success Story for Delaware Water Gap." Courier. Vol. 31, No. 6, June 1986. p. 10-11.

Heavy traffic prohibited from using Route 204 through the Delaware Water Gap National Recreation Area, the result of state (Pa.) and federal legislation.

ROADS--U.S.--NEW HAMPSHIRE

Clark, Tim. "The Kancamagus Highway, New Hampshire". Yankee. Vol. 49, No. 3, Mar. 1985. p. 54-59.

Travel editors name highway one of five most scenic highways in America.

ROADS--U.S.--VIRGINIA

"Citizens Seek Protection for Scenic Roads." Newsreporter. (Piedmont, Va., Environmental Council) Aug. 1986. p. 1-2.

ROADS, BRICK

Harmon, Kalynn. "Franklin Battles to Save Brick Streets." The Indiana Preservationist. No. 3, 1984. p. 2.

ROADS, BRICK

McCollum, Dannel. "Brick Street Protection." Illinois Heritage Association Newsletter. Vol. 2, No. 6, November/December 1984. Technical Insert #12. 2 pp.

ROADS, BRICK

Robinson, Michael C. and Simon, Mary. "Information Exchange ; (Column on Brick Roads." APWA Reporter. November 1981. p. 22.

ROADS, BRICK

Sorenson, Sharon. "Paved in Brick." Americana. Vol. 13, No. 1, Mar./Apr. 1985. p. 9.

ROMANESQUE REVIVAL (ARCHITECTURE)

Henry, Jay C. "The Richardsonian Romanesque in Texas: An Interpretation". Texas Architect. March/April 1981. pp. 52-59

ROOFING

Azevedo, J. "Metal Roofing: Sorting Through the Confusing Array of Metals, Patterns and Coatings.", Fine Homebuilding, No. 24, December 1984/January 1985, pp. 42-46.

ROOFING

Marshall, P.C. "Polychromatic Roofing Slate of Vermont and New York. The Association for Preservation Technology Bulletin, number 3 1979. pp. 77-87.

ROOFING

Marshall, Philip C. "Slated for Preservation." Landmarks Observer (Portland, Maine). p. 1.

ROOFS

"Nuts and Bolts, On the Roof." <u>Canadian Heritage</u>. February 1982. pp. 38-40.

ROOFS

Pierpont, Robert N. "Slate Roofing." <u>APT Bulletin</u>. Vol. 19, No. 2, 1987. p. 10-23.

ROOFS

Sim, Andrew. "The Changing Face of Thatch." <u>Traditional Homes</u>. Vol. 3, No. 8, May 1987. p. 42-44.

ROOFS

"Thatch As a Modern Building Material." <u>The Architects' Journal</u>. Vol. 184, No. 36, Sept. 3, 1986. p. 57-69.

ROOFS--MAINTENANCE AND REPAIR

Brunsman, Keith. "Repairing Slate and Tile Roofs", <u>St. Louis Home</u>, Vol. 5, No.1, 1985, p.33.

ROOFS--MAINTENANCE AND REPAIR

DeDominicis, Al. "Rebuilding a Victorian Bell Tower." <u>Fine Homebuilding</u>. No. 30, Dec. 1985 /Jan. 1986. p. 42-45.

ROOFS--MAINTENANCE AND REPAIR

Engle, Reed. "Restoration of a Roofing." <u>CRM Bulletin</u>. Vol. 8, No. 6, Dec. 1985. p. 4-5, 15.

Historic photographs verify a vernacular form of roofing employing biaxially tapered shakes.

ROOFS--MAINTENANCE AND REPAIR

Jowers, Walter. "Standing Seam Roofs." <u>The Old House Journal</u>. Vol. 13, No. 2, Mar. 1985. p. 35, 44-48.

ROOFS--MAINTENANCE AND REPAIR

Labine, Clem. "Roofing: Repair or replace?" <u>Old-House Journal</u>. February 1981. p. 29-32.

ROOFS--MAINTENANCE AND REPAIR

Leeke, John. "Caring for Wooden Gutters." <u>Landmarks Observer</u>. Vol. 12, No. 6, Nov./Dec. 1985. p. 12.

ROOFS--MAINTENANCE AND REPAIR

"Maintenance and Repair of Roofs." <u>City Limits</u>. Vol. 11, No. 5. May 1986. p. 15.

ROOFS--MAINTENANCE AND REPAIR

"Paint for Terne." <u>Old House Journal</u>. Vol. 13, No. 3, Apr. 1985. p. 68.

ROOFS--MAINTENANCE AND REPAIR

"Restoration and Maintenance Techniques for the Antique House." <u>The Old-House Journal</u>. April 1983. Special Issue.

ROOFS--MAINTENANCE AND REPAIR

"Slate roofs". <u>Old House Journal</u>. May 1980. p.49-55.

ROOFS--MAINTENANCE AND REPAIR

Waite, John G. "Tinplate and Terneplate Roofing: Preservation and Repair." Old-House Journal. March 1981. p. 53, 68-69.

ROOFS--MAINTENANCE AND REPAIR--U.S.--KANSAS

Rockhill, Dan and Terry Marmet. "Lane University Roof Trusses Repaired with Epoxy." Kansas Preservation. Vol. 8, No. 1, Nov./Dec. 1985. p. 1-3.

RURAL PLANNING

Environmental Comment, February 1979. Articles on rural land use and development.

ROW HOUSES

Massey, James C. and Shirley Maxwell. "From Elegant Townhouse to Plain Rowhouse: the Party Wall House." The Old House Journal. Vol. 13, No. 7, Aug./Sept. 1985. p. 154-155.

RURAL CONDITIONS

Dahms, Fred. "Wroxeter, Ontario: The Anatomy of a 'Dying' Village." Small Town. September-October 1983. pp. 17-23.

RURAL DEVELOPMENT

"Goodbye, West Loudoun? PEC says No." Piedmont Environmental Council Newsreporter. May 1987. pp. 1 - 2. Proposed subdivisions threaten Loudoun County, VA.

RURAL DEVELOPMENT

"New York Law Establishes New Rural Revitalization Program." Housing and Development Reporter. August 29, 1983. pp. 281-282.

RURAL DEVELOPMENT

Phillips, Patrick. " Growth Management in Hardin County, Kentucky, A Model for Rural Areas." Urban Land. Vol. 46, No. 6. June 1987. pp. 16 - 21.

RURAL DEVELOPMENT

"Rural Development, Historic Preservation Approved for Funding." Community Development Digest. No. 86-18, Sept. 23, 1986. p. 3-5.

RURAL DEVELOPMENT--U.S.--CALIFORNIA

Banham, Reyner, PhD. "The Greening of High Tech in Silicon Valley." Architecture. Mar. 1985. p. 110-119.

RURAL DEVELOPMENT--U.S.--LOUISIANA--BOGALUSA

Wagner, Fritz and Lee G. Gibson. "Revitalizing a Single Industry Town." Small Town. Vol. 14, No. 5, March-April 1984. pp. 22-24.

RURAL PLANNING

Altman, Ross J. "Historic Preservation Tied with New Development : Glenbrook, Nevada." Urban Land. October 1981. pp. 3-11.

RURAL PLANNING

Angevin, Susan. "Preserving the Rural West." American Land Forum. Vol. 6, No. 3, Summer 1986. p. 13-14.

RURAL PLANNING

Canagir, Mevlut and Steven Kraft. "Suburbia Meets Farm." Landscape Architecture. July 1983. pp. 79-80.

RURAL PLANNING

Environmental Comment May 1980.

CONTENTS: Miller, Robert E. "Jackson Hole:
A Fading Frontier" p.4-9
Stokes, Samuel N. "Rural Conservation"
p. 10-15.

RURAL PLANNING

"Farmland Protection Policy Act to Be
Strengthened." *Farmland Notes*. Vol. 6, No. 2.
Feb. 1987. p. 1.

RURAL PLANNING

Glenn, Jane. "Can This Province Be Saved?"
Planning. Vol. 51, No. 3, Mar. 1985. p. 22-23.

RURAL PLANNING

Hansen, Tim. "Entrances to Small
Towns: Front Door or Twilight Zone?"
Small Town. September-October 1983.
pp. 24-27.

RURAL PLANNING

Heimstra, Hal and Nancy Bushwick. "How
States Are Saving Farmland." *American Land Forum*.
Vol. 6, No. 2. Spring 1986. pp. 60-65.

RURAL PLANNING

Holding, Julie L. "A New View of the
Countryside--a Comparison of Countryside
Planning in England and Wales and Teton County,
Wyoming." *The Planner*. Dec. 1986. p. 19-22.

RURAL PLANNING

Lewis, Sylvia. "Circuit Riders: Locals
Love Them." *Planning*. May 1982. pp. 18-22.

RURAL PLANNING

Miller, Clara Gellermann. "Local History as
a Guide to Planning: A Case study of Trumansburg,
New York." *Small Town*. Vol. 10, Nos. 1-6.
Jul.-Dec. 1979. pp. 4-12.

RURAL PLANNING

Reeder, Marie. "McDonald's Farm." *Landmark*.
Vol. 3, No. 1. Summer 1986. pp. 22-23.

Vertical File

RURAL PLANNING

Reganold, John P. "Boundary Review Boards:
a Legislative Approach to Manage Growth Conflicts
in the Urban Fringe in Washington State."
Landscape and Urban Planning. Vol. 13, No. 3.
June 1986. (VF)

RURAL PLANNING

"Rural Heritage." *A Future for Our
Past*. No. 20-1983. Entire Issue.
CONTENTS: Neuwirth, Frank. The Urbanisation
of the Countryside--Crozet, Jacques. Rural
Europe and the Heritage--Council of Europe
Action and the Rural Heritage--Woollett,
Stephen. Village Ventures--Mosel, Manfred.
Public Awareness.

RURAL PLANNING

Tishler, William H. "Historic Preservation
in Tomorrow's Rural Landscape." *11593*. June 1980.
pp. 1; 5-8.

RURAL PLANNING

Topping, Kenneth C. "Thinking Big in
California." *Planning*. Ocotber 1982. pp. 16-
20.

RURAL PLANNING--CONSERVATION AND RESTORATION

"The Agricultural Land Preservation Issue:
Recommendations for Balancing Urban and
Agricultural Land Needs." *Urban Land*. July 1982.
pp. 18-26.

RURAL PLANNING--CONSERVATION AND RESTORATION

Blacksell, Mark. "The Spirit and Purpose of National Parks in Britain." Parks. January, February, March 1982. pp. 15-17.

RURAL PLANNING--CONSERVATION AND RESTORATION

"Columbia Land ConservancyOrganizes." Hudson River Heritage Newsletter. Vol. 12, No. 1, Feb. 1987. p. 6.

Newly-formed group will focus on "Preservation of farmland, open spaces and the rural character of Columbia County (NY)."

RURAL PLANNING--CONSERVATION AND RESTORATION

"The Farmyard Revival." Heritage Outlook. July/August 1982. pp. 103-106.

RURAL PLANNING--CONSERVATION AND RESTORATION

Koop, Michael H. and Steve McNeil. "Planning in Rural Dane County, Wisconsin: A Regional Perception of Historical Development in Five Communities." Pioneer America Society Transactions. 1982. pp. 45-53.

RURAL PLANNING--CONSERVATION AND RESTORATION

Kwong, Jo Ann. "Farmland Preservation: the Evolution of State and Local Policies." Urban Land. Vol. 46, No. 1, Jan. 1987. p. 20-23.

RURAL PLANNING--CONSERVATION AND RESTORATION

"Loudon Adopts Rural Plan, Approves Virginia's First Density Transfer." Piedmont Environmental Council Newsreporter. November 1984. pp. 1-4.

RURAL PLANNING--CONSERVATION AND RESTORATION

MacEwen, Malcolm. " Retreat from Conservation, Behind the Hedgerows of Britain's National Parks. And Then there were None. " Landscape Architecture. January 1982. pp. 86-91.

RURAL PLANNING--CONSERVATION AND RESTORATION

Patton, Phil. "The Brandywine Valley: preserving the pastoral for present and future." Smithsonian. Vol. 15, No. 12, Mar. 1985. p. 150-163.

RURAL PLANNING--CONSERVATION AND RESTORATION

"The Sautee and Nacoochee Valleys: A Preservation Study." Landscape Architecture. Sep./Oct. 1983. pp. 66-69.

RURAL PLANNING--CONSERVATION AND RESTORATION

Toner, Bill. "Ag Zoning Gets Serious." Planning. Vol. 50, No. 12, December 1984. pp. 19-25.

RURAL PLANNING--CONSERVATION AND RESTORATION

Turner, Tim. "Preservation Country Style." Architecture Minnesota. November/December 1983. p. 19.

RURAL PLANNING--CONSERVATION AND RESTORATION--GREAT BRITAIN

Sheppard, Stephen R.J. "Monitoring Change at the Grass Roots." Landscape Architecture. May 1983. pp. 53-55.

RURAL PLANNING--CONSERVATION AND RESTORATION--U.S.--ILLINOIS

"Rural Preservation Takes Root in Illinois." Landmarks Preservation Council of Illinois. Vol. 15, No. 1, Jan./Feb. 1986. p. 1, 4.

RURAL PLANNING--CONSERVATION AND RESTORATION--U.S.--INDIANA

Miles, Mark. "Conserving the Rural Landscape." The Indiana Preservationist. No. 6, 1984. p. 4-5.

RURAL PLANNING--GREAT BRITAIN

Brotherton, Ian. "Development Pressures and Control in the National Parks, 1966-1981." Town and Country Planning. October 1982. pp. 439-459.

RURAL PLANNING--GREAT BRITAIN

"Protecting the Countryside: Progress by Consensus and Consent." Country Life. Vol. 158, No. 4650, Oct. 2, 1986. p. 1006.

RURAL PLANNING--U.S.--OREGON

Daniels, Tom. "Directing Growth: Oregon Style." American Land Forum. Vol. 6, No. 1, Winter 1986. p. 5-8.

Discussion of land resource management to accommodate rural newcomers in a productive farm area without losing the land's productivity.

SAILING SHIPS

Foote, Timothy. "Working Sailboats: An Endangered Species." Smithsonian. Vol. 15, No. 9, December 1984. pp. 72-84.

SALVAGE (ARCHITECTURAL)

Donegan, Frank. "In the Marketplace: Architecturals." Americana. Vol. 12, No. 4, September/October 1984. pp. 18, 20-21, 34.

SALVAGE (ARCHITECTURAL)

Hammond, Margo. "Rubble with a Cause: Armed with Cross Bars and Flashlights, Youngsters from Bedford-Stuyvesant Are Turning Plunder into Profit." Metropolis. July/Aug. 1985. p. 26-27, 31.

Discussion of production of ornamental sculpture which is being saved from buildings to to be demolished.

SALVAGE (ARCHITECTURAL)

"Have I got a Gargoyle for You." Planning. November 1982. pp. 7-8.

SANDSTONE

Matero, Frank G. and Jeanne M. Teutonico. "The Use of Architectural Sandstone in New York City in the 19th Century." APT Bulletin. Vol. XIV, No. 2, 1982. pp. 11-17.

SAMPLING

"How to Select a Random Sample from your Files." Rehab Notes. Vol. 10, No. 4, May 1986. p. 1-2.

SANDSTONE--PRESERVATION

"Architectural Sandstone: Maintenance & Repair." The Brownstoner. February 1983. pp. 2-3.

SANDSTONE--PRESERVATION--U.S.--WASHINGTON, D.C.

Quenzel, Neale. "Rehabilitation Approaches to Severely Deteriorated Brown Sandstone at the Apex Building, Washington, D.C." Bulletin, APT. Vol. 17, No. 3&4, 1985. p. 65-68.

SCHOOL BUILDINGS

"Baldwin School." Neighborhood Quarterly. Vol. 7, No. 1, Winter 1987. p. 1, 3.

Neighborhood Housing Services of New Haven argues in favor of demolishing a school building and constructing townhouses rather than adaptive use of the building.

SCHOOL BUILDINGS

"Competition Converts Surplus School Site." Urban Innovation Abroad. August 1983. p. 7.

SCHOOL BUILDINGS

Gulliford, Andrew. "Country School Legacy." Utah Preservation/Restoration. Vol. III, 1981. pp. 42-51.

SCHOOL BUILDINGS

Hale, James. "School's Out: What do we do with redundant schools?" Canadian Heritage. October 1981. p.7-8.

SCHOOL BUILDINGS

Kindley, Mark M. "Little Schools on the Prairie Still Teach a Big Lesson." Smithsonian. Vol. 16, No. 7, Oct. 1985. p. 118-129.

SCHOOL BUILDINGS

Schroeder, Fred E. H. "Schoolhouse Reading: What You can Learn from Your Rural School." History News. April 1981. p.15-16.

SCHOOL BUILDINGS

White, Jane. "Lee Will Rise Again!" Riverside/Avondale Preservation, Inc., Community Newsletter. Apr. 1987. p. 4-5.

Community will restore 1926 highschool in Jacksonville, Florida.

SCHOOL BUILDINGS--ADAPTIVE USE

Anderson, Lee F. "Making the Most of Our Schools: New Uses for Old Spaces," Architecture Minnesota. Sep.-Oct. 1979. pp. 58-60.

SCHOOL BUILDINGS--ADAPTIVE USE

"Attending to the Inner Light in a Manhattan Brownstone." Architectural Record. August 1982. pp. 92-93.

SCHOOL BUILDINGS--ADAPTIVE USE

"Britain Reuses Surplus Schools." Urban Innovation Abroad. Vol. 8, No. 8, August 1984. p. 2.

SCHOOL BUILDINGS--ADAPTIVE USE

" The Charlestown High School. " Boston Preservation Alliance Letter. Vol. 8, No. 7. Jul./Aug. 1987. pp. 1 - 2.
A Boston High School has been converted into apartments.

SCHOOL BUILDINGS--ADAPTIVE USE

"Evanston Rehabs School into Municpal Building." Journal of Housing. July 1978. p. 371.

SCHOOL BUILDINGS--ADAPTIVE USE

"The Fall and Rise of a 19th Century School house." Architectural Record. Mid-February 1981. p. 70-73.

SCHOOL BUILDINGS--ADAPTIVE USE

Flynn, Barbara. "Bancroft and Rice Schools," Boston Preservation Alliance Letter, Vol. 5, No. 9, December 1984, pp. 3, 9-10.

SCHOOL BUILDINGS--ADAPTIVE USE

Gernand, Jean. "Determined Few Save Small-town School." The Indiana Preservationist. July-August 1983, p. 3.

SCHOOL BUILDINGS--ADAPTIVE USE

Humphrey, Leona. "Rural Redevelopment Creates Mixed-Use Project From Vacant School." Home Again. No. 4, Autumn 1984, pp. 22-3.

SCHOOL BUILDINGS--ADAPTIVE USE

"The Lincoln School: From Classrooms to Bedrooms." Revitalization. December 1981. pp. 4-5.

SCHOOL BUILDINGS--ADAPTIVE USE

"Living in a Schoolhouse"(Newtonville, Massachusetts) Architectural Record. July 1983. pp. 100-103.

SCHOOL BUILDINGS -- ADAPTIVE USE

McKenna, Barrie. "School's Out: How Three Vacant Montreal Schools became successful Housing Developments." Building Renovation. Vol.4, No. 3. May/June 1987. pp. 37 - 39.

SCHOOL BUILDINGS--ADAPTIVE USE

Miles, Mark. "School's Out; Condominiums In." The Indiana Preservationist. February 1983. p. 2.

SCHOOL BUILDINGS--ADAPTIVE USE

"Montgomery Firm to Host Reception at Renovated School." The Preservation Report (Ala.). May/June 1983. p. 4.

SCHOOL BUILDINGS--ADAPTIVE USE

Noser, Barbara. "Another Decommissioned School Finds Exiting New Use." The Indiana Preservationist. November/December 1983. p. 2.

SCHOOL BUILDINGS--ADAPTIVE USE

"Renovation Adds New Dimension to P.S. 78." Commercial Renovation. Vol 7, No. 6, Dec. 1985. p. 40-43.

SCHOOL BUILDINGS--ADAPTIVE USE

"School house in Michigan listed as Historical Site, turned into mini-mall." National Mall Monitor. May/June 1981. p. 68.

SCHOOL BUILDINGS--ADAPTIVE USE

"Schoolhouses Start Anew." Architecture Minnesota. Vol. 10, No. 5, September/October 1984. pp. 24-35.

SCHOOL BUILDINGS--ADAPTIVE USE

Talbot, Edward G. "How Our Schools Grew Up to be Scattered-Site Housing." Planning. October 1982. pp 21-23.

SCHOOL BUILDINGS--ADAPTIVE USE

Watts, Ellen. "The Mayer Art Center of the Phillips Exeter Academy: An Engaging Combination of Adaptive Reuse and New Construction." Technology and Conservation. Fall 1982. pp. 20-31.

SCHOOL BUILDINGS--ADAPTIVE USE--U.S.--GEORGIA--THOMASVILLE

"Changes Underway for East Side School." The Rambler, Newsletter of the Georgia Trust for Historic Preservation, Inc. Vol. 11, No. 4, Fall 1984. p. 9.

SCHOOL BUILDINGS--ADAPTIVE USE--U.S.--MASSACHUSETTS--BOSTON

Anderson, William V. "Preservation of the Oak Square School." Boston Preservation Alliance Letter. Vol. 6, No. 1. Jan. 1985. p. 3.

ROOFS

Koziol, Richard S. and Jerry G. Stockbridge. "Detecting Water Leaks in Slate and Clay-Tile Roofs." APT Bulletin. Vol. 19, No. 2, 1987. p. 6-9.

ROOFS

Hallock, Terry and Beverly. "How to Identify a Healthy Roof." Yankee. Oct. 1982. pp. 112-117.

ROOFS

"Cover Your Roof's Needs." The Medallion.
Vol. 24, No. 6, June 1987. p. 4.

ROOFS

"Cedar Shingles." The Architects'
Journal. Vol. 184, No. 37, Sept. 10,
1986. p. 53-59.

ROOFS

Black, David R. "Technical Tips: Slated
for Success." North Carolina Preservation.
No. 67. Spring 1987. pp. 20 - 21.
Repairing and replacing slate roofs.

SCHOOL BUILDINGS--ADAPTIVE USE--U.S.--MINNESOTA--
MINNEAPOLIS

Mack, Linda. "Fitting In." Architecture
Minnesota. Vol. 11, No. 6, Nov. 1985. p. 37-41.

Calhoun School developed into Calhoun
Square.

SCHOOL BUILDINGS--ADAPTIVE USE--U.S.--NEW YORK--
NEW YORK CITY

"Resurrection on Tenth Avenue." Architectural Record. Sept. 1985. p. 55.

SCHOOL BUILDINGS--ADAPTIVE USE--U.S.--OKLAHOMA--
Oklahoma City

Crosbie, Michael J. "School Turned Offices Rich
in Decoration", Architecture, January 1985, pp. 62-
69.

SCHOOL BUILDINGS--ADAPTIVE USE--U.S.--WASHINGTON
--SEATTLE

"Neighborhood Input in Reuse of Old Schools.
Urban Conservation Report. Vol. VIII, No. 13,
July 31, 1984. p. 2.

SCHOOL BUILDINGS--ADAPTIVE USE--U.S.--WASHINGTON--
SEATTLE

"The Rebirth of a Seattle School", Landmarks,
Magazine of Northwest History and Preservation,
Vol. 3, No. 3, Fall 1984, pp. 6-7.

SCHOOL BUILDINGS--ADAPTIVE USE--U.S.--WISCONSIN

"Earthly Delight." Architectural Record.
Mid-September 1984. pp. 118-119.

SCHOOL BUILDINGS--CONSERVATION AND RESTORATION--
U.S.--TEXAS

"Ozona Rehabilitates School", The Medallion,
Vol. 22, No.1, January 1985, p. 1.

SCHOOL BUILDINGS--U.S.--INDIANA

Davis, Ann. "Survey Find #2: Rural
Schoolhouses." The Indiana Preservationist.
No. 6, 1984. p. 2.

SCHOOL BUILDINGS--U.S.--PENNSYLVANIA--
PITTSBURGH

"The Evolution of Pittsburgh Public
School Design." PHLF News. No. 97, Spring 1986.
p. 7.

SCHOOL BUILDINGS--U.S.--TEXAS

"Special Issue: Historic Schools in Texas."
The Medallion. Vol. 22, No. 8, Aug. 1985.
Entire Issue. 6 p.

SCHOOL BUILDINGS--U.S.--VIRGINIA

McCleary, Ann. "Augusta County Schools
Selected for State's First Thematic Nomination."
Notes on Virginia. No. 26, Spring 1985. p. 28-
33.

SCULPTORS

Dryfhout, John. "Our Visual Heritage: Sharing the Fine Arts at Saint-Gaudens National Historic Site." CRM Bulletin. Vol. 8, No. 3 & 4, June/Aug. 1985. p. 1-4.

SCULPTORS

Galvin, Ruth Mehrlens. "Saint-Gaudens." American Heritage. Vol. 36, No. 4, June/July 1985. p. 42-53.

SCULPTORS

Hawkes, Pamela W. "Franklin Simmons, Yankee Sculptor in Rome." Antiques. Vol. 128, No. 1, July 1985. p. 125-129.

SCULPTORS

Olson, Sarah. "Remembering Saint-Gaudens: A Look at His Life and Time Through What He Left Behind". CRM Bulletin. Vol. 8, No. 1, Feb. 1985. p. 5-8.

SCULPTORS

Reynolds, Patrick T. "Art at Aspet." Americana. Vol. 13, No. 3, July/Aug. 1985. p. 50-54.

Saint-Gaudens life at home in Cornish, New Hampshire at Aspet, a National Historic Site.

SCULPTURE

Holser, Harold and Joseph Farber. "Sculpture of the United States Capitol, Part I: Architectural Sculpture." Antiques. July, 1979. pp. 146-159.

SCULPTURE

Jackson-Stops, Gervase. "New Deities for Old Parterres: the Painting of Lead Statues." Country Life. Vol. 181, No. 5, Jan. 29, 1987. pp. 92-94.

Restoration of outdoor lead statues sculpted by Carpentier.

SCULPTURE

Kreger, Gary. "How to Tell the Difference Between Real and Imitation." The Old News Is Good News Gazette. Vol. 3, No. 4, Jan. 1987. p. 8-9.

How to tell the difference between bronze and polybronze and marble and marblize casts.

SCULPTURE

Sellars, Richard West. "The Granite Orchards of Gettysburg." Courier. Vol. 31, No. 12, Dec. 1986. p. 20-22.

SCULPTURE--CONSERVATION AND RESTORATION

Leutwiler, Jenny. "Saving Face." St. Louis Home. Vol. 4, No. 10, October 1944. p. 41.

SCULPTURE--CONSERVATION AND RESTORATION

Matero, Frank G. "A Diagnostic Study and Treatment Evaluation for the Cleaning of Perry's Victory and International Peace Memorial." APT Bulletin. Vol. 16, No. 3 & 4, 1984. p. 39-51.

SCULPTURE--CONSERVATION AND RESTORATION

Panhorst, Michael W. "The Appreciation and Preservation of Monumental Bronze Sculpture." NPS, CRM Bulletin. Vol. 7, No. 2, July 1984. pp. 1-3; 5.

SCULPTURE--CONSERVATION AND RESTORATION

Van Zelst, Lambertus and Jean-Louis Lachevre. "Outdoor Bronze Sculpture: Problems and Procedures of Protective Treatment." Technology and Conservation. Spring 1983. pp. 18-24.

SCULPTURE--CONSERVATION AND RESTORATION

Veloz, Nicholas F. "Outdoor Sculpture in the Park Environment." NPS, CRM Bulletin. Vol. 7, No. 2, July 1984. pp. 4-7.

SCULPTURE, MODERN--19TH CENTURY

Bogart, Michele H. "In Search of A United Front: American Sculpture at the Turn of the Century", Winterthur Portfolio, Vol. 19, No. 2/3, Summer/ Autumn 1984, pp. 151-176.

SEASHORE--U.S.--NORTH CAROLINA--CAPE LOOKOUT

Black, Ann. "Cape Lookout: A Voyage to Discovery." National Parks and Conservation. July 1980. pp. 14-17.

SEPULCHRAL MONUMENTS

"Gravestones and epitaphs." Journal of Popular Culture. Spring 1981. p. 633-656.

CONTENTS: "Grinning Skulls, Smiling Cherubs, Bitter Words", M.A. Nelson and D.H. George. -- Ideologies in Stone: Meaning in Victorian Gravestones, K.L. Ames.

SEPULCHRAL MONUMENTS

Holton, Felicia A. " Death heads, cherubs, and shaded urns: gravestone markings enhance the precision of archeological study." Early Man. Autumn 1979. p. 5-9.

SHEET METAL

"Exhibition on Sheet Metal at NBM." Blueprints. Vol. 5, No. 1. Spring 1987. p. 16.
Exhibition planned at National Building Museum to heighten awareness of the signifi- cance of sheet metalwork.

SHIPPING--HISTORY

Kaiser, F.F. "Lumber North: Carolina Pine Teamed Up With Yankee Schooners." National Fisherman. April 30, 1980. p. 102-105.

SHIPS

Barbour, Alex and Ricahrd Fairweather. "What Do RBL's, Flour Mills, Hydrofoils, and Sailing Ships Have in Common." APT Bulletin. Vol. 18, Nos. 1 & 2, 1986. pp. 55-67.
The Machines and Vessels Section of Parks Canada is responsible for historic ships.

SHIPS

Benton, Nick. "The Sea Lion: Rigging a Sixteenth-Century Ship." Sea History. No. 42. Winter 1986-87. pp. 22-23.

SHIPS

"Chris Craft Archives donated to the museum." The Mariners' Museum Journal. Vol. 14, No. 1. Spring 1987. pp. 7 - 11.

SHIPS

Craig, James. "Restoring a Nineteenth Century Sailing Ship." Heritage Australia. Vol. 5, No. 2, Winter 1986. p. 38-39.

Restoration of a three masted barque.

SHIPS

Drummond, Maldwin. "The Iron Lady Comes Home." Country Life. Vol. 171, No. 28. July 9, 1987. pp. 118 - 120.
HMS Warrior, a late 18th Century battleship, has been restored and returned to Portsmouth, England.

SHIPS

"Interior Designates 27 WWII Ships As Historical Landmarks." Headquarters Heliogram. No. 175, March-April 1986. p. 4.

SHIPS

Johnson, Carol. "Algoma Central Railway." Inland Seas. Vol. 43, NR. 1, Spr. 1987. p. 2-7.

Oldest bulk steamship company, in continuity of name, began as a railroad.

SHIPS

Long, George C. "The Side-Wheel Carriers." American Heritage. Vol. 38, No. 2, Feb./Mar. 1987. p. 104-106.

SHIPS

Malley, Richard C. "The Titanic: An Unsinkable Tale." The Mariners' Museum Journal. Vol. 13, No. 1, Spring 1986. p. 7-9.

SHIPS

Napier, Rob. " The Ship 'Sooloo(II)' of Salem 1861-1887: History and Research for Building a model. " The American Neptune. Vol. 47, No. 2. Spring 1987. pp. 119 - 137.

SHIPS

"Nostalgia, Hard Work Routine for USS Prairie." Headquarters Heliogram. No. 182. Jan. 1987. p. 6.

The destroyer, USS Prairie, is the oldest Navy ship in continuous use.

SHIPS

Palmer, Richard F. "100 Years of Provisioning Great Lakes Ships-Oswego's Ship Chandleries." Inland Seas. Vol. 43, No. 1, Spr. 1987. P. 10-22.

SHIPS

"'Phantom Navy' in Reserve at Bay Area Mothball Fleet Base." Headquarters Heliogram. No. 177, July 1986. p. 8.

Nine cargo ships with historically significant pasts in San Francisco Bay.

SHIPS

Sands, John O. "The Last of the Bay Steamboats." The Mariners' Museum Journal. Vol. 13, No. 3. Fall 1986. p. 10.

SHIPS

"Ship Shape: Adopt-a-Boat Program Brings Luster Back to Small Craft Collection." The Mariners Museum Journal. Vol. 13, No. 4, Winter 1986. p. 15-16.

SHIPS

Thomas, Bill. "Tenth Year for National Maritime Museum: Successful Voyage for NPS through Stormy Seas of Ship Saving." Courier. Vol. 32, No. 6. June 1987. pp. 42 - 44.

SHIPS

Townley, John. "The Great Eastern." The Mariners' Museum Journal. Vol. 13, No. 1, Spring 1986. p. 5.

A huge passenger steamer had a stormy history.

SHIPS

Townley, John. "Summer in England, 1986, A Travelogue." The Mariners Museum Journal. Vol. 13, No. 4, Winter 1987. p. 6-7

SHIPS

"USS Arizona Takes the Prize". Courier. Vol. 31, No. 6, June 1986. p. 21.

The Society for History awarded the John Wesley Powell Prize to the National Park Service for the underwater survey/assessment of the U.S.S. Arizona.

SHIPS

"USS Olympia Contribution Slow." Headquarters Heliogram. No. 178, Aug. 1986. p. 5.

A shortage of contributors may scuttle project to save Admiral Dewey's flagship.

SHIPS

Warner, Robert J. "Battleship USS Missouri is Recommissioned." Headquarters Heliogram. No. 176, May-June 1986. p. 4.

The battleship U.S.S. Missouri is the historic site of the World War II Japanese surrender ceremony.

SHIPS--CONSERVATION AND RESTORATION

Koch, Carl. "End of an Era: the Preservation of a Lightship." Boston Preservation Alliance Letter. Vol. 7, No. 1, Jan. 1986. p. 4, 8.

One of the last two lightships decommissioned by the U.S. Coast Guard.

SHIPS--CONSERVATION AND RESTORATION

Laise, Steve. "Will the United States Sail Again?" Sea Heritage News. Vol. 2 #7. pp. 2-3.

SHIPS--CONSERVATION AND RESTORATION

Neill, Peter. "Shipwreck Preservation." Boston Preservation Alliance Letter. Vol. 5, No. 6, July/August 1984. p. 10.

SHIPS--CONSERVATION AND RESTORATION

Parker, Reuel. "A Story of Priorities." Wooden Boat. No. 65, July/Aug. 1985. p. 56-65.

How to prioritize, schedule, and limit cost of wooden craft restoration.

SHIPS--CONSERVATION AND RESTORATION

Steele, Peter. "To Rehabilitate a Warship." NPS, CRM Bulletin. Vol. 7, No. 2, July 1984. pp. 8-11.

SHIPS--CONSERVATION AND RESTORATION

"$10 Million Fund Drive Opens for USS Texas Preservation." Headquarters Heliogram. No. 173, Dec. 1985. p. 1, 12.

SHIPS--CONSERVATION AND RESTORATION

Walker, David. "The S.S. 'Acadia', A Case History in the Economics of Maintenance and Preservation of a Steel Ship as a Floating Artifact." APT Bulletin. Vol. 14, No. 2, 1982. pp. 2-10.

SHIPS--CONSERVATION AND RESTORATION--U.S.--TEXAS

"Battleship Focus of Study." The Medallion. Vol. 22, No. 4, Apr. 1985. p. 3.

SHIPS--HISTORY

Bellarosa, James M. "Built for Blazing Speed." Yankee Magazine. May 1984. pp. 126-139. (Clipper ships.)

SHIPS--HISTORY

Hansen, Moya. "The Titanic--Paradise Lost". Historic Denver News. April 1980. Special supplement.

SHIPS--HISTORY

Larson, Chiles T.A. "Chesapeake Log Canoes." Country Magazine. July 1981. pp. 14-17.

SHIPS, WOODEN

Brouwer, Norman. "The 1856 Packet Charles Cooper." Seaport. Fall 1981. pp. 18-21.

SHIPS, WOODEN

Brouwer, Norman. "The Last Clipper of Them All-Snow Squall." Seaport. Summer 1981. pp. 28-30.

SHIPS, WOODEN--CONSERVATION AND RESTORATION

Carlsen, Peter. "Sea Cloud: The Marjorie Merriweather Post Yacht Recommissioned." Architectural Digest. July 1981. pp. 126-132.

SHIPWRECKS

"Camera to Monitor Monitor." Headquarters Heliogram. No. 185. June 1987. p. 5.
The Navy will use an unmanned underwater camera to examine the wreckage of the USS Monitor.

SHIPWRECKS

Cummins, Gary T. "U.S.S. Arizona: A Cultural Resources Management Success Story." NPS, CRM Bulletin. Vol. 7, No. 1, April 1984. pp. 1,2, 4-5.

SHIPWRECKS

"Divers Search Pearl Harbor Hulk of Sunken USS Utah." Headquarters Heliogram. No. 180, Oct. 1986. p. 9.

SHIPWRECKS

"Excavation of Oldest Shipwreck." California Office of Historic Preservation Newsletter. Vol. 2, No. 2, May 1987. p. 1, 3.

SHIPWRECKS

"Fireworks at Shipwreck Forum." Place. Vol. 5, No. 3, Mar. 1985. p. 14.

SHIPWRECKS

Giesecke, Anne. "The Abandoned Shipwreck Bill: Protecting Our Threatened Cultural Heritage." Archaeology. Vol. 40, No. 4, Jul./Aug. 1987. pp. 50 - 53.

SHIPWRECKS

Hammersmith, Jack L. "Raising the battleship Maine." Industrial Archaeology. Winter 1980. p.318-329.

SHIPWRECKS

Hood, Graham. "The Wreck of the Geldermalsen." Colonial Williamsburg. Vol. 9, No. 2, Winter 1986-87. p. 40.

SHIPWRECKS

"Monitor artifacts awarded to The Mariners' Museum." The Mariners' Museum Journal. Vol. 14, No. 1. Spring 1987. p. 12.

SHIPWRECKS

"Proposed Legislation for the Protection of Historic Shipwrecks." Letter With News. (NTHP) Jan. 1986. p. 2-3.

SHIPWRECKS

Smith, Sheli, Kerry Shackelford and Linda Brown. "Yorktown Shipwreck Project." The Mariners' Museum Journal. Vol. 13, No. 2. Summer 1986. pp. 11-12.

Findings of the 1985 field season at the Yorktown Shipwreck Archaeology Project.

SHIPWRECKS

"Titanic Expedition Finds No Gash from Iceberg." Headquarters Heliogram. No. 178, Aug. 1986. p. 4.

SHIPWRECKS

Waldron, Sue. "Titanic Gets Memorial Designation." Headquarters Heliogram. No. 180, Oct. 1986. p. 9.

SHIPWRECKS

Wertime, Marcia Satterthwaite. "Sounding the Depths: an Encounter with the Titanic." Archaeology. Vol. 40, No. 1, Jan./Feb. 1987. p. 88.

SHOP FRONTS

State of West Virginia. "Art Deco Glass: History and Care." Culture & History. Vol. 1, No. 1, July-August-September 1984. pp. 30-1.

SHOP FRONTS

Wasama, Dougals R. "An 'Old Fashioned' Restoration." *Historic Kansas City Foundation Gazette*. Jan./Feb. 1983. p.5.

SHOP FRONTS--CONSERVATION AND RESTORATION

"Rare Commercial 'Pre-Fab' Restored." *Massachusetts Historical Commission Newsletter*. March 1983. pp. 4-5.

SHOP FRONTS--CONSERVATION AND RESTORATION--U.S. --TEXAS--AUSTIN

Freeman, Allen. "James H. Robertson Building Renovation." *Architecture*. Mar. 1986. p. 82-83.

SHOPPING CENTERS

"Architectural Design: Urban Shopping Centers." *Progressive Architecture*. July 1981. Entire Issue.

CONTENTS: Introduction: Shopping Goes to Town--Gratz, Roberta. Downtown Devitalized--Morton, David. Mall Modifications--Goldstein, Barbara. A Place in Santa Monica--Bazjanac, Vladimir. Energy Analysis--Stephens, Suzanne. As Troy Turns--Dixon, John M. Procession in Pasadena--Morton, David. Super-mercato--Roundtable on Rouse.

SHOPPING CENTERS

Gillette, Howard Jr. "The Evolution of the Planned Shopping Center in Suburb and City." *JAPA*. Vol. 51, No. 4, Autumn 1985. p. 449-460.

SHOPPING CENTERS

Mickens, Ed. "Instant Main Street : the Shopping Center Saga." *Urban Land*. Vol. 45, No. 6, 1986. p. 18-21.

Shopping centers from early days to the present.

SHOPPING CENTERS

Pulver, Glen C. and Robert A. Chase. "Assessing the Effects of Small Shopping Centers on Rural Communities." *Small Town*. January-February, 1983. pp. 9-13.

SHOPPING CENTERS

"Shopping Centers." *Architectural Record*. April 1982. pp. 124-139.

SHOPPING CENTERS--CONSERVATION AND RESTORATION

"Historic Shopping Center Reopens." *Pasadena Heritage*. Vol. 9, Nos. 3 & 4, Spring & Summer 1986. p. 5.

Hen's Teeth Square built in 1930 and one of the country's first drive-in shopping centers has been restored and reopened.

SHOPPING CENTERS--CONSERVATION AND RESTORATION

"New Life for Older Centers." *National Mall Monitor*. Vol. 11, No. 3. Jul./Aug. 1981. pp. 30-41.

Qualkinbush, Steve. Landscape Renovation Can Improve Older Center's Retail Potential--Leibler, Charles. Periodic Upgrading is Essential--Releasing and Remodeling Combine to Give Open Center Special Appeal--Mellinger, Barbara B. Urban Renovation Rtquire Cooperation,Careful Plans--Mall
(cont'd on next card)

SHOPPING CENTERS--CONSERVATION AND RESTORATION (Card 2)

Renovation Creates a 'New' Property--Dunham, Terry. Careful Planning Helps Renovation of Regional Open Center Succeed.

SHOPPING CENTERS--PLANNING

"Special Study: Downtown Beats Suburban Shopping Center Threat." *Downtown Idea Exchange*. July 1, 1981. pp. 2 - 5.

SHOPPING MALLS

"Enclosed Mall Turns Back the Clock." *National Mall Monitor*. July/August 1982. pp. 34-35.

SHOPPING MALLS

Fix, Michael. "The Impact of Regional Malls: Legal Questions." *Center City Report*. Mar. 1980. pp. 1-3.

SHOPPING MALLS

Hoss, Ann C. "Southdale, The First Mall of Them All." National Mall Monitor, Vol. 17, No. 4, May-June 1987. p. 193-198.

SHOPPING MALLS

Kowinski, William S. "Endless Summer at the World's Biggest Shopping Wonderland." Smithsonian. Vol. 17, No. 9, Dec. 1986. p. 34-43.

A huge enclosed mall in West Edmonton, Canada, will soon have 800 stores and also boasts the world's largest indoor amusement park, indoor water park and parking lot.

SHOPPING MALLS

McDonald, Michael S. "Conover Square: Piano factory turned specialty center is in constant state of growth". National Mall Monitor. January/February 1981. p. 90-92.

Vertical File
SHOPPING MALLS

Miller, Kay. "Southdale's Perpetual Spring." Minneapolis Star-Tribune Magazine. Sep. 28, 1986. pp. 8-13; 21; 23. (VF)

Southdale Mall turns 30.

SHOPPING MALLS

"Old Shopping Malls: A Bargain for Industry." Business Week. November 5, 1984. pp. 116-7.

SHOPPING MALLS

Phillips, Patrick. "Streets for Feet: Burlington, Vermont's Church Street Marketplace." Urban Land. Vol. 44, No. 11, Nov. 1986. p. 2-5.

SHOPPING MALLS--CONSERVATION AND RESTORATION

Raphel, Murray. "The Gordon's Alley Story: or How to Rebuild a Fading Center City Retail Section into an Exuberant, Healthy and Exciting Place to Shop." Challenge! Apr. 1979. pp. 22-24.

SHOPPING MALLS

Simson, John. "Two sides of a pyramid: the case against the Burlington mall; the case for it." Planning. May 1980. p. 24-27.

SHOPPING MALLS

"Stony Brook Preserves 19th Century Charm." National Mall Monitor. Vol. 17, No. 5. Jul./Aug. 1987. pp. 20 - 23.

SHOPPING MALLS

"UDAG Assisted Mall Threatens Historic Buildings, Existing Businesses." Urban Conservation Report. Vol. 9, No. 3, Mar. 1987. p. 6

SIDING (BUILDING MATERIALS)

Bock, Gordon. "Shingle Siding Repair." Old-House Journal. Vol. 14, No. 3, April 1986. p. 118-122.

SIDING

Conway, Brian D. "The Case Against Substitute Siding." Conservancy News. Vol. 4, No. 2. May/June 1987. p. 9.

SIDING (BUILDING MATERIALS)

Duncan, Bill. "Deciding on Siding." Cost Cuts. Vol. 3, No. 4, Jan./Feb. 1986. p. 1-3.

SIGNS AND SIGNBOARDS

"Blinded by the Blight." Sierra. Sept./Oct. 1986. p. 13-14.

34 percent of the 500,000 billboards on our federal highways are candidates for removal.

SIGNS AND SIGNBOARDS

"Center Signage: Developers' Restrictions Bring Back Neon and Old World Artistry." National Mall Monitor. Jan./Feb. 1982. p. 92.

SIGNS AND SIGNBOARDS

City of Annapolis Historic District Commission. Annapolis Historic District Design Guidelines for Signs. 1985. 33p. (VF)

SIGNS AND SIGNBOARDS

"The Clutter and Confusion of Sign Control." Zoning News. Aug. 1986. p. 1-3.

SIGNS AND SIGNBOARDS

Drucker, Johanna. "Language in the Landscape." Landscape. Vol. 28, No. 1, 1984. pp. 7-13.

SIGNS AND SIGNBOARDS

Duplantier, Michael. "Watch for Illegal Billboards." New Orleans Preservation in Print. Vol. 14, No. 4, May 1987. p. 7.

SIGNS AND SIGNBOARDS

"Failure of Federal Billboard Reforms." Zoning News. Nov. 1986. p. 3-4.

SIGNS AND SIGNBOARDS

Jenkins, Marlia. "Free Speech in Historic Commercial District Signage." Michigan Historic District Network. Jun./Jul. 1987. pp. 2 - 3.
Guidelines to regulating signage.

SIGNS AND SIGNBOARDS

Keenan, Robert J. "An Industry View of Sign Ordinances." Zoning News. Oct. 1986. p. 2-3.

SIGNS AND SIGNBOARDS

Leonard, King Patrick. "Planning Director's View of Revising a Sign Ordinance." Zoning News. Oct. 1986. p. 3.

SIGNS AND SIGNBOARDS

"Loop Elevated Signs Contested". Landmarks Preservation Council of Illinois. Vol. 14, No. 1, Jan./Feb. 1985. p. 3.

SIGNS AND SIGNBOARDS

"Montgomery County, Md., Bans Billboards." Zoning News. Oct. 1986. p. 3-4.

SIGNS AND SIGNBOARDS

"Signing Up for Billboard Control." Urban Outlook. Vol. 8, No. 19, Oct. 15, 1986. p. 7-8.

SIGNS AND SIGNBOARDS

"Signs of Success." Planning. Vol. 51, No. 7, July 1985. p. 25-30.

Sign news from various communities, including discussion of some local ordinances and of historic signs.

SIGNS AND SIGNBOARDS

Smith, Peter H. "Landmark Signs of Howard County Spared." The Society for Commercial Archeology News Journal. May 1982. p. 4.

SIGNS AND SIGNBOARDS--LAW AND LEGISLATION

Floyd, Charles F. "Double Standard." Planning. Vol 51, No. 7, July 1985. p. 21-24.

Discussion of various local and a federal effort to curb billboards.

SIGNS AND SIGNBOARDS--LAW AND LEGISLATION

"Signs of the Times: And Sign Controls." Downtown Idea Exchange. Vol. 31, No. 18, Sept. 15, 1984. pp. 3-4.

SIGNS AND SIGNBOARDS--LAW & LEGISLATION--U.S.-- NEW YORK--ALBANY

"City Sign Ordinance in Review." Albany Preservation Report. March/April 1984. p. 3.

Comprehensive ordinance under development.

SIGNS AND SIGNBOARDS--STANDARDS

"Sign Control: Rules, Aids and Guidelines." Downtown Idea Exchange. Vol. 31, No. 7, April 1, 1984. pp. 5-6.

SKYSCRAPERS

Anderson, Grace. "Five by KPF." Architectural Record. Feb. 1987. p. 126-135.

Five skyscrapers designed by Kohn Pedersen Fox Associates.

SKYSCRAPERS

Newman, M. W. "The Skyscraper Syndrome: the Height of Something or Other." Inland Architect. May/Juen 1979. pp. 16-21.

SKYSCRAPERS

Ricciotti, Dominic. "Symbols and Monuments: Images of the Skyscraper in American Art." Landscape. Vol. 25, No. 2. pp. 22-29.

SKYSCRAPERS

Robins, Anthony W. "Top this One: the Continuing Saga of the Tallest Building in the World." Architectural Record. Jan. 1987. p. 56-60.

SKYSCRAPERS--CONSERVATION AND RESTORATION

Hoster, Jay. "The Wyandotte: A Rehabilitation Effort." Urban Land. May 1979. pp. 3-8.

Economic and legal information on the rehabilitation and development of the Chicago-style Skyscraper in Columbus, Ohio.

SKYSCRAPERS--CONSERVATION AND RESTORATION-- U.S.--MASSACHUSETTS--BOSTON

Shrank, Elliot Jon. "Restoration of a Skyscraper: United Shoe Machinery Building." The Boston Preservation Alliance Letter. Vol. 5, No. 7, September 1984. pp. 1, 4-5.

SKYSCRAPERS--U.S.--LOUISIANA--NEW ORLEANS

Magill, John. "Early Skyscrapers." Historic New Orleans Collection Newsletter. Vol. 3, No. 3, Summer 1985. p. 6-7.

SKYSCRAPERS--U.S.--NEW YORK STATE--NEW YORK CITY

Ruttenbaum, Steven. "Visibility City." Metropolis. May 1985. p. 39-42.

The Ritz Tower, the first residential skyscraper, profiled.

SLATE

Clark, Edie. "Having a Roof of Stone." Yankee Magazine. May 1982. pp. 70.

SLIDES (PHOTOGRAPHY)

Dennison, Linda T. "Making It Special Every Time." Audio Visual Directions. July 1981. p. 22.

SLIDES (PHOTOGRAPHY)

Leps, A. Arvo. "Producing Single-Slide Multi-Imagery--The Basics." Audio Visual Directions. July 1981. p. 130.

SMALL TOWNS--AUSTRALIA

Hall, Robin. "An Australian Country Townscape". Landscape. 1980. vol24, no.2. p.41-48.

SMALL TOWNS

Hansen, Tim. "Small Town Entrances: A Strategy for Preservation." Small Town. Vol. 14, No. 6, May-June 1984. pp. 24-29.

SMALL TOWNS

McClung, William Alexander. "The Mediating Structure of the Small Town." Journal of Architectural Education. Vol. 38, No. 3, Spring 1985. p. 2-7.

SMALL TOWNS

Shiras, Ginger. "Eureka Springs: One Stop and You'll Never Want to Leave This Town in the Arkansas Ozarks." American Preservation. Apr./May 1979. pp. 44-57.

SMALL TOWNS--CONSERVATION AND RESTORATION

Marlin, William. "Marshall, Michigan: the Small Town Comes Back." Architectural Record, December 1979. pp. 108-113.

SMALL TOWNS--CONSERVATION AND RESTORATION

Paraschos, Janet Nyberg and Jack E. Boucher (photographer). "Madison: Historic Preservation is a Way of Life in This Indiana Town." American Preservation. Nov./Dec. 1979. pp. 7-22.

SMALL TOWNS--CONSERVATION AND RESTORATION-- IDAHO--MOSCOW

Driskell, Jeanette. "3rd & Main: a town plans its future". Small Town. January-February, 1980. p. 4-8.

SMALL TOWNS--CONSERVATION & RESTORATION-- N.Y.-- CORBETT

Williams, Harold and Natalie Hawley. " The Corbett Compact: Blueprint for Community Renewal". Small Town. January-February 1980, p. 15-22.

SMALL TOWNS--U.S.

Hummon, David M. "Popular images of the American small town". Landscape. 1980. vol.24 no.2. p.3-9.

SMALL TOWNS--U.S.--ILLINOIS--GALENA

Campbell, Thomas A., Jr. "Galena, 1820-1830: the Creation of a Mining Boom Town." Historic Illinois. Vol. 8, No. 1, June 1985. p. 8-13.

SMALL TOWNS--U.S.--MICHIGAN--GENESEE COUNTY

Leonard, Timothy. "An Urban County Rediscovers its Small Towns." Small Town. November-December 1980. p. 10-16.

SOCIETIES

Slade, Marilyn Myers. "Guardians of New England's Noble Houses." Yankee. Vol. 49, No. 6, June 1985. p. 36-45.

A discussion of the houses of the Society for the Preservation of New England Antiquities (SPNEA) on its 75th anniversary.

SOD HOUSES

Gulliford, Andrew. "Sod Houses: Cool in Summer and Warm in Winter." Fine Homebuilding. No. 31, Feb./Mar. 1986. p. 54-57.

SOD HOUSES

Noble, Allen G. "Sod Houses and Similar Structures: A Brief Evaluation of the Literature." *Pioneer America*. Vol. 13, 1981, No. 2. pp. 61-66.

SOLAR ENERGY

"Historic Districts: Solar in the Architectural Review Process." *SSEC News* March 1981. p.14-16.

SOLAR ENERGY

Holm, Alvin. "An Early Victorian Passive Solar System: Eleutherian Mills." *APT Bulletin*. Vol. XIII, No. 4, 1981. pp. 43-49.

SOLAR HEATING

"Reliability and Performance of Solar Collector Systems." *Building Research Establishment Digest*. October 1981,No. 254. pp. 1-8.

SOUTH CAROLINA--CHARLESTON

Rouda, Mitchell. "Charleston: by coupling development with urban planning, Charleston hopes to preserve its history without inhibiting growth". *Urban Design International*. May/June 1980. p.14-19.

SOUTH CAROLINA--CHARLESTON--DRAYTON HALL

George, Gerald. "The Great Drayton Hall Debate." *History News*. January 1984. pp. 7-12.

SOUTH CAROLINA--MIDDLETON PLACE--ARCHAEOLOGY

Lewis, Kenneth E. " Excavating a colonial rice plantation". *Early Man*. Autumn 1979. p.13-17.

SPACE FLIGHT

Butowsky, Harry. "Cape Canaveral Air Force Station." *CRM Bulletin*. June 1983. pp. 1-4.

SPACE FLIGHT

"Campaign Opens to Save Tower." *Headquarters Heliogram*. No. 174, Jan./Feb. 1986. p. 9.

SPACE FLIGHT

"8 Cape Canaveral Launch Sites Designated Landmarks." Council on America's Military Past, *Headquarters Heliogram*. No. 161, April-May 1984. p. 5.

SPACE FLIGHT

"$8 Million Eyed for Tower Project." Council on America's Military Past, *Headquarters Heliogram*. No. 161, April-May 1984. p. 4.

SPACE FLIGHT

"Help Space Preservation Interior Told." *Headquarters Heliogram*. No. 181, Nov. 1986.

The House Committee on Interior and Insular Affairs has been requested by the Secretary of the Interior to preserve the space launch towers at Kennedy Space Center, Florida.

SPACE FLIGHT

"22 Space Program Sites Now Landmarks." *Headquarters Heliogram*. No. 174, Jan./Feb. 1986. p. 9.

SPANISH MISSIONS--U.S.--TEXAS

The Medallion. Vol. 23, No. 8, Aug. 1986.

Entire issue devoted to Spanish missions in Texas.

SPORTS FACILITIES

"Old Wood and Brick Brushed with Color Transform Stanford's Old Pavilion into Handsome Offices." Architectural Record. September 1978. pp. 126-128.

SPORTS FACILITIES

"Recreation Buildings with Team Spirit." Architectural Record. November 1981. pp. 102-119.

PARTIAL CONTENTS: Recycling Introduces a New Game to an Old Building--A Girls' School Gym Wins Points for Playing by the Rules.

SPORTS FACILITIES--U.S.--ILLINOIS--CHICAGO

"Elevators Offer Challenge in Expansion of Wrigley Field's Services." Commercial Renovation Vol. 7, No. 4, Aug. 1985. p. 20, 22.

SQUATTERS

Kearns, Kevin C. "'Urban squatting' increases as Londoners'solution to nonavailability of housing". Journal of Housing. May 1980, p. 250-257.

STABLES--GREAT BRITAIN

Worsley, Giles. "London's Greatest Stable: the Royal Mews, Pimlico." Country Life. Vol. 180, No. 4640. Jul. 24, 1986. pp. 294-297.

STAINED GLASS

Raguin, Virginia C. "The Repair and Protection of Architectural Stained Glass." Connecticut Trust for Historic Preservation News. Vol. 10, No. 1, Winter 1987. p. 6-7.

STAINED GLASS

Sloan, Julie L. "Ask the Technical Preservation Services Center." Common Bond. Vol. 3, No. 1, Winter 1987. p. 8-10.

Evaluating the condition of stained glass windows.

STAIRCASES

Ireton, Kevin. "Traditional Stairways off the Shelf: About Manufactured Stair Parts, and How They Are Made." Fine Homebuilding. No. 36, Dec. 1986/Jan. 1987. p. 56-61.

STAIRCASES

Kitchel, Joseph. "Staircase Renovation." Fine Homebuilding. February/March 1981. p.14-18.

STAIRCASES

Nelson, Dale. "Newport Stairway Reproduction." Fine Homebuilding. No. 37, Feb./Mar. 1987. p. 30-33.

Rebuilding of staircase built in 1885 and destroyed by fire in 1983.

STAIRCASES

Poore, Jonathan and Patricia. "Repairing Wood Stairs--Anatomy of a Newel." The Old House Journal. July 1981. pp. 160-162.

STAIRCASES

Poore, Patricia. "Fixing Our Balustrade." The Old-House Journal. March 1982. pp. 58-62.

STAIRCASES

Poore, Patricia. "Repairing a Stair at Our Old House." The Old-House Journal. February 1982. p..27.

STAIRCASES

Poore, Jonathan and Patricia. "Repairing Wood Stairs: Balusters and Handrails." Old House Journal. June 1981. p. 138.

STAIRCASES

"Wooden Staircases." Old-House Journal.
March 1981. p. 64-65.

STATE PRESERVATION PLANNING

Adams, Katherine. "The Year in Review."
Statewide Information Exchange. Sept./Oct. 1985.
p. 2-10.

An assessment of the activities of the
statewide preservation organizations over the
last year.

STATE PRESERVATION PLANNING

American Society for Conservation
Archaeology. 1980 Proceedings. Vol. 7, 1980-81.

CONTENTS: Aten, L. Historic Preservation Planning--
Talmage, V. A Model for Management--Davis, H.A.
A State Plan for Archeology in Arkansas--Green, T.J.
State Planning for Archeology: The Idaho Example--
McManamon, F.P. Articulations between Federal
Regional Archeological Programs and State
Archeological Planning.

1980 Proceedings
(Card 2)

Rogge, A.E. The Evolution of Agency Compliance--
King, T.F. Resource Protection and the State
Plan: A Programmatic Relationship.

STATE PRESERVATION PLANNING

"Go to Your SHPO (State Historic
Preservation Office)." Old-House Journal.
Vol. XII, No. 7, August-September 1984.
pp. 159-162.

STATE PRESERVATION PLANNING

"Heritage Council Establishing Statewide
Network." Historic Hawai'i. Vol. 12, No. 8,
Sept. 1986. p. 6-7.

STATE PRESERVATION PLANNING--LAW AND LEGISLATION

"Governor Riley Proposes South Carolina
State Historic Preservation Trust Fund." The
New South Carolina Gazette. Vol. 17, No. 3,
Spring 1985. p. 4.

STATE PRESERVATION PLANNING--LAW AND LEGISLATION

"New Law Changes Maryland Historical Trust."
The Phoenix. Vol. 5, No. 4, Summer 1985. p. 1,
6.

STATE PRESERVATION PLANNING--LAW AND LEGISLATION

"State of Illinois Increases Preservation
Commitment". Landmarks Preservation Council
of Illinois. Vol. 14, No. 1, Jan./Feb. 1985.
p. 4.

STATE PRESERVATION PLANNING--LAW AND LEGISLATION
--U.S.--ALABAMA

"Preservationists Draft Statewide Enabling
Legislation." The Preservation Report. Vol. 13,
No. 4, Jan./Feb. 1986. p. 1.

STATE PRESERVATION PLANNING--LAW AND LEGISLA-
TION--U.S.--HAWAII

"Bill to lease historic sites for preservation passed." Historic Hawaii News. June 1985.
p. 1.

State owned properties may now be leased.

STATE PRESERVATION PLANNING--LAW AND LEGISLATION-
-U.S.--INDIANA

"Future of Heritage Law Linked to Fate of
School 5." The Indiana Preservationist. No. 2 &
3, 1985. p. 2.

State law upheld, particularly as state
owned property is protected. Partially demolished
facade of school building also ordered restored.

STATE PRESERVATION PLANNING--LAW AND LEGISLA-
TION--U.S.--MAINE

Shettleworth, Earle G. Jr. "The Case for
State Funding of Maine's Historic Properties."
Maine Citizens for Historic Preservation News-
letter. Vol. 10, No. 4, Winter 1985. p. 4-5.

STATE PRESERVATION PLANNING--LAW AND LEGISLATION--
U.S.--MARYLAND

"How Curatorship Works at Raincliffe."
The Phoenix. Vol. 5, No. 3, Spring 1985. p. 4-5.

Curatorship program for historic property
on state park land discussed.

STATE PRESERVATION PLANNING--LAW AND LEGISLATION--U.S.--MASSACHUSETTS

"Individual Landmark Designation Proposed Under Chapter 40C", Massachusetts Historical Commission Newsletter, Vol. 10, No. 4, Fall 1984, p. 9.

STATE PRESERVATION PLANNING--U.S.--FLORIDA

"Comprehensive Historic Preservation Planning Process Initiated." Florida Preservation News. Vol. 1, No. 3, Sept./Oct. 1985. p. 11-12.

A new statewide preservation plan is being developed.

STATE PRESERVATION PLANNING--U.S.--HAWAII

"Historic Hawai'i Board Approves 1986 Preservation Action Plan." Historic Hawaii. Vol. 12, No. 1, Jan. 1986. p. 4-5.

STATE PRESERVATION PLANNING--U.S.--HAWAII

Mullahey, Ramona K. "Statewide Directions for Preservation Emerge from Island-by-Island Conferences."Historic Hawaii. Vol. 12, No. 1, Jan. 1986. p. 2.

STATE PRESERVATION PLANNING--U.S.--MARYLAND

"Johns Hopkins University's Metro Center Reports on Preservation in Maryland." The Phoenix. Vol. 5, No. 3, Spring 1985. p. 1, 3.

STATE PRESERVATION PLANNING--U.S.--TEXAS

"Statewide Group Formed." The Medallion. Vol. 22, No. 10, Oct. 1985. p. 3.

STATE PRESERVATION PLANNING--U.S.--TEXAS

"Statewide Group Formed." Historic Dallas. Vol. 7, No. 17, Nov./Dec. 1985. p. 3.

Preservation Texas, a private non-profit statewide formed.

STATE PRESERVATION PLANNING--U.S.--WISCONSIN

"Historic Preservation Task Force Created to Study State Legislation and Preservation Program." Wisconsin Preservation. Vol. 10, No. 1, Jan./Feb. 1986. p. 1-3.

STATUES

Russell, John. "How Miss Liberty Was Born." Smithsonian. Vol. 15, No. 4, July 1984. pp. 46-55.

STATUES--CONSERVATION AND RESTORATION

Cliver, E. Blaine. "The Statue of Liberty: Systems within a Structure of Metals." APT Bulletin. Vol. 18, No. 3, 1986. p. 13-23.

STATUES--CONSERVATION AND RESTORATION

Crosbie, Michael J. "Restoring a Lady's Tarnished Beauty." Architecture. July 1984. pp. 44-54.

STATUES--CONSERVATION AND RESTORATION

Gale, Frances and John C. Robbins. "Removal of Interior Coatings at the Statue of Liberty." APT Bulletin. Vol. 16, No. 3 & 4, 1984. p. 63-65.

STATUES--CONSERVATION AND RESTORATION

"National Capital Restoration". CRM Bulletin. Vol. 8, No. 1, Feb. 1985. p. 12.

Dupont Fountain, Washington, D.C.

STATUES--CONSERVATION AND RESTORATION

"Renovating the Statue of Liberty." APWA Reporter. Vol. 53, NO. 6, June 1986. p. 10-11.

STATUES--CONSERVATION AND RESTORATION

"Statue a Beacon of Freedom." Historic Hawai'i. Vol. 12, No. 6, July 1986. p. 7-9.

Some history and details on the renovation of the torch of the Statue of Liberty.

STATUES--CONSERVATION AND RESTORATION

Taylor, Nick. "Restoration: On to 1986." Americana. Vol. 13, No. 4, Sept./Oct. 1985. p. 56-59.

The Statue of Liberty project discussed.

STATUES--CONSERVATION AND RESTORATION

Thomas, Bill. "Statue of Liberty." Courier. Vol. 30, No. 9, Sept. 1985. p. 1-3.

STATUES--CONSERVATION AND RESTORATION--U.S.-- NEW YORK--NEW YORK CITY

Britz, Billie S. "N.Y. Chapter Restoring Sherman Monument." The Victorian. Vol. 14, No. 2. Summer 1986. pp. 1-2.

Restoration and conservation of the St. Gaudens statue of General Sherman at the entrance to Central Park.

STATUES--CONSERVATION AND RESTORATION--U.S.--NEW YORK--NEW YORK CITY

Fisher, Thomas. "Liberty Update." Progressive Architecture. Mar. 1985. p. 95-99.

STATUES--CONSERVATION AND RESTORATION--U.S.-- NEW YORK--NEW YORK CITY

"HAER Sets Ms Liberty's Record Straight." Society for Industrial Archaeology Newsletter. Vol. 15, No. 2. Summer 1986. pp. 1-3.

Physical dimensions and structural statistics of the Statue of Liberty, plus HAER's role in documenting its renovation.

STEAMBOATS

Gerred, Jancie H. "Wreck of the Altadoc." Inland Seas. Vol. 42, No. 4. Winter 1986. p. 230.

The steamer Altadoc made into a tourist attraction after a storm put it out of active service.

STEAMBOATS

Alexander, Bill. "Romance, History, Beauty: It's the Delta Queen." The Old News Is Good News Gazette. Vol. 3, No. 3. Dec. 1986. pp. 1-2; 14.

STEAMBOATS

Harmon, J. Scott. "Recovering the Steamboat Bertrand: marine archeologists study the features and cargo of a unique time capsule buried since 1865 under 25 feet of river silt." Early Man. Autumn 1979. p. 10-12.

STEEL, STRUCTURAL

Nixon, Don. "A Simple Method for Measuring the Yield Strength of Steel in Heritage Buildings." APT Bulletin. Vol. 15, No. 2, 1983. pp. 17-19.

STENCIL WORK

Murphy, Barbara L. "Recreating the Victorian Ceiling." Utah Preservation/Restoration. Vol. III, 1981. pp. 37-41.

STENCIL WORK

Somers, Robert. "A Brief History of Stencil Decoration". The Clarion. Winter 1980. p. 46-63.

STENCIL WORK

Witsell, Rebecca. "Restoring 1919 Stencils." Old House Journal. Vol. 13, No. 3, Apr. 1985. p. 55-57.

STONE

Bristow, Ian. "Two exterior treatments used to imitate stone during the eighteenth and early nineteenth centuries." Transactions. v.4, 1979. p.3-6.

STONE

   Silcox-Crowe, Nigel. "Cobble Cottages."
Traditional Homes. Vol. 3, No. 1, Oct. 1986.
p. 98-102.

   Eighteenth and nineteenth century
flint cobble houses in Norfolk, England.

STONE--PRESERVATION

   Hatsagortsian, Zavene. "Methodes
d'essai pour l'evaluation de l'efficacite
de l'impregnation des pierres de
revetement avec des solutions hydrofuges
et stabilisatrices." Monumentum. June
1983. pp. 101-106.

STONE--PRESERVATION

   Korpan, Dean. "Composite Stone
Repairs at Drayton Hall, A Case Study
of Stone Restoration Techniques."
APT Bulletin. Vol. 14, No. 3, 1982.
pp. 36-41.

STONE--PRESERVATION

   Phillips, Morgan. "A Stone Porch
Replicated in Wooden Blocks, The Morse-Libby
House." APT Bulletin. Vol. 14, No. 3, 1982.
pp. 12-20.

STONE--PRESERVATION

   Uhlmann, Charles. "Love and Care of
Old Lava Rock." Historic Hawai'i News.
July/August 1983. pp. 4-5.

STONE--PRESERVATION

   Winkler, Erhard M. "Decay of Stone
Monuments and Buildings: The Role of Acid
Rain." Technology and Conservation. Spring
1982. pp. 32-36.

STONE-- PRESERVATION

   Winkler, Erhard M. "Historical Implications
in the Complexity of Destructive Salt Weathering -
Cleopatra's Needle, New York." APT Bulletin.
Vol. 12, No. 2, 1980. pp. 94-102.

STONE--PRESERVATION

   Winkler, Erhard M. "Stone Preservation, The
Earth Scientists's View." APT Bulletin. No. 2,
1978. pp. 118-121.

STONE CARVING

   Glover, Judy. "Arkansas Stonecutter."
Americana. Jan./Feb. 1986. p. 50-53.

   Stonemason in Eureka Springs, Arkansas aids
restoration of stone buildings.

STONE CARVING--U.S.--WASHINGTON D.C.

   Gurfein, Marion Reh. "Stone Beasties."
19th Century. Winter 1979. pp. 59-60.

STORE BUILDINGS--CONSERVATION AND RESTORATION

   "An Introduction to Storefront Rehabilitation."
Conserve Neighborhoods Supplement. Summer, 1979.
4p.: bibliography.

STORE BUILDINGS

   Flanagan, Barbara. "Box Americana."
Metropolis. Dec. 1985. p. 28-31, 36-37.

   A history of supermarket architecture.

STORE BUILDINGS--CONSERVATION AND
   RESTORATION

   "Profiting from the Past."
Architectural Record. January 1984.
pp. 97-113.

CONTENTS: Down to the Sea in Shops,
South Street Seaport, NYC--Main Street
Revival, Mill Street Revival, Aspen, Colo--
Pushcart Agora, Columbia Union Market,
Brooklyn, N.Y.--New Light on an Old
Subject, Miami, ▬ Fla.

STORE BUILDINGS--CONSERVATION AND RESTORATION

   "Upper-Story Conversions Find Strong Markets."
Center City Report. December 1981. pp. 5-6.

STOVES

Groft, Tammis. "Cast-iron stoves from the Upper Hudson Valley". 19th Century. Autumn 1980. p. 28-29.

STOVES

Pilling, Ron. "Restoring the Baltimore Heater." The Old-House Journal. Vol. XII, No. 9, November 1984. pp. 191, 206-209, 211.

STOVES

White, Frank G. "Stoves in Nineteenth-Century New England." Antiques. Sep. 1979. pp. 592-599.

STREET FURNITURE

Fleming, Ronald Lee. "Interpreting and Enhancing Townscape: Appealing to the Landscape of the Mind." Small Town. November-December 1981. pp. 18-24.

STREET FURNITURE

"Ring Out the Old." Country Life. Vol. 181, No. 18. April 30, 1987. p. 118-119.

Telephone boxes (booths) in Britain.

STREET FURNITURE--U.S.--MICHIGAN--SAGINAW COUNTY

"Historic Transit Shelter and Telephone Booth." Michigan Historic District Network. Dec. 1985. p. 1.

STREET LIGHTING

"Saving the Streetlights", The Landmark Society of Western New York, November 1984, p. 1.

STREET LIGHTING--HISTORY

Bolton, Kate. "The Great Awakening of the Night; Lighting America's Streets." Landscape. No. 3, 1979. pp. 41-47.

STREETCARS

Middleton, William D. "A Century of Cable Cars." American Heritage. Vol. 36, No. 3, Apr./May 1985, p. 90-101.

Includes list of companies and years of operation.

STREETCARS

Plous, F.K., Jr. "A Desire Named Streetcar." Planning. June 1984. pp. 15-23.

Restored or new streetcar systems help revitalize urban areas.

STREETCARS--U.S.--LOUISIANA--NEW ORLEANS

"Happy Birthday to the St. Charles Street-car Line." New Orleans Preservation in Print. Vol. 12, No. 7, Sept. 1985. p. 3-9.

A feature on streetcars in New Orleans presented on the occasion of the 150th anniversary of the still functioning St. Charles line.

STREETCARS--U.S.--TEXAS--DALLAS

"Perry to Head McKinney Ave. Trolley Fund-Raising Campaign." Historic Dallas. Vol. 7, No. 17, Nov./Dec. 1985. p. 4.

STREETS

Appleyard, Donald. "Livable Streets: Protected Neighborhoods?" Urban Design International. Jul./Aug. 1980. pp. 32-33; 39-40.

STRUCTURAL ENGINEERING

Koontz, Thomas. "Building Basics: What Makes Structures Stand Up, and Fall Down." Fine Homebuilding. No. 32, Apr./May 1986. p. 29-33.

Description of the structural systems of buildings with references to Frank Lloyd Wright's Fallingwater.

STUCCO

"It Looks Like Stucco..."
Progressive Architecture. December 1983.
pp. 83-87.

STUCCO--PRESERVATION

Gandee, Charles K. "In deference." Architectural Record. May 1985. p. 146-151.

The restoration of Santa Fe Museum of Fine Arts (1917) described.

STUCCO--PRESERVATION

Minnery, Catherine and Donald Minnery.
"Repairing Stucco." The Old-House Journal.
July 1979. pp. 73; 77-79.

SUBURBAN HOMES

Anderson, Jay. "Almost Gone, Historic Houses of Our Own Time." Museum News.
February 1983. pp. 45-53.

SUBURBS

Guter, Robert P. "Llewellyn Park: Landscape Landmark." Preservation Perspective NJ. Vol. III, No. 6, September/October 1984. p. 5.

SUBURBS

Stilgoe, John R. "The Suburbs." American Heritage. Feb./Mar. 1984. pp. 20-37.

SUBURBS

Wilk, Christopher. "American Arcadia."
Skyline. January 1982. p. 13.

SUBURBS

Yeager, David J. "Working Class, Looking for Elan in Levittown." Landscape Architecture.
January 1982. pp. 64-67.

SUBURBS--CONSERVATION AND RESTORATION

Berke, Arnold M. "An Experiment in Suburban Conservation." Place. Vol. 4, no. 3.
March 1984. pp. 1-4.

SURPLUS GOVERNMENT PROPERTY

"City Land Sales: Neighborhood Development Aided Thru Disposition Mechanisms." The Neighborhood Works.
April 1983. p. 1.

SURPLUS GOVERNMENT PROPERTY

Cooper, Terence K. "Disposition of City-held Properties: Six Cities Outline Techniques, Results." Journal of Housing. June 1978. pp. 287-289.

SURPLUS GOVERNMENT PROPERTY

"Program to Sell Federal Lands Sets Off Alarms." Conservation Foundation Letter.
April 1982. Entire Issue.

SURPLUS GOVERNMENT PROPERTY

Starr, Richard and Nathan Schloss. "Get the Most Out of Urban Land : Sell it or Lease it." Planning,
June 1979. pp. 14-17.

SURPLUS GOVERNMENT PROPERTY

"Surplus Property Can Be Development Tool."
Center City Report. April 1982. p. 1.

SURVEYS

Comp, Allen. "The Cultural Resources Inventory Comes to the Pacific Northwest Region." CRM Bulletin. September 1983. pp. 5-6.

SURVEYS

"First Annual Workshop on Survey and Registration." Newsletter, Society of Architectural Historians. Vol. 29, No. 4, July 1985. p. 7.

SURVEYS

Long, Nancy. "Before You Prepare a Nomination, Read This." The Indiana Preservationist. No. 2, 1982, p. 5.

SURVEYS--INDIA

Cooper, Ilay. "The Threatened Building of the Marwari Heartland." Intach. No. 7, Jan/March 1986. p. 2-7.

A survey of the painted havelis of the Marwari region of India.

SURVEYS--U.S.

CRM Bulletin. Vol. 9, No. 3, June 1986.

Entire issue on HABS and HAER.

SURVEYS--U.S.--ALASKA

Spude, Robert. "Historic American Building Survey/Historic American Engineering Record in Alaska." Heritage. No. 28. Apr.-Jun. 1986. p. 1.

SURVEYS--U.S.--ARKANSAS

"AHPP: Surveying the State's Historic Properties." Danch Directions. Vol. 4, No. 4, Fall 1985. p. 1, 4.

SURVEY--U.S.--CALIFORNIA--PASADENA

"ASID to Document Historic Interiors." Pasadena Heritage. Vol. 11, No. 1, Fall 1985. p. 8.

SURVEYS--U.S.--COLORADO

Gauss, Nancy V. "CRM Database." Colorado Heritage News. April 1983. p. 6.

SURVEYS--U.S.--GEORGIA--ATLANTA

Timmis, Gail Morgan. "City of Atlanta Historic Structures Inventory Update." Preservation Times. Vol. 5, No. 2, Fall 1985. p. 1, 3.

SURVEYS--U.S.--ILLINOIS

Seibert, Susan M. "Rural Survey Begins" Historic Illinois. April 1980. p. 12-13

SURVEYS--U.S.--INDIANA--COLUMBUS

Knight, Carleton III. "Return to Columbus." Architecture. June 1984. pp. 32-39.

SURVEYS--U.S.--IOWA--KEOKUK

Vogel, Neal. "Architectural Survey: Keokuk." The Bracket. Vol. 1, No. 3, Fall 1985. p. 1-3.

SURVEYS--U.S.--KENTUCKY--FLEMING COUNTY

Wells, Camille. "Survey of Fleming County, Kentucky: Suggestions for Recording Cultural Resources." 11593. Feb./Mar. 1980, p. 1-4.

SURVEYS--U.S.--MONTANA

"A Harvest of Survey Findings." Preservation. Nov./Dec. 1985. p. 1-3. Supplement to
Montana Post, Newsletter of the Montana Historical Society. Nov./Dec. 1985.

SURVEYS--U.S.--NEW YORK--ALBANY

Botch, Judith. "Significant Interiors:
State Street's Public Banking Rooms." Albany
Preservation Report. Summer 1985. p. 11.

SURVEYS--U.S.--OHIO

"Architectural Survey Underway in Two
Counties." Ohio Preservation. Vol. 6, No. 7,
July 1986. p. 1-2.

Survey of historic properties in Gallia
and Lawrence counties.

SURVEYS--U.S.--OHIO

"Lawrence County Survey Records 440
Historic Properties." Ohio Preservation.
Vol. 7, No. 2, Feb. 1987. p. 1-2.

SURVEYS--U.S.--TENNESSEE--NASHVILLE

"Taking Inventory Architecturally."
History-Gram. No. 38, Fall 1985. p. 1-2.

SURVEYS--U.S.--TEXAS--DALLAS

Emrich, Ron. "Resources Survey Nears Com-
pletion." Historic Dallas. July 1985. p. 4.

SURVEYS--U.S.--WASHINGTON, D.C.

"National Endowment for the Arts Funds
Downtown Study." D.C. Preservation League.
Winter 1986. p. 1.

Study of downtown Washinton D.C. will
deal with conflicting development needs and
incentives needed to encourage the preservation of small historic buildings.

SYNAGOGUES

Pearce, Sally. "Historic Synagogues Symbolize Perservance." Colorado Heritage News. April 1986. p. 5.

SYNAGOGUES--U.S.--CALIFORNIA--SAN FRANCISCO

"Ohabai Shalome Synogogue." Heritage Newsletter. Vol. 13, No. 2, Aug. 1985. p. 1.

SYNDICATES (FINANCE)

"Bank Holding Company, NHS, Team Up on
Syndicated Rehab in Chicago." Urban Conservation
Report. Apr. 29, 1983. p. 2.

SYNDICATES (FINANCE)

Blenko, David B. "Real Estate Syndication Investments: Risks and Rewards", Real Estate Issues,
Vol. 9, No. 2, Fall/Winter 1984, pp. 15-18.

SYNDICATES (FINANCE)

"Building Reversion Clause in
Land Lease Used to Stave Off
Displacement." Urban Conservation
Report. September 15, 1983. p. 2.

SYNDICATES(FINANCE)

"Charity + Syndication = Rent
Subsidies for Elderly Rehab in Boston."
Urban Conservation Report. January 28, 1983.
p. 3.

SYNDICATES (FINANCE)

"Cleveland Group Rehabs Historic Building
for Housing Through Syndicated Ownership."
Economic Growth and Revitalization Report. No.
85-24, Dec. 26, 1985. p. 1-2.

Cleveland's Near West Housing Corporation,
an ICVF grantee, portrayed.

SYNDICATES (FINANCE)

"Co-op Syndication, Rent Subsidy Trust Fund, Used in Adaptive Use in Maine." Urban Conservation Report. January 14, 1983. p. 2.

SYNDICATES (FINANCE)

"Nonprofit Syndication in Newton, Mass." Urban Conservation Report. February 29, 1984. p. 5.

SYNDICATES (FINANCE)

"Reversing Earlier Stand, IRS Tells Nonprofit it can Syndicate." Urban Conservation Report. October 31, 1983. p. 2.

SYNDICATES (FINANCE)

Roulac, Stephen. "Syndication Emerges to Transform the Real Estate Capital Market." Real Estate Finance. Vol. 1, No. 4, Winter 1985. p. 18-27.

SYNDICATES (FINANCE)

Sears, Cecil E. "The Growing Opportunities and Challenges of Syndications." Urban Land. June 1984. pp. 7-11.

SYNDICATES (FINANCE)

"Small-Scale Syndication Used in Neighborhood Commercial Revitalization." Housing and Development Reporter. March 28, 1983. pp. 948-949.

SYNDICATES (FINANCE)

"A Sweet Syndication." Urban Conservation Report. April 15, 1983. p. 3.

SYNDICATES (FINANCE)

Wetterer, Charles C. "Mortgage Loan Partnerships Fuel Industry Growth: Mortgage programs will soon be a major component of the syndication industry." Real Estate Finance. Vol. 1, No. 4. Winter 1985. pp. 81-84.

TALL BUILDINGS--U.S.--ILLINOIS--CHICAGO

Turak, Theodore. "Remembrances of the Home Insurance Building." Journal of the Society of Architectural Historians. Vol. 44, No. 1, Mar. 1985. p. 60-65.

TAX CREDITS

"Blaming Park Service Reversal, Developer Blanks Out Haas Mural." Architecture. May 1985. p. 72, 77, 82.

TAX CREDITS

Clark, Charles T. "Tax Credits Saved, but Developers Seek to Locate New Investors." Connecticut Trust for Historic Preservation News. Vol. 10, No. 1. Winter 1987. pp. 1; 11.

TAX CREDITS

"Eliminating Historic Tax Credits Doesn't Help Fund Rate Reduction, Says Trust President." Economic Growth and Revitalization Report. No. 85-12, June 27, 1985. p. 5.

TAX CREDITS

"Elimination of Historic Rehab Credit Will Hurt Projects and Cities, Trust President Says." Housing and Development Reporter. Vol. 13, No. 6, July 1, 1985. p. 92-93.

TAX CREDITS

"IRS Allows Historic Tax Credit on Private Renovation of Federal Building." Housing and Development Reporter. Vol. 12, No. 12, August 13, 1984. pp. 221-2.

TAX CREDITS

"IRS Issues Proposed Regulations for Rehabilitation Tax Credit." Housing and Development
Reporter. Vol. 13, No. 8, July 15, 1985. p. 131-
132.

TAX CREDITS

Kriviskey, Bruce. "Federal Standards for
Preservation." Architecture. Nov. 1986.
p. 114-115.

TAX CREDITS

McGrath, Roger. "Tax Credit, Tax Credit,
Who's Got the Tax Credit." St. Louis Home.
Vol. 6, No. 2, Feb. 1986. p. 6-7, 17.

TAX CREDITS

"New Tax Credit for Low-Income Housing
Should Spur Rehab." Community Development
Digest. No. 86-19, Oct. 7, 1986. p. 8-9.

TAX CREDITS

"Reagan's New Tax Plan." Urban Conservation Report. Vol. 9, No. 5, May 31, 1985.
p. 1-3.

TAX CREDITS

"Rehabilitation Tax Credit Update." The
Alliance Review. Vol. 2, No. 4, 1987. p. 1-2.

TAX CREDITS

Reilly, Ann. "Making the Best of Tax
Reform." Fortune. July 22, 1985. p. 86-88.

National Trust policy staffer Ian Spatz
quoted.

TAX CREDITS

"Relocated Old Buildings Should Not Lose
Rehab Tax Credits, IRS Panel Told." Community
Development Digest. No. 85-22, Nov. 19, 1985.
p. 11.

Former NT attorney Tom Coughlin testifies in
favor of allowing relocations of 30 and 40 year
old buildings to distressed areas.

TAX CREDITS

"Rostenkowski Pledges Transition Rules as
Real Estate Groups Criticize Tax Plan." Housing
and Development Reporter. Vol. 13, No. 8. July
15, 1985. pp. 116-117.

The testimony of National Trust Board Chairman Alan S. Boyd, in support of credits for
hsitoric rehabilitation is reported on.

TAX CREDITS

Schmertz, Mildred F. "Editorial: Rehabilitation investment tax credits - an endangered
achievement." Architectural Record. Feb. 1986.
p. 9.

TAX CREDITS

"Senate Tax Bill REtains Rehab Tax
Credits, LImits Use." Urban Conservation Report. Vol. 10, No. 5, June 1986.
p. 1-2.

TAX CREDITS

"Update on Investment Tax Credits
for Historic Preservation." Culture
& History. Vol. 2, No. 3, April-May-
June 1986. p. 26.

TAX CREDITS

"Using Tax Credits to Save Historic Buildings: An Update." Planning. January 1984.
pp. 24 - 27.

Act explained, statistics provided.

TAX CREDITS

Wells, John E. "Rehabilitation Tax Credits and
the Tax Reform Act of 1986." Notes on Virginia. No.
29, Fall 1986. p. 16-17.

TAX CREDITS--U.S.--Washington, D.C.

Arensburg, Walter W. "The Historic Approval Process: The Case of the Demonet", Urban Land, Vol. 43, No. 12, December 1984, pp. 6-10.

TAX INCENTIVES

"All You Ever Wanted to Know About Investment Tax Credits for Rehab., But Were Afraid to Ask and a Glossary of Preservation Terms." Historic Savannah Newsletter. Jan./Feb. 1984. pp. 8-9/

TAX INCENTIVES

Baxter, Cheryl. "Tax Increment Financing Remains a Viable Tool for Funding Public Projects." Journal of Housing. November 1981. pp. 549-554.

TAX INCENTIVES

Candee, Richard and Ward H. Jandl. "Forum on Preservation, Income Tax and Big Business." The Forum (SAH). October 1982. Entire Issue.

TAX INCENTIVES

Carpenter, Kimberly. "Landmarks are on Shaky Ground with Investors." Business Week. Aug. 26, 1985. p. 79-80.

TAX INCENTIVES

"Construction under threatened rehab tax credits tops $2 billion rate." Architectural Record. March 1985. p. 33.

TAX INCENTIVES

Coons, Richard A. "New Tax Law Offers Big Incentives for Renovation." Historic Hawai'i News. Nov. 1981. p. 7.

TAX INCENTIVES

Denhez, Marc. "Taxes." Canadian Heritage. May/June 1986. p. 37-41.

Heritage tax incentives may boost Canada's economy.

TAX INCENTIVES

Dora Moore Associates, Inc. "Rehab Tax Credit Aids Townhouses." Colorado Heritage News. Nov. 1983. p. 7.

TAX INCENTIVES

Forward, William. "New Tax Law Aids Preservation." (Statistics). New Jersey Historical Commission Newsletter. May 1983. p. 5.

TAX INCENTIVES

Friedman, Stephen B. "Local Incentives for Revitalization." Center City Report. July 1981. p. 1.

TAX INCENTIVES

Gilmore, Jann Haynes. "Tax Incentives for Historic Preservation." Practicing Planner, June, 1979. pp. 33-35, 48.

TAX INCENTIVES

Gleye, Paul H. "Canada Can Profit from Our Mistakes." Canadian Heritage. Vol. 12, Issue 4, Oct.-Nov. 1986. p. 2-3.

An American conservation planner discusses the creation of heritage tax incentives.

TAX INCENTIVES

"Historic Louisville Neighborhood Gets a Boost from Preservation Tax Credits." Local Economic Growth & Neighborhood Reinvestment Report. November 3, 1983. pp. 6-7.

TAX INCENTIVES

"Historic Rehabs Low Cost, High Benefit Says GAO." Urban Conservation Report. Vol. VIII, No. 7, April 24, 1984. p. 5.

TAX INCENTIVES

"Historic Tax Certification Backlogs Not a Problem, Says Interior Department." Housing and Development Reporter. August 1, 1983. p. 182.

TAX INCENTIVES

Huff, Nadine F. "Rehab Spurred by Equity Syndication." Urban Land. February 1983. pp. 28-29.

TAX INCENTIVES

"Leaseback Backlash." The Grants Manship Center News. July/August 1983. p. 13.

TAX INCENTIVES

Merritt, E.W. "Tax Increment Financing Can Aid Redevelopment." Center City Report. May 1982. p. 1.

TAX INCENTIVES

"Montana Sweetens Federal Preservation Tax Credits." Urban Conservation Report. January 14, 1983. p. 4.

Vertical File

TAX INCENTIVES

National Trust for Historic Preservation. A Tax Guide to Tax- Advantaged Rehabilitation. Washington D.C. 1986. 18p. (VF)

TAX INCENTIVES

"New Tax Act Strengthens Incentives for Rehabilitation." Notes on Virginia. Spring 1982. pp. 3-5.

TAX INCENTIVES

"Old Buildings and the Economic Recovery Act of 1981." Urban Conservation Report. Special Report, March 1982.

TAX INCENTIVES

Oldham, Sally G. "Historic Preservation Tax Incentives." Urban Land, December 1979. pp. 3-10.

TAX INCENTIVES

"Preservation Pays the Taxpayer." The Montgomery County Preservationist. Vol. 2, No. 4, Feb/Mar. 1987. p. 1, 5.

TAX INCENTIVES

"Sale of Tax Breaks, Foundation PRI: Keys to old 'Y' Renovation." Urban Conservation Report. December 17, 1981. pp. 4-5.

TAX INCENTIVES

"Tax Benefits - A Benefit for Virginia." Notes on Virginia. No. 26, Spring 1985. p. 4-7.

TAX INCENTIVES

"Tax Break Available for CA Restoration." The Society for Commercial Archeology News Journal. July 1983. p. 3.

TAX INCENTIVES

"Tax Incentives have Spurred Interest in Historic Preservation." AIA Journal. November 1982. pp. 19-21.

Vertical File

TAX INCENTIVES

Tax Policy and Administration: Historic Preservation Tax Incentives. U.S. General Accounting Office, Aug. 1986. 33p. (VF)

TAX INCENTIVES

Thompson, Terri. "Tax Reform Already Has Developers Spooked." Business Week. June 24, 1985. p. 42.

TAX INCENTIVES

"Twin Districts Fund Downtown Action." Downtown Idea Exchange. June 1, 1982. pp. 4-5.

TAX INCENTIVES

"Use of Historic Rehab Tax Credit Continues to Increase, Says Interior." Housing and Development Reporter. January 30, 1984. p. 744.

TAX INCENTIVES--U.S.--ARKANSAS--VAN BUREN

"Tax Incentives Provide Momentum for Revitalization After Federal Funds Run Out." Local Economic Growth and Neighborhood Reinvestment Report. July 19, 1984. No. 84-14. pp. 1-2.

TAX INCENTIVES--U.S.--COLORADO

Pfaff, Christine. "Survey Findings Support Rehab Tax Credits." Colorado Heritage News. Nov. 1985. p. 5.

Job creation, new housing and returning vacant buildings to service found among benefits of federal tax program in three Colorado cities.

TAX INCENTIVES--U.S.--HAWAII

Dressel, David L. "How to Get A Historic Home Tax Exemption." Historic Hawai'i News. January 1984. pp. 4-5.

TAX INCENTIVES--U.S.--ILLINOIS--STATE PROGRAM

"Private Homeowners Now Eligible for Rehabilitation Tax Incentives." Historic Illinois. Vol. 7, No. 1, June 1984. p. 4.

TAX INCENTIVES--U.S.--NEVADA--LAS VEGAS

Atchison, Sondra D. "A Renaissance That Tax Reform Could Smother." Business Week. June 24, 1985. p. 36D, 36H.

TAX INCENTIVES--U.S.--TEXAS

"Historic Rehabs: Little Cost to Federal Treasury, Big Gains for Local Economies." Urban Conservation Report. Vol. 9, No. 5, May 31, 1985. p. 3-4.

Summary of Shlaes & Co. study of the use of federal credits in Texas.

TAXATION

Brumbaugh, Mark B., Tho. J. Feichter and Lisa A. Winters. "Tax Reform Alternatives: Treasury II is Not the Only Game in Town." Real Estate Issues. Vol. 2, No. 3, Fall 1985. p. 59-73.

TAXATION

Downs, Anthony. "Impacts of the President's Proposed Tax Reforms Upon Real Estate." Urban Land. Vol. 44, No. 8, Aug. 1985. p. 7-14.

TAXATION

Guskind, Robert. "Tax Reform Blues." Planning. Vol. 51, No. 7, July 1985. p. 7-13.

TAXATION

Meltzer, Richard. "The New Tax Laws," Museum News, Vol. 63, No. 2, December 1984, pp. 38-40.

The 1984 tax act on charitable contributions discussed and the nature of additional change assessed.

TAXATION--LAW

Alexander, Laurence A. "TIF Equals Urban Renewal?" Downtown Idea Exchange. Vol. 33, No.22, Nov. 15, 1986. p.2-4.

Tax increment financing as a factor in urban renewal.

TAXATION--LAW

Bacot, Barbara SuRelle. "Changes in Tax Law Affect Historic Rehabilitation." New Orleans Preservation in Print. Vol. 14, No. 3, Apr. 1987. p. 12-13.

TAXATION--LAW

"Belgium, U.K. Move Ahead With Enterprise Zones." Urban Innovation Abroad. Vol. 8, No. 6, June 1984. p. 8.

TAXATION--LAW

Brumbaugh, Mark B. et al. "Special Report: The Deficit Reduction Act of 1984!" Real Estate Finance. Vol. 1, No. 3, Fall 1984. pp. 31-47.

TAXATION--LAW

Carlisle, Rick. "Tax Reform Plan Curbs Housing, CD Investments." NAHRO Monitor. Aug. 31, 1986. p. 7-13.

TAXATION--LAW

Friedman, Jack P. "Interest Rates on Seller-Financed Real Estate Under the 1984 Tax Act." Real Estate Finance. Vol. 1, No. 4, Winter 1985. p. 72-76.

TAXATION--LAW

Gottschalk, Earl C. Jr. "Tax Changes for Historic Rehabilitations Lead Syndicators to Seek Smaller Investors." The Wall Street Journal. Mar. 2, 1987.

TAXATION--LAW

Haaker, Anne. "Tax Reform Act of 1986 Aids Preservationists." Historic Illinois. Vol. 9, No. 5, Feb. 1987. p. 10-11.

TAXATION--LAW

"Historic Louisville Neighborhood Gets a Boost from Preservation Tax Credits." Local Economic Growth & Neighborhood Reinvestment Report. November 3, 1983. p. 6.

TAXATION--LAW

"Historic REhab Tax Provisions Alive and Well." North Carolina Preservation. No. 65, Sept.-Oct. 1986. p. 1.

TAXATION--LAW

"Low-income Housing Eggs All in Tax Credit Basket." Urban Conservation Report. Vol. 10, No.10, Oct. 31, 1986. p.1-3.

Effect of new tax law on rehabilitation of low-income housing.

TAXATION--LAW

"The 1981 Tax Act and Survival of Older Buildings." Urban Conservation Report--Special Report. August 18, 1981. 6 pages.

TAXATION--LAW

"Other Tax Law Changes: A Summary." Urban Conservation Report. Vol.10, No.10, Oct. 31, 1986. p.3-6.

The new tax laws effects on preservation and housing rehabilitation.

TAXATION--LAW

Shafroth, Frank. "1984 Tax Reform Act, Major Provisions of Interest to Cities." Nation's Cities Weekly. July 2, 1984. pp. 4-5.

TAXATION--LAW

Shenkman, Martin M. "1984 Tax Act: A Roster of Restrictions." National Mall Monitor. Vol. 14, No. 6, Jan./Feb. 1985. p. 68, 71-72.

TAXATION--LAW

Stoller, Linda A. "Tax Shelter Registration: When, How and What?: IRS Proposed Regulations give substance to the new registration requirements." Real Estate Finance. Vol. 1, No. 4, Winter 1985. p. 68-71.

TAXATION--LAW

"Tax Reform Act Trims the Good with the Bad." Farmland Notes. Vol. 5, No. 12, Dec. 1986. p. 1,3.

TAXATION--LAW

"Tax Reform and Housing Rehab: Part I." Rehab Notes. Vol. 10, No. 8, Sept. 1986. p. 1.

TAXATION--LAW

"Tax Reform and Housing Rehabilitation: City Partnerships Assess the Consequences." Economic Growth & Revitalization. No. 86-16, Aug. 28, 1986. p. 1-2.

TAXATION--LAW

"Tax Reform Passes." Preservation Progress. Vol. 1, No. 1, Winter 1986. p. 1.

TAXATION--LAW

"There is a 'Silver Lining' in Tax Reform for Community Groups: No Limit." Economic Growth and Revitalization. No. 86-24, Dec. 23, 1986, p.1-3.

TAXATION, ERTA, 1981

Feinschreiber, Robert. "New Tax Benefits from Old Buildings." Downtown Idea Exchange. Vol. 31, No. 12, June 15, 1984. pp. 2-4.

TAXATION, EXEMPTION FROM--U.S.--HAWAII

"Tax Exemption Takes Effect." Historic Hawaii News. June 1985. p. 1.

Real property tax exemption for homes on state register in effect.

TECHNOLOGY

Fidler, John. "High-Tech Diagnosis." Traditional Homes. May 1986. p. 58-62.

Use of fibre-optics, radiography, ultrasonics, etc. in the detection of structural defects.

TECHNOLOGY

Kevlin, Mary Joan. "Radiographic Inspection of Plank-House Construction." APT Bulletin. Vol. 18, No. 3, 1986. p. 40-47.

A veterinarian's portable x-ray unit used as a diagnostic tool to help uncover the skeletons of wood-frame buildings.

TECHNOLOGY

"Technologies for Prehistoric & Historic Preservation. Summary." Congress of the United States. Office of Technology Assessment. 1986. 39p. (VF)

TECHNOLOGY--HISTORY

Jones, Hervie P. "The Town Lattice Truss in Building Construction." APT Bulletin. Vol. XV, No. 3, 1983. pp. 39 - 41.

316

TECHNOLOGY--HISTORY

Pursell, Carroll. "The History of Technology as a Source of Appropriate Technology." The Public Historian, Winter 1979. pp. 15-22.

TECHNOLOGY--HISTORY--BIBLIOGRAPHY

Goodwin, Jack. "Current Bibliography in the History of Technology (1978)". Technology and Culture. April 1980. p. 281-355.

TENNESSEE--NASHVILLE--BELMONT

Cooney, Deborah. " Adelicia's House: Trophies of a Weekend Collector". 19th Century. Winter 1979. p. 49-51.

TERMINALS (TRANSPORTATION)

"The Golden Years in/of a Trolley Barn." Architectural Record. July 1982. pp. 88-89.

TERRA COTTA

Callahan, Carol. "Terra Cotta: A Worst Case History." Old House Journal. Vol 15, No. 4. Jul./Aug. 1987. pp. 52 - 54.

TERRA-COTTA

Fidler, John. "The Manufacture of Architectural Terracotta and Faience in the United Kingdom." APT Bulletin. Vol. XV, No. 2, 1983. pp. 27-32.

TERRA COTTA

Friends of Terra Cotta. Quarterly. Newsletter.

TERRA COTTA

Rastorfer, Darl. "Terra Cotta: Past to Present." Architectural Record. Jan. 1987. p. 110-111.

TERRA COTTA

Ryser, Edward E. "A History of the Terra-Cotta Roof." Friends of Terra Cotta. Vol. 3, No. 1, Spring 1984. pp. 16-18.

TERRA COTTA

Sites. No. 18, 1986. 64p. (Entire issue devoted to terra cotta.)

TERRA COTTA

Stockbridge, Jerry G. "Analysis of In-Service Architectural Terra Cotta: Support for Technical Investigations." APT Bulletin. Vol. 18, No. 4, 1986. p. 41-45.

TERRA COTTA

Tindall, Susan. "Terra Cotta: An Introduction to Its Manufacture, Inspection & Repair." Old House Journal. Vol. 15, No. 4. Jul./Aug. 1987 pp. 47 - 51.

TERRA COTTA

Tunick, Susan. "The American Terra Cotta Industry." SITES. No. 13, 1985. pp. 31-35.

TERRA COTTA--CONSERVATION AND RESTORATION

Fidler, John. "The Conservation of Architectural Terra cotta and Faience." Friends of Terra Cotta Newsletter. Fall 1983. Part I. pp. 10-13.

TERRA COTTA--CONSERVATION AND RESTORATION

Fidler, John. "The Conservation of
Architectural Terracotta and Faience."Part2.
Friends of Terra Cotta Newsletter.
Winter 1983-84. pp. 8-12.

TERRA COTTA--CONSERVATION AND RESTORATION

Fidler, John. "The Conservation of
Architectural Terra Cotta and Faience." Part
4, (7) The Soiling of Terra Cotta, (8) Cleaning.
Friends of Terra Cotta. Vol. 3, No. 2, Summer
1984. pp. 8-10.

TERRA COTTA--CONSERVATION AND RESTORATION

Fidler, John. "The Conservation of
Architectural Terra Cotta and Faience." Reprinted
from the Association for Studies in the Conservation of Historic Buildings Transactions, Vol.
6 (1981). Friends of Terra Cotta. Vol. 3, No. 1,
Spring 1984. pp. 12-16.

TERRA COTTA--CONSERVATION AND RESTORATION

Fidler, John. "The Conservation of Architectural
Terra Cotta and Faience: Maintenance, Repair
and Restoration", Friends of Terra Cotta Newsletter, Vol. 3, No. 3, Fall/ Winter 1984, pp. 18-25.

TERRA COTTA--CONSERVATION AND RESTORATION

Fidler, John. "The Conservation of
Architectural Terracotta and Faience."
Transactions. Vol. 6, 1981. pp. 3-16.

TERRA COTTA--CONSERVATION AND RESTORATION

Hunderman, Harry J. and Deborah J. Slaton Has-
brouck Hunderman, "Terra Cotta Restoration Part
I: Organizing the Successful Survey", Friends
of Terra Cotta Newsletter, Vol. 3, No. 3, Fall/
Winter 1984, pp. 11-16.

TERRA COTTA--U.S.--OREGON--PORTLAND

Hamrick, James. "Portland Terra Cotta
Seminar." Friends of Terra Cotta. Vol. 3,
No. 1, Spring 1984. pp. 1,19.

TERRA COTTA--U.S.--OREGON--PORTLAND

Junior League of Portland. "A Walking
Tour of Portland's Surviving Terra Cotta
Buildings." Friends of Terra Cotta. Vol. 3,
No. 1, Spring 1984. pp. 9-11.

TERRA COTTA--U.S.--PENNSYLVANIA--PITTSBURGH

Johnson, Julee. "Pittsburgh's Terra Cotta
Heritage." Friends of Terra Cotta. Vol. 3,
No. 1, Spring 1984. pp. 6, 18-19.

TEXAS--FORT WORTH

Chance, Piers. "Fort Worth: Blend of Old
and New." Center City Report. November 1983.
p. 264.

TEXAS--GALVESTON

"Galveston Report." Urban Design
International. March/April 1982. Partial Issue.

CONTENTS: Lewis, David. The Participation Process--
Galveston Group Therapy--Mitchell, George. The
Future Galveston--Samuels, John. Leadership in
Galveston.

TEXAS--GALVESTON--HOTEL GALVEZ

"Restoring the Grande Dame of the Gulf."
Buildings. December 1980. p.33-35.

TEXTILE FABRICS

Rufey, Celia. "Tails into Textiles." Country
Life, Apr. 9, 1987. p. 144-145.

History and use of haircloth.

TEXTILE FABRICS--CONSERVATION AND RESTORATION

Benson, Nancy C. "Quilt Conservancy."
Americana. Vol. 13, No. 1, Mar./Apr. 1985.
p. 11.

TEXTILE FABRICS--CONSERVATION AND RESTORATION

King, Rosalie R. and Richard Bisbee. "Preservation of Navajo Woven Textiles: Care and cleaning procedures for rugs and blankets". Technology and Conservation. Spring 1980. p. 40-43.

TEXTILE FABRICS--CONSERVATION AND RESTORATION

Perlingieri, Ilya Sandra. "How To Care for Textile Collections." History News. August 1981. pp. 42-44.

TEXTILE FABRICS--CONSERVATION AND RESTORATION

Schur, Susan E. "The Textile Conservation Center, Merrimack Valley Textile Museum." Technology and Conservation. Spring 1982. P. 20.

TEXTILE FABRICS--CONSERVATION AND RESTORATION--U.S.--RHODE ISLAND--NEWPORT

"Restoration Projects." Newport Gazette. No. 101, Feb. 1985. p. 2-4.

TEXTILE FABRICS--REPRODUCTION

"Experience the Elegance of Chintz." Colonial Homes. January-February 1982. pp. 49-55.

TEXTILE FABRICS--REPRODUCTION

Richards, Nancy. "Executed in Neatness of Patterns and Elegance of Colors." APT Bulletin. Vol. XII, no.1, p. 52-73.

TEXTILE FABRICS IN INTERIOR DECORATION

Nylander, Jane. "For Those Who Can Afford Decorative Textiles." Yankee. October 1981. p. 105.

TEXTILES

Farnam, Anne. "Household Textiles in the Essex Institute, Salem, Massachusetts." Antiques. Vol. 127, No. 4, Apr. 1985. p. 888-895.

THEATERS

Baylis, Jamie. "This Genuine Piece of Local Culture." The Washington Post. Sept. 28, 1986.

The closing of the Circle Theater.

THEATERS

Eppes, William D. "Alabama Shakespeare Festival the State Theatre, Montgomery." Marquee. Vol. 18, No. 3, 1986. pp. 8-12.

THEATERS

Gerber, Nancy. "Theater's Fate Uncertain." Preservation Perspective (NJ). Vol. 7, No. 4. May/June 1987. pp. 1; 6.
The fate of the 58 year-old Loew's Theater Jersey City is undecided.

THEATERS

Harris, Stephen. "Marquee Picture Portfolio: the Theatres of Birmingham." Marquee. Vol. 18, No. 3, 1986. pp. 16-22.
Picture essay of the Birmingham, AL, theaters built in the early twentieth century.

THEATERS

Headley, Robert K., Jr. "Source Records for Theater History." Marquee. Vol. 16, No. 2, Second Quarter 1984. pp. 12-15.

THEATERS

LaLanne, Bruce. "The 1870 MERCED Theater: The First Modern Theater in Los Angeles." Marquee. Vol. 19, No 2. Second Quarter, 1987. pp. 11-12.

THEATERS

"The Last Remaining Seats: Los Angeles and the Movies." Los Angeles Conservancy. Vol. 9, No. 4. Jul./Aug. 1987. p. 7.

THEATERS

Lewallen, Jim and Douglas Gomery. "Chronicling the Carolinas' Theaters." Marquee. Vol. 18, No. 3, 1986. p. 3-6.

THEATERS

"Lucas Theatre to be Restored." The Rambler. Vol. 14, No.1, Spring 1987. p. 9

THEATERS

Rae, Thomas. "Encore for Loew's Jersey." Preservation Perspective. Vol. 5, No. 6. Sep./ Oct. 1986. pp. 1; 6.

Efforts by preservationists to save a 1929 theater from demolition.

THEATERS

"Restoration of Hawai'i Theatre." Historic Hawai'i. Vol. 12, No. 11, Dec. 1986. p. 15.

Vertical File

THEATERS

Scherer, Herbert. "Marquee on Main Street." Journal of Decorative and Propaganda Arts. Spring 1986. p. 62-75. (VF)

Jack Liebenberg's art deco movie theaters.

THEATERS

Sheridan, Fifi. "Palaces Survive despite all odds". Federal Design Matters. Spring 1980. p. 6-7.

THEATERS

Stern, Robert A.M., John Massengale, and Gregory Gilmartin. "Setting the Stage : Herts and Tallent." Skyline. December 1981. pp. 32-22.

THEATERS

Swallow, Ann V. "Alexis Opera House Hometown Crowd Pleaser." Historic Illinois. Vol. 10, No. 2. Aug. 1987. pp. 1-4.

THEATERS

"Theatre Royal, Portsmouth: a Renewal in Many Parts." The Architects' Journal. Vol. 184, No. 39, Sept. 24, 1986. p. 77-87.

A classic Victorian theater is being restored.

THEATERS--ADAPTIVE USE

"Capital Mall: Miami's successful example of urban adaptive re-use." National Mall Monitor. May/June 1981. p. 76.

THEATERS--ADAPTIVE USE

Janick, Herbert. "Danbury." American Arts. January 1982. p. 18.

THEATERS--AUSTRALIA--MELBOURNE

Van Straten, Frank. "Her Majesty's Theatre." Trust News. Vol. 14, No. 10, May 1986. p. 2-3, 5.

Melbourne, Australia theater dates back one hundred years.

THEATERS--CONSERVATION AND RESTORATION

"Arlene Schnitzer Concert Hall Restoration, Portland Oregon", Portland Chapter/AIA 1984 Design Awards. Architectural Record. Feb. 1985. p. 77.

THEATERS--CONSERVATION AND RESTORATION

"Chicago Theater: LPCI Heralds Light at the End of the Tunnel in Curtain Raiser." Landmarks Preservation (Council of Illinois). Vol 14, No. 4, July/Aug. 1985. p. 1, 4.

THEATERS--CONSERVATION AND RESTORATION

"Down payment by Ramsey secures Option, 'Open Doors' of Hawai'i Theater; Purchase and Restoration Planned." Historic Hawaii. Vol. 12, No. 3, March 1986. p. 1.

THEATERS --CONSERVATION AND RESTORATION

"Eleven Years of Restoring at the Fox." The Rambler. Vol. 13, No. 1, Winter/Spring 1986. p. 19-20.

Atlanta's Fox Theatre, the first theater in the country to be designated a National Historic Landmark, continues to be restored to its former grandeur.

THEATERS--CONSERVATION AND RESTORATION

Federal Design Matters. Fall, 1981. Partial Issue.
PARTIAL CONTENTS: Johannesen, Eric. Clevelan, The Circle and the Square, Two Types of Cultural District Planning--Shinn, Dorothy. Akron, Akron Art Mueeum Relocates in Former Post Office and the Akron Civic Theater is Restored--Batten, Brenda. Indianapolis, Theater Renovation Includes Hotel Ballroom and Retail Shops Within the Theater Building--Price, Alfred. Buffalo, Downtown and

Federal Design Matters continued

Theater District Planning Linked--Sachner, Paul. New York, A Dance Theater At Last.

THEATERS--CONSERVATION AND RESTORATION

Fink, Carol. "Roundup of Opera Houses and Their Playbills." Americana. September/October 1981. p. 21.

THEATERS--CONSERVATION AND RESTORATION

George, Peter J. "Getting a Theatre Project Off Square One." Marquee. Vol. 15, no. 4. pp. 4-6.

THEATERS--CONSERVATION AND RESTORATION

Kirkham, Jane. "Playhouse Square Theatre Restoration." Urban Design. International. Summer 1983. pp. 14-15.

THEATERS--CONSERVATION AND RESTORATION

League of Historic American Theaters Bulletin. "Fundraising Basics". Vol. 8, No. 1 & 2, Jan./Feb. 1985. Entire issue.

THEATERS--CONSERVATION AND RESTORATION

Mackintosh, Iain. "Classifying Theaters - a Scenario for Act Two of the Preservation Drama." Marquee. Vol. 17, No. 2, Second Quarter 1985. p. 3-9.

THEATERS --CONSERVATION AND RESTORATION

Miles, Ann. "June '87 Opening Set for Renovated Hoosier Theater." The Indiana Preservationist. No. 5, 1986. p. 5.

THEATERS--CONSERVATION AND RESTORATION

Panzer, James, Carl Christianson, David Kahn. "Theatrical and Acoustical Systems for the Renovated Historic Theatre." Marquee. Vol. 15, no. 4. pp. 7-9.

THEATERS--CONSERVATION AND RESTORATION

Ryder, Sharon Lee. "Carnegie Hall: Better Than Ever." Architecture. Feb. 1987. p. 60-64.

THEATERS--CONSERVATION AND RESTORATION

Segan, Lenore. "New Faces on Old Spaces." Marquee. Vol. 18, No. 1, 1986. p. 3-29.

Historic theaters of New York State.

THEATERS--CONSERVATION AND RESTORATION

Sherman, Stratford P. "Movie Theaters Head Back to the Future." Fortune. Vol. 113, No. 2, Jan. 20, 1986. p. 90-94.

Old and historic movie theaters found to attract customers if well maintained, despite competition from VCR's.

THEATERS--CONSERVATION AND RESTORATION

Wiencek, Henry. "Preserving the Magnificent Faces of Dreamland." Americana. July/August, 1979. pp.42-45.

THEATERS--CONSERVATION AND RESTORATION

"The Wiltern, Part II Opens in L.A." Commercial Renovation. Vol. 6, No. 5, October 1984. pp. 48-53.

THEATERS--CONSERVATION AND RESTORATION--ENGLAND--LONDON

Pritchard, Barry. "Upon Reflection: the Architects' Account of the Restoration of the Old Vic Theatre." Bulletin, APT. Vol. 17, No. 3&4, 1985. p. 75-83.

THEATERS--CONSERVATION AND RESTORATION--FRANCE

Dixon, John M. "Theatrical Revival: Municipal Theater Renovation, Belfort, France". Progressive Architecture. 2:85. p. 94-101.

THEATERS--CONSERVATION AND RESTORATION--U.S.--CALIFORNIA--BERKELEY

"Orinda Theater, It is Not Saved Yet." Baha News, Berkeley Architectural Heritage Association. No. 50, Nov./Dec. 1984, Jan./ Feb. 1985. p. 9.

THEATERS--CONSERVATION AND RESTORATION--U.S.--CALIFORNIA--LOS ANGELES

"Wiltern Theater Reopens in Splendor." Pasadena Heritage. Vol. 11, No. 1, Fall 1985. p. 6-7.

THEATERS--CONSERVATION AND RESTORATION--U.S.--FLORIDA--MIAMI

Piazza-Zuniga, Jeannie. "Gusman Center: Downtown's Historic Star Shines Again." Preservation Today, Dade Heritage Trust. Vol. 1, No. 6, Fall 1985. p. 20-22.

THEATERS--CONSERVATION AND RESTORATION--U.S.--ILLINOIS

"At Issue: Illinois' Historic Theaters in Need of Restoration." Landmarks Preservation Council of Illinois. Vol. 15, No. 3. May-June 1986. p. 1.

THEATERS--CONSERVATION AND RESTORATION--U.S.--ILLINOIS--CHICAGO

Greer, Nora R. "Magnificence Made New: Mandel Assembly Hall, University of Chicago." Architecture. Jan. 1985. pp. 54-57.

THEATERS--CONSERVATION AND RESTORATION--U.S.--INDIANA--INDIANAPOLIS

"Rave Reviews for Indianapolis Theater Restoration." Architectural Record. Apr. 1985. p. 75.

THEATERS--CONSERVATION AND RESTORATION--U.S.--MINNESOTA--RED WING

"Red Wing Fund Drive to Save Sheldon Memorial Auditorium." Preservation Matters (Preservation Alliance of Minnesota). Vol. 1, No. 7, Oct. 1985. p. 1.

THEATERS--CONSERVATION AND RESTORATION--U.S.--NEW MEXICO--ALBUQUERQUE

Benson, Nancy C. "Pueblo Deco." Americana. Jul./Aug. 1984. pp. 36-40.

THEATERS--CONSERVATION AND RESTORATION--U.S.--OHIO--COLUMBUS

Schmertz, Mildred F. "Lobby for a Landmark." Architectural Record. Sept. 1985. p. 114-119.

The restoration of the lobby of the Ohio Theater described.

THEATERS--CONSERVATION AND RESTORATION--U.S.--
    OREGON--PORTLAND

"Victorian Phoenix." Architectural Record.
May 1985. p. 116-117.

The New Market Theater (1872) restored to
shops and office use.

THEATERS--CONSERVATION AND RESTORATION--U.S.
    --TENNESSEE--MEMPHIS

"Attention to Detail Revives Memphis'
Orpheum". Commercial Renovation. Vol. 7,
No. 1, Feb. 1985. p. 46-49.

THEATERS--CONSERVATION AND RESTORATION--WEST GER-
MANY

Blake, Peter. "Versatile Theaters in
a Restored Erich Mendelsohn Building." Architecture. September 1984. pp. 160-165.

THEATERS--CONSERVATION AND RESTORATION (18TH
    CENTURY)

Bush, Charles E. "Stage Struck, One Man's
Journey to the Theaters of the Past in an Effort
to Re-Create Them in the Future." Colonial
Williamsburg Today. Vol. VI, No. 2, Winter 1984.
pp. 11-13.

THEATERS--DECORATION

Glazer, Irvin R. "Symphony Hall, Boston,
Massachusetts." Marquee. Vol. 16, No. 4, 1984.
p. 15-18.

THEATERS--DECORATION

Miller, Michael R. "The Architecture and
Acoustics of Carnegie Hall." Marquee. Vol. 16,
No. 4, 1984. p. 10-14, 24.

THEATERS--DECORATION

Morrison, Craig. "The Academy of Music,
Philadelphia. Marquee. Vol. 16, No. 4, 1984.
p. 5-9.

THEATERS--U.S.--CALIFORNIA--LOS ANGELES

LaLanne, Bruce. "The 1920's Los Angeles
Neighborhood Theater Boom." Marquee. Vol. 17,
No. 1, 1985. p. 14-16.

THEATERS--U.S.--CALIFORNIA--SAN DIEGO

Karo, Steve. "The Balboa." Reflections,
The S-O-H-O Newsletter. Vol. 18, No. 1, Jan./
Feb. 1986. p. 4-6.

THEATERS--U.S.--CALIFORNIA--SAN FRANCISCO

"Where Does Heritage Stand on the Herbst?
Solidly Behind It, with All the Forces We Can
Muster to Ensure Preservation." Heritage Newsletter, The Foundation for San Francisco's Architectural Heritage. Vol. XII, No. 1, Winter
1984. pp. 1-3.

THEATRES--U.S.--HAWAII

Schmitt, Robert C. "Hawai'i's Historic
Movie Theatres." Historic Hawai'i News. Vol. 10,
no. 2. February 1984. p. 1.

THEATERS--U.S.--HAWAII--OAHU

Headley, Robert K., Jr. "The Theaters of
Oahu." Marquee. Vol. 17, No. 1, 1985. p. 3-8.

THEATERS--U.S.--HAWAII--OAHU--HONOLULU

Giza, Tom. "The Hawaii Theater, 1922-1983."
Marquee. Vol. 17, No. 1, 1985. p. 9-13.

THEATERS--U.S.--MISSOURI--ST. LOUIS

Marquee, Journal of the Theatre Historical
Society. Vol. 16, No. 1. First Quarter 1984.
Entire issue.

TILES

Dewhurst, C. Kurt and Marsha MacDowell, "The Conduit Tile Buildings of Grand Ledge, Michigan." <u>Pioneer America</u>. September 1983. pp. 91-103.

TILES

Freeman, John Crosby. "The Floor Designs." <u>Old-House Journal</u>. Vol. 14, No. 7, Sept. 1986. p. 336-337.

Tile laying patterns modeled on those used in the 1920's.

TILES

Herbert, Tony. "Floors of Clay." <u>Traditional Homes</u>. Vol. 3, No. 10. July 1987. pp. 10-19. History and Conservation of tile floors.

TILES

Lanham, Susan Warren. "Embossed Ceramic Tile." <u>The Old-House Journal</u>. Vol. 14, No. 2, Mar. 1986. p. 84-87.

TILES

O'Donnell, Bill. "New Life For Old Bathrooms." <u>The Old House Journal</u>. Vol. 13, No. 8, Oct. 1985. p. 165-167.

TILES

Palanza, William. "Mosaic Tile: for Restoration and Decoration." <u>Fine Homebuilding</u>. No. 36, Dec. 1986/Jan. 1987. p. 64-67.

TILES

"Preserving the Art of Hand Pressed Tiles." <u>Albany Preservation Report</u>. Vol. 5, No. 5, Summer 1986. p. 9.

An Albany business produces tiles using pre-industrial methods.

TILES

"Reproducing Embossed Tile." <u>Old-House Journal</u>. Vol 19, No. 10, Dec. 1986. p. 476-477.

TILES

"Reproducing Old Tile." <u>Preservation Perspective</u>. Vol. 5, No. 5, July/Aug. 1986. p. 4, 6.

TILES

" A Room With A View. " <u>Heritage Outlook</u>. Vol. 7, No. 3. May/June 1987. p. 63. The Victoria and Albert Museum acquire Victorian tile collection.

TILES

Saxe, Myrna. "The Transfer and Conservation of Long Beach Mosaic." <u>Bulletin</u>, The Association for Preservation Technology. Vol. 16, No. 2, 1984. p. 26-31.

TIMBER

Charles, F.W.B. "Contrasts in the Conservation of Timber Buildings." <u>ASCHB Transactions</u>. Vol. 9, 1984. p. 18-21.

TOOLS

Jones, Larry. "The Amazing Water Level." <u>The Old House Journal</u>. Vol. 13, No. 2, Mar. 1985. p. 42-43.

TOOLS

Riggio, John. "Keep on Toolin.'" <u>Saint Louis Home</u>. July 1984. pp. 20-31.

Historic tools.

TOPOGRAPHIC MAPS

Heppell, Roger C. "Topographic Maps and the Local Historian." Information sheet #68, Regional Conference of Historical Agencies. December 1982. Insert.

TOURISM

Alexander, Joseph. "Forging Partnerships in Marketing the Outdoors." Courier. Vol. 32, No. 6, June 1987. pp. 8 - 9.

TOURISM

Baker, Priscilla. "Tourism and the National Park Service." Courier. Vol. 32, No. 6. June 1987. pp. 4 - 5.

TOURISM

"Getting Organized." Economic Growth & Revitalization Report, No. 9, May 13, 1987. p. 4-6.

Organizing a local tourism program.

TOURISM

Minnucci, George. "Aiding the Tourism Industry: A New Destination for Cooperating Associations." Courier. Vol. 32, No. 6. June 1987. pp. 6 - 7.
National Park Service's new "Passport Program."

TOURIST TRADE

"Cultural Tourism and Industrial Cities." Environmental Comment. January 1981. Entire issue.

TOURISM--ECONOMIC ASPECTS

Patton, Spiro G. "Tourism and Local Economic Development: Factory Outlets and the Reading SMSA." Growth and Change. Vol. 16, No. 3, July 1985. p. 64-73.

TOURIST TRADE

Elder, Betty Doak. "Long Lines at the Pump...Shorter Lines at the Gate." History News. July, 1979. pp. 206-207.

TOURIST TRADE

Gay, Patricia. "Tourism and Cultural Resources." New Orleans Preservation in Print. Vol. 13, No. 8, Oct. 1986. p. 3.

The importance of cultural resources to the tourist industry.

TOURIST TRADE

"Historic Atmosphere Brings Most Tourists." Virginia Preservation. Feb. 1986. p. 1.

TOURIST TRADE

"Panel: Is Tourism Good for Heritage? Three Experts Say Yes, No, and Maybe." Heritage Canada. Aug. 1979. pp. 19-22.

TOURIST TRADE

Perry, Richard L. "Group Maneuvers: Bus Tours Increase Attendance at Historic Sites". History News. May 1981. pp. 12 - 15.

TOURIST TRADE

Pilling, Ron. "How to Hold a House Tour: Persuasion, Planning, Publicity." The Old House Journal. Vol. 13, No. 5, June 1985. p. 103-106.

TOURIST TRADE

Putz, Paul M., Sharon Waite and Dale Jahr. "The Impact of South Dakota Historic Sites on Tourist Activity". 11593. June 1980. p. 4, 20.

TOURIST TRADE

"Tourism and Rural Development: How Small Towns Can Develop Visitor Attractions." Economic Growth & Revitalization. No. 86-17, Sept. 15, 1986. p. 1-2.

TOURIST TRADE

"Tourism: Managing Regional Assets." Environmental Comment. December 1981. Entire Issue.

CONTENTS: Rifkind, Carol. The Prospects for Regional Tourism Development in New England--Martin, Thomas. Economic Needs: Factors that Influence Investment--Gunn, Clare. Physical Needs: Land Use Planning for Tourism.

TOURIST TRADE--CANADA

Dalibard, Jacques. "Has Cultural Tourism Become a Trivial Pursuit". Canadian Heritage. Vol. 11, Issue 1, Feb./Mar. 1985. p. 2-5.

History of heritage tourism and contemporary possibilities for enhancing same discussed.

TOURIST TRADE--ECONOMIC ASPECTS

Atchison, Sandra. "There's Not Much Joy in Leadville." Business Week. December 17, 1984. p. 68.

TOURIST TRADE--PLANNING

Brown, Peter A. G. "Back to the Drawing Board, Twenty-Seven Year-Old Information Center Redesigned to Meet Changing Visitor Needs." Colonial Williamsburg Today. Vol. VI, No. 2, Winter 1984. pp. 14-17.

TOURIST TRADE--PLANNING

Horowitz, Amy L. "Developing a Tourism Program." Main Street News. No. 10, Feb. 1986. p. 1-3.

TOURIST TRADE--PLANNING

"How Well are we Safeguarding Our Heritage?" Heritage Outlook. September/October 1983. pp. 134-136 and 146-147.

TOURIST TRADE--PLANNING

Lew, Alan A. "Bringing Tourists to Town." Small Town. Vol. 16, No. 1, July/Aug. 1985. p. 4-10.

TOURIST TRADE--PLANNING

Partners for Livable Places. Livability Digest. Vol. 1, no.1, Fall 1981.

CONTENTS : Rifkind, CArole. Tourism and Communities : Process, Problems, and Solutions.

TOURIST TRADE--PLANNING

Small Town. November-December 1983. Partial Issue.
CONTENTS: Manteo, North Carolina, Avoids the Perils of Boom-or-Bust Tourism--Playing Russian Roulette: Small Town Tourism Investment.

TOURIST TRADE--PLANNING

Special Focus on Tourism, Conserve Neighborhoods, No. 44, January 1985, entire issue.

TOURIST TRADE--U.S.

Doyle, M. Stannard. "Open House U.S.A." Town and Country. Mar. 1986. p. 156-159, 226-228.

Directory of spring and summer tours of private homes and gardens.

TOYS

Garrett, Elisabeth Donaghy. "Playthings of the Past: the Bernard Barenholtz Collection of American Antique Toys." Antiques. Vol. 129, No. 1, Jan. 1986. p. 220-231.

TOYS

Steinberg, Ina H. "Victoriana Revisited at the Perelman Antique Toy Museum in Philadelphia." The Victorian. Vol. 13, No. 1, 1985. p. 4-6.

TOYS--HISTORY

Levinsohn, Florence. "An Orphan After Her Own Heart, A Collector Treasures Her Little Orphan Annieabilia...." *Americana*. Vol. 12, No. 4, September/October 1984. pp. 52-54.

TRAFFIC

Bond, Evagene H. "The 'Woonerf' Solution to Traffic Control." *Place*. September 1982. pp. 4-7.

TRAFFIC

"By-Passes, Panacea or Pretence?" *Heritage Outlook*. January/February 1982. pp. 3-6.

TRAFFIC

"Lorry Action Areas." *Heritage Outlook*. November/December 1981. pp. 156-157.

TRAFFIC

The Neighborhood Works. December 18, 1981. Entire Issue.

PARTIAL CONTENTS : Community Traffic Safety Studies Reviewed. -- Cars and People Coexist thru Woonerven-- Street Barriers Which Alter Traffic Flow.

TOURIST TRADE--PLANNING

"Visitor Centers Can Boost Downtown Tourism." *Downtown Promotion Reporter*. Feb. 1983. pp. 10-11.

TOYS

Richter, Nora. "Construction Toys at the Octagon 'Just for Fun': an Exhibit in Washington, D.C., Combines Historic Examples with Contemporary Creations." *AIA Journal*. May 1979. pp. 70-71

TRAFFIC

Von Borstel, Edwin. "Controlling Neighborhood Traffic." *APWA Reporter*. Vol. 52, No. 11, Nov. 1985. p. 14-15, 32.

TRAFFIC

Whitehead, Cynthia. "Taming Automobiles in Neighborhoods." *Transatlantic Perspectives*. Sep. 1980. pp. 16-19.

TRAILS

Elliott, Malinda. "Trail Into Timelessness." *Americana*. Vol. 13, No. 5, Nov./Dec. 1985. p. 52-57.

The Santa Fe Trail is profiled.

TRAILS

Freeman, Kevin. "Restoring the Historic Mojave Road." *Trends*. 1983, Vol. 20, No. 4. pp. 24-28.

TRAILS

"Open Lands Help 5 Communities Realize the Benefits of Converting a Railroad Right-of-Way." *Terrain*. Vol. 9, No. 2, Aug./Sept. 1985. p. 1-2.

TRAILS

Trends, Spring 1979.

Note: Issue on "Trends in Rivers and Trails."

TRAILS

Westphal, Joanne M. and Stanley R. Leiber. "Predicting the Effect of Alternative Trail Design on Visitor Satisfaction in Park Settings." *Landscape Journal*. Vol. 5, No. 1, 1986. p. 39-44.

Cook County Forest Preserve, Chicago, Illinois, serves as the study site.

TRAILS--U.S.--DELAWARE

"Hagley Designated National Trail." Hagley Museum and Library Newsletter. Vol. 15, No. 2. Summer 1986. p. 1.

The trail system at the Hagley Museum (Wilmington, Delaware) has been designated a National Recreation Trail.

TRAILS--U.S.--IOWA--DUBUQUE

Roche, Art. "Volunteers Protect and Manage A Heritage." Land Trusts' Exchange. Vol. 4, No. 2, Summer 1985. p. 11, 16.

Establishment of 25 mile Heritage Trail discussed.

TRANSPORTATION

Anderson, Grace. "Eager Beaver." Architectural Record. Jan. 1987. p. 80-83.

Restoration of New York City's subway platforms and rebuilding of the kiosk entrances to the platforms.

TRANSPORTATION

Brenner, Douglas. "Cut and Recover." Architectural Record. Jan. 1987. p. 68-71.

Additions to and renovation of a San Francisco transit station.

TRANSPORTATION

"Gas Stations Are an Endangered Species." Urban Outlook. Vol. 9, No. 4, Feb. 30 (sic), 1987. p. 8.

Vertical File
TRANSPORTATION

Striner, Richard. "The Fight to Preserve the Greyhound 'Super Terminal' of Washington D.C." Lake County Museum Postcard Journal. Vol. 3, No. 3. Fall 1986. pp. 1-2. (VF)

TRANSPORTATION

"Trams Return to Brisbane in City Circle Plan." National Trust Queensland Journal. Dec. 1986. p. 21.

TRANSPORTATION

Zimmerman, Karl. "Ding, Ding, Ding." Americana. Vol. 15, No. 1, Mar./Apr. 1987. p. 59-60, 76-77.

Trolley cars are returning to some U.S. cities.

TRANSPORTATION--HISTORY--AUSTRIA--VIENNA

"World's Oldest Steam Tramway Reborn in Austria." Urban Transportation Abroad. Vol. 8, No. 3, Fall 1985. p. 7.

TREES

Biles, Larry E. "Trees for Today's Cities." APWA Reporter. December 1981. pp. 10-11.

TREES

Maciejak, Dan. "Selecting, Planting and Maintaining Street Trees." The Old-House Journal. August-September, 1983. pp. 154-157.

TREES

"Village Wages War Against Dutch Elm Disease." APWA Reporter. August 1983. p. 20.

TREES IN CITIES

Beatty, Russell. "Planning the Urban Forest." Landscape Architecture. July 1981. pp. 456 - 458.

TREES IN CITIES

Collins, John J. and Munsell, Ken. "Plant a Tree for Marshall: A Michigan Community Honors its Trees." Small Town. March-April, 1981. pp. 18-22.

TREES IN CITIES

Environmental Comment. Issue on urban forestry. November 1980.

TREES IN CITIES

"New York Tree Search." Place. Feb. 1985. p. 11.

Great tree search launched in New York City.

TREES IN CITIES

"Saving the Urban Tree: a Master Plan." Urban Land. Vol. 45, No. 2, Feb. 1986. p. 30-31.

TREES IN CITIES

Wrenn, Douglas M. "Urban Forests: Seeing More Than the Trees." Urban Land. Vol. 43, No. 3 March 1984. pp. 36-7.

TREES IN CITIES--U.S.--OREGON--PORTLAND

"Keeping an Urban Oasis Green." Conserve Neighborhoods. No. 56, Feb. 1986. p. 4-5.

Discussion of Ladd's Addition Conservation District, Portland, Oregon.

TREES IN CITIES

" Trends in Urban Forestry." Trends. Vol. 18, No. 4, 1981. Entire Issue.

PARTIAL CONTENTS: Crossman, E.R.F.W., Philip A. Barker and J. Alan Wagar. Cost Effectiveness in Managing Urban Forests-- Ng, Charmaine. Forests in the City--Pope, Lurrie V. Interpretation of Urban Natural Areas.

TROMPE L'OEIL PAINTING

Bland, John. "Architectural Trompe-1'Oeil in Quebec around 1900." APT Bulletin V.XII, no.3, 1980. p.13-19.

TROMPE L'OEIL PAINTING

Treeman, Allen. "Painting Architecture on Buildings." Architecture. Apr. 1985. p. 73-79.

TROMPE L'OEIL PAINTING

"Trompe L'oeil." Urban Land. August 1983. pp. 30-31.

UNDERDEVELOPED AREAS--CITY PLANNING

Porter, Douglas R. "Info on Infill," Urban Land, Vol. 43, No. 11, November 1984, pp. 32-33.

UNDERWATER ARCHAEOLOGY

Bentsen, Lloyd. Hon. "Salvage Laws Inadequate." The Medallion. Vol. 22, No. 4, Apr. 1985. p. 5.

UNDERWATER ARCHAEOLOGY

Giesecke, Anne G. "Management of Historic Shipwrecks in the 1980s." Journal of Field Archaeology. Vol. 12, No. 1, Spring 1985. p. 108-112.

Providing background to proposed federal law, this article also includes citations to state statutes and case law.

UNDERWATER ARCHAEOLOGY

Ellis, Gary. "Divers Document Shoreline Shipwrecks." The Indiana Preservationist. No. 1, 1985. p. 2.

UNDERWATER ARCHAEOLOGY

Doty, John. "Diving into History." The Courier (Tennessee Historical Commission). Vol. XXIII, No. 1, October 1984. p. 3.

UNDERWATER ARCHEOLOGY

"Diving for Doubloons." Fortune. Aug. 19, 1985. p. 10-11.

UNDERWATER ARCHAEOLOGY

"Divers View Revolutionary War Ship." Headquarters Heliogram. No. 182. Jan. 1987. p. 9.

Underwater archaeologists are working on a Revolutionary War ship sunk on the bottom of the York River.

UNDERWATER ARCHAEOLOGY

Green, Kevin W. "Building Bridges for Underwater Archaeology." Place. Vol. 4, No. 9, October 1984. pp. 1-4.

UNDERWATER ARCHAEOLOGY

Herscher, Ellen. "House Passes Historic Shipwriec Legislation." Journal of Field Archae-ology. Vol. 12, No. 1. Spring 1985. pp. 112-116.

Text of legislation and section-by-section analysis provided.

UNDERWATER ARCHAEOLOGY

Hitchings, Bradley. "Secrets of the Sunken Treasure Trade." Business Week. Aug. 19, 1985. p. 109-110.

UNDERWATER ARCHAEOLOGY

Kelly, Roger E. "Assessing USS Arizona." CRM Bulletin. Vol. 8, No. 6, Dec. 1985. p. 1-3.

UNDERWATER ARCHAEOLOGY

Marois, Denise. "Underwater archaeology: heritage vs. plunder." Place. Vol. 7, No. 4. Jul./Aug. 1987. pp. 3 - 10.

UNDERWATER ARCHEOLOGY

Miller, Edward M. "Management Strategies for the Monitor." Place. Vol. 4, No. 9, October 1984. pp. 5-7.

UNDERWATER ARCHEOLOGY

Moore, Christopher. "Shipwrecks: Plunder or Patrimony?: A New Diving Ethic Struggles to Emerge." Canadian Heritage. Vol. 11, No. 5, Dec. 1985/Jan. 1986. p. 14-20.

UNDERWATER ARCHAEOLOGY

Phillips, Charles. "Money and History." History News. September 1983. pp. 10-16.

UNDERWATER ARCHAEOLOGY

Skowronek, Russell K. "Sport Divers and Archaeology: the Case of the Legare Anchorage Ship Site." Archaeology. Vol. 38, No. 3, May/June 1985. p. 22-27.

UNDERWATER ARCHAEOLOGY

Smith, Roger C. and Donald H. Keith. "Ships of Discovery." Archaeology. Vol. 39, No. 2, Mar./Apr. 1986. p. 30-35.

Investigation of Caribbean shipwrecks.

UNDERWATER ARCHAEOLOGY

Trupp, Philip. "Ancient Shipwrecks Yield Both Prizes and Bitter Conflict." Smithsonian. October 1983. pp. 79-88.

UNDERWATER ARCHAEOLOGY

Watts, Gordon P. Jr. "Deep-Water Archaeologi-cal Investigation and Site Testing in the Monitor National Marine Sanctuary." Journal of Field Archaeology. Vol. 12, No. 3, Fall 1985. p. 315-332.

UNDERWATER ARCHAEOLOGY--NEW ZEALAND

McKinlay, J.R. and G.J. Henderson. "The Protection of Historic Shipwrecks: a New Zealand Case Study." Archaeology. Vol. 38, No. 6, Nov./ Dec. 1985. p. 48-51.

Vertical F:

UNDERWATER ARCHAEOLOGY--U.S.--NEW HAMPSHIRE

Switzer, David C. "Archeology Under New Hampshire Waters: The Present and the Future." Historical New Hampshire. Vol. 40, Nos. 1 & 2, Spring/Summer 1985. p. 34-46. (VF)

UNESCO

"The Convention Concerning the Protection of the World Cultural and Natural Heritage." World Cultural Heritage. Information Bulletin No. 18. Enitre issue.

UNESCO

Slatyer, Ralph O. "The Origin and Development of the World Heritage Convention." Monumentum. Special Issue 1984. pp. 3-7.

UNESCO--WORLD HERITAGE PROGRAM

Douglas, David. "UNESCO's World Heritage Program." National Parks. Nov./Dec. 1982. pp. 4-8.

UNITED STATES. CONSTITUTION.

"NPS Slates Nationwide Celebration of Constitution's Bicentennial." Courier. Vol. 31, No. 3, Mar. 1986. p. 1.

UNITED STATES. CONSTITUTION.

"1787: The American Experiment." Humanities. Vol. 7, No. 1, Feb. 1986. Entire issue.

U.S. DEPARTMENT OF HOUSING AND URBAN DEVELOPMENT

"HUD's Urban Environmental Design Awards - 1980." Challenge! Dec. 1980. pp. 10-21.

U.S. DEPARTMENT OF HOUSING AND URBAN DEVELOPMENT --COMMUNITY DEVELOPMENT BLOCK GRANTS

Przybycien, Frank E. "Block Grant Assistance Spurs Upper Mohawk Development". Challenge. May 1980. p.12-18.

U.S. DEPARTMENT OF HOUSING AND URBAN DEVELOPMENT-- SECTION 202

"Low-Interest Loans Under Section 202 Not Just for New Construction." Neighborhood Conservation and Reinvestment. June 26, 1980. p. 2.

U.S. DEPARTMENT OF HOUSING AND URBAN DEVELOPMENT-- URBAN DEVELOPMENT ACTION GRANTS

Greer, Nora Richter. "St. Paul and the Uses of UDAG." AIA Journal. Mar. 1981. pp. 82-85.

U.S. DEPARTMENT OF HOUSING AND URBAN DEVELOPMENT-- URBAN DEVELOPMENT ACTION GRANTS

Munkacy, Kenn and Jerome Rappaport. "The UDAG Program, Alive and Well and Taking Kickers." Urban Land. Dec. 1983. pp. 2-6.

U.S. DEPARTMENT OF HOUSING AND URBAN DEVELOPMENT-- URBAN DEVELOPMENT ACTION GRANTS

Myers, Phyllis. "Examing UDAG's Record." Urban Land. Oct. 1980. pp. 25-28.

U.S DEPARTMENT OF HOUSING AND URBAN DEVELOPMENT-- URBAN DEVELOPMENT ACTION GRANTS

Myers, Phyllis. "UDAG and the Urban Environment." APA Journal. Winter 1982. pp. 99-109.

U.S. DEPARTMENT OF HOUSING AND URBAN DEVELOPMENT--
URBAN DEVELOPMENT ACTION GRANTS

Silverman, Jane. "UDAG Funding in Four N.Y.
Cities." Urban Design International. May/June
1980. pp. 20-23; 40.

U.S. DEPARTMENT OF THE INTERIOR--NATIONAL PARK
SERVICE

Cahn, Robert. "The National Park System,
The People, the Parks, the Politics." Sierra.
May/June 1983. pp. 46-55.

U.S. DEPARTMENT OF THE INTERIOR--NATIONAL PARK
SERVICE

Dickenson, Russell. "Strategic Goals for
Cultural Resources." CRM Bulletin. Vol. 7, No. 3.
Oct. 1984. pp. 1-3; 6.

U.S. DEPARTMENT OF THE INTERIOR--NATIONAL PARK
SERVICE

Rogers, Jerry L. "The Integration of Law,
Policy and Technical Information in National Park
Service Cultural Resource Programs." CRM Bulletin.
Vol. 7, No. 3. Oct. 1984. pp. 8-9.

U.S. DEPARTMENT OF THE INTERIOR--NATIONAL PARK
SERVICE--HABS

Beaty, Laura. "The Historic American Buildings
Survey: For fifty years, HABS has traced the
shape of the nation's architecture." National
Parks. Mar./Apr. 1983. pp. 16-21.

U.S. DEPARTMENT OF THE INTERIOR--NATIONAL PARK
SERVICE--NATIONAL REGISTER

King, Thomas F. "Is There a Future for
the National Register?" The (SAH) Forum.
December 1982. Entire Issue.

U.S. DEPARTMENT OF THE INTERIOR--NATIONAL PARK
SERVICE--NATIONAL REGISTER

Shull, Carol D. and Keith A. Aculle.
"Response to The Forum on Is There a Future for
the National Register?" The Forum, Society of
Architectural Historians. Apr. 1983. Entire
issue.

U.S. GOVERNMENT--DEPARTMENT OF HOUSING AND URBAN
DEVELOPMENT--URBAN DEVELOPMENT ACTION GRANTS

"Adaptive Use of Vacant Buildings Figures
Prominently in Latest UDAGs." Urban Conservation
Report. Jan. 13, 1984. p. 5.

U.S. GOVERNMENT--DEPARTMENT OF HOUSING AND URBAN
DEVELOPMENT--URBAN DEVELOPMENT ACTION GRANTS

Byrne, Robert M., Douglas R. Porter, and
Elizabeth D. Baker. "Urban Development Action
Grants: An Investment Solution." Urban Land.
June 1980. pp. 3-4; 9-10.

U.S. GOVERNMENT--DEPARTMENT OF HOUSING
AND URBAN DEVELOPMENT--URBAN
DEVELOPMENT ACTION GRANTS

"UDAG Case Study: Guthrie,
Oklahoma." Partnership News. August 19,
1983. pp. 13-14.

UNIVERSITIES AND COLLEGES

"Campus Preservation: Focus of Successful
HAF - Sponsored National Conference." Albany
Preservation Report. March/April 1984. pp. 1-2,
8, 10.

UNIVERSITIES AND COLLEGES

"Let There Be Light." Progressive Architecture. June 1984. pp. 84-87.

Union Theological Seminary
Library renovation, New York.

UNIVERSITIES AND COLLEGES--BUILDINGS

Anderson, Grace M. "College Buildings".
Architectural Record. January 1981. p. 90-107.

CONTENTS: Case Western Reserve, student center;
Mount Holyoke, Newhall Center; Syracuse Univ.,
Hall of Languages; Yale, School of Organization
and Management, Commons.

UNIVERSITIES AND COLLEGES--BUILDINGS

Gaskie, Margaret. "Adding On, Fitting In."
(Building Types Study 607: College Buildings.*)
Architectural Record. October 1984. pp. 147-163.

Georgetown, Dartmouth, University of Colorado.

UNIVERSITIES AND COLLEGES--BUILDINGS

Lipstudt, Helene. "Exhibition Report: Collegiate Architecture and the Rise of American Modernism." Architectural Record. Nov. 1985. p. 89.

UNIVERSITIES AND COLLEGES--BUILDINGS

Merkel, Jayne. "Washington University : Campus Architecture As Suburban Prototype." Inland Architecture. July/August 1986. p. 45-50.

UNIVERSITIES AND COLLEGES--BUILDINGS

"Reasserting a Beaux-Arts Tradition: An expansion plan for Columbia's business school". Architectural Record. Feb. 1985. p. 61.

UNIVERSITIES AND COLLEGES--BUILDINGS

Russell, Stephanie. "When Campus and Community Collide." Historic Preservation. September/October 1983. pp. 36-41.

UNIVERSITIES AND COLLEGES--BUILDINGS--ADAPTIVE USE

Cox, Frederic. "A University Makes Preservation Pay Off." Place. October 1982. pp. 8-9.

UNIVERSITIES AND COLLEGES--BUILDINGS--CONSERVATION AND RESTORATION

Clancy, John M. "Austin Hall, Harvard Law School." The Boston Preservation Alliance Letter. Vol. 7, No. 3, Mar. 1986. p. 1, 3-4.

UNIVERSITIES AND COLLEGES--BUILDINGS--CONSERVATION AND RESTORATION

Knight, Carleton, III. "Significant Clients: Stanford Keeps its Special Character." Architecture. November 1983. p. 78-85.

UNIVERSITIES AND COLLEGES--BUILDINGS--CONSERVATION AND RESTORATION

Moore, Evelyn R. "Jubilee College, Philander Chase's Western Seminary," Historic Illinois, Vol. 7, No. 4, December 1984, pp. 1-7, 11.

UNIVERSITIES AND COLLEGES--BUILDINGS--CONSERVATION AND RESTORATION

"Preservation Paradox at Harvard." Progressive Architecture. November 1983. pp. 42-44.

UNIVERSITIES AND COLLEGES--BUILDINGS--CONSERVATION AND RESTORATION

"Renovation of Ames Courtroom, Harvard Law School." Architectrural Record. Mid-Feb. 1982. pp. 108-109.

UNIVERSITIES AND COLLEGES--BUILDINGS--CONSERVATION AND RESTORATION--U.S.--VIRGINIA--Charlottesville

"UVA Begins Restoration of Jeffersonian Buildings", Architecture, January 1985, pp. 37-38.

UNIVERSITIES AND COLLEGES--BUILDINGS--U.S.--CALIFORNIA--BERKELEY

Littlejohn, David. "Scattering of Buildings Softened by Landscape." Architecture. Dec. 1985. p. 72-81.

UNIVERSITIES AND COLLEGES--BUILDINGS--U.S.--CALIFORNIA--PALO ALTO--STANFORD

"Kaleidoscope." Architecture. Mar. 1985. p. 120-131.

Three new campus buildings discussed.

UNIVERSITIES AND COLLEGES--BUILDINGS--U.S.--CONNECTICUT--MIDDLETOWN

Crosbie, Michael J. "Varied Spaces in a Noble Shell." Architecture. Oct. 1985. p. 48-53.

1903 Laboratory building adapted as student center.

UNIVERSITIES AND COLLEGES--BUILDINGS--U.S.--
NEW YORK--ITHACA

"Fight to List Ag Quad on National
Register Succeeds". Newsletter, Preservation
League of New York State. Vol. 10, No. 6,
Nov./Dec. 1984. p. 2.

UNIVERSITIES AND COLLEGES--BUILDINGS--U.S.--
VIRGINIA--CHARLOTTESVILLE

Knight, Carleton III. "Mr. Jefferson and
His Successors." Architecture. Dec. 1985. p. 62-
71.

URBAN BEAUTIFICATION

Okerlund, Garland A. "Streetscape's
Identity Crisis." Urban Land. April 1983.
pp. 12-15.

URBAN BEAUTIFICATION

Partners for Livable Places. Place:
The Magazine of Livability. Vol. 1, No.1,
September 1981.

URBAN DEVELOPMENT ACTION GRANTS

"New Urban Program Launched in U.K."
Public Innovation Abroad. Vol. 11, No. 7.
July 1987. p. 1.

URBAN DEVELOPMENT ACTION GRANTS

"Washington Officials Look to Kill UDAG -
Again." Downtown Idea Exchange. Vol. 34,
No. 14. Jul. 15, 1987. p. 1.

URBAN DEVELOPMENT ACTION GRANTS

"Who Gains from UDAG Grants?" Center City
Report . February 1980. pp. 1-3.

Excerpts from January 8, 1980 discussion on
MacNeil/Lehrer Report", PBS.

URBAN HOMESTEADING

Challenge!, May 1979.

Note: Entire issue is devoted to the topic
of urban homesteading; includes articles on
economic, legal and international aspects.

URBAN HOMESTEADING

Finney, Angus. "Homesteading: New Reforms,
Old Problems." City Limits. Vol. 12, No. 1,
Jan. 1987. p. 18-20.

URBAN HOMESTEADING

Sumka, Howard J. and Anthony J. Blackburn.
"Multifamily Urban Homesteading: A Key Approach
to Low-income Housing." Journal of Housing.
July/August. 1982. pp. 104-107.

URBAN HOMESTEADING

Weinberg, Steve. "Ola Davis' One-Dollar House:
With Luck and Determination, this Washington, D.C.
Woman Won a Home of Her Own." American Preservation.
Apr./May 1979. pp. 38-43.

URBAN HOMESTEADING

Winkleman, Michael. "Urban Homesteading:
The New Frontier." Metropolis. August/September
1981. pp. 12-15.

URBAN HOMESTEADING--U.S.--NEW YORK--NEW YORK CITY

"Loisaida Homesteaders Buck the Odds." City
Limits. Vol. 10, No. 4, Apr. 1985. p. 9.

Efforts of the "Ahona" organization in the
Lower East Side described.

URBAN REDEVELOPMENT

Unger, Harlow. "Fusion: A Low-Cost
Formula for Urban Redevelopment." Building Renovation. Vol. 4, No. 4. Jul. 1987. p. 7.

URBAN RENEWAL

Knight, Carleton III. "Ed Logue, Hard-Nosed Houser. Reflections on Renewal in New Haven, Boston and New York." Architecture. Vol. 74, No. 7, July 1985. p. 60-61.

URBAN RENEWAL

Levine, Marc V. "Review Essay: The Political Economy of Urban Redevelopment." Urbanism Past & Present. Vol. 9, No. 18, Issue 2, Summer/Fall 1984. p. 34-41.

URBAN RENEWAL--U.S.--PENNSYLVANIA--PHILADELPHIA

Algatt, Jeffrey R. and Ann Lenney. "One Reading Center, Philadelphia". Urban Land. Vol. 44, No. 1, Jan. 1985. p. 8-10.

New office tower built using air rights transfer connects with Reading Terminal Headhouse (1893) (NHL).

URBAN TRANSPORTATION

Eager, William R. "Innovative Approaches to Transportation for Growing Areas." Urban Land. July 1984. pp. 6-11.

URBAN TRANSPORTATION

Henke, Cliff. "The California Rail Transit Conversion." Urban Land. July 1984. pp. 12-15.

URBAN TRANSPORTATION

"Marketing Transit -- A Basic Need." Downtown Idea Exchange. Vol. 32, No. 7, Apr. 1, 1985. p. 4-6.

URBAN TRANSPORTATION--HISTORY--U.S.--CALIFORNIA

Wachs, Martin. "Autos, Transit and the Sprawl of Los Angeles: The 1920's." Journal of the American Planning Association. Vol. 50, No. 3, Summer 1984. pp. 297-310.

URBAN TRANSPORTATION PLANNING

Orski, Kenneth C. "Transportation Planning as if People Mattered." Practicing Planner. Mar. 1979. pp. 22-25; 47.

URBANIZATION--HISTORY

Rees, Ronald. "Reconsidering Antiurban Sentiment." Landscape. Vol. 28, No. 5, 1985. p. 26-29.

UTOPIAS

Sprigg, June. "Hancock Shaker Village : The City of Peace." Antiques. October 1981. pp. 884-195.

UTOPIAS--U.S.--ILLINOIS--HANCOCK COUNTY

Posadas, Barbara M. and William B. Coney. "Hancock County's Cambre House, A Rare Survivor of Icarian Community". Historic Illinois. Vol. 7, No. 5., Feb. 1985. p. 6-7, 14.

UTOPIAS --U.S. ILLINOIS. NAUVOO.

Krohe, James, Jr. "A New City of Joseph: Joseph Smith's Nauvoo was the largest city in Illinois when the Mormons began their trek west in 1846. Today a 'Saintly steamroller' charts its rebirth." Americana. April 1980. pp. 56-61.

UTOPIAS--U.S.--MASSACHUSETTS--WEST ROXBURY

Hennessey, Alice. "Destruction by Default: the Loss of Brook Farm's Margaret Fuller Cottage." Boston Preservation Alliance Letter. Vol. 6, No. 8, Sept. 1985. p. 1-2.

Arson destroys last building of utopian colony.

VALUATION

"The Alpine Lakes Case." Landscape Architecture. Vol. 75, No. 5, Sept./Oct. 1985. p. 76-79.

The appraisal of land for its scenic beauty establishes new case law.

VALUATION

Avery, Jonathan H. "What, Why and Who: Guidelines for Selecting a Real Estate Appraiser." Real Estate Finance. Vol. 2, No. 3, Fall 1985. p. 93-95.

VALUATION

Brenner, Michael J. "Real Estate Valuation Data: Appraisals may effect your bottom line". Real Estate Finance. Vol. 1, No. 4, Winter 1985. p. 89-90.

VALUATION

Kozub, Robert M. and James P. Trebby. "Special Valuation of Farmland and Closely Held Business Realty for Estate Tax Purposes", Growth and Change, Vol. 15, No. 3, July 1984, pp. 25-29.

VALUATION

Listokin, David. "Appraisal of Designated Historic Properties." The Appraisal Journal. Vol. 53, No. 2, Apr. 1985. p. 200-215.

VANES

"The Art of the Weather Vane." Americana, January/February 1980. pp. 24-26.

VANES

Hegarty, Claire. "Lofty Tails." Traditional Homes. Vol. 3, No. 2, Nov. 1986. p. 28-31.

History of weathervanes.

VANES

Sessions, Ralph. "The Art of the Weathervane: catalogue to the exhibition at the Museum of American Folk Art December 5, 1979 to February 24, 1980." The Clarion. Winter 1980. p. 22-32.

VEHICLES

Stewart, Doug. "To Airstreamers, a Nomad's Life is the Good Life." Smithsonian. Vol. 16, No. 9, Dec. 1985. p. 74-83.

Early campers/trailers discussed.

VEHICLES

White, Roger B. "At Home on the Highway." American Heritage. Vol, 37, No. 1, Dec. 1985. p. 98-105.

70 years of history of trailers and mobile homes.

VENTILATION

Fitchen, John F. "The Problem of Ventilation through the Ages." Technology and Culture. July 1981, Vol. 22, No. 3. pp. 485-511.

VERMONT--SHELBURNE--SHELBURNE MUSEUM

Karp, Walter. "Electra Webb and her American Past." American Heritage. April/May 1982. pp. 16-29.

VERMONT--WOODSTOCK--WOODSTOCK HISTORICAL SOCIETY

McIntyre, Janet Houghton. "The Woodstock Historical Society, Woodstock, Vermont". Antiques. December 1980. p. 1232-1241.

VERNACULAR ARCHITECTURE

Gamble, Robert. "Plantation Plain: The "I"-Type House Was Popular Early Farm Dwelling." The Preservation Report (Alabama Historical Commission. Vol. XII, No. 2, Sept./Oct. 1984. pp. 2-3.

VERNACULAR ARCHITECTURE

Hind, Charles. "Patterns of Building." Traditional Homes. Aug. 1986. p. 8-15.

The influence of 18th century pattern books on provincial vernacular architecture.

VERNACULAR ARCHITECTURE

"Jottings from the Rockies: The Transmission of Cultural Phenomenon and a Message in the Stairs." Folklife Center News. April 1981. pp. 6 - 8.

VERNACULAR ARCHITECTURE

Kevlin, Mary Joan. "Plank House Construction in Ithaca, New York." Historic Ithaca, New Series, Vol. 2, No. 4, Fall 1984, (insert), 4 p.

VERNACULAR ARCHITECTURE

Low, Setha P. and William P. Ryan. "Noticing Without Looking: a Methodology for the Integration of Architectural and Local Perceptions in Oley, Pennsylvania." Journal of Architectural and Planning Research. Vol. 2, No. 1, Mar. 1985. p. 3-22.

VERNACULAR ARCHITECTURE

Tishler, William H. "Stovewood Architecture." Landscape. No. 3, 1979. pp. 28-31.

VERNACULAR ARCHITECTURE

Wilson, Richard Guy. "Learning from the American Vernacular." The Architectural Review. Vol. 180, No. 1077. Nov. 1986. pp. 77-84.

Influence of Richardson, McKim and Frank Lloyd Wright on the vernacular.

VERNACULAR ARCHITECTURE--BIBLIOGRAPHY

"Current Bibliography." Vernacular Architecture Newsletter. No. 22, Winter 1984-85. p. 7-22.

VERNACULAR ARCHITECTURE--BIBLIOGRAPHY

Vernacular Architecture Newsletter. Spring 1981. p. 5-9.

VERNACULAR ARCHITECTURE--GREAT BRITAIN--SCOTLAND

Allen, Nicolas G. "Documentary Research for Scotland's 'Buildings in the Countryside Survey'." APT Bulletin. v.XII, no. 3, 1980. p. 93-114.

VERNACULAR ARCHITECTURE--U.S.

Hubka, Thomas C. "In the Vernacular: Classifying American Folk and Popular Architecture." The Forum, Bulletin of the Committee on Preservation, insert in Newsletter, The Society of Architectural Historians. Vol. 30, No. 1, Feb. 1986.

VERNACULAR ARCHITECTURE--U.S.--MISSOURI/KANSAS

Shortridge, James R. "Some Relationships Between External Housing Characteristics and House Types." Pioneer America. Vol. 13, No. 2, 1981. pp. 1-28.

VERNACULAR ARCHITECTURE--U.S.--NORTH DAKOTA

Carlson, Alvar W. "German-Russian Houses in Western North Dakota." Pioneer America. Vol. 13, No. 2, 1981. pp. 49-59.

VIBRATION (TRAFFIC)

Rainer, J.H. "Effect of Vibrations on Historic Buildings: An Overview." APT Bulletin. Vol. 14, No. 1., 1982. pp. 3-10.

VIBRATION (TRAFFIC)

Sedovic, Walter. "Assessing the Effect of Vibration on Historic Buildings." APT Bulletin. Vol. 16, No. 3 & 4, 1984. p. 52-61.

VIBRATION (TRAFFIC)

"Vibrations: Buildings and Human Response." Building Research Establishment Digest. Oct. 1983, No. 278. 8 p.

VIDEO DISCS

    Cash, Joan. "Spinning Toward the Future: the Museum on Laser Videodisc." <u>Museum News</u>. Vol. 163, No. 6, Aug. 1985. p. 19-35.

VIDEO DISCS

    Cipalla, Rita. "The Video-Disk Advantage: How Video-Disk Technology has Revolutionized the Storage and Retrieval of Photographic Collections at the National Air and Space Museum." <u>History News</u>. Vol. 40, No. 8, Aug. 1985. p. 18-20.

VIDEOTAPES

    "Massie Center Offers Videotape." <u>The Rambler</u>. Vol. 14, No. 1, Spr. 1987. p. 14.

    Savannah heritage center chronicles development of K-12 program.

VIDEOTAPES

    Peters, James. "Video Comes Into Its Own." Planning Practice. <u>Planning</u>. Vol. 50, No. 9, September 1984. pp. 15-19.

VILLAS --AUSTRALIA

    Lucas, Clive. "The Villa in Australia." <u>Heritage Australia</u>. Vol. 5, No. 1, Autumn 1986. p. 13-18.

Australian villas of the mid-nineteenth century.

VIRGINIA--ALEXANDRIA

    Hurst, Harold W. "Decline and Renewal: Alexandria Before the Civil War." <u>Virginia Cavalcade</u>. Summer 1981. pp. 32-37.

VIRGINIA--CITY POINT

    "City Point". <u>CRM Bulletin</u>. December 1980. p.1, 6-7.

VIRGINIA--FAIRFAX COUNTY--GUNSTON HALL

    Brown, Bennie. "The Mysteries of An Old House: New Discoveries at Gunston Hall." <u>Fairfax Chronicles</u>. Feb./Apr. 1984. pp. 1-4.

VIRGINIA--HISTORIC HOUSES--POPLAR FOREST

    Nichols, Ashton. "Poplar Forest". <u>Country Magazine</u>. March 1981. p. 48-51.

VIRGINIA--HISTORIC HOUSES--STRATFORD HALL

    Cheek, Mary Tyler. "Stratford Hall, the Virginia Home of the Lees." <u>Antiques</u>. March 1981. p. 642-651.

VIRGINIA--MONTICELLO--LANDSCAPE

    Miller, Sue Freeman. "The Grove at Monticello". <u>Americana</u>. July/August 1980. p. 46-51.

VIRGINIA--RICHMOND COUNTY--SABINE HALL

    Rasmussen, William M. S. "Sabine Hall, a Classical Villa in Virginia". <u>Journal of the Society of Architectural Historians</u>. December 1980. p. 286-296.

VIRGINIA--WILLIAMSBURG

    Stapleton, Constance. "A House Fit for a President." <u>Americana</u>. March/April 1981. pp. 51 - 57.

VOLUNTEER WORKERS

    Brandes, Lisa. "The Balancing Act: a Business Technique Helps Managers Weigh the Costs and the Benefits of Volunteer Programs." <u>History News</u>. Vol. 41, No. 1, Jan. 1986. p. 21-25.

VOLUNTEER WORKERS

Corbett, Marjorie. "The Perfect Working Vacation." National Parks. Vol.60, No. 11-12, Nov./Dec. 1986. p.10-12.

Opportunities for volunteering with the American Hiking Society, the National Park Service, HABS/HAER, Appalachian Trail Conference and ICOMOS.

VOLUNTEER WORKERS

Hickerson, Ann T. "Is It Fun? Is It History?: A Teen-age Volunteer Corps Learns History and Lightens the Workload at Old Economy Village." History News. Vol, 40, No. 4, Apr. 1985. p. 30-33.

VOLUNTEER WORKERS

Keller, Shirley. "The New Volunteer." American Arts. July 1981. pp. 10 - 13.

VOLUNTEER WORKERS

Nickerson, Ann T. "How to Set Up a Corporate Volunteer Program." History News. Sep. 1983. pp. 34-37.

VOLUNTEER WORKERS

"Special Supplement on Volunteer Opportunities." Providence Preservation News. January-February, 1983. pp. 5-8.

VOLUNTEER WORKERS

Sullivan, Patricia. "Volunteers, How to Build Strong Support Staff for Your Institution." History News. October 1982. pp. 19-21.

VOLUNTEERS--U.S.--NEW YORK STATE

"Volunteers at New York State Historic Sites." Trends. 1983, Vol. 20, No. 4. pp. 43-47.

VOLUNTEER WORKERS

"Volunteers in Preservation." Historic Kansas City Foundation Gazette. September/ October 1982. pp. 5-8.

WALKING TOURS

Garrison, Joseph Y. "Planning and Producing Successful Historic Walking Tours." The Courier, Tennessee Historical Commission. Vol. 24, No. 1, Oct. 1985. p. 4-5.

WALKING TOURS

Triem, Judy. "Experiencing a City: Kansas City, Missouri--its Historical and Architectural Significance. The Public Historian. Spring 1979. pp. 72-76.

WALKING TOURS

"A Walking Tour Through Teneriffe." The National Trust Journal (Queensland, Australia). June 1986. p. 18-19.

The Teneriffe wool stores in Brisbane were the place from which wood was railed for shipping to Britain at the turn-of-the-Century.

WALKING TOURS--U.S.--CALIFORNIA--SAN FRANCISCO

"South of Market Street: a Brief Guide to Its Architecture." Heritage Newsletter. Vol. 13, No. 2, Aug. 1985. (Supplement) 8p.

WALKING TOURS--U.S.--CALIFORNIA--LOS ANGELES

"The Conservancy's Newest Walking Tour." Journal of the Society of Architectural Historians. June/July 1986. p. 1.

A tour of the commerical area on Seventh Street in Los Angeles.

WALKING TOURS--ILLINOIS--CHICAGO--OAK PARK

Barker, Catherine. "History Hikes: How to Put History in Your Walking Tour." History News. April 1981. p.10-11.

WALLPAPER

Bradbury, Bruce. "A Laymen's Guide to Historic Wallpaper Reproduction." APT Bulletin. Vol. XVI, No. 1, 1984. pp. 57-8.

WALLPAPER

Bradbury, Bruce. "Lincrusta-Walton, Can the Democratic Wallcovering be Revived?" The Old-House Journal. October 1982. pp. 203-206.

WALLPAPER

Brucksch, John P. "Great Cover-Ups: Reproduction Carpet and Wallpaper for National Park Service Historic Interiors." CRM Bulletin. Vol. 8, Nos. 3&4. Jun.-Aug. 1985. pp. 8-9.

WALLPAPER

"Decorative Discoveries." Traditional Homes. Vol. 3, No. 11. Aug. 1987. pp. 66 - 68; 71. Preservation of some recent wallpaper finds.

WALLPAPER

Flaherty, Carolyn. "Mid-19th Century Wallpapers." The Old-House Journal. June 1979. pp. 63-65.

WALLPAPER

Gilmore, Andrea. "Preserving Wallpaper in Historic Homes - Simple techniques for cleaning and maintaining non-historic wallpaper." CRM Bulletin. Vol. 8, No. 3 & 4, June/Aug. 1985. p. 18-19.

WALLPAPER

Kirsch, Francine. "Turn-of-the-Century Wallcoverings: The Rebirth of Wallpaper Borders." Victorian Homes. Vol. 6, No. 3. Summer 1987. pp. 7; 79 - 81.

WALLPAPER

Lynn, Catherine. "Decking Columbia's Walls: War, Patriotism, Nature, and Changing Taste-All Have Been Mirrored in our Wallpaper." American Heritage. December 1981. pp. 81-89.

WALLPAPER

Phillips, Morgan W. and Andrew L. Ladygo. "A Method for Reproducing Lincrusta Papers by Hand." APT Bulletin. v.XII, no. 2, 1980. p. 64-79.

WALLPAPER

"The Early American Look: Wallpapers." Early American Life. Vol. 17, No. 3, June 1986. p. 52-53.

WALLPAPER, VICTORIAN

Day, Nancy. "Giving Walls a Victorian Look." Americana. Vol. 12, No. 4, September/October 1984. pp. 64-69.

WALLPAPER, VICTORIAN

"Original Morris Wallpapers Available Again." Old House Journal. Vol. 13, No. 3, Apr. 1985. p. 69.

WALLPAPER, VICTORIAN

Schenk, Emmy Lou. "Victorian Wallpaper that shows how it really looked". Americana. July/August 1980. p. 37-40.

WALLPAPER, VICTORIAN

Stapleton, Ian et al. "St. John's Manse and its Wallpapers." Heritage Australia. Winter 1985. p. 12-17.

Method described for removal of 21 paper layers for study.

WALLS

"Installation of Wall Ties in Existing Construction." Building Research Establishment Digest. January 1982, #257.

WALLS

Santucci, R.M. "Up Against the Walls: Gypsum Board Savings Are Nailed Down One Piece at a Time." Cost Cuts. Vol. 2, No. 9, July 1985. p. 1, 4-6.

WALLS--CONSERVATION AND RESTORATION

"Assessment of Damage in Low-Rise Buildings with Particular Reference to Progressive Foundation Movement." Building Research Establishment Digest. July 1981, No. 251. 8p.

WALLS--CONSERVATION AND RESTORATION

"Interior Solutions-Some Wall Problems You Can Repair Yourself." Rehab Age. November 1981. pp. 44-57.

WAREHOUSES--ADAPTIVE USE

Anthony, Kathryn H. "Power in a Bowlful of Noodles." Planning. December 1981. pp. 16-17.

WAREHOUSES--ADAPTIVE USE

Atkin, Nigel. "The Terminal Warehouse: Canada's Largest Renovation Job." Housing Ontario. July/August/Sept/Oct. 1981. pp. 20-23.

WAREHOUSES--ADAPTIVE USE

"The Itasca." Architecture Minnesota. August/September 1981. pp. 52-53.

WAREHOUSES--ADAPTIVE USE

"Urbane Renewal: A Recycled San Francisco Waterfront Warehouse is the Site of Several Offices in Turn-of-the-Century Industrial Building." Interior Design, August 1979. pp. 182-193.

WAREHOUSES--ADAPTIVE USE

Vilades, Pilar. "Table Setting." Progressive Architecture. Sept. 1986. p. 110-113.

Conversion of an old carpet warehouse into a restaurant.

WAREHOUSES--ADAPTIVE USE--GREAT BRITAIN

Thorne, Robert and Dan Cruickshank. "Rebirth of a Rogue." AJ. No. 30, Vol. 184, July 23, 1986. p. 29-45.

History of the Skin Floor in London Docks from its original role as a tobacco warehouse and how the building is being restored and incorporated into a commercial development.

WAREHOUSES--CANADA--TORONTO

Anderson, Grace M. "A Warehouse Transmuted." Architectural Record. June 1985. p. 134-139.

1927 waterfront warehouse converted to mixed use.

WAREHOUSES--CONSERVATION AND RESTORATION

"Deco Warehouse Goes Condo." Architectural Record. July 1984. p. 55.

WAREHOUSES--CONSERVATION AND RESTORATION

"NEA Grant Project, The Warehouse Project." New Orleans Preservation in Print. Sept./Oct. 1983. Entire Issue.

WAREHOUSES--CONSERVATION AND RESTORATION

Sutton, Horace. "Who Said a Warehouse is Not a Home?" Challenge (HUD). January 1979. pp. 16-18.

WAREHOUSES--CONSERVATION AND RESTORATION--U.S
--ILLINOIS--CHICAGO

"Fitting the Pieces Together". Commercial Renovation. Vol. 7, No. 1, Feb. 1985.
p. 57-58.

WAREHOUSES--CONSERVATION AND RESTORATION--U.S.--
ILLINOIS--CHICAGO

Greer, Nora Richter. "Warehouse Becomes a
'House of Beauty'." Architecture. May 1985.
p. 216-219.

Helen Curtis Industries headquarters in 1912
warehouse.

WAREHOUSES--CONSERVATION AND RESTORATION--U.S.--
ILLINOIS--CHICAGO

"Landmark Warehouse Assumes Office Identity.'
Commercial Renovation. Vol. 6, No. 5, October
1984. pp. 40-43.

WAREHOUSES--CONSERVATION AND RESTORATION--
U.S.--MASSACHUSETTS--CAMBRIDGE

"Converted Warehouse Has Sunny Future."
Commercial Renovation. August 1984. pp. 50-51.

WAREHOUSES--CONSERVATION AND RESTORATION--U.S.--
NORTH CAROLINA--DURHAM

"Brickwork Bonanza." Architectural Record.
May 1985. p. 110-113.

The adaptive reuse of two National Register
listed warehouses discussed.

WAREHOUSES--U.S.--CALIFORNIA--BERKELEY

Woodbridge, Sally. "Awards Update: Warehouse
Rebound." Progressive Architecture. Nov. 1985.
p. 104-106.

WAREHOUSES--U.S.--CALIFORNIA--SAN FRANCISCO

"The Boutiquing on the Haslett Warehouse."
San Francisco Tomorrow. Issue 122. May 1986. p. 2.

WAREHOUSES--U.S.--CALIFORNIA--SAN FRANCISCO

Crosbie, Michael J. "Remnants of a Warehouse
as a Background for Airy Offices." Architecture.
Jan. 1985. pp. 74-75.

WAREHOUSES--U.S.--LOUISIANA--NEW ORLEANS

Amdal, Jim. "Warehouse District Update:
1985." New Orleans Preservation in Print. Vol.
12, No. 9, Nov. 1985. p. 7.

WATERFRONTS--U.S.--LOUISIANA--NEW ORLEANS

"The Future of the New Orleans Riverfront."
New Orleans Preservation in Print. Vol. 12, No.
9, Nov. 1985. p. 5-6.

WAREHOUSES--U.S.--MINNESOTA--MINNEAPOLIS--
BUTLER SQUARE

"Summing Up: A Big Old Warehouse
Uncrates a Rich Mixture of Activity and
Amenity." Architectural Record. December
1975. pp. 108-112.

WASHINGTON--SEATTLE

Land Polly. "Seattle: A Citizen-Watched
Pot on Constant Boil." Urban Land. Mar. 1983.
pp. 2-9.

WASHINGTON--SEATTLE--CITY PLANNING

Ryan, Dennis. "Urban Design in Seattle."
Environmental Comment. September 1981.
p. 14-19.

WASHINGTON, D.C.

"The Washington Landscape." Landscape
Architecture. November 1981. pp. 723-737.

CONTENTS: Jennings, J.L. Sibley. A Capitol Saga--
Coffin, Laurence E. A Capital Setting--Lockwood,
Grace S., Darwina L. Neal and James Van Sweden.
Favorite Places; Recent Works.

WASHINGTON, D.C.--DECATUR HOUSE

Brown, Joan Sayers. "Silver and Gold Owned by Stephen Decatur, Jr." Antiques. February 1983. pp. 399-405.

WASHINGTON--D.C.--DUMBARTON OAKS

Olmert, Michael. "Dumbarton Oaks: stately link from past to the present." Smithsonian. May 1981. p. 92-101.

WASHINGTON, D.C.--PENSION BUILDING

Smith, Janet Marie. "New Life for the Pension Building." Place. December 1981. pp. 8-10.

WASHINGTON, D.C.--U.S. CAPITOL

"Congress Sees Plan for Future Capitol Hill Area." Architectural Record. November 1981. p. 36.

WASHINGTON D.C.--WHITE HOUSE

"Architectural Digest Visits: President and Mrs. Reagan at the White House." Architectural Digest. Dec. 1981. pp. 104-121.

WASHINGTON D.C.--WHITE HOUSE

McDaniel, James I. "Twenty-eight coats of White House History." CRM Bulletin. Mar. 1981. pp. 1, 4-5.

WATER--LAW AND LEGISLATION

"Virginia Protects Rappahannock and Upper James; Other State Actions on Rivers Mixed So Far in 1985." American Rivers (American Rivers Conservation Council). Vol. 13, No. 1, Mar. 1985. p. 9.

WATER MILLS

Howard, Robert A. "A Primer on Waterwheels." APT Bulletin. Vol. XV, No. 3, 1983. pp. 26 - 33.

WATERFRONT

Allaby, Ian. "The Harbour-front Lands, Revitalizing Toronto's Waterfront." Urban Land. Vol. 43, No. 9, September 1984. pp. 22-25.

WATERFRONTS

Annual Design Issue. Waterfront World. Vol. 4, No. 6, Nov./Dec. 1985.

A variety of waterfront projects are showcased.

WATERFRONTS

Breen, Ann and Dick, Rigby. "SOS for the Working Waterfront." Planning. Vol. 51, No. 6, June 1985. p. 6-11.

WATERFRONTS

Breen, Anne, and Dick Rigby. " Waterfront Development in Review." Waterfront World. Vol. 6, No. 4. Jul./Aug. 1987. pp. 4 - 5. Factors underlying the recent urban waterfront development trend.

WATERFRONTS

Breen, Ann and Dick Rigby. "Waterfronts in the 1980's: An Overview." Journal of Housing. May/June 1984. pp. 78-9, 82.

WATERFRONTS

Greenwald, Susan. "America discovers its urban riverfronts." Inland Architect, August 1979. pp. 15-17.

WATERFRONTS

Nelson, Roberta and Steve Ellis. "Planning for First-class Waterfront Parks." Small Town. Vol. 17, No. 2, Sept-Oct. 1986. p. 11-17.

WATERFRONTS

Swain, William G. "Pittsburgh Launches a Public Boat Ramp", Place, January 1985, p. 5.

WATERFRONTS

Willmott, Gary, Richard Smardon and Rodney McNeil. "Waterfront Revitalization in Clayton, New York." Small Town. November-December 1983. pp. 12-19.

WATERFRONTS

Wrenn, Douglas. "Urban Waterfronts: Awash with Controversy." Urban Land. November 1982. pp. 14-23.

WATERFRONTS--CONSERVATION AND RESTORATION

Bachman, Geraldine, and Robert Knecht. "Waterfront: Rediscovering a Neglected Asset." AIA Journal. Feb. 1979. pp. 54-59.

Wilmington, N.C., finds that revitalization begins on the river.

WATERFRONTS--CONSERVATION AND RESTORATION

Catanese, Anthony James. "Recycling London's St. Katharine Dock." Urban Land. February 1981. p. 7-11.

WATERFRONTS--CONSERVATION AND RESTORATION

Cowey, Ann Breen and Richard Rigby. "On the Waterfront: Revitalization from Coast to Coast." Planning. Nov. 1979. pp. 10-13.

WATERFRONTS--CONSERVATION AND RESTORATION

Cummins, Joan. "Special Focus on Working Waterfronts: How Neighbors are Getting Involved." Conserve Neighborhoods. No. 51, Sept. 1985. Entire issue. 8 p.

WATERFRONTS--CONSERVATION AND RESTORATION

Douglas, William L. "Who Designs the Riverfront." New Orleans Preservation in Print. Vol. 11, No. 10, December 1984. p. 17.

WATERFRONTS--CONSERVATION AND RESTORATION

"Europe Makes Waves on Alexandria's Waterfront." Urban Innovation Abroad. April 1981. p. 1.

WATERFRONTS--CONSERVATION AND RESTORATION

Goldstein, Neil and Dana Rowan. "On the Urban Waterfront." Sierra. November/December 1981. pp. 33-39.

WATERFRONTS--CONSERVATION AND RESTORATION

Jones, Andrea L. and Peter Grenell. "Stearns Wharf." Environmental Comment. November 1981. pp. 11-12.

WATERFRONTS--CONSERVATION AND RESTORATION

"The Redevelopment of Britains Urban Docklands." Town and Country Planning. May 1982. Entire Issue.

CONTENTS: Hall, John. Docklands in the Metropolitan Economy--Sharman, Nick. Dock Decline and Job Replacement--Burton, Paul. LDDC-A New Broom--Hancock, Tom. In Place of Dereliction: Innovation!--Hebbert, Michael. The Five Problems of Dockland Redevelopement.

WATERFRONTS--CONSERVATION AND RESTORATION

"Rediscovering Urban Waterfronts." Terrain. Vol. 7, No. 2. Entire Issue.

WATERFRONTS--CONSERVATION AND RESTORATION

"The South Street Seaport News." *The Liveable City*. June 1981. Entire Issue.

WATERFRONTS--CONSERVATION AND RESTORATION

Shapiro, Mark and Tricia. "On Riverfront Development." *New Orleans Preservation in Print*. Vol. 11, No. 10, December 1984. p. 16.

WATERFRONTS--CONSERVATION AND RESTORATION

Stoloff, Judith G. "A Private Firm Renews a Seattle District." *Place*. January 1984. pp. 4-7.

WATERFRONTS--CONSERVATION AND RESTORATION

Wagner, Fritz, Robert Dupont, Jane Brooks and Ida Larson. "Down by the Waterfront: Focal Point for Revitalizing New Orleans". *Environmental Comment*. April 1981. pp 4 - 8.

WATERFRONTS--CONSERVATION AND RESTORATION

Ward, Richard. "St. Louis, Missouri, Riverfront Renaissance Meshes Old and New." IDEA, *Center City Report*. June 1984. pp. 1-2, 6.

WATERFRONTS--CONSERVATION AND RESTORATION

"Wilmington, N.C. : Revitalization Focuses on Downtown Riverfront." *Center City Report*. March 1981. p. 10-11.

WATERFRONTS--CONSERVATION AND RESTORATION

Zotti, Ed. "Cityfront Center: the 20 Year Venture." *Inland Architect*. Vol. 29, No. 6, Nov./ Dec. 1985. p. 50-53.

48 acre Chicago Dock and Canal Trust property to become multi-use office & residential site. Ogden Slip & North Terminal Bldg. to be renovated.

WATERFRONTS--CONSERVATION AND RESTORATION--U.S. --HAWAII--HONOLULU

"Hawaii Maritime Center: A bold concept to preserve ocean heritage." *Historic Hawaii News*. June 1985. p. 3-5.

WATERFRONTS--CONSERVATION AND RESTORATION--U.S.-- MASSACHUSETTS--BOSTON

Kashdan, Sandra. "Boom Begins in Earnest on Boston's Waterfront." *Waterfront World*. Vol. 4, No. 5, Sept./Oct. 1985. p. 1, 3-5.

WATERFRONTS--LAW AND LEGISLATION--U.S.--LOUISIANA --NEW ORLEANS

Anzalone, Kerry. "Legal-Ease On the Water-front." New Orleans *Preservation in Print*. Vol. 11, No. 8, October 1984. pp. 14-16.

WATERFRONTS--U.S.--CALIFORNIA--SAN FRANCISCO

Freeman, Allen. "An Explosion by the Waterfront." *Architecture*. Mar. 1985. p. 88-91.

WATERFRONTS--U.S.--CONNECTICUT--NEW HAVEN

Li, Gerald. "The Long Wharf Maritime Center: A Hybrid Plan Blossoms Among New Haven's Redevel-opment Efforts." *Urban Land*. Vol. 44, No. 6, June 1985. p. 22-25.

WATERFRONTS--U.S.--MINNESOTA--MINNEAPOLIS

"Banking on the Riverfront." *Architecture Minnesota*. Vol. 11, No. 2, Mar./Apr. 1985. p. 38-43, 68-69.

WATERFRONTS--U.S.--MINNESOTA--MINNEAPOLIS

Schwanke, Dean. "Riverplace, Minnesota: Mixed Use with a Good Splash of Housing." *Urban Land*. Vol. 44, No. 11, Nov. 1985. p. 2-7.

WATERFRONTS--U.S.--TENNESSEE

"Chattanooga riverfront park." Place. Feb. 1985. p. 13.

WATERPROOFING

Fisher, Thomas. "The Watery Underground." Progressive Architecture. Oct. 1985. p. 104-111.

Detailed comparison of methods included.

WEATHERING OF BUILDINGS

Farley, Clare. "The Rehab Corner." Neighborhood Quarterly. Vol. 6, No. 4, Fall 1986. p. 4.

Caulking and weatherstripping.

WINDOW TREATMENTS

Cotton, J. Randall. "Return to Awnings." The Old House Journal. Vol. 13, No. 6, p. 115, 126-130.

WINDOWS

"Aluminum Window Replacement in Historic Buildings: For Property Owners Seeking Federal Tax Benefits". Communique. Vol. 14, No. 1, Feb. 1985. Technical Notes 4, Insert, p. 9-10.

WINDOWS

Brunskill, R.W. "Skylights and Dormers." Traditional Homes. Vol. 3, No. 2. Nov. 1986. pp. 10-17.

History, development and maintenance of skylights and dormers.

WINDOWS

Clark, Susan. "Make Your Own Ornamental Wood Screens." The Old House Journal. July 1981. p. 149.

WINDOWS

Haynes, Wesley. "Windows: Techniques for Restoration and Replacement." Architectural Record. Vol. 175, No. 7. June 1987. pp. 150 - 165.

WINDOWS

"Helpful Information from the Window Conference." The Alliance Review. Vol. 2, No. 4, 1987. p. 2.

WINDOWS

"Hints for Successful Window Treatment in Historic Buildings." Florida Preservation News. Vol. 2, No. 4, July-Aug. 1986. p. 5.

WINDOWS

Marmet, Terry. "Historic Windows: Developing Appropriate Rehabilitation Treatments." Kansas Preservation. Mar./Apr. 1985, Vol. 7, No. 3. p. 3-4.

The first in a two-part series.

WINDOWS

Marmet, Terry. "Historic Windows: Repair or Replace?" Kansas Preservation. Vol. 7, No. 4, May/June 1985. p. 4-5.

Second in a two-part series on rehabilitation of historic windows.

WINDOWS

Marmet, Terry W. "New Glass Provides Sun Control." Kansas Preservation. November-December 1983. pp. 6-7.

WINDOWS

McConkey, James. "Fixing Double-hung Windows." The Old-House Journal. Dec. 1979. pp. 133; 138-139.

WINDOWS

Munroe, Kevin and Clifford Renshaw. "Window Treatments Affect Building Character and Performance." PPS News. September-October, 1981. pp. 8-9.

WINDOWS

O'Donnell, Bill. "Troubleshooting Old Windows: What to do with Neglected Double-Hung Windows." The Old House Journal. Vol. 14, No. 1, Jan./Feb. 1986. p. 16-23.

WINDOWS

The Old House Journal Technical Staff. "Historic Metal Windows: Maintenance & Repair." Old-House Journal. Vol. 14, No. 9, Nov. 1986. p.425-428.

WINDOWS

Peavler, Bill. "Rehabilitation Guidelines Series #7." Mistletoe Leaves. August 1983. p. 6.

WINDOWS

"Pittsburgh's Bigelow Hotel gets 2,400 Windows". Commercial Renovation. Vol. 7, No. 1, Feb. 1985. p. 30.

WINDOWS

"Preservation of Historic Windows." Culture & History. Vol. 3, No. 1, Oct.-Nov.-Dec. 1986. p. 17.

WINDOWS

Ruhling, Nancy A. "The Art of Window Dressing." Victorian Homes. Vol. 6, No. 2, Spring 1987. p. 54-65.

WINDOWS

"Special Window Issue." The Old-House Journal. April 1982. Entire Issue.

CONTENTS: Poore, Patricia. Replacing Old Windows--Jones, Larry. How To Install Weatherstripping--Poore, Patricia. Storm Windows.--Labine, Clem. Rescuing Those "Hopeless" Windows--Talk to Me of Windows, a glossary.

WINDOWS

"Specification Requirements for Proposed Window Replacement in Historic Buildings for Property Owners Seeking Federal Tax Benefits." APT Communique. Vol. XIII, No. 4, August 1984. pp. 9-10. (Technical Notes 3.)

WINDOWS

"Technique-Storms Help Fight Highwinds at Chicago Highrise.", Commercial Renovation, Vol. 6, No. 6, December 1984, p.26

WINDOWS

Trissler, Wayne and Charles E. Fisher. "Exterior Storm Windows: Casement Design Wooden Storm Sash." U.S. Department of the Interior, National Park Service, Preservation Tech Notes No. 3, 4 p. CRM Bulletin. Vol. 8, No. 2, Apr. 1985. Four page insert.

Lyndhurst gatehouse, Tarrytown, N.Y. case example.

WINDOWS

"Willits (FLW) Windows to be Removed." Landmarks Preservation (Council of Illinois). Vol. 14, No. 4, July/Aug. 1985. p. 5.

WINDOWS .

Wilson, H. Weber. "Decorative Windows in American Homes." Victorian Homes. Vol. 6, Issue 1, Winter, 1987. p. 56-59.

WOMEN IN THE ARTS

Roth, Darlene. "Feminine Marks on the Landscape: An Atlanta Inventory." Journal of American Culture. Winter 1980. p. 673-685.

WOOD

Anderson, Barbara. "Interior Woodwork Finishes Define the Character of Historic Buildings." Kansas Preservation. Vol. 9, No. 2, Jan.-Feb. 1987. p. 4-5.

WOOD

O'Donnell, Bill. "After You Strip, Before You Finish." Old-House Journal. Vol 15, No. 1, Jan./Feb. 1987. p. 43-47.

WOOD--DETERIORATION

Jagger, Allan. "Exterior Woodwork: Preserving Character." Landmarks Observer. Vol. 13, No. 1, Jan./Feb. 1986. p. 8.

WOOD--PRESERVATION

Elswick, Dan. "Preservation Pointers: Preparing Historic Woodwork for Repainting." The New South Carolina State Gazette. Vol. 19, No. 2, Winter 1987. p. 6-7.

WOOD--PRESERVATION

Graham, Robert D. "The Role of Fumigants in Log Preservation." APT Bulletin. Vol. 15, No. 1, 1983. pp. 20-21.

WOOD--PRESERVATION

Jones, Larry. "Wood Woes." Old-House Journal. Vol. 14, No. 7, Sept. 1986. p. 325-327.

Problems with Southern Yellow Pine and treated lumber.

WOOD--PRESERVATION

Labine, Clem. "Defeating Decay". The Old House Journal. May 1981. pp. 103 - 106.

WOOD--PRESERVATION

"Natural Finishes for Exterior Timber." Building Research Establishment Digest. 286, June 1984. 4 p.

WOOD--PRESERVATION

Newsletter, ICOM Committee for Conservation, Working Group on Waterlogged Wood. No. 4, June 1980.

WOOD--PRESERVATION

Prudon, Theordore H. M. "In-Situe Injection of Wood Preservatives." APT Bulletin. (Vol. XI, #1) 1979. pp. 75-80.

WOOD--PRESERVATION

Staehli, Alfred M. "The Preservation of Logs and Heavy Timbers in Historic Buildings by Using Volatile Chemicals." APT Bulletin. Vol. 15, No. 1, 1983. pp. 22-26.

WOOD--PRESERVATION

Szabo, T. and J.K. Shields. "Simple Remedial Treatment of Deteriorated Wood in Heritage Homes." APT Bulletin. (Vol. XI, #2) 1979. pp. 17-21.

WOOD FINISHING

Jones, Larry. "The Hand Rubbed Finish." The Old-House Journal. Vol. 14, No. 2, Mar. 1986. p. 70-74.

WOOD PRESERVATIVES

McNamara, Sarah J. "Seeing Through Opaque Stains." Old House Journal. Vol. 13, No. 3, Apr. 1985. p. 58-59.

WOODEN-FRAME HOUSES--CONSERVATION AND RESTORATION

Curtis, John Obed. "Salvage of Original Clapboards." The Old House Journal. Vol. 13, No. 7, Aug./Sept. 1985. p. 135, 156-158.

WOODEN FRAME HOUSES--CONSERVATION AND RESTORATION

Jones, Larry. "Minor Repairs of Clapboards." The Old-House Journal. Vol. XII, No. 4, May 1984. pp. 78-79.

WOODEN-FRAME HOUSING

Charles, F.W.B. "The Conservation of Timber Buildings: ICOMOS Wood Committee Meetings in Japan, Norway and Bulgaria." Association for Studies in the Conservation of Historic Buildings [England] Transactions. Vol. 10, 1985. pp. 16-22.

WOODWORK

Bock, Gordon H. "Removing Interior Wood-work: Clever Ways to Avoid Destroying Your Trim." The Old House Journal. Vol. 13, No. 5, June 1985. p. 97, 108-111.

WOODWORK

Byrne, Richard O. "Removing Fine Woodwork." Canadian Heritage. Dec. 1982. pp. 26-28.

WOODWORK

Johnson, Edwin R. "Restoring Woodwork in a Colonial Revival House." Victorian Homes. Vol. 6, No. 3. Summer 1987. pp. 56 - 59.

WOODWORK

Jones, Larry. "Wood Cornice: Restoration and Repair." The Old House Journal. Vol. 13, No. 7, Aug./Sept. 1985. p. 141-147.

WOODWORK

Labine, Clem. "Selecting a Clear Finish for Paint-Stripped Woodwork." The Old-House Journal. Vol. XII, No. 9, November 1984. pp. 197-199.

WOODWORK

Poore, Jonathan. "Woodwork Repairs." Old House Journal, Vol. 15, No. 3, May-June 1987. p. 32-37.

Repairs for minor woodwork damage.

WRECKING

Santucci, R.M. "Demolition: Be Selective, or you will tear up your savings, too." Cost Cuts. Vol. 3, No. 1, Sept./Oct. 1985. p. 8-9.

WROUGHT IRON

Alexander, Robert L. "Neoclassical Wrought Iron in Baltimore." Winterthur Portfolio. Autumn 1983. pp. 147-186.

X-RAYS

Clarke, Eric T. "Radiography of the Cape Hatteras Lighthouse: Non-Destructive Analysis of the Cast Iron Framework/Anchoring System." Technology and Conservation, Spring 1980. p.20-24.

X-RAYS

Firschein, William. "Computer Enhancement of Radiographic Films Used in Structural Investigation of an Historic Structure." APT Bulletin. Vol. XIV, No. 2, 1982. pp. 19-25.

X-RAYS

Rush, Richard. "Reading and Writing History with X-Rays; Hiegh Technology of Today and Tomorrow is Applied to the Build-ings of Yesterday. Architect David Hart Uses X-Ray Photos to Probe the Past of Historic Buildings." Progressive Architecture, November 1979. pp. 100-101.

ZONING

Babcock, Richard F. and R. Marlin Smith. "Zoning by the Numbers." Planning. Vol. 51, No. 6, June 1985. p. 12-16.

ZONING

Burnstein, Joseph and Leonard A. Zax. "Enterprise Zones: Congress Prepares to Debate the Issues." Journal of Housing. June 1981. pp. 325 - 329.

ZONING

"Cities Serve Up Fast Food Controls." Zoning News. Oct. 1985. p. 2-3.

San Francisco and D.C. statutes noted.

ZONING

Douthat, Carolyn. "More Review for Demolition Ordinance." Oakland Heritage Alliance News. Vol. 7, No. 1, Spring 1987. p. 9.

ZONING

Eagleton, Annette Kolis. "Recent Trends in Conditional Rezoning Validation." Urban Land. November 1981. pp. 21-23.

ZONING

Ellickson, Robert C. "Inclusionary Zoning: Who Pays?" Planning. Vol. 51, No. 8, Aug. 1985. p. 18-22.

ZONING

"FCC Limits Dish Regulations." Zoning News. Feb. 1986. p. 1-2.

ZONING

Haar, Charles M. and Jerold S. Kayden. "Zoning after 70 years." Zoning News. Jan. 1987. p. 1-2.

ZONING

Hinds, Dudley S. "Investment Risk in Older Buildings With Zoning Nonconformities: Updated Zoning Ordinances Place New Demands on Existing Structures." Real Estate Issues. Vol. 12, No. 1. Spr./Sum. 1987. pp. 36 - 41.

ZONING

Huff, Nadine. "Negotiating Rezoning Conditions in Fairfax County, Virginia." Urban Land. November 1981. pp. 13-15.

ZONING

Kendig, Lane H. "Developers and Performance Zoning." Urban Land. January 1982. pp. 18-21.

ZONING

Lieberman, Nancy C. "Contract and Conditional Rezoning: A Judicial and Legislative Review." Urban Land. November 1981. pp. 10-12.

ZONING

Mandelker, Daniel R. "Special Purpose Zoning." Urban Land. Vol. 43, No. 10, October 1984. pp. 34-35.

Special purpose zoning districts and neighborhood conservation districts are discussed.

ZONING

"Mixed-use Formula in San Francisco." Progressive Architecture. August 1982. pp. 30-31.

ZONING

Nellis, Lee. "Zoning's Vicious Cycle (And A Way Out)!" Small Town. Vol. 14, No. 6, May-June 1984. pp. 19-23.

ZONING

Nelson, Robert H. "Rethinking Zoning." Urban Land. July 1983. pp. 36-37.

ZONING

"New Rappahannock Zoning Ordinance." Piedmont Environmental Council Newsreporter. Jan. 1987. p. 1.

Rappahannock County, VA. adopts an ordinance to protect rural character.

ZONING

Phalen, Tam. "How Has Performance Zoning Performed." Urban Land. October 1983. pp. 16-21.

ZONING

Phillips, Patrick. "Environmental Comment: Sidewalk Solar Access: Downtown Zoning for Sun and Light." Urban Land. Vol. 44, No. 2, Feb. 1985. p. 36-37.

ZONING

Ponte, Robert. "New York's Zoning Solution." Planning. December 1982. pp.10-14.

ZONING

"Preservation Through Planned Unit Development in Evanston, Illinois." The Alliance Review. Vol. 2, No. 5, March 1987. p. 1.

ZONING

"Preserving Miami Beach's Art Deco District." Zoning News. July 1986. p. 4.

ZONING

"Proposition M Limits Downtown Development." Downtown Idea Exchange. Vol. 34, No. 5, Mar. 1, 1987. p. 7-8.

San Francisco voters approve limits to office building development.

ZONING

Ratcliffe, John. "Enterprise Zones in the United Kingdom." Urban Land. September 1981. pp. 14-17.

ZONING

Roeseler, Wolfgang C. and Brice W. McClendon. "Making Zoning Districts More Effective." JAPA. Vol. 52, No. 1, Winter 1986. p. 83-86.

ZONING

"San Francisco Adopts Chinatown Protections." Zoning News. June 1987. pp. 3 - 4.

ZONING

Sanders, Welford. "Zero Lot Lines Can Trim Housing Costs." Planning. April 1982. pp. 15-17.

ZONING

"Scottsdale, Arizona TDR Ordinance Ruled Unconstitutional." Farmland Notes. Vol. 6, No. 10, Oct. 1986. p. 3.

A zoning ordinance enacted to establish a conservation area through the transfer of development rights was ruled unconstitutional.

ZONING

Shilland, Kimberly. "Zoning and Historic Preservation." Boston Preservation Alliance Letter. Vol. 8, No. 3, Mar. 1987. p. 3-4.

ZONING

Stewart, Jon A. " Enterprise Zones: Tool of Urban Revitalization." Transatlantic Perspectives. January 1981. p. 2-6.

ZONING

"Summary of Enterprise Zone Proposal Obtained; Jobs, Housing, Business Incentives Offered." Urban Planning Reports. April 24, 1981. p. 1-3.

ZONING

"Survey of Big City Zoning Boards of Appeal." Zoning News. June 1985. p. 1-3.

Vertical File
ZONING

Thomas, Ron and Margaret Grieve. "Roa- noke Vision: A Public Process of Comprehensive Planning and Zoning for Preservation." UD Review. Vol. 9, No. 3, 1986. p. 6-9. (VF)

ZONING

Varoga, Craig. "The Preservationist Role of Safety and Permits." New Orleans Preservation in Print. Vol. 13, No. 10. Dec. 1986. p. 10.

ZONING

Wells, Roger. "Getting PUD Approvals in the '80s." Urban Land. February 1983. pp. 2-7.

ZONING

Wolf, Dick. "The Capitol Interest District Overlay Zone: Case 83-14 Before the District of Columbia Zoning Commission." News, Capitol Hill Restoration Society, Inc. April 1984. pp. 1,6.

ZONING

"Zoning Overlay Has Incentives for Preserving Harvard Square." Urban Conservation Report. Vol. 10, No. 9, Sept. 30, 1986. p. 2.

ZONING--U.S.--CALIFORNIA--PASADENA

Mossman, Sue and Linda Dishman. "New Overlay Zone in Pasadena." California Preservation. Vol. 8, No. 2, April 1984. p. 6.

ZONING--U.S.--CALIFORNIA--SAN DIEGO

"'Zoning' A Downtown District." Downtown Idea Exchange. Vol. 32, No. 19, Oct. 1, 1985. p. 4-7.

Discussion of Gaslamp Quarter.

ZONING--U.S.--CALIFORNIA--SAN FRANCISCO

"In Re-zoned Central San Francisco, Modesty is the Best Policy." Architectural Record. Sept. 1985. p. 59.

ZONING--U.S.--COLORADO--BRECKENRIDGE

Humphreys, John A. "Point Systems: Keeping Score: Breckenridge." Planning. Vol. 51, No. 10, Oct. 1985. p. 23-25.

ZONING--U.S.--LOUISIANA--NEW ORLEANS

"After the World's Fair." Zoning News. Sept. 1985. p. 4.

ZONING--U.S.--WASHINGTON, D.C.

"Zoning Commission Limits Fast Food Outlets in D.C. Neighborhoods." Urban Conservation Report. Vol. 9, No. 5, May 31, 1985. p. 6.

ZONING--U.S.--WASHINGTON--SEATTLE

"Seattle's Incentives for Downtown Housing." Zoning News. Sept. 1985. p. 3.

ZONING, MIXED-USE

Basile, Ralph J. "The Urban Environment." Environmental Comment. Sep. 1979. pp. 8-9.

ZONING BOARDS

"Survey of Zoning Boards of Appeals." Zoning News. May 1986. p. 1-3.

ZONING LAW

"Can a Civic Organization Be Aggrieved." Urban Conservation Report. Vol. 10, No. 7, July 9, 1986. p. 1-2.

Virginia Supreme Court ruling of June 13 declared that civic associations devoted to community improvement or preservation may not appeal zoning decisions.

ZONING LAW

"High Court Hears Another Takings Case." Zoning News. Nov. 1985. p. 1-2.

MacDonald, Sommer and Frates v. County of Yolo and City of Davis, California, question of whether a local government must compensate landowner unable to develop property to fullest because of local regulations, to be heard.

ZONING LAW

Kayden, Jerold S. and Leonard A. Zax. "A State Court Supports Low-income Housing." Place. November 1983. pp. 6-9.

ZONING LAW

"A Landmark Case Opens Up the Suburbs." Planning. November 1983. pp. 4-15. Partial Issue.

CONTENTS: Erber, Ernest. The Road to Mt. Laurel--Franklin, Herbert M. The Most Important Zoning Opinion Since Euclid--Rose, Jerome G. Questions Remain in the Wake of Mount Laurel II--Rabin, Yale. The Final Question: Who Benefits?

ZONING LAW

Netter, Edith M. "Hartford Adopts Incentive Zoning Regulations." Urban Land. June 1984. pp. 34-5.

Floor Area Ratio (FAR) Bonuses for preservation of historic buildings.

ZONING LAW

Pols, Cynthia. "FCC Plans to Preempt Local Zoning Laws on Satellite Antennae." Nation's Cities Weekly. Apr. 15, 1985. p. 7.

ZONING LAW--U.S.--FLORIDA--MIAMI BEACH

"Performance Zoning and Miami Beach's Small-Lot Problem." Urban Land. Vol. 44, No. 6, June 1985. p. 27.

ZONING LAW--U.S.--ILLINOIS--EVANSTON

"Preservation Through Planned Unit Development." Evanston Preservation News. Aug. 1986. p. 2-3.

ZONING--U.S.--MASSACHUSETTS--DUXBURY

Phillips, Patrick. "The Impact of Impact Zoning: Theory and Practice in a New England Town." Urban Land. Vol. 45, No. 8, Aug. 1986. p. 34-35.

ZONING LAW--U.S.--RHODE ISLAND--PROVIDENCE

"Report Defines Zoning Issues in Providence." PPS News. Jan./Feb. 1986. p. 5-6.

ZONING LAW--U.S.--VIRGINIA--FAUQUIER COUNTY

"Faquier Settles Suit Challenging Zoning Ordinance: Considers Reducing Rural Density." Piedmont Environmental Council Newsreporter. Sept. 1985. p. 1-2.

Management of growth pressures in rural county.

ZOOLOGICAL GARDENS

Douglas, William L. "New Orleans' Zoo Unveils a New Image." Place. Vol. 4, No. 9, October 1984. pp. 8-9.

ZOOLOGICAL GARDENS--U.S.--PENNSYLVANIA--PHILA-DELPHIA

Crosbie, Michael J. "The Making of a Magical Place." Architecture. Oct. 1985. p. 54-61.

A special children's space created in restored treehouse building (Antelope House, 1876, George Hewitt).

ZOOLOGICAL PARKS

Horowitz, Helen Lefkowitz. "Seeing Ourselves Through the Bars: A Historical Tour of American Zoos." Landscape. Vol. 25, No. 2. pp. 12-19.